Ha

THE CHURCH

IMAGE BOOKS

A Division of Doubleday & Company, Inc.

Garden City, New York

Image Books edition published by special arrangement with Sheed
  and Ward
Image Books edition published September 1976

Originally published under the title *Die Kirche* (Herder, Freiburg
  —Basle—Vienna)
© Verlag Herder KG Freiburg im Breisgau 1967
ISBN: 0-385-11367-6
English translation Copyright © 1967 Burns and Oates Ltd.
All Rights Reserved
Printed in the United States of America
            9 8 7 6 5

Brilliant, controversial, and outspoken, HANS KÜNG is highly regarded for his theological knowledge and insights not only among Catholics but by theologians of all religious persuasions. Born in Switzerland in 1928, he studied at the German College in Rome, at the Gregorian University, at the Institut Catholique and at the Sorbonne. In addition to a Doctorate in Theology, he holds honorary Doctorates in Law, Evangelical Theology, and Humanities. In 1962 Pope John XXIII named him official counselor on Theology at the Vatican Council. Since 1960 he has been Professor of Dogmatic and Ecumenical Theology and Director of the Institute for Ecumenical Studies at the University of Tübingen. He is the author of several significant and successful books—including *Infallible? An Inquiry; The Council; Reform and Reunion;* and *Why Priests?*

Of *The Church* Robert McAfee Brown, writing in *Commonweal,* had this to say:

> "Küng's most significant and enduring work thus far, which is saying a lot when one considers that in addition to the cluster of books Küng wrote before and during the Council, he has given us such substantial works as *Justification* and *Structures of the Church.* Nevertheless, *The Church* seems to me destined to become the work from which both Catholics and Protestants will begin new formulations of a doctrine of the church."

And theologian Avery Dulles, in a review for *America,* says:

> "*The Church* is a very important and valuable book. It brings together an almost unbelievable amount of exegetical and historical information, and effectively shows its bearing on the renewal of the Church today. Küng is profoundly committed to the renewal of the Church according to the gospel. This authentic evangelical motif should make this book as appealing to Protestants as it is necessary to Catholics."

TO
DR MICHAEL RAMSEY
Archbishop of Canterbury

ACKNOWLEDGMENTS

We wish to thank the following publishers for permission to reprint excerpts from their publications:

Alec R. Allenson, Inc.: *Essays on New Testament Themes,* by Ernst Kasemann, and *Promise and Fulfilment,* by W. G. Kummel. London, S.C.M. Press. Distributed in U.S.A. by Allenson's, Naperville, Ill.

T. and T. Clark, Publishers: *Church Dogmatics,* IV/1, by Karl Barth.

Guild Press, Inc.: Excerpts from The Constitutions, Decrees, and Declarations of the Ecumenical Council are taken from *The Documents of Vatican II,* published by Guild Press, America Press, Association Press, and Herder and Herder, and copyrighted 1966 by The America Press. Used by permission.

Harper & Row, Publishers, Inc.: *Two Types of Faith,* by Martin Buber.

Herder and Herder, New York: *God's Rule and Kingdom,* Vol. I 1952, Vol. II 1955, by Rudolph Schnackenburg.

Charles Scribner's Sons: *Theology of the New Testament,* Vol. I, by Rudolf Bultmann.

The Westminster Press: *Jesus,* by Martin Dibelius, translated by Charles B. Hedrick and Frederick C. Grant. The Westminster Press. Copyright 1949 by W. L. Jenkins. Used by permission.

All scriptural quotations are from *The Holy Bible, Revised Standard Version,* New York, Nelson, 1946, 1952. Copyrighted 1946 and 1952 by the Division of Christian Education of the National Council of Churches.

CONTENTS

E. THE OFFICES OF THE CHURCH

PREFACE

Though there is much talk nowadays about the Church in the secular world, there is not a corresponding awareness of what the Church is. One can only know what the Church should be now if one also knows what the Church was originally. This means knowing what the Church of today should be in the light of the Gospel. It is the purpose of this book to answer that question.

Whatever the disappointment we might feel in retrospect, Vatican II undoubtedly achieved a powerful breakthrough in terms of freedom, openness and flexibility on behalf of the Catholic Church. Catholics and non-Catholics alike, indeed the world as a whole, were happily surprised at this unsuspected evidence of a new lease of life so abruptly breaking through after centuries of reserve and isolationism. A fresh era was opening out, heralding new relationships between the Catholic Church and other Christian Churches, new attitudes to Judaism and the other world religions—in fact a new approach to the world in general.

But the rejoicing of the majority at this turn of events should not blind us to the concern many well-intentioned Catholics experienced precisely on account of their Church's newly declared goals of greater freedom, openness and flexibility. Some were disconcerted and feared unhappy consequences, and those not affected in this way should temper their enthusiasm with some understanding for the predicament of others. It was feared by some that the Church, that up to now had lived in consciousness of its role as the pillar and vessel of truth, was about to be dragged into the corruption and transience of earthly things. The new attitudes seemed to suggest that hitherto the Church had been travelling fast along the wrong road. And anyway, what guarantee was there that the new attitudes were milestones along the right road?

Relatively speaking, only a few people reacted to the Council in this way. We should not overestimate the importance of the handful of organized protest movements, which in fact have only small numbers of people behind them. In general the Catholic Church in every country welcomed the spirit and ambitions of Vatican II. Alert men throughout the Church sensed spontaneously that the change was for the better, that good would come of it.

Nevertheless, the concern some people have expressed must be taken seriously. It prevents us from escaping the vital question: by what criterion are we to judge that the Church is now headed in the right direction?

Is it enough to answer that the Church is on the right path so long as it adapts itself to the present? Evidently not, for that could mean adapting itself to the evil, the anti-God elements, the indifferentism in the world. What St Paul says in Romans 12:2 still applies: "Do not be conformed to this world but be transformed by the renewal of your mind, that you may prove what is the will of God, what is good and acceptable [to God] and perfect."

Or can one say that the Church is on the right path so long as it holds fast to the past? Again, evidently not, for that could mean ignoring what is good and acceptable and perfect, holding to what has gone simply because to do so is convenient, less disruptive. Clinging tenaciously to the past in this way is no less dangerous than a misdirected adaptation to the present. It is even possible that abiding by something good could be wrong, for instance when man's concerns are given priority over God's, when human tradition is preferred to God's word. Aware of man's reluctance to forgo his own tradition and that this is deaf to the freshness and perpetually recurring demands of God's will, Christ quoted Isaiah's warning: "This people honours me with their lips, but their heart is far from me; in vain do they worship me, teaching as doctrines the precepts of men" (Mark 7:6 f.). And Christ adds: "You have a fine way of rejecting the commandment of God, in order to keep your tradition! . . . thus making void the word of God through your tradition which you hand on" (7:9,13).

We can see, therefore, that where adaptation to the present is inadequate because it leads to modernism, clinging to the past is no better, for it leads to traditionalism. And so again we ask: How do we know when the Church is on the right path? Where is the golden thread?

The short answer to the question is that the Church is headed in the right direction when, whatever the age in which it lives, the Gospel of Jesus Christ is its criterion, the Gospel which Christ proclaimed and to which the Church of the apostles witnessed. The Church did not come about of itself. God himself called it into being as the *Ecclesia,* the body of those who answered the call, and this he did in the world, from among mankind. God himself convoked the Church in the call that issued through Jesus, the Christ. This call is an *Euangelion,* the good news: the news of the dominion of God over this world, the news that the hopes and desires of man should be directed to God alone, the news of God's love, and of man's love for God and his fellow men. It is this message, which Jesus lived out to the full, even to death, that arouses faith and acceptance in man. It is a message that has always found faith and within which the Church took life, the Church of the community of believers, of those who love God, of those who place their total trust in their glorified Lord and look for the coming of his kingdom.

The Church, therefore, is the pilgrim community of believers, not of those who already see and know. The Church must ever and again wander through the desert, through the darkness of sin and error. For the Church can also err and for this reason must always be prepared to orientate itself anew, to renew itself. It must always be prepared to seek out a new path, a way that might be just as difficult to find as a desert track, or a path through darkness.

There is, however, one guiding light it is never without, just as God's people in the desert always had a guide: God's word is always there to lead the Church. Through Jesus, the Christ, it has been definitively revealed to us. The word of Jesus Christ, as testified by the apostles, is the Church's guide. It is the word to which the Church appeals and according to which it must examine its activities in the confusion of this world.

With the message of Jesus Christ behind it, the Church is headed in the right direction. Thus armed, it is empowered to take new directions, indeed, now and again *must* do so in an attempt to perfect its fidelity to God's rule which it is so frequently inclined to forget. What conclusions are we to draw from this now that Vatican II is over?

Vatican II led the Church to a renewed consciousness of the Gospel of Jesus Christ. This is the unmistakable sign that the post-conciliar Church is on the right path, that it is truly guided by the Spirit of Jesus Christ. The Church today does not impenitently leave things as they were, but reforms and renews its life, structures and teaching, adapting itself to the world as it actually is. But it has not just developed a craze for modernity: it is also looking to its own origins, to the events that gave it life. This is the vital point that must be understood if one is to judge the Church's present development. This can be seen through the following examples.

The object of reforming the Mass liturgy is not to introduce a few box-office gimmicks but to reveal within the celebration of the Eucharist the original and so frequently obscured and forgotten meaning of the meal Christ ate with his apostles.

The reintroduction of the vernacular to the liturgy is not simply a condescension to modern tastes but is done so as to ensure that, as in the early Church, the good news of Christ is accessible to all, whether educated or not.

The examination of methods of pastoral care is not being conducted with a view to betraying inherited methods for the sake of new, untested ones, but with the object of enabling the Church to fulfil the Gospel's directive that it serve mankind, and this in a manner that is not at variance with the sensitivities of the times.

Contemporary theology is not striving to cook up new systems of man-made precepts, but to awaken a living consciousness of the word of God as witnessed in Scripture.

Ecumenical efforts spring not from indifferentism, much though this might suit our modern age, but from a new awareness of God's desire that all might be one.

In all cases it is now a question of pursuing the objective that Pope Paul demonstrated so unequivocally through his pilgrimage to Palestine: the Church must return to the place from which it proceeded; must return to its origins, to Jesus, to the Gospel. And as a direct consequence, this can only mean forward to a new future, the future God has in mind for mankind.

Our rôle in the secular world is not easy. Much hangs in the balance. More effort and more responsibility are required of the individual. But there is no reason for fear or timidity. On the contrary, we have every reason to rejoice and be grateful that it is permitted to us to live in such times as these, when the Church and the rest of Christendom have awakened to new life, new freedom and a new future.

Finally, I would like to say that it has been my pleasure to dedicate the English edition of this book to Dr Michael Ramsey, Archbishop of Canterbury. This will record my humble hope that there lies within the pages of this book a theological basis for a *rapprochement* between the Churches of Rome and Canterbury.

HANS KÜNG

Tübingen, 11 October 1967
Fifth anniversary of the Opening of the Second Vatican Council

FOREWORD

The problem of God is more important than the problem of the Church; but the latter often stands in the way of the former. This ought not to be the case. In this book an attempt is made to show that it does not need to be the case. To try to give a comprehensive picure rather than select individual topics at random is to be confronted with an almost overwhelming range of problems and a daunting mass of literature. For this reason it has been necessary to concentrate and restrict my attention, to put certain emphases, to deal with some aspects at length and others more briefly, with some more intensively and substantially, with others in a sparer and more outline fashion; and all this with an enthusiasm which does not preclude sober accuracy. What is the justification for dealing with the subject in this way rather than in any other? I have tried to allow the original Christian message to dictate the themes, perspectives and balance of the book, so that the original Church may light the way once more for the Church of today.

Taking this starting-point has certain consequences, the justification for which can only be found in the origins of the Church. Those who have doubts about this method may care to recall that it is the one which is expected of post-conciliar theology: "Dogmatic theology should be so arranged that the biblical themes are presented first"; from this starting-point it should pass to historical research, and thence to a systematic penetration of the mysteries of salvation (Decree on Priestly Formation, art. 16).

Structures of the Church (1962, English version 1964) is to be understood as a prolegomenon to this book.

The method followed here means that the systematic theologian was to an unusual degree dependent on the advice of the exegetical scholar. For this reason I am deeply grateful to my colleagues in Tübingen, Professor Karl Hermann Schelkle and Professor Herbert Haag, who read the whole or part of the manuscript, for their suggestions and encouragement which have been of great value to me. I am equally grateful to my colleague in Dogmatic Theology and fellow-editor of *Ecumenical Investigations*, Professor Joseph Ratzinger, for his valuable help. I should also like to thank my assistants, Dr Gotthold Hasenhüttl and Dr Alexandre Ganoczy, now Professor at the Institut Catholique in Paris, and all my colleagues at the Institute for Ecumenical Research, who gave me unstinting assistance both in the composition of the manuscript and in all the work of correction.

HANS KÜNG

Tübingen Sursee,
New Year 1967

A. *The Church as It Is*

I. HISTORICITY AND THE IMAGE OF THE CHURCH

1. ESSENCE AND HISTORICAL FORMS

The Church is rapidly approaching its third millennium. For the world in which the Church lives, the future has already begun. Science has begun to investigate both microcosm and macrocosm, both the atom and the universe; there are increasingly rapid and more efficient means of communication and transport; there is a wealth of new instruments, synthetic materials; methods of production are being rationalized; the expectation of human life has been increased by a decade or more; tremendous achievements have been made in physics, chemistry, biology, medicine, psychology, sociology, economics, historical research. All in all, despite those worldwide catastrophes and perils which have been the particular fate of our century, the story has been one of breathtaking progress. The highly industrialized nations of Europe and America have spread their knowledge throughout the world, the peoples of Asia and Africa have come to life; the world is becoming one and a single economic unit, a single civilization, perhaps even a single culture is emerging.

And what of the Church? Has the future begun for it too? In some respect perhaps, but in many others it has not. At all events we have surely come to realize that the Church cannot, even if it wants to, stand aside from this world-wide reorientation which heralds a new era; for the Church lives in this, not in another world. Our age, like all times of transition, is one of unrest. For all the triumphs of science and technology, there is a feeling of disquiet which finds expression in art, in films and in the theatre, in literature and in philosophy: it is an experience of individuals and nations alike. The Church too, behind its façade of seemingly timeless self-confidence, is affected by this unrest, since it affects the people who make up the Church. It is a healthy, even salutary, unrest and it should give us cause for hope, not anxiety. What looks like a serious crisis may mark the moment of new life; what looks like a sinister threat may in reality be a great opportunity.

Enormous tasks, both familiar and unfamiliar, confront a Church which sees itself as a part of this changed and changing world and claims to exist for the world. It must renew, reassemble and revitalize its people, who have often become stale and rigid because of traditional forms and formulas. It must preach the Gospel in countries which were once Christian but are now largely pagan, to educated and uneducated people who are today estranged from the Church and its message. It must achieve an ecumenical encounter and a reunion of separated Christians and Christian Churches. It must establish sympathetic dialogue with the great non-Christian religions, Islam, Buddhism, and Hinduism, in the context of a unified world. It must play its proper part in solving the world's enormous problems, helping to prevent wars and promote peace, to fight against famine and poverty, to educate the masses. There are many problems; there are many opportunities.

The Church cannot face these problems and use these opportunities if it is a prisoner of its own theories and prejudices, its own forms and laws, rather than being a prisoner of its Lord. As the prisoner of the Lord it is truly free, ready and willing to serve the constantly new requirements, needs and aspirations of mankind.

Our concept of the Church is basically influenced by the form of the Church at any given time. All too easily the Church can become a prisoner of the image it has made for itself at one particular period in history. Every age has its own image of the Church, arising out of a particular historical situation; in every age a particular view of the Church is expressed by the Church in practice, and given conceptual form, *post hoc* or *ante hoc,* by the theologians of the age. At the same time, there is a constant factor in the various changing historical images of the Church, something which survives however much the history of mankind, of the Church and of theology may vary, and it is on this that we must concentrate. There are fundamental elements and perspectives in the Church which are not derived from the Church itself; there is an "essence" which is drawn from the permanently decisive origins of the Church. This constant factor in the history of the Church and of its understanding of itself is only revealed in change; its identity exists only in variability, its continuity only in changing circumstances, its permanence only in varying outward appearances. In short, the "essence" of the Church is not a matter of metaphysical stasis, but exists only in constantly changing historical "forms". If we want to discover this original and permanent "essence", given that it is something dynamic rather than something static and rigid, we must look at the constantly changing historical "forms" of the Church. It is vital to distinguish permanent and continuing elements from changing and transient features, and to make this distinction we must take into account right from the start the fact that the Church's image contains impermanent features, conditioned by time.

The starting-point of the following discussion is the fact that the "essence" of the Church is expressed in changing historical forms. Rather than talking about an ideal Church situated in the abstract celestial spheres of theological theory, we shall consider the *real* Church as it exists in our world, and in human history. The New Testament itself does not begin by laying down a doctrine of the Church which has then to be worked out in practice; it starts with the Church as *reality,* and reflection upon it comes later. The real Church is first and foremost a happening, a fact, an historical event. *The real essence of the real Church is expressed in historical form.* There are two important points here:

1. Essence and form *cannot be separated*. The essence and the form of the Church should not be divorced from one another, but must be seen as a whole. The distinction between essence and form is a conceptual, not a real, distinction. There is not and never was, in fact, an essence of the Church by itself, separate, chemically pure, distilled from the stream of historical forms. What is changing and what is unchanging cannot be neatly divided up; while there are permanent factors, there are no absolutely irreformable areas. The relationship between essence and form is not simply that between core and skin. An essence without form is formless and hence unreal; a form without essence is insubstantial and hence

equally unreal. For all its relativity, historical form should not
be seen as totally irrelevant and contrasted with an essence
existing somewhere "beyond" or "above" it. It is all too easy
for us to retreat into harmless theologumena, remote from
real life, about the "essence" of the Church, and so try to
avoid having to make historical judgments and distinctions.
At the same time it is equally easy for us to disregard the essence of the Church which is dictated by its origins, to be
mentally lazy and uncritical and concern ourselves simply
with the present form of the Church, becoming absorbed with
ecclesiastical activity or even resigning ourselves to a totally
passive rôle. We can only glimpse the real Church if we see
the essence of the Church as existing in its historical form,
rather than as existing beyond and above it.

2. Essence and form *are not identical*. The essence and the
form of the Church should be not equated, but must be recognized and distinguished. Even if the distinction between essence and form is a conceptual one, it is none the less necessary. How else can we decide what is permanent in the
changing form of the Church? How else can we judge its actual historical form? How else can we establish a criterion, a
norm, which will enable us to decide what is legitimate in any
historical and empirical manifestation of the Church? No
form of the Church, not even that in the New Testament, embraces its essence in such a way that it is simply part and par-
cel of it. And no form of the Church, not even that in the
New Testament, mirrors the Church's essence perfectly and
exhaustively. Only when we distinguish in the changing forms
of the Church its permanent but not immutable essence, do
we glimpse the real Church.

The essence of the Church is therefore always to be found
in its historical form, and the historical form must always be
understood in the light of and with reference to the essence.

2. THE DEVELOPMENT OF THE IMAGE OF THE CHURCH IN CHURCH HISTORY

Ecclesiology, the theological expression of the Church's
image, varies, consciously, with the varying forms of the real

ecclesia. A few historical examples will suffice to illustrate this point.[1]

Even in the *ecclesiology of the primitive Church* there are significant distinctions and variations, as can be seen from the following simplified account. While the second-century apologists, with the exception of a few passages of Justin, scarcely use the word "ecclesia"—their apologetics were concerned with the one God and with Christ, not with the Church—the idea of the Church becomes important in the writings of the later Fathers. It is one of the main themes of their theological treatises and of their exegesis both of Old and New Testaments. The image of the Church in the first three centuries was determined by the opposition between a hostile pagan State and a Church which, under various kinds of persecution, knew both victory and defeat. In the following centuries, however, the image was determined by the harmony between an established Church, reaping the fruits of victory, and the Christian empire. Hippolytus of Rome, for example, saw the empire as a satanic imitation of Christ's kingdom, in complete contrast to the later imperialistic theology of Eusebius, the Church historian and court bishop. For him the empire was divinely ordained to prepare the way for Christianity, since both had arisen about the same time; he saw the Christian emperor as the Church's defender and protector against irreligion and false gods.

Ecclesiology varies according to whether, as is often the case in the writings of the apostolic Fathers, it is a means for the leaders of the community to edify their people, or, as is variously the case in Irenaeus, Cyprian and Augustine, it is a

[1] There is as yet no comprehensive history of ecclesiology. On the history of ecclesiology with regard to this and following chapters, cf., in addition to the works cited, the relevant passages in the histories of dogma (A. Harnack, F. Loofs, E. Seeberg) and the articles under "Church" or "Ecclesiology" in the standard works: LThK (J. Ratzinger, K. E. Skydsgaard, H. Bacht), RGG (A. Adam), EKL (U. Jaeschke, K. D. Schmidt), HTG (Y. Congar), DTC (E. Dublanchy), Cath. (M.-J. Le Guillou), ODCC. Valuable contributions to the history of ecclesiology may be found in S. Jaki, *Les tendances nouvelles de l'ecclésiologie*, Rome 1957; *L'Ecclésiologie au XIXe siècle*, Paris 1960; and in the Festschrift for Hugo Rahner, *Sentire Ecclesiam*, ed. J. Daniélou and H. Vorgrimler, Freiburg–Basle–Vienna 1961.

weapon for a frontal assault on heresy. A theologian who prefers to believe in the unobtrusive inner development of truth
and its gradual victory and who, living in the subtle intellectual atmosphere of the hellenistic world, regards refined
dogmatic formulas as the most effective, will produce a particular brand of ecclesiology, even if he is principally concerned with christology and trinitarian doctrine. A totally
different kind of ecclesiology will be produced by his Latin
contemporary, who belongs to a Church which sees itself as
acies ordinata, who interprets Christ and the Church in terms
of battles and victories, rewards and punishments, and who
erects his theology on the basis of strong ecclesiastical institutions, clearly defined rights and a smoothly running organization. A particular form of ecclesiology will be created if, in
the wake of Greek Neo-Platonism, the Church is seen principally as the school of truth and a fellowship of adepts; if the
pure apprehension of teaching of truth and the symbolic and
saving power of sacred rituals are seen to be all-important;
and if the Church's aim is seen as the establishing of a universal, all-embracing philosophy and the setting up of a culture
community on a religious basis. A very different form of
ecclesiology will result if, more on the basis of the pragmatic
popular philosophy of Roman stoicism, the Church is principally seen as a well-ordered community governed by laws; if
the holiness and obedience of Church members and an ecclesiastical order which imposes strict penitentiary discipline
and precise norms for daily life are seen as all-important; if
the Gospel is regarded as the "new law", preparing the way
for a holy State as part of God's kingdom on earth. In the
former case there is the danger that the Church will be
platonically hypostatized and made purely abstract; there is
the risk of interpreting Scripture ecclesiologically in an arbitrary and allegorical way, and a risk of ecclesiological triumphalism of a purely intellectual kind. In the latter case there
is the danger of a juridical approach in theory and practice,
of an ecclesiastical legalism which is purely formalistic; there
is the risk of clericalism and of ecclesiological triumphalism
of an authoritarian and traditionalistic kind.

Other differences in ecclesiology can be noted. Some ecclesiologies, as in Alexandrian theology of the third century,

and Origen in particular, will stress the priesthood of all believers, and draw a more important distinction between imperfect unthinking believers and perfect conscious gnostics than between laity and clergy; for them the holy doctors of the Church will basically hold the highest rank in the Church (ecclesiastical office is seen here primarily as a teaching office). Other ecclesiologies, as in the African and especially the Roman theology of the same time, will emphasize the idea of office and its legal character; they will ascribe the highest authority in the Church to the bishops (ecclesiastical office is seen here primarily as a governing office), and will minimize the importance of the priesthood of all believers and the charismatic element in the Church. The stress on ecclesiastical office can itself take different forms. In Roman theology, for example, the authority of the bishop is seen as derived solely from his official position, and as quite independent of his personal sanctity. The apostolic succession is primarily interpreted in an historical-canonical way and the achievements of a bishop are measured in terms of laws and correct formulations. An alternative view, taken by Cyprian, following Tertullian, is that the authority of the bishop depends essentially on the charismatic gift of the Spirit and hence on his personal sanctity. In this view the apostolic succession must also be a pneumatic succession, and the personal qualities of the bishop are taken fundamentally into account in measuring his success. There are also differences in the theologies of office. For some theologians it is the *episcopate* which is first and foremost the guarantee of unity; the person of Peter is regarded simply as a *sign* of Church unity and his successors are only accorded a kind of honorary primacy; this was the view of Cyprian and many other, especially Eastern, theologians. Other theologians see the *Roman bishop* as the primary guarantor of unity; the person of Peter is regarded as the *repository* of Church unity and his successors have a specific canonical primacy; Stephen I was the first pope to cite Jesus' words about the rock in Matthew 16:18 in this connection and these views were later held even more clearly by Siricius, Innocent I, Celestine I and Leo I.

The image of the Church in the first centuries shows enormous variations; see the writings of Hermas, Clement of Rome, Ignatius of Antioch, Irenaeus of Lyons and Hippolytus of Rome; Victor I, Stephen I, Leo I, Gelasius I and Gregory I; Clement of Alexandria, Origen and the Cappadocians; Tertullian, Cyprian and Augustine; Pachomius, the Egyptian monks, Benedict of Nursia and Western monasticism.

Changes and variations are equally striking in medieval ecclesiology. At some periods, as in the first millennium, ecclesiology arises unsystematically from the life of the Church, is not particularly emphasized, and is dealt with in conjunction with the doctrine of redemption. At other times, it becomes a special part of the Church's teaching, is dealt with consciously and systematically, and may even appear in the form of a separate and detailed tractatus, as became customary after Boniface VIII's quarrel with Philip the Fair, beginning with those theologians involved in the quarrel, James of Viterbo, Giles of Rome and John of Paris. There is an important difference between ecclesiologies which regard the legal constitution of the Church as relatively unimportant (cf. Rupert of Deutz, Joachim of Flora and others), and those which stress the legal and institutional aspects of the Church and the power and authority of the clergy, ideas which are especially expressed in systematic theology (cf., in addition to the medieval canonists, Thomas Aquinas in particular; for him submission to papal authority is necessary for salvation).

It is by no means unimportant whether an ecclesiology attributes to canon law a subordinate and serving function or whether it sees canon law as having a superior and dominating rôle, as something which provides ecclesiology with its materials and limits it with fixed concepts and formulas, as something which takes Church laws, laid down by men, as setting compulsory limitations on theological speculation. This latter view held sway particularly after the establishing of the faculty of canon law at Bologna in the twelfth century. Again, there are two completely different ways in which the power of the bishops can be strengthened. One, the method of the sixth-century Neo-Platonist who assumed the mask of Dionysius the Areopagite, disciple of Paul, was based on ver-

bose mystical interpretations of the Church's cult; the bishop
was held up as the bearer of mystical powers and the community was seen as bound to him above all by the cultic mysteries; the earthly ecclesiastical organization was depicted as
reflecting the heavenly hierarchy. A different method, as followed by the Frankish jurist at the beginning of the Middle
Ages, who was believed to be Isidore of Seville, was based on
ingenious forgeries of ecclesiastical laws; the bishop was seen
as the bearer of all legal powers and the community as bound
to him by the power of the keys. This latter view, in order to
guarantee the Church's independence of the State, decisively
strengthened papal primacy and decisively weakened the metropolitans and provincial councils. Under Charlemagne the
actual leadership of the whole Church is ascribed to the *emperor*, whom the Carolingian theologians called the defender
and guide of the Church; it is through him that the bishops
hold their sacred rights, can call councils and choose popes.
At a later point this leadership is ascribed to the *pope,* a view
presented with renewed vigour by Nicholas I, who referred to
the popes as princes of the whole earth. A different
ecclesiology is implied in each case. A similar contrast in
ecclesiologies is implied when on the one hand the Saxon and
Salic emperors of the pre-Gregorian period defend and
develop the idea of a harmony between *regnum* and *sacerdotium* and a sacral-priestly overlordship by a ruler ("the
Lord's anointed" and "the vicar of Christ"!) who appoints
bishops and can appoint and dethrone popes; and on the
other hand Gregory VII and the Gregorians in the so-called
Investiture contest put up the opposing view, confronting the
traditional rights of monarchy and nobility with a renewed
and centralized canon law, defending an hierarchical Church
which claims to be independent of the regnum and a pope
who is "prince of the kingdoms of the world", maintaining
that the pope has priestly sovereignty over political authorities
and can dismiss kings and emperors without being answerable
to anyone. Again an ecclesiology like that of the primitive
Church which comes "from below", from the Church as the
people of God, the Church which all ecclesiastical office is designed to subserve, will be very different from an ecclesiology
imposed "from above", beginning with the pope. In the latter

view, dating from about the time of Gregory VII, and partly
based on pseudo-Isidore, the pope is regarded as the head,
foundation, root, source and origin of all power and authority
in the Church.

The conciliar idea is another important expression of
ecclesiology, and here again we can trace remarkable variations. We have only to compare the writings of the decretists,
the commentators of the *Decretum Gratiani* in the twelfth
century (e.g., Huguccio, Johannes Teutonicus, etc.), with
those of the decretalists in the thirteenth century, who applied
company law concepts to the Church (especially Hostiensis,
also Tancred, Bernard Parmensis, etc.), and finally with the
actual conciliarists in the fourteenth century and at the time
of the Council of Constance (Conrad von Gelnhausen,
Heinrich von Langenstein, Dietrich von Niem, Jean Gerson,
Cardinal Pierre d'Ailly, Andreas of Randuf, Cardinal
Francesco Zabarella).

The medieval Church also presents a great variety of images of
the Church; how different are pseudo-Isidore and John Erigena;
Abelard and the Victorines; Peter Lombard and Bernard of Clairvaux; Gerhoh and Arno of Reichersberg and the great scholastics;
Leo IX, Gregory VII, Innocent III, Innocent IV, Boniface VIII
and Joachim of Flora and Francis of Assisi; William of Ockham
and the German mystics; Nicholas of Cusa and Torquemada!

Finally, there have also been great changes and variations
in the Catholic ecclesiology of recent times. Whereas in patristic and medieval times ecclesiology was marked by a considerable wealth of viewpoints and a breadth of perspective,
many controversial theologians of the Counter-Reformation
turned the theology of the Church into treatises on the various points of controversy.

The doctrinal statements of the Council of Trent consciously avoided the central controversial issue, that of the
papacy. After some initial hesitation, the First Vatican Council then grasped this nettle; it was the only one of all the outstanding ecclesiological questions that was the subject of a
declaration of dogma. Again, there are two different kinds of
ecclesiology in the background. That of the Gallicans was
largely determined by political considerations; it begins with

Philip IV's lawyers and pre-Reformation Gallicanism, is continued by Pithou, E. Richter and Bossuet under Louis XIV, and survives into nineteenth-century Gallicanism. Its basic inspiration, following seventeenth- and eighteenth-century researches into Church history, is the image of the primitive Church; it takes a stand on the autonomy of the national Church with its traditions, customs and usages, and hence on the autonomy of the national episcopate and local synods. The ecclesiology of the Ultramontanes on the other hand, which was equally conditioned by politics, was increasingly reduced to apologetic disquisitions on papal authority, in opposition to Protestants, Gallicans and Jansenists, as well as the various forms of episcopalism existing in Germany and Austria.

There is a world of difference between the ecclesiology of the Enlightenment which, basing itself on natural law, saw the Church from a juridical viewpoint as a *societas* having specific rights and obligations, and the later ecclesiology of Johann Michael Sailer which, under the influence of revivalist movements, mysticism and romanticism, concentrated above all on the religious and also the ethical side of the Church: the Church as the living mediatrix of a living spirituality. Similarly, there is a vast gulf in the nineteenth century between the reactionary ecclesiology of the Restoration period in France, as exemplified by de Maistre, and the new and influential ecclesiology of the Catholic Tübingen school, as exemplified by the young Möhler. De Maistre defended the idea of the absolute monarchy as the foundation of Christian Europe, in opposition to current democratic trends, and transferred his concept of the sovereignty of the absolute monarchy to the position of the pope in the Church. Möhler, on the other hand, rejected the alienated clericalistic ecclesiology of an official and institutionalized Church and saw the Church as a community of believers brought together in love by the Holy Spirit, a community which all ecclesiastical office was designed to subserve.

Again, what a contrast there is between the attitude of the First Vatican Council, when several of the fathers refused to take the "obscure" concept of the body of Christ as the starting-point for the schema on the Church, and that of the encyclical *Mystici Corporis,* which precisely tries to present the whole of ecclesiology in terms of the mystical body. What a contrast there is, finally, between the encyclical, which at several points is explicitly or implicitly polemical, and the more ecumenically orientated constitution of the Second Vatican Council, *De Ecclesia,* which has corrected a number of biases in previous ecclesiology. This constitution has given the oldest definition of the Church, the people of God, its rightful place at the beginning and the heart of ecclesiology, and by doing so has clarified the position of the laity as the Church and the clergy as its servants, as well as establishing the position of bishops in their relationship to the Petrine office.

Even in the post-medieval Church, then, there are many different images of the Church, as we can see if we compare Erasmus, Johannes Eck and Bellarmine; the *Imitation of Christ* and Ignatius of Loyola; the Spanish inquisitors and the mystics they persecuted; Suárez, the baroque scholastics and the German theologians of the Enlightenment; the French crown jurists, the theologians of the Sorbonne, Bossuet and Pascal; Drey, Möhler, Hirsch, Kuhn, Staudenmaier from Tübingen and Perrone, Schrader, Passaglia, Franzelin and Scheeben from Rome; Lamennais, Veuillot and Maret; Karl Adam, Emil Mersch and the bishops and theologians of Vatican II. To say nothing of the different images of the Church we find in Luther, Zwingli and Calvin, in the theology of the Lutheran and Reformed Churches, and in the various older or more recent Free Churches and revivalist movements.

Just as the real ecclesia is constantly evolving, so the ecclesiology of the ecclesia evolves too. The possibly rather confusing and sketchy list of historical details given above, which are intended to draw in, or rather to open up, the historical perspectives of ecclesiology, may look as though they refer to a vast series of distinct and atomized images of the Church. But in reality they are all part of the history of the real Church and its theology, from the beginnings of the Church down to the present day. Does this series of events, this process, mark a progression or a retrogression, or simply a movement of ebb and flow? Is its movement that of the pendulum, is it a circle or a spiral? No historical and philosophical pattern can adequately define this series of events, which has always been progression and retrogression at one and the same time; events have not come in waves of ebb and flow, but have always been different. There has always been a dialectical pendulum movement, and at the same time a circular return to the origins of the Church and a theologically orientated advance towards a future position; there have always been changing variations on a theme, using all kinds of different modulations and counterpoint—and yet the theme has remained constant, holding everything together even at times when it has been almost unrecognizable. This is what we mean when we say that ecclesiology is essentially historical, given that the ecclesia itself is made of and for men who exist at a particular time in a particular environment, in the unrepeatable present of their constantly changing world. The "essential nature" of the Church is not to be found in some unchanging Platonic heaven of ideas, but only in the *history* of the Church. The real Church not only has a history, it exists by having a history. There is no "doctrine" of the Church in the sense of an unalterable metaphysical and ontological system, but only one which is historically conditioned, within the framework of the history of the Church, its dogmas and its theology.

While we may be able to recognize certain ecclesiological types and styles, ecclesiology is always conditioned anew by history; this is a basic fact from which there is no dispensation. It is not just that every theologian sees the Church in a different perspective, from a different personal point of view. More important, since there are such things as supra-individual contingencies, is the fact that ecclesiology belongs to the world to which the Church also belongs. This means that ecclesiology is written in various specific places at specific points in history, in a constantly changing language and a constantly changing intellectual climate, in a changing variety of historical situations affecting the world and the Church alike. Ecclesiology is a response and a call to constantly changing historical situations. This requires repeated and determined attempts to mould, form and differentiate in freedom, unless ecclesiologists give up in despair at each new situation, close their eyes to them and simply drift. The Church's doctrine of the Church, like the Church itself, is necessarily subject to continual change and must constantly be undertaken anew.

It is not easy to find the middle way between the unthinking conservation of a *dead* past, an attitude which is unconcerned about the new demands of a new present, and the careless rejection of the *living* past, an attitude which is all too concerned with the transitory novelties of the present. An ecclesiology which takes a *traditionalist* view, which sees itself as something permanent and unchanged from the beginning of time and uncritically allows itself to be enslaved by a particular age or culture now past, misunderstands what historicity is. Historicity is also misrepresented by an ecclesiology which, taking a *modernist* view, adapts itself and becomes enslaved by the present age or culture, and so abandons itself equally uncritically to the disasters of total changeability. Ecclesiology, which is the Church's expression of its self-understanding, must not be enslaved by any particular situation, be it past, present or future, any more than the Church. It must not identify itself completely with the programmes and myths, illusions and decisions, images and categories of any particular world or era.

But precisely because it is historical, ecclesiology can and must be influenced by its origin, the origin of the Church. This origin does not simply lie in an historical situation, and still less in a transcendental "principle", fabricated or interpreted philosophically, which supposedly set the history of the Church in motion. Its origin is rather "given", "appointed", "laid down" quite concretely; according to the Church's understanding of faith through the powerful historical action of God himself, acting through Jesus Christ among men and for men and so finally through men. God's salvific act in Jesus Christ is the origin of the Church; but it is more than the starting-point or the first phase of its history, it is something which at any given time determines the whole history of the Church and defines its essential nature. So the real Church can never simply leave its origins behind or ultimately distance itself from them. Those origins determine what is permanently true and constantly valid in the Church, despite all historical forms and changes and all individual contingencies. The nature of the Church is not just given to it, it is entrusted to it. Loyalty to its original nature is something the Church must preserve through all the changing history of that world for the sake of which the Church exists. But it can only do that through change (*aggiornamento*), not through immobility (*immobilismo*); it must commit itself to each new day (*giorno*) afresh, accept the changes and transformations of history and human life, and constantly be willing to reform, to renew, to rethink.

3. THE CHANGING IMAGE OF THE CHURCH IN THE NEW TESTAMENT

The Church must constantly reflect upon its real existence in the present with reference to its origins in the past, in order to assure its existence in the future. It stands or falls by its links with its origins in Jesus Christ and its message; it remains permanently dependent, for the ground of its existence, on God's saving act in Jesus Christ, which is valid for all time and so also in the present. It must never cease to reflect upon those origins. Specifically, it must meditate on the original testimony of faith, which remains a constant point of reference for the Church in any century. This original testimony is unique, incomparable and unrepeatable and as such it is actively obligatory, binding and normative for the Church in all ages. The original witness, the original message, is given to us in the writings of the Old and New Testaments. These are the writings which the community of the Church itself, in a complex process lasting several centuries, has come to recognize officially as the original, valid and true witness to God's saving activity for mankind in Christ Jesus.

(*a*) The Church has obediently professed the word which was given to it, by collecting the New Testament writings, relating them to the Old Testament and excluding fanciful speculations and exaggerations. The result is the New Testament "canon",[2] a norm, a guideline and a boundary. The canon

---

[2] On the question of the canon and "early Catholicism", cf. Hans Küng, "'Early Catholicism' in the NT as a problem in controversial theology", in *The Living Church*, London, pp. 233–293, and in *The Council in Action*, New York, 1963, pp. 159–195, and the literature listed there, especially W. G. Kümmel, E. Käsemann,

represents a *via media*. The Church did not, like Marcion and some present-day Protestant theologians, want to narrow down the choice by radical reduction until only the true "evangelium" was left; nor, like the gnostics and some present-day Catholic theologians, did it want to make its choice as wide as possible, including apocryphal writings and "traditions". The New Testament canon was not selected on the basis of an *a priori* principle, but pragmatically; the living faith of the Christian communities was called upon to "discern spirits".

The Church listened in faith to the word of God, as given definitively by Jesus Christ in fulfilment of the old covenant, and as repeated through the human words of these New Testament writings. The fact that these human words are the original testimony of God's word of revelation is the reason why they are incomparable and unrepeatable, uniquely binding and actively obligatory. All other testimony in the tradition of the Church, however profound or sublime, can in essence do nothing more than circle round this original testimony of God's word, interpret, commentate, explain and apply the original message according to constantly changing historical situations. Because of these constantly changing situations facing the Church in its mission, the changing questions, problems and demands of everyday life, this original message is constantly plumbed for new depths. All commentaries and interpretations, all explanations and applications must always be measured against and legitimized by the message contained in Holy Scripture with its original force, concentrated actuality, and supreme relevance. Sacred Scripture is thus the *norma normans* of the Church's tradition, and tradition must be seen as the *norma normata*.

Even the original testimonies, however, did not simply fall from heaven, are not simply supra-temporal divine documents. Nor are they—as was the hellenistic Jewish view—the writings of ecstatics filled with a divine madness which ex-

---

H. Braun, H. Diem, H. Conzelmann, W. Marxsen, F. Mussner, P. Vielhauer, K. H. Schelkle. On recent writings and problems in the field, cf. also N. Appel, *Kanon und Kirche. Die Kanonkrise im heutigen Protestantismus als kontroverstheologisches Problem,* Paderborn 1964.

cludes all individuality and eccentricity, nor yet—as in the view of early Christian theologians—the writings of instruments, who simply transcribed, like secretaries, at the dictation of the Spirit. They are not men who are almost unreal in their persons and historical situation, but real men in all their humanity, historicity and fallibility, who bear witness to God's word in language that is often hesitant and in concepts that are often imprecise. Therefore, given that God's word can be proclaimed in human language, these testimonies are not sublime or above history, but are fundamentally historical testimonies. While Sacred Scripture is theologically normative for the believing Church, it has also, especially for the student of the Church, an historical and literary character: in this sense the Bible is the monument of a past era, a collection of ancient religious documents, which are subject to exegesis, to literary and form criticism, to the study of sources, ideas and themes, to all those disciplines which are a prerequisite of competent criticism.

For ecclesiology this means that the history of the Church, and also the history of the Church's self-understanding, began not *after* but *in* the New Testament, which itself cannot be understood without the Old Testament. The New Testament writings therefore give us more than just the antecedents and the founding of the history of the Church and of ecclesiology; they give us the first decisive phases of the by no means straightforward, indeed complex, history of the Church and its self-understanding. Different images of the Church arise not only after New Testament times, but in the New Testament itself. Indeed it is possible to say that the different emphases and perspectives, tensions and contrasts, which we can see in the ecclesiology of subsequent centuries, reflect to a very large extent the different emphases and perspectives, tensions and contrasts in the New Testament itself. This is due not simply to the individuality of the different writers and the traditions they drew on, but also their different theological attitudes and those of the communities they were part of, as well as the different missionary situations for which the writings were intended. This is something of which we have only a very fragmentary knowledge, especially since many New Testament writings are occasional and conversational in character and very much conditioned by their situation. Any development takes place along several lines with different traditions, and in no sense does the last writing offer an evolved and systematically reasoned ecclesiology.[3]

Within the New Testament there are so many different testimonies as there are witnesses and hearers of the testimonies. There are significant differences between the image of the Church which is adumbrated in Matthew and that in Luke, between the image of the Church in the gospel of St John and that in Ephesians and Colossians, between the image of the Church in Paul's four great epistles, which with the epistles to the Thessalonians are the oldest Christian documents, and that in the pastoral epistles which are among the latest writings in the New Testament canon. There is no doubt that

[3] On New Testament ecclesiology in general, cf. recent theologies of the NT (J. Bonsirven, R. Bultmann, M. Meinertz, E. Stauffer) and articles in LThK (R. Schnackenburg), RGG (K. Stendahl), ELK (N. A. Dahl), HTG (J. Schmid), also those in the DBS (A. Médebielle), in the *Bibellexikon* (W. Grossouw), in the *Bibeltheologisches Wörterbuch* (V. Warnach), in the *Vocabulaire Biblique* (P. H. Menoud) and in ThW (K. L. Schmidt). Cf. in particular two research reports; for the older literature O. Linton, *Das Problem der Urkirche in der neueren Forschung*, Uppsala 1932, and for subsequent research F. M. Braun, *Neues Licht auf die Kirche*, Einsiedeln–Cologne 1946. The following recent monographs are of importance: F. J. Leenhardt, *Etudes sur l'Eglise dans le NT*, Geneva 1940; N. A. Dahl, *Das Volk Gottes. Eine Untersuchung zum Kirchenbewusstsein des Urchristentums*, Oslo 1941; O. Michel, *Das Zeugnis des NT von der Gemeinde*, Göttingen 1941; George Johnston, *The Doctrine of the Church in the NT*, Cambridge 1943; W. Robinson, *The Biblical Doctrine of the Church*, St Louis 1948; Eduard Schweizer, *Church Order in the NT*, London–Naperville, Illinois 1961 (= Studies in Biblical Theology, no. 32); A. Oepke, *Das neue Gottesvolk in Schrifttum, Schauspiel, bildender Kunst und Weltgestaltung*, Gutersloh 1950; J. L. Leuba, *L'institution et l'événement*, Neuchâtel–Paris 1950; G. E. H. Aulen *et al.*, *Ein Buch von der Kirche*, Göttingen 1951; L. G. Champion, *The Church of the NT*, London 1951; H. Schlier, *Die Zeit der Kirche*, 4th edn, Freiburg 1966; A. T. S. Nygren, *Christ and His Church*, London 1957, Philadelphia 1956; P. S. Minear, *Images of the Church in the NT*, Philadelphia 1960; K. H. Schelkle, *Die Gemeinde von Qumran und die Kirche des NT*, Dusseldorf 1960; R. Schnackenburg, *The Church in the New Testament*, London and New York 1965; L. Cerfaux, *The Church in the Theology of St Paul*, London and New York 1959.

those images of the Church which throughout the centuries have been charismatic in character (whether of visionaries, reformers or Catholics) can appeal more to the great Pauline epistles, while those images of the Church in which office takes precedence (whether in the Catholic, Greek Orthodox, or Anglican sense) can lean more on the Acts and the Pastoral letters. Nor is there any doubt that the divergences between Pauline ecclesiology and that of the later Luke present one of the most difficult ecclesiological problems.

It is of course all too easy to play off one against the other, by contrasting the image of the Church in the two letters to the Corinthians, which are older even than the gospels we possess today, and that of the letters to Titus and Timothy, which belong to a much later stage of development, even though they claim Pauline authorship; this can be seen from the importance they give to the Spirit in the Church, to charism, to office and ordination, to preaching the word, etc. It is therefore very easy to disassociate the different images of the Church in the New Testament by simply gathering together different ecclesiological data and hypercritically setting them down side by side where there are points of conflict, without finding in ecclesiology a deeper unity in the context of the writings as a whole. In fact all of them aim to give a positive account of Christ and his Gospel, all in their different ways and according to their different situations seek to further the cause of Christ and to preach Christ, all have their focus, their common united point of contact in the saving event brought by Christ. On the other hand it is pointless to go to the other extreme, as Catholic theology often does, whether out of uncomplicated naïvety or out of the lethargy induced by systematic thinking; this way is to harmonize artificially the different New Testament images of the Church, by keeping to the apparently smooth surface of the texts instead of recognizing the contrasts that exist and probing seriously to the bottom of them. The whole art of the exegete consists in being able to make out, through the many voices of the witnesses, their unanimous testimony to Jesus Christ and his community, and to find that unanimity only through the multiplicity of the witnesses; he must be able to recognize in the many words the one Word, and the one Word only in the many words.

Only if we take the New Testament as a *whole* with *all* its writings as the positive witness of the Gospel of Jesus Christ, can we avoid the temptation to dissociate the contradictory ecclesiological statements of the New Testament, to "purify" the New Testament message and to make a selection, a *hairesis,* all of which is an attack on the unity of Scripture and of the Church. The reverse is also true. Only if we take the New Testament as a whole, with all its divergences and nuances, can we avoid the temptation to harmonize the conflicting ecclesiological statements of the New Testament, to level down its message and produce schematization and uniformity, all of which is an attack on the complexity of Scripture and of the Church. What is needed is not dissociation, but a discriminating study in depth; not harmonization but an outline which allows for variations. Ecclesiological study of the New Testament, in other words, needs, and it is no easy task, to combine catholicity, a breadth and awareness of tensions, with evangelical concentration. The "Catholic" approach will be able, like the early Church which laid down a single canon for the Church of later ages, to hear even in the secondary testimonies of the New Testament canon the authentic Gospel of Jesus Christ; the "evangelical" approach will refuse to attach more importance to secondary New Testament testimonies than to primary ones, and will avoid making what is peripheral the centre of the Gospel, and yet will be able to interpret the secondary sources in terms of the primary ones, and peripheral matter in terms of the centre. Here we must take into account three different kinds of originality, distinguishing them and yet combining them; that of chronology (I Corinthians is earlier than Ephesians), that of authenticity (I Corinthians is genuinely Pauline, Titus probably not) and that of relevance (I Corinthians is in content nearer to the Gospel of Jesus himself than James). The use of the word "gospel" in the New Testament itself, both by the synoptics and by Paul, indicates the right approach. On the one hand the word "gospel" is not restricted to a particular doctrine (as it were, the justification of the sinner), but is fundamentally open; on the other hand, the word "gospel" in the New Testament is indissolubly linked to the saving event in Jesus Christ. It was not the New Testament writers, but Marcion who first understood the concept in a limited sense. It is certainly possible to look impartially for a "centre" in Scripture, by working exegetically from the New Testament texts rather than dogmatically from established preconceptions. It is of course easier to establish such a centre in negative terms rather than in positive terms, to establish that certain things at any rate are not the heart of Scripture, are peripheral rather than central; but this in itself can be a gain. To establish a positive centre is more difficult because of the basic diversity of the individual New Testament writings. Yet, despite the differences, a discriminating and sensitive interpretation will be able to make out the decisive common links and a fundamental inner coherence between, for example, the idea of the beginning of the eschatological reign of God in Jesus Christ, which is central to the preaching of the synoptics, and the Pauline concept of the justification of the sinner through the grace of faith alone.

(*b*) Modern historical-critical method provides the theologian of today with a scholarly instrument for investigating the origins of the Church which an earlier generation of theologians did not possess.[4] Only with methodical historical thinking has it become possible to gain, to a limited extent at least, an overall view of the changes in the Church and in theology since New Testament times, of the shifts in perspective and emphasis, the improvements and deteriorations, the gains and losses. In addition, methodical historical thinking has for the first time made it possible for us to gain an insight into the extremely important changes which were taking place while the New Testament was being written (approximately between A.D. 50 and 150) and to some extent into the changes

---

[4] Bibliographies on biblical hermeneutics are given in the RGG article on hermeneutics (G. Ebeling) and the LThK article on biblical hermeneutics (A. Bea). For the development of Church doctrine, cf. especially the encyclical of Pius XII *Divino afflante spiritu* (1943); the *Instructio de historica evangeliorum veritate* of the Papal Commission on the Bible, 21.4.1964 (cf. the commentary by J. A. Fitzmyer in *Stuttgarter Bibelstudien* I, 1965) and the decree *De Revelatione* promulgated by Vatican II, 1965.

of the preceding years (from A.D. 30 to 50), to say nothing of the changes which took place during the two or three thousand years of Old Testament tradition.

Of course, the historical-critical method cannot help either the Church or individual Christians in their truly existential meditation on the word of God in Scripture, on the Gospel of Jesus Christ; at best such a method can assist and stimulate us. Our meditation must grow through God's grace from the basic roots of our Christian existence and of the Christian community, from their faith and love. But it is surely of immeasurable value for ecclesiology and thus also for the life and teaching of the Church that biblical scholarship has untiringly and painstakingly succeeded in performing, for the New Testament as well, such enormous labours, uncompleted and uncompletable though they are.

Despite the lack of original manuscripts and the fact that in many cases authentic readings were not fixed until a late date, *textual criticism* has succeeded in establishing, with the greatest possible certainty and exactitude, the original wording of biblical writings in the earliest form available to us. This has been done by external and internal forms of criticism, by taking linguistic and contextual considerations into account, and by drawing on textual history. *Literary criticism* has examined the literary integrity of the writings, elucidated differences in the legal, social and religious conditions which form the background to the writings, differences in language, chronology and in historical purpose, differences in ethical and theological conceptions. It has distinguished between oral and written traditions as sources of the writings and sorted out possible original material from later additions. It has established the age, origin, intended recipients and literary peculiarities of the writings; it has used the techniques of literary analysis to contrast them with uncanonical and contemporary Jewish and hellenistic literature, and so to determine their individuality. *Form criticism* has examined the question of their place in the lives of the community and of the individual. It has examined the genres of the writings, the framework of these small literary units, their original form, and tried to determine anew their historical reliability and the content of tradition. *Source criticism* has attempted to illuminate the pre-literary process. By analysing the oldest hymns, liturgical fragments, legal decrees, etc., and relating them to worship, preaching and catechesis, it has tried to trace the decisive origins of the Church and the first stage of its development. The vast amount of critical work which has been achieved along these lines, in the last 150 years in particular, and which has included the study of the history of ideas and themes, has always had its constructive side and its positive application. All serious biblical criticism leads automatically to hermeneutics, exegesis and biblical theology, in which the positive value of Scripture is brought out book for book, sentence for sentence, word for word, by all available means and in which great efforts are made to present these discoveries in a way comprehensible to the Church of today.

There are bound to be difficulties in all this. And it is in historical-critical research particularly—not only in exegesis, but also in the history of theology, of dogma and of the Church—that difficulties often assume such gigantic proportions, leaving us with the anxious feeling that we have lost our way in a jungle of problems, or are about to sink without trace in the changeability of everything historical. This much, however, is clear from the exciting story of modern exegesis and historical approach: what at first looks like wanton destruction will always, sooner or later, reveal its constructive potential. Wrong-headed or tendentious criticism has always been overcome by what is genuine and constructive. It is the greatest problems which have needed the greatest efforts to surmount them and have achieved the most fruitful results. Fear, and the fear of history in particular, has proved a poor counsellor in ecclesiology as elsewhere. Courage on the other hand, and particularly courage in historical thinking, has always proved of great value in the long run, even though it may have paid poor dividends at first. In ecclesiology courage means a respect for facts, and the determination to build theories on the basis of facts alone; but this honest courage must be combined with patience, a considered and thoughtful patience which recognizes that only the minutest problems can be settled in a day, and that none can be solved with a sledgehammer. We must realize that the theologian learns by his mistakes and that if he is prevented from making any, he is prevented from constructive thinking; that it takes time not only to find the truth but also for the truth to take effect in the Church generally, in the face of innumerable obstacles, of the prejudices and pretexts of an *opinio communis* which masquerades as genuine doctrine.[5]

(*c*) The Christian in the Church, even if he is an historian, does not approach the Bible without preconceptions. He cannot regard the New Testament simply as the literary document of a vanished era. For him, whether it is giving doctrine, commandments or simply history, it is *kerygma,* a message with force and relevance for the present day, God's call to contemporary man. Let us examine the implications of this.

We may say that the New Testament provides "doctrine". But the Church cannot regard it simply as a theoretical textbook in which truths about God and man's salvation in Christ, which are generally valid for its doctrine, have been "deposited". As against such doctrinalist misconceptions, it is clear that for the Church the New Testament is a proclamation, a preaching of God's saving act in Christ, which calls in turn for the Church to preach the message and to realize it in faith today. We may say that the New Testament provides "commandments". But it is far from being a practical book of laws, giving the Church a detailed moral, legal and spiritual code with rigid rules and calling on men to keep these rules in order to achieve self-justification by their own efforts. As against such moralistic misconceptions, it is clear that for the Church the New Testament is God's Gospel which sets us free from the law. It promises and proffers to all who believe and who renounce their own worth before God the free gift of God: the forgiveness of sins and a new righteousness. It proclaims how man is liberated to obedience to God's will through a life of love, which is the fulfilment of the law. We may say that the New Testament provides "history". But the New Testament for the Church is not simply the history book of salvation history, in which can be found a neutral, objective, chronological account of that history, together with appropriate historical comments on its continuing development. As against all such historical misconception, it is clear that

[5] On the problems of a critical theology, cf. Hans Küng, *The Theologian and the Church,* London 1965 (= Theological Meditations I)—*Freedom Today,* New York 1966, Chap. 3.

for the Church the New Testament is rather the preaching of a message, the accounts of which are always conditioned by theology. It tells of a self-revealing and merciful God who comes to meet us, who has acted once and for all in human history in Jesus Christ, and who expects from man not just an intellectual acquiescence to various historical facts but an existential decision of faith before God and for God.

In each case, then, we are concerned with the word of God. This word is testified to and made present in its full authority by human words, which themselves remain all along the line temporal and historically conditioned. The full import of what it has to say is only revealed to those who believe. It is not simply a written word which therefore belongs to the past; it is a word which always has to be preached and is therefore always actual. It is the living word of the Gospel, the saving message of God's love at work first in the Old Testament and then definitively in Jesus Christ, through his death and resurrection as the eschatological act of salvation.

From this it is very clear why, through all the changes of the times and the changes of the Church, we should reflect on the real Church of the New Testament, which was itself already in a state of change and already full of differences and variations. Not out of deference to a romantic ecclesiological love of the past, an attitude which automatically praises what is more ancient as being more perfect and sees the time of the primitive Church as the golden age of the Church. Such reflection is rather the grave duty of a theology which thinks historically and which, precisely avoiding the temptation of concentrating on any one age, even the earliest, concerns itself with the living eschatological word of God himself, the Gospel of Jesus Christ. It is this Gospel from which the Church of Jesus Christ took its origin and from which in its daily life the Church continues to take its origin. This is an attitude from which no Christian theology can possibly dispense itself.

To reflect on the New Testament, therefore, does not mean that we should try unhistorically to return to the Church's origins or try to imitate the New Testament community, as the Jewish Christians of the second century or the Anabaptists of the sixteenth century tried to do. The New Testament Church is not a model which we can follow slavishly without any regard to the lapse of time and our constantly changing situation. Nor is the recitation or reproduction of Jesus' words by itself of any effect. The letter kills, it is the spirit that gives life—in ecclesiology too. If the Church wants to remain true to its nature, it cannot simply preserve its past. As an historical Church it must be prepared to change in order to fulfil its essential mission in a world which is constantly changing, which always lives in the present, not the past.

On the other hand, reflection upon the Church of the New Testament will lead us to conclude that not all the subsequent developments in the Church can be authorized by its origins; there have been errors and false developments in its history. The New Testament message, as the original testimony, is the highest court to which appeal must be made in all the changes of history. It is the essential norm against which the Church of every age has to measure itself. The New Testament Church, which, beginning with its origins in Jesus Christ, is already the Church in the fullness of its nature, is therefore the original design; we cannot copy it today, but we can and must translate it into modern terms. The Church of the New Testament alone can show us what that original design was.

II. DISTORTIONS OF THE IMAGE OF THE CHURCH

1. THE CHURCH AS THE OBJECT OF ADMIRATION AND CRITICISM; THE NATURE AND "UN-NATURE" OF THE CHURCH

(a) By way of an introduction to this problem, it may be worth citing at length some words of Macaulay:

"There is not and there never was on this earth, a work of human policy so well deserving of examination as the Roman Catholic Church. The history of that Church joins together the two great ages of human civilization. No other institution is left standing which carries the mind back to the times when the smoke of sacrifice rose from the Pantheon, and when camelopards and tigers bounded in the Flavian amphitheatre. The proudest royal houses are but of yesterday, when compared with the line of the Supreme Pontiffs. That line we trace back in an unbroken series, from the Pope who crowned Napoleon in the nineteenth century to the Pope who crowned Pepin in the eighth; and far beyond the time of Pepin the august dynasty extends, till it is lost in the twilight of fable. The republic of Venice came next in antiquity. But the republic of Venice was modern when compared with the Papacy; and the republic of Venice is gone, and the Papacy remains. The Papacy remains, not in decay, not a mere antique, but full of life and youthful vigour. The Catholic Church is still sending forth to the farthest ends of the world missionaries as zealous as those who landed in Kent with Augustine, and still confronting hostile kings with the same spirit with which she confronted Attila. . . . Nor do we see any sign which indicates that the term of her long dominion is approaching. She saw the commencement of all the governments and of all the ecclesiastical establishments that now exist in the world; and we feel no assurance that she is not destined to see the end of them all. She was great and respected before the Saxon had set foot in Britain, before the Frank had passed the Rhine, when Grecian eloquence still flourished at Antioch, when idols were still worshipped in the temple of Mecca. And she may still exist in undiminished vigour when some traveller from New Zealand shall, in the midst of a vast solitude, take his stand on a broken arch of London Bridge to sketch the ruins of St Paul's."[6]

Have we not here the *real* Church? Macaulay's impressive rhetoric describes what many before him felt and what many have echoed since: admiration, whether strident or subdued, enthusiastic or hesitant. What do they admire? A uniquely continuous and consistent history, the blend of venerable age and vigorous youth, a powerful organization, sprung from humble roots, spread throughout the world, with hundreds of millions of adherents and a strictly ordered hierarchy, a cult rich in tradition and noble in its solemnity, a profound system of doctrine theology, the comprehensive cultural achievement, in the secular sphere, of building up and moulding the history of Christian Europe, modern social teaching. But Macaulay

[6] Taken from Macaulay's essay on L. von Ranke's *History of the Popes.*

and many others have admired the Catholic Church without wishing to be a part of it. It is possible to admire the Catholic Church without being a Catholic. And it is perhaps just as possible to be a Catholic without admiring it. At all events this admiration, which can be found both inside and outside the Catholic Church, is in no way decisive for a person's relationship to the Church. It is a neutral feeling, a psychological and sociological phenomenon without any essential relevance to the Christian faith, which occurs equally with reference to other historical institutions. In the same way one can admire the British Commonwealth, its impressive history, politics, organization and cultural achievements without being British. Admiration imposes no obligations; one can admire things without feeling that they are in any way binding on one's personal existence. In the same way, one can visit an imposing foreign church, walk round it and marvel at it with the clear consciousness that, while it is undeniably a great church, one does not belong to it; for all kinds of different reasons, it is not and never could be one's home.

This kind of admiration is basically directed towards a façade. The façade is a part of the Church and cannot be denied, but it is not the essence of the Church. The attitude one has towards this façade is unimportant: the Catholic Church would still be the Catholic Church if it had little or nothing to show of this admirable history and organization, art and scholarship, cultural achievement and cultic splendour. For centuries it was in fact without it and may, who knows, have to be without it again. Anyone who only sees this, does not penetrate beyond the superficial level—real though this is—to the true inner nature of the Church. To see this inner nature, it is not enough to be an historian or student of cultures, an aesthete, a sociologist or a politician. The inner nature within the outer structure can only be seen by the eye of the believing Christian.

(*b*) Sometimes this much admired exterior can, however, give scandal. It does not strike everyone as a portal which beckons one into the interior. In fact many people maintain that they find it an enormous barrier which prohibits any glimpse of an inner life. It is possible to look at the history of the Catholic Church in a positive light, as we have seen. But there are many who see it in a negative one: in all the Church's forming and controlling of history, they see only its seduction by history and capitulation to it; in all its influential organization the machinery of power operating with worldly means; in the serried ranks of the hierarchy an administrative authority avid for pomp and power; in the splendours of its cult a superficial ritualism rooted in the medieval-baroque tradition and foreign to the Gospel; in the clear, unified doctrinal system, a rigidly authoritarian scholastic theology, manipulating empty philosophical concepts, both unhistorical and unbiblical; in its cultural achievements in the West, its secularization and desertion of its true mission. . . . For them, this is what the Church is *really* like.

It should scarcely be necessary to remind those who admire the Church's wisdom, power and achievements, its splendour, influence and prestige, of the persecutions of the Jews and the crusades, the trials of heretics and burnings of witches, of ecclesiastical colonialism and "wars of religion", of the false condemnation of men and ideas, of the Church's frequent failures in the problems of slavery and war and in social questions, in its identification with certain systems of society, government and thought. Whatever its superficial brilliance, how can one overlook all these all-too-human features, all the cruelty, fear and narrowness, all the laziness, cowardice and mediocrity, all the lack of love? What is it worth, all that Macaulay and so many others praised, against all the things indicted by Kierkegaard and Dostoievsky in Macaulay's century, and in our own century by Karl Barth and Dietrich Bonhoeffer, Georges Bernanos and Reinhold Schneider, Heinrich Böll, Carl Amery and Rolf Hochhuth? How much they have to reproach the Church with, scientists and doctors, psychologists and sociologists, journalists and politicians, workers and intellectuals, practising Catholics and lapsed, young and old, men and women: with poor preaching, inadequate forms of worship, externalized piety, soulless traditions, authoritarian dogmatism mummified in its correctness, casuistic morality divorced from life, opportunism and intolerance, the legalism and self-aggrandizement of ecclesiastical functionaries at all levels, the lack of creative people in the Church. . . .

A few words about apologetics may not be out of place here. It is undeniable that many of the accusations directed against the Church are ignorant, exaggerated, biased, and

unjust, indeed they are often simply false or even malicious.
In all such cases an answer is appropriate: apology, defence
and justification are in order. But who can deny on the other
hand that most of the accusations directed against the Church
are justified, well-founded, in fact true? No apologia can answer these. What then can the Christian in the Church say to
the man who in all seriousness gives his reasons for not
belonging or no longer belonging to the Church, and explains
why he keeps his distance from it, perhaps not without sympathy, perhaps with feelings of indifference and impartiality,
perhaps in angry protest or even with hatred? And what can
this Christian in the Church say to himself, if he cannot prevent the doubt—an honest doubt—arising in his own mind, as
to whether his Church is more than just a religious society or
pious community, more than any other society or institution
formed to satisfy people's religious needs?

The Church can be the object of admiration and equally
well of scandal, or at any rate of criticism, whether disap-
pointed or disgruntled, sad or bitter. Just as the admiration
has a basis, so has the criticism. Just as one can admire the
Church without belonging to it, so one can criticize it without
leaving it. Like admiration, the criticism we find both inside
and outside the Church is not decisive for a person's attitude
towards the Church. It too is a neutral psychological and sociological phenomenon without real relevance to the Christian
faith and equally possible in the context of other historical institutions. Similarly one can criticize a State, its weaknesses
and failures, its history, its constitution and politics, and yet
belong to it and choose to belong to it.

(*c*) Criticism, like admiration, is often directed towards a
mere façade, however real. It attacks an external aspect of the
Church which may be part of its particular historical attributes but does not belong to its permanent nature. But there is
another factor here, something which is also a hidden objection to superficial admiration. The reality of the Church cannot adequately be described in terms of "essential nature"
and "forms".[7] The negative aspects which provoke criticism

[7] Cf. A I, 1.

and which superficial admiration overlooks or ignores are not simply the product of the historical "form" of the Church, which may be something completely positive. Nor are these negative aspects the product of the changing yet constant positive "nature" of the Church. They are rather the expression of the Church's evil "un-nature"; it is here, as real and unreal as always, that evil finds an outlet in the Church. The "unnatural" aspects of the Church are in conflict with the true nature of the Church, while depending on the latter for their existence. They represent the illegitimate as opposed to the legitimate side of the Church, the perversion of its true nature. They arise, as we shall see in more detail later, not from the holy will of God, but from the failings of the men who make up the Church. In all its historical forms the true nature of the Church is accompanied, like a dark shadow, by its "un-nature"; the two are inseparable.

Not that the discovery of an "un-nature" in this Church made up of human beings can serve as an excuse for all the dark corners of the Church's history. It should rather serve as a reminder to admirers and critics alike that this dark and unnatural side of the Church is something that we should reckon with from the start. Since we are dealing with a Church composed of men, it should surprise neither admirers nor critics. It is impossible to discern the permanent nature of the Church, which survives all changes, except through the changing historical forms of the Church; and in the same way it is impossible to discern the positive nature of the Church except through its negative "un-nature". Permanent nature and changing forms are inextricably interwoven; and in the same way good and evil, positive and negative, true nature and "un-nature" in the Church are interdependent things which cannot ultimately be worked out by human calculations. Even the most essential things can change. Even the essentials of the Church's true nature are subject to the effects of "un-nature". Sin is possible even in the area of the most holy. All ecclesiology must take as one of its bases, not merely the historicity of the Church, but the fact that the Church is historically affected by evil; and this fact must be accepted from the start without false apologetics and always taken into account. For this reason ecclesiology can never simply take the *status quo* of the Church as its yardstick, still less seek to justify it. On the contrary, taking once again the original message, the Gospel, as its starting-point, it will do all it can to make critical evaluations, as a foundation for the reforms and renewal which the Church will always need.

Only an abstract and idealistic ecclesiology, which is describing an ideal rather than the real Church, could overlook the "un-nature" of the Church. At best such an ecclesiology might attract unthinking admirers, but it would fail to move, perhaps might even repulse, a thoughtful critic. Certainly it could never be part of a sober, realistic and scholarly theology, which must aim to see the Church as it really is: its "nature" together with its historical "form" and at the same time its "nature" together with its "un-nature". Only a realistic and concrete view of the Church, as opposed to an idealistic and abstract one, will enable us to point out to the critic who only sees the negative side of the Church that the faults, whether real or imagined, do not touch what is most essential and profound in the Church. A man's shadow may be real but it is not the man himself. To attack the "un-nature" of the Church is to attack the real Church but not its real nature.

The negative critic, whether he is accurate or inaccurate, just or unjust, well-meaning or malicious, will not be able to see deeply enough to distinguish what is genuine from all the ungenuine features and divide the true nature from the false. He will be no more able than the superficial admirer of the Church to grasp the vital fundamental dimensions of the Church. Only the believing Christian can do that.[8]

[8] On systematic ecclesiology in general, cf. the recent handbooks of fundamental theology and dogmatics (P. Althaus, K. Barth, E. Brunner, F. Buri, H. Diem, W. Elert, Heppe–Bizer, A. Lang, L. Ott, R. Prenter, C. H. Ratschow, J. Salaverri, M. Schmaus, F. A. Sullivan, P. Tillich, W. Trillhaas, O. Weber, T. Zapalena) and the articles in LThK (J. Ratzinger, K. E. Skydsgaard), RGG (R. Prenter), EKL (J. Koukouzis, K. G. Steck, G. F. Nuttall), HTG (H. Fries, H. Küng), DTC (E. Dublanchy), Cath. (M. J. Le Guillou), and ODCC. The following recent monographs are important: R. Grosche, *Pilgernde Kirche,* Freiburg 1938; H. de Lubac, *Catholicism* (translated from 4th edn.), London–New York

2. THE CHURCH AS THE OBJECT OF FAITH

Admirers and critics of the Church alike must be aware that the men who, in a real sense, make up the Church are different from their fellows in one vital respect: they *believe*. They declare themselves to be a *fellowship of believers*. What they believe and hope for themselves, they want to believe and hope for others too. But those who, whether praising or blaming them, overlook the fact that they are a fellowship of

1950; Y. Congar, *The Mystery of the Church*, London–Baltimore 1960; K. D. Mackenzie, *The Way of the Church*, London 1945; Leclercq, *La vie du Christ dans son Eglise*, Paris 1947; G. Wehrung, *Kirche nach evangelischem Verständnis*, Gutersloh 1947; P. Broutin, *Mysterium Ecclesiae*, Paris 1947; G. Florowsky *et al.*, *La sainte Eglise universelle*, Neuchâtel–Paris 1948; H. Lutze, *Das Mysterium der Kirche Christi*, Gutersloh 1948; Y. de Montcheuil, *Aspects de l'Eglise*, Paris 1949; E. Brunner, *The Misunderstanding of the Church*, London 1952–Philadelphia 1953; R. N. Flew, *The Nature of the Church*, London 1952; L. Kosters, *The Church: Its Divine authority*, London 1938; L. Newbigin, *The Household of God*, 2nd edn., London 1964–New York 1954; H. de Lubac, *The Splendour of the Church*, London–New York 1955; O. Semmelroth, *Church and Sacrament*, Notre Dame 1965; B. Giertz, *Die Kirche Jesu Christi*, Göttingen 1954; C. Journet, *The Church of the Word Incarnate*, London–New York 1955; idem, *Théologie de l'Eglise*, Paris 1957; H. Fries, *Kirche als Ereignis*, Dusseldorf 1958; E. Kinder, *Der evangelische Glaube und die Kirche*, Berlin 1958; C. Welch, *The Reality of the Church*, New York 1958; O. Semmelroth, *Ich glaube an die Kirche*, Dusseldorf 1959; D. Bonhoeffer, *Sanctorum Communio* (translated from 3rd edn.), London 1963– *Communion of Saints*, New York 1964; H. U. von Balthasar, *Church and World*, New York 1967; H. Küng, *Structures of the Church*, London 1965–Camden, New Jersey 1963; P. Touilleux, *Réflexion sur le Mystère de l'Eglise*, Tournai 1962; B. C. Butler, *The Idea of the Church*, London–Baltimore 1962; Y. Congar, *Sainte Eglise. Etudes et approches ecclésiologiques*, Paris 1963; A. Hastings, *One and Apostolic*, London–New York 1963; H. Fries, *Aspects of the Church*, Dublin and Melbourne 1965–Westminster 1966; P. Glorieux, *Nature et mission de l'Eglise*, Tournai 1963; G. Wingren, *Gospel and Church*, Edinburgh–London 1964–Philadelphia 1965; A. Winklhofer, *Über die Kirche*, Frankfurt 1963. Two important anthologies: *Mysterium Kirche in der Sicht, der theologischen Disziplinen*, Salzburg 1962, and *De Ecclesia, Beiträge zur Konstitution 'Über die Kirche' des 2. Vatikanischen Konzils*, 2 vols., Freiburg–Frankfurt 1966.

believers, are in their view failing to understand them.[9] Indeed, these believers consider that the Church as the fellowship of believers is misunderstood, or at least that its fundamentals are not fully understood, by those who do not share their belief and their beliefs. The Church cannot be properly judged from outside, from the viewpoint of a neutral observer, but only from within, by those who live in and with the Church. As the Church of faith it calls all men to the faith of the Church.

It is therefore no historical accident that the Church, the ecclesia, was included in the creed, the confession of faith (D 2, 6, 14, 86, etc.); this credal statement was to provide a basis for understanding what the Church is. The Tridentine catechism speaks of the Church, whose "origin, mission and dignity we do not recognize by human reason, but perceive with the eye of faith", as being known "by faith alone" (*"Fide solum intelligimus"*).[10] Do we Christians then believe in the Church? No, that would be to take the Church too seriously; at most we would say this in a very loose sense. It is striking that in general the creeds speak of believing *in* God and *in* the Holy Spirit, but of believing *the* Church (D 2, 6, 86, etc.). Almost invariably in the third article of faith the Church is linked with the Holy Spirit. Particularly revealing is the third baptismal question in the oldest order we possess, the *Traditio apostolica* of Hippolytus of Rome, which dates from about 215 and is considerably older than the so-called Apostles' Creed.[11] Its wording is very precise: "Do you also believe in the Holy Spirit in the holy Church for the resurrection of the body?"[12] According to this, the Christian believes in God and in the Holy Spirit; the Church

[9] For references to the idea of the Church as the *congregatio fidelium* in Church tradition, cf. *Structures,* footnote on pp. 12–13, especially the references to Augustine, Thomas Aquinas and the Tridentine Catechism.

[10] *Catech. Trid.* I, 10, 20 f.

[11] Cf. B. Altaner, *Patrology,* Freiburg–Edinburgh–London 1960, pp. 47–48, 54–56 and the bibliography there.

[12] Cf. P. Nautin, *Je crois à l'Esprit Saint dans la Sainte Eglise pour la résurrection de la Chair, Etude sur l'histoire et la théologie du symbole,* Paris 1947.

is the place where the Spirit is at work; the resurrection of the flesh is the final act of the Spirit.

Hence it is no mere play on words to follow the lead of Augustine[13] in particular and draw a precise distinction[14] between the following: *credere Deum,* I believe that God exists; *credere Deo,* I believe on God's authority; *credere in Deum,* I believe by giving myself utterly to God (cf. Augustine: *credendo in eum ire*) in personal trust and confident self-surrender.

Faith in an ultimate and radical sense cannot properly be distinguished from love. It is a personal activity directed towards a personal recipient. Faith is never, in the final analysis, a matter of adherence to objects, rules, or dogmas, but is the sacrifice and self-giving of one person to another. "What seems to be decisive in any act of faith is the person to whose words approval is given."[15] But radical personal self-giving, something that in each and every case will be unconditional and irrevocable, can only be made to God; only God can be believed, in the fullest and most radical sense of the word. To believe in a man in this absolute and completely unconditional sense would be to make him into an idol; it would be a blasphemy against God, who alone is worthy of totally unconditional self-surrender; it would mean enslavement for the person who made himself an unconditional follower of another mortal and sinful being. The Christian only believes, in this sense of the word, in God and in him whom God has sent. The phrase "to believe in" (πιστεύειν, πίστις εἰς) does not occur in secular Greek usage or in the Septuagint. It is peculiar to the New Testament as a shorthand way of expressing the specifically Christian saving faith in the crucified and risen Christ and is the basis for a relationship with Christ analogous to our relationship with God.[16]

[13] Augustine, e.g. in Jo 29, 6; 48, 3 (CC 36, 287, 413).

[14] Cf. the numerous references in the footnotes to de Lubac, *The Splendour of the Church,* pp. 12–18; particularly important are the works referred to there by T. Camelot and C. Mohrmann.

[15] Thomas Aquinas, *S.th.* II–II, q.11, a.1.; cf. J. Mouroux, *I believe,* London–New York 1959.

[16] Cf. the article "πιστεύω" by R. Bultmann in ThW VI, especially pp. 203 f. and 209–214.

The Christian believes in God and in this sense believes in him alone. Can he then say for instance: "I believe in the holy Catholic Church"? "When we say '*in* the holy Catholic Church', this must be understood as referring to our faith in the Holy Spirit, who sanctifies the Church, and so the meaning is: I believe in the Holy Spirit sanctifying the Church. But it is better and in general more usual to say simply 'the holy Catholic Church'" (Thomas Aquinas).[17]

So for the Christian the Church is primarily there not to be admired nor to be criticized but to be believed. Neither admiration of the Church nor criticism of the Church really matters. What matters is the faith of the Church: that the Church, the communion of the faithful, itself believes (*genitivus subiectivus: ecclesia credens*) and that men believe the Church, rather than in the Church (*genitivus obiectivus: credens ecclesiam*). An admiration of the Church which is not rooted in faith can be of interest to the Christian but is not fundamentally Christian. Criticism of the Church which is not rooted in faith can be worth taking to heart but is not fundamentally Christian. Arising out of his faith an admiration of the Church is possible for the Christian in some circumstances, but it will always be a surprised admiration which sees the Church's "un-nature" and yet trusts in its good nature in spite of it. Arising out of his faith a critique of the Church is in some circumstances possible for the Christian, even necessary. But it will always be a balanced critique which attacks the "un-nature" of the Church and yet takes its good nature into account. Neither admiration nor criticism is absolute, but is essentially fragmentary, "dissolved", positively and negatively, in faith.

The Church as the object of faith: let us try to reach a deeper understanding of this idea by analysing more precisely why we believe *the* Church, rather than *in* the Church.

To say that we do not believe *in* the Church means that the Church is not God. The Church as a fellowship of believers is, in spite of everything positive that can be said about it, neither God nor a god-like being. Of course, the believer is convinced that God works in the Church and in the work of the

---

[17] *S.th.* II–II, q.1, a.9 ad 5; cf. also *Catech. Trid.* I, 10, 22.

Church. But God's work and the Church's are neither identical nor overlapping, there is indeed a fundamental distinction between them. God remains God. His work can never be superseded, made superfluous or redundant, by what he has already effected. The Church, however, is and remains something created. It is therefore not omniscient and omnipotent, not self-sufficient and autonomous, not eternal and sinless. It is not the source of grace and truth, it is not Lord, redeemer and judge, and there can be no question of idolizing it. The Church is the often threatened and endangered fellowship of the faithful and the obedient, which lives from God and for God, which places all its trust in him, which believes in God.

To say that we do not believe *in* the Church means that *we* are the Church. As the fellowship of believers the Church is in no way different from us. It is not a gnostic collective person, whom we can see to be separate from us. *We* are the Church, and we *are* the Church. And if we are the Church, then the Church is a fellowship of those who seek, journey and lose their way, of the helpless, the anguished and the suffering, of sinners and pilgrims. If *we* are the Church, then the Church is a sinful and pilgrim Church, and there can be no question of idealizing it. It is the fellowship of those who hear and believe, who make their pilgrimage through darkness and uncertainty, completely dependent on God's grace and truth, forgiveness and deliverance, putting their whole trust in God: as such this fellowship cannot be said to believe in itself.

To say that we believe *the* Church, however, means that it is from God's grace and through faith that the Church lives. A community that does not believe is not the Church. The Church does not exist of itself but in the actual men who believe. Just as there can be no country without people, no body without limbs, so there can be no Church without believers. The Church does not spring simply from God's ordinance but from the decision which is required of the men who must form the Church, the radical decision for God and his reign. This decision is faith.

To say that we believe the Church, however, means that faith comes from God's grace through the Church. God calls each man personally to believe. But without the community which believes, the individual would not attain faith. Faith does not exist by itself, but in the actual men who believe. And these men do not live as separate individuals, isolated believers. They do not derive their faith from themselves. Nor do they derive it directly from God. They have their faith through the community, which as a believing community proclaims the message to them and provokes the response of faith in them. This does not mean that the Christian always believes because of the Church. Today, in contrast with the time of Augustine for instance, it would be truer to say that men believe not because of but in spite of the Church, and they see it in its historical form. The Church is often simply accepted along with the faith they have in God and him whom he sent, if not simply tolerated as part of the bargain. And yet the Church as the fellowship of believers is not just the object of faith: it is at the same time the sphere, the home of faith. The faith of the individual is stimulated and developed, is constantly embraced and supported by the faith of the community. In this way the individual's faith shares in the community's faith and in the common truth. Precisely for us who live today, only too conscious of our historicity, relativity and isolation, it can be a relief as well as a burden to realize that despite our total individual responsibility our faith is part of the wider and richer, old and yet young faith of the believing community that is the Church.[18]

Ultimately, however, faith cannot simply be derived from the Church, nor the Church from faith. The Church does not exist as an objective entity independently of the individual's act of faith, nor can those who believe unite of themselves to make the Church. Faith and the Church are interrelated and react fruitfully upon one another in mutual service. But ultimately they have their foundations neither in one another nor in themselves; they have a common source in God's loving act of salvation. To ask which came first, faith or the Church, is like asking whether the flower comes before the seed or the seed before the flower. Neither faith nor the Church should be made absolute. Faith made absolute displaces the Church,

---

[18] Cf. Karl Rahner, "Dogmatic Notes on 'ecclesiological piety'" in *Theological Investigations* V, London–Baltimore 1966, pp. 336–365.

that is the Protestant danger. The Church made absolute disenfranchises faith, that is the Catholic danger. The vital fact is that God's saving act precedes both faith and Church.

3. VISIBLE AND INVISIBLE

The phrase *"credo ecclesiam"* refers to the Church as it is. The Church we believe is not an invisible Church of spirits but a visible Church of human beings. The words *"credo ecclesiam"*, while preventing us from opting for a visible Church as opposed to an invisible one, do not allow us to opt for an invisible Church in preference to a visible one. The old quarrel between the advocates of an *ecclesia invisibilis* and the advocates of an *ecclesia visibilis* is now long out of date.

(*a*) The Reformers, and before them Wyclif and Hus, were basically right to oppose the idea that the Church was simply the all too visible institution of the medieval Church, with its spiritual and political empire. Following Augustine and the New Testament, they stressed rather the invisible and hidden nature of the Church.[19] But what they aimed to do was to renew the visible Church rather than found an invisible one. There has never been such a thing as a completely invisible Church, neither at the time of its founding, nor in the time of the Fathers, nor at the time of the Reformation. The Reformation Churches, which soon became attached to particular principalities and rulers, were no less visible than the Roman Church. The little sects and spiritualistic groups which cut themselves off from the larger Churches were no less clearly visible.

A real Church made up of real people cannot possibly be invisible. The believing Christian least of all can harbour any illusions about the fact that the Church he believes is a real one and therefore visible. There is no place here for fantasies about a Platonic idea. The Christian's starting-point, which he may sometimes accept reluctantly, but he can surely also accept thankfully, is a real Church. The Church he believes is

[19] Cf. the literature referred to by E. Kinder, *Der evangelische Glaube*, p. 93.

visible as a human fellowship and through its acts as a community, through its preaching and teaching, its prayers and hymns, its confession of faith and its baptism, its works of mercy and consolation. The Church is more or less visible —preferably less than more in most cases—in its sermons and its worship, in baptism and the Lord's Supper, in its teaching and theology, its constitutions and orders.

It may of course often be irritating for the believing Christian to find that the Church he believes is unavoidably rooted in history, psychology and sociology, and can therefore be weighed up and compared with other institutions. The Church he believes can therefore, for all its desire to be something totally different, be considered on the same level as reputable or less reputable secular groups, communities, societies and organizations. But precisely because of his faith the Christian will accept this fact, indeed he will approve it, knowing as he does that the Church, visible like any group of people, any body or building, *must* be visible because it is composed of human beings and exists for human beings. By being visible the Church is being true, not false, to its essential nature. The fellowship of believing Christians, like the individual Christian, must exist in space and time, must exist visibly in order to fulfil the ministry to the world which is demanded and expected of it. Only a visible Church can be a home for human beings, a place where they can join in, give assistance, build.

No Protestant today would reject the visible aspect of the Church as something unimportant or as a necessary evil, like the enthusiasts of former times, least of all if he recalls the fate of Churches under totalitarian régimes. He will continue to lay great stress on the hidden and invisible aspects of the Church, but not as an absolute principle opposed to the idea of a human fellowship. Such stress will be relative, a necessary corrective to the constant dangers of ecclesiastical triumphalism and self-importance. Protestants today will agree with Luther that the Church is visible not only in the preaching of the word and in the administering of the sacraments, but also in the community's confession of faith[20] and

[20] Luther, "Propter confessionem coetus ecclesiae est visibilis", WA 39/2, p. 161.

they will be thankful that, instead of having to live their faith solipsistically, they can see it maintained, supported and furthered by a real communion of faith.

Today more than ever before Protestants will be concerned about the visible aspects of the Church: "If we say with the creed *credo ecclesiam,* we do not proudly overlook its concrete form; just as when we confess *credo resurrectionem carnis* we cannot overlook the real and whole man who is a soul and yet also a body, we cannot overlook his hope as though the resurrection was not also promised to him. Nor do we look penetratingly through this form, as though it was only something transparent and the real Church had to be sought behind it; just as we cannot overlook or look through the pleasing or less pleasing face of the neighbour whom we are commanded to love. We look at the visible aspect of the Church—this is the state of it. And as we look at what is seen— not beside it or behind it but in it—we see what is not seen. Hence we cannot rid ourselves in this way of the generally visible side of the Church. We cannot take refuge from it in a kind of wonderland. The *credo ecclesiam* can and necessarily will involve much distinguishing and questioning, much concern and shame. It can and necessarily will be a very critical *credo.* In relation to the side of the Church which is generally visible it can and necessarily will express what does not amount to much more than a hope and a yearning. But it does take the Church quite seriously in its common visibility—which is its earthly and historical existence. It confesses faith in the invisible aspect which is the secret of the visible. Believing in the *ecclesia invisibilis* we will enter the sphere of labour and conflict of the *ecclesia visibilis.* Without doing this, without a discriminate but serious participation in the historical life of the community, its activity, its upbuilding, its mission, in a kind of purely theoretical and abstract churchliness, no one has ever seriously repeated the *credo ecclesiam.*"[21]

(*b*) Catholic theology in the Counter-Reformation period, and in the preceding medieval period, was basically right, as has been made clear above, to insist on the visible aspect of the Church, in opposition to spiritualistic tendencies, and to insist on Church order, in opposition to enthusiastic tendencies. But it did not intend the impossible, to found a

21 Karl Barth, *Church Dogmatics* IV/1, Edinburgh 1965–Naperville, Ill., 1956, pp. 653–654.

purely visible Church. In as far as the Church is recognizable *fide solum*[22] it is hidden and invisible. Even at a time when Catholic Christianity was to an appalling extent committed to the visible aspects of the Church, it could never deny the implications of the words *credo ecclesiam,* the essentially hidden and invisible aspects of the Church.

The real Church is the Church we believe, and yet is visible; it is at once visible and invisible. Its visible aspects are therefore of a particular kind, having an equally essential invisible inner dimension. The decisive aspect of what is revealed remains hidden. The visible aspects of the Church are quickened, formed and controlled by the invisible aspects. This means that the Church is essentially more than what it appears to be. It is not an ordinary people or group, but a chosen people; it is not an ordinary body, but a mystical body; it is not an ordinary building, but a spiritual building. True, the Church can and must not deny that it is visible, essentially visible. It cannot hope to prevent the outside world taking it for what it appears to be as a visible entity: a religious organization among many other organizations, institutions and societies, something to be furthered, combated or tolerantly ignored, something to be taken seriously or not so seriously. At best the Church can protest and confess, quietly better than loudly, that it is more than it appears to be. And above all, by living in faith, it can confront the world with the disturbing question: is there more here than appears on the surface? But the Church will be heading for disaster if it abandons itself to its visible aspects and, forgetful of its true nature, puts itself on the same level as other institutions. It would be fatal for the Church to see itself primarily as a powerful factor in public life, as a high-powered combine, as a cultural or educational force, as the guardian of culture (Western culture, of course), as the bastion of "tradition" or the establishment, as a slightly more pious pressure group among many pressure groups, competing with others for power in politics, the arts, education and economics. If it did this the Church would be abdicating as a Church, forgetting the crucial element which alone can make its visible aspects

[22] *Catech. Trid.* I, 10, 21.

into a true Church: the Spirit, which invisibly controls the visible Church, making it spiritually alive, fruitful and credible.

No Catholic today who believes in the real Church would bluntly take the line of that champion of Counter-Reformation theology, Cardinal Bellarmine, and consider the Church to be as visible as the republic of Venice. He will continue to lay great stress on the visible aspects of the Church, but not as an absolute principle which would make faith irrelevant. Such stress will be a necessary corrective to the constant dangers of self-righteous enthusiasm. Catholics today will agree with the Tridentine catechism, that the vital element in the Church is hidden, recognizable only with the eye of faith,[23] and they will be thankful that through the power of faith they can see and be consoled by the fact that the Church is infinitely more than it seems to be in its all-too-human visible aspects.

Today more than ever before Catholics will be aware of the dangers of a Church which abandons itself to its visible aspects: "The Spirit of Jesus today can and will grant to his Church nothing but the Spirit of Jesus. That is to say, the spiritual nature of the Church today and always can be nothing more than spiritual. It cannot be worldly in the sense of secular power and secular achievements. The Spirit will not give to the visible Church new and promising secular methods of political, diplomatic, economic and sociological organization, which would assure it of greater independence, a more important voice in affairs, or stronger positions of power. It would still be a mistaken view, even if these promising secular methods were used in the first instance within the Church to tighten up discipline, to clean and oil the functional joints of the Church, to centralize administration, to speed up the channels of communication along which unified instructions and directives come, to raise the moral and intellectual standards of the clergy and, as far as possible, of the laity, who, it is thought, should be more rationally employed as active party cells or front-line troops in the ecclesiastical offensive. All these ideas are the slogans of integralism, something which, in the sense used here, is directly opposed to the activity of the Holy Spirit. In this respect there is a conflict within the empirical Church between two spirits, which Augustine, taking up the idea of the Bible with its old and

[23] *Catech. Trid.* I, 10, 19.

new covenants, describes as the struggle between two *civitates,* and the Spiritual Exercises, still more spiritually, envisages as the contrast between two attitudes: on the one hand the will to power, which is luciferian, on the other the will to poverty, humility and meekness, which is Christian. This confrontation between two attitudes must of course be fought out at its most conscious level within the individual Christian—hence the exercise of the "two banners" at the point where the most hidden and inward individual decision for Christ is at issue. The terrible thing about integralism is that it turns this confrontation into one between the visible Church and the visible non-Church, and then, since the battle is fought out over secular ground, uses the weapons of the non-Church for the Church."[24]

There are not two Churches, one visible and one invisible. Nor must we think, with Platonic dualism and spiritualism, of the visible Church (being earthly and "material") as the reflection of the real invisible Church (being spiritual and heavenly). Nor is the invisible part of the Church its essential nature, and the visible part the external form of the Church. The one Church, in its essential nature and in its external forms alike, is always at once visible and invisible. The Church which we believe is *one* Church: visible and invisible, or perhaps rather hidden, at once. This is the Church which believes and is believed. The *credo* does not remove the existence of the ecclesia, but gives it its foundation. The ecclesia does not give the lie to the *credo,* but supports it.

This then is the real Church: constant among all historical change, believing and believed despite its "un-nature". It is possible to live in the real Church. It is not an idealized Church, which self-confidently claims to be more than it is and therefore cannot fulfil its promises, it is not a minimalized Church, which despises itself, claims to be less than it is and therefore cannot make any promises. A man can live in the real Church, free from idealistic illusions and from depressing inferiority complexes, free to live his faith soberly and joyfully in the fellowship of believers. The real Church of the present has a future, in ministering to a world for which the future has already begun, although so many problems of the present still remain unsolved.

[24] H. U. von Balthasar, *Sponsa Verbi,* pp. 13 f.

For all that has been said above about the real Church, the vital question has not really been answered, or at best answered *en passant* without reflection. This believed and believing Church—in whom does it believe, this fellowship of believers? This Church with its historical existence—from whom does it take its origin, this community which journeys through history? Surely this historical Church must be a Christ-ian Church, this believing Church must be a fellowship of believers in Christ? What does this mean? All that has been said up till now has necessarily been provisional and sketchy: the following chapters will attempt to treat these difficult and fundamental questions.

B. *The Coming Reign of God*

I. THE PREACHING OF JESUS

1. THE APPEAL TO THE GOSPEL OF JESUS

Only twice—and, moreover, in two passages from the same gospel which are hotly disputed by exegetes (Mt. 16:18; 18:17)—does the word "church", or rather ἐκκλησία, appear in the gospels. On the other hand the words "kingdom of God" (βασιλεία του θεου) appear about a hundred times in the synoptic gospels. This is a disturbing fact for any ecclesiology, even today. Are we forced to agree with the ominous and often-quoted comment of Alfred Loisy: "Jesus proclaimed the kingdom of God, and what came was the Church"?[1]

It seems to be far from straightforward or without dangers for the Church to reflect seriously on the Gospel of Christ. Has it the right to appeal to the words of Jesus? Is it really founded on his Gospel? Or is it merely a substitute phenomenon, making do in place of something much greater which, despite Jesus' proclamation, has not yet come into being? It would do nothing but harm to the Church if questions like these, which are admittedly awkward ones and have never been adequately aired, were to be dismissed as stemming from the ill-will of critical exegetes and historians, who challenge an uncritical and unhistorical ecclesiological dogmatism which naïvely defends the *status quo*. Surely these questions indicate a fundamental Christian longing for the origins of Christianity, for the discovery of what Jesus really intended? What did Jesus really intend? Did he simply intend the Church we have today? Is the Church we have really backed up—in its essentials, not in its inessentials—by the message of Christ? Or is it not proudly basing the justification for its existence on the words of someone who would have opposed it from the start, just as he opposed the Jewish temple clergy

[1] A. Loisy, *L'Evangile et l'Eglise,* Paris 1902, p. 111: "Jésus annonçait le royaume, et c'est l'Eglise qui est venue." This quotation is always taken in the wrong, i.e. a negative sense; Loisy meant it as a positive statement.

and the theology of the scribes? Many people today must have the impression that the Church is a prisoner, so to speak, of its own history and traditions, of its own ideas and laws. All too often it seems to be defending itself against Jesus and the uncompromising challenge of his message. To many people the Church's frequent talk of "tradition" merely suggests it is afraid to investigate boldly and radically its own origins and the original message which brought it into existence; it seems to be unwilling to take serious steps to clear out of the way all the barriers which separate it from the source of its own existence. Does the Church too ask the same question which the Grand Inquisitor in Dostoievski's terrifying story puts to the returning Christ and to Christ's message: "Why do you come to disturb us?" There is no doubt that the message of Jesus has had, if not a destructive, at least a disturbing effect on the Church in any age, challenging it, rousing it, goading it into new life; in short, it has always been a "stumbling-block".

It is of course far from easy to gather the original message of Jesus himself from the source available. The gospels are not neutral historical chronicles, but committed and committing testimonies of faith. They are not written from the perspective of Jesus before his resurrection, but from that of the Church after his resurrection. And yet these testimonies of faith also include reports of Jesus and his message. The background to the gospels, and in particular the first three synoptic gospels, is not legend and speculation, but living experiences and impressions, reports handed down about the living Jesus of Nazareth. If not directly, at least through the evangelists' testimonies of faith we can hear Jesus himself speaking. Anyone who comes to these documents with essential rather than peripheral questions and puts them seriously rather than casually, will receive answers which are remarkably clear, consistent and original; answers which are obviously not just the product of a chance coincidence of various theological versions of the truth, but which—however much occasional details may seem historically dubious—speak to us with the original words of Jesus.

It is revealing that nowadays, precisely among followers of Bultmann, it is customary to affirm that, despite all the problems of the sources, "defeatism and scepticism should (not) have the last word and lead us on to a complete disengagement of interest from the earthly Jesus. If this were to happen, we should either be failing to grasp the nature of the primitive Christian concern with the identity between the exalted and the humiliated Lord; or else we should be emptying that concern of any real content, as did the docetists. We should also be overlooking the fact that there are still pieces of the Synoptic tradition which the historian has to acknowledge as authentic if he wishes to remain an historian at all. My own concern is to show that, out of the obscurity of the life story of Jesus, certain characteristic traits in his preaching stand out in relatively sharp relief, and that primitive Christianity united its own message with these. . . . The preaching of the Church may be carried on anonymously; the important thing is not the person, but the message. But the Gospel itself cannot be anonymous, otherwise it leads to moralism and mysticism. The Gospel is tied to him, who, both before and after Easter, revealed himself to his own as the Lord, by setting them before the God who is near to them and thus translating them into the freedom and responsibility of faith."[2]

"The time is fulfilled, and the kingdom of God is at hand; repent, and believe in the gospel." These lapidary phrases from the start of St Mark's gospel (Mk. 1:15) are a telling summary of what Jesus really intended. The *basileia* (meaning "kingdom" or better, because of the misleading concrete associations, "reign") of God or, in the secondary formulation of Matthew, whose Jewish respect for the name of God led him to avoid it but who means exactly the same thing, the "basileia of heaven"—or simply "the basileia" by itself—this basileia of God is the ruling, central concept of Jesus' preaching, which affects all stages of the synoptic tradition from Jesus himself via Mark and the sayings of source Q up to the writing of Matthew and Luke. The kingdom of God is *at hand:* all exegetes are agreed that this fact is at the very heart of Jesus' preaching, that this approaching kingdom of

[2] Ernst Käsemann, *Essays on NT Themes,* London–Naperville, Ill. 1964 (= Studies in Biblical Theology No. 41), pp. 45–46. For recent developments on the subject of the quest for the historical Jesus, cf. J. M. Robinson, *A New Quest of the Historical Jesus,* London–Naperville, Illinois 1959.

God is the centre and the horizon of his preaching and teaching, whatever the precise interpretation put on the idea of "nearness" may be.

We have come a long way from the era of liberal Protestantism, when Jesus was seen as a gentle moral preceptor, an exemplar of humanitarianism, and the "kingdom of God" was interpreted as a worldly, ethical kingdom, a "religious idea", a "moral ideal"; man's "chiefest good"; for Albrecht Ritschl,[3] the "father of liberal Protestantism", who wrote under the influence of Kant and Schleiermacher, and for his school, which dominated German theology at the end of the nineteenth century, the kingdom of God was a universal moral community which could be achieved by men working together in neighbourly love, and was thus the final goal of the divine plan for the world and of man himself. It was Ritschl's son-in-law Johannes Weiss[4] and then Albert Schweitzer[5] who gave the death-blow to this conception of the kingdom of God by the rediscovery, startling at the time, of the essentially eschatological, other-worldly and transcendental nature of the kingdom of God, which is not to be achieved by the ethical actions of men, but is an act of God which is shortly to make its apocalyptic irruption into history and bring it to a close (eschatology here in the sense of anticipation of an imminent end). But we have also come a long way from the time when eschatological elements in Jesus' message were recognized, but their relevance to the present time remained obscure, since the parousia (an apocalyptic illusion!) had not occurred—this was the case precisely in Schweitzer's (and Martin Werner's)[6] "consistent eschatology": the eschatological message was the shell, but only the ethical kernel was still valuable. The First World War and the upheavals in all spheres of life which it brought with it destroyed the alliance between theology and bourgeois rationalism, belief in progress, and optimism about the course of civilization; a new atmosphere was engendered in which the eschatology of the New Testament once again made sense. Karl Barth not only succeeded in making eschatology seem of contemporary relevance, he made it his dominant theological theme: "Christianity which is not totally and entirely

[3] A. Ritschl, *Rechtfertigung und Versöhnung* I–III, Bonn 1870–1874; *Geschichte des Pietismus* I–III, Bonn 1880–1886.

[4] J. Weiss, *Die Predigt Jesu vom Reich Gottes*, Göttingen 1892.

[5] Albert Schweitzer, *The Quest of the Historical Jesus*, London 1910–New York 1961.

[6] M. Werner, *The Formation of Christian Dogma*, London–New York 1957.

eschatology has separated itself totally and entirely from Christ."[7] At the same time he increasingly gave eschatology a radically christocentric interpretation: "Jesus Christ is himself the established kingdom of God."[8] Form-criticism, and above all Rudolf Bultmann, took up the lines indicated by Schweitzer and Barth, and suggested a positive evaluation of eschatology based on a new human self-awareness.

The more detailed interpretations of the reign or kingdom of God, especially with reference to its "nearness", show considerable differences, the more extreme and characteristic of which may be briefly mentioned. There is Schweitzer's "consistent eschatology" according to which the kingdom of God which was announced was for Jesus a universal catastrophe along the lines of Jewish apocalyptic thinking and hence no longer meaningful for us today; on the other hand there is the "realized eschatology" of Charles Dodd,[9] according to which the kingdom of God was a present reality for Jesus and therefore is a reality for us too. At the present time there is a marked divergence between Bultmann's "existential eschatology", according to which cosmic and apocalyptic expectations of a future event must be demythologized, since they are no longer meaningful for us today, and the reign of God must be interpreted with reference to the eschatological moment and a new existential view (existential in the sense of a moment of challenge, a conscious decision of commitment to God); and on the other hand the "salvation-historical eschatology" of several exegetes, both Protestant (especially Oscar Cullmann[10]) and Catholic (especially Rudolf Schnackenburg[11]), who hold that the kingdom of God came with Jesus, but is still awaiting its fulfilment.

[7] Karl Barth, *Der Römerbrief*, 2 edn., Munich 1922, p. 298. Eng. tr. *The Epistle to the Romans*, Oxford 1933, not quoted as inaccurate at this point.

[8] Karl Barth, *Church Dogmatics* II/2, Edinburgh–Naperville, Illinois 1957, p. 177.

[9] C. H. Dodd, The Apostolic Preaching and its Developments, New York, 1936.

[10] O. Cullmann, *Christ and Time*, London 1962–Philadelphia 1964; *Heil als Geschichte, Heilsgeschichtliche Existenz im NT*, Tübingen, 1965.

[11] R. Schnackenburg, *God's Rule and Kingdom*, Edinburgh–London–New York 1963.

2. THE GOSPEL MESSAGE OF THE REIGN OF GOD

"The time is fulfilled and the kingdom of God is at hand": despite the divergences mentioned above, all the current interpretations of the reign of God share the same fundamental perspectives:[12]

[12] In this section reference will be made particularly to two books by leading representatives of Protestant and Catholic exegesis: R. Bultmann, *Theology of the New Testament*, London–New York 1952 (vol. I) and 1955 (vol. II), and R. Schnackenburg (see n. 11 above). The older works on the life of Jesus are given in Schweitzer's book (see n. 5 above). The most important books on Jesus after Schweitzer are those by P. Wernle, W. Heitmüller, A. Schlatter, R. Bultmann, K. Bornhäuser, K. L. Schmidt (RGG[2]), A. C. Headlam, J. Klausner, P. Feine, F. C. Burkitt, M. Goguel, F. Prat, K. Adam, T. W. Manson, R. Guardini, G. Ricciotti, M. Dibelius, R. Otto, W. Grundmann, R. Meyer, A. T. Cadoux, C. J. Cadoux, H. J. Cadbury, F. Büchsel, W. Manson, V. Taylor, E. Percy, G. Bornkamm, E. Stauffer, L. F. Church, H. Conzelmann (RGG[3]), J. R. Geiselmann. For discussion in the Bultmann school, cf. J. M. Robinson and his bibliography. Important collections of essays: *Der historische Jesus und der kerygmatische Christus*, ed. H. Ristow and K. Matthiae, Berlin 1960; *Der historische Jesus und der Christus unseres Glaubens*, ed. K. Schubert, Vienna 1962. Cf. in addition the articles on the Kingdom of God in: LThK (H. Fries, R. Schnackenburg), RGG (H. Conzelmann, E. Wolf, G. Gloege), EKL (L. Goppelt, J. Moltmann), HTG (P. Hoffmann), ODCC; also the articles in the *Bibellexikon* (P. van Imschoot), in the *Bibeltheologischen Wörterbuch* (R. Schnackenburg), in the *Vocabulaire Biblique* (H. Roux) and especially in ThW (H. Kleinknecht, G. von Rad, K. G. Kuhn, K. L. Schmidt). The works of theology and dogmatics listed above under A I, 3 and A II, 2 may also be consulted. Finally, the following more recent monographs should be added to the list given above under B I, 1: O. Cullmann, *Königherrschaft Christi und Kirche im NT*, Zollikon–Zürich 1941; K. Buchheim, *Das messianische Reich. Über den Ursprung der Kirche im Evangelium*, Munich 1948; H. Ridderbos, *Coming of the Kingdom*, Nutley, N.J. 1962; A. N. Wilder, *Eschatology and Ethics in the Teaching of Jesus*, 2 ed., New York 1950; R. Morgenthaler, *Kommendes Reich*, Zürich 1952; W. G. Kümmel, *Promise and Fulfilment*, London–Naperville, Illinois 1957 (= Studies in Biblical Theology No. 23); T. F. Glasson, *His Appearing and His Kingdom*, London 1953; R. H. Fuller, *The Mission and Achievement of Jesus*, London 1954; H. Roberts, *Jesus and the Kingdom of God*, London 1955–Naperville, Illinois 1954; J. Bonsirven, *Le Règne de*

(a) The "reign of God" to which Jesus refers does not mean the constant universal reign of God, which is a consequence of the creation and which Jesus in his message takes for granted on the basis of the Old Testament. It means the eschatological, that is the fully realized, *final and absolute reign of God at the end of time, which as an event is now "at hand"* (Mk. 1:15): it has "come upon you" (Mt. 12:28; Lk. 11:20), it will "come" (Lk. 22:18; cf. Mk. 14:25, Mt. 26:29), "come with power" (Mk. 9:1). The concept is nowhere defined by Jesus; he assumes a knowledge and understanding of it and interprets it in his own way. Its eschatological character is evident from the historical setting of Jesus' preaching: the eschatological call to repentance and baptism of John the Baptist, of which Jesus is seen as the fulfilment, and then the eager eschatological expectations of contemporary Jewry and in particular the Qumran sects. But it is also evident in many details of Jesus' preaching itself— the phrases including the word "basileia" which are attributed to Jesus and the sayings which include the words ἐγγύς, ἐγγίζειν and ἔρχεσθαι, as well as from the overall perspectives: only this eschatological significance will make sense of the stress on the present time, on a specific hour, the hour of decision; it is also the key to the radical moral demands made by Jesus, in the "Sermon on the Mount" for example, which are a precondition of entry into the eschatological kingdom of God.

The strictly eschatological nature of the reign of God, as an event, is undeniable: "It must be insisted emphatically that the idea of God's reign in his (Jesus') mouth referred always to God's

Dieu, Paris 1957; E. Grässer, *Das Problem der Parousieverzögerung in den synoptischen Evangelien und in der Apostelgeschichte*, Berlin 1957; H. Conzelmann, *The Theology of St Luke*, London–New York 1960; T. Blatter, *Die Macht und Herrschaft Gottes*, Fribourg 1961; F. Mussner, *Die Botschaft der Gleichnisse Jesu*, Munich 1961; W. Trilling, *Das wahre Israel*, Munich 1964. For the development of the idea of the Kingdom of God in Church tradition, cf. the work in several volumes of E. Staehelin, *Die Verkündigung des Reiches Gottes in der Kirche Jesu Christi*, Basle 1951 ff. Further bibliographical material will be given in subsequent chapters.

eschatological kingship, though he was familiar with the notion of God's continuous government of the universe and took it for granted. But when he refers to the 'reign of God' he is not dealing with this. His ordinary usage of this term applies to God's eschatological kingship, and the texts should not be explained or toned down in a non-eschatological sense."[13] "Reign of God is an eschatological concept. It means the régime of God which will destroy the present course of the world, wipe out all the contra-divine, Satanic power under which the present world groans—and thereby, terminating all pain and sorrow, bring in salvation for the People of God which awaits the fulfilment of the prophets' promises."[14]

What is it then that makes the message of Jesus so disturbing, so tremendously urgent? "The time is *fulfilled* and the kingdom of God is *at hand*" (Mk. 1:15).

(*b*) The "reign of God" is not in the preaching of Jesus— as it was in that of several rabbis—something that could be brought about or achieved by faithful adherence to the law; it appears as a powerful *sovereign act of God himself*. There is no one who can invite himself to the eschatological banquet. The Father issues the invitations. It is he who makes the seed grow, by his power and his grace. It is *his* reign. "Thy kingdom come": in these words man may *pray* (Mt. 6:10; Lk. 11:2). He may cry to God day and night (Lk. 18:7), he may seek God's kingdom (Mt. 6:33; Lk. 12:31), he may seek to enter it (Lk. 13:24; cf. Mt. 7:13), he may prepare himself and hold himself in readiness like the wise virgins (Mt. 25:1–13) and the wakeful servants (Lk. 12:35–37; cf. Mt. 24:44). But it is not man, it is God who "gives" the kingdom (Lk. 12:31). He "appoints" it (Lk. 22:29 f.), decides whose it shall be (Mt. 5:3, 10; cf. Lk. 6:20; Mk. 10:14). He is unshakable and unfathomable, sovereign and free, the God who acts like a king, acting in fulfilment of his unconditionally free will. It is not man but God himself who administers his rule in this way. Man cannot storm for himself the kingdom of God, he can only receive it like a child (cf. Mk. 10:15).

[13] Schnackenburg, *op. cit.*, p. 81.
[14] Bultmann, *op. cit.*, I, p. 4.

The idea of the kingdom of God as a divine and sovereign gift has been generally recognized: "The coming of God's reign is a miraculous event, which will be brought about by God alone without the help of men."[15] ". . . admission or exclusion, reclining at table (Mt. 8:11; Lk. 13:29; cf. Mt. 22:10 f.) and also eating of bread (Lk. 14:15), drinking of the fruit of the vine (Lk. 22:18; Mk. 14:25). All these images portray the basileia as a saving benefit in the future, of which God alone can dispose. The reign of God is an event that is to occur for men, a good offered to them, a privilege that is also a challenge. It is never something of which they can dispose, or that they can compel or insist upon. . . . Furthermore, certain turns of phrase which have become current are not found on the lips of Jesus: 'to build up the kingdom of God', 'to work at it', 'to assist in its construction', etc."[16]

How can we then be sure of this future reign? It is not the work of men, but of God alone: "the kingdom of *God* is at hand" (Mk. 1:15).

(*c*) The "reign of God" is not for Jesus—as it was for certain groups of the people, especially the Zealots, who fought against the enemies of God in order to free their people from Roman domination—an earthly, national and religio-political theocracy. It is rather a *purely religious kingdom*. Jesus is always at pains to refute the misapprehensions of his people, but also and especially of his disciples, that he had come to free them from misery and foreign domination and to set up once more the earthly kingdom of Israel. He rejects any splendid earthly expectations (Lk. 19:11; 23:42; 24:21; Acts 1:6), the pursuit of positions of honour in the kingdom (Mk. 10:35–45 par.), any violent actions (Mk. 14:17 par.; Lk. 13:1–3; 22:38). Peter is roundly rebuked for his failure to understand Jesus' way of suffering (Mk. 8:31–33 par.). In general Jesus' picture of the kingdom, if we exclude passages of editorial framework and decoration borrowed from apocalyptic material, is remarkably restrained in comparison with apocalyptic literature. Apocalyptic calculations as to when the end will come are rejected, for "the kingdom of God is not coming with signs to be observed" (Lk.

[15] Bultmann, *op. cit.*, I, p. 4.
[16] Schnackenburg, *op. cit.*, pp. 85–86.

17:20), only the Father knows the day and the hour (Mk. 13:32). Judgment, resurrection of the dead and future glory are not painted in detail. Images like that of the feast are not literal descriptions of the kingdom of God, but are intended to emphasize its reality: they point not to pleasures of the table but to communion with God and with one's fellow men. In the last analysis all details of the kingdom of God are unimportant (cf. Mk. 12:24–27) by comparison with the single fact that it represents the time when God will reign. Hence the term "basileia" should not be taken to mean a kingdom, an area of dominion situated in place and time, but simply God's rule: the reign of the king.

The purely religious character of the reign of God is not in dispute. It is based on the most firmly authenticated sources of Old Testament belief: "These texts show us that Israel experienced Yahweh's kingship in the historical action of its God. This is no 'kingdom' and no 'sphere of dominion' but a kingly leadership and reign which develops from Yahweh's absolute power and shows itself in the guidance of Israel. This original meaning, namely that Yahweh as King actively 'rules', must be kept in mind through the whole growth of the *basileia* theme. God's kingship in the Bible is characterized not by latent authority but by the exercise of power, not by an office but a function; it is not a title but a deed."[17] With regard to Jesus' eschatological message it is important to note the following: "With such a message, Jesus stands *in the historical context of Jewish expectations about the end of the world and God's new future*. And it is clear that his thought is not determined by the *national* hope then still alive in certain circles of the Jewish people, in which the time of salvation to be brought in by God was thought of as the restitution of the idealized ancient kingdom of David. No saying of Jesus mentions the Messiah-king who is to crush the enemies of the People, nor the lordship of Israel over the earth, nor the gathering of the twelve tribes, nor the joy that will be in the bounteous peace-blessed Land. Rather, Jesus' message is connected with the hope of other circles which is primarily documented by the *apocalyptic* literature, a hope which awaits salvation not from a miraculous change in historical (i.e. political and social) conditions, but from a cosmic catastrophe which will do away with all conditions of the present world as it is. . . . However, it is free from all the learned and fanciful spec-

[17] Schnackenburg, *op. cit.*, p. 13.

ulation of the apocalyptic writers. . . . Everything is swallowed up in the single thought that then God will rule; and only very few details of the apocalyptic picture of the future recur in his words."[18]

Why is the purity, clarity and directness of Jesus' message so appealing, and why was it rejected by a large part of his nation, in particular by its religious and political leaders? The kingdom of God which he proclaims is not a political empire of earthly goods, but the reign of God, which must be preceded by repentance and faith: "the *kingdom of God* is at hand; repent, and believe in the gospel" (Mk. 1:15).

(*d*) The "reign of God" is not for Jesus—as it was for many of his contemporaries, including the communities of Qumran—a judgment of vengeance on sinners and godless men: it is rather a *saving event for sinners*. Jesus' call to repentance does not invoke, as John the Baptist's did, God's anger, but God's mercy. The message of the reign of God is not one of threats and coming disaster, but of salvation, peace, joy. It is a positive, not a negative message, an εὐ-αγγέλιον (Mk. 1:15), not a δυς-αγγέλιον. Whether Jesus himself used the *word* εὐαγγέλιον or not (the noun, as distinct from the verb, is only used in this sense in the New Testament), at all events he preaches the "good news", the "gospel" of which Deutero-Isaiah speaks (52:7): "How beautiful on the mountains are the feet of *one who brings good news* (LXX: εὐαγγελιζόμενος), who heralds *peace*, brings *happiness*, proclaims *salvation*, and tells Zion: '*Your God is king*'." And this gospel is not only intended for the powerful and the rich, but also and especially—as illustrated by the Sermon on the Mount—for the poor and the sorrowful, the despised and the downtrodden. And it is not addressed only to the just and the righteous, but also and especially—how many parables and narratives indicate this— to the sinners and the godless. This is the stumbling-block for the "righteous" and the "god-fearing": Jesus chooses to consort with notorious sinners, with Samaritans, tax-gatherers and prostitutes. Even when threats and warnings are used,

---

[18] Bultmann, *op. cit.*, I, pp. 4–5.

they are not an end in themselves; they are intended to point to the great offer of God's grace which precedes judgment. God's grace and mercy and forgiveness are preached to all and are made visible in Jesus' actions: the revelation of God's love for sinners is a sign of the coming reign of God.

The basically salvational character of the reign of God is obvious: "Now is no time to mourn and fast; this is a time of joy like a wedding (Mk. 2:18 f.). So he now cries his 'Blessed are you' to the waiting, expectant ones: 'Blessed are you poor, for yours is the Reign of God! Blessed are you that hunger now, for you shall be satisfied! Blessed are you that weep now, for you shall laugh!' (Lk. 6:20 f.). Satan's reign is now collapsing, for 'I saw Satan fall like lightning from heaven' (Lk. 10:18)."[19] In Jesus' message salvation is always especially salvation for the sinner: "With Jesus, weal and woe are more than the warnings they are with the prophets. His preaching is not merely an appeal for conversion as was that of the great Baptist from Jordan. He proclaims salvation as something already present and operative though not yet fully and perfectly realized. He assured many persons that their sins were immediately forgiven and his jealous enemies understood that he was laying claim to divine power (Mk. 2:1–12 par.). This revealed God's mercy and salvific will to men and showed that the prophecies were fulfilled. . . . The direct revelation of God's love for sinners as a mark of his eschatological reign, the grace bestowed upon all who accept the salvific gospel of Jesus and are converted, God's delight in forgiveness and the generous outpouring of his saving graces: all this is an original and unique feature of Jesus' gospel of the *basileia*. But there is another facet of his thought and another element in his preaching that distinguishes him from representatives of later Judaism. For him the whole content of salvation was found in the reign of God; all hope of salvation reaches its fulfilment here."[20]

Why is Jesus' preaching about the reign of God so uniquely "good news"? Because God's salvation is offered to all men, sinners included, under the one condition: "repent, and believe in the *gospel*" (Mk. 1:15).

(*e*) Jesus' proclamation of the "reign of God" does not involve a demand for men to follow a new, improved moral

19 Bultmann, *op. cit.*, I, p. 6.
20 Schnackenburg, *op. cit.*, pp. 88–89, 92.

code. It demands rather a *radical decision for God*. The choice is clear: either God and his reign or the world and its reign. Nothing must prevent man from making this radical decision between God and the world. Jesus himself left behind family and career, house and home. And he summoned other men to leave their family and social settings and accompany him as his disciples. He did not call all to leave family, career and home; he was not a social revolutionary. But each one individually he confronted with a radical decision: where in the last analysis did his heart lie—with God or with the goods of this world? The world and its goods must be seen, in the perspective of the coming reign of God, as part of an inner dialectic, as both positive and negative. The world is evil, man is wicked; and yet there remains God's creation, man is still the child of God the Father. The man who accepts the coming reign of God must turn away in metanoia from the evil of the world and of man; but at the same time he must turn back to the world and to his fellow men in a new way, in love. Jesus did not preach—as the communities of Qumran did—an ascetic withdrawal from the world; he founded no monasteries. Nor did he wish to separate off new areas of the "sacred" in time and place, accessible through cultic initiation, distinct from the "profane" world and its history. No, man must accept radical obedience towards the will of God, while remaining in the world and working for his fellow man. But though living in the world man must wait for the coming of God's reign and give his heart finally and solely to God: not to money and possessions (Mt. 6:19–21, 24–34; Mk. 10:17–27), nor to rights and honours (Mt. 5:39–41; Mk. 10:42–44), nor even parents and family (Lk. 14:26 f.; Mt. 10:34–39). God does not demand only external acts which can be codified as laws, he requires a certain inward disposition and state of mind; anger as well as murder, evil desires as well as adultery, deceitfulness as well as perjury are all offences against God's commandments: "You have heard that it was said to the men of old. . . . But I say to you. . . ." (Mt. 5:21–48).

Thus the decision for God is irrevocable: "No one who puts his hand to the plough and looks back is fit for the kingdom of God" (Lk. 9:62). God wants the entire man, wants his heart. Man is not to leave the world, but is to hold himself in readiness, unhampered by the world. Readiness for what? Readiness to fulfil God's will, in order to be ready for the kingdom of God: "Whoever does the will of God is my brother, and sister, and mother" (Mk. 3:35). And what does the will of God demand? Not merely the negative rejection of the world, but a positive commitment; not the fulfilment of a vast number of commandments, but basically only one thing: love. While the Sermon on the Mount and similar sayings of Jesus explain and illustrate the requirements of the reign of God, in a variety of ways, these requirements are no more than a summary, uniquely simple, of the main commandment of love of God and of one's neighbour. Jesus formulated no new laws and laid down no new detailed precepts. He is concerned with the one great and concrete demand which embraces the whole of human life in its totality and yet is directly applicable to each individual case: "You shall love the Lord your God with all your heart and with all your soul, and with all your mind. This is the great and first commandment. And a second is like it, You shall love your neighbour as yourself. On these two commandments depend all the law and the prophets" (Mt. 22:37–40). Perfection is shown above all by loving one's enemies: "Love your enemies and pray for those who persecute you, so that you may be sons of your Father who is in heaven; for he makes his sun rise on the evil and on the good, and sends rain on the just and on the unjust. . . . You, therefore, must be perfect, as your heavenly Father is perfect" (Mt. 5:44 f., 48). Who then is ready for the reign of God? The man who lives, free from any worldly enslavement, in a state of readiness for God and his demands which confront him every day in the world in his neighbour.

This is what is involved in *repentance* (μετανοειτε, **Mk.** 1:15), the repentance which the proclamation of the reign of God demands of men: not an outward repentance with sackcloth and ashes, but a radical and total inward change of the entire man, a change of direction towards God. This too is what is involved in *faith* in the message of salvation (πιστεύετε ἐν τῷ εὐαγγελίῳ, Mk. 1:15), which comes to the same thing as repentance: radical change is made possible by faith that the time of salvation is fulfilled and the reign of God at hand; conversely, radical faith is possible only through repentance which recognizes personal guilt and the need for grace and expresses a readiness for the radical fulfilment of the will of God.

It is impossible to overlook the fundamentally challenging and demanding character of the reign of God: "The announcement that the reign of God is at hand swells to a mighty appeal to men to subject themselves to God alone. A survey of the full range of the discourses and sayings of Jesus in the synoptic gospels shows how this urgent note is in the forefront of his teaching. The divine sovereignty manifested in the actions of Jesus compels men to make their decision. The critical situation created by its presence and power in the words and deeds of Jesus, with the assurance of fulfilment in the future, necessarily involves an imperative, at once curt and comprehensive as in Mk. 1:15, 'Be converted and believe the gospel', or metaphorically in the passages about entering into the kingdom of God."[21] "All that man can do in the face of the Reign of God now breaking in is this: keep ready or get ready for it. Now is the *time of decision,* and Jesus' call is the *call to decision.* . . . Now the question is whether a man really desires God and His reign or the world and its goods. . . . *God demands the whole will of man* and knows no abatement in His demand. . . . Man, upon whose self God's demand is made, has no freedom towards God; he is accountable for his life as a whole—as the parable of the talents teaches (Mt. 25:14–30 par.). *He may not, must not, cannot raise any claim* before God, but is like the slave who only has his duty to do and can do no more (Lk. 17:7–10)."[22]

What then is the necessary and fundamental condition of entry into the coming reign of God? *"Repent,* and *believe* in the gospel" (Mk. 1:15).

II. THE FOUNDATION OF A CHURCH

1. THE "NEARNESS" OF THE REIGN OF GOD IN JESUS

How "near" for Jesus is the reign of God which is "at hand"? It is still temporally distant, but brought closer to us

[21] Schnackenburg, *op. cit.,* p. 104.
[22] Bultmann, *op. cit.,* I, pp. 9, 13–14.

in prophetic perspective, or is it really imminent, or has it already been achieved? It is on this point that the interpretations of the exegetes diverge and it is not our aim here to enter into the debate about the detailed exegetical question of "immediate expectation" or "distant expectation". In the context of the present work it must suffice to set out the limits of our position, without detailed arguing of the case, simply in as far as this is essential for the rest of our thesis.

(a) *Futurist or presentist eschatology?* Exegetical discussion about the "nearness" of the reign of God has so far shown that very different positions can be supported by following only *one* of the lines of thought suggested by the synoptic kerygma of the reign of God; this one line merely has to be extracted, and strengthened by interpretation, while others are either rejected as non-genuine or disregarded as unimportant or—much more commonly—interpreted in such a way as to make them support the single line pursued. In this way an impressive, unequivocal and consistent picture of Jesus' preaching can be drawn, which, seen from the totality of the synoptic preaching only, leaves one question unanswered: how far does this impressive, unequivocal and consistent picture of Jesus' preaching tally with reality, the complete reality of the preaching of Jesus handed down to us? Can we in fact be sure that this picture does not do violence —not by what it brings out but by what it passes over in silence —to the original message?

If, for example, we follow Albert Schweitzer or Charles Dodd and suppose that all Jesus' teaching about the reign of God can be interpreted with reference to a single time-scale —whether futurist or presentist—then without much difficulty an impressive picture of Jesus' preaching emerges. For Schweitzer[23] Jesus invokes a *consistent* eschatology which *will be realized* in the immediate future (the final and definitive kingdom of God at the end of time is not yet present, but is awaited in the immediate future, during Jesus' lifetime, or subsequently as linked to his death). For Dodd,[24] Jesus in-

[23] Similar views are held by M. Werner, F. Buri, etc.
[24] Similar views are held by W. Grundmann, A. T. Cadoux, T. F. Glasson, etc.

vokes a *consistent* eschatology which *has already been realized* (the final and definitive kingdom of God at the end of time is no longer anticipated, it is already present).

However, Dodd, with weighty texts drawn from the oldest parts of the synoptic tradition behind him, is able with justice to refute Schweitzer on the grounds that it is impossible to interpret all the eschatological sayings of Jesus in a futurist sense, and that there are quite clearly several *presentist* sayings about the existing reign of God, and that several apparently futurist sayings, which speak of a reign of God yet to come, should be interpreted presentistically, in the light of the fulfilment which has already occurred. On the other hand, Schweitzer could have replied to Dodd, with the support of no less weighty and old-established synoptic texts, that it is impossible to interpret all the eschatological sayings of Jesus in a presentist sense, which would dilute their message, and that there are quite clearly several *futurist* sayings about the reign of God which is to come in the immediate future, and that several apparently presentist sayings, which speak of a reign of God which has already come, should be interpreted futuristically, in the light of a reign of God yet to come.

Here it would seem to be a case of extremes not so much touching—as the phrase goes—but cancelling each other out. So it is not surprising that these extreme positions have lost favour.

This is especially true of Schweitzer's view, which form-criticism has made untenable: "There is scarcely a New Testament scholar who would still share Schweitzer's view: namely that Jesus, inspired by an ardent expectation of the imminent end of time, sent his disciples on a hasty mission throughout Palestine and himself proclaimed an interim ethic, and then finally, when his hopes were deceived, attempted to force the intervention of the Almighty by his journey to Jerusalem and thereby lost his life."[25]

(*b*) *A futurist-presentist eschatology:* A majority of exegetes—at least on the continent of Europe—is convinced that the eschatological sayings of the synoptic tradition are diverse and many-faceted, and that only an interpretation which

[25] Ernst Käsemann, *Exegetische Versuche,* II, 107 f.

avoids extremes and makes differentiations can hope to do justice to the findings of exegesis. Such different exegetes as Bultmann, Cullmann, Jeremias, Käsemann, Kümmel, Vögtle and Schnackenburg are agreed that in the authentic preaching of Jesus the reign of God is announced both as something to come and as something present, that futurist and presentist eschatology are united in this preaching; hence the question as to the "nearness" of the reign of God can only be answered simultaneously in terms of a "not yet" *and* "but already" dialectic.

The "not yet" has already been briefly described: the reign of God is for Jesus essentially not yet fulfilled, it has a futurist-eschatological character. But on the basis of the oldest sections of the synoptic tradition the "but already" is also undeniable: the reign of God is already effective in the present through and in Jesus, it already has power in the present and its influence is already apparent. It is a reign of God which is fulfilled, if not yet completed, in Jesus.

Fulfilment has already begun: the eschaton is effective in the *victory over demonic forces,* which is achieved by the power of God; for Jesus as for his contemporaries numerous illnesses were attributed to the power of demons: "If it is by the finger of God that I cast out demons, then the kingdom of God has come upon you" (Lk. 11:20). That Satan has been bound by Jesus (Mk. 3:27) and robbed of his power (cf. Lk. 10:18), is a sign that the future he preaches is already present in him, that it has already begun.

Similarly in his *saving acts,* which are the fulfilment of the messianic prophecies of salvation (cf. Is. 19:18 f.; 35:5 f.; 61:1), the reign of God is already effective: "The blind receive their sight and the lame walk, the lepers are cleansed and the deaf hear, and the dead are raised up, and the poor have good news preached to them" (Mt. 11:5 par.). Jesus' healing work testifies to the eschatological salvific will of God. The proclamation of salvation and the saving actions of Jesus prove that in Jesus eschatological salvation has already begun.

How far the symbolic actions of Jesus during his time in Jerusalem—the entry into Jerusalem, the purification of the temple and the Last Supper—are also indications of the presence of the reign which is at hand, is a matter of controversy; but there are good grounds for seeing them in this way. At all events the old aeon has passed with the coming of Jesus. That the reign of God is already present is indicated not least by the fact that it can be opposed. This is evident from Mt. 11:12 f. and Lk. 16:16, whatever the exact sense of this saying, which exists in different versions and has been much discussed, may be: "From the days of John the Baptist until now the kingdom of heaven has suffered violence, and men of violence take it by force. For all the prophets and the law prophesied until John"; "The law and the prophets were until John; since then the good news of the kingdom of God is preached, and everyone enters it violently." Jesus appears here as the end of the law and the prophets, an idea which is made clear and concrete in the antitheses of the Sermon on the Mount, where Jesus both aligns and contrasts himself with Moses (cf. also Mk. 10:1–9 par.).

Thus Jesus himself is the great sign of the times (cf. Lk. 12:54–56; Mk. 13:28 f.). His coming and his work are signs of the reign of God which has already begun; in him future perfection is already present. And hence Jesus is in his own person the *challenge to decision* (cf. Mt. 8:22 par.; Lk. 9:62; 14:26 f. par.). His Gospel is the last word of God before the end, the urgent call to unavoidable and radical decision for God and his reign. The hour of decision is not at some vague time in the future, but *now*. Now, confronted by him, it is a question of believing or not believing, repenting or not repenting, obedience or disobedience. And according to how men receive or reject him, they are decisively marked for the eschatological judgment of God (Mk. 8:38; Mt. 19:28). Blessed therefore are those who in the words and actions of Jesus can recognize and experience the eschatological time of salvation in Jesus: "Blessed are your eyes, for they see, and your ears, for they hear. Truly, I say to you, many prophets and righteous men longed to see what you see, and did not see it, and to hear what you hear, and did not hear it" (Mt. 13:16 f.; Lk. 10:23 f.). If the queen of the South once came to hear Solomon: "Behold, something greater than Solomon is here"; and if the men of Nineveh repented at the preaching of Jonah: "Behold, something greater than Jonah is here"

(Lk. 11:30–32 par.): "Blessed is he who takes no offence at me" (Mt. 11:6 par.).

The claim of Jesus is unique and goes far beyond the category of the prophetic. Bultmann and others have disputed the idea that Jesus had any consciousness of his messianic rôle. But Bultmann's pupil Käsemann among others has pointed out that Jesus, by setting his authority beside and against that of Moses, in fact puts himself above Moses, and hence ceases to be a rabbi, since rabbis have only an authority derived from Moses.

"To this there are no Jewish parallels, nor indeed can there be. For the Jew who does what is done here has cut himself off from the community of Judaism—or else he brings the Messianic Torah and is therefore the Messiah. Even the prophet does not stand alongside Moses but under him. The unheard-of implication of the saying testifies to its genuineness. It proves, secondly, that while Jesus may have made his appearance in the first place in the character of a rabbi or a prophet, nevertheless, his claim far surpasses that of any rabbi or prophet; and thirdly, that he cannot be integrated into the background of the Jewish piety of his time. Certainly he was a Jew and made the assumptions of Jewish piety, but at the same time he shatters this framework in his claim. The only category which does justice to his claim (quite independently of whether he used it himself and required it of others) is that in which his disciples themselves placed him—namely, that of the Messiah."[26]

Other Protestant and Catholic exegetes have gone further and suggested that there are sufficient grounds for showing that Jesus himself—in hidden terms in order to avoid misunderstanding, but clearly enough for those who understood—claimed to be the Messiah, in a purely religious sense. He himself is the "Son of man", who will come "with power" in order to set up the perfect cosmic-universal reign in the name of God and according to God's sovereign will. He is, moreover, the obedient servant of God, who despite the rejection of his message of salvation by most of the old people of God achieves, by his representative death of atonement, a new pe-

[26] Ernst Käsemann, *Essays on NT Themes*, pp. 37–38.

riod of grace: a new possibility of salvation for all men, including the unbelieving Jews.[27]

This is sufficient to indicate that the reign of God of which Jesus speaks is not *only* a future but an already present entity. His preaching is therefore not merely a variant on later Judaic apocalyptics, pointing forward to future events at the end of time. On the other hand, as we have seen, it is not just one way of interpreting the present time, completely separate from any of the contemporary apocalyptic ideas, proclaiming simply the present fulfilment of apocalyptic expectations. Jesus' preaching is situated between the two poles of "not yet" and "but already", and represents therefore a futurist-presentist eschatology. At the same time, these two poles should not be confused with two *periods* of preaching (first presentist and then futurist or *vice versa*), for the texts show no development in Jesus' eschatological thinking. On the contrary, many passages combine presentist and futurist perspectives (Mk. 8:38; Mt. 19:28; Lk. 12:31: man decides now, God judges then). The reign of God is a future which confronts us as present. Jesus' preaching of the reign of God is at once an expectation of the future and a proclamation of the present.

2. BETWEEN ALREADY AND NOT YET

How near for Jesus is the reign of God which is at hand? While not yet present, it irrupts into the present, takes on in the present power and effect in Jesus, is fulfilled if not completed in him. If these are our answers, we are led to assume a futurist-presentist eschatology.

But this is not a complete description of the nearness of the reign of God. Can no definite point in time be fixed? *Futurist*-presentist reign of God: does that imply an imminently expected end, an eschaton? It would be easy to link this to a strong emphasis on the presentist character of the reign of God. But then Jesus' preaching would after all be no more than one variant of the Jewish apocalyptics. Futurist-*presentist* reign of God: does that imply an end, an eschaton,

27 These theses are argued in detail by Schnackenburg, *op. cit.*, pp. 114–177.

which is happening here and now? This would not exclude certain futurist perspectives. But then Jesus' preaching would after all be no more than a form of simple interpretation of the present.

Characteristically, Rudolf Bultmann combines both views and eliminates neither the futurist nor the presentist perspectives. In contrast to Dodd, and following Schweitzer, he sees the apocalyptic expectation of an imminent end as a determining—but in the last analysis secondary—impulse of Jesus' preaching, and like Schweitzer he regards this expectation, which after all was not realized, as having no permanent significance. For Bultmann it is a part of that mythical world-view which has become scientifically, philosophically, and theologically valueless for us, and it must therefore be demythologized and interpreted existentially. On the other hand Bultmann differs from Schweitzer and supports Dodd in recognizing the presentist impulses of Jesus' preaching about the reign of God, and like Dodd he regards these presentist aspects as being decisive for Jesus and as having continuing value for us today. They reveal a new existential understanding of man and the myth of an expected end must be interpreted in these terms. The kerygma of the reign of God demands faith, not mythological thinking, and man is challenged to submit himself totally and obediently to the will of God. For the believer the eschaton takes place in the present, in the past, and in his decision which has constantly to be reviewed. In this case too there is no room for a detailed analysis of our position and a brief outline must suffice.

(*a*) The expectation in the New Testament that the end of time is near is a question of the greatest importance which needs examination. In particular there are three classic passages which seem to indicate an expectation that the end is near not merely on the part of the early Church, but on the part of Jesus himself. Does it not seem as though Jesus himself expected the coming of the reign of God to take place during the lifetime of living generations? "Truly, I say to you, there are some standing here who will not taste death before they see the kingdom of God come with power" (Mk. 9:1 par.). "Truly, I say to you, this generation will not pass away before all these things take place" (Mk. 13:30 par.). "When they persecute you in one town, flee to the next; for truly, I say to you, you will not have gone through all the towns of Israel, before the Son of man comes" (Mt. 10:23). Other passages, although they indicate no precise time, point in the same direction, especially the parables of the ten virgins, of the waiting servants, of the faithful and unfaithful servants, of the thief in the night. In all these passages the reign of God seems disturbingly and threateningly close. It is therefore not surprising that most exegetes incline to the view that Jesus himself felt that the end of time was near.

Interpretations of these three sayings have admittedly been very divergent: often they are not associated with the parousia, but have been seen as pointing to the transfiguration, the resurrection, Pentecost, the destruction of Jerusalem, etc. But even among those interpreters who refer to the parousia, considerable differences in detail are apparent. Thus in Mk. 13:30 par., for example, the words γενεὰ αὕτη have been taken as referring to the present generation, or the Jewish people, or the wicked and misguided people, and ταυτα πάντα has been seen either as the totality of eschatological events or as merely those events which *precede* the parousia. In view of the direct sense of the three texts, any interpretations which do not point to the imminent coming of the reign of God seem artificial and unconvincing, and are particularly weak with regard to Mk. 9:1 par. Surely no interpretation should overlook the eager apocalyptic expectations of the time of Jesus? Apologetic tendencies should not be decisive in interpretation. If the three sayings are seen in context, in the situation of the times, and are read according to their straightforward sense, then they point clearly (especially in the original Marcan wording) to the expectation of an imminent end. This does not exclude the fact that the exact day, a day on the calendar so to speak, is not and indeed cannot be given. The urgent summons to watchfulness is linked to the words "you know neither the day nor the hour" (Mt. 25:13; cf. 24:43 f.; Mk. 13:33, 35). Of particular importance is the undoubtedly genuine phrase which suggests that Jesus himself can know nothing about the precise time: "But of that day [i.e., day of Yahweh] or that hour [Mt.: and that hour] no one knows, not even the angels in heaven, nor the Son, but only the Father" (Mk. 13:32; Mt. 24:36). Any calculations in advance are similarly excluded by the words: "The kingdom of God is not coming with signs to be observed" (Lk. 17:20 f.; cf. 17:24; Mk. 13:21 par.).

If we attribute to Jesus the idea that the end was near, we can at all events take it for no more than an idea of expectation, conditioned by the age in which he lived, the meaningfulness of which did not lie in the giving of a *terminus ad quem*. For Jesus the question of precise times, which was so important for contemporary apocalyptics, was in no sense a central problem. The central question for him was: What does the reign of God, which is already irrupting into the present, mean for the concrete existence of mankind, what meaning does it give to man's life here and now? The apocalyptics thought of the kingdom of God in terms of the situation of man and of the world, and hence were concerned about the precise hour of its arrival. Jesus, on the other hand, thinks about the situation of man and of the world in terms of the reign of God already dawning. He is not concerned with the kingdom, with its nearness or with the moment of its arrival—for it is already dawning—but with man, his repentance, his faith, his decision for God and for his reign, here and now.

Jesus does not therefore see it as his task to satisfy human curiosity, to date and localize the kingdom of God, to reveal apocalyptic events and mysteries, to foretell the apocalyptic drama; his task is the proclamation of the approaching reign of God, in prophetically urgent and abbreviated terms; his task is to challenge man to a decision. Precisely because the reign of God, which is to come in the future, is already irrupting into the present, man has no time to bother about apocalyptic calculations, which always come too soon or too late; he must concern himself with his repentance and with doing the will of God, now, without any delay or hesitation. The direct confrontation of man with the reign of God is not something that will happen at some determinate or indeterminate future time, but something that is happening now, in these last days: the time is fulfilled *now* (Mk. 1:15), the hour of decision has struck *now*. It is time now for man to free himself from his slavery to money, power, instincts, the world, and give his heart to God the Lord. It is time now for him to give up deceit, hardness of heart, hatred and all wrongdoing, and devote himself to radical love for God and his neighbour. The presence of Jesus is the limited time of grace, is the final time of decision at the end of time. Here and now man experiences—as the beatitudes of the Sermon on the Mount indicate—his eschatological salvation.

We must therefore agree wholeheartedly with Bultmann's view that the decisive element of Jesus' message lies not in the expectation of an imminent end, but in the challenge to decide here and now for the reign of God. But in rejecting the expectation of an imminent end—and here Bultmann would undoubtedly agree in his own fashion—we should not reject any kind of expectation. The fact that the expectations of an imminent end were not fulfilled should not lead us, like the mockers of II Peter 2:3, to conclude that any expectations of something in the future are misplaced. If we stress the presentist character of the reign of God and the importance of a decision which always has to be made here and now, must we then conclude that the whole future of the reign of God must be dissolved into the present? Does the "now" of an already fulfilled reign of God exclude a future "then", a reign of God which God himself will complete in the future? Jesus himself does not resolve the tensions between presentist and futurist eschatologies, neither by reducing presentist eschatology to futurist eschatology, like the apocalyptics of his time, nor seeing futurist eschatology exclusively in terms of presentist eschatology, as Bultmann and in a different way A. N. Wilder does.[28] Bultmann, as we have seen, does not deny the elements of futurist eschatology in Jesus' preaching, but he is convinced that precisely this aspect of Jesus' message needs demythologizing.

(*b*) This is not the place for a debate about the word "demythologize".[29] If it means that Jesus' message about the

[28] Cf. A. N. Wilder, *Eschatology and Ethics.*

[29] For discussion of this issue, cf. above all the various volumes in the series *Kerygma und Mythos,* ed. H. W. Bartsch, Hamburg 1948, etc. (selections published in English under the title *Kerygma and Myth,* London 1953–New York 1962, etc.); of especial importance are the contributions by R. Bultmann, G. Harbsmeier, E. Lohmeyer, J. Schniewind, H. Thielicke, E. Stauffer, R. Prenter, F. Buri, C. Hartlich, W. Sachs, W. G. Kümmel, A. Oepke, H. Jaspers, H. Ott; from the Catholic viewpoint K. Adam, J. de Fraine,

kingdom of God ought to be translated out of the situation of that time and out of the mythological world-view current at the time into the language of our present situation and of our present world-view, then we not only may agree, we are bound to agree, out of respect for the original message and out of concern for man today. Our preaching of the reign of God today should not include the preaching of an outmoded view of life, for fear of its effect on the message itself and on those who hear it. This is especially true of times which are not subject to historical observation and control—the beginning and the end of time. From this viewpoint we have to demythologize *eschatology* as much as *protology,* something with which we are familiar in the context of Genesis exegesis. Protology is not an eyewitness account of bygone events

H. Fries, J. Hamer, A. Kolping, R. Schnackenburg, F. Theunis. Cf. also the following collections of essays: *Il problema della demitizzazione,* ed. E. Castelli, Rome 1961, with essays by K. Kerényi, J. Daniélou, P. Ricoeur, H. G. Gadamer, H. Lotz, H. Bouillard, V. Fagone, R. Lazzarini, A. Caracciolo, R. Panikkar, F. Bianco; *Kerygma and History. A Symposium on the Theology of R. Bultmann,* ed. C. A. Braaten and R. A. Harrisville, New York–Nashville 1962; *New Frontiers in Theology,* vols. 1 and 2, ed. J. M. Robinson and J. B. Cobb, New York 1963, etc.; with essays by G. Ebeling, J. Dillenberger, R. W. Funk, A. N. Wilder, A. B. Come, C. Michaelson, S. M. Ogden, etc. The following recent monographs are important: Karl Barth, "Rudolf Bultmann, An attempt to understand him," in *Kerygma and Myth,* vol. II, London 1962; E. Buess, *Die Geschichte des mythischen Erkennens. Wider sein Missverständnis in der "Entmythologisierung",* Munich 1953; F. Gogarten, *Demythologizing and History,* London 1955; H. Ott, *Geschichte und Heilsgeschichte in der Theologie R. Bultmanns,* Tübingen 1955; R. Marlé, *Bultmann et l'interprétation du NT,* Paris 1956; L. Bini, *L'intervento di Oscar Cullmann nelle discussione Bultmanniana,* Rome 1961; G. Hasenhüttl, *Der Glaubensvollzug. Eine Begegnung mit R. Bultmann aus katholischem Glaubensverständnis,* Essen 1963; G. Greshake, *Historie wird Geschichte. Bedeutung und Sinn der Unterscheidung von Historie und Geschichte in der Theologie R. Bultmanns,* Essen 1963; E. Hohmeier, *Das Schriftverständnis in der Theologie R. Bultmanns,* Berlin–Hamburg, 1964; A. Anwander, *Zum Problem des Mythos,* Würzburg 1964; F. Vonessen, *Mythos und Wahrheit. Bultmanns "Entmythologisierung" und die Philosophie der Mythologie,* Einsiedeln 1964. For the latest statement of his position by Bultmann himself, cf. *Glauben und Verstehen* IV, Tübingen 1965.

which has been handed down to us; and similarly eschatology is not an anticipatory report of events to come. The six days of creation and the narrative of the creation of man are, as we are well aware today, *images* which do not describe the scientific course of the origin of the world; they proclaim—and still proclaim to man even today—the splendour and uniqueness of the Creator and the greatness, simplicity and goodness of his work. In the same way the descriptions of the end of the world we find in the synoptic material, which were taken over from the prophets (especially Isaiah and Daniel) and from contemporary apocalyptic thinking, and which should not unquestioningly be attributed to Jesus himself—these descriptions of the stars falling from the sky, the darkening of the sun and angels blowing trumpets are not describing the scientific course of the end of the world, but proclaim the final completion and revelation of the reign of God at the end of time, as something which is beyond our comprehension and which can only be achieved by the power of God. In these various synoptic (or Pauline) descriptions, which incidentally do not agree at all, we must distinguish clearly between image and meaning, form and content.

Jesus himself spoke in the language and the imagery of his age; precisely because of this he was able to make the nearness and the certainty of the reign of God seem so real and so urgent. But he not only specifically dismissed predictions about the time of eschatological fulfilment; he reduced to a minimum, in comparison with later Judaic apocalyptic writings, pictorial descriptions of the reign of God, and directed attention towards man's decision for God, here and now. Images like that of the feast are not an end in themselves, but are intended to preach the message of salvation and demand a metanoia here and now. Jesus does not give *descriptions*, but *images* of the reign of God—as "life" (Mk. 9:43–47; cf. 10:17), "glory" (Mk. 10:37), "joy" (Mt. 25:21–23), "light" (Lk. 16:8). It is not the calculations as to when, or descriptions as to how the reign of God will come about that are important, but the absolutely certain fact that the reign of God will be perfected and completed. God reigns already; this much is revealed, made tangible, comprehensible and certain in Jesus. But God will also reign

in a quite different and new way, which will be revealed to
the whole world: namely, to quote a Pauline phrase which
also sums up the fact and not the manner of the future reign,
when God is not only in everything but is "everything to everyone" (I Cor. 15:28).

This perspective of a reign of God which has begun, but
nevertheless belongs to the future, is not something which
must be abandoned along with a mythological world-view; it
is a *decisive perspective of the New Testament kerygma itself.*
Just as we must distinguish between the protological myth
and the protological event of the creation, so also we must
distinguish between the eschatological myth and the eschatological event of consummation; for just as the Old Testament links its protological myths to history, so the New Testament links its eschatological myths to history. Not only
Jesus' own message, but the whole of the New Testament,
while concentrating on the idea of a reign of God which has
already begun and on the necessity for a decision here and
now, maintains the perspective of future fulfilment and futurist eschatology—not just unreflectively, but in full consciousness of the significance of this perspective. This is not
only true of Luke and the "early Catholic" writings. Paul
himself is full of the idea of living in an interim period, albeit
a short one. It would be wrong to talk in this context of "sur-
vivals of apocalyptic thinking". According to Paul the tension
between "already" and "not yet" is what conditions not only
the existence of the individual, but the whole history of this
interim epoch. Christian existence is lived between an indicative and an imperative, between present and future; the Christian community also lives in this tension, as the body of
Christ and the people of God, as consecrated and yet sinful;
the Holy Spirit has been given to it, but only as a guarantee
(II Cor. 1:22; 5:5), as the firstfruits (Rom. 8:23); baptism
and the Lord's Supper are at once remembrance of things
past and anticipation of things to come. All this is unthinkable without the idea of a real future, which belongs to God
and to God alone and which Paul obviously and ardently
hoped was imminent. The history of the individual, the history of Israel and of the Church are all directed towards the
ending of this interim period.

In remarks which are clearly directed against ideas prevalent in his own school, E. Käsemann writes: "It is perfectly plain that Paul is quite unable and unwilling to speak of an end of history as something that has already happened; but he sees the final epoch of time as having already begun. This is particularly the case since the resurrection of Christ, because since that time the cosmic forces have been under subjection. Paul in fact takes up the presentist eschatology of the enthusiasts, but unlike them he anchors and limits it apocalyptically. For Paul presentist eschatology is not an alternative to, but an essential part of a futurist eschatology, to put it in technical terms. Its realm is referred to as the basileia of Christ. . . . Presentist eschatology by itself, without the elements of futurist eschatology, is for the Christian nothing other than the hubris of the flesh, as enthusiasts of all ages have amply illustrated. It would be illusion, not reality. It is precisely Paul's apocalyptics which give reality its due and oppose a mere pious illusion."[30]

In the fourth gospel presentist eschatology is clearly much more important than elsewhere in the New Testament, and presentist and futurist eschatology is not combined in the same organic way as in Paul. But this does not prove that the original writer of the gospel had abandoned the communal faith of the original Church. In John too—provided that one does not dismiss the awkward passages as interpolations, as Bultmann does, without convincing exegetical or literary grounds—there are sayings which unequivocally point to the future and announce a final event to come on the "last day": 5:25–69; 6:39–40; 4:4; 5:4; 11:24; 12:48. But it is not so much an analysis of these passages in isolation as a view of the fourth gospel as a whole which provides the important evidence.

Recent interpretations such as those of L. van Hartingsveld[31] and J. Blank[32] bring out once again the strongly presentist-*futurist* character of the fourth gospel. "The interim period is extended here, as in Luke, in comparison with Jesus and Paul; as in Luke a

[30] E. Käsemann, *Exegetische Versuche* II, pp. 127 f. and 130.
[31] L. van Hartingsveld, *Die Eschatologie des Johannesevangeliums*, Assen 1962.
[32] J. Blank, *Krisis. Untersuchungen zur johanneischen Christologie und Eschatologie*, Freiburg 1964.

longer era of the paraclete and of the community is envisaged. But it would be wrong to think that it is no longer regarded as an interim period. All the teaching of the last discourses about the time of the Church is only comprehensible against a background of a futurist eschatology, and in the sayings of chapter 11 (vv. 25 f.) we may even discern a reference to the fate of the dead during this interim period. A view of the fourth gospel as a whole obliges us to give a *temporal* sense to the clear emphasis on the idea that the last days are *already here*. . . . But in this case presentist sayings only have meaning if they include the presupposition that what *has happened* now in him who has appeared in the flesh, *will happen* at the end of time."[33]

(c) We may therefore conclude that demythologization, or existential interpretation, is justified and necessary if we are to translate the message of Jesus unimpaired from the language of the mythological world-view of his time into the language of our present world-view, in order to accommodate it to man today, his language, his thinking about the world and about history, his capacity for understanding and the limitations of his understanding. It is only unjustified when it offers modern man an interpretation which has not only banished elements of an outmoded world-view, but has also eliminated what are consistent, fundamental and central perspectives of Jesus' message and of the whole New Testament. In stripping away the elements of an expectation of an imminent end, which belongs to the thinking of the time, we must not also excise the idea of expectation, a constant expectation of the reign of God which will only be completed in the future. An eschatology of this kind would lead to an entirely present-orientated view, to de-eschatologization, an eschatology without hope.

[33] O. Cullmann, *Heil als Geschichte*, p. 266; cf. also E. Ruckstuhl, *Die literarische Einheit des Johannesevangeliums*, Fribourg 1951, pp. 159 ff.; S. Schulz, *Untersuchungen zur Menschensohn-Christologie im Johannesevangelium*, Göttingen 1957, pp. 109 ff., 159 ff.; Kümmel–Feine–Behm, *Einleitung in das NT*, 12th edn., Heidelberg 1963; R. Schnackenburg, "Kirche und Parusie" in *Gott und Welt* I (Festschrift for Karl Rahner), Freiburg 1964, pp. 555 f., and bibliography; idem, *Das Johannesevangelium* I, Freiburg–Basle–Vienna 1965, pp. 38–40. Cf. also D. Holwerda, *The Holy Spirit and Eschatology in the Gospel of John. A Critique of R. Bultmann's Present Eschatology*, Kampen 1959.

An eschatology without future fulfilment indicates a *misunderstanding of the human situation:* "The reference to a real future yet to come, involving all the aspects of man's being, may be omitted; or it may be eliminated in favour of an existential actualism in the course of an ostensible 'de-mythization'; or it may be forgotten that man has a physical, spatio-temporal, bodily existence, even in matters of salvation and that the nature of man and of his one and total fulfilment must also be envisaged in the light of these things. But if so, man and his self-understanding have been really mythologized, because his linear direction in time towards what is still to come in time, and hence the dimension of his historicity, has been omitted. And since it is there that he works out his salvation with his God, his salvation would not take place where we really are."[34] An eschatology without future fulfilment also indicates a *misunderstanding of God:* "Since the New Testament announces as its central message an act of God at a definite moment in history to be a final redemptive act, the mythological form of the conception cannot simply be detached from this central message; for it would mean that the New Testament message itself is abrogated if a timeless message concerning the present as the time of decision or concerning the spiritual nearness of God replaces the preaching of the eschatological future and the determination of the present by that future. For this would result in a complete disintegration of Jesus' message that man through Jesus' appearance in the present is placed in a definite situation in the *history* of salvation advancing towards the end, and the figure and activity of Jesus would lose their fundamental character as the *historical* activity of the *God* who wishes to establish his kingdom. Therefore it is impossible to eliminate the concept of time and with it the 'futurist' eschatology from the eschatological message of Jesus (and from the New Testament altogether) . . ."[35]

Is everything in the biblical message which seems, to our modern view of life, "alien" and "impracticable", which "no longer appeals to us" or runs counter to our approach to the problems of today, simply myth? Even Bultmann would not maintain this. The idea of a stumbling-block, a *skandalon*, to any human conception of existence is an essential part of the New Testament message, and we must look for it where the

[34] Karl Rahner, *Theological Investigations* IV, London–Baltimore 1966, p. 331.

[35] W. G. Kümmel, *Promise and Fulfilment,* London–Napier, Ill. 1957, p. 148.

New Testament writers saw it, accepting the challenge of the new and alien problems it poses. It is not just the message of *future* fulfilment which is "alien" to men today; the message of the *cross* is already something alien—and this is why in his earlier writings F. Buri, in contrast to Bultmann's demythologization, called—mistakenly—for a consistent de-kerygmatization.[36] Why should it in fact be more alien to believe in a future revelation than to believe in a decisive revelation in the early years of the first millennium and hence, through the preaching of the message, in the present? Both make a radical claim upon our faith, and there is no sense in debating which demands "more". Both are ultimately in the world's eyes "foolishness"; and Acts 17:19–32 shows, lest we should be inclined to overestimate our modernity, that the difficulty existed long before the modern world and its conception of existence.

In contrast to Buri's demand for de-kerygmatization, Bultmann has continued to insist absolutely on the unique and decisive saving act of God in Jesus, which Buri in his earlier writings regarded as a "mythological remnant", an "illusion of exclusiveness", a "Christ-myth". And this insistence distinguishes Bultmann—a fact that is often overlooked—from the superficial theological liberalism of the nineteenth century. It is not surprising that Bultmann, being consistent in a completely opposite direction from Buri, should have accepted, on the basis of the whole New Testament, a new eschatological act of God, not only in the past, or rather in the present, but also in the future, in the time of fulfilment. The presupposition for such a view is faith in a living God with sovereign power to act in human history, a God who has in his power a future which is beyond the power of man, a future both limitless and incomprehensible.

As has just been suggested, the positive aspects of demythologization and existential interpretation must be recognized. The kerygma of the future consummation of God's reign is not a kind of objective prediction of mysterious events, a prophecy which aims to satisfy man's curiosity about the future. It is not an "appendix", a basically

---

[36] F. Buri, "Entmythologisierung oder Entkerygmatisierung der Theologie" in *Kerygma und Mythos* II, Hamburg 1952, pp. 85–101.

superfluous addition to a reign of God which is already present. The kerygma of future consummation, precisely because it is the consummation of something that already exists, is an appeal, a challenge, a call to decision, a call to faith and to the enhancing and fulfilling of our existence in the *present,* in the context of an ultimate future which is itself revealed to us in the *present.* Eschatological present and eschatological future: however little they may overlap, they are irrevocably linked and perpetually interact.

1. The present points to the future: the final period of history begins with Jesus. But this final period—a period which despite everything is only too obviously temporary, for precisely when we see with the eyes of faith we cannot overlook all the wretchedness and sin, the suffering and death of the present time—is directed towards a specific goal, as the whole New Testament kerygma makes plain; it is a time hastening towards its end. Only our expectations of a future *eschatological* action give us, in the darkness of the present, the certainty of faith; faith that God's saving act is not exhausted in the imperfect, temporary and uncertain present, but is directed towards a perfect, permanent and revealed future (cf. I Cor. 13:9–12). Faith, that is, that God's reign will not remain on the drawing-board, but will be carried out and consummated, in a future which is both the real present, from moment to moment, and a real future. Precisely the preaching of the *nearness* of the reign of God affirms the certainty that God's saving act is directed towards definitive consummation at the end of time. Since the reign of God has been preached, has begun, and is already effective—through and in Jesus—in the present, the hope for a consummated and revealed reign of God is not an empty and unfounded hope directed to the future alone; but a hope, rooted in already fulfilled realities, for the future consummating of this present reality through the eschatological saving act of God, which is the same and yet new. The decisive moment of the final period of time has already occurred, and so the ending of that period is inevitable. The present reality of the reign of God is already open to man's experience, and so its future is assured; it has begun with Jesus, it will be consummated in Jesus. God acts in the present *and* in the future; the one is de-

pendent on the other, and hence faith and hope belong together as different perspectives of one and the same acceptance of God's gracious will in the present and in the future.
Because we believe in the present, we can, against all hope,
hope for a future; and because we hope for a future, we can,
against any *skandalon*, believe in the present.

2. The present points to the future, but the future also
points back to the *present:* man's decision must not simply
be a consolation for the future, and an excuse for neglecting
the present world; it is rather a reason for changing it. As we
have seen, the hour is *now*. Precisely because of the real future which we await, but which is already dawning in the
present, the *present* time is not a time without salvation, a
time of mere waiting, but a time of salvation, the time for a
unique decision. Precisely in the light of a future goal, not
something that has begun but something that will be completed, the future reign of God, man in the *present* is challenged to a radical decision, the present is for him the "last
days", the eschaton. Both in relation to the future and in relation to the present man must decide between belief and
unbelief. As Martin Dibelius writes:[37] "Only, the decision
now is not whether or not those apocalyptic hopes are ade-
quate, but whether or not one recognizes in the radical nature
of the Gospel and of the One who proclaimed it the genuine
sign of the actuality of God. The man who affirms this will at
the same time realize that this actuality is not something in
space and time; but he will know that it exists, and he will believe that it must some time, somehow or other, come to pass
—otherwise God would not be the ruler of the world and of
history. But the man who recognizes in the tradition about
Jesus the Christ contained in the New Testament the true
'sign' of God will also recognize that this actuality has already
begun to come to pass, precisely in the event whose record is
the New Testament."

But what—the question which can no longer be ignored—
has all this to do with a Church? The word "Church" (community) is not important, as far as Dibelius' book about Jesus
is concerned. What need is there to interpose something be-

[37] Martin Dibelius, *Jesus,* London 1963–Philadelphia 1949, pp.
134–135.

tween God and man, between the reign of God and the decision of faith? Did Jesus have anything to do with a Church? Did he intend a Church at all?

3. JESUS AND THE BEGINNING OF THE CHURCH

In dealing with this question, too, it is far from easy to face up to the evidence of history. It would be far easier, as is often done in both Catholic and Protestant dogma, simply to repeat dogmatic statements and comment on them. And yet we must take the more difficult course if we are to face up to the historical truth about the formation of the Church. We have long since passed the stage when it was possible to relate the history of the Church by re-telling, with commentary, the Acts of the Apostles, and filling in the story with other New Testament and related material.

After some early attempts during the time of the Enlightenment (J. L. von Mosheim), it was Ferdinand Christian Baur, one of the Tübingen school, who first tried to write a complete history of the early Church on a purely *historical* basis. He was followed by other members of the Tübingen school—influenced like Baur by the philosophy of Hegel—and then by members of Ritschl's school, under the influence of neo-Kantianism and with tendencies towards positivism (E. von Dobschütz, R. Knopf, H. Lietzmann, J. Weiss, C. Weiszäcker and especially A. von Harnack); finally after the turn of the century by the comparative religion school (W. Bousset, W. Heitmüller, P. Wernle, H. Weinel, W. Wrede), which contributed to the form-criticism school (R. Bultmann and M. Dibelius). Pure historicism was defeated, not only by the Bultmann school, but also by scholars more interested in "salvation history" (J. T. Beck, J. C. von Hofmann, G. Kittel, J. Schniewind, T. Zahn and finally A. Schlatter) and by English and American scholars (P. Carrington, C. T. Craig, A. C. McGiffert, B. H. Streeter), who, while not denying the importance of historical research, were anxious to give full weight once more to the content of revelation in the New Testament.

But the view of the New Testament writings as kerygma—not as purely historical documents, but as writings subserving the practical preaching of the faith—makes it particularly difficult to find a satisfactory solution to the problems con-

cerning Jesus and the Church. It is hard to draw a dividing
line in individual matters between history and its interpretation, between historical report and kerygmatic presentation, between records of facts and theological reflection and
application, between words spoken before the first Easter and
realizations which followed it. What is true hermeneutically
of the whole New Testament is also true of the words and
events which may be taken to be ecclesiologically significant;
and especially true of the words of commission which the
gospels and the Acts report as words of the risen Christ.
There are marked divergences in these reports as to time and
place, as to those who were addressed, as to the exact words
and their content—differences which are difficult to sort out
historically. There can be no doubt that the form of these
texts was considerably influenced not only by the original
writer or editor of the texts, but also by the whole situation of
the early Christian community, its worship and its preaching,
its discipline and its mission. In consequence, exegetical interpretations are similarly very divergent. Catholic exegesis in
particular has generally avoided this, the most difficult aspect
of the ecclesiological problematic of the New Testament, and
preferred to write countless treatises about the theology and
the form of the New Testament Church; a fact which makes
systematic investigation particularly difficult. The line which
we intend to follow here is that pursued both critically and
constructively by two more or less representative specialists in
the matter, Anton Vögtle on the Catholic side[38] and Werner

[38] Anton Vögtle, "Ekklesiologische Auftragsworte des Aufer-
standenen", in *Sacra Pagina* II, Paris–Gembloux 1959, pp. 280–294;
"Jesus und die Kirche", in *Begegnung der Christen* (Festschrift
for Otto Karrer), Stuttgart–Frankfurt 1959, pp. 54–81; "Der
Einzelne und die Gemeinschaft in der Stufenfolge der Christus-
offenbarung", in *Sentire Ecclesiam* (Festschrift für Hugo Rahner),
Freiburg 1961, pp. 50–91; "Exegetische Erwägungen über das
Wissen und selbstbewusstsein Jesu", in *Gott und Welt* I (Festschrift for Karl Rahner), Freiburg 1964, pp. 608–667. Cf. also
J. Betz, "Die Gründung der Kirche durch den historischen Jesus",
in ThQ 138 (1958), pp. 152–183; O. Kuss, "Bemerkungen zum
Fragenkreis: Jesus und die Kirche im NT", in ThQ 135 (1955),
pp. 28–55; R. Schnackenburg, *God's Rule and Kingdom*, pp. 215–
270; idem, the article "Kirche" in LThK VI, pp. 167–172; H. Ried-
linger, *Geschichtlichkeit und Vollendung des Wissens Christi,*

G. Kümmel on the Protestant.[39] Our objective must be to discern, in the welter of problems thrown up by this centuries-old controversy, some measure of agreement. What common ground can be found between these exegetes?

(*a*) In the *pre-Easter period,* during his lifetime, *Jesus did not found a Church:*

In his preaching and ministry Jesus never addressed himself merely to a select group separated from the mass of the people. There were plenty of such select groups in Jesus' time. The Qumran texts in particular document the claim of this community to be the holy remnant, the pure community of God's elect, the chosen community of the new covenant. In preaching the coming reign of God, Jesus could not avoid dealing with the vital problem of the eschatological people of God, in particular with the question of who would inherit salvation and on what conditions. To this last question Jesus frequently gave an answer.

It is striking that Jesus, while aware, even painfully aware, of the decisive and divisive effect of his message and the fact that it was rejected by the majority of his people, never bases his preaching on the idea of the remnant, as the other select groups of his time did. He stresses a public ministry and rejects withdrawal from the world; his love for sinners, which excludes no one and is a source of scandal, is an urgent protest against any religious separatism and exclusiveness. Jesus supports neither the banding together of the Pharisees with its exclusivist tendencies, nor a community or sect in the manner

Freiburg 1966. For further bibliography, cf. A I, 3 and B I 2 above, also the literature for Matthew 16:18.

[39] W. G. Kümmel, *Kirchenbegriff und Geschichtsbewusstsein in der Urgemeinde und bei Jesus,* Uppsala 1943; *Promise and Fulfilment,* London–Naperville, Ill. 1957 (with bibliography); "Jesus und die Anfänge der Kirche" in *Studia Theologica* 7 (1953), pp. 1–27; "Die Naherwartung in der Verkündigung Jesu" in *Zeit und Geschichte* (Festschrift for R. Bultmann), Tübingen 1964, pp. 31–46. Cf. also A. Oepke, "Der Herrenspruch über die Kirche in der neueren Forschung", in *Studia Theologica* 2 (1948), pp. 110–165; P. Nepper-Christensen, *Wer hat die Kirche gestiftet?*, Uppsala 1950; O. Cullmann, *Peter,* London–Philadelphia 1962. For further bibliography, cf. A I, 3 and B II, 2 above, also the literature for Matthew 16:18.

of the Essenes. He is aware that his mission is not to gather up the "just", the "righteous", the "pure", but to gather up the *whole* of Israel. To be sure, the idea of the Messiah necessarily includes that of the messianic community. But Jesus does not allow himself to be pressed into a premature sundering of the good from the wicked, the wheat from the tares. He sees the whole of Israel as a unity, as a pitiable flock lacking a shepherd. It is this total Israel, rather than a holy remnant or community, which he sees as called to be God's people in the last days. To the very last, despite all his lack of success, Jesus addressed himself to *all* the ancient people of God.

What then of the founding of the circle of twelve? This too illustrates precisely not the singling out of the select few, but the calling of Israel as a whole. The twelve were to represent Jesus' call to the whole people of the twelve tribes and therefore to have the rôles of rulers and judges in the time of eschatological consummation. The wider circle of disciples called to follow Jesus personally is similarly entrusted with the mission to Israel as a whole. It is true that its missionary task makes particular demands on this group, but in spite of this there is no specific rule of life nor is membership a condition of salvation. Neither the circle of his disciples nor even those Israelites who showed themselves ready for repentance were ever organized formally into a society by Jesus.

It is not surprising then—indeed it is an argument for the authenticity of the gospel accounts, which in this respect were certainly not inflated by the primitive Christian community— that the gospels do not report any public announcement by Jesus of his intention to found a Church or a new covenant or any programmatic call to join a community of the elect. Such statements would have been interpreted as the founding of a separate synagogue and would have minimized and confused the uniqueness of Jesus' preaching. The alarming message that the eschatological act of God had really begun and that the demand of the hour to each man to repent was imperative would have been weakened, had Jesus formed his supporters into a visible organization. Nothing in the gospel accounts gives us to infer that Jesus ever publicly demanded more from men, as a condition of entry into the reign of

God, than the obedient acceptance of his message of salvation and the immediate and radical submission of the individual to the will of God. The saying at Matthew 16:18, of which authenticity and interpretation have been much debated—and which in any case was not a public utterance—is the only time in the gospels when Jesus speaks of an ecclesia as a total Church; and these words precisely situate the building up of a Church not in the present but in the future. Neither those Jesus had called to repentance and who now followed him nor the smaller circle of his special disciples was the "Church of Christ" or even the "new people of God". Jesus does not separate them from the rest of Israel nor contrast them, as a new people of God, with the ancient people of God. The believers among the Israelites who followed Jesus' public ministry are not referred to in the New Testament as the "new people of God", nor are the "twelve" or the "disciples" referred to as the inner circle or kernel of this new people of God. The new people of God—as distinct from the old and as its eschatological continuation—in the first place is revealed by the preaching of the apostles; but it is also the Church which is made possible by the death and resurrection of Jesus. For all the New Testament writers the Church is conditioned by the death and resurrection of Christ. Not until Jesus is risen from the dead do the first Christians speak of a "Church". The Church (and in this sense the new people of God) is therefore a post-Easter phenomenon. The statistical evidence that the word ἐκκλησία only appears at Matthew 16:18, or perhaps also with reference to the individual community at Matthew 18:17, is therefore completely irrelevant. So the idea of the Church remains unaffected by the question of whether these sayings are authentic.

It must be noted in passing that the easy solution of deducing the idea of the Church from the central concepts of Jesus' preaching does not work. Such a deduction from a collective, or rather individual-collective, interpretation of the title "Son of Man" is unfounded, as closer examination shows;[40] nor

---

[40] For arguments against the collective interpretation put forward above all by F. Kattenbusch, and in English by T. W. Manson, C. J. Cadoux and V. Taylor especially, cf. A. Vögtle, *Der Einzelne*, pp. 54–65; on the idea of the remnant, cf. pp. 80–83.

can it be deduced from the reign of God described in the parables (of the fish-net, the leaven, or parables of seeds and growth), for this reign of God is always seen in the gospels as a future entity created solely by the gift and the act of God, not as a worldly, temporal reign of God on earth which would develop organically through our human actions, would grow intensively and extensively, become institutionalized and finally be more or less specifically identifiable with the Church.[41] The reign of God cannot be identified with the people of God, the Church, any more than the saving act of God can be identified with man's reception of salvation.

(*b*) In the *pre-Easter period,* Jesus, by his preaching and ministry, *laid the foundations* for the emergence of a post-resurrection Church. It is no accident that all the gospels are interested in Jesus' preaching and ministry in the pre-Easter period down to the last detail. The emergence of the Church after Easter is directly connected with Jesus' pre-Easter ministry; how is this? Jesus revealed the reign of God, promised for the future, in the present through his person and in his ministry; he revealed sufficient to confront men with the hour of decision, the decision for belief or unbelief, obedience or disobedience. In this way he called the whole nation to belief in his message of good news and to repentance. At the same time the effect of his message was a divisive one and, although he did not form them into a group, those Israelites who accepted his message in faith are decisively distinguished from those who rejected it as far as the coming reign of God is concerned. These are the sole aspirants to salvation, who belong to the future community of salvation at the end of time. Apart from the twelve he chose a greater number of disciples who shared a way of life with him; the later members of the Church are those who were formerly disciples of Jesus of Nazareth. Jesus proclaimed both the dawning of the reign of God and the emergence of the eschatological messianic people, to which he claimed his disciples belonged. He reckoned with an interim period between his death and the parousia, even though an historical study of the texts does

[41] On exegesis of the parables of growth, cf. Schnackenburg, *op. cit.,* pp. 143–159.

not permit us to draw the definite conclusion that Jesus saw this period as lasting for generations and centuries. And since Jesus foresaw that Jerusalem, which was called to salvation, would reject it and that instead the heathen would be called to the eschatological feast, he proclaimed a new people of God, one not based simply on ethnic origins, which would take part in the eschatological completion. "There can be no question that Jesus reckoned upon his disciples gathering together again after his death and resurrection and sharing in a common meal and that, waiting and persecuted, they would be opposed by the great mass of the unbelieving members of the ancient people of God. The common experience of personal communion with the living Jesus, especially as a result of communal meals, would inevitably have led, in addition to the common experience of the resurrection, to a new alliance between the disciples. It was their common allegiance to Jesus, to the 'man' now hidden, but who would soon reveal himself in glory, which according to Jesus' expectation would remain a constant factor for the disciples, even after his death, and would continue to bind them together. The fact that Jesus would then no longer be among them as an earthly human being, but that they could believe that through his resurrection he had already entered into God's glory, would not only strengthen them in their waiting for the parousia, but also in their certainty that the coming eschaton had already irrupted into the present in the person of Jesus."[42]

(c) The Church has existed *from the time of faith in the resurrection.* As soon as men gathered together in faith in the resurrection of the crucified Jesus of Nazareth and in expectation of the coming consummation of the reign of God and the return of the risen Christ in glory, the Church came into existence. Not in the pre-Easter period, but certainly in the post-Easter period, primitive Christianity speaks of the "Church". Thus there was never—as was widely held at the beginning of this century—an original Church-less, enthusiastic period, which was only gradually succeeded by a Church with all its limitations. At the same time the Church was from

[42] W. G. Kümmel, *Jesus und die Anfänge,* pp. 26 f.

the first moment of faith in the resurrection seen as something *given by God*. As a work of God it was regarded as essentially different from other human groups and communities and took on similarly a very different form. This stress on the act of God, working in and through Christ, is revealed in the language of the primitive Church. The most often used phrases are "church *of God*" (ἐκκλησία του θεου), "people of God" (λαὸς του θεου); even though the Church, in its very earliest interpretations of itself outside the gospels, is undeniably christocentric and founded on the life of Christ, it is only occasionally described as the Church of Christ (ἐκκλησία του Χριστου) (Rom. 16:16; cf. Gal. 1:22).

(*d*) The *origins* of the Church do not lie solely in the intention and the message of Jesus in the pre-Easter period, but in the whole *history of Jesus' life and ministry:* that is, in the entire action of God in Jesus Christ, from Jesus' birth, his ministry and the calling of the disciples, through to his death and resurrection and the sending of the Spirit to the witnesses of his resurrection. Not the words and instructions of Jesus in the time before Easter alone, but the action of God in resurrecting the crucified Christ and in pouring out the Spirit, turned the group of those who believed communally in the risen Jesus into a community of those who, in contrast to the unbelieving ancient people of God, could claim to be the new eschatological people of God. Precisely through giving full weight to this idea of the saving action of God, expressed in the whole life and ministry of Christ, can we see that the validity of individual sayings of Christ which have ecclesiological importance, especially post-Resurrection sayings, does not depend on whether historical criticism can demonstrate their authenticity as sayings of Jesus (even the Pauline doctrine of baptism, "Christ-mysticism" and the concept of the Body of Christ do not stem directly from actual words of Jesus). It was not any particular words of Jesus, nor ultimately his teachings, but his person as the hidden Messiah and as the risen Christ, which historically speaking constitutes the roots of the Church.

As far as these basic ideas are concerned, most exegetes, as represented here by Kümmel and Vögtle, would seem to be in agreement, however differently they may view individual points such as the imminent expectation of an end.

While a few exegetes, out of what may be regarded as exaggerated historical scepticism, would go somewhat less far, others go much further. Vögtle himself, supporting J. Jeremias, goes beyond Kümmel in assuming, without sufficiently weighty grounds, that Jesus, as a result of the deadly hostility of the spiritual leaders of his people and the rejection of his message of salvation by Israel as a whole, was led to see the meaning of his fate as a prophet in terms of the representative sufferings of the servant of God, suffering on behalf of Israel and hence for the salvation of "the many", Israel and the Gentile nations. In his view, the gospel accounts are authentic in relating how after a certain time Jesus began, admittedly only in the circle of his disciples, to talk about his death of atonement (especially on the occasion of the Last Supper). This atoning death, leading to a new covenant, would explain the idea of the founding of a Church, as at Matthew 16:18. "That Jesus regarded his violent death, which he foresaw as an atoning death for 'the many' (that is, for all people from all nations) and ascribed to it the power to create a new covenant, led to a completely new situation, seen in terms of the economy of salvation. The proof that Jesus understood his death in this way is the really decisive point in the question of the founding of a Church. Seen from this viewpoint, his death brought an entirely new prerequisite for 'entry into the kingdom of God', for membership of the community of aspirants to salvation, or rather the community of the saved at the completion of God's reign; it also laid new foundations for the message and means of salvation in the future situation, which would be fundamentally different from the pre-Easter one. This interpretation of his death as a redeeming death created an entirely new situation in salvation-history; but Jesus only spoke of it—understandably and fittingly, as we can now see—to the specifically constituted circle of the twelve and beyond any doubt at the Last Supper (J. Jeremias; J. Betz). It is here that Jesus uses the word 'covenant', which in this situation is revealed for what it is, as completely different from all other contemporary attempts to realize the idea of the covenant; 'new', as it is clarified in the Pauline–Lucan tradition. Among these same disciples, to whom was revealed the meaning and purpose of his dying, Jesus announced the future building of 'his Church'—whether at the same time or earlier is immaterial, certainly under similar suitable conditions;

the 'Church' which is to be the new community of the heirs of salvation, purified from sin by his death."[43]

This short and systematic investigation of the beginnings of the Church, supported by the sound opinions of representative exegetes, has naturally not attempted to answer all questions and remove all the difficulties which are posed by present-day exegesis and source-studies—for example those connected with Matthew 16:18. But we hope to have indicated a possible way which neither denies the validity of historical data nor bypasses them with the aid of *a priori* dogmatic assertions, but attempts to understand and come to terms with them. It is a middle way—not in the sense of a compromise, however—and one which is supported by the present state of critical research. It is distinct from the one-sided ecclesiology of a scholastic dogmatism which is too uncritical of its presuppositions and which would take Jesus as having, in the pre-Easter period, the intention of founding an organized Church (as envisaged for example by modern Catholic canon law), or indeed maintain that he did found it, formally and juridically. It is equally distinct from a one-sided exegesis, similarly uncritical of its presuppositions, which regards the pre-Easter Jesus and the community of the Church as two totally different things. The most orthodox theologian is not necessarily he who, looking at the sayings of Jesus in the gospel accounts, takes as *many* of them as possible to be authentic. The most critical theologian is not necessarily he who takes as *few* of them as possible to be authentic. Uncritical belief misses the point in theology as much as unbelieving criticism. True faith strengthens rather than hampers criticism. True criticism fructifies rather than destroys faith.

All we have, in fact, done in this chapter is to explain, make

---

[43] A. Vögtle, *Der Einzelne,* p. 90; for further discussion of this hypothesis, cf. A. Vögtle, *Exegetische Erwägungen,* pp. 642–643; J. Jeremias, *The Eucharistic Words of Jesus,* London–New York 1966, pp. 210–229. On the dogmatic consequences, cf. Karl Rahner, "Dogmatic Reflections on the knowledge and self-consciousness of Christ", in *Theological Investigations* V, London–Baltimore 1966, pp. 193–215.

precise and give theological background (starting from the present state of research) to the fundamental and, by contrast with earlier doctrinal statements (especially anti-modernist ones), cautiously worded par. 5 of the Constitution *De Ecclesia:* "The mystery of the holy Church is manifest in her very foundation, for the Lord Jesus inaugurated her by preaching the good news, that is, the coming of God's Kingdom, which, for centuries, had been promised in the Scriptures: 'The time is fulfilled, and the kingdom of God is at hand' (Mk. 1:15; cf. Mt. 4:17). In Christ's word, in His works, and in His presence this kingdom reveals itself to men. The word of the Lord is like a seed sown in a field (Mk. 4:14). Those who hear the word with faith and become part of the little flock of Christ (Lk. 12:32) have received the kingdom itself. Then, by its own power the seed sprouts and ripens until harvest time (cf. Mk. 4:26–29). The miracles of Jesus also confirm that the kingdom has already arrived on earth: 'If I cast out devils by the finger of God, then the kingdom of God ha come upon you' (Lk. 11:20; cf. Mt. 12:28). Before all things, h wever, the kingdom is clearly visible in the very person of Christ, Son of God and Son of Man, who came 'to serve, and to give his life as a ransom for many' (Mk. 10:45). When Jesus rose up again after suffering death on the cross for mankind, He manifested that He had been appointed Lord, Messiah and Priest forever (cf. Acts 2:36; Heb. 5:6; 7:17–21), and He poured out on His disciples the Spirit promised by the Father (cf. Acts 2:33). The Church, consequently, equipped with the gifts of her Founder and faithfully guarding His precepts of charity, humility, and self-sacrifice, receives the mission to proclaim and to establish among all peoples the kingdom of Christ and of God" (CE 5).

In this way a critical path is opened up which ecclesiology can follow in a critically sound and acceptable manner to show what the concept of "Church" means in the New Testament. We have seen that against the background of eschatological expectation there is a quite legitimate way from the message of the reign of God to the Church. At the same time it would be illusory to try and establish historically that Jesus' own preaching includes the constituting and ordering of a Church or gives a basis for taking the elements of constitution and order which may be discerned in the New Testament as forming a closed system. On the other hand, this does not exclude the fact that Jesus' preaching includes elements which the young Church, during its time of complex development, could recognize as factors of order of the first importance.

But while stressing the historical problems, we must not overlook existential ones. What is important is whether we today can regard the transition from Jesus of Nazareth and his message to the early Church and its message as historically legitimate. But apart from the fact that the decisive factor in this transition—the significance for salvation of the cross and the resurrection of the crucified Christ—can only be recognized in faith, the important question affecting the acceptability of the Church is whether it is *factually* connected with the message of Jesus and hence with Jesus himself: did it receive his message in faith and live it convincingly? If not, then to prove a historical connection is of little value. Only if the Church lives the message of Jesus can it be acceptable for the man who is at the very least open to the message of Jesus himself. Only then can a positive answer be given to Dostoievski's question quoted at the beginning of this chapter and echoed by so many others. The rest of this section is devoted to a study of the relationship between the message of Jesus and the Church.

III. THE ESCHATOLOGICAL COMMUNITY OF SALVATION

1. THE EKKLESIA AS CONGREGATION, COMMUNITY, CHURCH

Without the raising of Jesus from the dead, Christian preaching and Christian faith is futile (I Cor. 15:14–20). More than that: without the raising of Jesus from the dead the community of believers, the Church, is meaningless. Only the certainty that the crucified Christ lives on as the risen Christ, glorified by God, gives us the solution to the riddle of Jesus as a person and makes the Church possible and real. The different accounts of the resurrection, which, in contrast with the apocryphal writings, is not described by the canonical gospels, do not agree in detail, as a brief comparison between the various New Testament accounts shows. Only by doing violence to the texts could they be artificially harmonized. But this kind of agreement is not their aim; they are not police reports. As texts which belong to the preaching of the Church, they are kerygmatically inspired, elaborated and applied. But they agree in one decisive point: Jesus who had been crucified is alive and lives in the glory of God; as the glorified Christ he revealed himself to the disciples. The precise how, when and where is unimportant; what matters is the fact of his resurrection.

The oldest circle of Jesus' disciples based its account, with considerable emphasis, on meetings which they really and unquestionably had with Jesus, whom God had raised from the dead. The Church sprang not from imaginings, not out of a baseless credulity, but from real experiences of encounters with one who was truly alive; from the standpoint of unbelief these encounters may be challenged, but no interpretation of the disciples' witness can explain them away. Certainty replaces anticipation, affirmation replaces doubt. Jesus the preacher becomes Jesus the preached, the bearer of the message becomes the central substance of the message. Jesus is now recognized and acknowledged to be what he has now revealed himself to be: the Messiah (the anointed king, the Christos, a word which was later attached like a second name to that of Jesus), the Son of Man descended from heaven, the Son of David, the Servant and Son of God, the Kyrios, the Lord (the name especially used in the hellenistic world).

With this affirmation of faith a *new community* is born. The scattered disciples congregated once more in Jerusalem, the focal point of the coming reign of God. The experience of this new community is a cause of joy and gratitude for the disciples; the sources nowhere suggest that there was any disappointment, as might be if this community were only a temporary solution in view of the postponed parousia. The disciples celebrated their communal meal, their "breaking of bread", with "glad hearts" (Acts 2:42–47), in eschatological joy. The new community applies to itself the Old Testament prophecies concerning the last days. In fulfilment of ancient prophecies the special gift of the last days, the *spirit of God* is bestowed on them: this is the significance of the account of Pentecost. This spirit, which the Jews regarded as having deserted Israel after the time of the last prophets, but which was promised again for the last days, is effective in a variety of ways in the new community: in the new prophets, in the gift of tongues and acts of power, in finding the right words when on trial. From the beginning the initiation rite of the new community is baptism, as prefigured by John: a bath of purification from the guilt of sin, witnessing to repentance and looking forward to the coming reign of God and administered now in the name of Jesus.

Thus in many ways the new group of disciples may be seen as the *eschatological community of salvation*.[44] More and more clearly and profoundly the coming of Jesus is recognized as the single decisive event, as the truly eschatological event. The faith born of Easter overcomes the stumbling-block of the cross and renews its decision for Jesus by seeing his death as a death for sinners. Through faith in the risen Christ the disciples can interpret what appeared as a curse—this is how the Jews understood crucifixion—as an event of salvation, as *the* saving event. The death and resurrection of Christ are seen as the decisive eschatological action of God. The earthly past of him who came and the future of him who should come was seen in a new light. But the power of the risen Christ does not reveal itself to the community only in a future not yet present, but already in the new present, the time which dates from the resurrection. Jesus, whose earthly ministry the community now sees in a new light, whose coming as the Son of Man it looks forward to, this Jesus already reigns as the Christ glorified by God.

In this way the new community of disciples comes to see itself as the eschatological community called and chosen by God. The renewed decision of the disciples for Jesus, which the death on the cross made necessary, was only made possible by God's eschatological action in Jesus. Thus the members of the community rightly bear the title: "the elect" (ἐκλεκτοί), "the saints" (ἅγιοι). They form a community which can with justice take over the great title of the Old Testament and equally of the eschatological community

[44] Cf. the bibliography given above for A I, 3.

of God: *kehal Yahweh,* the "community of God". This name had been used by the Jews to describe not only Israel, but also the eschatological people of God, which would be revealed by the gathering up of the still scattered and hidden Israel. The corresponding Greek word, which became established as the name of the community, was "Ekklesia of God" (ἐκκλησία του θεου) today simply called the "Church".

The word "Church" has, through varied usage in the course of centuries, developed a variety of meanings and nuances. The usual word in *Germanic* languages ("Church", German *"Kirche"*, Swedish, *"Kyrke"*, cf. Slav *"carkov"*), does not come from *"curia"*, as Luther supposed (which contributed no little to his dislike of the word as opposed to the word "community" or "congregation", *Gemeinde*). The word did not stem from Rome, but was carried up the Danube and down the Rhine from the Gothic kingdom of Theodoric the Great. Its origin was the Byzantine Greek form κυρική (for κυριακή, supply: οἰκία) which means "belonging to the Lord", or in its full form "Belonging to the house of the Lord"; this might be briefly rendered as "kyrios-community". By contrast with the Germanic languages, the Romance languages kept a direct connection with the word used in the New Testament: Latin *ecclesia,* Spanish *iglesia,* French *église,* Italian *chiesa.* All stem from the Greek ἐκκλησία. What does this word mean?[45]

The word ekklesia is also used in Greek in secular contexts, as is shown by the story of the riot against Paul at Ephesus in Acts 19:32 and 39 f. When Thucydides, Plato, Xenophon and later Greeks speak of ekklesia, when Greek citizens read inscriptions about the ekklesia, the meaning was immediately clear: the citizens are the ἔκ-κλητοι, those called out and summoned together by the herald; the ek-klesia is therefore "those who have been called out", the gathering of "those who have been summoned together": a meeting of the people. For all its religious undertones, ekklesia refers to a political meeting, not to a cultic or sacred meeting. And ekklesia only refers to the actual congregation, each particular "ses-

---

[45] Cf. the article "ἐκκλησία" by K. L. Schmidt in ThW III. pp. 502–539, and the articles in the various biblical and theological dictionaries.

sion"; there is no ekklesia in the intervals between them. The difference between this ekklesia and ekklesia meaning Church is evident. It is therefore impossible to relate New Testament usage of the word directly to its secular Greek usage.

The important thing for the New Testament ekklesia is not Greek etymology, but the use of the word in the Greek translation of the Old Testament. In the Septuagint the word occurs about a hundred times, almost always as a translation of the basically secular Hebrew word *kahal*, that is, a meeting of the people summoned together (the word *"eda"*, the community of the people as a juridical or cultic community, is usually translated by συναγωγή). The important references are those where the word ἐκκλησία is qualified by the phrase "of the Lord" (of Yahweh). Here too the process of congregating has not been forgotten, but in this case it is not a congregation of anybody for any purpose: God gathers together and the ekklesia therefore becomes a community *of God* (often also the case when the word ekklesia is used by itself without qualification). The ekklesia of God is more than an arbitrary congregation of arbitrary people, and more than the process or occasion of such a congregation. The ekklesia is the congregation of those previously chosen by God, who gather round God as their centre. The word is therefore used in the Septuagint in a religious and cultic sense, and is increasingly given an eschatological sense, as the admittedly rare use of the word *"kahal"* in the Qumran writings indicates (e.g. 1 QSa 1:4; 2:4; Dam 12:6). Ekklesia comes to mean the true eschatological community of God.

By taking over the term ekklesia, the early Christian community made its claim to be the true congregation of God, the true community of God, the true eschatological people of God. Although the word does not occur in the gospels (except for Mt. 16:18; 18:17), nor in Titus, II Timothy and Jude (but cf. I Tim. 3:5 and 15; 5:16), nor in I John and II John (but cf. III Jn. 6 and 9 f.), nor even in I Peter and II Peter (but cf. the equivalents at I Pet. 2:9 f.), the word is of special importance in Acts and in the Pauline writings.

In Acts the word is used to refer to the ekklesia in Jerusalem (Acts 5:11; 8:1, 3; but used referring to the people of Israel in the wilderness at 7:38), and then of the ekklesia in the whole of Judaea, Galilee and Samaria (9:31). In this latter passage some textual traditions have *"ekklesiai"* in the plural, and this is the common reading in other passages (15:41 with few exceptions; especially 16:5). In later chapters reference is made to the ekklesia in Antioch, and those in Caesarea and Ephesus (20:28 is especially important). In each case the reference—even though only once made explicit, it is implicit elsewhere—is to the ekklesia *of God;* it is God who gathers his people together (cf. 20:28).

Paul too speaks on numerous occasions of the Church in the plural (e.g. I Cor. 11:16; 14:33; II Cor. 8:18; 12:13; Gal. 1:2, 22; Rom. 16:4, 16). Singular and plural are often interchangeable; sometimes the article is used, sometimes not. The place of the ekklesia is often mentioned. Frequently it is a town: Thessalonica (I Thess. 1:1; II Thess. 1:1), Corinth (I Cor. 1:2; II Cor. 1:1), Cenchreae (Rom. 16:1), Laodicea (Col. 4:16). But is also often a district: Asia (I Cor. 16:19), Galatia (I Cor. 16:1; Gal. 1:2), Macedonia (II Cor. 8:1), Judaea (Gal. 1:22; I Thess. 2:14). By contrast, even small house communities are referred to by Paul as ekklesia (Rom. 16:5; Philem. 2; cf. Col. 4:15), and may be listed alongside larger communities (I Cor. 16:19). Paul also uses the word with especial reference to the community gathered together for worship (I Cor. 11:18; 14:23, 24; the concrete idea of congregation is specifically mentioned at I Cor. 11:18 and 20 and 33 f.; 14:23; cf. 14:26). Only in Ephesians does the Church as a whole occupy the central place in Paul's reflections, particularly in the context of the one Church composed of Jews and Gentiles. But whatever form the ekklesia may take, it remains and is often specifically called the ekklesia of God (cf. I Cor. 12:28). God acts through Jesus Christ. Thus the Churches of the New Testament are congregations of God in Christ, are Churches in Jesus Christ (I Thess. 2:14; Gal. 1:22) or Churches of Jesus Christ (Rom. 16:16). The Germanic words for "Church" are, seen in this light, accurate translations of the New Testament ἐκκλησία. Factually speaking, ekklesia is precisely the community of the Lord.

What conclusions may be drawn from this necessarily brief

analysis of the New Testament usage of the word *ekklesia?* The following basic points seem to emerge:[46]

(*a*) Ekklesia, like "congregation", means both the actual *process of congregating* and the *congregated community* itself: the former should not be overlooked. An ekklesia is not something that is formed and founded once and for all and remains unchanged; it becomes an ekklesia by the fact of a repeated concrete event, people coming together and congregating, in particular congregating for the purpose of worshipping God. The concrete congregation is the actual manifestation, the representation, indeed the realization of the New Testament community. Conversely the community is the constant source of the constantly repeated event of congregating. In many languages the word "church" is still used today in the sense of the act of coming together—"it is time for church", "before (after) church", "at church" or "in (as opposed to in the) church"—here the sense is always that of the actual congregating of the community, their worship.

(*b*) *"Congregation"*, *"Community"*, *"Church"* are not mutually exclusive terms, but should be seen as interconnected: the undeniable fact that the New Testament itself always uses the same word "ekklesia" where we should say "congregation", "community", or "Church", should warn us against trying to invent contrasts here. The three words are not in competition, but complement one another in translating the very rich and many-faceted "ekklesia". "Congregation" expresses the fact that the ekklesia is never merely a static institution, but one that exists through the repeated event of a concrete coming together. "Community" emphasizes that the ekklesia is never merely an abstract and distant superorganization of functionaries set above the concretely congregated community, but is a fellowship of people who meet regularly at a given place and a given time for a given purpose. "Church" makes it plain that the ekklesia is never merely a disconnected jumble of isolated and self-sufficient religious groups, but the members, united through their indi-

[46] Cf. the bibliography given above for A II, 2.

vidual service, of an all embracing fellowship. Generally these three words, especially the last two, are interchangeable, while it remains true that "congregation" emphasizes a concrete event, "community" a constant local group, "Church" a supra-local fellowship, and hence in translating ekklesia different words may be chosen in different cases. But fundamentally they are interchangeable, and one may speak of a local Church as well as of a local community, and of a total community as well as a total Church.

(c) Each individual ekklesia (each individual congregation, community or Church) is not *the* ekklesia (the whole Church, community or congregation); but none the less fully represents it: this means two things. Firstly: the local ekklesia is not a "section" or a "province" of the whole ekklesia. It is in no way to be seen as a sub-division of the real "Church", which as the wider unit must therefore be regarded as senior in rank and more important. It is an unfortunate fact that the word "Church" is habitually used to describe the whole ekklesia—this is one consequence of an abstract and idealizing concept of the Church, as though the Church were not *wholly* present in every place, endowed with the *entire* promise of the Gospel and an *entire* faith, recipient of the *undivided* grace of the Father, having present in it an *undivided* Christ and enriched by the *undivided* Holy Spirit. No, the local Church does not merely *belong* to the Church, the local Church *is* the Church. The whole Church can only be understood in terms of the local Church and its concrete actions. The local Church is not a small cell of the whole, which does not represent the whole and which has no purpose in itself. It is the real Church, to which in its own local situation everything is given and promised which it needs for the salvation of man in its own situation: the preaching of the Gospel, baptism, the Lord's Supper, different charisms and ministries. Secondly: The "whole ekklesia" is not a "collection" or "association" of local Churches. In the New Testament the word ekklesia is used to describe the various communities in their different localities, and both singular and plural forms are variously used. At the same time, both in Acts and in Paul's writings, especially in Ephesians, the word ekklesia is used in a supra-local sense. Even though the relationship between the local Churches and the whole Church is not laid down, either theologically or juridically, in the New Testament, it is certain that the individual local Churches are united by more than a common term, by more than some external union, by more than an organization which is superior to the individual Churches. All individual communities receive one and the same Gospel, all receive the same mission and the same promise. All are subject to the grace of one and the same Father, have one and the same Lord, are inspired by one and the same Holy Spirit in their charisms and their ministries. They believe one and the same faith, are sanctified by one and the same baptism, and refreshed by one and the same meal. Through all these things—and what could be more important than these?—they are not just linked together externally, but internally united; they form not just an ecclesiastical organization, but one Church. The Church is not a limited company or organization of individual communities; the ekklesia is not made by adding together the local Churches nor can it be broken down into them. Rather, *the* ekklesia of God exists in each place. There is not a Corinthian ekklesia (or an ekklesia of the Corinthians, or an ekklesia of Corinth), but: "the ekklesia of God, which is at Corinth" (I Cor. 1:2; II Cor. 1:1). Each ekklesia, each congregation, community, Church, however small, however poor, however insignificant, is a full and perfect manifestation of *the* ekklesia, the congregation, the community, the Church of God.

(d) It is as a congregation that the ekklesia of men is *God's* congregation: it is a meeting together of people who in faith acknowledge their fellowship. Hence one may speak of an "ekklesia of the Thessalonians" (I Thess. 1:1; II Thess. 1:1)—but ultimately only "in God the Father and the Lord Jesus Christ", as Paul at once adds. Ekklesia is more than the congregation, it is the congregated fellowship of faith. This gathering of people does not take place arbitrarily or idiosyncratically. They have been summoned together to the "ekklesia of God". Even where this genitive is not explicitly supplied, it is unquestionably implicit. Both the whole ekklesia and single ekklesiai—the genitive is attached to plural and singular alike—are "of God". The beginnings of the Church do not lie with men as individuals. The Church is not composed by the free association of individuals; it is more than the sum of its members. Naturally it cannot exist without the decision and the faith of individuals; but these are preceded by God's call. This is what creates the Church and makes the response of faith possible in the first place. Man has no control over this divine summons. The ekklesia is, in spite of institutionalistic misconceptions, the fellowship of believers; it is also, in spite of mistaken religio-sociological ideas, the foundation and creation of the God who calls: the *congregatio fidelium* only exists as *con-vocatio Dei*, the *communio sanctorum* only exists as *institutio Dei*.

This whole matter can be summed up in the words of Vatican II: "This *Church* (ecclesia) of Christ is truly present in all legitimate *local congregations* of the faithful (*fidelium congregationes locales*) which, united with their pastors, are themselves *called churches* (*ecclesiae*) in the New Testament. For *in their own locality* these are the *new people called* (*vocatus*) *by God*, in the Holy Spirit and in much fullness (cf. I Thess. 1:5). In them the *faithful are gathered together* (*fideles congregantur*) by the preaching of the gospel of Christ, and the *mystery of the Lord's Supper* is celebrated, 'that by the flesh and blood of the Lord's body the whole brotherhood may be joined together' (Mozarabic prayer). . . . In these communities, though frequently small and poor, or living far from any other, Christ is present. By virtue of Him the one, holy, catholic, and apostolic Church gathers together" (CE 26).

This then is the "ekklesia, the congregation, community, Church of God in Jesus Christ", made possible and real through God's raising of the crucified Jesus of Nazareth to life and to dominion and through the gift of the Holy Spirit. For this Church—and here all parallels with later Judaism and with the Qumran communities break down—the decisive eschatological turning-point has already begun with Jesus the Christ. The promises of God have been fulfilled, his faithfulness affirmed: "But when the time had fully come, God sent forth his Son" (Gal. 4:4). The eschatological time of salvation has begun and will soon be consummated. This eschatological period between fulfilment which has come and consummation which is to come is the temporary, interim period of the Church. It is precisely its expectation of the coming parousia which unites the Church and gives it its distinctive form. Precisely because the Church confesses Jesus as Lord, it has confidence that the Lord himself during this interim period will lead the new community and with it the world to its predestined goal. Hence the Church from the very beginning saw itself as an eschatological phenomenon.

But things did not remain so: the fire of eschatological expectation soon grew cold, the Church's eschatological self-interpretation of itself soon petered out. Christ becomes less and less the expected Lord; he is increasingly taken over by the Church as its present possession. The Church sees itself less and less as a temporary community. It establishes firm roots in this world. The period soon begins in which the Church identifies itself with the kingdom of God, an identification which was made over and over again during the succeeding centuries, and provoked an extreme reaction whereby any link between Church and kingdom was denied. The time has come, on the basis of the above analysis, to examine more closely the relationship between the Church and the reign of God.

2. SIMILARITIES AND DIFFERENCES BETWEEN CHURCH AND REIGN OF GOD

Is it not the case—and this could serve as an excuse for many things in the history of the Church and of theology—that even in the New Testament the original message of Jesus about the reign of God is very quickly overlooked in the Church and by the Church? A simple statistical check is again revealing and at the same time disturbing: in Luke's gospel the phrase "the reign of God" occurs around forty times, but only seven times in the whole of Acts, where it is often specifically associated with the name of Jesus; in all the missionary sermons which are quoted the phrase does not occur once. Moreover, the references to the basileia are very general, even stereotyped, in tone.

But in this context it is vital to note that Luke himself evidently saw no contradiction in mentioning the basileia in so many passages of his gospel and at the same time failing to emphasize it in Acts, where it would have been easy to bring it into some of the missionary sermons. Why this clear difference between the gospel and Acts? What lies between the two? The answer is simple: Easter. The verbs of preaching (εὐαγγελίζεσθαι, κηρύσσειν) themselves reveal that now something else has become of more importance; for the object of these verbs is now much more frequently Jesus Christ than the basileia. The preaching of Jesus is not of course contradicted, it is maintained. But through his death and resurrection Jesus the preacher has become Christ the preached. He is now the centre of the apostolic message: the crucified Messiah, raised by God from the dead and raised to the glory of God, the Christ in whom the Scriptures have been fulfilled. The reign is now his, the Lord's. Certainly the post-Easter community did not forget the reign of God; but it interpreted it in a new light: the reign of God has become decisively operative in the reign of the glorified Jesus. In his reign the coming completed reign of God is proclaimed and in his reign it is already effective: through the eschatological gift of forgiving sins, through the pentecostal gift of the Spirit to everyone who believes and is baptized. Thus the christological interpretation of the reign of God, which is already associated in Matthew and Luke with the reign of Christ (or of the Son of Man), is taken up again and developed further by Luke in Acts.

The evidence of Acts is confirmed in the writings of Paul. He too speaks noticeably rarely of the reign of God, only eight times in the uncontroversial Pauline letters, and four of those are merely the stereotyped phrase "to inherit the kingdom of God" (I Cor. 6:9, 10; 15:50; Gal. 5:21; cf. Eph. 5:5). The future eschatological basileia stands in the foreground (cf. also I Thess. 2:12; II Thess. 1:5; cf. Col. 4:11), but Paul does not overlook the fact that the reign of God is effective and can be experienced in the present: "For the kingdom of God does not consist in talk but in power" (I Cor. 4:20); "For the kingdom of God does not mean food and drink but righteousness and peace and joy in the Holy Spirit" (Rom. 14:17). It is not surprising that Paul speaks specifically of the present reign of the glorified Lord in the time between resurrection and parousia: the reign which Christ will deliver to God the Father at the end, after destroying every rule and every authority and power; for he must reign until he has put all his enemies, including the last enemy, death, under his feet (I Cor. 15:24-28; cf. Col. 1:13; Eph. 5:5; II Tim. 4:1, 18; Heb. 1:8; II Pet. 1:11). That will be the new fully redeemed humanity and the new world, in which God will be everything to everyone: the completed reign of God.

For Paul too what the reign of God is becomes clear in the light of Easter: it is the present reign of Christ, in which the coming completed reign of God—which for Paul unequivocally includes the final and revealed victory of Christ, the conversion of Israel and the resurrection of the dead—is revealed and becomes effective in the present: for his preaching too the central element is Jesus as the Christos and Kyrios. This is the reason why in preaching the "Lord Jesus Christ" the concept of the reign of God becomes of secondary importance; because the glorified Kyrios shows in himself the meaning of the reign of God in which the Church lives. This also explains why Paul's preaching does not contrast the reign of God and the reign of Christ, indeed does not even consciously distinguish between them. At work in the reign of the glorified Jesus Christ is the reign of God himself; God exercising his dominion over the Church and the world in a hidden but totally effective way through Christ. So Paul clearly anticipates what Luke is later to describe as "the good news about the kingdom of God and the name of Jesus Christ" (Acts 8:12) and so Luke rounds off his great bipartite work with the words: Paul preached "the kingdom of God and taught about the Lord Jesus Christ quite openly and unhindered" (Acts 28:31). We find similar words at Acts 28:23: "And he expounded the matter to them from morning till evening, testifying to the kingdom of God and trying to convince them about Jesus both from the law of Moses and from the prophets." (With reference to the claim to kingship in John, where other terms as well as basileia are used, with the exception of 3:3 and 5, especially "[eternal] life", cf. in particular, John 18:36 f., but also 3:35; 5:35; 5:27; 10:28; 14:3; 17:2.)[47]

(*a*) Christ as Lord proclaims and brings about the reign of God in its full meaning. For this very reason the danger exists that in the interim period the basileia is identified with the Church. The *identification* of Church and basileia is suggested by the fact that the reign of God, for all its futurist quality, has at the same time a presentist dimension; it irrupts into the present and hence could easily be taken to be simply a "kingdom of God",[48] both present and developing.

With Irenaeus, who placed the kingdom of God in the context of salvation-history, and Clement of Alexandria, with his markedly spiritualistic and ethical conception of the kingdom of God, as his forerunners, *Origen* took the kingdom of God as meaning above all the "kingdom of God within us", as referring to the autobasileia of Christ in the soul of each individual, and saw the Church platonically as the earthly image of a heavenly kingdom of God. Not until the historical turning-point in the reign of Constantine did the "Christian" religio-political idea of an empire emerge, as developed by the Byzantine court theologians (Eusebius of Caesarea) under the slogan: "one God, one Logos, one Emperor, one Empire". In this view the *Christian imperium* is the fulfilment of the messianic time of salvation. As a result the Church became a State Church, subordinate to the imperium. This Eastern imperial theology of the kingdom of God is not so very different from the episcopal theocracy of the West, as supported by Athanasius, Ambrose, Hilary and the Roman bishops in opposition to Byzantine caesaro-papalism. For the idea of a theocracy also implied an extensive identification of the kingdom of God with earthly realities, in this case with an hierarchical Church. However, the idea of a theocracy was strong enough to outlive the collapse of the Roman empire.

It was *Augustine* whose genius purified the theology of the kingdom in this time of decadence, by making clear the distinctions between it and the political theology of the empire, as well as contemporary apocalyptics. Christendom ruled over by the emperor

[47] For further examination of the biblical evidence, cf. the bibliography given above for B I, 2, and especially Schnackenburg, *God's Rule and Kingdom*, pp. 271–347.

[48] On the historical development, cf. the bibliography given above for A I, 2.

was not for him simply the temporary earthly representation of the final realm of God. He sees both State and Church as being in a state of tension with regard to the consummated eschatological realm of God, which will comprise the full number of the elect. The Church, or rather its hidden kernel (the elect), appears as no more than the beginning of the kingdom of God, in so far as the elected faithful partake with angels and saints in the reign of Christ. On the other hand Augustine includes apocalyptic chiliasm in his view of the Church, in as far as the Church is seen as the historical form of the thousand-year kingdom and hence as the kingdom of Christ. World history cuts across salvation history: it is the sixth age since Adam and in the Church the historic struggle of the kingdom of God, the *civitas Dei,* against the kingdom of darkness, the *civitas diaboli,* is taking place; the outcome of this struggle at the end of time will be the definitive victory of the kingdom of God and the attainment of heavenly peace.

Augustine's profound view of the kingdom, which is very roughly outlined above, had an immense influence during the whole *medieval* period, but precisely its differentiations were not pursued. The Middle Ages are characterized by an often massive consciousness of a real kingdom of God present on earth, the full achievement of which was, in the early medieval view, to be the work of the emperors, in the later medieval view, the work of the popes (Dante had other ideas). Detailed interpretations changed and varied, but for the theology both of the Carolingian and the Papal imperium, Christendom, the *corpus christianum* guided by *regnum* and *sacerdotium,* was for all practical purposes identical with the *civitas Dei.* The members of the *civitas diaboli* included all outsiders: heretics, Jews and pagans. Hence the crusades equally with the missions could be seen as an extension of the kingdom of God.

This identification of the kingdom of God with an increasingly secularized Christendom produced various *reactions*—some of which suggested new identifications. There is the reaction of the apocalyptic movements, to which we shall return later; the reaction of *mysticism,* which from Eckhart via Tauler, Suso and Ruysbroeck down to the *devotio moderna,* regarded the kingdom of God as something totally inward and identified it with God himself, as experienced in the depths of the individual soul; the reaction of *humanism* (Erasmus, for example), which gave a moral interpretation to the idea and saw it developing, according to the ideal of Christ, in virtue, knowledge and human progress towards a "golden age"; finally the most violent reaction of the *Reformation.* Zwingli took up the humanist interpretation of the kingdom of God, and a number of Anglicans (Whitgift, later Hooker) extended this towards an identification of the kingdom of God and the Christian community (*civitas Christiana,* Christian commonwealth). Luther, on the other hand, while his concept of the kingdom of God is extremely complex, revives a number of Augustine's views: for him the kingdom of God is the hidden realm of faith, realized by the saving action of the crucified Christ in the forgiveness of sins, extended solely through the word of preaching. But at the same time Luther sees the kingdom of God operative as the spiritual rule of God in the world, which extends in a hidden manner through the reign of Christ. From this standpoint he could defend himself against the enthusiasts who claimed to base their views on him, and give a theologically strong position to secular authority, which was to lead finally to widespread State control of the Church. Calvin, who among all the reformers worked out the most extensive theology of the kingdom of God, extends his conception in the opposite direction towards Church control of the State (Geneva): the function of a christocracy is to penetrate the whole of human society, Church and State alike. The kingdom of God is the area in which God establishes his reign in Christ, through justification and sanctification, and finally leads dynamically to its completion. But like the other reformers Calvin too overlooked the importance of the decisively eschatological character of the reign of God, which fundamentally rules out any identification either with an institutionalized or with a hidden Church.

The *modern age* produced various and contradictory views of the kingdom of God, with marked differences in the Lutheran and Reformed traditions, in pietism and enlightenment, and in the Catholic Tübingen school (J. S. von Drey, J. B. Hirscher). But as a whole there is a clear tendency to take a moralizing and immanent view, which leads to secular and speculative interpretations of the idea of the kingdom of God. A long but not inconsistent line leads from the Enlightenment and from Kant, through Fichte, Schelling, Hegel and Schleiermacher (for whom the kingdom of God always plays an important part) to *R. Rothe,* who considered that Christ ought to be liberated from the Church, in order that the kingdom of God be realized in the State, as the highest embodiment of morality and religiosity, and to *A. Ritschl,* who saw the kingdom of God as the religious idea revealed through Jesus Christ, and as the moral ideal of the Christian, a chief good which it must be the community's task to fulfil; it is to be fulfilled within the natural order of man's place and rôle in society out of brotherly love; Church and State are the means whereby moral spirit and moral perfection are created.

Thus, both through adopting and through reacting against the idea of a kingdom of God which was identified with the Christian imperium and the Christian Church, an idea of the kingdom of God emerged which was largely identifiable with Christian bourgeois society and culture, the worldly and ethical kingdom of liberal Protestantism, for which eschatological expectation was a meaningless idea. It was only with the shock rediscovery of the strictly eschatological and transcendental character of the basileia by *Johannes Weiss* and *Albert Schweitzer* (other English deists, Reimarus and D. F. Strauss, had pointed the way) that the diastasis between the reign of God and Christian society, between the reign of God and the Church, was once more recognized and given its proper weight.

In the light of the New Testament message, as it has been rediscovered for us by modern exegesis,[49] it is impossible to speak of Christian society or even of the Church as being "God's kingdom on earth", the "present form of the kingdom of God", the "forerunner of the kingdom of God". But it would also be wrong to suggest—however well-intentioned the suggestion—that the Church builds up the kingdom of God, extends it throughout the earth, or works for its realization. The Church, after all, prays, not "Let us realize thy kingdom!" but "Thy kingdom come!" The transcendental and eschatological character of the reign of God, as the reign of *God*, makes any identity or even continuity out of the question. There can be no question of identity (Church=kingdom of God), for the reign of God according to the New Testament is the universal, final, and definitive basileia. There can be no question of continuity ("The kingdom of God emerges from the Church"), for the reign of God is not the product of an organic development, of a process of maturation or interpenetration, but of a wholly new and unprepared perfecting action of God. Man's part is the way of readiness and openness, obedience and watchfulness, faith and repentance.

So far from stressing identity, we should be concerned to stress the basic *difference* between the Church and the reign of God. To apply to the Church what is said in the New Testament about the reign of God will inevitably lead to an intol-

[49] Cf. the bibliography given above for B I, 2.

erable glorification of the Church, the presentation of an *ecclesiologia gloriae* with the Church as its end. This is to forget that the power and the glory of the reign of God are still to come, that the promises made through and in the Church have not yet been fulfilled, that the Church is called to pilgrimage, not to rest. It is to forget that the Church is composed of men, and sinful men at that; it is to forget that the Church's preaching, its baptism and its Lord's Supper are announcing something that has not yet been fulfilled.

While ekklesia is something essentially of the present, something finite, basileia is something which, although it has irrupted into the present, belongs fundamentally to the future. Ekklesia is a pilgrimage through the interim period of the last days, something provisional; basileia is the final glory at the end of all time, something definitive. Ekklesia embraces sinners and righteous, basileia is the kingdom of the righteous, of the saints. Ekklesia grows from below, can be organized, is the product of development and progress and dialectic, in short is definitely the work of man; basileia comes from above, is an unprepared action, an incalculable event, in short is definitely the work of God. God is the subject of this reign, he himself as the Lord and Father acting in kingly freedom and sovereignty. The reign of God is *his* kingly dignity, his act and his domain.

It is not the Church but the consummated reign of God which is reflected in so many parables: those of the tree overshadowing the earth, of the rich harvest, of the feast given by God, of the eschatological marriage feast. It is not the Church but the consummated reign of God which is the goal of creation: the new creation, in which the distinctions between Church and world will be overcome. The term "God's kingdom", which indicates something finished and complete is apposite, not for the basileia which has irrupted into the present, but for this consummated cosmic basileia and the images used for it.

(*b*) The identification of God's reign with the Church can very easily lead to *dissociation*. Countless varieties of apocalyptical utopianism have arisen, protesting against the Church as the "kingdom of God on earth", invoking future judgment and the coming reign of God against the existing Church. In these cases the kingdom of God is seen not as something distinct from the Church, an opposite pole, but as an opponent and enemy. At the same time we should not forget that the apocalyptics, for all their bizarre or erroneous notions, were better able to understand the crucial character of the reign of God than their opponents, who were ready to employ force and violence to defend the ecclesiastical establishment.[50]

The idea of an apocalypse, drawn from the New Testament and often linked with the expectation of an imminent end and with speculation about the thousand-year empire of the apocalypse (chiliasm) was at first, in the writings of the apostolic Fathers (Letter of Barnabas, Ignatius) and the apologists (Justin) for example, not directed against the Church. But criticism developed as the Church became more institutionalized. In Montanism and for *Tertullian,* however, the enthusiastic-pneumatic idea of the kingdom of God was directed against the Church as a whole, while Donatism and Novatianism emphasized the pneumatic element in the Church. The increasingly clericalized Church of the empire provoked more and more determined opposition. In particular this was true in the middle and late medieval period, from the spiritualists connected with the abbot Joachim of Flora, who looked forward to the "third age of the Holy Spirit", down to the eve of the Reformation, with the execution of the Dominican Savonarola. During this time the secularized imperial Church was opposed by an ideal of the kingdom of God that was apocalyptic and chiliastic, and finally allied even overtly to the idea of social revolution. There is a clear line from the spiritualists round Joachim of Flora to the Hussite Taborites and on to the Bohemian Brethren and the enthusiasts of the Reformation period.

The enthusiasts of the Reformation period can therefore be regarded as a continuation of the medieval enthusiasts, though they were given new and decisive impetus by Luther. For some the apocalyptic notion of the kingdom of God led to a revolutionary struggle against order, against State and Church (Th. Müntzer, M. Hofmann, and the Baptists of Münster), for others it led to a mystical lack of concern with the world (C. Schwenckfeld, S. Franck). Numerous links connect the enthusiasts of the Reformation period with modern *apocalyptic sects* (Irvingites, Adventists, Mormons, Jehovah's Witnesses), but also, and this is no less im-

[50] On the historical development, cf. the bibliography given above for A I 2.

portant, with secularized imperial utopias, with the socialist eschatology of Marx, Engels and the Russian revolutionaries and to the messianism of National Socialism (Hitler's Third Reich as the thousand-year Reich). All these movements were radically anti-ecclesiastical. On the other hand, the beginnings of *research into the life of Jesus,* and in particular the rediscovery of the basic eschatological dimension of Jesus' preaching by English deists, and by Reimarus, Strauss and the advocates of "consistent eschatology", also had a clear anti-ecclesiastical tendency. From their standpoint the Church was no more than an ersatz affair, an attempt to solve the problem of a reign of God, prophesied by Jesus, which had not arrived; and it was in this sense that Loisy's phrase, quoted at the beginning of the chapter, was usually taken. But this brief sketch of the history of enthusiasm shows that dissociation from the Church does not necessarily lead nearer to the reign of God, even though it remains true that most of these movements, apart from "accidents" of personality or locality, have arisen because of the failure of the secularized Church to fulfil Jesus' message of the reign of God. A total dissociation of the reign of God from the Church can only be avoided if the Church does not set itself up as the kingdom of God, and make Jesus' challenge into the possession of the church.

The message of Jesus, as far as we can see it today,[51] allows for neither identification of Church and reign of God, nor dissociation between them. Seen from the New Testament, it is impossible for the Church, provided it remains true to the original charge entrusted to it, to be regarded as a contradiction to the idea of the reign of God. As an eschatological community of believers, the Church is not a fill-in, a compromise solution, and ersatz kingdom for the kingdom of God which was awaited in vain. The eschatological community of believers is not in opposition to the reign of God, nor are the two unconnected; the Church is directed towards and belongs to the coming reign of God. In this context therefore it is important to stress not dissociation but the connection between the two. The eschatological community of believers comes from the preaching of the reign of God—the reign of God is its beginning and its foundation. And it moves towards the revealed consummation of the reign of God—the reign of God is its goal, its limitation, its judgment. The Church is not

[51] Cf. the bibliography given above for B I, 2.

the kingdom of God, but it looks towards the kingdom of God, waits for it, or rather makes a pilgrimage towards it and is its herald, proclaiming it to the world.

The Church on its pilgrimage is not deserted or forgotten by God; it is not wandering totally in the dark. Even though it is not the kingdom of God which is to come, it is already under the reign of God which has begun; though looking forward to the final victory of the reign of God, it can look back to the decisive victory: in Jesus the Christ; while still wandering in the shadow of death, it has the resurrection not only ahead of it, but in its decisive form behind it: in Jesus the risen Kyrios. This living Kyrios is with it, remains with it, all days until the consummation of the world, until the coming of the kingdom of God in glory. Until that time it is under the reign of this Kyrios, the reign of Christ, which will also continue until the coming of the reign of God. The reign of Christ, the hidden ruler of the whole world, is already effective in the Church: in the preaching of the word, which already has power to forgive sins, to renew men and so to proclaim the consummation of all things; in the giving of baptism, a visible sign and action which makes men members of the eschatological community, in which the old man is buried in penance and the new man arises in faith to become part of the new creation; in the celebration of the Lord's Supper which proclaims and represents the eschatological meal of salvation in the glory of the Father and is shared by the heirs of God's kingdom until the Lord comes again. The Church has already been granted the Holy Spirit, if only as a guarantee. So at work in the Church, though constantly in jeopardy, is the love which will remain with it and in it always.

Thus the Church as the eschatological community of salvation lives and waits and makes its pilgrim journey under the reign of Christ, which is at the same time, in Christ, the beginning of the reign of God. Thus the promises and powers of the coming reign of God are already evident and effective, through Christ, in the Church, which so partakes in a hidden manner in the dawning reign of God. Thus the Church may be termed the fellowship of aspirants to the kingdom of God. But it should not be regarded as a preparatory stage in the journey to the kingdom of God. There is no continuity from stage to stage, from the Church to the final reign of God, and belonging to the Church is no guarantee, in this era of temptation, of belonging to the final kingdom of God.

The Church is not a preliminary stage, but an *anticipatory sign* of the definitive reign of God: a sign of the reality of the reign of God already present in Jesus Christ, a sign of the coming completion of the reign of God. The meaning of the Church does not reside in itself, in what it is, but in what it is moving towards. It is the reign of God which the Church hopes for, bears witness to, proclaims. It is not the bringer or the bearer of the reign of God which is to come and is at the same time already present, but its voice, its announcer, its *herald*. God alone can bring his reign; the Church is devoted entirely to its service.

But does the Church really serve the reign of God? The Church as we actually know it? Is the Church's service of the reign of God a fact, or only a theory, a programme? At all events this is the duty and calling of the Church: to serve the reign of God.

3. IN THE SERVICE OF THE REIGN OF GOD

The New Testament, particularly the synoptic kerygma, shows that despite the preaching of Jesus as the crucified and risen Lord, the *message of Jesus himself* was not forgotten. While the Church proclaims the message of Jesus as the Lord, it also takes over the message of the reign of God in concentrated form: it becomes the voice of Jesus himself. It takes over the radical demands of Jesus, preaches them to others and practises them. For the early Christians Jesus remains the preacher of the reign of God, the preacher of the necessity of total submission, without compromise, to the will of God. The same divine demands which Jesus had preached under the heading "the reign of God", the Church now preaches under the heading "Jesus the Lord", because this same Jesus fulfilled all the demands of the reign of God in an exemplary way and was thus raised to the glory of the Father. The Church is preaching the same as Jesus preached; his preaching of the reign of God is genuinely continued by the Church's preaching of the reign of Christ. The Church is given an understanding of the mystery of the reign of God (Mk. 4:11). The reign of God, fulfilled, realized, and personified in Christ, remains the horizon of the Church, and the focal point of its own life and which it strives to bring to the world.

If the Church wants to be a *credible* herald, witness, demonstrator and messenger in the service of the reign of God, then it must constantly repeat the message of Jesus not primarily to the world, to others, but to itself; the Church must accept in faith the message of the coming reign of God which has irrupted into the present, and constantly accept anew and in obedience the reign of God which is already present, God's gracious and demanding salvific will. Its credibility—and no amount of energetic and busy activity can replace that vital factor—depends totally on its remaining faithful to the message of Jesus. The five perspectives of the preaching of the reign of God through Jesus which we examined at the beginning of this chapter, thus become ecclesiological imperatives.

(*a*) *Jesus* preached that the reign of God is a decisive, *future, final event at the end of time*. If the *Church,* following Christ, preaches the reign of God as something future and final, there are certain inevitable consequences.

The Church should not make itself the focal point of its preaching in these last days; its task is to point from the fulfilled reign of God in Christ to the coming reign of God, towards which it looks as the crucial consummation of its mission. The Church is moving towards the revelation of God's victory and glory, a revelation which will be universal, not particular, definitive, not temporary. It should not pretend to be an end in itself or appear to claim for itself the glory which rightly belongs to God. It must not give the impression that man's decision is for the Church, rather than for God, for Jesus the Christ. It must not give the impression that the *Church* itself is the end and consummation of world history, something definitive, or that it is the *Church's* definitions and declarations, rather than the word of the *Lord,* which stand for ever; or that the *Church's* institutions and constitutions, rather than the reign of God, outlast all ages. It must not give the impression that man exists for the Church, rather than the Church for mankind, and hence for the reign of God.

A Church which in these last days forgets that it is something temporary, provisional, and interim, makes too many demands upon itself; it grows tired and weak and will fail because it has no future. A Church, on the other hand, which is constantly aware that its goal is not in itself, but can only be found in the kingdom of God, can survive, knowing that it has not demanded too much of itself, that it does not need to pretend it is something definitive, an abiding city; it is not surprised when in its temporary state it is shaken by doubts, deterred by obstacles and weighed down with cares. The Church would certainly despair if it considered itself something final and definitive; it is precisely because it is only something provisional that it can hope. Christ's promise to the Church was that the gates of hell shall not prevail against it.

(*b*) *Jesus* preached that the reign of God is *an all-powerful act of God himself.* If the Church, following Christ, preaches the reign of God as an all-powerful act of God himself, there are again certain inevitable consequences.

The Church in these last days must not try, however great its efforts in the service of the reign of God, to create the kingdom of God by itself. God creates it *for* the Church, which must put its whole trust in his act, not in its own. The Church of itself has not achieved and will not achieve the reign of God; it can only testify to it. Can the Church do more in these last days than pray for it and look for it and through its ministry and its sufferings prepare itself and the world intensively for it? Can it ever have any say in the coming of his kingdom? Ought it ever to glorify itself and boast before God and men of its own power to give life and form? Ought it to make claims with regard to God through its decisions, measures and ideas, rather than support God's claims in the world? Can it ever, supposing that it knows better, mistrust God's grace and further its own self-made greatness and power? Can it ever suppose that of its own accord it bestows grace, rather than being constantly in need of it? Must it not always accept grace trustingly and unconditionally, like a child with empty hands? And even if it performs its duty, must it not always regard itself as an unworthy servant?

A Church which imagines that in these last days it is the *Church* itself which makes the decisive moves and can out of its own strength inaugurate and build up the kingdom of God, is a Church that will scatter and destroy, because it lacks unselfish and trusting faith in God's decisive action. But a Church which in trusting faith is convinced that it is God who inaugurates, gives support to and rules over this interim period, and that God will bestow on the world and on men their new perfected reality, is a Church which will indeed gather together and build up, for strength will be given to its humility and confidence. Such a Church will know that, whatever efforts it makes, its theory and practice is in the last analysis not what matters; it will know that a list of its achievements or wonderful statistics will not guarantee the coming of the kingdom of God and that therefore no lack of response need discourage it from continuing to call and no failures dishearten it. The Church would lose heart if it had to fight the decisive battle by itself. But if the final victory is given from above independent of its actions, it can in confidence and faith do its uttermost and so change the world. For the Church was promised that its faith would move mountains.

(*c*) *Jesus* preached the reign of God as a *purely religious reign*. The *Church,* following Christ, must preach the reign of God as a purely religious reign.

The Church in these last days must under no circumstances present itself as a religio-political theocracy. Its rôle is the spiritual diakonia. Instead of establishing an imperium of spiritual and temporal power, it has been granted the grace to perform its ministerium in the guise of a servant: the service of God as a service to men, the service of men as a service of God. How could it ever in these last days take refuge in methods common to the secular seizing and maintenance of power, of political strategy and intrigue? How could it radiate worldly splendour and pomp or distribute places of honour left and right or hand out titles and decorations? How could it wish to hoard the goods of this world, money and riches, beyond a bare necessary minimum? How could it ally itself with the powers of this world, or identify itself with any secular unit, political party, cultural organization, economic or social pressure group, or give uncritical and unqualified support to a particular economic, social, cultural, political, philosophical or ideological system? How could it fail constantly to disturb and alienate and challenge these secular powers and systems with its revolutionary message, question their very existence and so experience their resistance and their attacks? How could it evade suffering, scorn, slander, persecution? How could it attempt to turn the way of the cross into a triumphal progress? How could it continue to see outsiders as enemies to be hated and destroyed, rather than as its neighbours, to be embraced in an understanding and helpful love?

A Church which in these last days overlooks the fact that it is called to the selfless service of humanity, of its enemies and of the world, loses its dignity and rank and the very justification of its existence, since it thereby abandons the true discipleship of Christ. But a Church which remains aware that it is the reign of God, not the Church, which is coming in "power and glory", will find in its insignificance its true greatness. Such a Church knows that it is great precisely when it is without pomp and majesty, that it can only in a limited and conditional way reckon with the support of the rulers of this world, that its existence will constantly be ignored, neglected or merely tolerated, or even regretted, accused and cursed; that its activity will constantly be mocked, suspected, disapproved and hampered; but that far above all other powers the reign of God exists, beyond the reach of all attacks. The Church would lose heart in the world altogether, if its worldly power were its only strength. But if its strength lies in the cross of Christ and in its own cross, then its weakness is its strength and it can go on its way fearlessly, conscious of the victory of the resurrection, guaranteed from the beginning. For the Church was promised that only in losing its life would it find it.

(*d*) *Jesus* preached the reign of God as a *saving event for sinners*. So the *Church,* following Christ, must also preach the reign of God as a saving event for sinners.

Despite the gulf which separates it from the world and its

powers, the Church in these last days can never behave as though it were a menacing, intimidating institution, devoted to preaching doom and inculcating fear. It should preach not warnings of doom, but the message of salvation, not menaces but the joyful good news, not a declaration of war but words of peace. The Church exists, not for the pious and righteous, but for sinners and godless men. It must not judge and condemn, for all the gravity of its message, but heal, forgive, save. Its inevitable warnings must not be an end in themselves, but a reminder of the offer of grace held out by God. It can never, despite all the graces it has received, indeed precisely because of the grace it has received, pretend to be a self-righteous caste or class of pure and holy men. It can never assume that unholy, godless and evil things exist only outside itself. There is no part of the Church which is perfect, no element which is not endangered, frail, unstable, constantly in need of correction and improvement. The front-line between the world and the reign of God passes directly through the centre of the Church, through the heart of every individual member.

A Church which in these last days does not realize that it is composed of sinful men and exists for sinful men, must grow hardhearted, self-righteous and without compassion, deserving neither the mercy of God nor the confidence of men. But a Church which is genuinely aware that only the perfect reign of God can divide wheat from tares, good fish from bad, will be granted the grace of holiness and righteousness which it cannot create for itself. Such a Church will know that it has no need to affect a high moral tone for the world's benefit, as though everything in it were as good as it possibly could be; it will know that its treasures are stored in very earthly vessels, that its lights are dim and flickering, its faith weak, its knowledge lacking, its confession of faith halting. It knows that there are no sins and omissions to which it cannot be tempted and to which it has not, in one way or another, yielded and that however much it continues to keep sin at a distance, it has no reason to keep the sinner at a distance also. The Church would be unable to enter the kingdom of God justified, if it looked down self-righteously on publicans and sinners. But if the Church, as the fellowship of those who are called to righteousness and holiness, remains aware of its guilt and sin, then it may live in joyful assurance of forgiveness, then in the dawning reign of God its unholy members will be saints, then it need have no fear despite the almost irresistible temptations to which it is exposed and despite its constant failures and mistakes. For the Church has been promised that he who humbles himself shall be exalted.

(*e*) *Jesus* required for the reign of God that man should make a *radical decision for God*. The *Church,* following Christ, must make a similar demand, with important consequences for itself.

The Church, too, in these last days is confronted with a decision: between God and his reign and the world and its reign. The Church, too, must not be distracted by anything from its radical decision for God. The Church must constantly turn away from the message of the world in metanoia and accept the coming reign of God, so that it can turn next in love to the world and to men. It must not shut itself off from the world in a spirit of asceticism, but live in the everyday world, inspired by the radical obedience of love towards God's will; it must not try to escape from the world, but work in the world. The Church cannot evade this radical obedience to the will of God. It cannot assume that all the demands of the Gospel are directed towards the "evil world" rather than the constantly secularized Church. It cannot assume that by obeying its own commands it can dispense itself from obedience to God's holy will. It cannot pretend that its own liturgical, dogmatic and legal codes and precepts, traditions and customs are commandments of God or are equal or even superior to the will of God as revealed in Jesus Christ. It cannot raise its own temporary and time-conditioned stipulations to the rank of eternal norms, so that they have to be adapted to each changing situation by means of artificial and painful reinterpretation. It cannot allow itself to "swallow camels" in the things that matter, and "strain at gnats" with petty casuistry in other things. It cannot allow itself to load men with the burdens of countless laws and regulations which they cannot bear. It cannot, in place of the obedience of the heart, born of the love for God, demand blind obedience born of fear, an obedience not born of understanding and approval, but simply in response to a command, which would not exist if the command did not exist. It cannot allow itself to care more for external legality than inward state of mind, more for tradition than the "signs of the times", more for lip-service than purity of heart, more for the "commandments of men" than for the absolute and uncurtailed will of God.

The Church which in these last days forgets to whom its obedience is due, which tries to seize power for itself, tries to establish its own sovereignty, to play the master, must finish by enchaining and enslaving itself. But the Church which, despite all failures, is continually concerned for the coming of God's reign, which knows whose it is, for whom it has made its decision, and for whom it must constantly renew its uncompromising and vital decision, such a Church becomes truly free: free to imitate Christ's service to the world, free for the service of God by which it can truly serve men, free for the service of men by which it serves God, free to overcome suffering, sin and death through the cross of the risen Christ, free for an all-embracing creative love which changes and renews the world, free for an unshakable and resolute hope for the coming kingdom of God, the kingdom of complete justice, of eternal life, of true freedom and cosmic peace, free to hope for the final reconciliation of men with God and the end of all godlessness. The Church would make men unhappy, miserable slaves, if its heart is given to the world or to itself. But if the Church has given its heart to God the Lord and to him alone, then through the free grace of God it can make prisoners free, make sad men rejoice, make poor men rich, make weak men strong, make the unloved loved. The Church has been promised that, if it makes itself ready and keeps itself so, God will make *all things new* and become all in all.

It is hardly necessary to emphasize, in conclusion, that the Church can only fulfil its enormous task if it prays for that fulfilment anew every day. What it cannot achieve of itself, can be granted to it by God's grace: "Thy kingdom come" (Mt. 6:10); and as several texts add: "For thine is the kingdom and the power and the glory, for ever and ever"

(Mt. 6:13). Or, as it says in the Didache, in the words of the very early Church:

> Remember, O Lord, your Church,
> save it from every evil
> and perfect it in your love.
> Gather it together from the four winds
> and lead it sanctified
> into your kingdom you have prepared for it. (10:5).

Jesus returns again and again to his Church with his message and the power of his spirit. Not in order to "disturb" it, unless it thinks with the Grand Inquisitor that it can do better without him and his message. But to arouse a Church which, tired and listless, is always on the point of sleep; to light the way for a Church which is so often on the point of losing the path on its pilgrimage; to strengthen a Church which so often, confronted by difficulties, obstacles and opposition, is on the point of failing; to bring new life to a Church which in so many places and in so many members is on the point of death; to rescue for the kingdom of God a Church which so often, in sight of the promised land, is on the point of giving up. Not "Why do you come to disturb us"; but "Lord, make haste to help us."

Has the Church a future, a future in this modern world? This was the question we asked ourselves at the beginning. The fundamental answer has already been given: *if* the Church believes, preaches and lives, convincingly and actively, the message of Jesus Christ, then it has a future in the modern world and in humanity. For then it will be granted not *a* future, above and beyond any modern age, but *the* future, the only perfect future: the kingdom of God. No one can promise or grant more.

The aim of this chapter has been to make clear what Jesus' real intention was and how far and in what sense the Church can appeal to him as its founder. It has also tried to make clear that even after the saving event of Jesus Christ's death and resurrection the world has been given time in these last days; time for the preaching of the Gospel, time for a response, for faith, for repentance, for active service in love. This is the time of the eschatological community of those who believe and love, the time of the Church: a limited but genuine time of grace.

This chapter has also aimed to point out what is most important about the nature of the Church in its changing forms, about the Church's task despite its "un-nature" working against it. Is it too much to hope that at least so far—and this would in itself be a great deal—the larger part of divided Christianity might be in agreement on the *fundamental* issues, so that remaining differences are not necessarily ones that would divide the Churches? There remain, of course, sufficient grounds for the Churches to be divided. But it is to be hoped that a broad consensus might similarly be obtained on the basic structure of the New Testament community—an analysis of which follows—leaving out of account the countless differences which exist between theological *schools* and which often cut right across confessional differences. How did this ekklesia, this eschatological community of salvation, which so far we have only traced in brief general terms, see and interpret itself? How does it see its own nature in more precise terms?

C. *The Fundamental Structure of the Church*

I. THE CHURCH AS THE PEOPLE OF GOD

1. BEYOND JUDAISM?

To refer to the post-Easter fellowship of the disciples of Jesus as the eschatological community of salvation, as the ekklesia of God, as the congregation, community or Church of God— are not these descriptions somewhat exaggerated? We may ask whether the reality of this "Church" did not look very different, and whether, as far as its external appearance and its everyday practical actions were concerned, this "Church" was really more than a sect of Jews who believed in the Messiah and had a particular creed. How much more were they than the Zealots, who called for political revolution, or the Pharisees, who called for moral reform according to the law, or the Essenes, who withdrew, regarding themselves as the elect community, into the desert? Were they more than people with a particular religious slant, with a particular conception of religion in theory and practice, but retaining otherwise their links with Judaism?[1]

Even the Acts of the Apostles, which often idealizes facts

[1] Cf. the relevant sections of the histories of the early Church (see also the authors mentioned at the beginning of B II, 3), the biblical and theological dictionaries, the theologies of the NT (esp. Bultmann) and the commentaries on Acts (esp. the more recent ones by F. F. Bruce, E. Haenchen, B. Reicke, G. Stählin, A. Wikenhauser, C. S. Williams); survey of research by E. Grässer in *Theologische Rundschau*, 26 (1960), 93–163. Of recent studies of the apostolic and post-apostolic time with extensive bibliographies the most important are: from the Protestant side, L. Goppelt, *Die apostolische und nachapostolische Zeit. Die Kirche in ihrer Geschichte*, ed. by K. D. Schmidt and E. Wolf, I 1962; from the Catholic side K. Baus, *From the Apostolic Community to Constantine*, vol. I "Handbook of Church History" series, ed. H. Jedin, London–New York–Freiburg 1965; *Geschichte der Kirche*, ed. by L. J. Rogier, R. Aubert and M. D. Knowles. Vol. I, "Von der Gründung der Kirche bis zu Gregor d. Gr." by J. Daniélou and H. J. Marrou, Einsiedeln–Zurich–Cologne 1963 (English trans. London 1964). For NT ecclesiology cf. the bibliographies at A I, 3 and B II, 3; for the historical development of ecclesiology see A I, 2.

(cf. Paul's letters) and can be used as an historical source only with caution—the synoptic gospels, more indirectly, also give us an idea of the differences between communities—clearly reveal that the fellowship of Jesus' disciples even after Pentecost appeared to be no more than a religious party within the Jewish nation: "the sect of the Nazarenes" (Acts 24:5; cf. 24:14, 28:22). They were a kind of separate synagogue, of which there were several at the time, or a group of disciples with their own master.

A number of points seem to support this view. The disciples of Christ did not withdraw from life as much as, for example, the Essenes. They met in the temple (Acts 2:46), apparently approved Jewish sacrificial customs (cf. Mt. 5:23 f.) and the paying of the temple tax (cf. Mt. 17:24–27) and apparently submitted themselves to the judgment of the synagogues (cf. Mk. 13:9; Mt. 10:17). Despite their Master's critical attitude and his relative freedom *vis-à-vis* the cultic and ritual dictates of the law, they seem to have complied fully with the Old Testament law (cf. Mt. 5:17–19); observation of the law seems to have been enjoined on all members of the community as a basic condition of their sharing in salvation. How far indeed could the disciples of Jesus claim to be the chosen people of the eschatological age without this observance of the law? Again it is Acts which tells us that at first the disciples definitely did not take up a mission to the Gentiles, and both Acts and Paul's letters agree on the fact that at first the Gentiles were required to be circumcised and so to follow the law (with possible exceptions, e.g. Cornelius, Acts 10?). But for this initial requirement there would have been no dispute—a dispute presumably first of all with the hellenistic, diaspora-Jewish Christians in Jerusalem, who were critical of traditional Jewish piety (cf. Acts 6–7), then with the hellenistic communities (in Antioch above all) and with Paul and Barnabas in particular, who rejected the idea of circumcision and obedience to the law for Gentiles. Can we not assume that the first disciples of Jesus Christ were fully and entirely members of the people of Israel, whose religious and legal practice marks a continuation of their life as part of the Jewish nation?

The disciples of Jesus saw themselves as the *true* Israel. But this was equally true of the Pharisees, the Sadducees, the Zealots and the Essenes. Clearly it took time and various historical experiences before the disciples saw themselves clearly as not only the true, but the *new* Israel. The foundations for this view had already been laid: the faith, rooted in their personal encounter with the risen Christ, that with the death and resurrection of Jesus the crucial and decisive eschatological saving event had occurred. In contrast to all other "parties" the fellowship of those who believed in Christ could look back to this decisive event; for them the Old Testament promises had been fulfilled, the eschatological spirit had been bestowed on them, they had been given hope, based on the fact that the Messiah had really come, of the coming consummation of the reign of God. They *were* already the new Israel, even if externally little different from the old. In the light of this saving event which had already occurred they could remain members of the people of Israel, share in its cult, keep its laws, affirm its history and its expectation—and yet see all these things in a fundamentally new way because of Jesus Christ. They could retain Jewish forms and yet give them an entirely new content, because of Jesus Christ; and this new content was bound, sooner or later, to burst the bounds of the old forms.

Thus the true and new Israel was already realized within the old; externally little different, inwardly already very different, but still waiting for the metanoia and the faith of the *whole* people of the promise. But precisely because this expectation of the whole people of Israel was not fulfilled, the new Israel was revealed more and more clearly in its differences from the old. The early Christian community, for all its links with the Jewish nation as a whole, already possessed certain peculiar forms which pointed to a distinctive development:

1. *Baptism,* as a sign of repentance and the purification from sin, was given with reference to the coming reign of God in the name of Jesus; from the first this is the initiation rite of the new fellowship (Acts 2:38, 41; 8:12, 16, 36, 38; 9:18; 10:48, etc.; cf. I Cor. 12:13; Gal. 3:27; Rom. 6:1–11). This rite shows that the eschatological community is not just a vague movement or a mere fellowship of like-minded peo-

ple, but is a community with historical forms: a Church. Baptism is already a mark of separation from the Jewish nation as a whole and it takes on even more fundamental importance when it does not have to be preceded by circumcision as a rite of initiation.

2. The communal *service of prayer,* as a community or in smaller groups in private houses (Acts 2:46; 12:12), was an occasion for saying the Lord's prayer together, for interpreting sacred texts, for recalling the words of Jesus and studying his life in the light of the Old Testament. In all this lay the seeds of later separation from Judaism; but especially and fundamentally the title given to the risen Christ: "our Lord" ("Maranatha", I Cor. 16:22), which indicated a new cult community with a new cult object, which sooner or later would have to split off from Judaism. This service of the word, which took over features of the synagogue service, naturally became a service in its own right in places where the disciples of Jesus were excluded from the synagogue services.

3. The communal eschatological *meal* of the community was celebrated, probably often in association with the simple service of prayer, in memory of the meals shared with Jesus and particularly his last supper (cf. the synoptic traditions and I Cor. 11:20–29). It was a joyful meal of memory and expectation, probably what is referred to as the "breaking of bread" with eschatologically "glad hearts" (Acts 2:42–46). This shared meal which consciously recalls the Last Supper—there is no evidence for shared meals which did not have this function—marks another point of division between the early Christians and the unbelieving nation as a whole. As a meal which recalls the Lord before his death and looks forward to the Lord who is shortly to come in glory, it continually recreates the community's sense of belonging to the eschatological people of God, of being called to share in the reign of God. When the Jewish passover-meal—Jesus' Last Supper was in all probability a passover-meal—ceased to be important for the Gentile Christians, there remained this eschatological meal of the community, which Paul was then to see more profoundly as "the Lord's Supper".

4. The community had its *own leaders,* composed at first—always in co-operation with the community—of the twelve,

the representatives of the eschatological Israel of the twelve tribes, among whom, according to synoptic, Pauline and Johannine tradition alike, Peter had the chief rôle to play. Soon others also had an important authority, notably John the son of Zebedee and James the brother of the Lord—Paul calls these three "pillars" (cf. Gal. 1:18; 2:9). After Peter left, James was the chief figure in Jerusalem (Acts 12:17; 21:18; Gal. 2:12). From early times there seems to have been a council of elders, formed on the Jewish pattern, as well as the twelve (Acts 11:30; 15; 21:18). In association with Peter, the disciples and the community, we find the power "to bind and to loose" (Mt. 16:18 f.; 18:15–18; Jn. 20:22 f.). Even an undeveloped, rudimentary ordering of the community would have been bound to lead to a separation of the eschatological community of salvation from the nation as a whole. But in fact the tasks of the leaders of the community grew as the young Church became more and more independent, with its extension beyond the frontiers of Jewish influence.

5. The community was a living *fellowship of love;* the koinonia (Acts 2:42) linked together all members in a brotherly fellowship, which found expression in mutual help, shared sufferings and to a certain extent in common ownership (Acts 2:45; 4:32–36). This fellowship was tested and proved during the friction between Jerusalem and the Gentile Churches.

In the primitive community ecclesiastical forms were barely developed at all; the expectation of the imminent completion of the reign of God and the return of the Lord prevented the community from developing into an "institution for salvation". But although at first the eschatological community of salvation was limited to the Jewish nation, it did not remain so for long; it is unthinkable that it should never have crossed this frontier, that it should have become simply a Jewish sect. The community was, as we have seen, well prepared for this process of liberating itself from Judaism. The process was begun by the development of a Christianity freed from Judaic laws, and, after a few decades, completed by the destruction of Jerusalem and the ending of the temple cult.

1. The development of a *Gentile Christianity freed from Judaic laws*. This began with the mission of hellenistic Jewish Christians who, partly from fear of persecution, had fled from Jerusalem (Acts 8:4; 11:19–21); it was supported by the determined efforts of Paul and Barnabas, and received the approval of the early Church at the "Apostolic Council" (Gal. 2:1–10; Acts 15; 21:25). These Gentiles had not accepted circumcision or obedience to the Mosaic law. They did not become Jews; they kept to the Old Testament, although they interpreted it very differently as time went on (cf. Paul —Hebrews—Epistle of Barnabas—first Epistle of Clement— Justin).

By contrast with many of his contemporaries, Jesus' whole attitude and especially his eschatology was never influenced by ideas of hatred or revenge against the Gentiles (and Samaritans). He did not automatically exclude them from salvation—quite the reverse. It is true that during the time of his public ministry—exceptions prove the rule—Jesus limited his activities and those of his disciples rigorously to Israel. There is no historical evidence to show that he spoke of his intention that the Gospel should also be preached in missionary manner to the Gentiles; all passages which refer to this idea are disputed by experts. The behaviour of the primitive Christian community scarcely indicates that it had received a general missionary brief. At the time of the beginning of the mission to the Gentiles, no appeal to the words of Jesus as support is reported, even by Acts. The versions we have of the (post-Easter) missionary commandments of Jesus presumably dated from the time after the mission to the Gentiles had already begun.

On the other hand, we must not overlook the fact that Jesus, when he spoke of eschatological consummation, anticipated a new people of God (eschatological pilgrimage of the peoples to Mount Sion?), not composed merely of those who were directly descended from Abraham. For all practical purposes his message was completely universal: not descent from Abraham and the confirmation of the promise through Moses, but faith and metanoia and doing the will of God with love is required for a salvation which is God's act alone. God has absolute claim on man; man has no claim he can present to God, neither on the basis of his origins nor of his fulfilment of the law. The distinction between the people of God and a racial community was clearly drawn and had serious consequences when the Christian message was rejected by the mass of the Jewish people.

Yet the eschatological *community* itself still had to become aware of the concrete implications and consequences of the universalism of Jesus' message; this awareness was won through historical experiences and serious conflicts. The mission to the Gentiles was not the central problem here; the Pharisees too conducted missions to the Gentiles. The question was the form of initiation into the new community, whether circumcision and obedience to the Mosaic law was necessary. The community retained its link with the ancient people of God through its confession of faith in Jesus as the crucified and risen Messiah, as the Messiah of their people. But this very confession also laid the foundations of a distinction between it and the unbelieving nation. The external division occurred at the moment when Gentiles were accepted into the community without circumcision and acceptance of the Mosaic law, without the detour through Judaism. Paul was the first to explain theologically that by the cross and resurrection of Jesus Christ the law as a way to salvation was no longer essential and that faith in Jesus Christ was the only thing that mattered. Before Paul the hellenistic communities had begun to develop the Jerusalem gospel of Jesus as the promised Messiah of Israel—a gospel which left the validity of the Mosaic law unchallenged—into a gospel for Jews and Gentiles alike, while retaining links with the Old Testament. But it was Paul who, on the strength of a revelation from Christ, as he emphatically states, had developed this idea of a gospel for Jews and Gentiles alike and laid the essential foundations for Gentile Churches freed from Judaic laws. These Churches, despite the opposition and counter-propaganda of the zealous Jewish Christians, the Judaists (cf. Galatians), were after a relatively short time spiritually and soon numerically the leaders of the early Church.

2. The *destruction of Jerusalem* and the *end of the temple cult*. The situation had changed rapidly: the primitive community had been purely Judaeo-Christian, if also in part

hellenistic. Then mixed communities developed outside Jerusalem. Gradually Jewish Christianity becomes less and less important, and Gentile Christianity becomes dominant. This process of separation reached its external culmination with the catastrophe of the Jewish war in the years 66–70. With the destruction of the temple the Jews lost, in addition to the self-government which the Romans had hitherto allowed them, their cultic centre. The temple taxes were changed by the Romans into a tax for the Jupiter Capitolinus in Rome.

At the same time Jerusalem ceased to be the ecclesiastical centre of early Christianity. The Christians in Palestine had not taken part in the insurrection against the Romans. Persecuted as traitors, they fled into the lands east of Jordan and spread the Christian faith in the Syrian and Arab frontier-areas. Only a few returned to Palestine after the end of the war and this decimated Church could no longer claim to be the mother Church of Gentile Christendom, the centre of the whole Church. Leadership of the Church was transferred from Jerusalem to Rome. Even at the time of Nero's persecution in 64 the world as a whole regarded the Church as a religious community which had separated itself from Judaism. After the destruction of Jerusalem in the year 70 Jewish Christianity was of very little importance. The history of the Church from this point is the history of a Gentile Christian Church. The last act of the tragedy—after the revolt of the Jewish diaspora, particularly in Mesopotamia and Egypt in 116–117, which dealt a violent blow to the economic, political and spiritual power of hellenistic Jewry—came with the Jewish revolt in Palestine in 132–135, led by Bar-Kochba: Jerusalem, the holy city of Israel, was rebuilt as a purely hellenistic city and named Aelia Capitolina. Jews and (circumcised) Jewish Christians were forbidden to enter the town and its environs, and circumcision was forbidden, under pain of death. Much later, from the third century, Jewish pilgrims were allowed to visit the west wall of the temple (the Wailing Wall) once a year, on the anniversary of its destruction.

Thus in the course of a dramatic history the Church made up of Jews had become a Church of Jews and Gentiles and finally a Church of Gentiles. Jewry, which had rejected Jesus, now began to be hostile also to the young Church. The Church, at that time still weak, responded to countless attacks chiefly with intercession; but apart from the Palestinian-Syrian area, any real attempts to convert the Jews had ceased by about 80. The Jews expelled the Christians from the national community; possibly as early as the second century the curse on "heretics and Nazarenes" was included in the principal daily rabbinic prayer (*Schmone 'Esre*).

In the course of this dramatic history the ways of Israel and the Church totally diverged. Yet the two remain, whether they like it and know it or not, indissolubly bound together. This is inevitable, since the Church claims to be the new *Israel*, the new *people of God*.

2. FROM THE ANCIENT TO THE NEW PEOPLE OF GOD

The new Israel, the new people of God, was founded as such before it described itself as such. It was founded when Jesus' disciples began not merely to preach the message of Jesus, but to preach in faith Jesus himself as the fulfilment of this message; when they began to exhort their hearers to accept that message—not to abandon Israel, but to fulfil it in the eschatological kehal Yahweh, the true eschatological community of salvation. But since the majority of the people of Israel rejected the message of the disciples, it became inevitable that the latter should describe themselves as that which they really were: the true and new "ekklesia of God", the true and new "Israel", the true and new "people of God". By taking over the venerable Old Testament title of "ekklesia of God" for themselves, the disciples had already in practice applied to themselves the basically interchangeable titles of "Israel" and "people of God".

(a) *"Israel"*[2] originally meant "God reigns" and is the

2 Cf. the histories of Israel (A. Alt, M. A. Beek, J. Bright, E. L. Ehrlich, P. Heinisch, G. Riciotti, C. Schedl and esp. M. Noth), the OT theologies (W. E. Albright, O. J. Baab, A. B. Davidson, W. Eichrodt, P. Heinisch, E. Jacob, P. van Imschoot, G. A. F. Knight, L. Köhler, A. Lods, O. Procksch, G. von Rad, H. H. Rowley, E. Sellin, N. H. Snaith, T. C. Vriezen) and the biblical

name of the union of the twelve tribes. It was then transferred to their ancestor Jacob, when the people had become accustomed to seeing their election prefigured in their ancestors. Israel implies at once membership of a nation and of a religion. It becomes the sacral name for those chosen by Yahweh and united in his worship. After the splitting up of the Davidic empire in 932 B.C. only the northern tribes still formed the kingdom of Israel, while the southern tribes took over the title of Judah. But after the collapse of the northern kingdom and the deportation in 722, the name Israel is transferred to the remaining southern kingdom and is again a term used to describe the whole nation: a term which is now no longer primarily of political significance, but a religious description which the chosen people of God applied to itself, although now as before only those who were members by race formed part of this empirical nation. Especially in the post-exilic period this new interpretation was linked to a growing expectation of the eschatological time of God's salvation, which was to reconstitute the kingdom of Israel of the twelve tribes. Thus "Israel" is increasingly interpreted in eschatological terms, with an eye to the eschatological re-establishment of the people of God.

In the New Testament too the word "Israel" is used to describe the Old Testament people of God; it can either be the common description of the people, without any religious emphasis, or it may—as in the synoptic gospels, especially Matthew and Luke, in John, Acts and Paul's letters—emphasize the specific nature of this people as God's chosen people. In so far as the name "Israel" describes the Jewish people in its character as the people of God, it is different from the term "Jew", which while it is not necessarily disparaging in its use, invariably, in New Testament usage as in that of the pre-Christian Gentile world, stresses its apartness. None of the gospels suggests an extension of the word "Israel" to cover the new people of God, the Church; but such an extension seems possible in Acts, since Israel remains the name for the people of God, on whose behalf Christ is to "restore the kingdom" (1:6; cf. 28:20) and

_____

and theological dictionaries, esp. ThW III, 356–394 (G. von Rad, K. G. Kuhn, W. Gutbrod); for the New Testament, see C I, 1.

since, moreover, the Israel to which the promises were made and the Israel to which fulfilment was given, remains one and the same people of God (cf. 13:23).

Paul too generally uses the word in its specific religious sense for the ancient people of God (cf. especially Rom. 9–11). But faced with the unbelief of the majority of his people he sees the painful necessity of drawing a distinction: membership of the people of Israel by descent and race is not sufficient for real membership of the people of God (Rom. 9:6). Hence Paul calls the unbelieving Israel "Israel after the flesh" (I Cor. 10:18 A.V.) without going on to use the parallel expression "Israel after the spirit". Only at one point in the New Testament is the name Israel applied to the new people of God, and that only polemically and in parentheses: this must be the meaning of the phrase "the Israel of God" (Gal. 6:16).

This exegetical investigation shows two things. The name Israel still applies to the ancient people of God, even after Christ, and cannot be taken away from it and simply transferred to the New Testament ekklesia. On the other hand the New Testament ekklesia clearly remains, outwardly and historically as well as inwardly and actually, linked to Israel, the ancient people of God. The transference of the name "Israel" to the Church can therefore never be exclusive in character, but at best an extended application according to Paul's parable of the olive tree (Rom. 11:17–24), the Jews are the rightful bearers of the title and the Gentiles are only the grafts onto the old stem. All this becomes clearer if we examine the biblical use of the title "people of God".

(*b*) *"People of God"*:[3] the corresponding Greek word in

[3] Cf. the OT and NT theologies as well as the biblical and theological dictionaries, esp. ThW IV, 29–57 (H. Strathmann, R. Meyer), as well as the bibliographies at A I, 3 and C I, 1; especially important are the monographs by N. A. Dahl, *Das Volk Gottes*, Oslo 1941; A. Oepke, *Das neue Gottesvolk*, Gütersloh 1950; F. Asensio, *Yahveh y su Pueblo*, Rome 1953; H. J. Kraus, *The People of God in the OT*, London–New York 1958; H. Wildberger, *Jahwes Eigentumsvolk*, Zurich–Stuttgart 1960; R. Schnackenburg, *The Church in the NT*, London–New York–Freiburg 1965; W. Trilling, *Das wahre Israel. Studien zur Theologie des*

the Septuagint and the New Testament for the Hebrew word *am* (people) is λαός. While the other Hebrew word for people, *goj,* is generally used for the Gentile peoples, *am* or λαός is fairly regularly used for Israel, in the Greek Bible even more clearly than in the Hebrew. The word λαός in the Septuagint, according to its chief usage, has a different sense from that of non-biblical Greek; it means "people", not in the sense of population, the mass, people in general, but in the sense of nation and national community. With few exceptions it is deliberately and clearly restricted to describing the people of Israel. Why? To indicate the especial dignity of Israel by using a special word, to indicate that it is the people *of God.* The phrase "people of God" is used over and over again (λαὸς θεου) and the old-fashioned and solemn word λαός has the same overtones even if the genitive θεου is not added.

The concept of the people of God is at the heart of Judaism. Fundamentally the whole faith of Judaism can be summed up in the single phrase: Yahweh is the God of Israel and Israel is the people of Yahweh. This is true from the moment when Israel was led out of Egypt by God's merciful call and came to see itself as a national and religious unity. This is the meaning of the mission of Moses: "I am the Lord, and I will bring you out from under the burdens of the Egyptians, and I will deliver you from their bondage, and I will redeem you with an outstretched arm and with great acts of judgment, and I will take you for my people, and I will be your God" (Ex. 6:6 f.). This is also the meaning of God's revelation on Sinai: "Now therefore, if you will obey my voice and keep my covenant, you shall be my own possession among all peoples; for all the earth is mine, and you shall be to me a kingdom of priests and a holy nation" (Ex. 19:5 f.). It is also the meaning of the covenant: "And I will have regard for you and make you fruitful and multiply you and will confirm my covenant with you. And I will make my abode among you and my soul shall not abhor you. And I will walk among you and will be your God, and you shall be my people" (Lev. 26:9; 11–12).

Yahweh as the God of Israel and Israel as his people—this

Matthäus-Evangeliums, Munich [3]1964; L. Cerfaux, *The Church in the Theology of St. Paul,* London–New York–Freiburg 1959.

is the thought which underlies the other writings too of the Old Testament. It is systematically and theologically worked out in Deuteronomy (cf. especially 4, 7, 6–12); it is hymned in the Psalms (e.g. Ps. 135) and the theme is subject to endless variations in the writings of the prophets.

Specific references are superfluous for an idea which runs through the whole Old Testament: Yahweh, the Lord of the earth and of all nations, is the God of Israel, the God of Abraham, Isaac and Jacob, the God of our forefathers, our God. He is the Lord, the father and creator, the king and judge of Israel, its helper and redeemer, its shield and defence, its rock and stronghold. Conversely Israel is the people of Yahweh, his people, his possession, his own. It does not own itself, it is the property of Yahweh, a people set apart and hence holy, belonging to the Lord. Yahweh's name resounds throughout Israel. Israel is the servant, the son of Yahweh. The Israelites are his servants, his sons and daughters. Israel is the vine, the vineyard, the flock, the bride of Yahweh. The Israelites are the chosen people, holy and righteous, just and upright; they know Yahweh, cry to him, seek him, fear and love him, trust and wait for him. God and his people belong together, linked by that covenant which God in his free and powerful mercy has made with this small, insignificant, weak and sinful people: a covenant that is more than a contract, that means a way of life and a community. The cause of the people is God's cause; God's cause is theirs. The victory and success of the people is the praise and honour of God. Life and blessings are given by God to the people of the covenant. To the God of the covenant Israel owes honour and obedience.

The union between God and his people does not, therefore, depend on natural necessity, but on the free historical activity of God in the history of his people. Israel interpreted everything in terms of God's free choice, his mercy, love and faithfulness. God acts, in the very dawn of history, by choosing the forefathers of the nation and giving them his promises. He acts by freeing the tribes from Egyptian slavery, an action which binds together Israel as a nation for the first time, and by making the covenant and giving them the law at Sinai, an action which establishes them as the people of the covenant.

He acts also in the occupation of Canaan, in the foundation of states, in the founding and guiding of the kingdom, in blessings of his presence in the temple of Sion. His historical action determines the covenant and the cult, law and justice, war and peace. He makes tiny Israel the centre of the earth, the focal point of history and the goal of creation, by giving his word to Israel through his prophets who continually proclaim his word anew.

And yet Israel's answer by no means always corresponds to the acts of God. The history of Israel is a story of repeated failures and betrayals, backslidings and loss of faith: a story of sin. Israel found itself more and more in a crisis, which was also a religious and political crisis and culminated in the destruction of the state, an event which was interpreted as judgment and punishment for the sins of the people. It was the prophets who continually announced God's judgment and rejection to his faithless people and who preached God's mercy and his renewed election of them to a defeated and demoralized Israel.

When Israel has fallen away from God, the idea that they are the people of God is a theme of threats and judgments: "Call his name (the son) Not my people; you are not my people and I am not your God" (Hos. 1:9). When Israel has turned to God, on the other hand, the idea is a theme of promise and consolation: "Behold, the days are coming, says the Lord, when I will make a new covenant with the house of Israel and the house of Judah, not like the covenant which I made with their fathers when I took them by the hand to bring them out of the land of Egypt, my covenant which they broke, though I was their husband, says the Lord. But this is the covenant I will make with the house of Israel after those days, says the Lord: I will put my law within them, and I will write it upon their hearts; and I will be their God, and they shall be my people. And no longer shall each man teach his neighbour and teach his brother, saying, 'Know the Lord', for they shall all know me, from the least to the greatest, says the Lord; for I will forgive their iniquity and I will remember their sin no more" (Jer. 31:31–34).

In this way the accent of the prophetic message shifted increasingly from the present to the future, in which a new eschatological action of Yahweh was expected. The greater their misery, the greater their hope for a new Israel recreated by God: "And I will give them one heart, and put a new spirit within them; I will take the stony heart out of their flesh, and give them a heart of flesh, that they may walk in my statutes and keep my ordinances and obey them; and they shall be my people and I will be their God" (Ez. 11:19–20; cf. 14:11; 36:28; Jer. 7:23; 24:7; 30:22; 32:37–40).

What was formerly valued as a present possession became, after the numerous failures of the people of the covenant, something promised and longed for in the future. Israel, the people of God, becomes an eschatological concept: Yahweh *will* once again be Israel's God, Israel *will* once again be Yahweh's people. The eschatological age will recapitulate the first days again, and Yahweh will once again free Israel from slavery, save and redeem and win it over. He will have mercy on his people and forgive them their sins. The Israelites will be called "sons of the living God" (Hos. 1:10), "the priests of the Lord", "ministers of our God" (Is. 61:6). They will be a new people with a new heart and a new spirit, the Lord will pour out his spirit on all mankind (Joel 2:28–32) and circumcision of the heart will replace circumcision of the flesh (Jer. 4:4; 9:24 f.; cf. Deut. 30:6).

The hopeful expectation of eschatological fulfilment goes beyond limited national feelings; even though thoughts of punishing and destroying the heathen are not forgotten and there is no attempt to reconcile the two, the hope is now expressed that the heathen too will receive grace and salvation: "Sing and rejoice, O daughter of Sion; for lo, I come and will dwell in the midst of you, says the Lord. And many nations will join themselves to the Lord on that day, and shall be my people; and I will dwell in the midst of you, and you shall know that the Lord of hosts has sent me to you" (Zech. 2:10 f.; cf. Is. 19:21–25; 25:6 f.; 42:6; 55:4 f.; 66:18–24). It will be the task of the servant of Yahweh to be a "covenant of the people and light of the nations" (Is. 42:6; cf. 49:6). All eschatological hope culminates in the expectation of the Messiah, the anointed king of the blessed people of God.

(c) In the light of the Old Testament it is not at all surprising that, despite all the misunderstandings of the idea of the people of God in Later Judaism (nationalistic, rabbinistic, hellenistic and apocalyptic misinterpretations), the Old Testament conception of the people of God should have been applied to the eschatological community of salvation, which had gathered together in their faith in Jesus as the Messiah. This community realized more and more clearly that through faith in Jesus as the Messiah it was the *true* Israel, the *true* people of God. And as a consequence of the rejection of their message by the Jews and the acceptance in faith of their message by the Gentiles, the disciples of Jesus realized more and more clearly that they were at the same time the *new* Israel, the *new* people of God: the new eschatological people of God. Thus they did not balk at applying to themselves the old, pregnant and central idea of the people of God. It was not the name "disciples" (μαθηταί) nor the name "Christians" (χριστιανοί) (first given to the members of the community, as Acts 11:26 tells us, in Antioch and by outsiders) which are the characteristic names for the believers in Christ, but the ancient titles of Israel. First and foremost beside "ekklesia", that of the "people of God". The idea of the people of God is the oldest and most fundamental concept underlying the self-interpretation of the ekklesia. Images such as those of the body of Christ, the temple and so on, are secondary by comparison. The many-layered basic structure of the Church must be understood in the light of the people of God. It should never be forgotten that the living consciousness of the Church precedes the more or less theoretical characterization of the Church.

In the New Testament the word λαός is at first used in the same way as in the Septuagint: people in the sense of nation and (especially in Luke) in the sense simply of the crowd, the populace, the people; and then in the specific sense of the people of God, to describe Israel as opposed to the heathen, the ἔθνη (for special reasons this distinction is abandoned, in part at least, in Luke and John). In the New Testament too this technical use of the term λαός has a religious basis: the idea that Israel and Israel alone has been chosen, as is stated explicitly in many places, to be "his people", "God's people".

But then the New Testament goes a decisive step further

than the Septuagint: λαός is used for the fellowship of the disciples, for the community of Jesus Christ. This is the case not—as is scarcely surprising in view of the almost total absence of the word ekklesia—in the gospels, but in the other New Testament writings. Not that the title is ever withdrawn from Israel. But in addition to Israel another people of God is envisaged, a people of God—and this is the revolutionary idea—composed of Jews and Gentiles. The brief review above of the history of the Old Testament idea of the people of God makes it apparent what a tremendous matter it was for the young Church to apply to itself the basic formula of the whole Old Testament. It is now to the *Church* that the words are spoken: "I will live in them and move among them, and I will be their God, and they shall be my people". Paul writes in words (II Cor. 6:16) that echo phrases from Sinai (Lev. 26:12) and from prophecy (Ez. 37:27). The writer of the letter to the Hebrews similarly applies words from Jeremiah (31:31–34) to the people of the new covenant (Heb. 8:10–12); finally the vision of the new Jerusalem (Rev. 21:3) is based again on the passage from Ezekiel (37:27). Elsewhere the idea of the people of God is directly applied to the community of Christians. A striking example is found in the words of James (Acts 15:14), which must have sounded terminologically paradoxical and scandalous to Jewish ears: "God has visited the Gentiles, to take out of them (ἐξ ἐθνῶν) a people (λαός) for his name" (cf. 18:10). In addition there is Paul's daring application of two passages from Hosea (2:23; 1:10), originally referring to Israel, to the Church of Jews and Gentiles: ". . . us whom he has called, not from the Jews only but also from the Gentiles, as indeed he says in Hosea: 'Those who were not my people I will call "my people", and her who was not beloved I will call "my beloved". And in the very place where it was said to them "You are not my people", they will be called "sons of the living God"'" (Rom. 9:24–26). Finally there are examples in later New Testament writings: "a people of his own" (Tit. 2:14), "my people" (Rev. 18:4), and in particular "a holy nation, God's own people" and "God's people" (I Peter 2:9 f.).

(d) More important than the word λαός, which is comparatively rarely used for the New Testament community, is the reality of the people of God. On the basis both of Acts and of the Pauline letters it is in fact possible to trace a development and clarification of a theology of the people of God.

It is difficult to avoid the conclusion that it is the new people of God to which Paul is referring in the oldest surviving New Testament writing, I Thessalonians, where the words "Israel" and λαός are not used, but in the opening verse the community is addressed with the ancient title of the Old Testament people of God, as "ekklesia" (I Thess. 1:1; cf. II Thess. 1:1). What is the "ekklesia of God in Christ Jesus" here (I Thess. 2:14) and elsewhere if not the congregated "people of God in Christ Jesus"? The "ekklesia in Christ" is surely the fulfilment of the Old Testament "ekklesia of God". The new people of God, like the old, depends on God's "choosing" (I Thess. 1:4), and hence we may infer that Paul's idea of election is here in fact associated with the idea of the people of God. Surely the sharp and in this case wholly negative criticism of the Jews who do not believe in Christ (I Thess. 2:14–16), of the Jews who have thereby set the seal on the manifold backslidings of the people of the old covenant, is only comprehensible in terms of the idea of the people of God?

It is clear that at the time of the founding of the Church there were more important things to do than describe the nature of the Church, which was presumably anyway not a theme of actual missionary preaching. But confronted with misunderstandings which developed and false directions which were taken, Paul found it necessary to clarify the idea of the Church to counteract the Judaists (in Galatians) and the enthusiasts (in Corinthians). In all three letters, written to existing communities, the idea of the people of God is of great importance.

In Galatians the main issue is that of the true sonship of Abraham. Paul draws the clearest distinction here not between Church and Old Testament but, with reference to the Old Testament, between Church and synagogue. He finds an image of this distinction in Isaac, the son of the free woman, born through promise, and Ishmael, the son of the slave, born according to the flesh (Gal. 4:21–31). It is not the continuity of race or blood, but God's faithfulness to his promises, fulfilled in Christ, which maintains the true people of God. For Judaism physical descent is the essential basis of the sonship of Abraham; for Paul it is righteousness before God, a righteousness which is given to men, as it was to Abraham the father of the people of God, in response to their faith and not in response to the works of the law (3:1–7). Faith, not circumcision, is essential for membership of the true people of God. On the basis of faith Gentiles too, without having to accept Jewish law, can enter into the new people of God, the Israel of the promise. Therefore it was promised to Abraham, the father of the faithful, that in him all nations would be blessed (3:8 f.). The "Israel of God" (6:16) is not the community of the law, but the community of faith (3:15–4:7). As the community which has been freed from the law, its calling is to walk in the spirit.

In the two letters to the Corinthians also, the idea of the people of God is important. The "Israel after the flesh" (I Cor. 10:18 A.V.) is held up as a warning example to the new people of God, the people of God "after the spirit", as we may call it. The new people of God can fall away from God and be exposed to judgment, as the old was (10:1–13); here the continuity between old and new peoples of God is stressed rather than denied. The things which were given to the old people of the covenant in the form of images and parables, as "prefigures", are now given to the Church in their full reality. Just as the Israelites in the wilderness, by their journey under the cloud and their passage through the sea were baptized into Moses and thus became the people of God; and just as they were fed and sustained by the supernatural food of manna and the supernatural drink of water, so Christians are baptized into Jesus Christ, become the people of God and are sustained by the spiritual food of the Lord's Supper. Or as Paul explains elsewhere (II Cor. 3): Just as the old people of the covenant received the temporary revelation of God, so the new people receives a lasting and final revelation. And yet the community of the new covenant is not a community of perfect men, as several of the Corinthian enthusiasts supposed. To the Galatians Paul had to make it clear above all that even without the law they were true children of Abraham and belonged to the true people of God; to the Corinthians, rather the reverse of the coin, Paul had to make it clear that, even though they had been liberated by Christ, they were still on their pilgrim journey, that they, like Israel in the wilderness, could fall and be judged. The resurrection is still to come, meanwhile they have to keep and live out their faith in Christ according to the spirit. This explains Paul's warnings about their worship, services of the word (I Cor. 14) and the Lord's Supper (I Cor. 11:17–34); it explains also his warning against idolatry, fornication, quarrelling, etc., and his exhortations to a spiritual way of life—exhortations to the community rather than to individuals. All this is founded on an indicative and its consequent imperative:

You are God's people (II Cor. 6:16), therefore you must live as God's people (6:17) in order to be God's people (6:18).

The issue touched on in all these three letters is more extensively and positively discussed by Paul in the letter to the Romans: what is the relationship between the historical Israel and the Church of Jews and Gentiles? We shall return to this later. The idea of the people of God is not forgotten in the later New Testament writings even after Paul. Nowhere is it more vividly and emphatically expressed than in the *letter to the Hebrews;*[4] the idea of the people of God may be described as a leitmotif of this letter. With the use of typological images from the Old Testament, and using "Alexandrian exegesis", the New Testament "people of God" (4:9; cf. 2:17; 11:25; 13:12) is discussed. The idea of the people of God is applied to the Church, and the idea of the new covenant is established, not in opposition to the old covenant itself, which was something that looked to the future, but against the old covenant as misunderstood by contemporary Judaism, as a conservative and absolute idea, closed to the future.

Israel's journey through the wilderness is the typological image, which prefigures and provides a contrast with the people of the new covenant (cf. especially Heb. 3:7–4:13). The new people of God like the old received the "word" of revelation (4:12 f.) not in order to rest content with it as a possession, but in order to be challenged by it, and hence to set out on the way in obedience and faith. The new people of God, like the old, has no security, but must make its way through temptation and sin, threatened by lassitude, failing faith, and dwindling hope. Like the old, the new people of God has been given a promise that after all the toils and tribulations of the long journey, after a long time of faith, of perseverance and firmness of purpose, of firm confidence and unshakable assurance, despite struggles, suffering and death, they will enter into their rest.

---

[4] Cf. in addition to the more recent commentaries (esp. J. Hering, O. Kuss, O. Michel, C. Spicq, H. Strathmann) the monographs cited in C I, 1b. For the concept of the people of God in Hebrews, see: E. Käsemann, *Das wandernde Gottesvolk*, Göttingen 1961; F. J. Schierse, *Verheissung und Heilsvollendung. Zur theologischen Grundfrage des Hebräerbriefes*, Munich 1955.

But the difference between type and antitype is considerable and vital: the "word" of revelation given to the new people of the covenant is no longer a provisional one, but the final and definitive word. Threats and dangers can never overwhelm the new people of God, as they did the old; it has the assurance of salvation in spite of all its failings. The promise given to the new people of God (already in part fulfilled, but still awaiting its decisive completion), is the eschatological promise, which cannot be reversed, which is quite definitely guaranteed by a better covenant between God and his people and gives them a real consolation on their journey.

Thus the old covenant, image and parable of the coming covenant, is confirmed and at the same time dissolved and exceeded. This is the result of the eschatological saving action of God which has occurred in Jesus Christ, the leader and perfecter of the faith of his people. He is the "pioneer of salvation", who as Son brings "many sons" and as brother brings his "brethren" to glory (2:1–18). He is the "Son" who was not only, like Moses, faithful in God's house (the community of God), but is faithful over God's house which he has built (3:1–6). He is the new Moses, who leads the new people of God into the promised land, into the Sabbath peace (3:7–4:11). He is above all the true high priest of the new covenant, who once for all has, by the sacrifice of his own blood, entered the heavenly sanctuary, has opened the way to his people and appears in the presence of God on their behalf (4:14–5:10; 7:1–10:18). Thus the pioneer of salvation and his brethren, Son and sons, the mediator of the covenant and the people of the covenant, the sinless high priest and sinful people, belong together. The individual is never isolated or alone. He is taken up into membership of the "people of God" (4:9) having a "share in Christ" (3:14). Only within this fellowship, which is essentially a cultic fellowship, is revelation granted; only within it does the individual find faith and life and the strength to journey onwards. The individual must not isolate himself from the people of God on its journey, or he risks losing his way and remaining finally lost in the wilderness of the world. And precisely in this world the people of God has no abiding city; it journeys towards the future city of God. They are strangers and exiles on the earth, a great cloud of witnesses, seeking together a better country, a heavenly one (chapter 11): "Mount Zion, the city of the living God, the heavenly Jerusalem" (12:18–22).

The writer of the letter to the Hebrews paints a magnificent fresco of the journeying people of God, of the old and new covenants. References to the people of God in Acts, in the pastoral letters and in the letter of James pale by comparison. But one other passage must be mentioned in conclusion, the concentration of which has made it a *locus classicus* of the theology of the people of God. Here we find an accumulation of all the titles and dignities given to Israel in the Old Testament (drawn especially from Ex. 19:6; Is. 43:20; Hos. 2:23, not of course Hos. 1:9), applied almost exuberantly to the Church of the Gentiles: "But you are a chosen race, a royal priesthood, a holy nation, God's own people, that you may declare the wonderful deeds of him who called you out of darkness into his marvellous light. Once you were no people but now you are God's people; once you had not received mercy but now you have received mercy" (I Pet. 2:9–10).

There can be no clearer expression than this of the application of the idea of the people of God to the New Testament Church, indeed to the Church of the Gentiles. Separation from ancient Israel seems—almost with too much emphasis—to be completed here. The whole of the Old Testament will in future, as far as its positive statements are concerned, be referred to the Church. The Church now knows with complete certainty, and without thinking too much about the ancient Israel (now rejected?) which lives on, that it is the new eschatological people of God, in which all God's promises to the ancient Israel have been fulfilled. The Church is thus the true Israel of God (Gal. 6:16; Rom. 9:6), the true seed of Abraham (Gal. 3:29; cf. Rom. 9:7 f.), the true circumcision (Phil. 3:3), the true temple (I Cor. 3:16). We shall come back to the question of the relationship of the new people of God to the ancient Israel.

First we must ask: what does it mean for the Church today when it sees itself as the new people of God.[5]

[5] In addition to the works cited in A II, 2 see esp.: A. Vonier, *The People of God,* London 1937–Westminster, Maryland 1952;

3. THE CHURCH, THE PEOPLE OF GOD TODAY

(a) *All* the faithful belong to the people of God; there must be no *clericalization* of the Church.

If we see the Church as the people of God, it is clear that the Church can never be merely a particular class or caste, a group of officials or a clique within the fellowship of the faithful. The Church is always and in all cases the *whole* people of God, the *whole* ecclesia, the *whole* fellowship of the faithful. Everyone belongs to the chosen race, the royal priesthood, the holy nation. All members of the people of God have been called by God, justified by Christ, sanctified by the Holy Spirit. All members of the Church are equal in this. And all members of the people of God have been called by the message of Jesus Christ to faith, obedience and complete devotion in love; in this, too, all members of the Church are equal. This fundamental parity is much more important than the distinctions which exist in the people of God and which it would be foolish to deny.

If the Church is the true people of God, it is impossible to differentiate between "Church" and "laity", as though the laity were not in a very real sense *"laos"*. This would be a *clericalizing misconception* of the Church: the Church is directly or indirectly identified with the clergy, perhaps not with regard to duties, but at any rate with regard to rights and privileges. It is striking that the word λαός with the meaning "people of God" is so often used for the Christian community, whereas the word λαϊκός, "layman", whether in the Gentile meaning of the "uneducated masses" or in the Jewish meaning of one who is neither priest nor Levite, simply does not occur in the New Testament. It would have been impossible to use it ecclesiologically, since in the New Testament no reference is made to a group, but only to the whole company

M. D. Kloster, *Ekklesiologie im Werden,* Paderborn 1940; *Volk Gottes im Wachstum des Glaubens,* Heidelberg 1950; J. Ratzinger, *Volk und Haus Gottes in Augustins Lehre von der Kirche,* Munich 1954; H. Asmussen, H. Gross, I. Backes, etc., *Die Kirche— Volk Gottes,* Stuttgart 1961; F. B. Norris, *God's Own People,* Baltimore 1962.

of "the elect", "saints", "disciples", "brethren", all having one Lord and one Master alone. The word λαός in the New Testament, as also in the Old Testament, indicates no distinction *within* the community as between priests ("clerics") and people ("laity"). It indicates rather the fellowship of all in a single community. The distinction it implies is one *outside* the community, between the whole people of God and the "non-people", the "world", the "heathens". Not until the third century do we find any distinction between "clerics" and "laymen".

Of course, there are within the New Testament people of God certain differences which we shall discuss later; there are different charisms, services, tasks and functions. But however important these differences may be, they are never characterized with the words λαός or λαϊκός, and they are secondary by comparison with the idea of fundamental equality. Whatever special function a man may have, the vital thing for him is whether he is accepted by God, who is no respecter of persons and who recognizes no precedences of blood or race, of standing or office; the vital thing is whether a man believes and obeys, hopes and loves. The holding of an office in the Church, of whatever kind, is unimportant compared to whether, in exercising that office, a man is truly one of the "faithful"; whether he lives in faith and obedience, in love and hope.

" 'Behold, the days shall come, saith the Lord, and I will make a new covenant with the house of Israel and with the house of Judah. . . . I will give my law in their bowels, and I will write it in their heart: and I will be their God, and they shall be my people. . . . For all shall know me, from the least of them even to the greatest, saith the Lord' (Jer. 31:31–34). Christ instituted this new covenant, that is to say, the new testament, in His blood (cf. I Cor. 11:25), by calling together a people made up of Jew and Gentile, making them one, not according to the flesh but in the Spirit. This was to be the new People of God. For, *those who believe in Christ,* who are reborn not from a perishable but from an imperishable seed through the Word of the living God (cf. I Pet. 1:23) not from the flesh but from water and the Holy Spirit (cf. Jn. 3:5–6) are finally established as 'a chosen race, a *royal priesthood,* a holy nation, a purchased people. . . . You who in times

past were not a people, but are now the people of God' (I Pet.
2:9–10). That messianic people has for its head Christ, 'who
was delivered up for our sins, and rose again for our justification'
(Rom. 4:25), and who now, having won a name which above all
names, reigns in glory in heaven. The heritage of this people are
the *dignity and freedom of the sons of God,* in whose hearts the
Holy Spirit dwells as in His Temple. Its law is the new commandment to love as Christ loved us (cf. Jn. 13:34)" (CE 9; cf. 10 f.;
39 f.).

(*b*) Everyone belongs to the people of God *through God's
call:* there must be no attempt to make the Church private
and exclusive.

If the Church sees itself as the people of God, then clearly
it can never be merely a free association of like-minded religious people. The Church is always and everywhere dependent on the free choice and call of God, who wills the salvation of all men. Without God's free grace and love there can
be no Church. Conclusions which can be drawn in a general
sense from the idea of the ecclesia are given concrete form in
the history of the old and new covenants. God's call to men is
his decisive initiative for their salvation. This is clear from the
Old Testament stories—the calls to the prophets, as related by
them in vivid imagery (Isaiah, Jeremiah, Ezekiel) or sometimes briefly reported (Hosea, Amos); the calls to other
men of God, the patriarchs (especially Abraham), to Moses,
Gideon, Samson and Samuel, to the kings Saul, David,
Solomon, Jeroboam, Jehu. These calls are not some kind of
privilege, a personal honour given to individuals; God calls
them to the service of his people. For the people is the called
and chosen people, chosen from the time of Abraham, Isaac
and Jacob ("Israel"), from the time above all of Moses and
its freeing from Egyptian slavery. The same is true of the new
covenant: the calls to the individual disciples, whether nar-
rated at length or briefly reported, are above all calls to service, service of the *eschatological* people of God, which like
the ancient people of God is also called as a whole, and is as
a whole a "chosen race" (I Pet. 2:9). Thus the whole people of God is made up of those who "have received mercy"
(I Pet. 2:10) and are "called to belong to Jesus Christ",
"called to be saints" (Rom. 1:6 f.; I Cor. 1:2) and "chosen

in Christ before the foundation of the world, that we should be holy and blameless before him" (Eph. 1:4). And God's choice is free. He calls those who seem to the world foolish and weak, so that no one can boast in the presence of God (I Cor. 1:25–31). Like the calling of Paul (cf. Acts 9:1–31; 18:10), the calling of the Gentiles is the free work of God (cf. Acts 15:14; Rom. 9–11). Thus the whole people is called to the service of God—to praise him, witness to him, glorify him—and to the loving service of men. This vocation is the key to an understanding of the whole life of the people of God, and especially the covenant, whether old or new: God and his people do not make a covenant *together,* as equals; it is *God* who makes the covenant with his people. The covenant, like their vocation as a whole, is God's grace and free gift to his people.

If the Church really is the people of God, it is impossible to see the origins of the Church in individuals, in believing Christians. This misconception reduces the Church to something private, to an agglomeration of pious individuals. But the essential difference and superiority of the Christian message, when compared to other oriental religions of redemption is that its aim is not the salvation of the individual alone and the freeing of the individual soul from suffering, sin and death. The essential part of the Christian message is the idea of salvation for the whole community of people, of which the individual is a member. Closely linked to the idea of the Christian's message is the outward sign which is at once a sign of grace and vocation for the individual and of his reception into the community of the people of God: baptism (cf. Eph. 4:1–5). Since God's call precedes any action and any faith on the part of the individual, and since this call is addressed to the whole people of God, the individual never stands alone, but within the community, just as the individual communities are part of the one community, the Church. The Church begins, not with a pious individual, but with God. The pious individual cannot by himself achieve the transformation of isolated sinful men into the people of God. How could an atomized crowd of pious individuals be a home for the homeless and isolated men of today?

True, the Church is made up of individuals. But the

Church can only be seen in terms of the individuals, in as far as the individual is a member of the Church from *God's* point of view. It is not the individual as such, but the individual who has been *called* by God who becomes and remains a member of the Church; and this Church is more than the sum of the individuals which compose it and more than the product of an urge towards religious fellowship. For this reason different groups, which otherwise were often in opposition, could find their way to the Church: Jews and Gentiles, free men and slaves, men and women. God himself gathers his people around him, from every nation and class, from every town and village. The initiative lies with God. In this sense it is possible to speak of the Church as a "foundation", an "institution", in spite of all the misleading overtones of the word. To say this is to affirm that the Church does not originate simply in a common will or a common spirit among its members. The existence and the nature of the Church is determined in advance by the will of *God,* and unlike other human foundations where the founder retires after a time, it remains completely dependent on him. So the Church is not just an "institution"; it is "God's institution".

"At all times and among every people, God has given welcome to whosoever fears Him and does what is right (cf. Acts 10:35). It has pleased God, however, to make men holy and save them *not merely* as individuals without any mutual bonds, *but by making them into a single people,* a people which acknowledges Him in truth and serves Him in holiness. He therefore chose the race of Israel as a people unto Himself. With it He set up a *covenant.* Step by step He taught this people by manifesting in its history both Himself and the decree of His will, and by making it holy unto Himself. All these things, however, were done by way of preparation and as a figure of that new and perfect covenant which was to be ratified in Christ, and of that more luminous revelation which was to be given through God's very Word made flesh" (CE 9).

(*c*) We all belong to the people of God through our *human decision:* there must be no *hypostatization* of the Church.

If the Church is the people of God, it is clear that the Church can never be merely a super-entity poised above real human beings and their real decision. The Church is always and in all cases dependent on free human assent. True, the

Church is decreed by God. But there can be no Church without men. Just as the Church is impossible without the merciful and loving call and election of God, so too, at the same time and dependent on it, there can be no Church without the reply and assent of men in faith and obedience. God's free grace and love is necessary to the people *of God;* the free faith and obedience of men, which must constantly be renewed and lived out in our lives, is necessary to the *people* of God. The people of God is anything but a flock of sheep with no will of their own.

Here again, conclusions which could generally be drawn from the idea of the ekklesia become quite specific when we look at the history of the old and new covenants. The stories of the calling of the patriarchs, of Moses and the people in Egypt and in the wilderness, of kings and prophets in the Old Testament, and of Mary and the disciples in the New Testament, testify to the overwhelming grace and mercy of God's call; but they also indicate the necessity of assent on the part of the people called. Mary's fiat, "Let it be to me according to your word" (Lk. 1:38), is expected from all who have "found favour with God" (1:30). There could have been no Church without the fiat of Mary and of the disciples. Men are called, they must respond; they are chosen, and must assent. To the call of God they must reply "Amen"—and "saying Amen" means in the original Hebrew form the same things as "believing", "trusting". So in Romans 4 Abraham is held up as the archetype of faith in the Old Testament, and in Luke Mary is held up as the archetype of faith for the New Testament: "blessed is she who believed" (Lk. 1:45). In neither case is faith an independent discovery or creation of the human being; it is a humble and selfless response to God's word, a willingness to receive grace with empty yet open hands. Thus both are a *typus ecclesiae,* the Church as the fellowship of believers. Belonging to the Church is not a matter of birth, race or tradition without personal faith. Baptism, especially infant baptism, should not be seen as a means of circumventing this personal decision of faith. On the contrary, baptism is a sign both of the grace of God and of the faith of man (*sacramentum fidei*): a sign of faith, which must be personally ratified by man at the time, or, in the case of children, at a later stage.

If the Church really is the people of God, it is impossible to see it as a quasi-divine hypostasis between God and man. This would be a *hypostatizing misconception* which would dissociate it from the real people who make up the Church and make it into something in its own right—an *ecclesia quoad substantium*, a suprapersonal institution mediating between God and man. Certainly the Church is always more than the sum of its individual members; but it is and remains the fellowship of its believing members, which God has gathered into his people. There can be no Church without this people of believers. *We* are the Church—not God, not Christ, not the Spirit. Without us and outside us the Church has no reality. There is a constant danger that we let our distinctions and differentiations—valid enough in themselves—become too important, and finish up by dividing things which in reality cannot be divided. It is right to distinguish between the "structure" and the "life" of the Church, but wrong to assign to "structure" faith, sacraments and offices, and endow them with a particular importance as spiritual riches, while we pigeonhole the fellowship of believers under "life". There can be no faith, sacraments and offices, nothing of an institutional nature, without men, they cannot precede or be superior to men. All these things only exist in the fellowship of believers, who *are* the Church; it is this fellowship, which is identical with the new people of God, which constitutes the *basic structure* of the Church.

"All the elect, before time began, the Father 'foreknew and predestined to become conformed to the image of his Son, that he should be the firstborn among many brethren' (Rom. 8:29). He planned to assemble in the holy Church all those who would believe in Christ" (CE 2). "God has gathered together as one all those who in faith look upon Jesus as the author of salvation and the source of unity and peace, and has established them as the Church that for each and all she may be the visible sacrament of this saving unity" (CE 9).

(*d*) The people of God is an *historical* people: there must be no *idealization* of the Church.

If the Church really sees itself as the people of God, it is obvious that it can never be a static and supra-historical phenomenon, which exists undisturbed by earthly space and historical time. The Church is always and everywhere a living people, gathered together from the peoples of this world and journeying through the midst of time. The Church is essentially *en route,* on a journey, a pilgrimage. A Church which pitches its tents without looking out constantly for new horizons, which does not continually strike camp, is being untrue to its calling. The historical nature of the Church is revealed by the fact that it remains the pilgrim people of God. It renews and continues the history of the ancient people of the covenant and fulfils it in the new covenant. At the same time it journeys through history, through a time of complex imperfection, towards the final perfection, the eschatological kingdom of God, led by God himself. It is essentially an interim Church, a Church in transition, and therefore not a Church of fear but of expectation and hope: a Church which is directed towards the consummation of the world by God.

If the Church is really the people of God, then it is impossible to see it as something set apart from everything earthly, from error and sin. This would be an *idealizing misconception* of the Church, by which it would become an unreal, distant ideal surrounded by a false halo, rather than a real historical Church. Such an ideal Church would have no faults or blemishes, would know nothing of error and sin, and so would need no repentance and penance. It would be perfect in itself. But the only perfect being without error and sin is God, there can be no other. The ideal Church does not exist empirically in this world, as we constantly rediscover to our sorrow; but equally it does not exist in Scripture. For Scripture the Church is the people of God, which, following the Old Testament people of God, is always a people of sinners, constantly in need of forgiveness. The Church journeys through the darkness of failures and wrong turnings, constantly in need of God's grace and mercy. Constantly exposed to temptation, it has every cause for its constant attitude of humility and metanoia. The phrase *"ecclesia semper reformanda"* is not just a slogan for times of especial difficulty, but God's everyday demand to his people as it journeys, the repeated

demand for greater faithfulness towards him. It is no accident
that the words *"populus tuus"* in the liturgy are so often associated with penance. The people of God has constantly to
prove itself. Even when it is in full possession of his promise,
it can fall away from God. The people of God, the Church, is
not the same as the community of the elect in the consummated kingdom of God. The Church is still under God's judgment. It is therefore exhorted, on its journey towards the
peace of its Sabbath, to "lift drooping hands and weak knees"
(Heb. 12:12), as "aliens and exiles to abstain from the passions of the flesh" (I Pet. 2:11), to avoid loving the transient world and its "lust" and to do the will of God (I Jn.
2:15–17), to "contend" against the demonic "powers" of this
world (Eph. 6:12), to "repent" once again of evil works
(Rev. 2:5). The way of the people of God is not easy, but
its struggles and its tribulations, its persistence and its trust
can all be seen in the context of God's promise of certain victory.

"While Christ, 'holy, innocent, undefiled' (Heb. 7:26) knew
nothing of sin (II Cor. 5:21), but came to expiate only the sins of
the people (cf. Heb. 2:17), the Church, embracing sinners in her
bosom, is *at the same time holy and always in need of being
purified,* and incessantly pursues the path of *penance and renewal.*
The Church, 'like a pilgrim in a foreign land, presses forward
amid the persecutions of the world and the consolation of God'
(Augustine), announcing the cross and death of the Lord until He
comes (cf. I Cor. 11:26). By the power of the risen Lord, she is
given strength to overcome patiently and lovingly the afflictions
and hardships which assail her from within and without, and to
show forth in the world the mystery of the Lord in a faithful
though shadowed way, until at the last it will be revealed in total
splendour" (CE 8).

But, it may be asked, are we not speaking too glibly about
the people of God, about the *Church* as the people of God?
What of Israel and the Jews? Hitherto we have spoken only
of the ancient, pre-Christian Israel; it is now time to turn our
attention to the continuing, existing Israel.

4. THE CHURCH AND THE JEWS

(a) *The burden of the past.*[6] For long centuries the Church simply dismissed Israel. The Jews were a *quantité négligeable*, both numerically and influentially. For Paul the relationship between the Church and Israel was still a central problem,

[6] The literature on Christianity and the Jews is extensive. There are good bibliographies in Freiburger Rundbrief series 12 (1959/60), 101–116 (special publication) and by A. L. Rueff in *Israel und die Kirche*, Zurich 1961, 85–93. Also noteworthy are the specialist series (Judaica, Studia Delitzschiana, Studia Judaica) and periodicals (*Freiburger Rundbrief, Der Zeuge, The Bridge, The Hebrew Christian, Cahiers sioniens*). Particularly important are two volumes of collected essays: *The Christian Approach to the Jew. Addresses delivered at the Pre-Evanston Conference at Lake Geneva, Wisconsin,* New York 1954; *Juden-Christen-Deutsche*, ed. by H. J. Schultz, Stuttgart–Olten–Freiburg 1961, with important contributions on the historical aspects by D. Brachfeld, F. Heer, J. H. Kraus, R. Pfisterer; on the fundamental relationship between the Christians and Jews by H. U. von Balshasar, H. Gollwitzer, A. Rosenberg, E. Rosenstock-Huessy; on the basic theological problems by F.-X. Arnold, S. Ben-Chorin, G. Ebeling, E. Käsemann, O. Michel, K. Rahner, F. Schubert, F. Stier, P. Tillich, C. Westermann, P. Winter, H. W. Wolff, W. Zimmedi; on the Jewish personal viewpoint by H. G. Adler, M. Buber, H. Bergmann; and finally also *Der ungekundigte Bund. Neue Begegnung von Juden und christliche Gemeinde*, ed. by D. Goldschmidt and H. J. Kraus, Stuttgart 1962. More recent writings are: K. Barth, *Church Dogmatics*, II/2, pp. 195–506, Edinburgh–Naperville, Illinois 1957; III/3, pp. 210–226, 1961; IV/3/2, pp. 876–878, 1962; C. Journet, *Destinées d'Israel*, Paris 1944; H. Schmidt, *Die Judenfrage und die christliche Kirche in Deutschland,* Stuttgart 1947; J. M. Oesterreicher, *The Apostolate to the Jews,* New York 1948; J. Jocz, *The Jewish People and Jesus Christ*, London 1949–Naperville, Illinois 1954; *A Theology of Election. Israel and the Church,* London–Naperville, Illinois 1958; P. Démann, *La catéchèse chrétienne et le peuple de la bible,* Paris 1952; G. Dix, *Jew and Greek,* London–Chester Springs, Pa. 1953; W. Maurer, *Kirche und Synagoge. Motive und Formen der Auseinandersetzung der Kirche mit dem Judentum im Laufe der Geschichte,* Stuttgart 1953; L. Goppelt, *Christentum und Judentum im 1. and 2. Jahrhundert,* Gütersloh 1954; G. Hedenquist, etc., *The Church and the Jewish People,* London–Edinburgh 1954; F. Lovsky, *Antisémitisme et mystère d'Israel,* Paris 1955; E. Sterling, *Er ist wie Du. Aus der Frühgeschichte der Antisemitismus,* Munich 1956; H. U. von Balthasar, *Martin Buber and Christianity. A dialogue between Is-*

but in the later New Testament period it became a peripheral question. Was this simply because of the fall of the Jewish metropolis Jerusalem and the consequent almost total disappearance of Jewish Christianity? The Fathers of the Church could not ignore the fact that the Jewish people still existed; but they came to regard it in an increasingly anti-Jewish spirit. Here then, in the earliest Christian centuries, begins that hostility to the Jews which later was—but only towards the end of the last century, and erroneously, since Arabs are also semitic—to be known as anti-Semitism. This original hostility to the Jews was not, however, as in modern times, based on racial ideas but resulted from different views of revelation. It was not until the time of the imperial Church of Constantine that Gentile hostility to the Jews, which had existed before Christianity, was continued as something "Christian" and was later to become intensified during the Middle Ages.

Gentile hostility to the Jews, especially as a result of the religio-political non-conformism of the Jews, existed before Christianity. The same complaints were made about Christians up to the third

rael and the Church, London 1961–New York 1962; H. Gollwitzer, *Israel-und wir,* Berlin 1958; G. Jasper, *Stimmen aus dem neureligiösen Judentum in seiner Stellung zum Christentum und zu Jesus,* Hamburg 1958; F. W. Foerster, *The Jews,* London 1961–New York 1962; W. Sulzbach, *Die zwei Würzeln und Formen des Judenhasses,* Stuttgart 1959; E. Peterson, *Frühkirche, Judentum uns Gnosis,* Freiburg 1959; M. Barth, *Israel und die Kirche im Brief des Paulus an die Epheser,* Munich 1959; K. Kupisch, *Das Volk der Geschichte,* Berlin 1960; H. Diem, *Das Rätsel des Antisemitismus,* Munich 1960; D. Judant, *Les deux Israel,* Paris 1960; *Israel und die Kirche. Eine Studie im Auftrag der Generalsynode der Niederländischen Reformierten Kirche,* Zurich 1961; W. Marsch and K. Thieme, eds., *Christen und Juden,* Mainz 1961; G. Dellinger, *Die Juden im Catechismus Romanus,* Munich 1963; G. Baum, *The Jews and the Gospel,* London 1961; W. Seiferth, *Synagogue und Kirche im Mittelalter,* Munich 1964. Also see the numerous textbooks and works on the history of Judaism and especially the interpretative works by Jewish authors (L. Baeck, S. Ben-Chorin, M. Buber, H. Cohen, E. L. Ehrlich, A. Gilbert, J. Klausner, F. Rosenzweig, H. J. Schoeps, P. Winter). Finally the encyclopaedia articles on Judaism and Jewish Christianity. See also the bibliography below for Romans 9–11 and that given for C I, 2.

century, but nevertheless the enmity between Jews and Christians increased. Various interacting factors played an important part in this: (1) the increasing distance of the Church from its Old Testament roots as a result of the hellenization of the Christian message; (2) the exclusive commandeering of the Old Testament by a Church which no longer valued the Old Testament in its own right, but by means of typological and allegorical interpretation turned it almost entirely into a prophecy of the Christian religion; (3) guilt for Jesus' crucifixion and death, which was generally attributed to the Jews and to all Jews, and taken as the reason why the whole race had been cursed, rejected and condemned to dispersion; (4) the breakdown of any dialogue between Church and synagogue, growing isolation, and the substitution for dialogue of an apologetic monologue.

The formation of the *imperial Church under Constantine* brought a further development. On the basis of the uniqueness of their God as revealed in the Old Testament, and especially on the basis of their expectation of a Messiah and the kingdom of God, the Jews had always rejected the hellenistic and Roman imperial cult and the whole myth of the empire—an essential reason for *Gentile* hostility to the Jews. In the same way they now rejected the christianized ideology of the empire, according to which the emperor and his rule was an image and continuation of the heavenly reign of God. Specifically Gentile hostility to the Jews was now taken over by the imperial Church, which had conveniently forgotten its own days of persecution, and strengthened considerably by the introduction of Christian ideas. The laws of the imperial Church effectively banished Jews from the sacral kingdom, to which entry could only be obtained through the sacraments: mixed marriages were forbidden, as was the holding of official posts by Jews, the building or extension of synagogues, etc. So the Jews within the empire were in practice living *outside* the empire. While some theologians like Augustine still saw the Church as having a missionary duty towards the Jews, others, like Chrysostom, were already making inflammatory attacks upon the Jews in the style of later anti-Jewish preachers. The *Corpus iuris civile* of Justinian, which intensified the anti-Jewish measures of Theodosius in particular, became a cornerstone of all medieval laws about the Jews. While the papacy, as it grew in strength, and Gregory I in particular, conducted a moderate policy towards the Jews and condemned enforced baptisms, there were also more violent measures against them, even if until the Crusades they remained the exception rather than the rule. In France and Spain especially there was violence (cf. Isidore of Seville's anti-Jewish polemic) and the Arab conquest of Spain was hailed by the Jews as a liberation.

It is true that the period of more than a thousand years in which Christians and Jews lived in close contact had more positive aspects, and both parties were often enriched by it. But in the High Middle Ages, coinciding with fierce attacks on heretics (such as the Albigensians), the crusades especially (1096–1215) marked a turn for the worse in the position of the Jews. They were put on the same level as the Moslems. During the first three crusades there were terrible slaughters of Jews in France, in the Rhineland, in Bohemia and in Palestine, where the crusaders were determined to settle with the "enemies of Christ". The great Pope Innocent III, and the most important of the medieval councils, the Fourth Lateran Synod of 1215, were noted for their anti-Jewish measures. A special dress was prescribed for the Jews, they were forbidden all public office and prohibited from going out during Holy Week. As a result of their sufferings during the crusades countless German Jews emigrated to Poland and Russia. The institution of the inquisition, and the work of the Dominicans, who were put in charge of it and whose aim was the "conversion" of all Jews, had terrible effects. Clement IV attempted to impose the ghetto system.

But it was precisely the Church, which with the help of the secular arm suppressed and persecuted the Jews, which never doubted that it was the successor, representative and heir of the now finally rejected Israel. The Jews were seen as the rejected Israel, and all the *judgments* and *curses* of the Old Testament were applied to them. But the Church was "Israel", inheritor of all the *promises* of the Old Testament: the true and spiritual Israel, *the* people of God. After the crucifixion of Jesus, for which the Jews were responsible, the people of the Jews had ceased, so the Church thought, to be the people of God. And the Jews had to pay for this in the course of centuries of sufferings unparalleled in history. These powerful and ingrained prejudices were not the least of the reasons why the centuries which followed the crusades were for the Jews centuries of condemnations, expulsions, lootings, tortures and murders. Only gradually, and not through the Reformation, did an improvement in the situation begin in more modern times, to be reversed in the most hideous way in our own century by unparalleled mass madness and mass murders which wiped out a third of all Jews.

The *historic prejudices* against the Jews which were repeated right down to most recent times are in part very old, in part of medieval origin; their lack of foundation is well known: "Jews are only interested in money" (cf. the colloquial sense of the word "Jew"). But it was the *Christians* who drove the Jews out of their official posts, out of the judiciary and the army, and in addition denied to them farming and crafts. Jewish landowners were not allowed to use Christian workers, Christian guilds closed all crafts to the Jews. In this way they compelled them to take up trading in money, as the only way they could eke out their existence. Almost everything—the right to come and go, to buy and sell, to communal prayer, to marry and to bear children—the Jew had to pay for in cash. Only in recent times, with the setting up of the State of Israel, has the old idea that Jews were incapable of farming and craft-work been clearly refuted.

"The Jews are damned to perpetual homelessness" (cf. the legend of the wandering Jew Ahasuerus, condemned because of Jesus to wander and never die). But the Jewish diaspora had begun several centuries before the death of Jesus. At the time of Jesus' birth only a fraction of Jews were living in Palestine. On the other hand, a large number of Jews continued to live in Palestine both after the destruction of Jerusalem by the Romans and after the revolt of Bar-Kochba. It was not until the crusaders came that they were reduced to a tiny remnant who lived a penurious existence as dyers. Here again the foundation of the State of Israel has demonstrated the untruth of this legend.

"The Jews are criminals" (cf. the fables of ritual murders, of the poisoning of wells; of sacrilege against the sacred host; or the dangerousness of Jewish doctors, cf. the "plot" of Jewish doctors on the life of Stalin in 1953). But all these general accusations are without foundation, in the Old Testament and the Talmud alike we find a horror of defilement through blood; medieval emperors like Frederick II and popes like Innocent IV defended the Jews against attacks of this kind centuries ago.

These often laughable, but at root highly dangerous prejudices and legends cost countless Jews their lives. In 1348–9, the time of the worst persecutions of the Jews in the Middle Ages, about 300 Jewish communities in Alsace and in the Rhineland, in Thuringia, Bavaria and Austria were destroyed, and the rest lived there on sufferance. Why? The rumour had started in southern France that Jews had poisoned the wells and were therefore responsible for the plague which had broken out. In 1290 the Jews were expelled from England, in 1394 from France, in 1492 from Spain, in 1497 from Portugal.

But the terrible persecutions, expulsions and mass murders of the later Middle Ages by no means ended with the Reformation. Luther particularly, in his later writings, wrote more violently against the Jews than many of his predecessors. In his notorious pamphlet "The Jews and their lies" (1543) he called for the burning of their synagogues, the destruction of their houses, the confiscation of their sacred writings; he proposed that they should be forbidden on pain of death to teach or hold services, that safe-conduct should be denied them, that their possessions should be seized. Even though Calvin's whole theology emphasized the unity of the covenant, and even though in the Reformed Churches as a whole there was a respect for Judaism, under the influence of humanism, this did not materially affect the preaching and cate-chetics of these Churches.

Significant changes were brought about by *humanism,* which went back to Hebrew sources (Reuchlin, Scaliger) and tried to interpret Jewish history without prejudice, and later *pietism* (Zinzendorf), which particularly in the foundation of the Institutum Judaicum at Halle attempted to approach Judaism factually and in brotherly love; finally the *Enlightenment* (the Toleration Edict of the Emperor Joseph II, and the declarations of the rights of men made in America and by the French Revolution), which with its principles of humanity and tolerance led to the emancipation of the Jews and their gaining equal rights of citizenship. This external emancipation was frequently followed by internal assimilation and by the reform of synagogue worship and religious teachings in liberal Judaism. In opposition to assimilation there developed Zionism, which led to the founding of the State of Israel and hence to a new form of emancipation.

But despite these changes hostility to the Jews had by no means been overcome in the Church and in society at large. In the East there were numerous violent persecutions of the Jews and as a result of the Russian and Polish *pogroms,* many Jews fled to the West and to America. For German idealism, notably for Hegel, Judaism figured as the manifestation of the evil principle. It needed merely the race-theories of men like Gobineau and Houston Stuart Chamberlain to provide the ideological basis for a racist "anti-semitism". As a result of various economic, political and ideological factors this led to the unparalleled and fearful explosion of "anti-semitism" in National Socialism. The Nazi atrocities reduced the number of Jews in Europe by two-thirds, and that of all the Jews in the world by a third. About six million Jews, men, women and children, were gassed and annihilated. At the turn of the century 80 per cent of all Jews lived in Europe; in 1958 34 per cent.

We may wonder how this centuries-long history of horrors, of suffering and death, culminating in the murder of millions by the Nazis, could come about. We could ask this question as historians and examine the historical origins of hostility to the Jews; or we could ask it as psychologists and analyse the effective psychological impulses in anti-semitism (breakdown of personality structure, hostility to outside groups, scapegoat-thinking, fear of alien things, counter-ideal, etc.). But we ask this question here simply as Christians, as members of a community which distinguishes itself from the old people of God by calling itself the new people of God. How could all this happen? Shame and guilt must be our silent reply—would we wish to speak above the enforced silence of millions?

We could, of course, try to justify ourselves with apologetic arguments of various kinds: moral (the Jews also made mistakes—of course!) or historical (things must be understood in their historical context—everything?) or theological (it was not the true Church acting in these cases—but where and what then is this true Church?) or even political (it was a question of choosing between evils, it was more opportune to do nothing about it—but was it Christian, was it evangelical?). The weight of guilt is too heavy by far to be balanced by such self-justifications. The Church preached love, while it sowed the seeds of murderous hatred; it proclaimed love, while it prepared the way for atrocities and death. And these acts were perpetrated against the compatriots and brothers of him who taught the Church: "What you did to one of the least of these my brethren, you did to me" (Mt. 25:40). The Church that stood between Israel and Jesus prevented Israel from recognizing its Messiah.

At this point mention should be made of the declaration made by the Second Vatican Council in the name of the Church: "The Church repudiates all persecutions against any man. Moreover, mindful of her common patrimony with the Jews, and motivated by the gospel's spiritual love and by no political considerations, she deplores the hatred, persecutions and displays of anti-Semitism directed against the Jews at any time and from any source" (DR 4).

Of course, not all the guilt for the sufferings of the Jews can be laid at the door of the Church. They were often caused by heathens, both then and now, who were against Israel's God. And in spite of all the heathen elements which crept into the Church, there has always been, particularly in recent times, vocal Christian protest and courageous opposition to all "anti-semitic" hatred and all inhumanity. But too often this protest was made by individuals or outsiders, while official representatives of the Church, and often its highest dignitaries, withdrew into cautious, politic and opportunistic silence, or spoke only hesitantly and softly, in words which were diplomatically shrouded in qualifications, and failed to display any prophetic power or spirit of commitment; words, in short, which fell short of the Gospel of Jesus Christ. But it is important to see beyond the individual case and to realize that Nazi anti-semitism, however much it may have been primarily the work of godless and criminal men, would have been impossible without the preceding two thousand years of "Christian" hostility to the Jews, which hampered Christians in offering convinced and energetic resistance to it on a broad front.

It was no accident that Catholic commentators on the Nazi race laws appealed to their "unshakable faith that they were acting in accordance with the will of the omnipotent creator", nor that one of the leaders of the Nazi persecution of the Jews should have referred to Martin Luther during the Nuremberg trials. It is fair to say—in the interests of precision not of excusing the inexcusable guilt—that none of the anti-semitic measures of the Nazis were new. The use of special clothing as a distinguishing mark, exclusion from certain professions, banning of mixed marriages, seizing of Jewish goods, expulsion and concentration camps, burning and butchering—all these things existed in the "Christian" Middle Ages and during the "Christian" Reformation. The only new things were the racist arguments as a foundation for these acts, and the hideous thoroughness of the organization, the technical perfection and the terrible "industrialization" of the killings.

(b) *Present tasks:* Only one thing is of any use now: a

radical metanoia, repentance and re-thinking; we must start on a new road, no longer leading away from the Jews, but towards them, towards a living dialogue, the aim of which is not the capitulation but simply the understanding of the other side; towards mutual help, which is not part of a "mission", to an encounter in a true brotherly spirit.

The Second Vatican Council was not content with a mere admission of guilt: "Since the spiritual patrimony common to Christians and Jews is thus so great, this sacred Synod wishes to foster and recommend that mutual understanding and respect which is the fruit above all of biblical and theological studies, and of brotherly dialogues" (DR 4).

The Council expressly dismissed the widespread theological misinterpretation which has caused most disaster in the Church's history—the idea that the Jews, they alone and as a whole, bore the guilt of Jesus' death on the cross: "True, authorities of the Jews and those who followed their lead pressed for the death of Christ (cf. Jn. 19:6); still, what happened in His passion *cannot be blamed upon all the Jews then living, without distinction, nor upon the Jews of today*. Although the Church is the new people of God, the Jews should not be presented as *repudiated or cursed by God*, as if such views followed from the holy Scriptures. All should take pains, then, lest in catechetical instruction and in the preaching of God's Word they teach anything out of harmony with the truth of the gospel and the spirit of Christ" (DR 4). Jesus' death occurred because of the sins of *all men*: "Besides, as the Church has always held and continues to hold, Christ in His boundless love freely underwent His passion and death because of the sins of *all* men, so that *all* might attain salvation. It is, therefore, the duty of the Church's preaching to proclaim the cross of Christ as the sign of God's all-embracing love, and as the fountain from which every grace flows." (DR 4).

Any time would have been a good time for this encounter, but today is especially apt, so soon after the most terrible catastrophe in the history of the Jewish people and after the unexpectedly hopeful new beginning of the State of Israel. Now after thousands of years this old and yet surprisingly young people has begun its own life as a State again; this is an event which ranks as the most important in Jewish history since the destruction of Jerusalem and of the temple and one with religious consequences, both positive and negative, which it as yet is too early to assess.

This weak people which has survived the centuries, this decimated people which is now starting life anew, stronger than ever, has always been a riddle to the world and often to itself. What are these Jews? A race, and yet, as a result of frequent intermingling and the fact that it has no undisputable distinguishing features, not a race. A linguistic community and yet, since only part speaks Hebrew, not that either. A religion, and yet, since many Jews have become completely secularized or been baptized, not a religion. A State, and yet, since a vast majority is not citizens of this State, not that either. A people, and yet, since a majority has become assimilated into other peoples, not a people. Thus the Jews are a puzzling fated fellowship, mostly accepted by individual Jews, but rejected by some; this enigma is perhaps an indication of the hidden *secret* of the Jews. Their secret, which believing Jews and believing Christians alike accept, is their vocation to be a people of God in the midst of other peoples. This vocation was never questioned, even at a time when the Church regarded Israel as no more than an outmoded earlier form of the true people of God. Today we must think more deeply about this continuing character of the people of the Jews as a people of God, if we are to determine more positively the relationship between the Church and Israel.

In many ways there is a better basis today for a dialogue between Jews and Christians, seen from both points of view, than at any time during previous centuries when it was almost but not quite non-existent.

From the Christian side: before the crimes of the Hitler regime opened the eyes of Christians to the suffering and misery of the Jews, Christian theology had already begun to investigate the Old Testament and the Hebrew world of ideas seriously. In contrast to earlier studies, the unity of the Old and New Testaments rather than the distinctions between them was stressed and its impact traced in similar attitudes towards God, men and the world. The result of historical-critical studies was that the Old Testament was no longer simply interpreted in an over-neat allegorical way as a preparation for the New Testament, but was put once again into its individual and real historical setting. Instead of being seen as a spiritual entity, Israel, both as a people and as a country, was studied as something actual. Comparisons with the Greek and hellenic worlds, which were now possible, showed the great strength of Hebrew thinking: its greater historical dynamism, its appreciation of totalities, its sympathy, born of its faith, for the world, for the body, for life, its eschatological orientation towards the coming kingdom of God. Seen in this light, the figure of Christ no longer appeared as the fulfilment of isolated and sporadic Old Testament prophecies, but as the fulfilment of the old covenant as a whole and of the saving purpose of God, linked to Israel and the Torah.

From the Jewish side: here, as is shown in particular, by the remarkable reconstitution of Israel as a separate sovereign State, the position has also greatly changed. The rabbis and their casuistic devotion to the law have lost their influence over large numbers of Jews today, above all among the younger generation, and this is a great aid to dialogue. As against the previously dominant authority of the Talmud, the Bible has, at least in the lives of a small élite, re-established its central position. Beginnings have been made with common Jewish-Christian Old Testament studies. Jewish worship has been revised and made more vital, just as Christian worship has been, and the relationship between the two has thus become more apparent. There are signs that a mutual consciousness of a common Jewish-Christian basis is beginning to develop. Some Jews are now reading the New Testament and as regards the person of Jesus hatred and scorn have begun to give place to appreciation and respect for him as a great son and prophet of Israel, even though his claim to be the Messiah is, in general, as fanatically rejected as it ever was. There is a long list of books about Jesus of Nazareth which have been published in recent years in the State of Israel. Leading spirits of Judaism—women like Simone Weil and Edith Stein, men like Hermann Cohen, Martin Buber, Franz Rosenzweig, Leo Baeck, Max Brod, Hans Joachim Schoeps, Schalom Ben-Chorin, and more indirectly men like Freud, Einstein, Kafka and Ernst Bloch have helped to make the particular nature of Jewishness more comprehensible to the Gentile world of the twentieth century.

The dialogue between Christians and Jews, if it is to be serious and not mere superficial fraternization, must be based on the *Bible*. This does not make things easier. The dialogue between Christians and Jews is clearly much more difficult than that between separated Christians who at least have a common basis in the *Bible,* whereas the conflict between

Christians and Jews cuts across the heart of the Bible and divides it into two testaments, each one preferred by a different group. There is no point in trying to overlook the real centre of controversy here: Jesus of Nazareth, who appears in the New Testament as the Messiah promised in the Old Testament and is rejected by the greater part of Israel. There is no question of two "ways of belief" here—that would be easier for discussion—what divides us is Jesus, who is for us the Messiah, his death and resurrection. Between Jews and Christians, an apparently unsurmountable barrier to reconciliation, there stands the cross, a stumbling-block for Jews, the sign of God's power and wisdom for Christians. The *cross,* and this point cannot be argued away, imbues the whole New Testament with a militant anti-Jewish atmosphere; this is as true of the gospel as of Paul's letters. We may well wonder whether the New Testament itself was not at least used as an authority for later anti-semitism on the part of the Church. This is less of a problem with Jesus' own preaching than with Paul's, for it was Paul who led and won the battle for a Gentile Church in the first days of Christianity. We must therefore turn—we have already examined earlier writings—to the letter to the Romans; chapters 9–11 of this letter have become a *locus classicus* for the relationship between the Church and Israel. The following lines of thought may fruitfully be stressed, but only seen together are they a reflection of the whole truth.[7]

(c) *Hope for the future:* (1) The promise of Israel. Did Israel lose its special position as the people of God after the death of Jesus? Not at all, according to Paul. God's faith-

[7] Cf. the more recent commentaries on the letter to the Romans: P. Althaus, H. Asmussen, C. K. Barrett, J. Huby–St Lyonnet, J. Knox, O. Kuss, F. J. Leenhardt, A. Nygren, K. H. Schelkle, and particularly O. Michel; and in addition: E. Weber, *Das Problem der Heilgeschichte nach Rom. 9–11,* Leipzig 1911; F.-W. Maier, *Israel in der Heilsgeschchte nach Rom. 9–11,* Münster 1929; K. L. Schmidt, *Die Judenfrage im Lichte der Kapitel 9–11 des Römerbriefes,* Zollikon–Zurich 1943; G. Schrenk, *Der göttliche Sinn in Israels Geschich,* Zollikon–Zurich 1943; *Die Weissagung uber Israel im NT,* Zurich 1951; W. Vischer, *Das Geheimnis Israels,* Zurich 1950 = *Judaica* 6, 2; K. H. Schelkle, *Paulus, Lehrer der Vater,* Dusseldorf 1956; J. Munck, *Christus und Israel. Eine Auslegung von Rom. 9–11,* Copenhagen 1956.

fulness to Israel persists, even when Israel is unfaithful (Rom. 3:3). The vocation of this people of God is continuous, irrevocable, indestructible. The Jews are and remain God's chosen and beloved people. The new brotherhood in the Church does not destroy the old (9:3). To the Jews—here addressed with their historical, vocational title as "Israelites" (9:4)—belongs "the sonship": the people of Israel is God's "first-born son" (cf. Ex. 4:22); to Israel belongs "the glory": the glory of the presence of God with his people; and "the covenant": the covenant of God with his people which was continually renewed and confirmed; and "the giving of the law": the way of life prescribed by God to his people as a sign of the covenant; and "the worship": the true worship of the priestly nation; and "the promises": the promises of God's grace and salvation; and "the patriarchs": their ancestors of old in the fellowship of the one true faith; and finally, far more important than all the others, "the Christ", the Messiah, Jesus Christ, born of Jewish flesh and blood, belongs first and foremost to the people of Israel (cf. 9:4 f.).

The Second Vatican Council affirms: "As this sacred Synod searches into the mystery of the Church, it recalls the spiritual bond linking the people of the New Covenant with Abraham's stock. For the Church of Christ acknowledges that, according to the mystery of God's saving design, the beginnings of her faith and her election are already found among the patriarchs, Moses, and the prophets. She professes that all who believe in Christ, Abraham's sons according to faith (cf. Gal. 3:7), are included in the same patriarch's call, and likewise that the salvation of the Church was mystically foreshadowed by the chosen people's exodus from the land of bondage. The Church, therefore, cannot forget that she received the revelation of the Old Testament through the people with whom God in his inexpressible mercy deigned to establish the Ancient Covenant. Nor can she forget that she draws sustenance from the root of that good olive tree onto which have been grafted the wild olive branches of the Gentiles (cf. Rom. 11:17–24). Indeed, the Church believes that by His cross Christ, our Peace, reconciled Jew and Gentile, making them both one in Himself (cf. Eph. 2:14–16). Also, the Church ever keeps in mind the words of the Apostle about his kinsmen, 'who have the adoption as sons, and the glory and the covenant and the legislation and the worship and the promises; who have the fathers, and from whom is Christ according to the flesh' (Rom. 9:4 f.), the son of the Virgin Mary. The Church recalls too that from the Jewish people sprang the apostles, her foundation stones and pillars, as well as most of the early disciples who proclaimed Christ to the world" (DR 4).

All these things still belong to the Jews, even though they rejected Jesus as the Messiah, a fact which fills Paul with "great sorrow" and "unceasing anguish", as his "conscience bears witness in the Holy Spirit"; so much so that he would gladly offer himself as an atoning sacrifice for his people, just as Moses, David and the prophets suffered on behalf of their people. From this standpoint any kind of anti-semitism is radically impossible. Paul the Jew does not cease to be a Jew now that he is a Christian. He fulfils his Jewishness, as an inheritor of the Old Testament, and fills it with a new, freer, more all-embracing spirit, in the light of a new and unexpected action on the part of God, who in the old covenant too had always acted in a new and unexpected way. The God who in Jesus of Nazareth has acted in a decisively new way on his people's behalf and whom Paul proclaims in his teaching, is none other than the God of Abraham, Isaac and Jacob. The God of the Church of Christ is and remains the God of Israel. And this God's message, the new like the old, is given first of all to Israel. The Church becomes a part of the people chosen in Abraham. God's plan for Israel is still effective in the New Testament.

For this reason the Church can never seriously take up the task of "missionizing" the Jews. The Gospel cannot be presented to the Jews as something alien and external to them. The Jews were never previously guilty of a false faith; before the Church existed they believed in the one true God and before the Church existed, not simply through the Church, the Gospel was preached to them. They were and remain those to whom God addresses himself first. The young Church comes from the Jews. But have they not, for the most part, rejected that Gospel?

(2) Israel's guilt and duty: According to Paul's account the truth cannot be hidden: the Jews, for the most part at

least, rejected the Gospel, thereby denying their "sonship", their especial election and vocation, at the decisive moment. They did not recognize the "glory" as it was revealed in Jesus the Messiah. They rejected the new "testament" in his blood. They did not accept the fulfilment of the "law" which God wanted to write upon their hearts. They failed to recognize the true "worship" made possible through his spirit. They were blind to the fulfilment of the "promises" in the figure of the suffering servant of God and expelled and handed over to the Gentiles the man for whom their "fathers" had been waiting. Paul does not baulk, so serious is the matter, at speaking here, as the prophets had spoken before him, of "blindness", "hardness of heart", "obduracy", "a spirit of stupor", even of "rejection".

The fact remains that the failure of his people does not mean that "the word of God had failed" (9:6). But it is also clear that the rejection of Jesus as Messiah has created a division within Israel: "Not all who are descended from Israel belong to Israel" (9:6). God's promises, Israel's prerogatives, are by no means the inalienable saving possession of every Israelite, which he may boast of in comfort. A distinction must be made—as it was basically already made in the Old Testament, but now with eschatological urgency—between an Israel of the flesh and an Israel of the promise, between an Israel that has been chosen and one that has not (cf. 9:8–13). Here we cross the frontier of purely human decisions. Here God's sovereign freedom and inexplicable grace is at work, unfathomable, indeed a stumbling-block to man (cf. 9:14–29). It is true that the guilt of man is presupposed here, indeed it is explicitly affirmed by Paul; but it is included within God's sovereign act. In freedom God chooses Isaac, not Ishmael, Jacob, not Esau, Moses, not Pharaoh. Man cannot quarrel with God about this. But Paul here is not concerned with the election or rejection, the salvation or damnation of *individuals,* as was mistakenly understood from Augustine through the Middle Ages to Luther and Calvin. In his historical and theological perspective here he is concerned with the election of a *community* as such, with the election of the people of God, Israel. God is sovereign even with regard to Israel's prerogatives. God's plan of salvation includes free choice, even though his promises are offered to the whole nation. He freely chooses and rejects, without in the least abandoning his purposes of grace and love, his aim to lead Israel as a whole to salvation. The prerogatives of Israel remain in force, but they must, precisely in keeping with the prophetic message, be interpreted anew in the light of the cross of Christ, the cross which unmasks all human self-righteousness, all works intended to ensure salvation, all self-confidence claims and shows them as the impious illusions of pious men.

God separated off only a "remnant" (9:27), a "seed" (9:29 A.V.) which would be saved, as he had promised. But God (in his unbounded mercy) executes his decree, by making a rejected people, the Gentiles, into a chosen people (9:22–26). Israel "after the flesh", as Paul knew and understood it, had sought to replace selfless and trusting faith in God's promises with its own pious works and deeds. In this way it had thought to justify itself before God through its *own* righteousness instead of putting its trust in God's promises alone like Abraham and with him all of ancient Israel "after the spirit".

Now in the preaching of the Gospel it is above all *God's* righteousness which is revealed for *everyone* who *believes,* whether Jew or Gentile. The crucified Christ is the test of faith. He is the stumbling-block set by God to cause the downfall of those who look for righteousness on the merits of their own pious works. But he is also the sign of salvation for all who put their faith and trust in him (cf. 9:30–33). So a distinction is drawn between the righteousness of works and the righteousness of faith, between works as merit and faith without merit, between self-glory and the glory of God. Christ is the end of the law. He is the new sign of the covenant. Through him the promises are no longer tied to the law. The reign of the law is over, the new reign of grace for all who believe has begun. It is Christ who now stands where the law formerly stood (cf. 10:1–13). Precisely in the terms of the old covenant Israel is unpardonable, because of its lack of faith and disobedience and because it did not recognize the fulfilment of the promise (10:14–21).

But Israel's abandonment of God furthers the election of the Gentiles. "Has God rejected his people? By no means! . . . God has not rejected his people whom he foreknew" (11:1 f.). True, God has hardened the hearts of Israel, with the exception of a "remnant" (cf. 11:2–10), has given them a spirit of stupor and darkened their eyes, but not rejected them: they are still a part of his plan of salvation. They still have a part to play: the judgment of his righteousness is the judgment of his mercy. God confirms his election, though not as Israel had anticipated. "So I ask, have they stumbled so as to fall? By no means! But through their trespass salvation has come to the Gentiles, so as to make Israel jealous" (11:11) (Jerusalem Bible: in a way the Jews may now well emulate). The believing "remnant", the Jewish Christians, are the proof that God's promises have not failed. Israel's blindness is only temporary and its stumbling not final. The stumbling of the mass of Israel has served to convert the Gentiles. Certainly, superiority on the part of Judaism is unfounded, for it is not racial descent and not good works of any kind, but solely faith in Jesus Christ which decides who belongs to the people of God. But arrogance on the part of Gentile Christians would be even less well founded, for the Gentile has still fewer prerogatives than the Jew, his only claim to belong to the people of God is his faith in Jesus Christ. Gentile Christians have therefore no grounds at all for acting arrogantly, still less for acting inimically towards Israel. Self-glorification, scorn, mockery, pride, any sort of revenge against the Jews (or Jewish Christians), any kind of anti-semitism indicates a total misunderstanding of the situation. It is not up to men to judge guilt; that is for God alone. And this God will turn his judgment on Israel to mercy. The tree is not chopped down, even when branches are broken off it and only a few remaining branches represent Israel which does believe. It is not the wild branches, the Gentiles, artificially grafted on to the tree, which give strength to the root, but the other way round. The election of the Gentiles is pure mercy. "But if some of the branches were broken off, and you, a wild olive shoot, were grafted in their place to share the richness of the olive tree, do not boast over the branches. If you do boast, remember it is not you that support the root, but the root that supports you" (11:17 f.). Moreover, the Gentiles, just like the Jews, can be broken off. All are under judgment, and each belongs to the tree only through faith, trusting not in himself and his own strength, but in God and his mercy (11:19–22). And finally the most surprising sentence: "And even the others (the Jews), if they do not persist in their unbelief, will be grafted in, for God has the power to graft them in again" (11:23). Just as there is a final possibility of failure for the Gentile who today believes, so there is a final possibility of salvation for the Jew who today does not believe. Election is and remains pure grace, not a legal entitlement.

(3) The salvation of all: here the perspectives become much wider, since on the way to salvation the Jews are linked to the Gentiles as much as the Gentiles to the Jews and since Israel's vocation is no longer an unconditional privilege, but has become a promise of unlimited grace and mercy for the *whole human race,* of which Israel is a part. If Israel's "trespass" has meant such "riches for the world", if Israel's "failure" has meant such "riches for the Gentiles", what blessing their full eschatological inclusion will mean (cf. 11:12)! And if the "rejection" of Israel means "the reconciliation of the world", how much more will their "acceptance" bring "life from the dead" (11:15)! Hence the ordering of salvation has been totally reversed: Christ is the dividing line. The narrowing down and restriction of the old covenant to a remnant has given place to a more and more all-embracing inclusiveness.

This is Paul's eschatological "mystery": "all Israel will be saved" (11:26). Israel's obduracy is given time, until the full number of the Gentiles shall be saved. Israel's partial obduracy will result through God's free mercy in the saving of the "full number of the Gentiles", and from this will result, again through God's mercy, the saving of "all Israel", of Israel as a whole (11:25 f.). Paul is speaking here not of individuals as individuals, nor of a magic guarantee of salvation, but of groups within salvation history as a whole and of their merciful election.

We can therefore only speak of the Jews in dialectic terms. "Enemies" of God, who make possible the salvation of the Gentiles by their rejection of the Gospel, they remain nonetheless "beloved" for the sake of their forefathers (11:28).

For God is constant and faithful: "The gifts and the call of God are irrevocable" (11:28). Just as previously the Gentiles were disobedient, so now are the Jews. But just as God had mercy on the Gentiles, so he will also have mercy on the Jews. The Jews' lack of faith brought about the salvation of the Gentiles, and the faith of the Gentiles will bring about the salvation of the Jews. Gentiles and Jews alike are guilty before God, only God is righteous. His mercy alone can justify and save Gentiles and Jews alike. Israel exists not just for its own sake, but for the sake of the Gentile Church, and the Gentile Church similarly exists not just for its own sake, but for that of Israel too. In this way God's unchanging and consistent will for the salvation of all men will be fulfilled in his people. God's mercy and grace, which embraces the whole of mankind, will triumph over the disobedience of the whole of mankind: "For God has consigned *all* men to disobedience, that he may have mercy upon *all*" (11:32).

This all-embracing hope is also taken up by Vatican II: "As holy Scripture testifies, Jerusalem did not recognize the time of her visitation (cf. Lk. 19:44), nor did the Jews in large number accept the gospel; indeed, not a few opposed the spreading of it (cf. Rom. 11:28). Nevertheless, according to the Apostle, the Jews *still remain most dear to God* because of their fathers, for He does not repent of the gifts He makes nor of the calls He issues (cf. Rom. 11:28–29). In company with the prophets and the same Apostle, the Church awaits that day, known to God alone, on which *all peoples* will address the Lord in a single voice and 'serve him with one accord' (Zeph. 3:9; cf. Is. 66:23; Ps. 65:4; Rom. 11:11–32)" (DR 4).

The fate of Jews and Gentiles, of Israel and the Church is mysteriously interwoven. No one has any reason for pride, we all have grounds for hope. For all of us there will come at the end the common eschatological salvation, in which election and rejection, rejection and election will be balanced out. The horizon of the new as of the old people of God is bounded, in the darkness of the present, by the bright hope which is common to both: the coming of salvation for the whole of mankind. The final aim of God's plan of salvation is not the salvation of the Gentiles, nor the salvation of the Jews, but the salvation of *all men,* the salvation of the one and entire people of God composed of Gentiles and Jews. Paul can do no more than end with a song of praise which combines both Old Testament and hellenistic formulas, a song in praise of God's revealed yet still mysterious and inscrutable decree of salvation: "O the depth of the riches and wisdom and knowledge of God! How unsearchable are his judgments and how inscrutable his ways! 'For who has known the mind of the Lord, or who has been his counsellor?' 'Or who has given a gift to him that he might be repaid?' For from him and through him and to him are all things. To him be glory for ever. Amen." (Rom. 11:33–36).

We are a long way here from any hostility to the Jews, which would see them as a rejected people; for here Paul is writing in all earnestness of Israel's election, which no failure has been able to reverse. And yet we must ask whether a Jew would be able to understand the Jew Paul; and here we must have no illusions. In order to understand the Jew Paul, a Jew would have to follow Paul: without ceasing to be a Jew, without being a deserter or renegade to a "different faith", but precisely in full loyalty to the God of Abraham and Isaac and Jacob, he would have, like Paul, to become a Christian, to confirm anew his faith in the one true God, who in the Jew Jesus of Nazareth acted, decisively and eschatologically, for the salvation of Israel and of the whole world. Then he would be able to understand how the new people of God is a continuation, despite the change of direction, an eschatological fulfilment, despite the new creation, of the ancient people of God.

Even today Jews do not recognize in Jesus' message the essence of the preaching of the prophets, nor in Jesus himself, in his freedom, in his absolute power, in his self-giving, the Messiah, the Christ. But it is a consoling sign of mutual understanding that Jesus has once more become a matter of concern for leading Jewish thinkers. Two examples of this follows:

Martin Buber: "From boyhood I have thought of Jesus as an elder brother. That Christianity has regarded, and still regards him as God and Redeemer has always been a matter of the utmost importance to me, something that for his sake and for mine I must try to comprehend. . . . My own open and brotherly relationship to him has become increasingly strong and free with time, and today I can regard him more strongly and freely than ever. I am now more certain than ever that he holds a significant place in the history of the faith of Israel and that this place cannot be defined by any of the usual categories."[8]

Schalom Ben-Chorin: "Even if Jesus of Nazareth is not all that many of you hold him to be, he is nonetheless, for me too, for me as a Jew, a central figure whom I cannot exclude from my life—and in particular from my Jewish life. Martin Buber's phrase, that from boyhood he thought of Jesus as an elder brother, has become famous. I should like to adopt the phrase, for myself, but add this to it: that the further I have gone along the road of life, the nearer I have come to the figure of Jesus. At every turning of the road he has been standing, repeatedly putting the question he asked at Caesarea Philippi: 'Who am I?' And repeatedly I have had to give him an answer. And I am convinced that he will continue to go with me, as long as I go along my road, and that he will constantly come to meet me as he once came to meet Peter on the Via Appia, so legend tells us, and as he once came to meet Paul, as the Acts of the Apostles relate, on the Damascus Road. Again and again I meet him, and again and again we converse together on the basis of our common Jewish origins and of Jewish hopes for the coming kingdom. And since I left Christian Europe and went to live in Jewish Israel, he has come much closer to me; for I am now living in his land and among his people, and his sayings and parables are as close and as alive for me, as though it was all happening here and now. When at the passah meal I lift the cup and break the unleavened bread, I am doing what he did, and I know that I am much closer to him than many Christians who celebrate the Eucharist in complete separation from its Jewish origins."[9]

A new era in relations between Israel and the Church has begun. From all that has been said above, two things are clear. (1) The Church, being the new people of God, cannot possibly speak or act in any way against the ancient people of God. It is a sure sign that we are opposed to the one true God, if we are opposed to the Jews. Israel remains a living witness of the reality of the living God. The Father of Christ and of the Church remains the God of Israel. (2) The Church, being the new people of God, must seek in

---

[8] M. Buber, *Two Types of Faith*, London 1951–New York 1961.
[9] Schalom Ben-Chorin, "Judische Fragen um Jesus Christus", in *Juden–Christen–Deutsche*, 147 f.

every way to enter into sympathetic dialogue with the ancient people of God. Even from Paul's viewpoint this dialogue was not concluded, but remained open, and we today do not need to rest content simply with Paul's viewpoint. The common basis of Israel and the Church is evident: it is one and the same God who leads them both. Their origins are one, their ways are one, their goals are one. Like Israel and following Israel the Church sees itself as the journeying people of God, constantly being delivered from bondage, constantly wandering through the wilderness of this age, constantly maintaining the tension between thankful commemoration and hopeful expectation and preparing itself for its entry into the promised land, the messianic kingdom, the goal that always lies in the future.

Only one course of action is permitted to the Church on this common journey—not "tolerating", not "missionizing", not "converting", but only "making Israel jealous" (cf. Rom. 11:11, 14, παραζηλουν). The Church can make Israel jealous of the "salvation" it has received (Rom. 11:11), in order to spur Israel to emulate it. But how? The Church, in its whole existence, must be a token of the salvation it has received. In its whole existence it must bear witness to the messianic fulfilment. In its whole existence it must vie with Israel in addressing itself to a world which has turned its back on God, and in demonstrating to it, with authority and love, the word that has been fulfilled, the righteousness that has been revealed, the mercy that has been accepted, the reign of God which has already begun. Its whole life, lived in a convincing way, would be a call to all men to believe the good news, to experience a change of heart and to unite themselves with its Messiah.

This is how Israel and the Church must confront one another—not in theoretical debate, but in existential dialogue; not in an uncommitted battle of words, but in committed competition. By its whole life the Church must witness to the reality of redemption. Is this the case? Is this the witness of the Church? The Jews do not think so. For them the claims made by the Church are unconvincing. The reality of redemption asserted by the New Testament seems to them, particularly in the light of the Old Testament, to have been an illusion.

"We must then question, in the light of the Bible, whether the message of the Old Testament which the New Testament claims has been fulfilled, has in fact been fulfilled in history, in the history lived and suffered by us and our ancestors. And here, my dear Christian readers, we give a negative reply. We can see no kingdom and no peace and no redemption. The dawning of the kingdom of God, the 'malchuth schaddaj', still lies hidden in the future, whether near or far, at a time which both Jews and Christians believe can be determined by no man."[10]

The unredeemed state of the world and of the Church is the reason why the Jews deny Jesus as the redeemer who has already come. The Church of Christ is also convinced that the final and revealed redemption of the world, that is, the kingdom of God, has not yet come. The Church too, like Israel, insists on a "not yet", and prays with Israel for the future and long-awaited coming of the kingdom. But this "not yet", as far as the Church is concerned, presupposed a crucial "but already". The Church believes that in Jesus the Christ the world has already been redeemed, though this redemption is still hidden; and this redemption is also, indeed first of all, for Israel, even though it does not share the Church's belief. And because of this belief the Church looks forward in hope with Israel and ultimately for Israel to the revealed and final redemption of the world.

But is the Church not deluded if it believes in a redemption which has already occurred? This is the continuing question which Israel puts to the Church, a question which carries us further into the Church's essential nature, into its basic structure.

[10] Schalom Ben-Chorin, *op. cit.*, 142.

II. THE CHURCH AS THE CREATION OF THE SPIRIT

1. THE NEW FREEDOM

Are Christians redeemed and free people? Do they show it? "They would have to sing better songs to make me believe in their Redeemer: his disciples would have to look more redeemed! . . . Truly, their Redeemers themselves did not come from freedom and the seventh heaven of freedom!"[11]

In the early Church the message of Christ was preached, received and experienced as redemption, as a setting free. So Paul says: "For freedom Christ has set us free" (Gal. 5:1), and John promises: "So if the Son makes you free, you will be free indeed" (Jn. 8:36).

This freedom is not an illusion for the believer, but a reality. And it is not only an empty formal freedom *from* something, but also a rich and definite freedom *for* something. We must examine what this means in the light of Paul's teaching.[12]

(a) Who is free? This is a question men have always asked. Is a man free if he is independent of any kind of tyranny and thinks and acts accordingly? This was the view of the classical Greeks, who measured freedom above all by the standards of the Greek *polis*. Or is a man not rather free if as a thinking man—quite apart from whether he is free politically and socially or not—he can liberate himself from the tyranny of passions and emotions? Such was the view of the Stoics, when the political freedom of the Greek State no longer existed. Or is a man not rather free if he is inde-

[11] F. Nietzsche, *Thus spake Zarathustra*, London 1961, II, 4, p. 116.
[12] Cf. the exegetical and theological dictionaries on the keywords: freedom, sin, law, death. Basic details are given by H. Schlier in the article ἐλεύθερος in ThW II, 484–500 (bibl.); on the perfect law of freedom: *Die Zeit der Kirche*, Freiburg 1955, 193–206; and R. Bultmann, *Theology of the New Testament*, London 1952–New York 1951, 227–259, 330–345 (see biblio.).

pendent of the evil world and the demonic powers which control man's fate? So thought the hellenistic gnostics, who hoped to find salvation in mystery religions, either through ascetic abstinence from the good things of this world, or through an intemperate indulgence in its life.

Who, then, is truly free? It should be clear enough that man is far from being free simply because he has thrown off threats and pressures outside himself. The real threat to his freedom, as the Stoics rightly observed, comes from within, from himself. It is in his own soul that a man must fight for and win his freedom. But is this freedom something a man can win? Is man in reality the ideal, purely rational being the Stoics saw him as, someone who can really follow the dictates of reason? Is man in reality the superior and free being he so often likes to pretend to be? If man faces up to himself as he really is, he surely looks very different—not at all independent, superior and sovereign, but constantly trapped and enslaved, enslaved to the things and the pleasures, the possessions and powers of this world. Above all he seems to be chained to himself, to what he has so far made of himself. "I can will what is right, but I cannot do it. For I do not do the good I want, but the evil I do not want is what I do. . . . So I find it to be a law that when I want to do right, evil lies close at hand. . . . Wretched man that I am! Who will deliver me from this body of death?" (Rom. 7:18–24).

Man constantly fails to do the good which he ought to do and is constantly drawn to the evil which he ought not to do. Instead of living "in the flesh" but "according to the spirit", he lives "according to the flesh": his heart is fixed on transient, futile, earthly, purely human things. He falls a prey to the world, its goods and its pleasures, and to himself. He lives in conflict with himself. He seeks the source of life in places where he can never find it: in the created world, in its goods, in himself. He becomes a slave of the created world, which cannot give him the strength to live or the norms to live by. In this way he refuses his service to God, to whom he and the world owe their life. By turning in on himself and the world he is overlooking the fact that he and the world are creatures and denying God as the creator. Instead of depending on God, he tries to depend on himself, either by ignoring or disobeying God's commandments in pleasure-seeking amorality, as heathens tend to do, or by attempting to fulfil God's commandments on his own through incessant moral activity and trust in worldly achievements. In either case man fails to find life and falls away from God. This turning away from God to the created world, to the powers of this world and to human strength, and the disobedience towards God's will and enmity towards God himself which follows (Rom. 8:6–8), is what we mean by sin.

Who, then, is free? The man who is free from *sin* (cf. Rom. 6:18–23; Jn. 8:31–36), the man who lives, not by himself and through himself and for himself, but the man who lives in God and so for his fellow man. But can man possibly pull himself out of the mire of unfreedom by his own bootstraps? How can he shake off his own enslaved and sinful self by his own efforts, and win a new and free self? "Wretched man that I am! Who will deliver me from this body of death?" (Rom. 7:24). This is the reply of faith: "Thanks be to God through Jesus Christ our Lord!" (Rom. 7:25).

God himself must free the man who is unfree and incapable of winning his own freedom, must free him for freedom. He can turn "slaves of sin" into "slaves of God", who have been "set free from sin" (Rom. 6:20, 22). God does this for the man who believes, whether Jew or Gentile, through his eschatological act of salvation in Jesus Christ. In Christ, the new free man, God promised and revealed and created the way to a new and true freedom. Sinful man thinks he can find freedom by self-confidently controlling himself and his own life. But he is warned that he can only win freedom by abdicating this control to another—not to men, who would reduce him to the rank of a slave, but to God, who will accept him as his child. To be able to do what one wants is only the appearance of freedom; true freedom is to will what God does. Freedom from the power of sin does not of course imply an automatic state of sinlessness nor exclude serious temptations to sin. Man may sin as before, but he does not have to. Sin has no more power over him. Over against all compulsion to sin he now has the possibility of acting according to God's merciful commands. This possibility is no mere abstract theory or empty illusion. The freedom for which

Christ has set us free can be experienced and lived. How different is the life of a self-reliant slave of the world, and that of a free child of God in the world!

The enslaved man is "anxious": "he is anxious about worldly affairs" (I Cor. 7:33). But can he make his life and his future by his anxiousness? The free man is not anxious about worldly things, but about "the affairs of the Lord" (I Cor. 7:32), and so has no anxiety "about anything" (Phil. 4:6). The enslaved man on the other hand "desires evil" (I Cor. 10:16). But can he find peace and contentment from his desires in the "works of the flesh" (Gal. 5:19)? The free man does not desire the works of the flesh, but "to be with Christ" (Phil. 4:6 f.). The enslaved man "boasts": he "boasts" of his own strength, his own achievements and works (I Cor. 4:7). But with all his boasting can he claim that his achievements are his own? The free man does not boast of his own achievements, but "of the Lord" (II Cor. 10:17), and hence of the "things that show his weakness" (II Cor. 11:30). The enslaved man "puts his trust in the flesh": he "relies on himself" (II Cor. 1:9). But for all his self-reliance can he ultimately depend upon himself alone? The free man does not rely on himself, but "on God who raises the dead" (II Cor. 1:9).

The man freed in Christ knows that "he is not his own" (I Cor. 6:19). He lives "not according to the flesh, but according to the spirit" (Rom. 8:4), trusting not in visible and transient things but in invisible and permanent things: he lives for God. At the same time it is clear that the new freedom is in no sense the same as unrestrained and unlimited self-indulgence: "For you were called to freedom, brethren; only do not use your freedom as an opportunity for the flesh" (Gal. 5:13). Freedom means the obligation of living not according to this world but according to the will of God (cf. Rom. 12:2). The new freedom means a new "service" (Rom. 7:6), the service of a "living and true God" (I Thess. 1:9) and of "Christ" (Rom. 14:18; 16:18), and hence of "one another" (Gal. 5:13; cf. I Cor. 9:19). For the Christian freedom means an attitude of openness and service towards God and our neighbours. The man who is no longer anxious about himself loses his "fear" (Rom. 8:15) and is granted "peace and joy" (Rom. 14:17; 15:13; Gal. 5:22).

(*b*) But can the *law* not prevent evil? If God's law is kept, does it not become a way to salvation? Paul admits to his fellow Jews: "The law is holy, and the commandment is holy and just and good" (Rom. 7:12).

The law is intended to lead man to "life" (Rom. 7:10; cf. 10:5; Gal. 3:12); it is "the embodiment of knowledge and truth" (Rom. 2:20), it is "spiritual" (Rom. 7:14). The "giving of the law" is one of Israel's marks of excellence (9:4). Paul includes in the "law" the moral commandments as well as the cultic and ritual commandments of the Old Testament. Indeed he refers to the whole of the Old Testament as "law", since he sees it as God's command, to which man must respond in obedience. The Gentiles too are under God's command, although they have no written law; the most important part of the law, its moral requirements, in particular the decalogue (cf. Rom. 2:1–3, 20; 13:8–10; Gal. 5:14), can also be accepted by them. The works required by the law are written in their hearts and their conscience bears witness to them (Rom. 2:14 f.). So Jews and Gentiles alike are judged according to their works (Rom. 1:18–3:20; I Cor. 3:12–15). "It is not the hearers of the law who are righteous before God, but the doers of the law who will be justified" (Rom. 2:13). The Christian must therefore reflect that "we must all appear before the judgment seat of Christ, so that each one may receive good or evil, according to what he has done in the body" (II Cor. 5:10).

Can the law therefore be equated with slavery? Is the law not the way to freedom, to redemption? This would seem to explain the rabbinical view that a single day of perfect fulfilment of the law on the part of the entire people would bring the day of Yahweh, would bring redemption.

Paul with the greatest emphasis constantly rejects this idea, that the law can be the way to salvation, to justification, to God. After his long discussion of the ways to salvation of the Gentiles and the Jews (Rom. 1:18–3:20), Paul sums this up in the brief conclusion: "No human being will be justified in God's sight by works of the law" (Rom. 3:20; cf. Gal. 3:10). On the contrary, the beneficial law of God is shown in practice to be a "law of sin and death" (Rom. 8:2), a "dispensation of death", a "dispensation of condemnation" (II Cor. 3:7, 9); "the written code kills" (3:6).

Can no one, may no one attain salvation through works of

the law? No; for "if it is by grace, it is no longer on the basis of works; otherwise grace would no longer be grace" (Rom. 11:6). God's grace has been revealed in Jesus Christ, in his cross and resurrection, and has become effective for everyone who puts his trust, not in himself, the law and his works, but in God and his grace, for everyone who believes, whether he is subject to the written code of the law or not, whether he be Jew or Gentile. Therefore "Christ is the end of the law, that everyone who has faith may be justified" (Rom. 10:4). And conversely: "You are severed from Christ, you who would be justified by the law; you have fallen away from grace" (Gal. 5:4).

If Paul's attitude seems unnecessarily severe here, we must remember that his attitude to the law is a direct consequence of his attitude to sin. Sin and law are interdependent. The law leads to sin, by stimulating man's desire to break the law; "if it had not been for the law, I should not have known sin" (Rom. 7:7; cf. 7:8–13; 3:20). Moreover, the law seems to offer man the possibility of misdirected zeal in fulfilling the law with his own strength, and to lead to the arrogance of self-justification. "If a law had been given which could make alive, then righteousness would indeed be by the law" (Gal. 3:21; cf. 3:22–25). Both those errors spring from self-reliance and selfishness and a consequent denial of God: the anarchy of disobeying the law and the self-pride in doing works according to the law.

Thus sin is increased by the law (Rom. 5:20), precisely so that man might be confronted by God's grace, which is not to be attained through works, but only through faith: "Where sin increased, grace abounded all the more" (5:20). Thus it is precisely the *negative function* of the beneficial law and the beneficial activity of God which contains its *positive finality:* "So that the law was our custodian until Christ came, that we might be justified by faith. But now that faith has come, we are no longer under a custodian" (Gal. 3:24 f.).

Who then is free? The man who is *free from the law*. In being free from sin, we are also free from the law. This above all is the meaning of the words: "For freedom Christ has set us free" (Gal. 5:1). That is the freedom to which "you are called" (5:13), which we "have in Christ Jesus" (2:4). The law, like sin and the flesh, has lost its power over the man who believes in God's merciful saving act in Christ: "Sin will have no dominion over you, since you are not under the law but under grace" (Rom. 6:14; cf. 7:5 f.). Any attempts to turn the law once again into the way of salvation for the man who believes in Christ must be energetically resisted: "Stand fast, therefore, and do not submit again to a yoke of slavery" (Gal. 5:1). Christ is now the way of salvation.

The Christian has to fulfil the will of God in the secular world. He does not need to renounce the good things of the world; but he must never give himself into their power. The Christian can only give himself to God. He must remain in the world without falling a prey to it, setting not an external spatial distance between himself and the things of this world, but an inner personal distance. If the man freed from the law can say of himself: "All things are lawful for me" (I Cor. 6:12) he must also say "I will not be enslaved by anything" (*ibid.*). In the world "nothing is unclean in itself" (Rom. 14:14; cf. Tit. 1:15: "To the pure all things are pure"). But I can lose my freedom to anything in the world and allow myself to be ruled by it, as by an idol. For while "all things are lawful for me", it remains true that "not all things are helpful" (I Cor. 6:12). A second point is important here: even things that are lawful *and* helpful can be harmful to a man. For while "all things are lawful" it remains true that "not all things build up. Let no one seek his own good, but the good of his neighbour" (I Cor. 10:23 f.). Freedom for the Christian who follows Christ can be the freedom to renounce: "For though I am free from all men, I have made myself a slave to all" (I Cor. 9:19). This is not the denial, but the ultimate affirmation of Christian freedom.

True freedom is never unthinking: "Take care lest this liberty of yours somehow become a stumbling-block to the weak" (I Cor. 8:9). The Christian is a servant of all (I Cor. 9:19; Gal. 5:13), but not in a way that denies his freedom: "do not become slaves of men" (I Cor. 7:23). In the last analysis the Christian is not limited by the opinions and judgments, the traditions and values of others: "For why should my liberty be determined by another man's scruples?"

(I Cor. 10:29). "My own conscience, as arbiter of good and evil, is what binds me" (I Cor. 8:7–12; 10:25–30).

The Christian's freedom, with its paradoxical harmonization of independence and duties, power and renunciation, autonomy and service, dominion and slavery, is a mystery to the world. The solution to this mystery, for the Christian, is the core of his freedom: love. Love, in which faith becomes effective (Gal. 5:6), in which the differences between circumcision and uncircumcision are removed, in which the master becomes a slave and the slave a master, independence becomes obligation and obligation independence. To be available for others, to exist for others, to live in selfless love is the only way to realize freedom: "For you were called to freedom, brethren; only do not use your freedom as an opportunity for the flesh, but through love be servants of one another. For the whole law is fulfilled in one word: 'You shall love your neighbour as yourself'" (Gal. 5:13 f.). Whatever God demands through the law is a demand for love. Love is the fulfilment of the law: "Owe no one anything, except to love one another, for he who loves his neighbour has fulfilled the law. The commandments, 'You shall not commit adultery, You shall not kill, You shall not steal, You shall not covet', and any other commandment, are summed up in this sentence: 'You shall love your neighbour as yourself'. Love does no wrong to a neighbour; therefore love is the fulfilling of the law" (Rom. 13:8–10). The "law of Christ" is nothing but the freedom of love; "Bear one another's burdens, and so fulfil the law of Christ" (Gal. 6:2). The man who is bound to God and hence to his neighbour is set free for real freedom.

(c) In all his sinful anxiety, desires, boasting and self-reliance man is seeking for life, but he seeks it in the world and in himself, blindly trusting his own efforts. This apparent life is deceptive, for beneath its surface lurks the emptiness of death. By stubbornly looking for the source of life where it is not to be found, rather than looking for it where it really is, man misses life and runs headlong into death. God is life and he alone gives life. By not aiming at God, but dallying instead with the things of life and with himself, man loses God, the source of life, and his own life too. His existence disintegrates, because he has fallen a prey to the world and to himself and hence to death.

In the Old Testament we find death as a *punishment* for man's sins. Sinners "deserve to die" (Rom. 1:32). In Paul's view sin comes from the law, and death from sin: "The sting of death is sin, and the power of sin is the law" (I Cor. 15:56); "the written code kills" (II Cor. 3:6; cf. 3:7). Death is the "wages" with which sin pays its servant, man (Rom. 6:23). Or conversely: sinful man pays for his guilt with death (6:7). And this death is not merely temporal death (cf. 5:12–21), but at the same time God's final condemnation of man to perdition (2:6–11).

Desire, aroused by the law, leads man through the law to his death; sin deceives man into thinking he can win life through his desires, instead of which, without knowing what he is doing, man wins death, which is present for man in sin (7:7–25). Thus we see that death is not only the external punishment of sin but its *inward consequence*. "He who sows to his own flesh will from the flesh reap corruption" (Gal. 6:8). By clinging to transient, futile, mortal and valueless things, man will pass away together with them: "for if you live according to the flesh you will die" (Rom. 8:13). Man's sin even affects nature, which draws its meaning from man; God's absence from the life of man is revealed in the groaning and travail of the whole creation in its creaturely corruptibility (Rom. 8:19–23). Sin bears death within itself. Fleshly, sinful life brings death as its fruit: "While we were living in the flesh, our sinful passions, aroused by the law, were at work in our members to bear fruit for death" (7:5). The end of the life of sin is death (6:21).

Who is ultimately free? The man who is *free from death*. The man of faith, who in faith accepts the message of Christ's death and resurrection, who acknowledges the crucified Christ as his Lord and submits himself to his glory, the man who follows his Lord, takes up the cross and allows it to become the determining power of his existence, he is the man who shares in Christ's new life. The freedom from sin and law given to man in Christ is also freedom from death, which is the wages and fruit of sin. Being freed from sin, the believer is freed from the decay which threatened his existence. Being forgiven, he has also been given life, a new life for God which has put death behind it: "For if we have been united in him with a death like his, we shall certainly be united with him in a resurrection like his. We know that our old self was crucified with him so that the sinful body might be destroyed, and we might no longer be enslaved to sin. For he who has died is freed from sin. But if we have died with Christ, we believe that we shall also live with him. For we know that Christ being raised from the dead will never die again" (Rom. 6:5–9; cf. I Cor. 15:20–22).

Freedom from death will only be revealed in the *future*. Not until the "day of our Lord Jesus Christ" (I Cor. 1:8, etc.) will ultimate redemption be manifest in the resurrection of the dead: the beginning of the glory of God in which death will be overcome and God will be everything to everyone (I Cor. 15:20–27). This future condition is described in detail by the Jewish apocalyptics and in gnostic mythology, but not by Paul. He describes it in general terms as a "being with Christ" (I Thess. 4:17, etc.), as walking by sight as opposed to faith (II Cor. 5:7), as looking not into a mirror dimly but face to face, not knowing in part, but understanding fully (I Cor. 13:12), as a revelation of glory (II Cor. 4:17; Rom. 8:18). Only then will the "glorious liberty of the children of God" be revealed (Rom. 8:21), only in the future will full redemption come (Rom. 8:23)—after a time of faith, of sufferings and sorrow. "In this hope we were saved" (Rom. 8:24). Only at the end of this last time will death, the last enemy, be destroyed (I Cor. 15:26).

And yet this last time has already begun in the *present* as a time of resurrection and new life—with the resurrected and newly living Christ, who is not only the beginning but the origin of resurrection and life (I Cor. 15:21 f.). The believer can already utter the paradoxical words: "It is no longer I who live, but Christ who lives in me" (Gal. 2:20). The old man with his passions and desires *has* been crucified already (Rom. 6:6; Gal. 5:24; 6:14). The new man *is* reality already: "Therefore, if anyone is in Christ, he is a new creation; the old has passed away, behold, the new has come" (II Cor. 5:17). Hence we are admonished: "So you also must consider yourselves dead to sin and alive to God in Christ Jesus" (Rom. 6:11).

Suffering too is fundamentally overcome along with death. Suffering reminds the believer of the rule of death and the transience of all earthly things; it calls upon him to rely on God and not on himself, to let God's grace be sufficient and not to exalt himself, to boast of his weakness, in which God's power may be made perfect (II Cor. 12:7–9): "For when I am weak, then I am strong" (II Cor. 12:10). By sharing in the sufferings of Christ, the Christian becomes like Christ in his death (Phil. 3:10; Gal. 6:17). Weak in Christ, the Christian will live with him by the power of God, in communion with other sufferers, so that no one is alone in his sufferings any more (II Cor. 13:4). Thus the believer welcomes the resurrection in and through his sufferings. The Christian's freedom culminates in his freedom from suffering, which is turned into grace, and his freedom from death, which has lost its sting and its victory: "If God is for us, who is against us? . . . Who shall separate us from the love of Christ? Shall tribulation, or distress, or persecution, or famine, or nakedness, or peril, or sword? . . . No, in all these things we are more than conquerors through him who loved us. For I am sure that neither death, nor life, nor angels, nor principalities, nor things present, nor things to come, nor powers, nor height, nor depth, nor anything else in all creation, will be able to separate us from the love of God in Christ Jesus our Lord" (Rom. 8:31–39).

(*d*) Is the Christian truly redeemed and freed? Despite the fact that the revelation and perfection of his redemption is still in the future, for which he, like the Jew, is still justified in hoping, the believing Christian can already be a redeemed person, freed from sin, law and death. This can of course only be understood in the context of faith, and certainly only lived in the context of faith. But *if* a man has accepted in faith the message of freedom in Christ, and *if* he strives to live in that faith, then he truly experiences freedom, he is a free man in the way that a Jew waiting for his salvation under the law cannot be. A Jew might have many objections to raise to Paul's arguments, but surely he would find it hard to refuse his respect, perhaps even agreement and faith, to a testimony of faith which is backed up not by mere words, but by a life, by sufferings and death.

Paul is speaking of a superior *freedom in living,* a wholly committed freedom, which rejoices with those who rejoice, weeps with those who weep (Rom. 12:15), which is familiar with all things in this life, and knows how to live in abundance as in want (Phil. 4:11–13), and which through its commitment to God maintains an ultimate independence in the world.

". . . Let those who have wives life as though they had none, and those who mourn as though they were not mourning, and those who rejoice as though they were not rejoicing, and those who buy as though they had no goods, and those who deal with the world as though they had no dealings with it" (I Cor. 7:29–31).

Paul is speaking of a consoling *freedom in suffering,* which by no means tries to pretend that suffering is not there, but which patiently affirms it and thus reveals its true freedom in weakness.

"When reviled, we bless;
when persecuted, we endure;
when slandered, we try to conciliate" (I Cor. 4:12 f.).
"We are treated as imposters, and yet are true;
as unknown, and yet well known;
as dying, and behold we live;
as punished, and yet not killed;
as sorrowful, yet always rejoicing;
as poor, yet making many riches;
as having nothing, and yet possessing everything" (II Cor. 6:8–10).

Paul is speaking of a victorious *freedom in dying,* for which Christ's living and dying is gain (Phil. 1:21), which does not live for itself nor die for itself (Rom. 14:7–9), which can be separated neither by life nor death from the love of God which is in Christ (Rom. 8:38).

"For all things are yours . . .
whether the world or life or death
or the present or the future,

all are yours;
and you are Christ's;
and Christ is God's" (I Cor. 3:21–23).

Such is the daring testimony of Paul, who in phrases of breathtaking dialectic gives us a picture of freedom, drawing on the best of the Old Testament—unconditional trust in God —and yet bursting open all the limitations of Judaism; it is the Jew Paul who in the early Church is *the* witness to the freedom for which Christ made us free. What then—a question asked by Christians as well as Jews—of the *Church itself?* Is Paul not an idealistic, enthusiastic but solitary voice, which has been taken up by all too few? Is the Church really a fellowship of free men, of men truly freed from sin, law and death? Was the Church then, and is it today, really like that?[13]

The question needs to be taken seriously. Freedom in the Church was already seriously threatened in Paul's time, not so much from outside as from within (cf. Galatians, Rom. 14, I Cor. 8:10), and it has remained threatened. There are few reproaches which have so frequently and so passionately been levelled at the Church than this, that the Church is a place of unfreedom. What about freedom from sin? We see profound sinfulness in the Church, all human vices *and* the abuse of what is most sacred; not only offences against moral standards, but a falling away from the Gospel on which the Church is based. What about freedom from the law? We see a new spirit of legalism in the Church: a legalism flying Christian colours, authoritarianism, absolutism, even totalitarianism; personality cults, blind obedience, servility. What about freedom from death? We see in the Church a profound and deceitful confidence in life, an ecclesiastical triumphalism all too little concerned about the transience and decay of all earthly things, and an all too solidly established and secularized institutionalism.

It is not enough to protest against the one-sidedness and injustice of such charges. They may often be one-sided and unfair—often, but unfortunately by no means always. It is not

[13] Cf. H. Küng, *The Church and Freedom,* London 1965; in *Freedom Today,* New York 1966.

enough to say, in defence against these very real charges, that the Church is a reality of faith. True, the Church is a reality of faith, and freedom from sin, law and death is only convincing for the believer. But this freedom must be apparent and must be radiated, and at least must be a challenge and an invitation to faith. It is not enough to appeal, as a defence against the irrefutable proofs of lack of freedom in the Church, to the human make-up of the Church. An honest and unvarnished admission of guilt for its sins against the freedom of the children of God is something that the Church will constantly have to make, and it would have been better had it done so more often in the past. But even an admission of guilt is not enough, if it is not backed up by action.

The Church can only be credible as the place and home of the new freedom if it constantly shows to men of good will and men of good faith its light and freedom rather than its darkness and unfreedom. It is true that the Church, composed as it is of sinful men, is never simply at a distance from the freedom of the world. The dividing line between freedom and unfreedom does not run between the Church and the world, but through the heart of each individual. And yet, for this very reason, the Church must continually demonstrate that it is what it claims to be: the fellowship of free men, a Church of freedom, a Church not in the image of Hagar, the slave, bearing children for slavery, but in the image of Sarah, the free woman, and of the free Jerusalem above, bringing forth children of the promise (Gal. 4:21–30). "We are not children of the slave but of the free woman" (Gal. 4:31). It is up to the Church to witness in its entire existence to the freedom of the saving grace of God, rather than to the slavery of sin; to witness to the freedom of the reign of God and the service of man, rather than to the compulsion of the law; to witness not to the power of death but to eternal life in the reign of God.

We can see with gratitude that the splendid freedom of the children of God has constantly been testified to and experienced and lived in the Church—generally in inconspicuous ways that have not directly affected world history, and by small people rather than by the great. Despite all shortcomings, countless believers from apostolic times down to the present day have accepted this freedom in faith and obedience, lived it in love and joy, suffered and struggled and waited for it in hope and patience. In great and small decisions of life, in tribulation, distress and persecution, in hunger and nakedness, peril and death, countless unknown people have found in this freedom their stay and consolation, strength and hope, joy and peace. A remarkable freedom, which poses the question again and again: where did this strength, this superhuman strength, as it often seems, have its origin?

2. THE CHURCH OF THE SPIRIT

Freedom is demanded of the Church precisely because freedom has been given to the Church. The indicative precedes and makes possible the imperative: ultimately it is not because freedom has to be struggled for and won that it is granted, but it is because it has been granted that it can and must be lived. True freedom is not rooted in man's existence, but comes to him from outside.

Freedom is a gift, a gift of God. The basis and origin of man's freedom lie not in man himself but in the freedom of God, in the freedom of his grace which freed us in Christ. "For freedom Christ has set us free" (Gal. 5:1)—Christ lived a life of service to others and of obedience to God's will which included his death, and he was then freed and glorified by God. How does this freedom come to men? Through the call of the Gospel: "For you were called to freedom" (Gal. 5:13). It is also the work of the *Spirit,* who takes possession of us in word and sacrament and awakens his freedom in us: "where the Spirit of the Lord is, there is freedom" (II Cor. 3:17). The *Spirit* gives the believer this threefold freedom from sin, law and death: "For the law of the Spirit of life in Christ Jesus has set me free from the law of sin and death. . . . To set the mind on the flesh is death, but to set the mind on the Spirit is life and peace. . . . But you are not in the flesh, you are in the Spirit, if the Spirit of God really dwells in you. Anyone who does not have the Spirit of Christ does not belong to him. But if Christ is in you, although your bodies are dead because of sin, your spirits are alive because of righteousness. If the Spirit of him who raised Jesus from the dead dwells in you, he who raised Christ Jesus from the dead will give life to your mortal bodies also through his Spirit which dwells in you" (Rom. 8:2–11). Freedom is given to us when we accept the spirit which supports us, the Spirit of God, the Spirit of Christ. Man is flesh in his state of slavery to the world, but "we have received not the spirit of the world, but the Spirit which is from God, that we might understand the gifts bestowed on us by God" (I Cor. 2:12). The Spirit of God turns man away from the world and from himself and places him under God's grace. The reign of the world is finished, the true reign of Christ begins. The Spirit of the Lord takes possession of us, and opens to us intransient things, life and the future. He gives us a recreated childhood: a new freedom from sin, law and death in peace, joy and life. But the Spirit is only given to the individual through being given to the community, the Church. What significance does this have for the Church? What is the significance of this Spirit which has been given to it?[14]

(a) *The Spirit as an eschatological gift.* In the messianic time of salvation, according to the prophetic expectation of

[14] For the biblical idea of the Holy Spirit, see the dictionary articles by H. Kleinknecht, F. Baumgarten, W. Bieder, E. Sjoberg and especially E. Schweizer in ThW VI, 330–453 (Lit.); E. Käsemann in RGG II, 1272–1279; F. Mussner in LThK VIII, 572–576; among the theologies of the New Testament see in particular R. Bultmann; as well as the older works by H. Bertrams, F. Buchsel, E. Fuchs, H. Gunkel, H. Leisegang, W. Reinhard, P. Volz, N. A. Waanink. The following more recent monographs are important: C. K. Barrett, *The Holy Spirit and the Gospel Tradition,* London–New York 1947; E. Schweizer, *Geist und Gemeinde im NT,* Munich 1952; S. Zedda, *L'adozione a figli di Dio e lo Spirito Santo,* Rome 1952; H. von Campenhausen, *Kirchliches Amt und geistliche Vollmacht in den ersten drei Jahrhunderten,* Tübingen 1953; N. Q. Hamilton, *The Holy Spirit and Eschatology in Paul,* London 1957; R. Schnackenburg, *The Church in the NT,* London–New York–Freiburg 1965; I. Hermann, *Kyrios und Pneuma. Studien zur Christologie der paulinischen Hauptbriefe,* Munich 1961; K. Stalder, *Das Werk des Geistes in der Heiligung bei Paulus,* Zurich 1961. L. Cerfaux, *The Church in the Theology of St Paul,* London–New York–Freiburg 1959; also cf. the commentaries on Acts and the Pauline letters. For the literature on charisms see C II, 3.

salvation, not only individual prophets and wise men, warriors, singers and kings, were to be fulfilled by the spirit of God, by God's creating power and strength of life; it was to be given to the whole people.

"For I will pour water on thirsty land, and streams on the dry ground; I will pour my Spirit upon your descendants and my blessing on your offspring" (Is. 44:3; cf. 63:14). "And I will put my spirit within you, and cause you to walk in my statutes and be careful to observe my ordinances" (Ez. 36:27; cf. Zech. 4:6).

The early Christian communities, the Pauline communities as well as that in Jerusalem, saw the expectation of the prophets as having been fulfilled in reality. The pouring out of the Spirit is the signal for the beginning of the eschatological event—the pouring out of the Spirit upon *all* mankind: on sons and on daughters, on old men and young men, on menservants and maidservants, as well as on their masters (Joel 2:28 f.). Spirit in this context, in the Old and New Testament alike, is not used, as the word often was, in the sense of breath, or angel or demon (or ghost or spirit of the departed), nor in the sense of soul or source of life, nor in the sense of the seat of knowledge and volition, the living ego of a man. No, in this context the Spirit of *God* is referred to, the *Holy* Spirit; its holiness separates it distinctly from the spirit of man and of the world. This Spirit is not some magical, mysteriously supernatural aura of a dynamistic kind, nor a magical being of an animistic kind, but God himself in his especially personal and self-giving aspect: as a power which gives itself to man, but cannot be controlled by man, as a power which creates life. The Spirit is God himself, a merciful power establishing his reign over man's heart, over the whole of man, inwardly present to man and apparent in his workings to man's human spirit.

It is not the place here to go into the discrepancies in the interpretation of the idea of the Spirit which are apparent in the New Testament. We can sum them up briefly as follows: the *Judaic Old Testament* tradition starts more from "animistic" conceptions: spirit is imagined as a self-contained person-like subject, which can take possession of a man and enable him to carry out particular feats of strength; the workings of the Spirit are here rather thought of in terms of particular situations and actions rather than in terms of a permanent situation. The *hellenistic* conception, on the other hand, starts from a more "dynamistic" viewpoint: spirit is imagined as an impersonal power or divine substance, which fills men with a kind of aura, not temporally but permanently.

But these differences are not crucial, for: (1) the two conceptions are not mutually exclusive, but complementary; there are traces at least of animistic conceptions in the hellenistic tradition, and dynamistic conceptions in the Old Testament; (2) in the New Testament a clear distinction between the two traditions is impossible, for they are never contrasted; on the contrary, we very often find them used by one and the same writer; (3) in the New Testament any kind of magic naturalism is generally avoided, and where it seems to be invoked, it is always with a view to expressing the power and effect of the spirit in man in his totality; (4) in the New Testament, despite the difference between the origins of the two traditions, there is a significant uniformity in basic conceptions: (a) Pneuma in the New Testament is not opposed in a platonic or idealistic way to the body or to nature, but is the miraculous divine power as opposed to all things human; (b) Pneuma in the whole of the New Testament is seen as an eschatological gift, albeit in different ways.

The Spirit is God's eschatological gift with which the community, and the individual who is incorporated into the community through baptism, is blessed in the last days. In Mark and Matthew we find relatively few sayings about the Spirit, mostly christological ones; they are concerned not to present Jesus as the first pneumatic of the community, which they might well have done, but rather to express Jesus' unique eschatological position, namely that God himself is uniquely present in Jesus. Only John the Baptist speaks of a more general eschatological outpouring of the Spirit: "I have baptized you with water; but he will baptize you with the Holy Spirit" (Mk. 1:8). Not until after Jesus' resurrection did the community experience the sending of the Spirit, God's sign which sealed them as the eschatological community.

Whereas in Mark and Matthew the coming of the Spirit is generally regarded, as in the Old Testament, as something exceptional, the hellenistic Luke, who is concerned less with the parousia of Christ than with the missionary history of the

Church, sees the Spirit as given permanently to all members of the community. The gift of the Spirit is often seen as a natural consequence of believing, or of baptism (Acts 2:38 f.; 9:17; 10:44; 19:6). The basis for Luke's widely ranging narrative of Pentecost, to which several historical objections have been raised, is a decisive experience of the sending of the Spirit in the early Church, evidently connected with the ecstatic speeches of the disciples: "they were all filled with the Holy Spirit" in order to "tell of the mighty works of God" (Acts 2:4, 11). According to rabbinic teaching the Spirit had disappeared with the last Old Testament prophets; the apocalyptics concealed their pneumatic gifts under pseudonyms, and there were only a few isolated prophets among the Zealots. But the Acts of the Apostles proclaims the outpouring of the Spirit on the whole community. The ecstatic praises of God in which the eschatological Spirit finds utterance, reveals the community of the disciples as the eschatological community of salvation, in whom the prophecy of Joel about the eschatological outpouring of the Spirit has been fulfilled (Acts 2:14–21; cf. Joel 3:1–5). Even for Luke, of course, Pentecost is not the moment of the Church's birth: that is Easter, and for Luke too the community of Jesus Christ existed before Pentecost (Acts 1:15). And according to the fourth gospel, which like the other gospels and Paul's writings, makes no mention of a pentecostal event *after* Easter, the Spirit was already given at the time of Easter (Jn. 20:22). But through the giving of the Holy Spirit the community recognized itself and testified to itself as the eschatological community. Thus the time of the Church, for Luke an essentially missionary Church, is the time of the Spirit. The Spirit bestows power, authority and legitimacy. The Spirit as divine authority links communities to the one Church and gives continuity; he guides the early Church and its missionaries, gives offices (Acts 20:28), sends out ecclesiastical decrees through the Church (15:28), is connected with the laying-on of hands (6:6; 13:2 f.) and legitimizes the testimony of the Church (5:32). Numerous miracles further strengthen the Church and the legitimacy of its messengers.

By contrast with the Acts of the Apostles, Paul makes it clear that the Spirit is not just a special gift for a special external action, but that he determines fundamentally the existence of the believer. In Acts the Spirit is given to the faithful; in Paul's writings prayer itself is an act of the Spirit; for Paul there can be no new eschatological existence at all without the Spirit. If there is no Spirit, it does not mean that the community lacks its missionary commission, but that there is no community at all. "For all who are led by the Spirit of God are sons of God. For you did not receive the spirit of slavery to fall back into fear, but you have received the spirit of sonship. When we cry 'Abba! Father!' it is the Spirit himself bearing witness with our spirit that we are children of God, and if children, then heirs, heirs of God and fellow heirs with Christ, provided we suffer with him in order that we may also be glorified with him" (Rom. 8:14–17). So the Spirit is in a much profounder way the eschatological saving gift of God (cf., among the writings which draw on Paul, Heb. 6:4 f.; I Pet. 1:2).

How does Paul come to add this dimension of profundity to his conception of the Spirit? He thinks of the Spirit wholly in the light of the decisive saving event, the great eschatological turning point: the death and resurrection of Christ. The giving of the Spirit is linked to this eschatological event, in which God himself acted in Jesus Christ. So for him the Spirit is no obscure and nameless power such as it was for hellenistic gnosticism, but is, being the Spirit of God acting in *Christ*, the Spirit of Christ (Rom. 8:9), the Spirit of Jesus Christ (Phil. 1:19), of the Son (Gal. 4:6), of the Lord (II Cor. 3:18). By his resurrection Jesus became the glorified Kyrios, with power over the Spirit and the freedom to impart that Spirit. The Pneuma is so much his own, that he too can be seen as Pneuma, and phrases such as "in the Spirit" and "in Christ", or "the Spirit" and "Christ in us" are parallel ones. Christ himself is called "the spiritual rock" (I Cor. 10:4 A.V.). It is the resurrection of Christ which has fundamentally altered the situation, for through it Christ became a "life-giving spirit" (I Cor. 15:45), indeed "the Lord is the Spirit" (II Cor. 3:17). Paul does not mean here the absolute identity of two personal entities, but rather that the Kyrios appears in the mode of existence of the Pneuma. The Kyrios is identical with the Pneuma as soon as he is seen not in isolation but in his actions both with regard to the community and the individual. This explains why the Kyrios and the Pneuma can at the same time be put on the same level, and the Pneuma seen as subordinate to the Kyrios (II Cor. 3:17 f.). The encounter between the believer and "Theos", "Kyrios" and "Pneuma" is ultimately one and the same encounter: "The grace of the Lord Jesus Christ and the love of God and the fellowship of the Holy Spirit be with you all" (II Cor. 13:14; cf. I Cor. 12:4–6; Gal. 4:4–6; Rom. 5:1–5). In each case it is the action of the one God.

The Spirit is thus the earthly presence of the glorified Lord. In the Spirit Christ becomes Lord of his Church, and in the Spirit the resurrected Lord acts both in the community and in the individual. The power of his resurrection is more than a power of ecstasy and miracle; it produces a new creation. The Spirit opens up for the believer the way to the saving action of God in Christ. He does this not as a magic power which man cannot resist; he creates the possibility of man's replying with a responsible and conscious affirmative. He gives him, through the knowledge of the crucified Christ, the realization that in Jesus Christ God acted for him. The Spirit gives faith in the cross and resurrection of Christ and gives the power to live a life of faith. He is the "spirit of faith" (II Cor. 4:13; cf. II Cor. 5:5, 7). The Spirit is not man's own potential, but entirely the gift, the power and strength of God. The Holy Spirit, as *God's* Spirit, must be distinguished from *man's* own spirit, his human self; he should not be confused with man's spirit, since he is the *Holy* Spirit, free from all sin. The Holy Spirit is always entirely God's Spirit and is not absorbed into the individual spirit of man (cf. Rom. 8:16; I Cor. 2:10 f.). At the same time, God's Spirit can win power and dominion over man, so that he becomes man's inner self, so that a man no longer lives by his own strength, but by God's (cf. Rom. 8:9–15, 26 f.). In this way God's Spirit does not work, as in the gnostic view, as an automatically divinizing substance. The Spirit is the power which creates faith, and the norm according to which the believer is constantly summoned to live: "If we live by the Spirit, let us also walk by the Spirit" (Gal. 5:25; cf. 6:8). The pneumatic existence of the believer is lived in the dialectic between an indicative and an imperative.

The Spirit makes the believer a part of Christ's body. It is he who creates the unity of this body, which consists of many members, with different gifts of the Spirit (cf. I Cor. 12). By becoming a part of Christ through the Spirit, the believer guarantees his pneumatic existence. Not only does God assure the believer, through his Spirit working in the risen Christ, of eternal life in the *present*—since the resurrection of the crucified Christ means a final victory over death; but also God will, through the same life-giving Spirit, give him eternal life in the *future* too: "If the Spirit of him who raised Jesus from the dead dwells in you, he who raised Christ Jesus from the dead will give life to your mortal bodies also through his Spirit which dwells in you" (Rom. 8:11). The Spirit is the power of future life. The work of the Spirit of God in Christ will be perfected—again a difference from the gnostic view— in the future, in the redemption of our bodies (Rom. 8:23), so that at the end all things are put in subjection under Christ and the Father (cf. I Cor. 15:27 f.).

So the Spirit of God, given to the Church and the individual, the Spirit of the risen Lord, is the sign that the last days have begun and have been fulfilled, but have not been finished and consummated. Since the resurrection of Jesus the community of believers can regard the resurrection of all men at the end of time not as an uncertain hope, but as a firm certainty. The reality of the present Spirit guarantees the reality of future glory. By contrast with the Qumran community, which also speaks of an outpouring of the Spirit in the present, the Christian community sees the Spirit as a guarantee and seal of that perfection which is to come but which has already begun: God has "put his seal upon us and given his Spirit in our hearts as a guarantee" (II Cor. 1:22; cf. 5:5). "We ourselves, who have the firstfruits of the Spirit, groan inwardly as we wait for adoption as sons, the redemption of our bodies" (Rom. 8:23). "In him you also, who have heard the word of truth, the gospel of your salvation, and have believed in him, were sealed with the promised Holy Spirit, which is the guarantee of our inheritance until we acquire possession of it, to the praise of his glory" (Eph. 1:13

f.). "And do not grieve the Holy Spirit of God, in whom you were sealed for the day of redemption" (4:30; cf. Tit. 3:6 f.).

The ecclesia is the eschatological people of God, the people of God of the last days: we have been looking at this fact from an entirely new perspective. God has not called and gathered his people simply as an alien being, an outsider. He has not made a new covenant, with his people as a distant party to an agreement, completely uncommitted in his personal existence. No, God has revealed himself in his entire living power, and it is through his self-giving power that he makes his claim to reign over his people. He himself is, through his Spirit which is at the same time the Spirit of Jesus Christ, present and efficient in the ecclesia. There are no limits to his self-giving power, which has been revealed to his people and has transformed its whole existence, indeed recreated it anew. His power sustains it and leads it towards its goal. The young communities of the Church, as we can see not only in the Acts but in Pauline and Johannine writings as well, were consoled and strengthened in joy and hope by their *experience* of God's power in his Spirit, whatever historically explicable differences there may have been in the actual phenomena of these experiences. This, as they recognized, was the essential difference between them and other religious groups in Judaism (the apocalyptic sects and the Qumran community) and in the hellenistic world (gnosticism and the mystery religious): only the community of Jesus Christ had received through their glorified Lord the Spirit of God as the guarantee and firstfruits of salvation. Only they could therefore make "demonstration of the Spirit and power" (I Cor. 2:4; cf. I Thess. 1:5).

This then is the biblical background to what Vatican II had to say about the Spirit which sanctifies the Church: "When the work which the Father had given the Son to do on earth (cf. Jn. 17:4) was accomplished, the Holy Spirit was sent on the day of Pentecost in order that He might forever sanctify the Church, and thus all believers would have access to the Father through Christ in the one Spirit (cf. Eph. 2:18). He is the Spirit of life, a fountain of water springing up to life eternal (cf. Jn. 4:14; 7:38 f.). Through Him the Father gives life to men who are dead from sin, till at last

He revives in Christ even their mortal bodies (cf. Rom. 8:10 f.). The Spirit dwells in the Church and in the hearts of the faithful as in a temple (cf. I Cor. 3:16; 6:19). In them He prays and bears witness to the fact that they are adopted sons (cf. Gal. 4:6; Rom. 8:15 f., 26). The Spirit guides the Church into the fullness of truth (cf. Jn. 16:13) and gives her a unity of fellowship and service. He furnishes and directs her with various gifts, both hierarchical and charismatic, and adorns her with the fruits of His grace (cf. Eph. 4:11 f.; I Cor. 12:4; Gal. 5:22). By the power of the Gospel He makes the Church grow, perpetually renews her, and leads her to perfect union with her Spouse. The Spirit and the Bride both say to the Lord Jesus, 'Come!' (cf. Rev. 22:17). Thus, the Church shines forth as 'a people made one with the unity of the Father, the Son and the Holy Spirit' (St. Cyprian, St. Augustine and St. John of Damascus)" (CE 4). This text also contains some ideas which must be examined further, again in the light of the New Testament.

(*b*) *The Church as the temple of the Spirit:* The Church is the work and the tool, a sign and a witness of the Spirit of God which fills it. It is, to use the scriptural image, a temple, a building filled and reigned over by the Spirit: *a building of the Spirit.* How are we to understand this scriptural image of the Church? The idea of the Church as a temple built by God, by Christ or by the Holy Spirit, is one we find at various points in the New Testament (cf. Mt. 16:18; Mk. 14:58; Jn. 2:19; Heb. 3:2–6; 10:21; Rev. 21:22). Three classic texts give us important perspectives for the link of this particular image with the Spirit.

1. The *individual community* is built by the Spirit (I Cor. 3:16 f.). The image of the temple is not an idealized picture of an ideal Church. This is made clear by the fact that its first use in the New Testament shows it being applied to an individual community, to the community in Corinth in fact, about which we know a good deal. We know in particular that the "saints" in Corinth had, as Paul's two letters reveal, only too often acted in an unsaintly manner. It is this community of unsaintly saints which Paul addresses—by way of an admonition—as a temple of the Spirit: "Do you not know that you are God's temple and that God's Spirit dwells in you?" (I Cor. 3:16).

To refer to the Church as a temple, therefore, does not mean referring to the Church in a spiritualized sense. These people, this community with all its evident human failings, is the temple of God. Although it must be admonished to live according to the Spirit, this Church is nonetheless in the Spirit, or rather, the Spirit dwells in it: God's moulding power and life-giving strength has through Christ taken possession of it, has overwhelmed and penetrated it in its entire existence. In the Spirit, God himself and the Kyrios are effectively present in the community of believers despite all their human weaknesses. The Church is the place of God's special presence on earth. Just as God was once thought of as dwelling in a stone temple, both in the Jewish and Gentile religions, he now lives in the community of Christ. It no longer needs a stone temple, it is itself the new spiritual temple. For this very reason the community has the responsibility of maintaining the temple in brotherly unity. "If anyone destroys God's temple, God will destroy him. For God's temple is holy, and that temple you are" (I Cor. 3:17). Any Church which like the Corinthians destroys the unity of the community by making factions drives out the Spirit. Anyone who drives out the Spirit destroys the temple, destroys the community and ultimately destroys himself. The fact that the Church, the community, is a building of the Spirit, implies a charge upon the members of the community: since they are spiritual, they must lead spiritual lives.

2. The whole Church is a building of the Spirit (Eph. 2:17–22). In these verses from Ephesians[15] the remarks quoted above from I Corinthians are extended to cover the whole Church, in accordance with the total salvation-historical conception of the letter, and with special reference to the Jews and the Gentiles, those who are "far off" and those who are "near": "And he came and preached peace to you who were far off and peace to those who were near; for through him we both have access in one Spirit to the Father. So then you are no longer strangers and sojourners, but you are fellow citizens with the saints and members of the house-

[15] Among the more recent commentaries on Ephesians cf. especially H. Schlier, *Der Brief an die Epheser*, Düsseldorf ²1958, 118–145.

hold of God, built upon the foundation of the apostles and prophets, Christ Jesus himself being the chief cornerstone, in whom the whole structure is joined together and grows into a holy temple in the Lord; in whom you are also built into it for a dwelling-place of God in the Spirit."

Here we have a more detailed description of the inner structure of the building of the Spirit. The "foundation" of this spiritual building is the "apostles and prophets", that is, the prophets of the New Testament, of whom Paul often speaks, as do also Acts, Revelation and the Didache; the directly commissioned apostolic authorities, and the charismatic prophetic authorities—all those who had the word directly from Christ (who elsewhere is himself described as the foundation of the Church, cf. I Cor. 3:11). The "stones" are the members of the Church, all those who believe in Christ; not only Jews, but Gentiles too, who were previously strangers and sojourners but are now citizens and members of the household of God, all are "built in" to the dwelling-place of God in the Spirit. The "cornerstone" is "Christ Jesus", or rather, he is the "keystone", as most modern exegetes prefer to read, by contrast with I Cor. 3:10 f.: the keystone which rounds off and holds together the whole arch. The temple as a whole is "a holy temple in the Lord" or "a dwelling-place of God in the Spirit", which means the same thing; "in the Lord" and "in the Spirit" are parallel phrases. The "Lord" holds the building together, gives it a basis and a purpose; the "Spirit" gives the power and strength by which the building exists. The Church is a building which exists in the Spirit and through the Spirit and by virtue of the Spirit of the Lord. The glorified Lord sends his Spirit and turns his fellowship of disciples into a Church. It is through the Spirit that the reconciliation effected by Christ between Jews and Gentiles becomes effective and fruitful. In *one* Spirit and in *one* body they all have access to the one God. The Spirit therefore makes the Church a completely pneumatic reality. For "dwelling-place, temple, building in the pneuma" we could also read "pneumatic temple, building, house". And it is the "pneumatic house" to which the third classic text refers.

3. The faithful are *built up* and *themselves build* the building of the Spirit (I Pet. 2:4–7). The image of the corner-

stone, even more than that of the keystone, emphasizes the fundamental importance of the risen Lord for the Church as a building of the Spirit or, as it is called here, a "spiritual house": "Come to him, to that living stone, rejected by men but in God's sight chosen and precious; and like living stones be yourselves built into a spiritual house, to be a holy priesthood, to offer spiritual sacrifices acceptable to God through Jesus Christ. For it stands in scripture: 'Behold, I am laying in Zion a stone, a cornerstone chosen and precious, and he who believes in him will not be put to shame.' To you therefore who believe, he is precious" (I Pet. 2:4–7).[16] Here again the indicative precedes the imperative: the Church is God's house, a spiritual house. Christ is the cornerstone, as the quotation from Isaiah makes clear, the stone at the corner which supports the whole house: a living stone, since Christ, rejected and crucified, is now the risen and living Christ. Only through the living Christ are Christians living stones, freed from death. The Church is built up of believers on the foundation-stone of Christ—as a *spiritual* house; not a material earthly temple, nor yet a completely spiritualized temple, but as a pneumatic temple which lives by the Pneuma and of which all the members are filled and vivified by the Pneuma.

Because we are living stones, we must *let ourselves be built up;* whether the original Greek form is indicative or imperative, the meaning at all events is imperative. Not that Christians as pious people can build up the house by themselves; another builds with them. They must in faith put themselves at the builder's disposal; as believers they must serve the house. How? The image of the spiritual house, the spiritual temple is transposed into that of the temple-priesthood: the believers must offer sacrifices to God. But here again the writer is not thinking of material earthly offerings, animals, meats and incense, but pneumatic offerings: prayer, praise and thanks, penitence, fruits of faith and love. These sacrifices are not to be offered by the believers, but by the High Priest, Christ; then they will be well pleasing to God and their acceptance is certain. Then the believers will become a true "holy priesthood".

[16] Among the more recent commentaries on I Pet. see esp. K. H. Schelkle, *Die Petrusbriefe,* Freiburg–Basle–Vienna 1951, 57–63.

Vatican II has this to say about the image of the building of the Spirit: "The Church has more often been called the edifice of God (I Cor. 3:9). Even the Lord likened Himself to the stone which the builders rejected, but which became the corner stone (Mt. 21:42 par.; cf. Acts 4:11; I Pet. 2:7; Ps. 117:22). On this foundation the Church is built by the apostles (cf. I Cor. 3:11), and from it the Church receives durability and solidity. This edifice is adorned by various names: the house of God (I Tim. 3:15) in which dwells His family; the household of God in the Spirit (Eph. 2:19–22); the dwelling-place of God among men (Rev. 21:3); and, especially, the holy temple. This temple, symbolized by places of worship built out of stone, is praised by the holy Fathers and, not without reason, is compared in the liturgy to the Holy City, the New Jerusalem. As living stones we here on earth are being built up along with this City (I Pet. 2:5). John contemplates this Holy City, coming down out of heaven from God when the world will be made anew, and prepared like a bride adorned for her husband (Rev. 21:1 f.)." (CE 6)

The Spirit of God communicated through the glorified Lord is thus seen to be, in various ways, the basis of the Church's existence, its source of live and controlling power. The Church is filled and vivified, sustained and guided by this Spirit, the power and strength of God. The Church owes to the Spirit its origin, existence and continued life, and in this sense the Church is a *creation of the spirit*. But this expression does not only suggest a *unity* of Spirit and Church, a unity which seems explicitly emphasized in the images of the spiritual building; to refer to the Church as a creation of the Spirit also emphasizes a distinction which is taken for granted in Scripture and on occasions referred to explicitly. It is important in the Church today, especially as regards Church unity, to stress this distinction.[17]

[17] In addition to the general systematic works on the idea of the Church (see A II, 2) and the relevant sections in the dogmatics (esp. K. Barth, *Church Dogmatics*, Edinburgh–Naperville, Illinois 1956, IV/1, 643–650) there are the more recent monographs on the relationship Spirit-Church: A. Vonier, *The Spirit and the Bride* (Coll. Works, II, London 1952); Westminster, Md., 1952; P. Nautin, *Je crois à l'Esprit Saint dans la Sainte Eglise*, Paris 1947; R. Prenter, *Le Saint-Esprit et le renouveau de l'Eglise*, Neuchâtel–Paris 1949; K. Rahner, *The Dynamic Element in the Church*, London–New York 1964; J. G. Davies, *Der Heilige Geist*,

(*c*) *The Church under the reign of the Spirit.* The distinction between Spirit and Church has its basis in the divine nature of God's Spirit or, as we can also put it, in its freedom. Spirit and Church, however closely linked, are not on the same plane; the Church is subordinate to the Spirit of God. This distinction of freedom can be summed up in four sentences:

1. The Spirit *is not* the Church. It would be dangerous to try and identify the Church and the Holy Spirit; for the Holy Spirit is the Spirit of God, not of the Church; hence the fundamental *freedom* of the Holy Spirit. Just as the Holy Spirit, although he dwells in a Christian, is not identical with the Christian's spirit, so the Spirit is not the Spirit of the Church but of God. There is no mention in the New Testament of the Holy Spirit as the "Spirit of the church", only as the "Spirit of God", as the "Spirit of Jesus Christ". This Spirit proceeds not from the Church nor from an individual Christian, but from God. He is not the possession or property of the Church, nor its power and strength, but God's. Through him God acts *in* the Church, reveals himself and comes *to* the Church, provides a foundation *for* the Church and sustains it. He governs the Church, but never becomes the Church's own spirit, nor merges with it. He remains God's own Spirit and for this reason is and remains the *free* Spirit.

We are the Church, we the fellowship of men who believe in Christ. We, the Church, are a human structure. But the Holy Spirit is divine, not human. For all the links between them there is no identity, but rather a fundamental distinction between the Spirit of God and the human structure of the Church. This difference is not merely a general and abstract one, the ontic difference between the divine and the human. The real Church, of which we are speaking, is not only a Church composed of people, but of sinful people. The real

die Kirche und die Sakramente, Stuttgart 1958; S. Tromp, *Corpus Christi quod est ecclesia,* vol. I–III, Rome 1957 ff.; O. Ertis, *Die Erneuerung der Gemeinde durch den Geist,* Kassel 1960; H. Volk, *Gott alles in allem,* Mainz 1961, 86–112; P. Brunner, *Pro Ecclesia,* Berlin–Hamburg 1962, I, 213–224; W. Mühlen, *Der Heilige Geist als Person,* Munster 1963; *Una mystica persona. Die Kirche als das Mysterium der Identität des Hl. Geistes in Christus und den Christen,* Munich–Paderborn–Vienna 1964.

Church is not only human, but also sinful. We are the Church, justified but sinful men, we, the fellowship of the righteous who are yet constantly dependent on forgiveness: *communio sanctorum* indeed, but also regrettably always the *communio peccatorum*. So the Church is sinful. The Spirit of God on the other hand is not sinful, but the Holy, the completely Holy, Spirit. Hence the Spirit is in this very much deeper sense also the *free* Spirit, truly free from sin, guilt and death.

This free Spirit of God is essential for our understanding of the Church, as well as for our understanding of the believer as a man made free by God's Spirit. But the free Spirit of God in no sense belongs to the Church and must in no way be confused with it.

To avoid confusing the Spirit and the Church, it would be better not to speak of the Church as a "divine" reality. The individual believer, after all, does not become a "divine" reality because he is filled with and governed by the Spirit. It would also be better not to speak of an organic development of the Church and its spirit. The romantic and idealistic view of Church history overlooks the fundamental difference between the perfect Spirit of God and an imperfect Church. It is because of the distinction between the Spirit and the Church that its development often includes developments in the wrong direction, and progress often includes retrogression. Finally, to avoid confusing the Spirit and the Church, it would be better not to speak of the "sense of the faithful" (*sensus fidelium*) in the Church as though it were a revelation of the Holy Spirit. The Church's sense of the faith can never be a source and a norm of the revelations of the Spirit. On the contrary: revelations of the Holy Spirit provide the source and norm of the Church's sense of the faith. These concrete examples show that the Holy Spirit in the Church is and remains a free Spirit.

It is obvious how important this distinction is. The Church does not *per se* and in each case represent the Holy Spirit; the Church has to prove its holiness in action. Only by accepting the distinction can we truly face up to the all too human aspect of the Church, its failures and shortcomings, its sin and guilt, in a proper liberating way. A Church which identifies itself with the Holy Spirit cannot say the *Confiteor*. It cannot, may not, confess that it has sinned in thought, word and deed, through its fault, through its most grievous fault. It will be forced into unsound theological prevarications and apologetics which convince no one. In short, it will fall prey to an idealistic and triumphalist conception of the Church which is full of illusions. And it will therefore not be a *free* Church.

Only by drawing this distinction can we really listen to God's word in the Holy Spirit and be obedient to the Holy Spirit, in a truly liberating way. A Church which identifies itself with the Holy Spirit has no need to listen, to believe, to obey. It turns itself into a revelation, it knows and does everything. It needs only to listen to itself, to obey itself and believe in itself, and urge others outside the Church to listen, believe and obey. In short, it will fall prey to a self-glorifying and egocentric conception of the Church, and again it will be anything but a *free* Church.

But a Church which distinguishes between itself and the Holy Spirit can face up to sin and failure in the Church soberly and humbly, but also with the liberating hope of those already justified that they will be forgiven anew. A Church which draws this distinction will believe, obey and hope without putting its trust in itself, but precisely in God's Holy Spirit. A Church which proudly identifies itself with the free Spirit of God is a Church which for all its vaunted strength is ultimately weak, for all its imagined freedom is ultimately unfree. But the Church which humbly distinguishes itself from the free Spirit of God is for all its undeniable weakness strong, and for all its apparent unfreedom ultimately free.

So it is that we believe *in* the Holy Spirit (*credo in Spiritum Sanctum*); by contrast we believe *the* holy Church (*credo sanctam ecclesiam*). We do not believe *in* the Church, in the final analysis we never believe in ourselves. We, the Church, believe in the Holy Spirit just as we believe in God, from whom the Holy Spirit cannot be distinguished. In this faith in the Holy Spirit the holy Church is best taken care of.[18]

2. The Spirit *precedes* the Church. The Holy Spirit is not an external extra to the Church, as though the Church could exist without the Holy Spirit, although perhaps only in an imperfect and unvital way. When Scripture refers to the Church

[18] Cf. A II, 2.

as a spiritual house, as a temple of the Holy Spirit, it does not mean that the Church is the outward form or framework into which the Spirit, the living content, then entered. The Church is not something which competent and clever ecclesiastical organizers, administrators and big business men can work out and set up, *after* which the Holy Spirit can find in it a centre of operations or even a resting-place.

The Spirit of God comes first; and through the Spirit God in his freedom *creates* the Church, and constantly creates it anew from those who believe: "No one can say 'Jesus is Lord' except by the Holy Spirit" (I Cor. 12:3). Through the operation of the Spirit the Church is created and created afresh each day: *emitte spiritum tuum—et creabuntur!* There is no Christian existence which is not created and must constantly be created; and none is created without the operation of the Spirit. There is no Church which is not created and must constantly be created; and none is created without the operation of the Spirit. Of course, there is no Church without the decision of believers and their free gathering together. But the believers who congregate in the Church do not summon themselves. They do not even summon themselves to faith. God himself calls them through the word of Christ in the power of the Holy Spirit to faith and hence to the Church as the fellowship of the faithful. God in the Holy Spirit acts in perfect freedom. The beginning is his, as is the continuation and the end. Everything is his, who in the freedom of his power and strength remains the sovereign Lord of the Church.

3. The Spirit works *where* he wills. The Spirit of God cannot be restricted in his operation by the Church; he is at work not only in the offices of the Church, but where he wills: in the whole people of God. He is at work not only in the "holy city", but where he wills: in all the churches of the one Church. He is at work not only in the Catholic Church, but where he wills: in Christianity as a whole. And finally he is at work not only in Christianity, but where he wills: in the whole world.

The power of the Spirit of God can pass through *all* walls, even church walls. It is true that the Holy Spirit has his dwelling and his temple in the Church, which he fills and which he governs. Here his power is especially revealed, since in the Church and through the Church the word of God is preached and his sacraments are administered. But the Spirit of God, if domiciled in the Church, is not domesticated in it. He is and remains the free Spirit of the free Lord not only of the "holy city", not only of Church offices, not only of the Catholic Church, not only of Christians, but of the whole world.

Certain questions arise here. Might *Christians* not be more cautious, more open and just in their judgments and attitudes towards the great non-Christian religions of the world if they were completely convinced of the fact that the Holy Spirit, who is revealed in and through the Church, is the free Spirit of the Lord of the whole world, who is at work where he wills? Might *Catholics* not be more restrained, more open and friendly in their judgments and attitudes towards the other Christian Churches if they were completely convinced that the Holy Spirit, in whom as Catholics they put, or ought to put, their whole trust, is also the hope and strength of the whole of Christendom and desires in freedom to be so? Might *Church leaders* not be more modest, more open and humble in their judgments and attitudes towards other Christians if they were completely convinced that the Holy Spirit, who is certainly promised to those who hold office in the Church, is not a Spirit of office reserved for the privileged few, but is the Spirit of God, who has been poured out in the hearts of all who believe and love and who acts and desires to act freely in all hearts and minds? The free Spirit is at work where *he* wills.

4. The Spirit is at work *when* he wills. The Spirit of God is not, of course, a Spirit of arbitrariness or apparent freedom, but of real freedom; he is a Spirit of order, not chaos; peace, not contradictions, in the Church as well as in the world. This is what Paul had to remind the Corinthians, who, proud of their spiritual gifts, had neglected order in the Church: "God is not a God of confusion but of peace" (I Cor. 14:33). Arbitrariness, disorder and chaos in the Church cannot be the work of the Holy Spirit.

At the same time, God's Spirit does not blow when he *must*, but only when he *wills*. No decrees of the Church, in doctrine or practice, can force him to act or not to act at a given time. True, God is absolutely free, and is thus free even with regard to his freedom. He is so overwhelmingly free, that he can bind himself, as he does indeed in word and sacrament. But by being bound to word and sacrament he affirms not his limitations or unfreedom, but his all-powerful, abundant freedom.

God's Spirit knows no law but that of his own freedom, no authority but that of his own grace, no power but that of his own faithfulness. God's Spirit is at all events not bound by the laws or authority or power of the *Church*. God's Spirit is not ruled by ecclesiastical laws or authority or power. He himself reigns and rules sovereign over them. Anyone in the Church who supposes he can dictate to the Spirit on the basis of law, authority or power must necessarily fail. The Church cannot take over the Spirit, or in any real sense "possess" him, control or limit, direct or dominate him.

The Church cannot do any of these things, either through its word or its sacraments. God binds himself in the Spirit to word and sacrament, not on the basis of the Church's law, but on the basis of his own freedom; not on the basis of the Church's authority, but on the basis of his free grace; not on the basis of the Church's power, but on the basis of his faithfulness. The fact that God binds himself to word and sacrament of the Church, lays an obligation not on him but on us. We do not demand something of him, he demands something of us: our unconditional *faith*. Neither word nor sacrament works automatically; where there is no faith, they are not operative. Anyone who thinks that the Spirit can be compelled with word or sacrament, or with law and authority, power or order, is leaving out of account precisely that faith which the Spirit demands of him: faith not in his or the Church's law, authority, power or order, but in God's free grace and faithfulness. It is true therefore of the Church too that the Spirit blows not when he must, but when he wills.

Here again certain questions arise. Might not Catholic doctrine on the sacraments be more discriminating and more accurate in its theory of *opus operatum* if it took as its starting-point the fact that even the *opus operatum* cannot compel the *Spiritus operans,* but must be subject to him in faith? Might not Catholic canon law manipulate all its canons and tenets more restrainedly (for example, in its view of the sacraments), if it constantly realized that its canons and tenets, provided they are meaningful and appropriate, can be seen as the concrete presentation of God's demands upon us, but can never be seen as demands of the Church upon the Holy Spirit, as though to compel him to act at a certain time in a certain manner? Might Catholic judgments with regard to the preaching and sacraments of other Christian Churches (for example, with regard to the validity or invalidity of marriage rites, ordination or Eucharist) be more cautious, if their starting-point were the freedom of the Holy Spirit, who blows when and where he wills, that freedom which in nearly all cases would make a definite *negative* judgment impossible?

The Church cannot dictate to the Spirit or regiment it. It can only pray and beg: *Veni!* God's Spirit may dwell in the spiritual house of the Church, and remain with the Church and work through it. But he dwells and remains and works there not on the basis of a law, because he must, but on the basis of his faithfulness, because he wills. "He who calls you is faithful, and he will do it" (I Thess. 5:24).

We, who are the Church, must never forget that we are sinners, albeit justified, and must constantly be aware of the fact; we live therefore in contradiction to God's Spirit, we "grieve" him and can, from our viewpoint at least, lose him. We must not forget that our faith though it may give us certainty, is constantly threatened and challenged; we can only trust in God's faithfulness and grace. It is by no means automatic that the Spirit should remain with us, the Church. All we can do is to pray penitently, not only *"veni sancte Spiritus"* but also *"mane sancte Spiritus"*, remain with us, despite our faithlessness, because of your faithfulness. The Church, despite its constant failures, has never lost the free Spirit of God in all its members; this is not something to be taken for granted, it is the miracle of God's faithfulness, which we can never take for granted but must constantly believe and pray for anew.

But the work of the Holy Spirit is not only to be seen in these general terms. It is true that the Spirit is given to the *community*. But the community is composed of individual believers, received into it through baptism. The operation of God in the Spirit is directed towards these individuals in the Church, it is something concrete and individual. This becomes clear when we describe the pneumatic reality of the Church in terms of what may be called its charismatic structure.

3. THE CONTINUING CHARISMATIC STRUCTURE

There seem to be two reasons why for such a long time Catholic theology and the Church overlooked the importance, both in theory and practice, of the charismatic structure of the Church. *First* a certain clericalism and legalism, which in recent times has been much criticized within the Catholic Church itself. A clericalistic attitude can only recognize real and decisive activity and initiative in the Church if it comes from the clergy rather than from other members of the people of God. Juridical thinking is deeply mistrustful of any movements of the free Spirit of God, the Spirit which is operative in the Church where and when he wills, which cannot be regimented.

Secondly, the fact that the ecclesiology of Catholic textbooks was exclusively based on the ecclesiology of the pastoral epistles (and of Acts), and largely overlooked the specifically Pauline ecclesiology of the letters which were undoubtedly written by Paul, although it often formally cited Pauline texts. The variety and the inner tensions of the New Testament were ignored or harmonized in an unreliable way. But, as we have already seen, the various differences that there are in conceptions of the Church, of the Spirit, of the charisms, are undeniable. Here it is helpful to examine how the word "charisma" is used.

The oldest New Testament document—earlier even than Mark or Matthew—is, along with the two letters to the Thessalonians, the first letter to the Corinthians. No other New Testament writing gives such original and detailed information about the external and internal ordering of a Church. This first letter to the Corinthians, which like all uncontested Pauline letters speaks neither of "elders" or "bishops" (with the sole late exception of the reference to "bishops and deacons", Phil. 1:1), nor of ordination or the laying-on of hands, repeatedly refers to the "charismata" or "pneumatika" which, according to Paul, are bestowed on each Christian according to the measure of his faith; the letter also contains long chapters about the charismatic structure of the Church, which is a presupposition of Paul's other letters and occasionally may be glimpsed in them. By contrast, in the pastoral letters, which are among the latest New Testament writings, the Pauline view that each Christian has received the Spirit and his gifts is overlaid by a strongly emphasized theology of Church office. The Spirit is given in ordination. Despite the obvious references to Paul, the pastoral letters, significantly enough, do not use the Pauline word πνευματικός at all, nor does it appear in Luke's Acts of the Apostles, which chronologically comes between the Pauline and the pastoral letters. Moreover, the word "charisma", which does not appear in Acts either, is only used twice in the pastoral letters (I Tim. 4:14; II Tim. 1:6), in each case, we may note, in connection with ordination. This is one of the numerous and weighty differences between the Pauline and the pastoral letters, which have caused even Catholic exegetes to doubt the Pauline authorship of the pastoral letters—a question to which, as is well known, there can only be historical, not dogmatic answers.

Although Catholic theologians are convinced that the pastoral letters, along with other "early Catholic" writings were not included by the early Church in the canon of the New Testament without good reason, they may not draw from this the same conclusions as several Protestant theologians have done: namely that the pastoral letters can best be seen as a "contrast" to the real "gospel" as it was preached by Jesus and interpreted by Paul at his most profound. Catholic hermeneutics demand that the New Testament καθ' ὅλου, as a *whole*, in all its writings, should be taken seriously, and that the whole truth of the New Testament should be accepted as it stands. Thus the "early Catholic" writings as much as Acts and the pastoral letters, demand scholarly and positive study. Any exegesis must, of course, take note of the fact that the Pauline letters have a primacy of originality, not only because of the authenticity of the apostolic author and his temporal closeness to the Gospel of Jesus, but also because of his thematic closeness to the Gospel. The Acts of the Apostles on the other hand, and the pastoral letters, both of which are often based on Paul, are evidently *secondary* testimonies. But precisely as such they should be seriously and positively examined, which should not be difficult for the theologian who thinks historically.[19]

This hermeneutic introduction makes it abundantly clear why an ecclesiology based primarily on Acts and the pastoral letters, which merely acknowledge the Pauline texts or used them to support arguments drawn from elsewhere, necessarily neglected the charismata of all Christians, and why only the "hierarchical" rather than the pneumatic and charismatic structure of the Church was examined. The rediscovery of the charisms is a rediscovery of specifically Pauline ecclesiology, the importance of which for the problems of Catholicism and ecumenism cannot be overestimated. Rigorous theological investigation is needed to show how fruitful Pauline ecclesiology could be in the contemporary situation; in the present context it will help us to throw light on the continuing charismatic structure of the Church. Before examining charisms in detail, three recurring misconceptions about them must be discussed.[20]

[19] Cf. A I, 3.

[20] In addition to the literature cited in C II, 2 and the articles on charisms and the Spirit in the dictionaries of the Bible and of theology, cf. esp. F. Grau, *Der neutestamentliche Begriff. Seine Geschichte und seine Theologie,* Diss. Tübingen 1946; J. Brosch, *Charismen und Ämter in der Urkirche,* Bonn 1951; E. Lohse, *Die Ordination im Spätjudentum und im NT,* Berlin 1951; H. von Campenhausen, *Kirchliches Amt und geistliche Vollmacht in den ersten 3 Jahrhunderten,* Tübingen 1953; K. Rahner, *The Dynamic Element in the Church,* London–New York–Freiburg 1964; E. Schweizer, *Gemeinde und Gemeindeordnung im NT,* Zurich 1959; R. Bultmann, *Theology of the New Testament,* London [3]1965; E. Käsemann, *Ministry and community in the NT, in Essays on NT themes,* London–Naperville, Illinois 1964, 63–94; G. Eichholz, *Was heisst charismatische Gemeinde? 1 Cor 12,* Munich 1960; O. Perels, *Charisma im NT,* in Fuldaier Hefte 15, Berlin 1964, 39–45; H. Schürmann, *Die geistliche Gnadegaben,* in *De Ecclesia. Beiträge zur Konstitution "Über die Kirche" des 2. Vatikanischen Konzils,* ed. by G. Barauna, Freiburg–Frankfurt a.M. 1966, 494–519. The details which follow are drawn from my article, "The Charismatic Structure of the Church", *Concilium* 4/1, April 1965.

(*a*) *Exceptional or everyday phenomena?* It is a misconception to think of charisms as principally exceptional, miraculous or sensational phenomena. The prototypical charism in that event—apart from the driving out of demons, healings, acts of power, miracles—would be glossolaly, which is often quoted in this connection; speaking ἐν γλώσσῃ or ἐν γλώσσαις (I Cor. 12–14; Acts 10:46; 19:6; Mk. 16:17), the ecstatic language of the spirit which may be unintelligible, unarticulated sounds (I Cor. 14:6–11, 23) and which is uttered in praying or singing, praising or giving thanks (I Cor. 14:15 f.; cf. Eph. 5:19; Col. 3:16).

What is Paul's attitude to these exceptional charisms, such as were also found in mystery religions outside the Church? Speaking with tongues was a feature of hellenistic ecstatic mysticism, as for example the Delphic Pythia and the Sibyls, who murmured ominous phrases in their mantic trances.

It would be wrong to suppose that Paul rejected or even mistrusted these exceptional gifts on principle. He welcomes all gifts of the Spirit, and he himself is apparently specially gifted in speaking with tongues (I Cor. 14:18). But he emphatically reduces in importance this sensational gift, by insisting that it is nothing compared with the charism of interpretation; it is not of itself edifying for the community, nor does it clarify the understanding of the man who prays. It is thus less valuable than prophecy and is to be used in the community only within certain limitations (I Cor. 14). In the list of charisms (I Cor. 12:28) it takes last place. In his letter to the Romans, probably written in Corinth, Paul in a list of charisms does not mention it at all (Rom. 12:6–8).

In addition to minimizing the importance of such charisms of enthusiasm, Paul criticizes the miraculous hellenistic "pneumatika", the powers of ecstasy and wonders and, instead of the very common hellenistic expression, he usually substitutes, on purpose we may suppose, the word "charisms". When he uses the word "pneumatika" (I Cor. 12:1; 14:1) he points out their distinctive Christian features. Demons and dumb idols may also because of their power have an irresistible attraction for people (I Cor. 12:2), signs and wonders can also occur outside the Church, and can be done by Antichrist. There are lying prophets and lying apostles as well as true ones. The obvious conclusion to be drawn from this is that the signs and wonders are not unequivocally signs of the Holy Spirit, of the real charism.

Since there are different spirits and spiritual phenomena, it is essential that there should always be "the ability to distinguish between spirits" (I Cor. 12:10). Paul establishes two principal criteria for recognizing the Spirit which comes from God. The first is stated at the beginning of his detailed discussion of charisms (I Cor. 12:2 f.): the Spirit which comes from God enables a man to affirm that Jesus is the Lord. Only "in the Holy Spirit" can a man assert that "Jesus is Kyrios". The Spirit which comes from God binds men to Jesus and to his reign. Jesus Christ is the centre of all preaching and all actions of the community. This is how Paul distinguishes the specifically Christian element: where Jesus, rather than any person or power of this world, is the Lord, the Spirit is from God (cf. I Jn. 4:2 f.).

The second criterion is the element of service attached to the charism. The true charism is not simply a miracle; it is something in the service of the community, giving a sense of responsibility towards the community and the desire to edify and benefit it. Charism is directly connected with the community. "To each is given the manifestation of the Spirit for the common good" (I Cor. 12:7). Paul also mentions less striking charisms, such as exhortation and acts of mercy (Rom. 12:8), service (Rom. 12:7), teaching (Rom. 12:7; I Cor. 12:28 f.), the utterance of wisdom and knowledge (I Cor. 12:8), faith (I Cor. 12:9), discernment of spirits (I Cor. 12:10), helping and administration (I Cor. 12:28), and so forth.

Charisms are by no means only exceptional things, they are everyday phenomena in the life of the Church. Christians should desire earnestly the higher charisms, and these are not striking ones like speaking with tongues, but everyday ones. "But earnestly desire the higher gifts. And I will show you a still more excellent way", says Paul at the conclusion of his list of charisms (I Cor. 12:31). And this "more excellent way", the best and greatest of the charisms, is the least sensational, the most everyday of gifts: love. Without love, speaking with tongues and prophecy, even faith or the renunciation of all property or martyrdom, is nothing: "If I speak in the tongues of men and of angels, but have not love, I am a noisy gong or a clanging cymbal. And if I have prophetic powers, and understand all mysteries and all knowledge, and if I have all faith, so as to remove mountains, but have not love, I am nothing. If I give away all I have, and if I deliver my body to be burned, but have not love, I gain nothing" (I Cor. 13:1–3). This charism which is above all others, and regulates all others, is revealed unobtrusively in the thousand very unsensational situations of everyday life, and effects what man of his own nature can never hope to achieve: "Love is patient and kind; love is not jealous or boastful; it is not arrogant or rude. Love does not insist on its own way; it is not irritable or resentful; it does not rejoice at wrong, but rejoices in the right. Love bears all things, believes all things, hopes all things, endures all things. Love never ends" (I Cor. 13:4–8).

The Constitution "On the Church" of Vatican II refers explicitly to "charismatic gifts, whether they be the most outstanding or the more simple and widely diffused", and adds the warning: "Still, extraordinary gifts are not to be rashly sought after, nor are the fruits of apostolic labour to be presumptuously expected from them". At the same time it is stressed that true charismatic gifts "are exceedingly suitable and useful for the needs of the Church" (CE 12).

The everyday nature of charisms will become clearer when we examine the various kinds of charismatic gifts.

(*b*) *Uniformity or diversity?* A second misunderstanding of the charism would be to suppose that there is only one particular kind of gift, for example, that connected with some kind of ordination. The only charism mentioned in the pastoral letters, and mentioned with emphasis, is "the gift of God that is within you through the laying on of hands" (II Tim. 1:6), "the gift you have, which was given you by prophetic utterance when the elders laid their hands upon you" (I Tim. 4:14). If this were the only real charism of the Spirit, we should have to assume that charisms were exclusively "sacramental" or institutionalized in some way or another, rather than being a manifold variety of gifts of the Spirit designed for diverse services.

That this is not the case is revealed by the fact that those letters of Paul in which the charism plays an extremely important part contain no references to ordination at all. Nothing could have been further from his mind than to sacramentalize or make uniform the charism, and hence the workings of the Spirit. On the contrary, the workings of grace and of the Spirit of God are characterized for him by richness, variety, exuberance: "in every way you were enriched in him . . . so that you are not lacking in any spiritual gift . . . (I Cor. 1:5, 7); "as you excel in everything" (II Cor. 8:7); "God is able to provide you with every blessing in abundance, so that you may always have enough of everything" (II Cor. 9:3).

A glance at the lists of charisms which Paul gives in various places (especially I Cor. 12:28–31; Rom. 12:6–8; Eph. 4:11 f.) is enough to show how diversified they are. Apart from the gifts of speaking with tongues, of miraculous healing and exorcism, there are the following groups of gifts:[21]

(1) Charisms of *preaching:* these include the functions of apostles, prophets, teachers, evangelists and exhorters;

(2) Charisms of *service:* these include the functions of deacons and deaconesses, of those who give alms and tend the sick, and of the widows who are in the service of the community;

(3) Charisms of *leadership:* "first converts", elders, bishops, pastors.

But this is not the sum of the charisms, by any means. Even though the word itself may not be used in the immediate context, it is clear that Paul regards suffering as a charism (II Cor. 4:7–12; cf. Col. 1:24). Ultimately *every "vocation"* is an *"assigning"* (cf. I Cor. 7:17) of the charism (cf. Rom. 12:3, 6): "Each has his own *special gift* from God, one of one kind and one of another . . . ; let everyone lead the life which the Lord has *assigned* to him, and in which God has *called* him" (I Cor. 7:7, 17). Charism is different from a gift for music or mathematics, for example,

21 Cf. E. Käsemann, *op. cit.,* 68–70.

which one either "has" or does not have. Charism is bestowed, assigned, distributed not on one's own behalf, but on behalf of others; it is not a natural talent, but a call of grace, a call to service. In this sense, of course, even natural talents can become charisms; indeed Paul seems even to regard one's state of life—being married or unmarried (I Cor. 7:7), circumcised or uncircumcised (I Cor. 7:18–20), being a free man or a slave (I Cor. 7:20–24)—as a potential charism: as a call to service. From this viewpoint we can see why Paul can so easily transfer from talking about the apostolate and public functions in the community to talking about private virtues when he is listing various charisms (cf. I Cor. 12:28–30; Rom. 12:6–8). Charisms are potentialities which are appealed to, aroused and created by the Spirit of God.

Any gift of the Spirit, any vocation is therefore a charism. Even eating and drinking can become charisms—not of themselves, but when they are done "in the Lord" and "for the Lord"; eating or fasting out of obedience to or love of the Lord, keeping or not keeping certain regulations, living or dying (cf. Rom. 14)—the same is true of everything, provided it is done in faith, in conscience (Rom. 14:22 f.). So the *whole* man with all his human gifts is enlisted in the Lord's service; new gifts are given to him by the Spirit of God, and his life is given a goal.

The Constitution "On the Church" emphasizes that charisms are assigned to Christians according to the free will of God in his grace: "allotting his gifts 'to everyone as he will' (I Cor. 12:11)." The charisms thus prepare us to discharge the *variety* of services which the community has need of: through his gifts the Holy Spirit "makes them (the faithful) fit and ready to undertake the various tasks or offices advantageous for the renewal and upbuilding of the Church". Charisms are explicitly distinguished from sacraments (which include ordination).

Since charisms take such varied forms, they are necessarily spread generally throughout the Church.

(c) *Charisms: for the few or for all?* A third misunderstanding of the nature of the charism is to suppose that charisms are limited to a small group of people, that there is a special rank or class of charismatics. But it is far from the case that the great variety of charismatic gifts is concentrated and centralized in a few individuals, the leaders of the community for example (elders, bishops, elder-bishops).

Charisms, as has been made clear above, are a general rather than a specific phenomenon in the Church. Since they are so various, and everyday, they must be general.

On the evidence of the New Testament it would be impossible to limit charisms to those who hold office in the Church. For a start, Paul gives a very different answer to the question of order and rank in the "hierarchy" than we would usually give today. Carefully numbering them, he lists as follows: "God has appointed in the Church first *apostles,* second *prophets,* third *teachers,* then workers of miracles, then healers, helpers, administrators, speakers in various kinds of tongues. . . . But earnestly desire the higher gifts" (I Cor. 12:28, 31).

In this charismatic order of preference the *apostles* come first, which for Paul include more than the original twelve (cf. Rom. 16:7; I Cor. 9:5); they are the original witnesses of the risen Lord, sent out by him and authorized to preach in his name. Second the *prophets* who are mentioned elsewhere (Eph. 2:20) together with the apostles as the foundation of the Church; they light up the road of the individual and the community, in present and in future, by the freedom of their Spirit-inspired proclamations; they too have been chosen and authorized by God. Third come the *teachers,* who hand on and interpret the message of Christ, shedding light on the tenets of faith and the commandments of that message, and interpreting the Old Testament according to the ideas of the young Church. Like the prophets, they derive their message from the original testimony of the apostles, and direct the present and the future of the community, but instead of intuitive proclamations their work is rather the systematic and theological development of ideas.

But the Church which receives these charisms is in the interim situation between "not yet" and "but already". No member of the community has a plenitude of all charisms. In making his lists Paul is concerned to show that no one can be all things to the community, even though he knows that in individual cases one person might have a number of special gifts, as was true of Paul himself. The nature of these gifts means that the community can never be a one-man band, since charisms are variously distributed: "Are all apostles? Are all prophets? Are all teachers? Do all work miracles? Do all possess gifts of healing? Do all speak with tongues? Do all interpret?" (I Cor. 12:29 f.).

The fact that no one person can do everything is particularly true for Christians with the function of leadership. We may notice that the gift of leadership (κυβερνήσεις, the art of the steersman, of the guide) is not mentioned first, but next to last, together with the helpers, in Paul's list. It is difficult to determine what functions are involved here. Paul urges the Corinthians to be subject to "first converts" (the "first converts in Achaia", I Cor. 16:15 f.; cf. the "first convert in Asia", Rom. 16:5). In the first verse of Philippians, probably one of his last letters, Paul sends a greeting to "bishops and deacons", but we know nothing of their rôle in the community. Much earlier, Paul speaks of those holding authority in the Church (cf. I Thess. 5:12; Rom. 12:8), who are to be recognized and revered: "But we beseech you, brethren, to respect those who labour among you and are over you in the Lord and admonish you, and to esteem them very highly in love because of their work" (I Thess. 5:12 f.).

The charisms of leadership in the Pauline Churches did not at all events produce a "ruling class", an aristocracy of those endowed with the Spirit who separated themselves from the community and rose above it in order to rule over it. The entire New Testament carefully avoids using secular terms of office to describe functions in the community (ἀρχή, τιμή, τέλος), because all of them express a relationship of rulers and ruled. Instead, and by direct contrast the New Testament speaks of "service" (διακονία). Still more inclusive, for Paul, is precisely the concept of charism (cf. Rom. 12:6–8), which, as we shall see, describes with theological precision all the services and functions in the Church. The charism cannot be subsumed under the heading of ecclesiastical office, but all Church offices can be subsumed under the charism.[22]

[22] See under Chap. E.

This makes it clear that charisms are not limited to a particular set of persons but are given to each and every Christian. Each Christian has *his* charism. Each Christian is a charismatic. *"Each* has his own special gift from God, one of one kind and one of another" (I Cor. 7:7); "To *each* is given the manifestation of the Spirit for the common good" (I Cor. 12:7); "as *each* has received a gift, employ it for one another, as good stewards of God's varied grace" (I Pet. 4:10).

According to Acts, chapter 2, the Spirit has been poured out "on all flesh". And whoever has a share in the Spirit has a share in the gifts of the Spirit. So charisms are not special marks of distinction belonging to a chosen few, whether on account of their enthusiasm or of their office in the Church, but a distinguishing mark of the whole Church, of the fellowship of all believers. In a Church or community where only ecclesiastical officials rather than all the members of the community are active, there is grave reason to wonder whether the Spirit has not been sacrificed along with the spiritual gifts.

The Constitution "On the Church" emphasizes the general distribution of charismatic gifts: "Allotting his gifts 'to everyone according as he will' (I Cor. 12:11), He (the Holy Spirit) distributes special graces *among the faithful of every rank"*. Here again the text is quoted: "To each is given the manifestation of the Spirit for the common good" (I Cor. 12:7). However, the sentence which the Constitution seeks to apply to those "who preside over the Church" is spoken by Paul, as the text shows beyond any doubt, to the whole community and hence to each individual Christian: "Do not quench the Spirit . . . but test everything; hold fast what is good" (I Thess. 5:19–21).

(*d*) *The charismatic community.* We have seen that charisms are everyday rather than fundamentally exceptional phenomena, that they are various rather than uniform in kind, and that they are found throughout the Church rather than being restricted to a particular group of people. These conclusions lead to others; that they are phenomena not exclusive to the early Church, but present and contemporary ones; and not peripheral phenomena, but central and essential elements in the Church. Hence one can speak of a *charis-*

matic structure of the Church, which *includes but goes far beyond the hierarchical* structure of the Church. The theological and practical implications of this are evident.

The prime importance of the idea of charism for Pauline ecclesiology is underlined by the fact that it is, as no other so definitely is, a *specifically Pauline idea.*[23] The Greek word has no Hebrew equivalents, and is difficult to trace, though it may have existed, in pre-Christian times. The word was used, outside the Pauline tradition and in no way as a technical term, for a present or a mark of favour; but Paul, so far as we know, was the first to give a technical sense to this rare word and introduce it into theology.

On the basis of all the foregoing evidence we can attempt a theological description of what charism means; in its widest sense it signifies *the call of God, addressed to an individual, to a particular ministry in the community, which brings with it the ability to fulfil that ministry.* We have seen how interconnected charism, vocation and service are; terminologically they seem to merge together; thus "charisms" can alternate with "services" (I Cor. 12:4–6), or with "vocation" (Rom. 11:29; I Cor. 7:7). Prerequisites for "services" are "charisms" and "vocation".

Taking charism in this widest sense, rather than seeing it as a strange, exceptional and miraculous power, we can translate the word simply as "gift of grace" (in secular language there is often an overlap between the ideas of a "gift" for something and a "vocation" for something). But charism as a "gift of grace" must never be seen as something autonomous, as distinct from the giver. All charisms are expressions of God's grace and power, in the Spirit. They all point to the one great charism of God, the new life which has been given to us in Christ Jesus; "The charism of God is eternal life in Christ Jesus our Lord" (Rom. 6:23; cf. Rom. 5:15 f.). In the fullness of Christ's grace the riches of spiritual gifts are revealed to us (cf. I Cor. 12:4–6; Eph. 4:8, 11; Jn. 1:16). Whether a man is an apostle, a prophet, teacher, evangelist, a bishop or a deacon, whether he consoles, exhorts, forgives, loves—all these things are gifts in Jesus Christ and point to

[23] Cf. E. Käsemann, *op. cit.,* 63–64.

him who is and does all these things in his own person. Charisms are the revelations, in concrete and individual form, of the charis, the power of God's grace, which takes hold of us, leads us to our appointed service and gives us an individual share in the reign of Christ. And to the extent that we have a present share in the grace and the reign of Christ in the Spirit, our charisms are expressions of power (ἐνεργήματα), "the manifestation of the Spirit" (I Cor. 12:6 f.): "All these are inspired by one and the same Spirit, who apportions to each one individually as he wills" (I Cor. 12:11). Charisms are pure gifts of the Spirit, and yet the Christian can and must "earnestly desire" the higher charisms (I Cor. 12:31), can and must pray for them (cf. I Cor. 14:13).

In this way we have found an answer to the question: how, given the tremendous variety of charisms which fills the Church, can there be unity; and how, given the freedom of the Spirit, can there be order? The fundamental answer is that the Spirit creates unity and order: "There are varieties of gifts, but the same Spirit . . . to each is given the manifestation of the Spirit for the common good" (I Cor. 12:4, 7).

Unity and order are not created, for the men who have these charisms, by levelling out their variety. It is important for the unity and order of the community that each person has *his* charism. *To each his own:* that is a fundamental principle of the charismatic ordering of the Church. No individual can set himself above others and attempt to seize or subjugate everything; by taking rather than leaving to each his own, he will create not order but disorder (I Cor. 12:12–30). At the same time each one has his charism not for himself but for his fellows. *With one another for one another:* this is a second principle of the charismatic ordering of the Church. More than the "fruits of the Spirit" (Gal. 5:22), which are rather directed towards the sanctification of the individual (love, joy, peace, patience, kindness, goodness, faithfulness, gentleness, self-control), the charisms exist for the "edification of the Church" (I Cor. 14:12; cf. Eph. 4:12 f.). The Christian is not to use his charism as a weapon with which he can seize power and position in the Church, but as a gift for the service of others and of the whole community. Hence the first fruit of the Spirit (Gal. 5:22) and the greatest of the charisms is love (I Cor. 13); charism summons us to follow the way of the cross, the way of service and love. *Obedience to the Lord:* this is a third principle of the charismatic ordering of the Church—we recall the criterion for the discernment of spirits. Order in the Church means for the individual Christian living in one spirit with his individual charism, living a life of love and mutual service, obedience to the one Lord.[24] All charisms have their origin in one and the same giver: God himself through Christ in the Spirit. All charisms are subject to one and the same "law", the law of love. All charisms have one and the same goal: the edification of the community.

The charismatically orientated ordering of the Church does not therefore mean either enthusiasm, which ends in anarchy and disorder, nor legality, which petrifies into mediocrity and uniformity; neither anarchy nor uniformity, neither too much order nor too little, but order in freedom: "where the Spirit of the Lord is, there is freedom" (II Cor. 3:17). Even evidence of hierarchical structures in the early Church—the appointing of elders (an idea borrowed from the Jewish synagogue structure in the Palestinian tradition), which appears to have occurred early on in the Pauline communities (cf. the elder-bishops in Acts, and the indications in Philippians 1:1), and to have solved the problem of the succession to the apostles—even this must be seen not as the beginnings of a clerical ruling system, but against the background of the fundamentally charismatic structure of the Church.[25]

But even this fundamental charismatic structure is only a temporary thing, part of the "not yet" of the eschatological period. It belongs to the "imperfect" things of this interim period and will be replaced by the fullness of perfection: "When the perfect comes, the imperfect will pass away" (I Cor. 13:10).

On this basis of New Testament understanding, we can now appreciate and understand in its complete context the principle text of Vatican II (there are countless other references) on the

[24] Cf. E. Käsemann, *op. cit.*, 76–78.
[25] See Chap. E.

charisms: "It is not only through the sacraments and Church ministries that the same Holy Spirit sanctifies and leads the People of God and enriches it with virtues. Allotting His gifts 'to everyone according as he will' (I Cor. 12:11), He distributes special graces among the faithful, whatever their position. By these gifts He makes them fit and ready to undertake the various tasks or offices advantageous for the renewal and building up of the Church, according to the words of the Apostle: 'The manifestation of the Spirit is given to everyone for profit' (I Cor. 12:7). These charismatic gifts, whether they be the most outstanding or the more simple and widely diffused, are to be received with thanksgiving and consolation, for they are exceedingly suitable and useful for the needs of the Church. Nonetheless, extraordinary gifts are not to be rashly sought after, nor are the fruits of apostolic labour to be presumptuously expected from them. In any case, judgment as to their genuineness and proper use belongs to those who preside over the Church, and to whose special competence it belongs, not indeed to extinguish the Spirit, but to test all things and hold fast to that which is good" (Cf. I Thess. 5:12, 19–21) (CE 12).[26]

If the charisms of individual Christians were discovered and furthered and developed, what dynamic power, what life and movement there would be in such a community, such a Church. "Do not quench the Spirit, do not despise prophesying" (I Thess. 5:19 f.). But Paul's next sentence indicates that these workings of the Spirit and of men filled with the Spirit can lead to tensions and difficulties: "But test everything; hold fast what is good, abstain from every form of evil" (5:21 f.). We must here turn to a phenomenon which has played a rôle throughout the history of the Church from the beginning: enthusiasm.

4. THE CHURCH AND THE ENTHUSIASTS

The Johannine writings also see the Spirit as an eschatological gift, but there is a new stress. Spirit is no longer, as in common Christian use, the divine power to do unusual deeds, nor in Paul's sense the power and the norm of Christian existence.

[26] Cf. Card. L. Suenens, "The charismatic dimension of the Church," in *Council Speeches of Vatican II,* ed. by Y. Congar, H. Küng, D. O'Hanlon, London–New York 1964, 18–21.

For John the Spirit is the power of Christian preaching and knowledge in the community. Although the "Paraclete" of the leave-taking discourses (Jn. 14:16, etc.) can be taken, in accordance with Jewish tradition, as an intercessor, or, in accordance with gnostic tradition, as a helper or supporter, he fulfils these functions primarily as the "Spirit of truth" (14:17; 15:26; 16:13; I Jn. 4:6). What does this mean? The Spirit works by "teaching all things" (Jn. 14:26), by "guiding into all truth" (16:13), so that those filled by him "know the truth" (I Jn. 2:20 f.) and "have no need that anyone should teach them" (I Jn. 2:27). The things that Jesus could not yet say to them were to be revealed by the Spirit: "I have yet many things to say to you, but you cannot bear them now. When the Spirit of truth comes, he will guide you into all the truth" (Jn. 16:12 f.).

It is small wonder that enthusiasts of all periods have chosen to base their ideas on John in particular. From these and similar Johannine sayings they have concluded that the Spirit teaches a particular wisdom which exceeds what Jesus said himself. They have claimed that the Spirit working in them has revealed the truth to them personally and directly. The revelation was direct in two senses, indicative of the opposition to them which took on different forms and emphases in history: directly as opposed to a revelation which is fundamentally linked to the *word of Scripture;* and directly as opposed to a communication of the Spirit, which is supposed to come only through *ecclesiastical office.*

We are taking the word "enthusiast" here not in the narrow sense (in contrast to, say, Quakers and Baptists), but in its widest sense, to include all variants, from pure Quakerism, to which the Inner Light is paramount, to social revolutionary enthusiasm, which regards the Spirit as at work in external things too. All have in common the idea of a direct working of the Spirit, all consider that the biblical message is only conditionally normative, and that they possess a revelation which goes beyond that of Christ and the New Testament.

Movements of enthusiasm are as old as the Church itself. Paul himself was waging a battle on two fronts: not only against Jewish (and hellenistic) legalism, but also against hellenistic (and Jewish) enthusiasm. In Corinth in particular he was up against gnostic enthusiasts who boasted of their possession of the Spirit. The first great inner crisis which the Gentile Christian community had to overcome in the second century—and overcame with the help of creeds, a scriptural canon and a reinforced ecclesiastical office—was hellenistic Christian gnosticism, which wanted to draw the Christian faith into a combination of other religions and make it a syncretistic mystery religion. It offered a higher, mythological and philosophical wisdom, a gnosis which would uncover all the secrets of the world and belonged to initiates, as opposed to the simple *pistis* of the community; it offered a revelation based on its own prophets, its own sacred texts, its own cult, its own secret and esoteric mystery traditions and learned theological investigations. But even after this first outbreak of enthusiasm, which led to a clear consolidation of doctrine, cult and constitution, there were constant outbreaks of an enthusiasm which claimed direct contact with the Spirit. It is clear that enthusiasm cannot be dismissed as an unimportant and peripheral aspect of the life of the Church. These assaults questioned the very nature of the Church, by questioning its view of the Spirit and of revelation. It is equally important for the state of the Church today to examine briefly some typical outbreaks of enthusiasm in ancient, medieval and modern times—a complete history of enthusiasm would be far too extensive to be attempted here.[27]

[27] In addition to the bibliography at A I, 1 and the relevant sections on individual authors in the standard works on the history of dogma and of the Church and the dictionary articles on the subject, see the following works: R. A. Knox, *Enthusiasm*, London–New York 1950; W. Maurer, "Luther und die Schwärmer" in *Schriften des theologischen Konverts Augsburgischen Bekenntnisses*, Vol. 6, Berlin 1952; K. G. Steck, *Luther und die Schwärmer*, Zollikon–Zurich 1955; *Der linke Flügel der Reformation, Glaubenszeugnisse der Täufer, Spiritualisten, Schwärmer und Antitrinitärier*, ed. by H. Fast, Bremen 1962; H. Grundmann, *Ketzergeschichte des Mittelalters*, Göttingen 1963; A. Hilgenfeld, *Die Ketzergeschichte des Urchristentums, urkundlich dargestellt*, Darmstadt 1963, reprint of 1884 edition; E. Benz, *Ecclesia spiritualis. Kirchenidee und Geschichtstheologie der franziskanischen Reformation*, Darmstadt 1963, reprint of 1934 edition. Specialist works on Montanism: N. Bonwetsch 1881; P. de Labriolle 1913, W. Schepelern 1929; on Joachism: H. Grundmann 1927, 1950,

The following may be taken as typical examples:

1. *In ancient times:* After the elimination of gnosticism, the next major crisis within the Church was provided by *Montanism*. This movement, which started in Phrygia (Asia Minor) some time after the middle of the second century, was begun by Montanus, who, according to Jerome, was a former priest of the *magna mater*. The most significant thing about it is the name which it usually gave itself: "the new prophecy". The Montanists believed that Montanus himself was the "paraclete", who would bring a higher and final revelation. The oracles of the new prophecy improve on and far outdo the revelations of the Old and New Testaments. Prophetesses (Maximilla and Priscilla) were instrumental in renewing enthusiastically the early Christian expectation of the parousia, which had grown dim, and the imminent end of the world was proclaimed in ecstatic and visionary language. This end was to be prepared for by extreme austerity of morals; the ascetic rigorism of Montanus made the fasting laws more severe, put a ban on marriage (later on second marriages), and encouraged martyrdom.

The Montanist movement spread like wildfire through the Roman empire and gave the Church numerous difficulties, especially when in Carthage at the beginning of the third century the great Tertullian joined it. At the same time the expectation of an imminent end became less important than more extreme penitential practices, and they began to rebel against the action of the magisterium in expelling those who claimed to possess the Holy Spirit and administered forgiveness of sins. It is noteworthy that opponents of Montanism (the "Alogians") strongly rejected the fourth gospel and the apocalypse as being gnostic.

2. *In the Middle Ages:* The most important apocalyptic and prophetic enthusiast movement of the Middle Ages was *Joachism*. Its founder was the distinguished abbot Joachim of Flora (1145–1202). The basis of his apocalyptic view of history was a detailed historical-typological interpretation of Scripture, characterized by number mysticism (the numbers seven and three) and calculations. Joachim worked out a large-scale doctrine of the three ages of history: the age of the Father, with its Old Testament and Judaistic atmosphere, its domination by married people and laymen, was followed by the age of the Son, with its New Testament and clerical atmosphere and domination by priests; this was

H. Bett 1931, E. Buonaiuti 1931, J. C. Huck 1938, F. Russo 1954, 1959; on Müntzer: P. Wappler 1908, E. Bloch 1921, H. Böhmer 1922, J. Zimmermann 1925, A. Lohmann 1931; A. Meusel 1952, C. Hinriche 1952, M. S. Smirin 1956, W. Elliger 1960.

to be followed, in the year 1260, by the age of the Holy Spirit, with a monastic and spiritual atmosphere, dominated by monks (Joachim had himself founded an order which existed in various forms up to the seventeenth century). The Church of this third age is not to be clerical or Petrine but Johannine, a reformed Church of the Spirit akin to the early Church. Then the "eternal gospel" (Rev. 14:6) will be proclaimed and the new spiritual, pneumatic view of Scripture established; the Sermon on the Mount will be the rule of life and the spirit of poverty triumph; there will be no more war, the Eastern and Western Churches will be reunited and the Jews will be converted.

Honorius Augustodunensis, Rupert of Deutz and Anselm of Havelberg had prepared the ground for this doctrine of the three ages (and the connected schema based on the number seven); the ideas of Gerhoh and Arno of Reichersberg on reform were similar to those of Abbot Joachim. Joachim himself was not basically opposed to the hierarchy; he wanted to interpret traditional Church doctrine "spiritually". Hence he was highly regarded as an exegete and as a prophetic thinker by popes and kings alike. The situation only became critical when on the one hand Joachim's ideas were taken up by the Ghibellines (who were hostile to the Pope, and who identified Antichrist not with the Emperor, as Joachim had, but with the Pope), and on the other, the more austere aspects of his ideas were taken up by the young Franciscan order. For these *"spirituales"* the writings of Joachim were the "eternal gospel"; the popes took action against them. In 1260 there was a great flagellant pilgrimage in Italy, and a community of enthusiasts called the "Apostolic Brethren" grew up. They saw themselves as the Church of the poor and the Roman Church as the Babylonian harlot of the apocalypse; their founder Segarelli was banished, and a crusading army sent out against his followers. Later there developed the sects of the Amalricians and the "Brotherhood of the Free Spirit", and other similar sects in France and Germany. Cola di Rienzo on the other hand turned away from the spiritualistic and apocalyptic aspect of these ideas and sought to establish a political reformation. This kind of political messianism was to have many successors. The effects of Joachism can be traced as far as German idealism (philosophy of the spirit, kingdom of the spirit, a preference for the fourth gospel) and the totalitarian systems of the twentieth century: the secularized idea of a "Duce" (the *novus dux* of Joachim) and of the "third Reich" (empire).

3. *In Protestantism:* The early years of the Lutheran reformation were characterized by violent outbreaks of enthusiasm. Having first defended himself against Rome, Luther soon had to de-

fend himself no less against the "mobs and enthusiasts", represented by such figures as Karlstadt, Thomas Müntzer, Schwenckfeld and Franck. These enthusiasts can of course be regarded as a continuation of medieval ideas, but it must not be forgotten that in the writings of the early Luther in particular they found ideas which helped them on their way. From Karlstadt to the Antinomians all the enthusiasts of the time took Luther as their vindication. The enthusiasts (and the Peasants' Revolt connected with them) forced Luther after 1525 to secure his defences on this side and to moderate some of his originally radical positions.

A revealing figure in this context is that of Thomas Müntzer (d. 1525). Like Luther he was an educated monk and an inspiring preacher, and he had read Joachim of Flora. Luther himself had recommended him for the post of vicar in Zwickau in 1520, where Müntzer came under the influence of the "Zwickau prophets". The latter tried to replace Scripture with the direct enlightenment of the Holy Spirit and justification by faith with experience of the cross, that is—spiritual sufferings. So instead of Luther's ideas on interpreting Scripture we find in Müntzer a belief in the Spirit (the word of God as an inner, supernatural illumination, visions and dreams, all combined with fantastic interpretations of Scripture). From his faith in the Spirit and his experience of the cross Müntzer found a basis for practical and then for political action. Dismissed from his post in 1521, he fled to Bohemia; in his "Prague manifesto" he emphasizes the gifts of the living Spirit, which alone can turn the dead letters of Scripture into living words. Instead of a Church of "priests and monkeys", he calls for a Church "of the elect friends of God".

Müntzer pressed for the realization of his ideas. In 1523, back in Germany again, he at once took up violent opposition to Luther, claiming that external baptism was not necessary, but only an inner baptism "in water and the Holy Spirit". After failing to win over the princes to his plans, he exploited the revolutionary tendencies of the German peasants for his purely religious and enthusiastic purposes. The last phase of world history, the age of the Holy Spirit, had in his view already begun. Linked to his expectation of an imminent end of the world were his hopes for the establishing of a theocracy. Luther was impelled to write to the princes of Saxony a "Letter concerning the spirit of revolt"; Müntzer replied to Luther with his "Defence and reply against the unspiritual and self-indulgent flesh in Wittenberg". But Müntzer became more and more involved in the political turmoils of the time. He roused the peasants to war with his preaching, and put himself at the head of the army as their prophetic leader. He was captured and executed after cruel tortures.

Only by violent measures was Luther able to settle with the enthusiasts, who regarded him as one of their spokesmen. Their common ground was after all very extensive: the idea of individual interpretation of Scripture under the guidance of the Spirit, a particular interpretation of the idea of the priesthood of all believers, the devaluation of the sacraments and of ecclesiastical office. What the enthusiasts did was to give a radical twist to Luther's tentative beginnings—and appealed in doing so to the authority of the free Holy Spirit.

There is no doubt that in fact enthusiasm very largely triumphed over Luther. There were countless other enthusiasts in the sixteenth century apart from those mentioned above, such as the vast groups of "Baptists" who, starting from Zurich, spread quickly as far as Moravia and the Netherlands (Mennonites). They based their views on the "inner light", their own prophetic illumination, and rejected infant baptism; both in the early days when they were regarded as rebellious sects, and later on when they were peaceful communities, they were cruelly persecuted by Protestants and Catholics alike, and thousands of them were martyred. Then there were the mystical and speculative spiritualists like Sebastian Franck (later Valentin Weigel, Giordano Bruno and Jacob Böhme) and the sects of the Familists and the Schwenckfeldians (expelled, and later in Pennsylvania), and finally the radical religious movements like the Anti-trinitarians (Michael Servetus, burned alive under Calvin, and the Socinians). The continuing influence and the constant forming of new enthusiast movements cannot be traced any further here. The most outstanding among them, however, were: radical Pietism in Germany, the Congregationalists, the Baptists and Quakers and later the Irvingites and Plymouth Brethren in England, and finally the different revivalist movements in America, down to the time of the Mormons and the Seventh Day Adventists. Many of these different sects have been able to win large numbers of adherents. In the present context the "Pentecostal Church" is of particular interest. It began in America, where in 1906 "the fire of God" descended on a congregation of the faithful in Los Angeles. This reception of the Spirit was accompanied by curious phenomena and speaking with tongues, and aroused widespread attention. Soon this baptism by the Spirit was seen as the third and greatest work of the Spirit, after the experience of justification and sanctification. The Pentecostal movement today has many hundreds of thousands of active adherents in North and South America and in Europe.

One of the most highly debated questions in contemporary Protestant theology is worth noting here: "How did it happen that the enthusiasts in fact triumphed over Luther? A large measure of blame may perhaps be attributed to the way in which the struggle against the Roman Church was conducted. Essential matters were neglected during the struggle against Rome, simply because they were seen to be present in the Roman Catholic Church. As a result the Lutheran Church became exposed to dangers from the other direction, a threat that has often been overlooked." These remarks were made at a Lutheran theological congress, following a paper by W. Maurer on "Luther and the enthusiasts".[27]

4. *In post-Tridentine Catholicism:* The previous remarks should not lead to the mistaken supposition that enthusiasm is a feature of Protestantism only. There were enthusiasts within Catholicism after Trent as well as in ancient times and in the Middle Ages. True, specifically Catholic enthusiasm takes different forms from Protestant enthusiasm; it appears to be more domesticated within the Church and hence less dangerous. But here too we find appeals to a higher revelation, a new prophecy, something that earlier was too much to bear, but which has now been revealed: a special revelation which goes beyond that brought by Christ. In these circles reports and books about new "revelations", "apparitions", and "wonders" were much more avidly read and absorbed than the original Christian message given in Scripture. There is a direct relationship between these two things: as Scripture became less important, the new revelations were more attentively read, and the more these new revelations became popular, the less important Scripture seemed. This development began in the Middle Ages; we may note in passing how much it was aided by the polemical attitude of Counter-Reformation theology (now happily corrected by Vatican II) and by bans on reading the Bible in the vernacular, which were constantly reiterated right down to the nineteenth century.

More important in the present context is the fact that these new revelations not only overshadowed the Bible and the Gospel, but also him whom the Gospel proclaims and to whom the Bible bears witness. It is striking how rarely Christ appeared in all these "revelations", "apparitions" and "wonders". He took second place to the "saints", and was often simply replaced by the founder of a new order or the foundress of a new congregation. This brand of enthusiasm did not even need to appeal to the Holy Spirit to justify its existence. For the new and direct revelation it was enough to have a holy man who could figure as the new "paraclete" to

[27] *Op. cit.,* 89.

lead men into the new truth and say things which previously would have been too much for men to bear.

The aim of this enquiry is not to deny the truth of mystical experiences, miraculous events, mysterious insights. The matter does, however, become a problem for the Church when (1) those who have these revelations claim that they are not only valid for the individual in question but for the Church as a whole; (2) these revelations are in fact put on the same level as the original revelation in Christ, and in practice often on a higher level. There were countless Catholics in the post-Tridentine period who followed in the wake of every new "revelation", which often turned out to be fantasy or deceit, who read large tomes about new promises and indulged their desire for sensation by looking for the latest reports of miracles—and yet who had never once in their whole lives read the Scriptures from cover to cover. There were countless Catholics in the post-Tridentine period who found much greater satisfaction in all kinds of prayers, novenas and devotions to some saint or other than in sharing in the eucharistic meal, Catholics for whom Christ, as the only mediator between God and *all* men, had simply ceased to exist. Despite the often admirable apostolic zeal and effort of the time there was the very real threat of a decentralization and paganization of the Christian faith, the more dangerous because it was often sincere and went unnoticed.

This becomes clearer if we examine briefly the relationship between post-Tridentine forms of Catholic enthusiasm and the other forms of enthusiasm already discussed and observe a few parallels: (1) Like *Montanism* the post-Tridentine enthusiasts were often dominated by apocalyptic ideas (prophecies of the imminent end of the world, of a great war, of an apocalyptic catastrophe or of the conversion of Russia), which—and this is the key to their often astounding successes—contrive to frighten as well as to attract and fascinate pious people. Like the Montanists the post-Tridentine enthusiasts often made markedly rigorous moral demands on their followers: the world was condemned out of hand and very severe external works of penitence were enjoined on them under threat of dire punishment. As in Montanism there were also prophetesses at work, who made predictions and were the recipients of special revelations. (2) Like *Joachism* post-Tridentine enthusiasm, especially when it made inroads into theology, specialized in arbitrary typological and allegorical interpretations of Scripture; the Old and New Testaments were made the basis for the most remarkable speculations. If the texts could not provide what was wanted, the Holy Spirit was appealed to, who had hidden other things away in the Bible and who was now revealing what originally was too much to bear. As in Joachism, there was much play with number mysticism and calculations of future events; important events often occurred on the thirteenth of the month; many things happened—or had to happen—three, seven, twelve or thirty times in succession. As in Joachism a new congregation was often regarded as essential for the spreading of these ideas, for which, in contrast to the great traditional orders, a special kind of piety (a holy picture, a devotion, a medallion) was just as important as the word of God revealed in Scripture. (3) As in *Protestant enthusiast movements* post-Tridentine enthusiasm often neglected the word of Scripture, and also—as in Müntzer's case—neglected baptism. A special "consecration" to a saint, for which terminology was often borrowed from baptism, or a vow upon joining an order, in which the baptismal name was given up, often had the effect of overshadowing the importance of baptism in the minds of individuals. Relations with the ecclesiastical office were often, as for the Protestant enthusiasts, a difficult matter. On the one hand there were many who could not do enough out of "loyalty to the Church", and were only too ready to condemn as "disloyal" those who did not share their ideas of a particular "revelation" or devotion to a particular "means to salvation". But as soon as the magisterium moved in an opposite direction—as for example at Vatican II—then this superficial "loyalty to the Church" was shattered to its foundations and in many cases turned into the complete opposite. Very quickly a much-vaunted obedience was forgotten, and particular promises and forms of devotion were invoked in opposition to the Council and the Pope. While many critically-minded Catholics remained loyal to their Church even in difficult times, these enthusiasts frequently abandoned their loyalty as soon as the magisterium had once decided against them.

How should enthusiasm be countered? The first answer is: *not by negative opposition*. There are three reasons for this. (1) Negative opposition is usually unsuccessful. Enthusiasts can be decimated, but rarely rooted out even by force. This was Constantine's experience when he tried to impose laws against the Montanists, and Augustine's, when with his *"compelle intrare"* (Lk. 14:23!) he invoked the power of the State against sects. Innocent III, who supported the terrible wars and the inquisition against the Albigensians; Alexander IV, who condemned a number of Joachist minorities to life imprisonment in a monastery; Luther and Calvin, who demanded the death penalty for enthusiasts; and Paul III who revived the inquisition to combat Protestant movements in Italy—all shared this experience. (2) Negative opposition leads to the formation of sects. Groups of enthusiasts within the Church, as soon as they are negatively opposed, feel themselves misunderstood and outcast, quickly form into sects and defend themselves against all attacks; this is no solution to the problem. (3) Negative opposition overlooks the positive nature of the challenge. Outbreaks of enthusiasm are always signs of a crisis, usually a crisis of scriptural doctrine or of Church order. The Montanists and many ancient sects reacted, and rightly so, against the overshadowing of the idea of eschatological expectation and against the growing worldliness of the early Church. Joachism and many medieval movements of enthusiasm protested, and rightly so, against a Church which had become a centre of power, had become unspiritual, involved in politics and too institutionalized. The enthusiasm of the Reformers was directed, and rightly so, not only against the externalism, the sacramentalism and ritualism of the medieval Church, but also against the identification of the Reformed Churches with particular political systems, with the forces of social reaction, with the "establishment". Post-Tridentine enthusiasm pointed, directly and indirectly, to a number of short-comings and false developments in the medieval and post-Tridentine Church: new devotions and forms of piety arose, often of a peculiar kind, because the official liturgy of the Church had become torpid, lifeless and incomprehensible. New revelations were over-valued because Scripture had become neglected to a frightening degree both in theology and preaching. Curious forms of charismatic phenomena appeared, because the Church's life and order had become extraordinarily petrified. Was negative criticism the right answer in all these cases? The workings of the Spirit may often, as once in Corinth, produce unattractive side-effects; but have we the right to quench the Spirit when we can only set the letter of the law against it? The only answer is to accept the challenge of enthusiasm and make what is good better.

How should enthusiasm be countered? The real answer must obviously be: *by concentrating on the Gospel of Jesus Christ.* Instead of negative polemics, the Gospel, the *whole*

Gospel must be positively preached and positively lived. The demands of the enthusiasts which are truly rooted in the Gospel must be energetically taken up and put into practice. If we do this the enthusiasts will realize, provided they are not inhibited on other grounds (psychological, sociological, political) from the realization, how infinitely richer and deeper and higher the whole Gospel is than what is offered to them as "new revelation" and "higher wisdom". They will realize that nothing which later prophets and prophetesses, whether true or false, can proclaim offers more height and depth, strength and consolation, than what Jesus himself proclaimed and did, and the original Christian community testified to and lived; and that all new revelation, if and in as far as it is true, can at best only be more or less successful confirmation and support of that Gospel which is itself the *"evangelium aeternum"*; and that finally our salvation can only be found in Jesus Christ, the crucified and risen Lord and in no other person, that he alone is *"the* way, *the* truth, and *the* life" (Jn. 14:6) and that he alone can bestow the Holy Spirit, which is his own Spirit.

These "revelations" of private pious persons pale into insignificance when compared with John's gospel of the revealed Logos. How dull are all the reports of miraculous apparitions by comparison with a single one of Paul's letters! How empty are all the sensational prophecies and promises by comparison with the incomprehensible promises of the Sermon on the Mount! It is not surprising that so many have rejected all this secondary material and resolutely held to the one revelation, apparition and miraculous event which God offered to man "once for all" in Jesus Christ.

For all the freedom of the Holy Spirit to work where and when he wills, he is not a Spirit of wild enthusiasm, but a Spirit bound to the definitive eschatological saving action of God in Jesus Christ. This is precisely what John's gospel, in unparalleled concentration, makes clear: the Spirit is bound to Jesus Christ's word of revelation.[28] Many other aspects of

[28] Among the more recent commentaries on John, cf.: C. K. Barrett, R. Bultmann, E. C. Hoskyns, R. H. Lightfoot, R. Schnackenburg, H. Strathmann, M. C. Tenney, as well as the relevant sections in the New Testament theologies. General literature on the

the Pneuma do not appear in John (the link with resurrection and the body, the charisms), and others play little part (the link with baptism and with the Church). But, on the other hand, this one connection is unquestionably central to the Gospel: the connection between Spirit and Word. The Spirit appears as the power of Christian preaching, which leads to our knowledge of Jesus as the redeemer and hence to our knowledge of the living God. The Spirit is the power over which man himself has no control, but which enables man to know what of himself he cannot know: that here God confronts him in reality. God testifies to himself in the testimony of the Spirit (cf. I Jn. 5:6–12). Only through the Spirit does the word give life (Jn. 6:63; 3:6). What the flesh, what earthly things cannot create is created by the Spirit through the word: faith, rebirth, eternal life. The Spirit is not simply identical with Jesus; he only comes to the community after Jesus' departure (16:7; 7:39) and he will remain with the believers as the "other paraclete" (14:16). But through the coming of the paraclete after Jesus' departure as Jesus' representative, Jesus himself comes in truth to his own (16:12–24).

Through preaching, the knowledge which the Spirit has given is once again made alive; through preaching, the revelation of the Spirit is repeated once more: the Spirit "will bear witness to me; and you also are witnesses" (15:26 f.). But this makes it clear that even for John, and precisely for John, the Spirit is never a *deus ex machina*, which justifies things that could not be justified on the basis of the original word of revelation. It is the very words about the Spirit leading the Church into all truth, the words which above all have served as a basis for enthusiasts in their doctrines and lives, which show unmistakably how much the Spirit and the word of Jesus are inseparable (Jn. 16:12 f.). These words have to be protected from misunderstandings in the Church in two directions, not only against modernistic enthusiasts but also against traditionalist orthodox believers. The words have been abused

---

biblical concept of the Spirit is given at C II, 2. For the concept of the Spirit in John, see the biblio. in R. Bultmann, *Theology of the New Testament*, London 1965[3]; E. Schweizer, ThW VI, 436–443 (biblio.).

by those who, appealing to the sure guidance of the Church by the Holy Spirit, have been content to sit back and let everything continue as before; they have also been abused by those who, on the contrary, have appealed to the same Spirit to justify the idea that all innovations in the Church are revelations of the Spirit and should be accepted as such. Both parties give a different sense to the words from that originally intended.

The first group, the traditionalist *"orthodox"*, who defend the *status quo* in the Church by referring to the Spirit, overlook the words which come *immediately before* the statement that the Spirit will guide the Church into all truth. There we read that the Spirit will come again "to convince the world (here meaning the evil, sinful world alienated from God) of sin and of righteousness and of judgment" (16:8). The world, indeed, but also the Church, which is in this world and all too often becomes worldly. The Spirit must come again and again to uncover the guilt of the worldly Church, and open its eyes to sin, righteousness and judgment. To sin, which is at root unbelief in Jesus Christ; to righteousness, which consists in overcoming the world through Jesus Christ; to judgment, which in the death and resurrection of Christ has already been passed on the world. This is the way in which the Spirit demonstrates his freedom.

The Church, we the Church, have every reason to ask ourselves, constantly, whether we live up to our faith in Jesus Christ, whether we live according to his righteousness, whether we reckon with the judgment that has been passed. The Church has constantly every reason to confess its sins, to reflect on itself and to resolve upon greater loyalty, upon a renewed "abiding in him" (15:4).

The Church which believes in the free Spirit of Christ leading it constantly into truth, knows that the Spirit must also constantly confront it with its own sin, with the righteousness of Christ and with judgment. It knows that in this way the Spirit is challenging it to new faith in Christ, to greater loyalty to his Gospel, to a more dedicated life in accordance with his message. Hence the Church which is under the Spirit cannot simply rest content with the *status quo,* but must constantly allow itself to be renewed in that Spirit which renews the face of the earth and also the face of the Church, the

Spirit of him of whom it is written: "Behold, I make all things new" (Rev. 21:5).

The statement that the Spirit will lead the Church into all truth has also been misunderstood by those who take it as a justification for seeing all innovations in the Church as the truth of the Spirit. These in one way or another modernistic *enthusiasts* overlook the words which *immediately follow* that statement. We read there that the Spirit "will not speak on his own authority, but whatever he hears he will speak, and he will declare to you the things that are to come. He will glorify me, for he will take what is mine and declare it to you. All that the Father has is mine; therefore I said that he will take what is mine and declare it to you" (16:13–15).

What the free Spirit of God has to reveal to the Church is therefore not *new* revelations, *new* doctrines, *new* promises, which go beyond things that Jesus himself said or even complement and add to them. It is not said of the Spirit that he will lead the Church into *new* truth, but into *all* truth. This is a basic conviction of the evangelist: Jesus' word is the absolutely decisive word, which decides life and death. "No man ever spoke like this man!" is the excuse offered by the officers to the chief priests for not arresting Jesus (Jn. 7:46). He is not like one of the Old Testament prophets, whose words had *on each occasion* to be inspired by the Spirit anew; here speaks one who *constantly* speaks and acts in unity with God. No prophet has absolute importance; prophets follow one another in their turn. But Jesus is followed by no new revealer: in him, once for all, the revelation of God is given to the world.

This revelation is of course inexhaustible. But the new insights bestowed on the Church by the Spirit do not add to or surpass what Christ himself revealed. They can only be a recollection of what Jesus said: the Spirit will "bring to remembrance" what Jesus said (14:26); he will not speak "on his own authority", but only say what he has "heard" (16:13); he will "take what is mine" (16:14); he will "bear witness" to Jesus (15:26) and "glorify" Jesus (16:14). The Spirit cannot say *more* than Jesus; for in his leave-taking Jesus says: "all that I have heard from my Father I have made known to you" (15:15).

The Spirit cannot give a *new revelation,* but through the preaching of his witnesses he will cause everything that Jesus said and did to be revealed *in a new light.* The Spirit is not needful because Jesus' teaching was quantitatively not complete, but because Jesus' teaching must qualitatively become a new revelation through the Church's preaching. Revelation is not a closed doctrinal system, nor is it a completed history, but through the Spirit it must constantly be made a new reality, a new event. Jesus says not only "I made known . . ." but also "I will make known . . . that the love with which thou hast loved me may be in them, and I in them" (17:26). What would be the value of revelation if it were no more than a kind of garland of Jesus' sayings, which would have to be read out constantly anew and interpreted anew for our edification? Revelation must constantly present a new challenge to the believer, take hold of him, and find faith, not just as human words, but as God's word. And this can only happen through the witness of the Spirit himself, who does not bring us sensational novelties nor a higher revelation, but who in his uncontrollable power "recalls" Jesus' words to us, so that we constantly have to seize them anew in faith. God's revelation in the words of Jesus remains the same. But being always the same it must always be made new for those who hear and those who believe.

An enthusiasm which looks beyond Jesus' words and appeals to the "Spirit", may indeed be able to appeal to some kind of spirit, but certainly not to the Spirit of Jesus Christ. Hence John, like Paul, calls for the individual and the whole community to distinguish between spirits: "Beloved, do not believe every spirit, but test the spirits to see whether they are of God; for many false prophets have gone out into the world. By this you know the Spirit of God: every spirit which confesses that Jesus Christ has come in the flesh is of God, and every spirit which does not confess Jesus is not of God. This is the spirit of antichrist, of which you heard that it was coming, and now it is in the world already" (I Jn. 4:1–3).

The Spirit is bound to the word. This is what stands against all enthusiasm. But the Spirit is not confined to the word. So much must be granted enthusiasm. A Church which abandons the link with the word and tries to rely only on the Spirit falls a prey to all the evils of spiritualistic enthusiasm. Conversely, a Church which tries to rely only on the word and tries to reduce the Spirit to the word, falls a prey to all the evils of a verbalistic enthusiasm. And both the Spirit and the word, if they are isolated, can turn into a myth. The New Testament recognizes no single route alone: together with the Son there is the Spirit, with faith there is love, with justification sanctification, with preaching the active help, with the word the image, or—and this is our next concern—with the word the sacrament. In speaking of the Church as ecclesia, people of God, creation of the Spirit, we have referred frequently to baptism and the Lord's Supper, without which there is no Church. We must now turn in more detail to these two aspects of the Church, and discover a fresh perspective: the Church is not only the people of God and a creation of the Spirit, it is also—and we are speaking of the same thing, only in different terms—the body of Christ.

III. THE CHURCH AS THE BODY OF CHRIST

1. MEMBERS THROUGH BAPTISM

(*a*) No Church without baptism;[29] is this statement histori-

[29] For the doctrine on baptism: in addition to the dictionary articles (esp. LThK: R. Schnackenburg, B. Neunheuser; RGG: E. Dinkler, F. H. Kettler, E. Sommerlath, W. Kreck; EKL: M. Barth, W. Andersen, W. Kreck; ThW I: A. Oepke), and the biblical theologies and the textbooks of dogmatics and the history of dogma, see among the more recent monographs: H. G. Marsh, *The Origin and Significance of the NT Baptism*, Manchester 1941; F. J. Leenhardt, *Le baptême chrétien*, Neuchâtel 1946; K. Barth, *Teaching of the Church Concerning Baptism*, Naperville, Illinois 1958; O. Cullmann, *Baptism in the NT*, Naperville, Ill. 1958; W. F. Flemington, *The NT Doctrine of Baptism*, London–Naperville, Illinois 1948; R. Schnackenburg, *Baptism in the Thought of St Paul*, New York 1964; P. Brunner, *Die evangelisch-lutherische Lehre von der Taufe*, Berlin 1951; J. Beckmann, *Die Heilsnotwendigkeit der Taufe*, Stuttgart 1951; G. W. H. Lampe, *The Seal of the Spirit*, London–New York 1951; F. Gruenagel, ed., *Was ist Taufe?*, Stuttgart 1951; M. Barth, *Die Taufe—ein Sakrament?*, Zollikon–Zurich

cally justified? We may have doubts when we consider that Jesus himself, and even the disciples in the pre-Easter period —according to the synoptic gospels, John 4:2 suggests otherwise—did not baptize. Moreover, the commandment of the Lord after Easter to baptize does not, in the view of many exegetical scholars, give any clear evidence, since Mark 16:15 f. comes from the "longer ending" added at a later stage to the gospel, John 3:5 is not definitely authentic and the end of Matthew's gospel, precisely in its trinitarian form, is based in the view of many exegetes, including leading Catholic scholars (Schmid, Schnackenburg, Vögtle), on a tradition or a practice of the community. It is certainly curious that apart from these passages there is no reference in the whole apostolic period to baptism as having been instituted by Jesus.

But this fact does not exhaust historical consideration of the matter. Even critical exegetes like Bultmann are nowadays of the opinion that there was never a time right at the beginning of the Church when there was no baptism, an assumption which was formerly made in certain quarters. It is evident that the early Church began to baptize very shortly after Easter. It is true that nothing is told us of the baptism of the apostles themselves, apart from the fact that several disciples of Jesus had been baptized by John and that others, Paul in particular, were baptized immediately after their conversion

1951; J. Schneider, *Baptism and Church in the New Testament*, London 1957; A. Benoît, *Le baptême chrétien au 2e siècle des Pères*, Paris 1953; H. Schlier, *Die Zeit der Kirche*, Freiburg 1956, 47–56, 107–129; B. Neunheuser, *Baptism and Confirmation*, London–New York–Freiburg 1964; J. Jeremias, *Infant Baptism in the first four centuries*, London 1960–Philadelphia 1961; also: *Origins of Infant Baptism*, Naperville, Illinois 1963; A. Stenzel, *Die Taufe. Eine genetische Erklärung der Taufliturgie*, Innsbruck 1958; A. Gilmore, ed., *Christian Baptism. A Fresh Attempt to Understand the Rite in terms of Scripture, History and Theology*, London–Valley Forge, Pa. 1959; P.-Th Camelot, *Spiritualité du baptême*, Paris 1960; H. Mentz, *Taufe und Kirche in ihrem ursprünglichen Zusammenhang*, Munich 1960; E. Käsemann, *Essays on NT themes*, London–Naperville, Illinois 1964, 149–168; G. Delling, *Die Zueignung des Heils in der Taufe*, Berlin 1961; *Die Taufe im NT*, Berlin 1963; K. Aland, *Did the early Church baptize infants?*, London 1963; G. R. Beasley-Murray, *Baptism in the NT*, London 1962–New York 1961.

(Acts 9:18; cf. I Cor. 12:13). But the testimony of Paul is of prime importance here. In the spring of 56 or 55 or perhaps even 54, in all probability, Paul wrote from Ephesus (I Cor. 16:8) to the community at Corinth: "For by *one* Spirit we were all *baptized* (ἐβαπτίσθημεν) *into one body*—Jews or Greeks, slaves or free—and all were made to drink of *one* Spirit" (I Cor. 12:13). This testimony takes us back biographically to somewhere around the year 33, that is, the time immediately after Jesus' death. This statement is confirmed in Romans (written probably in Corinth in spring 56 or 57): "Do you not know that all of us who have been baptized into Christ Jesus were baptized into his death?" (Rom. 6:3). There seems to be a problem here, of reconciling on the one hand the fact that Jesus gave no historically verifiable commandment to baptize and on the other the fact that at no time, at the very beginnings of the Church, was there no baptism. What are the roots of baptism?

The roots of Christian baptism, according to all the evidence we have, lie not in the hellenistic but in the Judaic sphere, and the gospels themselves point to the prototype: the baptism of John. It is characteristic of John's baptism that it is conditioned by eschatological expectation, that it is the call to repentance, that it takes place through the baptizer, not through the baptized, that it only happens once rather than repeatedly, that it is not the foundation of a sect but is demanded for the whole people. It is no wonder that the young community of Christ, filled with the Spirit, saw themselves as the fulfilment of John's eschatological expectation of the coming of a Messiah and the creation of a pure people of God.

The clear parallels between the baptism of John and Christian baptism make any comparison with the immersions of atonement of the Qumran community pale into insignificance, not so much because the links between John and the Dead Sea sects have still not been conclusively proved, but above all because the self-immersion in Qumran (a repeated and esoterically exclusive immersion) was practised on ritual rather than eschatological grounds. The parallels to the Jewish baptism of proselytes are also very slight, not so much because there is no clear evidence of these baptisms before A.D. 80 (though they may have occurred), but above all because these baptisms had no eschatological character and were principally the ritual and legal occasion of the reception of the individual into the community. At most the baptism of proselytes could have had a secondary influence on the development of Christian baptism; but the latter seems overall to have been a completely original creation of John, who was not for nothing called "the Baptist".

This name was apparently invented for John the forerunner and used exclusively for him. The noun τὸ βάπτισμα is found solely in Christian usage. The verb βαπτίζειν (meaning "to immerse repeatedly" in secular Greek) is used in the New Testament solely in the technical sense of baptism. The associated word ὁ βαπτισμός is, however, only used for ritual washings. This distinctive use of particular words is an indication of the special character of baptism.

That Jesus was baptized by John (Mk. 1:9–11 par.) is generally agreed even by the most critical exegesis. The considerable importance of this fact for the concept of baptism, is that Jesus thereby approved the prophetic activity of John. He himself follows the Baptist's eschatological call to penitence and gives it a radical basis in his preaching of the dawning reign of God, and his demands that all men should subject themselves in faith to the will of God. In this way the community is convinced of the fact that Jesus approved this "baptism of repentance for the forgiveness of sins" (Mk. 1:4), by being baptized himself and subsequently confirming this divine mission of the Baptist (cf. Mk. 11:27–33) to seal willing men for the new people of God by this sign of repentance and forgiveness of sin. In John's gospel this is expressed in the idea that Jesus himself, or at any rate his disciples, baptized (3:22; 4:2).

The community baptizes, therefore, in memory not only of John's baptism, but also in memory of Jesus himself, who himself approved and accepted this baptism. Easter then gave this baptism a completely new meaning: Jesus is now the risen Messiah and Lord, and the action of the Baptist appears as no more than a provisional preparation. Eschatological salvation has become reality through the death and resurrection of Jesus, and although baptism still remains indeed a "bap-

tism of repentance for the forgiveness of sins" it takes on a
new meaning because "God has made him (Jesus) both
Lord and Christ" (Acts 2:36). Repentance must now mean
a turning to *Christ,* and the forgiveness of sins reveals that
Christ has now the authority to do this; for God *through
Christ* has given man the promised salvation, has created the
new eschatological community of salvation and bestowed on
it his Holy Spirit.

So now baptism is administered "in the name of Jesus", as
Acts (2:38; 8:16; 10:48) and Paul (I Cor. 1:13–15; Gal.
3:27; Rom. 6:3) equally report. This distinguishes the baptism of the Christian community from the baptism of John,
or baptism of proselytes or in the Qumran community, to say
nothing of parallels in other non-biblical religions. In the
phrase "in the name of Jesus", the word "name" is a legal
concept, signifying authority and competence. By being baptized in the name of Jesus, a person becomes a subject of
Jesus, and is committed to the rule and to the care of the
risen Lord. He becomes the property of the risen Lord and
has a share in him, in his life, his Spirit, his Sonship of God.
Thus the trinitarian formula reported only by Matthew
(28:19) is an expansion of the true content of the
christological formula.

Baptism, whatever historical view we take of the commandment to baptize, is therefore far from being a product of the
imagination, an invention or an arbitrary act on the part of
the community. The community believes, on the contrary,
that it is fulfilling its Lord's will—whether a specific injunc-
tion on his part had been made or not—by baptizing in memory of the action of John the Baptist, as approved by Jesus, in
memory of Jesus' baptism itself, in response not to an explicit
command but to Jesus' preaching as a whole, which called
men to repentance and faith and promised the forgiveness of
sins and salvation. The young community baptizes according
to the Lord's intentions, in fulfilment of his will and in response to his word, and baptizes in his name, in his authority,
according to his command. The central feature of baptism is
"his name", into which men are "immersed", in which men
are "baptized". In Jesus the reign of God has already begun,
in him had been given the call to a radical decision of faith in

God and his reign, in him man is challenged, in opposition to the law, to fulfil his will in love of God and his neighbour. In him God's reign, God's challenge, God's will, God's word and hence God himself has been revealed. This is the significance of the trinitarian baptismal formula; baptism is given in the name of him, in whom God himself through the Spirit has his dwelling among us.

In this way man is taken up into the eschatological saving event, or rather he enters voluntarily into it. The visible sign, like the proclaimed word, makes this saving event present for the believer; and the visible sign is itself principally made up of the proclaimed and administered word, which is addressed, not to water which is to be "consecrated" but to the believer himself. Baptism is not a sign without words, but a word-sign, not a magical or cultic action, but an action which proclaims and which demands the response of faith. In the early days baptism probably always meant total immersion. This gave real and visual expression to what baptism originally meant: a bath of purification from the guilt of sin, undertaken in penitence, an indispensable condition of entry into the holy eschatological community and into fellowship with the Lord. "And there is salvation in no one else, for there is no other name under heaven given among men by which we must be saved" (Acts 4:12). "He who believes and is baptized will be saved; but he who does not believe will be condemned" (Mk. 16:16).

We can also see from this that baptism by itself is of no value. Baptism and metanoia, baptism and faith go together. Faith alone is not the basis of baptism; baptism is more than a sign of faith and confession, designed merely to confirm faith. Conversely, baptism alone is not the basis of faith; faith is not the natural consequence or the automatic fruit of baptism. The New Testament does not allow us to take either view. The real reason for this is that faith and baptism do not have their bases in themselves, but alike in the saving act of God in Christ; the eschatological saving act includes and provides a basis for both. On this common basis the two are linked: baptism comes from faith, and faith leads to baptism. In more precise terms: on the one hand *faith*, as man's act of radical self-offering and trusting acceptance of grace, is a *con-*

dition of baptism. This act of full personal self-giving to God and the acceptance of his grace is required for baptism and made possible by God's grace itself. On the other hand, *baptism* as the visual sign and testimony of faith and as the guarantee and presentation of God's justifying grace is a *consequence* of faith. From the human viewpoint baptism is the individual, spiritual and corporeal visible expression of repentance and trust, of self-giving and confession of faith; the individual visibly demonstrates and testifies to his faith in the presence of the community before entering the community. From the divine standpoint baptism is the visible sign of grace, directed towards this one individual person, and the guarantee and presentation of God's justifying grace proclaimed and given to the believer.

It is then an essential feature of Christian baptism that it is not only a human action, an act of faith and confession which man must decide upon, but also an action of God. The believer does not baptize himself, but offers himself for baptism. And according to the testimony of the New Testament he receives in baptism something he could not win for himself, something that he can only accept with empty but open hands from God's grace, in faith: the forgiveness of sins, the sealing with the name of Jesus as a sign of allegiance, the giving of the Spirit. At the same time Paul warns us that baptism has no magic effect and cannot of itself guarantee salvation. "Therefore let anyone who thinks that he stands take heed lest he fall" (I Cor. 10:12)—this is his admonition to the enthusiasts of Corinth, reminding them of the Jews in the wilderness who were baptized into Moses in the cloud and in the sea, and yet were overthrown (10:1–11).

The origins of the idea, which Paul also mentions, that baptism gives a share in the death and resurrection of Christ, is a matter of controversy. In the hellenistic world the fact that baptism could be seen as a rite of initiation into the community led to parallels being drawn between it and hellenistic initiation rites and the idea of a dying and a rising again with the divinity. But nowadays more attention is paid to the Old Testament and Judaic background of the idea. Thus in a more profound way baptism is seen in connection with the eschatological saving event of the death and resurrection of

Christ. "Do you not know that all of us who have been baptized into Christ Jesus were baptized into his death? We were buried therefore with him by baptism into death, so that as Christ was raised from the dead by the glory of the Father, we too might walk in newness of life. For if we have been united with him in a death like his, we shall certainly be united with him in a resurrection like his. We know that our old self was crucified with him so that the sinful body might be destroyed, and we might no longer be enslaved to sin" (Rom. 6:3–6). In this way the new life is present as well as future: baptism is a realization of the saving action in Christ. The future is already a present which makes demands on us: "So you also must consider yourselves dead to sin and alive to God in Christ Jesus" (Rom. 6:11). He who is in Christ is already "a new creation" (II Cor. 5:17). Thus in the Pauline tradition (Tit. 3:5; cf. I Pet. 1:3 and 23) as well as in the Johannine tradition (Jn. 3:3–5) baptism can be seen as a rebirth. Christian existence is conditioned in a new way by the once-for-all (Rom. 6:10) saving event of Christ's death and resurrection. But precisely because it has a share in the death and resurrection of Christ, our baptized state is not something final and assured, but is movement towards its goal, our own resurrection (cf. Phil. 3:10–14).

But baptism is never just an individual act concerning only Christ and the man baptized. A man does not baptize himself, he is baptized in the presence of the community and for the community. By being baptized, he becomes a member of the community; by having his sins forgiven, he is included in the communion of saints; by being sealed with the name of Jesus as a sign of his allegiance, he becomes a member of the community which as a whole owes its allegiance to Jesus; by receiving the Spirit, he becomes a living stone in the spiritual house of the community; by sharing in Christ's death and resurrection, he becomes a part of the post-Easter fellowship of those who believe and love. In this way baptism is the entry into the community; baptism is the *seminarium ecclesiae*. This is why public confession of faith is a part of baptism; credal statements originally belonged to the rite of baptism, and only later did this baptismal symbol become distinct from it.

The believer becomes a member of the community through

baptism. This indicates that entry into the community is not
like joining a club, something a man can do on his own decision, on the basis of his own faith, as it were. Nor is one born
into the community; membership of it is not a kind of citizenship. True, man's decision to enter the community must be a
free decision in faith (or in the case of infant baptism he
must ratify his entry into the community in some way subsequently, by a conscious act of faith). But this action is only
possible in response to God's call. The man who freely offers
himself for baptism has been drawn and is inspired by God's
grace. The believer does not therefore make himself a
member of the community, but he is made a member. What
baptism expresses is that men do not have to create the community by their own efforts; they can only help to build it up
because it already exists. On the other hand the "visible"
word of baptism unmistakably expresses the fact that this
event of grace is directed towards this one man and no
other, that membership of the community has been granted
to him and no other.

Baptism is therefore not only a condition but also a guarantee of being made a part of the Church. Man is removed
from the loneliness of his own ego, and finds a home in the
community. On the basis of this sign he can be sure and
proud of his membership. By the sign of water the word of
grace which is effective in him is confirmed. Baptism gives
such a radically new character to man, that he can only receive it once. Baptism cannot be revoked or repealed or removed; a man can only acknowledge his baptism or deny it.
Even those who leave the Church retain a continuing relationship, albeit a wrong one, with the Church; if they return, they
do not have to be baptized again. The same baptism which is
the basis of a man's certainty that he is a member of the
Church is the basis for his re-acceptance.

Paul, in a manner characteristic of him, goes on to give a
new dimension to the idea that men become members of the
Church through baptism; we find this already introduced in
Galatians. Here Paul explains how the reign of the law was
ended through Christ and faith in him (3:1–25). What does
this mean for the believer? All those who have become sons
of God through faith in Jesus Christ (3:26) have put on

Christ in baptism: "For as many of you as were baptized into Christ have put on Christ" (3:27). This means for the community the enriching experience of a new fellowship in which all natural differences lose their meaning: "There is neither Jew nor Greek, there is neither slave nor free, there is neither male nor female; for you are all one in Christ Jesus" (3:28). The close links between those who have been baptized, indeed their unity, is summed up in the words "one in Christ Jesus". The word "body" is not used here; but we are surely reminded of a similar passage, also concerned with baptism, where the word is explicitly used: "For by one Spirit we were all baptized into one body—Jews or Greeks, slaves or free—and all were made to drink of one Spirit" (I Cor. 12:13).

"In the human nature which He united to Himself, the Son of God redeemed man and transformed him into a new creation (cf. Gal. 6:15; II Cor. 5:17) by overcoming death through His own death and resurrection. By communicating His Spirit to His brothers, called together from all peoples, Christ made them mystically into His own body. In that body, the life of Christ is poured into the believers, who, through the sacraments, are united in a hidden and real way to Christ who suffered and was glorified. Through baptism we are formed in the likeness of Christ: 'For in one Spirit we were all baptized into one body' (I Cor. 12:13). In this sacred rite, a union with Christ's death and resurrection is both symbolized and brought about: 'For we were buried with him by means of Baptism into death'. And if 'we have been united with him in the likeness of his death, we shall be so in the likeness of his resurrection also' (Rom. 6:4–5)." (CE 7).

We must now examine this conception of the community, of the Church as a body, which forms the background to Paul's understanding of baptism.

2. UNITED IN THE FELLOWSHIP
OF THE LORD'S SUPPER

No Church without the Lord's Supper:[30] can we be certain

30 On the doctrine of the Lord's Supper: In addition to the relevant dictionary articles (esp. LThK: H. Schürmann, Abendmahl,

that right from the beginning the last meal of Jesus with his
disciples was repeated? We should first note the antiquity of
the Last Supper tradition, which has four variant versions: I
Cor. 11:23–25; Mk. 14; 22–25; Mt. 26:26–29; Lk.

Einsetzungsbericht; J. Betz, *Eucharistie*; RGG: E. Schweizer–H.
Grass–E. Sommerlath–W. Kreck, *Abendmahl*; EKL: W. Marxsen–W. Pannenberg, *Abendmahl*), the biblical theologies and the
textbooks on dogmatics and the history of dogma, see the following more recent monographs: E. Gaugler, *Das Abendmahl im NT*,
Basle 1943; O. Cullmann, *Early Christian Worship*, London 1953–
Naperville, Illinois 1956; *La foi et le culte dans l'Eglise primitive*,
Neuchâtel 1955; G. Söhngen, *Das sakramentale Wesen des Mes-
sopfers*, Essen 1946; F. J. Leenhardt, *Le sacrement de la sainte
cène*, Neuchâtel 1948; *Ceci est mon corps*, Neuchâtel 1955;
W. Marxsen, *Die Einsetzungsberichte zum Abendmahl*, Diss. Kiel
1949; *Das Abendmahl als christologisches Problem*, Gütersloh[2]
1965; H. de Lubac, *Corpus mysticum. Eucharistie et l'Eglise au
Moyen Age*, Paris[2] 1949; K. Rahner, *Die vielen Messen und das
eine Opfer*, Freiburg 1951; *Theological Investigations IV*, London–
Baltimore 1966, 260–320; A. J. B. Higgins, *The Lord's Supper*,
London 1952; H. Schürmann, *Der Paschamahlbericht Lk 22, 7–18*,
Münster 1953; *Der Einsetzungsbericht Lk 22, 19–20*, Münster
1955; *Jesu Abschiedsrede Lk 22, 21–38*, Münster 1957; E. L. Mas-
call, *Corpus Christi*, London–New York 1953; H. Lessig, *Die
Abendmahlsprobleme im Lichte der ntl. Forschung seit 1900*, Diss.
Bonn 1953; F. Heiler, *Das Sakrament der kirchlichen Einheit*,
Basle 1954; R. Erni–H. Haag, etc., *Das Opfer der Kirche. Ex-
egetische, dogmatische und pastoral-theologische Studien zum
Verständnis der Messe*, Lucerne 1954; A. Tamborini, *L'eucaristia*,
Milan 1954; J. Betz, *Die Eucharistie in der Zeit der griechischen
Väter*, Freiburg 1955 ff.; E. Bizer–W. Kreck, *Die Abendmahl-
lehre in den reformatorischen Bekenntnisschriften*, Munich 1955;
A. Piolanti, *Il misterio eucaristico*, Florence 1955; N. Moccia,
*L'istituzione della S. Eucharistia secondo il metodo della storia
delle forme*, Naples 1955; H. C. Schmidt-Lauber, *Die Eucharistie
als Entfaltung der Verba Testamenti*, Kassel 1957; R. Koch, *Erbe
und Auftrag. Das Abendmahlsgespräch in der Theologie des 20.
Jhs.*, Munich 1957; A. Piolanti ed., *Eucharistia*, Rome 1958;
G. Bornkamm, *Studien zu Antike und Urchristentum II*, Munich
1959, 138–176; M. Thurian, *Eucharistic Memorial*, Richmond
1961; H. Schillebeeckx, *Christ, the Sacrament of Encounter with
God*, London and NY 1963; P. Neuenzeit, *Das Herrenmahl.
Studien zur paulin. Eucharistieauffassung*, Munich 1960; B. Neun-
heuser ed., *Opfer Christi und Opfer der Kirche*, Düsseldorf 1960;
J. Jeremias, *The Eucharistic Words of Jesus*, Oxford 1955–New
York 1966; E. Käsemann, *Essays on NT Themes*, London–
Naperville, Illinois 1964, 108–135; *Pro Mundi Vita. Festschrift*

22:15-20. Apart from the fact that the passage in Matthew seems quite clearly to be an edition of Mark's account, there is considerable controversy about the priority of these texts and the historical development of the tradition. At all events it is clear that the oldest biblical version of the Last Supper narrative (and the oldest reported direct saying of Jesus himself) which we possess, in Corinthians, dates fairly probably from the years 54–56. This passage also refers to the fact that Paul handed on this tradition to the Corinthians at the beginning of his missionary activity in Corinth (probably in A.D. 49). But Paul states that this tradition comes directly from the Lord himself, and that he was its origin. Whether we think that Paul's account originates with the community in Damascus (Gal. 1:17) or in Jerusalem (Gal. 1:18), or at the latest in Antioch, the account which he gave to the Corinthians could at all events have been compared with the account of eye-witnesses who were still alive (among others probably Peter, with whom one part of the Corinthian community had a special connection, I Cor. 1:12). Paul himself lived for many years with members of the Jerusalem community (Barnabas, Mark, Silas) and took part in the Lord's Supper in various communities. His account must have agreed in its essentials with those of eye-witnesses, and was derived either indirectly or probably directly from the earliest community itself. The more strongly semitic flavour of

zum Eucharistischen Weltkongress 1960, ed. by the theological faculty of the University of Munich; P. Meinhold–E. Iserloh, *Abendmahl und Opfer,* Stuttgart 1960; M. Schmaus ed., *Aktuelle Fragen zur Eucharistie,* Munich 1960; D. C. Fandall, *The Essence of the Eucharistic Sacrifice,* River Forest, Ill. 1961; G. Sola, *Tractatus dogmaticus de eucharistia,* Barcelona 1961; H. U. von Balthasar, *Sponsa Verbi,* Einsiedeln 1961, 502–524; The Sartory, ed., *Die Eucharistie im Verständnis Konfessionen,* Recklingshause 1961; E. Schweizer, *Neotestamentica* Zurich 1963, 344–396; V. Vajta, *Kirche und Abendmahl,* Berlin 1963; J. Galot, *Eucharistie vivante,* Bruges 1953; J.–M. R. Tillard, *L'eucharistie, pâques de l'Eglise,* Paris 1964; A. Winklhofer, *Eucharistie als Osterfeier,* Frankfurt/Main 1964; W. L. Boelens, *Die Arnoldshainer Abendsmahlsthesen. Die Suche nach einem Abendsmahlkonsens in der Evangelischen Kirche in Deutschland 1947–1957 und eine Würdigung aus katholischer Sicht,* Assen 1964; O. Koch, *Gegenwart oder Vergegenwärtigung Christi im Abendmahl,* Munich 1965.

Mark's account has led exegetes to see its wording as still closer to the original than Paul's. The differences between the Pauline and Marcan accounts in particular are too great for us to assume a common Greek source. On the other hand the agreement between them in content is so great that we must assume a common (Aramaic or Hebrew) source. Naturally the reports were recast, particularly under the influence of their liturgical use (note the command to repeat the Lord's actions, which is strikingly absent from the Mark-Matthew report, yet appears twice in Paul). But the essential kernel of the reports is part of a unanimous tradition.

It is impossible to go into the extremely complex exegetical problems of tradition history here: The Lucan short text in Codex D is nowadays almost always regarded as secondary; far-reaching conclusions based on this short text are therefore irrelevant. There is no evidence for two different types of Lord's Supper (Jerusalemic and Pauline, or Jerusalemic and Galilean). The hypothesis that the Lord's Supper was celebrated in the hellenistic communities as a meal in memory of the dead has also now been largely abandoned. As regards the lack of any account of the Last Supper in John various theories have been put forward (the widespread esotericism of the time which sought to protect sacred formulas from profanation, etc.). The view that Jesus' words about the living bread, the combination of the skandalon of the incarnation (Jn. 6:51–58), are an editorial addition is one that has proved untenable (cf. also 19:34b; 21:13; I Jn. 5:6–8). Many parts of the accounts of the Last Supper which used to be regarded sceptically have received new validation through the discovery of the existence at that time of a "community of the new covenant" in the Qumran texts, which also held meals with the blessing of bread and wine (cf. Dam. 20:12; 1 QS 6:4–6).

The meal of Jesus which the various witnesses report was the last of a long series of daily meals which Jesus shared with his disciples. For Orientals shared meals have always signified peace, trust, community of living. But the shared meal with Jesus, as all the gospels agree in emphasizing, was more than that; he shared meals with tax-collectors, sinners and outcasts, as a sign of the reign of God which had begun and of the love which it demanded. But this last meal was something special; according to the synoptics it was a ritual

Passover meal (John is different here), or—perhaps one night earlier (according to John)—a festive farewell meal, which was already overshadowed by thoughts of the Passover and at all events was celebrated with a view to the coming kingdom of God. Whether it was a Passover meal or not, Jesus' particular words over the bread and wine fitted easily into the ritually ordered course of the Jewish meal: the words over the bread recalling the grace before the main meal, at which the father of the house would speak the words of praise over the loaves of bread, break off a piece for each and distribute it; the words over the wine recalling the prayer of thanks which the father of the house would speak over the cup. It is probable, therefore, that Jesus took a form which already had religious importance and gave it new content. In this way his words were immediately comprehensible to the disciples; he interpreted bread and wine as himself, meaning his own person: This is my body, this is my blood. Knowing of his coming death, which he was now confronting, he speaks of himself as a sacrifice, just as the unleavened bread is broken, so my body will be broken; just as the red wine is poured out, so my blood will be poured out. For what purpose? All four texts agree that Jesus' death is an atonement and is the founding of a new covenant. "Body" is already seen in Mark (Matthew), as a parallel to "wine-blood", as the material for sacrifice (i.e. "flesh"); this is made clearer in Paul by the words "for you", and Luke adds "given for you". "Blood" is already described in Mark (Matthew) as "blood of the new covenant, which is poured out for many" (Matthew: "for the forgiveness of sins"); Paul and Luke even stress the "new covenant in my blood". The Jews regarded every death, but particularly an innocent death, innocent blood, as having the character of atonement. Jesus was bound to see his innocent sufferings in this way.

Two fundamental Old Testament ideas are here referred to. One is the idea of the sacrifice of the covenant in Exodus: "And Moses took the blood and threw it upon the people, and said, 'Behold the *blood of the Covenant* which the Lord has made with you in accordance with all these words'" (Ex. 24:8); thereupon followed a meal on Sinai for Moses, Aaron and the elders: "They beheld God, and ate and drank"

(24:11). The phrase *"new* covenant" refers to Jeremiah 31:31–34. The second idea is that of the atoning sufferings of the servant of God in Isaiah 53: ". . . because he *poured out* his soul to death, and was numbered with the transgressors; yet he bore the sin of many, and made intercession for the transgressors" (53:12). Jesus' death therefore appears as the saving event of him who as the servant of God will make atonement for the many (i.e. for the totality, which embraces the many), will establish the new covenant by his blood and will bring the beginning of final redemption. The disciples therefore appear as the representatives of the new people of the covenant.

But Jesus' words are more than a parable, more than teaching. He does not only speak, as he speaks he gives gifts to be eaten and drunk. When at a Jewish meal the gifts were distributed while the blessing was being said, those eating and drinking also shared in the blessing. By not only speaking the blessing, but giving to his disciples the broken bread and the red wine as his flesh and blood, for them to eat and drink, Jesus was indicating that he was giving them a share in his sacrificed body and outpoured blood, a share in the power of his death to make atonement and establish the new covenant, a share in the saving work of his death. It is a familiar idea to the Oriental that eating and drinking communicated divine gifts; eschatological imagery, particularly in the New Testament itself, draws frequently on the images of bread, cup, wine, the meal of salvation which communicates the saving gifts of God. Thus this last meal is related both to the imminent death of Jesus and to the future kingdom of God, presented in the image of the eschatological shared meal.

Throughout the whole New Testament Christ's death on the cross is seen as an atoning sacrifice for sins, a sacrifice offered by Christ to the Father, or offered by the Father himself through the giving of his Son on the cross. This unique sacrifice cannot therefore be interpreted in an Old Testament or pagan sense. This sacrifice is not intended to pacify and influence an angry God. It is not God who must be reconciled, but man; and the reconciliation depends entirely on God's initiative: "All this is from God, who through Christ reconciled us to himself" (II Cor. 5:18). This reconciliation is not effected by removing personal hostility, but by removing the real basis of enmity between God and man, which is sin. Man can only *receive* this reconciliation (Rom. 5:11) and accept it (II Cor. 5:20). Christ's death is the end of all sacrifices made by men to appease God. The sacrifice of Christ is not an offering of outward gifts, fruits or animals; Christ sacrifices himself, makes a personal offering of himself (cf. the word "himself" Phil. 2:7 f.). Christ's death is the end of all sacrifices of atonement. The Epistle to the Hebrews takes this knowledge, which runs through the whole New Testament, and gives it new clarity by describing Jesus' sacrifice as the perfect sacrifice *once for all* (ἐφάπαξ), which unlike the Old Testament sacrifice makes all other sacrifices of atonement superfluous. The glorified Lord does not sacrifice himself again; as he who was sacrificed on the cross once for all, he is the eternal high priest, who constantly intercedes with God for his people.

Jesus' unique sacrifice has a continuing effect on the community he founded. God gives the community a share in the sacrifice of atonement which Christ achieved for it once for all. Christ gives himself in the Lord's Supper to the community which he won through his own blood. And in the different gifts of bread and wine he gives himself as the one who sacrificed his life for it. By giving it a share in his unique sacrifice of atonement and hence in his victory, he includes the community in the new covenant, founded by the sacrifice of his blood for the many. This is why sacrificial terminology is used in the reports of the Last Supper. The Lord's Supper gives a share in the unique sacrifice of Christ on the cross and is therefore not a repetition of or addition to or a surpassing of this unique sacrifice of atonement. The Lord's Supper repeatedly points to the unique sacrifice of Christ's cross, makes it present once more and allows it to become effective. The gifts of the Lord's Supper signify and are Christ's dedication of his sacrifice to his community.

But in the light of Christ's sacrifice the community is also required to make sacrifices; again, not external offerings, but the offering and sacrifice of man himself is required; not a material but a spiritual sacrifice of praise and thanks, of faith and obedience and love: an offering of praise and thanks which is not limited to the particular act of worship of the congregation, but must be a daily offering in everyday life. The community is not thereby putting a second sacrifice of atonement beside that of Christ, but gives praise and thanks for Jesus' unique sacrifice, in which it has a share through the Lord's Supper.

Easter gave the disciples the certainty that the crucified

Christ was alive and had risen, and that the glorified Lord lived on among them. Easter gave them the impetus to begin their shared meals again, and they celebrate these occasions in the assurance that the risen Christ will make good his promise to be present among those who are gathered together in his name (cf. Mt. 18:20). The meals previously shared with Jesus now have a new meaning. The new fellowship which met to share meals was according to the New Testament characterized by eschatological joy (cf. especially Acts 2:46): joy in the experience of this new fellowship, joy especially in the awareness of fellowship with the glorified Christ who would be present in the meal of the community, joy above all in their excited expectation of the approaching kingdom of God.

In the context of the present study it is not important to examine in detail the original form of Jesus' words at the Last Supper and the precise way in which they developed, a subject which because of the very complex exegetical problems involved has led to highly conflicting opinions. It is impossible to say precisely to what extent Jesus expressed in his words at the Last Supper the idea of the coming of the consummated reign of God, the idea of handing on to his disciples the power of his death to make atonement and establish the new covenant, the idea of the coming shared meal in the future kingdom. The remarks above were intended to show that there are sufficient grounds for assuming an essential continuity, however we understand it, between the Last Supper and the meal celebrated by the community after Easter. This indeed is the only satisfactory explanation of why the apostles repeated this meal and why the later communities referred to the actions of Jesus at the Last Supper as the pattern and authority for what they did. The Lord's Supper is not an invention or an arbitrary act on the part of the community. The community is, on the contrary, convinced that it is fulfilling the Lord's will—however we like to regard the historicity of the commandment to repeat his action—and responding to his words by continuing the idea of the shared meal with him, the Lord's Supper. Our main purpose must therefore be to find out what theological meaning was attributed to the Lord's Supper in the preaching of the early Church. In all four variants of the traditions we see three constant motifs which from the first, whether explicitly or not, were connected and which are developed theologically in the New Testament itself along three different lines:

1. The perspective of the *past:* the Lord's Supper is a meal of *recollection* and *thanksgiving.* In the Lord's Supper the community always looks back to something that has happened. The Lord's Supper itself, and not just the words which may have been proclaimed at the same time, is a proclamation of the death of Jesus: "For as often as you eat this bread and drink the cup, you proclaim the Lord's death" (I Cor. 11:26). But this death which is proclaimed is always seen as the death of the risen Lord (cf. I Cor. 15). And the death of the risen Lord is proclaimed in all four reports as having occurred "for" the participants in the meal: in this way the saving fruits of this death are assured and dedicated to them. The Lord's Supper as celebrated after Easter was never a meal of mourning, it was a meal of joy.

2. The perspective of the *present:* the Lord's Supper is a meal of fellowship and of the covenant. In the Lord's Supper the community looks at the present. In the covenantal blood of Jesus' death the new covenant has been established; he himself is present again in the Lord's Supper. At each meal the covenant of God with the community is proclaimed and sealed anew. This covenant is revealed in the fellowship of those who share the meal, not with one who is dead and gone, but with one who is alive and present. Through his call to metanoia Jesus had summoned those who had fallen away from God to a new fellowship with God, and by eating and drinking with sinners and outcasts he revealed God's mercy and grace. And God showed his approval of his Messiah who was a friend of sinners by raising him from humiliation and glorifying him. In the Lord's Supper the community also recalls those earlier meals which Jesus shared, while their fellowship with the glorified Lord is experienced at the same time, as a fellowship among all those taking part. The Lord's Supper as celebrated after Easter was not a solitary meal of the individual, but a meal of the community held in love: a love-feast.

3. The perspective of the *future:* the Lord's Supper is an

anticipation of the eschatological meal of the Messiah. In the Lord's Supper the community looks towards the future. In addition to proclaiming the death of Jesus it also proclaims his second coming: "For as often as you eat this bread and drink the cup, you proclaim the Lord's death *until he comes*" (I Cor. 11:26). According to the synoptics Jesus will "not drink again of the fruit of the vine until that day when I drink it new in the kingdom of God" (Mk. 14:25; Mt. 26:29; Lk. 22:18). The idea, widespread in later Judaism, of the expectation of an eschatological meal is taken up here, just as in Acts 2:46 the basic mood of the early Christian community at the breaking of bread is described with the typically eschatological word "gladness". Because of the link it provides with the risen, living and perfect Lord, the Lord's Supper becomes for the community the beginning of the fulfilment of the eschatological meal. Christ's presence in the Lord's Supper is the presence of something that is to come. In this idea there may be echoes of the old Aramaic cry "Marana-tha" (I Cor. 16:22; cf. Didache 10:6), "Our Lord, come!" The Lord's Supper as celebrated after Easter was not a meal looking back in memory of the dead, but a meal which looked forward to the future, full of confidence and hope.

We have used here the term "Lord's Supper", because it is equally apposite for all the three perspectives mentioned above, and is, moreover, the term used in the oldest account of the occasion which we possess (I Cor. 11:20: κυριακὸν δεῖπνον). Whether the "breaking of bread" (Acts 2:42, 46; 20:7, 11) is a technical (esoteric?) term for the Lord's Supper or not is disputed.

The expression "agape" is not used for a meal (love-feast) in the New Testament, apart from Jude 12, though it is used by Ignatius. As we see from the synoptics and Paul, the Lord's Supper was combined with an ordinary meal. The original sequence seems to have been: words over the bread—ordinary meal—words over the cup (cf. I Cor. 11:23–26, which describes the situation at around A.D. 55). The second phase of development was to eat the ordinary meal by itself first (Mk. 14:22–24?; Didache 9 f., in the first half of the second century). The third phase was the complete separation of the Lord's Supper and the ordinary meal (cf. Justin, around 150). The term agape was now used for the common meal of Christians, an expression of brotherly love, companionship and generosity which was arranged by more well-to-do members of the community.

The equally pertinent name *"eucharistia"* (thanksgiving) is not used in Scripture for the Lord's Supper, but in Didache 9 and 10, and by Ignatius and Justin. In the second century the word was used to refer to the great prayer of thanks in the Lord's Supper for the saving acts of God, which culminated in the account of its institution, directly followed by the distribution of the gifts to all the community. At this time the Lord's Supper still consisted simply of a far from rigid form of the eucharistic prayer which provided the kernel of the later "canon of the Mass", although it was then broken up by the addition of petitions (*memento vivorum, mortuorum, martyrum*) which obscured the essentials of the original. The oldest fixed formula of the eucharistic prayer in its original unified state that we have in the Roman liturgy comes from Hippolytus of Rome (*circa* 215). From early times a service of the word was often combined with the Lord's Supper, as we can see from Justin.

Finally the name "Mass"; this is easily the youngest and by far the least suitable expression for the Lord's Supper. The late Latin word *"missa"* means *"missio, dimissio"*, a dismissal after a meeting. *Missa* became the term in ecclesiastical usage for the final blessing, then at the end of the fourth century for the blessing in general and then, since every act of worship included a blessing, for any act of worship. From the middle of the fifth century, the word *missa* came to be used for the eucharistic celebration in particular, and from the sixth century onwards it became the usual term and largely superseded other terms (*eucharistia, oblatio, sacrificium*, etc.). The rite of the Roman Mass went a long way, from the simple and easily comprehensible vernacular house-eucharists of the second century community, to the much more ceremonious but still vernacular basilica Mass of the fifth and sixth centuries, and from there to the Mass or Masses ("read" for the people simultaneously in the same church in unfamiliar Latin) of the High Middle Ages, at which only the priest received the sacrament, and then to the medieval Mass of the Counter-Reformation restored by the Council of Trent. It was left to the Second Vatican Council to go back to the origins of the Mass and to make clear once more the connection between it and the Lord's Supper celebrated in the early Church.[31]

There have been repeated controversies in the history of the Church about the force of "is" in the words "This is my

[31] J. A. Jungmann, *The Mass of the Roman Rite*, New York 1951.

body, this is my blood". Jesus himself, as far as we can judge today, almost certainly never used the word, since the copula was not used in Aramaic. The New Testament nowhere goes into the question of the elements. But from both the Jewish and hellenistic viewpoints there was from the first the possibility of understanding or misunderstanding the Lord's Supper. Jewish thinking, strongly influenced by juridical categories and with a strong aversion to the idea of drinking blood, was in danger of seeing the Lord's Supper as a purely symbolic action. Hellenistic thinking, much more used to natural categories and tending to conceive every power concretely, was in danger of seeing the Lord's Supper as a magic transformation. In fact, the two modes of thought complement and correct one another; from hellenistic thinking we can see that the Lord's Supper is not merely an image for something quite different, which we could equally well have without the image; from Jewish thinking we can realize that the Lord's Supper is not a mysterious natural process which can be described in natural categories. Yet on the one hand Jewish thinking was able to see the Lord's Supper as a making present of Christ and his saving act, since Judaic worship had always celebrated Yahweh's acts not as belonging to the distant past but as something really present. On the other hand hellenistic thinking, and here Paul is an example, was able to confront the danger of a magical misunderstanding, just as John places the clear warning at the end of Jesus' words about the bread of life: "It is the spirit which gives life, the flesh is of no avail; the words that I have spoken to you are spirit and life" (Jn. 6:63).

The *word* is decisive in the Lord's Supper as in baptism. The elements by themselves have no significance, and it is in the light of the word that we should understand the Lord's Supper. The word here has not primarily the function of consecrating and transforming, but of proclaiming and testifying. It is a word which carries the promise of God, it is God's word and as such efficacious, *verbum efficax*. A purely symbolic interpretation of the Lord's Supper is not sufficient, for the words of Jesus, like those of Paul and John, clearly imply more than that. Certainly bread and wine *are* "symbols", but they are symbols *filled with reality*. They are *signs*, but *effective* signs, containing what they represent. But should we go to the opposite extreme and try to understand them in a wholly material and realistic sense? Paul rebukes the self-confident assurance of the Corinthians, who thought these gifts communicated the fullness of salvation and completely removed any possibility of temptation and sin. In John's gospel Jesus rebukes the misunderstanding of the people of Capernaum who took his words about eating flesh and drinking blood in a completely literal sense. What Christ offers is his reality, his self. But for this very reason his gift is not a controllable "something", a magic object, or an autonomous gift quite independent of the giver. His gifts give us a share in the Lord himself; precisely because of this, they are not an assurance against our falling away from him and our consequent rejection by God; they are not guarantees of salvation, but a call to obedience to the Lord, a call which gives us the power to be obedient (cf. I Cor. 10:1–13).

Christ becomes present not through the power of the bread or the wine, but through the word which is proclaimed at the Lord's Supper, the word which is an efficacious act. In the proclaimed word he comes to us himself, he becomes, anew each time, really and spiritually present through the Spirit. Christ is, of course, made present by the word of preaching. But he is present in a particular way in the Lord's Supper, as a bodily presence associated with the corporality of Jesus. And the response of the believer is bodily, total, in a quite different way in the Lord's Supper, namely through eating and drinking in faith. The Lord's Supper is, to use an Augustinian formula, a "visible word" (*verbum visibile*), and in receiving it—much more clearly than with the "audible word" (*verbum audibile* or *sacramentum audibile*)—I can be absolutely certain that it is intended for me and for no one else. Under the forms of bread and wine the Lord reveals his presence for the believer in a visible way, which goes beyond the mere hearing of the word. And by eating and drinking in faith the believer shows that his faith is part of his whole existence, a part not just of his spirit, but of his very flesh and blood. But this is not done by the individual as an individual; it is done by the community as a community. And in this way it is made visibly clear that through the bread and wine the community has a share in the body and blood of Christ, in fact a share in Christ himself, that it lives under the reign and blessing of Christ. In the Lord's Supper the reign of the Kyrios is established and recognized and the community constantly reaffirms its dominion.

The Lord becomes present in a particular way in the Lord's Supper. He is there, if one wishes to use this terminology, in a real presence, a spiritual presence and a personal presence. Bread and wine are the signs of his real and effective presence. In the Lord's Supper I encounter not merely bread and wine, not merely body and blood, but the Lord acting in the present time in the community and thus in me. The giver of the gifts bestows himself on the believer in the gifts he has given, he is at once giver and gift. Obviously the Lord is not present in the Lord's Supper in the way he was present as an historical person on earth, nor is he so completely present as he will be when he comes again as the glorified Lord. But he is present as he who acts through the Lord's Supper in the Spirit, which is his Spirit. The essential thing is our approval and affirmation of the fact that Christ is present and active in a particular way in the Lord's Supper, in the eating and drinking of his body and blood; theological description of how that happens is secondary by comparison. Theological curiosity has always been aroused by the question of "how it happens", but it has always very quickly reached the frontiers of mystery. The presence of Christ is at all events a real and not an apparent presence. But the Lord's Supper is not about a matter of fact, but about an event of grace; not about sacred objects effective of themselves, but about an encounter with a person; not about a miraculous natural process, but about the action of Jesus Christ himself in the faithful gathered together to eat in fellowship and thus in the individual. The offerings should not be dissociated from the event of the Lord's Supper. They do not exist for themselves, to be looked at or marvelled at, but are there for the community's meal, to be eaten and drunk. The Lord's Supper is not, any more than was Jesus' own Last Supper, an individual giving and taking, but a coming together of many people to form a real fellowship of sharers in a meal, for common prayer, for giving, taking and distributing, eating and drinking. The meal is there not for the individual but for the community and therefore for the individual too. If the offerings are taken to an individual, a sick member of the community for example, this is because he is absent through no fault of his own and still remains a member of the fellowship of the meal. "Communion of the sick" is, properly understood, not an individual feeding of the soul as distinct from the communal meal, but an extension of the community's meal and the celebration which accompanies it. The same is true of the sacred species which are reserved in church.

We must receive the Lord himself, by eating and drinking his body and blood, in faith. Without faith no one can receive the blessing of the Lord's Supper. And yet the presence of the Lord in the Lord's Supper does not depend on the faith of the individual. It is not the faith of the recipient, nor the community's confession of faith which makes Christ really present, but the promise and the assurance of the glorified Lord himself, who gives himself in the offerings of bread and wine and who awakens faith through his own word. Man's lack of faith cannot destroy God's promises or make the Lord's presence not happen. But the man who lacks faith eats and drinks not to his salvation, but to his judgment: "Whoever, therefore, eats the bread or drinks the cup of the Lord in an unworthy manner will be guilty of profaning the body and blood of the Lord. Let a man examine himself, and so eat of the bread and drink of the cup. For anyone who eats and drinks without discerning the body (i.e. distinguishing the Lord's body from other food) eats and drinks judgment upon himself" (I Cor. 11:27–29).

Every believer in the community is called upon to eat and drink, to share in offering thanks and praise and petitions. The community constantly receives anew its share in the atoning death of Jesus: "The cup of blessing which we bless, is it not a participation in the blood of Christ?" (I Cor. 10:16). The community is constantly united anew with Christ and with one another: "The bread which we break, is it not a participation in the body of Christ?" (10:16). Paul goes on once again to add a yet more profound dimension here—this is no doubt why he reverses the double formula: "Because there is *one* bread, we who are many are one body, for we all partake of the one bread" (10:17).

The Lord's Supper is then essentially a *fellowship, koinonia, communio,* and in a double sense. First and foremost the Lord's Supper is a *fellowship in Christ:* Christians are called to fellowship with the Son, the Lord (I Cor. 1:9). Communio with the glorified Lord, a profound and an intimate relationship, which Paul expresses in numerous compounds formed with συν-: living with Christ (Rom. 6:8; II Cor. 7:3), suffering (Rom. 8:17) and being crucified with him (Rom. 6:6; Gal. 2:19), dying (II Cor. 7:3; cf. Rom. 6:8) and being buried with him (Rom. 6:4; Col. 2:12), being glorified (Rom. 8:17) and raised with him (Col. 2:12, 3:1; Eph. 2:6), being made alive (Col. 2:13; Eph. 2:5) and reigning with him (cf. II Tim. 2:12). This fellowship with Christ in life and death is manifested in a particular way in the Lord's Supper. Here the fellowship founded in faith and baptism is realized in a new way as the "participation in the body of Christ" and "participation in the blood of Christ" (I Cor. 10:16). Just as those who take part in pagan sacrificial meals, the "table of the demons" (I Cor. 10:21), become "partners with demons" (10:20) (mystery rites?), so those who share in the Lord's Supper, the "table of the Lord" (10:21), become partners of Christ. The Lord's Supper is fellowship with Christ, and so *fellowship with other Christians;* their common union with Christ naturally leads to a union of those who share the Lord's Supper, a communio of Christians among themselves. The one is not possible without the other, because they all partake of the same bread, Christ (10:17); the fellowship of Christians with one another is often expressed in the verb κοινωνειν. For this reason the Lord's Supper has been called a "synaxis", a joining together of Christians, which reveals the true nature of the community. By the meal they share members of the Church are united with the Lord and with each other.

So much is clear: the Lord's Supper is the centre of the Church and of its various acts of worship. Here the Church is truly itself, because it is wholly with its Lord; here the Church of Christ is gathered for its most intimate fellowship, as sharers in a meal. In this fellowship they draw strength for their service in the world. Because this meal is a meal of recollection and thanksgiving, the Church is essentially a community which remembers and thanks. And because this meal is a meal of covenant and fellowship, the Church is essentially a community, which loves without ceasing. And because finally this meal is an anticipation of the eschatological meal, the Church is essentially a community which looks to the future with confidence. Essentially, therefore, the Church must be a meal-fellowship, a koinonia or communio, must be a fellowship with Christ and with Christians, or it is not the Church of Christ. In the Lord's Supper it is stated with incomparable clarity that the Church is the ecclesia, the congregation, the community of God. In the Lord's Supper in fact the Church is constantly constituted anew. If the Church owes to baptism the fact that it *is* a Church, and does not have to become a Church through its own pious works, the Church owes to the Lord's Supper the fact that it *remains* a Church, despite any falling away and failure. From God's viewpoint this means that while baptism is the sign of electing and justifying grace, the Lord's Supper is the sign of sustaining and perfecting grace. From the human viewpoint it means that while baptism is above all the sign of the response of faith and obedience, the Lord's Supper is the sign of the response of love and hope.

But Paul is saying something more in his sentence: "Because there is *one* bread, we who are many are *one body*" (I Cor. 10:17). By their communio the sharers in the meal are made into one *body*, because the bread is the body of Christ. Those who eat the body of the Lord themselves become a body. By receiving the body of the Lord, the community reveals itself as a body; their share in the body of the Lord makes the believers who eat it into the body of the Lord. In the Lord's Supper the community is constituted as a body. Not that the community is only the body of Christ when it shares in the Lord's Supper; but it is in the meal, in which all eat one bread, the one body of the Lord, that the fact that the community is the body of Christ appears in concrete form as nowhere else. For this reason it is vitally important for Paul that the Lord's Supper is a real meal. Where there is no fellowship in the meal, where there are divisions, where each one eats his meal in advance, where some are hungry, some drunk and no one waits for the other (11:17–34), then there is no real fellowship and there can be no real Lord's Supper; all alike are exposed to "judgment" (11:34). In the Lord's Supper it is also a matter of proclaiming the word, a "proclamation" (11:26); but over and above this proclamation the common meal gives concrete and visible expression to the fact that the believers belong together, form a real fellowship and—in Paul's characteristic image—form one body.

"Truly partaking of the body of the Lord in the breaking of the Eucharistic bread, we are taken up into communion with Him and with one another. 'Because the bread is one, we though many, are one body, all of us who partake of the one bread' (I Cor. 10:17). In this way all of us are made members of His body (cf. I Cor. 12:27), 'but severally members of one another' (Rom. 12:5). As all the members of the human body, though they are many, form one body, so also are the faithful in Christ (cf. I Cor. 12:12)". (CE 7)

We must now examine the idea of the community, the Church, as the body of Christ, which forms the background to Paul's understanding of the Lord's Supper.

3. THE LOCAL COMMUNITY AND THE WHOLE CHURCH AS THE BODY OF CHRIST

The Church—people of God or body of Christ? The differences between these two conceptions are considerable, as we shall see. In the idea of the "people of God" temporal categories are supremely important; as the people of God the Church is making a journey from Old Testament election through the present towards the future. The notion of the "body of Christ" is dominated by spatial categories: the union of the Church with its glorified Lord as the continuing present.

But the fact that both ideas are typical of Paul's thinking and are integrated in his writings shows that they are not necessarily contradictory. Both concepts of the Church seek to express the union of the Church with Christ and the union of its members among themselves. It is, however, important that in seeing the Church as the body of Christ we should not base our view on an abstract of the body, but see it as the people of God placed by Christ in history. It is fundamental from every point of view to see the Church as the people of God; this idea is found not only in Paul, but is the oldest term to describe the ecclesia, and it emphasizes the crucial continuity between the Church and Israel and the Old Testament. Only by seeing the Church as the people of God can we understand the idea of the Church as the body of Christ; then we shall see that the concept "body of Christ" describes very fittingly the new and unique nature of this new people of God. The Church is only the body of Christ insofar as it is the people of God; but by being the new people of God constituted by Christ it is truly the body of Christ. The two concepts of the Church are linked precisely through their Jewish roots.[32]

There have been many and very varied conjectures about the *origins* of the body of Christ idea in Paul during the course of lengthy discussions on the matter. These origins have been sought

---

[32] For the biblical concept of *soma* see the general ecclesiological bibliography at A I, 3, esp. the following dictionary articles: H. Schlier, in LThK VI, 907–910; *idem*, in *Reallexikon für Antike und Christentum*, Stuttgart 1957, III, 437–453; (by the same author: *Der Brief an die Epheser*, Düsseldorf[2] 1958, esp. 90–96, reviewed by E. Käsemann, in *Theol. Lit. Zeitung* 86, 1961, 1–8); E. Schweizer, F. Baumgärtel, in ThW III, 1024–1091; and in this connection too E. Schweizer, *Die Kirche als Leib Christi in den paulinischen Homologumena*[8]; *Die Kirche als Leib Christi in den paulinischen Antilogomena*, both in one volume: *Neotestamentica* Zurich 1963, 276–316; more recent monographs are: A. Wilkenhauser, *Die Kirche als der mystische Leib des Christus nach dem Apostel Paulus*, Münster[2] 1940; L. S. Thornton, *The Common Life in the Body of Christ*, London 1942–Naperville, Illinois 1963; E. Percy, *Der Leib Christi in den paulinischen Homologumena und Antilegomena*, Lund 1942; W. Goosens, *L'Eglise Corps du Christ d'après Saint Paul*, Louvain 1949; T. Soiron, *Die Kirche als der Leib Christi*, Düsseldorf 1951; J. A. T. Robinson, *The Body*, London–Chicago 1952; R. Bultmann, *Theology of the NT*, London 1965; E. Best, *One Body in Christ*, London 1965; F. Mussner, *Christus, das All und die Kirche*, Trier 1955; J. J. Meuzelaar, *Der Leib des Messias;* L. Cerfaux, *The Church in the Theology of St. Paul*, Edinburgh–London–New York 1959.

in hellenistic ideas (in the gnostic myth of a redeemer, or in stoic imagery) and also in the Old Testament, in the idea of a race or people as a total personality, and in rabbinic speculation about Adam, or finally in the New Testament itself (in Jesus' words about the temple of his body, or in the Last Supper). It is important therefore to keep to what can be proved historically and to avoid suppositions and hypotheses which cannot be based on any definitely pre-Christian texts. A study of the sources shows with regard to the idea of the Church as σωμα Χριστου two things:

In *Gnosticism* there is not a single parallel to Paul's use of σωμα; these are only to be found in literature directly dependent on Paul (Ignatius, the *Shepherd* of Hermas, the second Epistle of Clement). The very rare, late and even then still not fully clear passages about the idea of the "perfect man" who contains redeemed men within himself, similarly provides no evidence as to the source of Paul's idea. Gnosticism seems to know nothing about an identity of the redeemer with the redeemed.

On the other hand, indisputably contemporary and pre-Christian documents of *Later Judaism* reveal conclusively the existence of certain eschatological expectations: (*a*) The eschatological host of the elect, after judgment and purification from sin, will regain the splendour of the original man Adam (Qumran); (*b*) divine wisdom will appear as a revealer and will recall to man his divine origins which he has forgotten; (*c*) a new father of a new race (Enoch, Noah and especially Jacob-Israel) will appear, after the end of a guilty and lost mankind, to lead a new people of God in the eschatological age; (*d*) the whole race is imaged as an individual man.

Even before Paul Jesus as the Son of Man had probably been linked with Adam, the first man. At all events Paul himself sees the Son of Man as the eschatological Adam, whose fate would be shared by all his people (Rom. 5:15; I Cor. 15:21 f., 45–49). On the basis of later Judaistic thinking, Paul may therefore have been led to create the concept of the "body of Christ", which is his own original creation; only in the Pauline writings and in writings directly influenced by him does the expression occur. What led Paul to adopt this image which was so familiar in hellenistic usage?

After the encounter between later Judaism and Hellenism, temporal concepts (this world—the world to come) were very commonly reinterpreted in spatial terms (below—

above). In hellenistic language it was common to express with the word "body" the unity of anything which consisted of various members (e.g. the State, the cosmos, a speech, a melody, a vine); for many of the Stoics indeed the congregation of the people, the ecclesia, was a "body" made up of many members. The application of the concept "body" to the ecclesia of Christ must have come all the more easily to Paul, since the "blood of Jesus" (i.e. his sacrificial death) had already, before Paul, been invested with a continuing saving effect for the community of the present. When Paul does the same thing for the parallel expression "body of Jesus", we must not forget that for Paul the risen body is also the crucified body, in so far as the latter has a continuing efficaciousness. Thus it is possible for Paul to use the words "body of Christ" to refer to Jesus' body hanging on the cross, as well as to the body made present in the Lord's Supper, and as well as finally to the Church which is made a member of the crucified body. It is in the body of Christ on the cross that the event of his saving death occurs. It is in the body of Christ in the Lord's Supper that the event of his death becomes fruitful. It is in the body of Christ, the Church, that the area is indicated in which the blessing and the dominion of this death is and remains efficacious. Through baptism in which they are buried and made alive with Christ, the believers have a share in the one body of the crucified and risen Christ. In the Lord's Supper, by eating and drinking, the baptized believers identify themselves bodily with the same body. By identifying themselves with this one body the believers are united among themselves, they become themselves "one body in Christ", "the body of Christ".

We must now examine what the idea of the body of Christ means in connection with the Church. Who is the "body of Christ"? According to those letters generally accepted as being by Paul, which are among the oldest, this is unequivocal; the body of Christ is the local community.

(*a*) *The local community as the body of Christ.* It is clear that Paul is referring to the local community in the text already quoted in connection with the Lord's Supper (I Cor. 10:16 f.) as well as in the text quoted in connection with baptism (I Cor. 12:13; cf. 12:12, 14–27; 6:5–17). Neither of these statements is abstract or general, but each is directed to the community in Corinth; it was this community which had been founded through baptism and realized through the Lord's Supper as the body of Christ. The third classic Pauline text about the body of Christ is also addressed to a local community, that in Rome (Rom. 12:4 f.).

The members of the body of Christ are always seen as the bearers of charisms. I Corinthians 12 and Romans 12 are the classic texts on the charismatic structure of the Church, and what Paul has to say about the Church as a creation of the Spirit must be presumed for the study of the Church as the body of Christ; in fact the statements about the scriptural creation and the body of Christ are interwoven with and complement one another. By linking his teaching about charismata with that about the body of Christ Paul at all events made clear that the Church is never—as some people in Corinth seem to have supposed—a gathering of charismatics enjoying their own private relationship with Christ independently of the community. According to Paul, all charismatics are part of the body of Christ, of the community. The fact that all charismatics are members of one body does not of course mean uniformity, but on the contrary a variety of gifts and callings. But fundamentally all individual members, having been baptized, are equal. But, by contrast with this fundamental equality all differences are ultimately without importance (cf. I Cor. 12:12 f.).

It is striking that Paul's remarks about the community as the body of Christ never appear in the context of christology or soteriology or even of an explicitly theoretical ecclesiology. The context is rather that of an admonition, a paranesis. However much Paul learned and drew from the ideals and conceptions of the world around him, he never loses himself in superficially ingenious speculations. He is not concerned with using mysterious mystical expressions for their own sake. Rather he is concerned with this idea of the body of Christ to help the members of the community to live their concrete lives in a bodily way, but in the light of Christ. Just as Menenius Agrippa, according to Plutarch's account, tried to persuade the plebs, who had retired away from the city to the *mons sacer,* to return, by telling them the well-known fable of the stomach and the other parts of the body; so Paul, by presenting the image of the body, wants to admonish the members of the community to live in unity, with mutual help and sympathy: "For just as the body is *one* and has many members, and all the members of the body, though many, are *one,* so it is with Christ. For by *one* Spirit we were all baptized into *one* body—Jews or Greeks, slaves or free—and all were made to drink of *one* Spirit. For the body does not consist of *one* member but of many. If the foot should say, 'Because I am not a hand, I do not belong to the body' that would not make it any less a part of the body. And if the ear should say, 'Because I am not an eye, I do not belong to the body,' that would not make it any less a part of the body. If the whole body were an eye, where would be the hearing? If the whole body were an ear, where would be the sense of smell? But as it is, God arranged the organs in the body, each one of them, as he chose. If all were a single organ, where would the body be? As it is, there are many parts, yet *one* body. The eye cannot say to the hand, 'I have no need of you', nor again the hand to the feet, 'I have no need of you'. On the contrary, the parts of the body which seem to be weaker are indispensable, and those parts of the body which we think less honourable we invest with the greater honour, and our unpresentable parts are treated with greater modesty, which our more presentable parts do not require. But God has so adjusted the body, giving the greater honour to the inferior part, that there may be no discord in the body, but that the members may have the same care for one another. If *one* member suffers, all suffer together; if *one* member is honoured, all rejoice together. Now you are the body of Christ and individually members of it" (I Cor. 12:12–27; cf. Rom. 12:4 f.).

Only once does Paul, in the generally acknowledged letters, use the expression "body of Christ" (I Cor. 12:27), and that without an article, somewhat undeterminately. Otherwise Paul simply says *"one* body", or *"one* body *in* Christ". In this way he is drawing on common Greek usage. In none of these passages is he concerned to determine ontologically the relationship of the body to a head. He is rather concerned with the proper relationship of the one body to the many members, and of the members among themselves in the concrete historical life of the community. When he starts speaking about the relationship between head and feet, in order to warn against feelings of superiority, the head here is just one among many members. In these letters Christ is never spoken of as the head of the Church.

The members of the community *ought* to be "one body". They *ought* to be "one body", because they already *are* "one body" in Christ. This idea must have been strange to the Greeks, who would be unfamiliar with the idea of a fellowship having an historical dependence on an historical body (and on one executed on a cross). As is true of the existence of the individual believer, Paul's view of the Church as the body of Christ presents an imperative which is founded on an indicative. Because the believers, through baptism and in the Spirit, are members of the body of Christ, because through the Lord's Supper they *are* united in one body, then they *ought* in their everyday lives to live as members of the one body and realize the unity of the one body. The body of Christ is not the result of the efforts of individual members of the community, who have formed themselves together into one body and thereby, through their love and desire for unity, constitute the body of Christ. The body of Christ has been constituted by Christ and in this sense pre-exists. Thus the admonitions quoted above begin with an indicative sentence: "For just as the body *is one* and has many members, and all the members of the body, though many, *are one* body, so it is with Christ" (I Cor. 12:12). Christ makes the believers into one body; seen from their origins, they are one *through* Christ; seen as a present reality, they are one *in* Christ. They are one, to express it in the briefest possible terms, like Christ. The body of Christ itself is present wherever the community lives "in Christ", wherever it lives in the realm of the saving death of the risen Christ, under his blessing and under the reign which he has established. To be "in Christ" (Rom. 8:1; II Cor. 5:17; Gal. 2:17)—this is not primarily a christological but an ecclesiological formula, and refers not primarily to an individual and mystical union with Christ, but to the state of being a part of the body of Christ (cf. Gal. 3:28; 1:22; Rom. 16:7, 11; I Cor. 1:30; I Thess. 2:14). The body on the cross is made present and efficacious in the present within the community itself. So all are *"one* body *in* Christ", as Romans 12:5 says. The phrase "so it is with Christ" (I Cor. 12:12) probably contains a further idea which Paul makes explicit at the end of his remarks about the body, by using the phrase: "you are the body of Christ" (12:27). The community is included in the destiny and the way of Christ, just as race and people were included in the destiny and the way of the ancestor of the race. The connection between Christ and the Church as his body is not a physical substantial one, as in gnosticism, nor a symbolic metaphorical relationship such as the Stoics would have understood, but an actual historical relationship in the Old Testament sense.

"As all the members of the human body, though they are many, form one body, so also are the faithful in Christ (cf. I Cor. 12:12). Also, in the building up of Christ's body there is a flourishing variety of members and functions. There is only one Spirit who, according to His own richness and the needs of the ministries, distributes His different gifts for the welfare of the Church (I Cor. 12:1–11). Among these gifts stands out the grace given to the apostles. To their authority, the Spirit Himself subjected even those who were endowed with charisms (cf. I Cor.14). Giving the body unity through Himself and through His power and through the internal cohesion of its members, this same Spirit produces and urges love among the believers. Consequently, if one member suffers anything, all the members suffer it too, and if one member is honoured, all the members rejoice together (cf. I Cor. 12:26)" (CE 7).

(*b*) *The whole Church as the body of Christ.* In I Corinthians and Romans the body of Christ is the individual community; in Colossians and Ephesians it is the whole Church. Exegetes, as is well known, have divided views on the question of the Pauline authorship of Colossians, and particularly of Ephesians, where the doctrine of justification, eschatology and anthropology seem to be neglected, and there is a concentration, unusual for Paul, on ecclesiology. The question cannot be debated here and in this context is not essential. At all events the very considerable differences be-

tween these letters and those generally accepted as Pauline—
particularly with regard to the conception of the body of
Christ—should, even if we agree that Paul wrote them, be attributed not so much to the "mature wisdom" of the apostle as
to the very different ecclesiastical situation he faced at the
later period. In Ephesians and Colossians Christ is seen as the
reply to the problem oppressing these communities, namely
that the cosmos seems to have slipped out of man's hands. In
order to show that the whole cosmos is in the hand of Christ,
it is not sufficient to think simply in terms of the local
Churches. Hence the body of Christ in these two letters is the
world-wide Church—admittedly in very idealized form, and
the central perspective is not so much the relations of the individual members to each other, but the relationship between
the body and its head. Christ is now explicitly named as the
"head" (κεφαλή) of the Church.

We may presume that the background to Colossians in particular includes a cosmic interpretation of the body of Christ.
The basis for Colossians 1:15–18 seems to be a cosmic hymn,
which has been adapted by the author in order to put it into a
correct historical context, the context of the death of Christ
on the cross as the decisive saving event. The body of Christ
is not understood cosmically here, but ecclesiologically. True,
Christ is also the head of the world, but it is not the cosmos
but the Church which is called the body of Christ (Col.
1:18, 24; 3:15; cf. 2:19). The reconciliation of the cosmos is
something that does not happen ontologically, namely through
the preaching of the Gospel among all peoples (1:23). In
this way the Church, the body of Christ, grows out into the
world (cf. 1:6; 1:23–29; 2:19).

In Ephesians, too, Christ is the ruler of the cosmos (1:22
f.). But despite the cosmic perspectives of this letter the word
"body" again does not refer to the cosmos, but to the Church
(1:22 f.; 2:12–16; 4:4, 12–16; 5:23, 30). Here again the
body of Christ grows through the mission to all peoples and
more generally through the service of the Church in the
world (cf. 2:21 f.; 4:11 f., 15 f.). As the body of Christ the
Church is the "fullness", the pleroma of him who fills "all in
all" (1:22); through all the powers of life which come from
him, Christ, whose body is the Church, reigns over the whole

cosmos. This does not refer to a Greek kind of total unity in a pantheistic sense, but a penetration of the cosmos through dominion of it, corresponding to the Jewish idea of subjection, which implies service and obedience.

These two letters give us considerable insight into the relationship between Christ and his Church in several ways. (1) By describing Christ and the Church as head and body, their indivisible interrelationship is stressed (Eph. 1:22 f.; Col. 1:18, etc.). This interrelationship, this community of fate confirms the use of συν-compounds which were quoted above, and which are particularly frequent in these two letters: "God . . . made us alive together with Christ (by grace you have been saved), and raised us up with him, and made us sit with him in the heavenly places in Christ Jesus" (Eph. 2:5 f.; cf. Col. 2:12 f.; 3:1). (2) Christ as the head is the origin and the goal of the Church's growth: "Rather, speaking the truth in love, we are to grow up in every way into him who is the head, into Christ, from whom the whole body, joined and knit together by every joint with which it is supplied, when each part is working properly, makes bodily growth and upbuilds itself in love" (Eph. 4:15 f.; cf. Col. 1:18; 2:19). (3) Christ reigns superior over the Church, as the head over the body, and the Church as body is subject in obedience to Christ the head: God's "great might" was "accomplished in Christ when he raised him from the dead and made him sit at his right hand in the heavenly places, far above all rule and authority and power and dominion, and above every name that is named, not only in this age but also in that which is to come; and he has put all things under his feet and has made him the head over all things for the Church, which is his body, the fullness of him who fills all in all" (Eph. 1:20–23; cf. 5:24; Col. 1:18; 2:10, 14 f., 19).

"The Head of this body is Christ. He is the image of the invisible God and in Him all things came into being. He has priority over everyone and in Him all things hold together. He is the Head of that body which is the Church. He is the beginning, the firstborn from the dead, so that in all things He might have the first place (cf. Col. 1:15–18). By the greatness of His power He rules the things of heaven and the things of earth, and with His all-surpassing perfection and activity He fills the whole body with the riches of His glory (cf. Eph. 1:18–23). All the members ought to be moulded into Christ's image until He is formed in them (cf. Gal. 4:19). For this reason we who have been made like unto Him, who have died with Him and been raised up with Him, are taken up into the mysteries of His life, until we reign together with Him (cf. Phil. 3:21; II Tim. 2:11; Eph. 2:6; Col. 2:12, etc.). Still in pilgrimage upon the earth, we trace in trial and under oppression the paths He trod. Made one with His sufferings as the body is one with the head, we endure with Him, that with Him we may be glorified (cf. Rom. 8:17). From Him 'the whole body, supplied and built up by joints and ligaments, attains a growth that is of God' (Col. 2:19). He continually distributes in His body, that is, in the Church, gifts of ministries through which, by His own power, we serve each other unto salvation so that, carrying out the truth in love, we may through all things grow up into Him who is our head (cf. Eph. 4:11–16, Greek text). In order that we may be unceasingly renewed in Him (cf. Eph. 4:23), He has shared with us His Spirit who, existing as one and the same being in the head and in the members, vivifies, unifies, and moves the whole body. This He does in such a way that His work could be compared by the holy Fathers with the function which the soul fulfils in the human body, whose principle of life the soul is" (CE 7).

But this does not exhaust the rich treasury of ideas about the body of Christ that we find in Ephesians. The writer lays especial weight on two points. One is *unity,* which is seen in two aspects. There must be unity between the many members, who have received various gifts and who perform various ministries: ". . . with all lowliness and meekness, with patience, forbearing one another in love, eager to maintain the unity of the Spirit in the bond of peace. There is *one* body and *one* Spirit, just as you were called to the *one* hope that belongs to your call, *one* Lord, *one* faith, *one* baptism, *one* God and Father of us all, who is above all and through all and in all. But grace was given to each of us according to the measure of Christ's gift" (Eph. 4:2–7; cf. 4:11–13). There must in particular be unity between the two formerly divided groups, Jews and Gentiles, which Christ has reconciled into *one* body through his death on the cross: "For he (Christ) is our peace, who has made us both one, and has broken down the dividing wall of hostility, by abolishing in his flesh the law of commandments and ordinances, that he might create in himself *one* new man in place of the two, so making peace, and might reconcile us both to God in *one* body through the cross, thereby bringing the hostility to an end. And he came and preached peace to you who were far off and peace to those who were near; for through him we both have access in *one* Spirit to the Father" (Eph. 2:14–18; cf. 3:6; 4:4). In this way the body of the crucified and risen Christ expands through the Spirit to the ecclesiological "body of Christ". The "one new man" is Christ in his entirety, "head" and "body" (cf. 4:13).

The second important aspect is that of *love,* which in the image of the marriage between man and wife is presented as the most profound mystery of the unity of Christ and his Church (Eph. 5:22–32). For all the difference which remains between Christ and his Church, for all the continuing reign of the head over the body, the relationship is ultimately one of unity in mutual self-giving. The writer here adopts the image of the "holy marriage" which was widespread later on in ancient times and which in its subjection of the wife to the husband is an expression of those times. Christ and the Church are like man and wife; the wife appears as the body of the man, who is the head (in I Corinthians 6:12–20 the relationship between Christ and the community had already been envisaged in sexual terms). "The church is subject to Christ" (Eph. 5:24), and is to "respect" Christ, as the wife does her husband (cf. 5:33). But this act is not one-sided. Just as the Church must give itself to Christ, so Christ first loved it and gave himself for it. He is not only the "head", but the "saviour of his body" (5:23). He "loved the church and gave himself up for her, that he might sanctify her, having cleansed her by the washing of water with the word, that the church might be presented before him in splendour, without spot or wrinkle or any such thing, that she might be holy and without blemish" (5:25–27). Christ "nourishes and cherishes" the Church. The washing with water, which the Church like a bride undergoes, is baptism; it is possible that the food with which the Church is "nourished" is a reference to the Eucharist. The love between man and wife, that great mystery, points to the love between Christ and his Church:

"He who loves his wife loves himself. For no man ever hates his own flesh, but nourishes and cherishes it, as Christ does the church, because we are members of his body. 'For this reason a man shall leave his father and mother and be joined to his wife, and the two shall become *one*'. This is a great mystery, and I mean it in reference to Christ and the church" (Eph. 5:28–32; cf. II Cor. 11:2).

"Having become the model of a man loving his wife as his own body, Christ loves the Church as His bride (cf. Eph. 5:25–28). For her part, the Church is subject to her Head (cf. Eph. 5:22–23). 'For in Him dwells all the fullness of the Godhead bodily' (Col. 2:9). He fills the Church, which is His body and His fullness, with His divine gifts (cf. Eph. 1:22–23) so that she may grow and reach all the fullness of God (cf. Eph. 3:19)" (CE 7).

(*c*) *Christ and the Church.* To avoid misunderstanding which might have far-reaching consequences, we must now attempt to define more closely the relationship between Christ and his Church, on the basis of the biblical sources. The following points must be borne in mind throughout and at the same time:[33]

[33] In addition to the general systematic works on the nature of the Church (see A II, 2) and the relevant sections in the standard dogmatics, see the more recent systematic monographs on the concept of the body of Christ: S. Tromp, *Corpus Christi quod est ecclesia*, I–III, Rome 1937; C. Feckes, *Die Kirche als Herrenleib*, Cologne 1949; H. de Lubac, *Corpus mysticum*, Paris[2] 1949; E. Mersch, *Theology of the Mystical Body*, St Louis 1951; *The Whole Christ*, Milwaukee 1938; A. Mitterer, *Geheimnisvoller Leib Christi nach St. Thomas von Aquin und Papst Pius XII*, Vienna 1950; E. Sauras, *El cuerpo mistico de Christo*, Madrid 1952; E. L. Mascall, *Corpus Christi*, London–New York 1953; F. Garcia Martinez, *El cuerpo mistico de Cristo*, Barcelona 1959; C. Mac-Gregor, *Corpus Christi*, London 1959; H. Schauf, *De Corpore Christi Mystico sive de Ecclesia Christi Theses. Die Ekklesiologie des Konzilstheologen Clemens Schrader . . .* Freiburg 1959; F. Malmberg, *Ein Leib–ein Geist*, Freiburg 1960; A. Cervia, *Unica persona mystica*, Rome 1960; P. L. Hanley, *The Life of the Mystical Body*, Westminster 1961; E. Mersch, *Le Christ, l'homme et l'univers. Prolégomènes à la théologie du corps mystique*, Bruges 1962; M. J. Le Guillou, *Le Christ et l'Eglise. Théologie du mystère*, Paris 1963; K. E. Skydsgaard, etc., *The Church and the Body of Christ*, Notre Dame, Indiana 1963; H. Mühlen, *Una mystica*

1. *Christ is present in the Church.* The crucified Jesus is present in the Church as the risen Lord. Christ does not exist without the Church, the Church does not exist without Christ. Christ is for the Church not only an event in a constantly receding past, nor only an event in the future, whether near or distant. He who is the Kyrios over all mankind, whether they know it or not, is present in his Church. The Church does not derive its life only from the work which Christ did and finished in the past, nor only from the expected future consummation of his work, but from the living and efficacious presence of Christ in the present. The preaching of the Gospel is not merely an account of the historical saving act of God in Christ; Christ himself is at work in the word which is preached. Where two or three are gathered in his name, there he is in the midst of them (Mt. 18:20); he is with us all days until the end of the world (28:20). It is not the fruits of his life on earth, not the significance of his historical existence which is at work in the Church; he himself in person works in and through the Church, and all its existence is based upon and directed towards him.

Christ is present in the entire life of the Church. But Christ is above all present and active in the *worship of the congregation* to which he called us in his Gospel, and into which we were taken up in baptism, in which we celebrate the Lord's Supper and from which we are sent again to our work of service in the world. In this congregation there occurs in a special way God's service to the Church and the Church's service before God. Here God speaks to the Church through his word, and the Church speaks to God by replying in its prayers and its songs of praise. Here the crucified and risen Lord becomes present through his word and his sacrament, and here we commit ourselves to his service: by hearing his Gospel in faith, by confessing our sins, by praising God's mercy and by petitioning the Father in Jesus' name, by taking part in the meal of the Lord who is present among us and by providing the basis for our service of one another by our pub-

persona, Munich–Paderborn–Vienna 1964; of the systematic articles in the encyclopaedias, see esp. J. Ratzinger in LThK VI, 910–912; cf. finally the commentaries on Pius XII's encyclical, *Mystici Corporis.*

lic confession of faith and by praying for one another. This is fundamentally where the Church is, where the Church, the community, the congregation, happens. Here God's new people is reminded of the great deeds and promises of God, which are proclaimed aloud in thankfulness and joy—the creation and preservation of the world and of man, the calling and guiding of Israel up to the eschatological saving act in Christ's death and resurrection and on to the consummation of the world and of mankind. Here, on Christ the living cornerstone, those who are baptized in faith are built as living stones into the spiritual house, and become part of the building and temple of the Holy Spirit. Here we are built up as a body, as the body of Christ, by remembering, thanking and looking forward, by sharing in the meal of joy, love and hope to which Christ has invited us, and by receiving the body of Christ himself.

Since Christ is *entirely* present in every congregation of worship, every congregation of worship held by the local community is in the fullest sense God's ecclesia, Christ's body. The individual local community is of course not simply *the* ecclesia, *the* body of Christ, since there are other communities which are just as much God's ecclesia and Christ's body. But each is truly God's ecclesia and Christ's body because the Lord is present in each, truly, wholly and undivided. And because it is the same Lord who is truly, wholly and undividedly present in each community, these communities do not exist side by side in isolation, nor even in a loose federation, but they are all together in the same Spirit the one ecclesia of God, the one body of Christ, and through koinonia, communio, fellowship with him they are in koinonia, communio and fellowship with one another.

What then is the relationship between Christ and his Church? The two are not distinct entities, linked by some ethical bond, nor in a state of polarity, with Church and Christ opposite one another like subject and object. There is rather a *unity* between Christ and his Church, in as much as Christ is *present inwardly* and personally in the Church. But this is only half the truth.

2. *Christ is not wholly contained in the Church.* The New Testament statements about the body of Christ which refer to

body *and* head are concerned not so much with the Church as the body, but with Christ as the head of the Church. In Colossians and Ephesians the accent falls not on the Church as the body which represents Christ, but on Christ as the living and active head of the Church; any reflection on the Church as the body is made only to stress the unity of the body, given by the head through the Spirit.

True, there is an inner unity between Christ and the Church, but the relationship can never be reconstructed to make the Church the head of the body, its own head. In this sense there can never be autocephalous or autonomous Churches. Christ gives himself to the Church, but he is never wholly contained in it. Christ is the head, and he remains the head, which controls the body. The concept of head always carries overtones of the ruler. The body can only exist in total dependence on him. It is of vital importance for the Church that it allows Christ to be its head; otherwise it cannot be his body.

Despite his continuing presence in the Church Christ is and remains the Lord of the Church. To develop the idea simply from organic images (head—body; vine—branches, etc.) will give a one-sided view and overlooks the fact that any biblical image, if taken in isolation and made autonomous, becomes false. The organic images of the relationship between Christ and the Church must always be complemented and corrected by the personal images (bridegroom—bride; man —wife), for the living relationship involved includes a personal encounter. The Church receives from Christ its life and at the same time his promises and his direction, or rather his promises and his direction, and *therefore* its life. The Church is and remains bound to Christ as its norm. Its whole autonomy consists in this heteronomy.

It is mistaken and misleading, therefore, to talk of the Church as a "divine-human" being, a "divine-human" reality, phrases which stress the unity but overlook the difference between Christ and the Church, and suggest that Christ is simply a part of the Church rather than its Lord, the head of the body. Christ is not wholly contained in the Church. There is no hypostatic union between Christ and the Church any more than there is between Christ and the individual Christian. The Church remains the fellowship of believers, believers *in Christ;* this relationship of faith is never altered. The Church remains the Church which has been sanctified by Christ but is always composed of sinful men and is itself therefore sinful; with good reason it says its *Confiteor* and repeats "Lord, I am not worthy".

Since the Middle Ages it has been customary to talk of the Catholic Church as the *"corpus Christi mysticum";* the word "mystical" here, in accordance with Ephesians 5:32, simply means "mysterious" (in contrast to the *"corpus Christi naturale"* on the cross and the *"corpus Christi sacramentale"* in the Lord's Supper, each of which remains however the *"corpus Christi verum")*. To talk of the "mystical" body of Christ is misleading, since the word is very often taken in the sense of what we nowadays understand by mysticism; this gives rise to a view of the Church as united with the divinity in a way that overlooks human creatureliness and sinfulness, and suggests a direct relationship with Christ, an identity with Christ, which is quite wrong.

True, head and body cannot in reality be divided, but still less can they simply be identified. For all the intimacy of the relationship Christ and the Church remain distinct, and the distinction is never overcome. The Church remains constantly and in all things dependent on Christ, in every moment of its existence, and constantly needs his grace and forgiveness. The Church lives, but not the Church but Christ lives in it. It is strong only in him who can make it strong through its weakness. It is free only in him who every day makes it free anew.

What then is the relationship between Christ and the Church? There is no physically necessary identity between Christ and his Church, nor an ontic identity in which Christ and the Church merge their several individualities; rather there is a union between them, in which despite Christ's presence in the Church the personal *differences* between them are maintained. It is a peculiar and unique union, which can only be described in *different* images: a union in duality and a duality in union. But this relationship exists not ontologically and statically, but historically and dynamically. We must pursue this thought by examining the historical perspective more clearly.

3. The Church *develops in obedience* to Christ. It is an im-

portant aspect of Colossians and Ephesians that the body of Christ grows. It grows *from the head,* "from whom the whole body, nourished and knit together through its joints and ligaments, grows with a growth that is from God" (Col. 2:19). Christ as the "head of the body", as the "firstborn from the dead", is the "beginning" of growth (Col. 1:18). And the body grows *towards its head,* growing "in every way into him who is the head, into Christ" (Eph. 4:15). Christ as the "perfect man", in whom all members are joined together, is the goal of growth (Eph. 4:13). The body of Christ grows *inwards,* in the growth of faith, knowledge, love, and in "sufferings", which "complete what is lacking in Christ's afflictions for the sake of his body, that is, the church" (Col. 1:24). And the body grows *outwards,* through new members who have been incorporated in baptism on the basis of the preaching of the Gospel. In this way the Church is "the fullness of him who fills all in all" (Eph. 1:23); it is the fullness of Christ, who fills all things with his body.

At the same time, this tells us that the growth of the body of Christ is not *organic,* not something that happens with ontological necessity. An optimistic and idealistic view of the Church and its history would see a Church in constant development, unfolding and becoming more perfect, constantly making progress and improving itself. But this is not a view the New Testament allows us to hold, still less Church history. Given that Christ is the head of the Church and hence the origin and goal of its growth, growth is only possible in *obedience* to its head. If the Church is disobedient to its head and his word, it cannot grow, however busy and active it may seem to be, it can only wither. Its development, no matter how spectacular, will prove basically misdirected; its progress, no matter how grandiose, will prove ultimately a disastrous retrogression. The valid movements in the Church are those that are set in motion by God's grace. The Church does not grow automatically and ontologically, but only historically. Real growth in the Church occurs when Christ penetrates the world by the activity of his Church in history, whether outwards, through missions to the pagans which reveal the mystery of Christ and the election of all mankind in him, or inwards through men of faith and love in whom Christ establishes his reign over the world, who act in faith and love in every sphere of their everyday life and reveal the world as the kingdom of Christ from which all demons have been banished, and as the creation of God. This precisely is the message of Colossians and Ephesians. The New Testament message gives no basis at all for ideas about the development of the Church which play down or even domesticate the idea of the reign of Christ. It is extremely misleading to speak of the Church as the "continuing life of Christ" or as a "permanent incarnation". In such views the Church is identified with Christ, so that Christ as its Lord and head takes second place to his Church, which pretends to be the Christ of the present in constantly new incarnation. Christ is thereby seen as having abdicated in favour of a Church which has taken his place and become his autonomous representative in everything, and so has gone a long way towards making him superfluous. Christ's work in and through the Church is made the work of the Church itself. This "continuing Christ" has need of the original Christ only as a dead figure of the past. The *truly* "continuing Christ" is of course the glorified Christ in the glory of his Father, who so far from having abdicated in favour of the Church, has firmly established his reign over the Church and the world by his resurrection, and will not abandon it until he hands it over to the Father at the end of the world (cf. I Cor. 15:20–28).

Of course the Church which pretends to be the continuing Christ does not seek to deny Christ, but on the contrary affirms him by identifying itself with him; men have only to keep to the Church and thereby they will be keeping to Christ himself. But such a Church, despite its apparent selflessness, is trying to emancipate itself, for all its pose of humility is trying to be self-reliant, for all its modesty is trying to be autonomous. A knowing Church has replaced a believing Church, a possessing Church has replaced a needy Church, total authority has replaced obedience. Not in theory or principle, perhaps, but in fact and in reality. It has become its own mistress and no longer needs a master. As the continuing Christ it is only responsible to itself, its all too human directives are given out as the directives of Christ; human commandments are turned into divine commandments. Such a

Church is a caricature of itself. Is there such a Church? It would surely be hard to deny that such a Church always exists, at least as a powerful temptation, the temptation to become an autonomous and autocratic Church which puts itself in the place of Christ.

The Catholic Church in particular is often accused of having "taken over" Christ, by identifying itself with Christ and his revelation in the course of a long and complex process, and by altering the *original* testimony of the revelation of Christ, the Bible. Instead of recognizing Scripture as a unique and fundamental authority, the Church has added to it its own ecclesiastical tradition, and then extended the ground covered by this tradition more and more, until finally the whole life of the Church, especially the present life of the Church, came to be regarded as tradition. In the course of time the existing Church and its magisterium has come more and more to be taken for tradition. At Trent tradition ousted Scripture, at Vatican I real historical tradition was in turn ousted by the present magisterium of the Church. Trent said that tradition shows what Scripture teaches; Vatican I said that the Church teaches what tradition is. The "teaching of the Church", understood in this way, and hence the Church itself was made identical with the revelation of Christ. A Church which is identical with Christ stops listening, and merely teaches; or rather, it only needs to listen to its own teaching to know what God says. In this way it becomes Christ as he speaks, reigns, acts and decides today. J. A. Möhler defined the Catholic Church accurately when he called it "the Son of God continually among men in human form . . . the continuing incarnation of Christ". Such a Church has no option but to usurp for itself the prerogative of God, infallibility. All Vatican I had to do was simply decide the question of the range of the Church's competence in concreto; it was already identical with Christ and infallible. These are the accusations very sharply directed at the Catholic Church, particularly by Karl Barth, and by Loofs, Rückert, Diem, Ebeling, and von Löwenich among others. I have attempted a reply elsewhere.[34] For the purposes of the present context, and with special reference to the modern development of the problem, it should suffice to note here the following four points. (1) Though *J. A. Möhler* was not trying to define the Church (which he defines as the fellowship of believers!) in the remarks quoted, but rather to make clear the continued activity of *Christ* in the Church, his remarks are admittedly open to misin-

[34] See *Structures*, 305–351.

terpretation and better avoided.[35] (2) *Vatican I* did not take up the idea of the "continuing presence of Christ", and indeed a majority voted against basing a description of the Church on the idea of "the body of Christ". The task of the Petrine office was seen as "preserving whole and pure . . . the saving teachings of Christ" (D 1836); the support of the Holy Spirit was promised to Peter's followers not so that they might "reveal new teachings", but so that they might "keep sacred and faithfully interpret the revelation handed down by the apostles" (D 1836). (3) *The encyclical "Mystici Corporis"* regrets the "insidious growth of a false mysticism which, with its attempt to obliterate the inviolable frontiers between things created and their Creator, falsifies the Sacred Scriptures".[36] (4) Vatican II cautiously affirms that "by an excellent analogy" (that is, a likeness where dissimilarity is greater than similarity) the Church "is *compared* to the mystery of the incarnate Word". There is no question of an identification here. "Just as the assumed nature inseparably united to the divine Word serves Him as a living instrument of salvation, so, in a similar way, does the communal structure of the Church *serve* Christ's Spirit, who vivifies it by way of building up the body (cf. Eph. 4:16)" (CE 8). The "sense of the faithful" (*"sensus fidei"*, cf. CE 12), does not mean that the faith of the faithful represents the revelation of Christ, engenders it and gives norms to it, rather than the converse, namely that the faith of the faithful is engendered and directed by the revelation of Christ. The Constitution "On Revelation" was not, as is obvious, sufficiently stringent with the problems raised by Barth. But chapter 6, "Sacred Scripture in the life of the Church", is a new and positive beginning. In the present context it is also worth noticing the statement: "The teaching office (of the Church) is not above the Word of God, but serves it" (De Revelatione 10).

With regard to Christ and his revelation the Church is in a position of obedience, which it can never abandon; no development of Church history can ever change this position into one of domination, in which the Church controls Christ and his word. The Church always suffered shipwreck whenever it tried, often in very curious and roundabout ways, to "take over" Christ and his word as though it were its own "posses-

[35] Cf. W. Kasper, *Die Lehre von der Tradition in der Römischen Schule,* Freiburg 1962, 141 f.

[36] Pius XII, Encyclical *Mystici Corporis,* in *Acta Apostolicae Sedis* 35 (1943) 197.

sion". But the Church has always found new life, usually against great opposition, whenever it has tried to find its way back to Christ and his word and has accepted the authority of his word in order to become once more what it is: the possession and property of Christ, his body. The teaching authority of the Church can never be its own first-hand teaching; it must always be derived from Christ and his word. Christ's word, which can never be absorbed or domesticated by the Church, is the basis as well as the frontier of all Church teaching. By divinizing its own teaching authority, the Church robs it of substance, because then it is no longer subject to Christ's word, the very spring which gives it life. By accepting the authority of the word of Christ humbly, modestly and gratefully, by hearing, preaching and living not its own but Christ's word, the Church will win an authority which men cannot give to it. The Church does not need to be a "continuing Christ"; this is a role which exceeds its strength. But it must be, and fully be, the body of Christ.

4. THE CHURCH AND THE HERETICS

The body of Christ, in I Corinthians and Romans as much as in Colossians and Ephesians, means, essentially, *unity: one* body. The Church *is* one body and *must be* one body. The conclusion here that the Church is one embraces the admonition that the Church should always be one, and reminds us that the unity of the body of Christ is always endangered. It is endangered by *heresy*.[37] If we are considering the Church as the body of Christ as a real and historical phenomenon rather than as an abstract notion, we must consider the

[37] See the textbooks of fundamental theology (esp. A. Lang, M. Nicolau–J. Salverri, T. Zapelene) and canon law (esp. Eichmann–Mörsdorf) and the articles in LThK (heresy: J. Brosch; history of heresy: K. Rahner), RGG (heresy: I. E. Wolf), EKL (E. Altendorf), HTG (O. Karrer), ThW (H. Schlier); also W. Bauer, *Rechtgläubigkeit und Ketzerei im ältesten Christentum*, Tübingen 1934² 1964; W. Nigg, *Das Buch der Ketzer*, Zurich 1949; H. E. W. Turner, *The Pattern of Christian Truth. A Study in the Relation between Orthodoxy and Heresy in the early Church*, London–Naperville, Illinois 1954; J. Brosch, *Das Wesen der Häresie*, Bonn 1956; A. Böhm ed., *Häresien der Zeit*, Freiburg–Basle–Vienna 1961, esp. the contribution by Karl Rahner.

fundamental threat to the body of Christ which heresy signifies. The Church and the heretics: this is a difficult topic, which is too often dealt with in an aggressive and one-sided manner. We have already laid the basis for investigating it by looking at related topics such as the Church and the Jews, and Church and the enthusiasts.

The very fact that the young Church was itself regarded as "heretical" must have made it cautious and wary in its relations with heretics. The greater number of believers is not automatically a sign of true faith; God is not, after all, on the side of the big battalions. The primitive Church, small and unimportant, was regarded as a Jewish "heresy", the "sect of the Nazarenes" (Acts 24:5; cf. 24:14; 28:22). As we have seen, it was in all outward appearances at first little different from Judaism. Αἵρεσις literally means choice, selection, a minority opinion, and was used in the Greek world to describe a self-chosen philosophical doctrine, a school or tendency, in Judaism to describe a religious school or party like the Pharisees, the Sadducees and the Essenes (cf. Acts 5:17; 15:5; 26:5).

Much more startling than the fact that the young Church was regarded as a "heresy" is the fact that from the very beginning there were heresies *within* the Church. This shows that heresy is not a chance historical phenomenon, but something that is bound up with the nature of the Church. In Galatians Paul finds it necessary to include among the works of the flesh, alongside enmity, strife, and dissension, "party spirit" ("heresies" in A.V.) (5:20). And there seems to be a tone of resignation in his words: "There *must* be factions ("heresies") among you in order that those who are genuine among you may be recognized" (I Cor. 11:19). Later we find the warning that Christians are to have nothing more to do with a man who is "factious" ("heretic": A.V.) after he has been admonished once or twice (Tit. 3:10), and in the second letter of Peter, at the end of the New Testament period, it is announced with considerable rigour: "But false prophets also arose among the people, just as there will be false teachers among you, who will secretly bring in destructive heresies, even denying the Master who bought them, bringing upon themselves swift destruction. And many will follow their licentiousness, and because of them the way of truth will be reviled" (II Pet. 2:1 f.). Warnings against false prophets and teachers recur throughout the whole New Testament, from the synoptic gospels to the Johannine letters.

(*a*) When the expression "heresy" is used in the New Testament, not in a neutral sense, meaning "school" or "party", but in a definitely negative sense, it implies something more than the related word *"schisma"* (cf. I Cor. 1:10; 11:18; 12:25), which indicates a "split" in the community based above all on personal quarrellings. "Heresy" means a fellowship which questions the whole basic faith of the ecclesia by presenting "another gospel" (cf. Gal. 1:6–9), and which is therefore in opposition to the ecclesia. It is condemned not, as in philosophy, by reference to a supposedly correct (ὀρθός) system, but by reference to the true message of salvation. Heresy occurs, when "someone comes and preaches another Jesus than the one we preached, or if you receive a different spirit from the one you received, or if you accept a different gospel from the one you accepted" (II Cor. 11:4; cf. Gal. 1:6–9). According to the first letter of John the "children of God" can be recognized by their true confession of faith in Christ (2:22; 3:14; 4:2 f.; 5:1), and at the same time by their brotherly love (2:9–11; 3:14; 4:20 f.; 5:2). False prophets are recognized by the wickedness of their behaviour as a whole, their bad "fruits" (Mt. 7:15–20).

The heretical groups in opposition to the early Church were connected either with Jewish parties or with the hellenistic schools of philosophy. Enthusiasts, who claim to have a direct revelation from the Holy Spirit, are often regarded as heretics, but are not necessarily heretical unless they hold a confession of faith different from that of the Church. The Fathers considered the Samaritan Simon Magus the first heretic (Acts 8:9–25). He attempted to buy the power of the Holy Spirit with money and gave his name to "simony", which was later always regarded as one kind of heresy. After the time when the unity of the Church was threatened by the opposition between the strict Jewish Christians and the Gentile Christians, which led to a number of small breakaway Jewish sects (Ebionites, etc.), there were heretical movements of especial importance in Church history: the different Gnostic and Montanist groups, which were referred to in connection with enthusiasm, and then—a heresy which is most useful in reaching a definition of what heresy is—the anti-Church of Marcion.

After Simon Magus, it was *Marcion*[38] above all whom the Fathers regarded as the arch-heretic: "the first-born of Satan" (Polycarp). This rich, cultured and clever ship-owner from Sinope in Pontus was not intent on heresy, but on reforming the Church: the Judaized Church needed to rediscover its origins! He regarded as essential a radical concentration on the Gospel of Jesus, which in turn was only possible by a radical reduction along Pauline lines. For Marcion Paul was the only apostle who really understood Jesus, while the other twelve were Judaizers (cf. Gal. 2:11–16). Paul teaches Christians to distinguish between the Gospel and the law. This for Marcion meant a complete rejection of the Old Testament *and* its God. The God of the Jews is the demiurge, the creator of the world, the one who made this wretched world and acts as a God of justice according to the principle of "an eye for an eye, a tooth for a tooth". The Christian God is wholly different, unknown to creation and the creator alike, the *alien* God, who out of pure grace has mercy on human beings who are not really his concern. This true God of love appears in Christ. In his apparent, material body he is crucified by the God of the Jews, an action which puts this God of justice in the wrong. Now the God of love reigns, the law is discarded and salvation depends on faith alone. Marcion's ideas were put forward in his "Antitheses", of which only fragments remain.

Armed with these ideas Marcion boldly undertook his own biblical criticism, in a spirit of radical Paulinism, and replaced the rejected Old Testament by a canon of the New Testament which consisted of the "Evangelion" (i.e. the presumedly Pauline gospel of Luke, duly purged of all Judaisms), and the "Apostolikon" (i.e. 10 similarly purged letters of Paul; Marcion was the first to reject the pastoral letters as unpauline).

In 138–139 Marcion came to Rome, where in 144 (?) he was

[38] See the standard works on the history of dogma (esp. A. Harnack) and also cf. the monographs on Marcion by A. Harnack 1920, ²1924. Reprint 1960; R. S. Wilson 1933; A. Hollard 1935; J. Knox 1942; E. C. Blackman 1949; and the article by G. Bardy in: DBS V, 682–877.

excluded from the community after discussions with the elders. Thereupon, in a very short time and with remarkable organizing ability, Marcion formed an anti-Church, which in the second and third centuries stretched from the Euphrates to the Rhône and presented a considerable challenge to the Catholic Church. Whether Marcion ranks as a Gnostic depends on one's definition of the word. His basic approach was not Gnostic; he did not appeal to a gnosis superior to simple pistis; his authority is not derived from mystical traditions, speculation about the ages of the world or the magic of mystery cults, but from the Gospel of Jesus and from Paul. In the way they are worked out his ideas do, however, overlap with Gnostic ideas (influence of Kerdon?): rejection of the Old Testament, assumption of two Gods, hostility to creation, matter and body, rigorous asceticism (marriage, eating meat and drinking wine are banned), rejection of the belief in the resurrection of the dead.

It would be fascinating, although not germane in the present context, to show to what an extent many modern and indeed contemporary movements have remarkable parallels with Marcion's system, especially as regards hermeneutic principles leading to an exaggerated Paulinism (cf. A. von Harnack's view of Marcion as "the first Protestant"). In the present context it is more important to take this first obvious heresy, which developed into an "international" anti-Church, as a basis for deductions about the nature of heresy: what does it suggest about the relationship between Church and heresy?

The following points concerning the relationship between the Church and heresy, or the Church and heretics, are useful as a basis for discussion:

1. *The element of truth in heresy.* Whenever a believer clearly deviated from the original message, he was rejected by the Church, even though in its early days the Church is characterized by extraordinary diversity. This rejection is apparent in the first apostolic community (cf. Mt. 7:15–23; 24:11), in Paul's writings (Gal. 1:6–9) and in John's (cf. I Jn. 4:1–6). Those who deviated from the true message were often connected with particular trends of the time which in fact conflicted with the message.

But the question of heresy is not settled simply by the Church's excluding it. Can a heresy exist solely on the basis of error? We are not talking here about sects which attempt to make their own individual destiny into a general law. *True* heresy does not draw its strength solely from error, or else it would be very short-lived. And heresies are by no means short-lived; indeed they seem ineradicable. Why? Because they draw their strength from part of the truth, often indeed, as closer examination reveals, from a good deal of the truth.

Marcion was in error in a number of his ideas—his dialectic of two Gods, his modalistic and docetist christology, his dualism and opposition to matter, his moralistic rigorism, his anti-Judaism, on a religious, not a racist basis. And yet on the other side, it appears that Marcion was highly sensitive to the uniqueness of the Gospel, to the wholly "other" aspect of the Christian view of God, to the incomprehensibility of God's merciful love and the incomparability of the figure of Christ, to the basic contradiction between law and Gospel and the Church as a fellowship of love. In him we find someone rare for that time: a man who, in complete contradistinction to the apologists of the time, those worthy founders of Christian theology, had a penetrating and far-seeing eye for what is specifically Christian and specifically Pauline, for the totally different and new aspects of the Christian message. It was his intention, by critically analysing and compiling the writings of primitive Christianity, to focus attention on what was central in those writings—and the fact that the Catholic Church ever drew up a New Testament canon is due in no small measure to Marcion. It is true that Marcion exaggerates and overdoes everything; he is idiosyncratic in his selection and his juxtaposition alike. He overlooks what is "evangelical" in the Old Testament, and the Old Testament elements in the Gospel of Jesus; above all he fails to comprehend Pauline dialectic. These are all errors. But perhaps we should be ready not to approve but to excuse this great heretic, excusing what is untrue in his ideas for the sake of what is true in them, just as, on the other hand, we have to excuse his countless orthodox opponents for ideas which, although they may not have been opposed to formal orthodoxy, may nevertheless, on closer inspection, be seen to have offended against both the richness and the concentration of the Christian message.

"Do not believe, brethren, that heresies are produced by insignificant souls! Only great men have produced heresies".[39] Selectivity, which is the essential feature of heresy, does not

[39] Augustine, *Enarrationes in Ps.* 124 (5), in CC XL, 1839.

only lead to error; it can very often lead to an impressive degree of concentration, in which a single trait, perhaps a vital trait, and even, as in the case of Marcion, the real centre of the Christian message, can be brought out in a new way that is all too often neglected by the Church. This brings us to a second and complementary aspect of the problem.

2. *Error in the Church.* The statement that the Church potentially preserves all truth is as abstract as the statement that each man is potentially everything (*anima est in potentia omnia*). Heresy too could claim this, in so far as it has unlimited potential for development and has indeed on occasion developed in such a way that only verbally was it separated from the Church (e.g. during the struggles about Arianism certain homoiousians developed increasingly homoousian tendencies).

When the Church says that it fundamentally preserves all truth, this is primarily a statement of intent, and a good one, indeed the best possible one. Everything will depend on how much this intention is realized. What use are buried talents, undiscovered treasures, unconscious insights, unfulfilled tasks? Moreover, since the Church as much as heresy is composed of men, sinful men, the Church's treasure has always been concealed among dross and even dirt, its unknown truths always co-existed with some errors, its unfulfilled tasks with sin and vice. This was, if not the only, often the decisive reason for heresy, the point at which it mounted its attack.

From the standpoint of the original Christian message the Church was right to defend itself against the Gnostic cosmogony and soteriology of Marcion, his rejection of the Old Testament, and his latent polytheism. But in the interests of historical justice we can surely not allow ourselves to overlook the fact that the second-century Church had already undergone not insignificant changes, and had certainly become somewhat shallow. With alarming rapidity the core of Pauline theology, the doctrine of justification, had become obscured, and Paul's teaching on the believer's freedom from the law had been overlaid by a new legalism. It was not until Augustine that these themes were once again taken up, albeit in a different perspective. In the time of the apostolic Fathers stress was already being laid on monotheism and Christianity's high moral code to such an extent that the Christian faith had come to look like a "new law", with Christ as the revealer of monotheism and the new "lawgiver". Many Christian apologists seem to have regarded the faith as a kind of Christian philosophy, a higher wisdom, a revealed "teaching" *about* God and the Logos, about the world and mankind.

This was not, of course, error. On the contrary, the taking over of hellenistic concepts, attitudes and methods was quite simply an inevitable process. Compared with pagan polytheism the teaching of the apologists represented a significant liberation, but compared with the original Christian message it was a dilution. Essential aspects of Jesus' original message and of the preaching of Paul and John were not allowed to bear their full fruit. False accents were placed and false developments took place, especially in a religion which was increasingly governed by laws. Marcion was able to put his finger on these weaknesses of the Church of his time, and this is why his heresy, with all its errors, had such a success. Marcion was wrong to suppose that there had been a "conspiracy", wrought by evil powers, against the truth of the Gospel, but there had certainly been a development, which was both hellenizing and judaizing, that is, intellectualizing and moralizing in tendency, and which was only devalued by the historical research of the present and previous century.

Augustine remarked that heretics carry away from the Church truths which belong to it. This can only happen if these truths are not sufficiently regarded and respected within the Church. In all ages the Church has been partly responsible for the rise of great heresies, and nearly always by neglecting or even by obscuring and distorting the Gospel. Truths can be abandoned by letting them grow dry and dusty as much as by denying them. From this viewpoint heresy fulfils the function of warning and admonishing the Church. This does not justify its existence. But the Church is not justified in overlooking this function of heresy, as a challenge to self-criticism, reform and renewal according to the Gospel. This is the only way in which the Church can seriously come to grips with heresy, something that it always needs to do. It is the only way in which it can be honest with erring men without, of course, compromising with their error. Before coming to terms with heresy, the Church must humbly acknowledge that *every* Christian within the Church is a potential heretic, and that the Church itself is full of "cryptogamous heresies".

3. *The good faith of the heretic.* Why do people become heretics? This is a question which the opponents of heresy have asked relatively rarely, and then always found a quick answer. It was always accepted as a matter of fact that the reasons for becoming a heretic must be basically dishonest. Why do people become heretics? It is the work of Satan, who brings about apostasy from orthodox doctrine—this was the answer of the early opponents of heresy (Justin, Ignatius, Irenaeus, etc.). And they added: through doubt and lack of faith, especially where Greek philosophy is concerned, so adding psychological motives too. In consequence there was soon no insult and no injury bad enough for condemning heretics on moral grounds, and the heretic was turned into a terrifying and repellent figure. To accuse a man of heresy was to strike a moral blow at his whole person. This resulted in countless good ideas and impulses in the Church being stifled before they could develop at all.

But as we have seen, light and darkness are not equally distributed between Church and heresy. Or do we wish to try and maintain that the power of evil is only effective *outside* the Church, and that faith only exists inside it? What of the faith of the heretic? In order to defend heretics, who found it difficult to defend themselves against categorical moral disqualifications, several modern scholars have found a different explanation for the origin of heresy. In their view heresy arises from the struggle between majorities and minorities in the Church, in which victorious majorities classify defeated minorities as heretics. But the disputes in the history of the Church are surely not decided so fortuitously; the question of who bases his view on the original Christian message is surely not irrelevant in the forming of a majority and the outcome of any struggles. One thing at least should be taken into account when we consider the extreme simplification of such a solution: almost without exception the early accounts of heresy—from Irenaeus, Hippolytus, and Zephyrinus, via Epiphanius, Theodoret, Filaster and Augustine down to Liberatus and John of Damascus, Germanus I and the later Byzantine and Counter-Reformation accounts of heresy—were written from the standpoint of those who triumphed in the history of the Church, and served, in a perfectly honest way, the aim of self-justification. It is instructive to consider what the same accounts—*audiatur et altera pars!*—would look like from the standpoint of the vanquished.

Why do people become heretics—what answer would heretics themselves give? We must here address ourselves not to self-centred sect-builders or pathological malcontents, who have always been plentiful in this area, but to the genuine great heretics. Leaving aside all detailed and technical points and any psychological motivation, they would surely reply that they wanted the best for the Church, that they acted in good faith. But most ancient heretics in particular can no longer speak to us; their writings were callously destroyed, and it is easy to deny that they were in good faith. But ought the Christian to do this? Surely he must presuppose such a good faith—*interpretatio benigna must* apply to heretics as well—particularly knowing that he himself cannot *prove* his own good faith to anyone at any time? There are certain indications to guide us. It is striking that the great heretics rarely took an easy road, they committed themselves *totally* to their ideas, without counting the cost; they subordinated everything to their faith and sacrificed everything to it: this was how they were able to make their tremendous impact. In this the great heretics were very like the great saints. Neither group has ever been understood by lukewarm believers, by shrewd ecclesiastical tacticians and by the diplomats of the Church, great and small, who are not born for martyrdom.

It is remarkable how often one reads of Marcionite martyrs. It was not the pagan State, but the Church, or alternatively the Christian State, which put them to death. The heretics had innumerable martyrs, tortured and killed by the Church as well as by the pagans. Still greater is the number of *confessores*, famous or little-known confessors to their faith. We may wonder how many of them were inspired by God in the very depths of their being, and inspired by the message of the Gospel, like Marcion—and like Arius and Pelagius, Gottschalk and Erigena, Wyclif and Hus, Giordano Bruno and Blaise Pascal. And we must ask ourselves what, in the last analysis, counts in God's eyes.

The heretic does not submit to the authority of the Church. This is what distinguishes him from the saint, who although he may often be in conflict with the authority of the Church will finally accept it patiently and humbly. The heretic rebels, feels he must stick to his conviction, and decides on opposition. To do otherwise, according to his conscience, would be to betray the truth and abandon himself. Here no man can be a *final* judge. The decision confronting a man's conscience is never an easy one; it brings with it an internal and external crisis, struggle and tragedy and often death. We cannot judge erring men in the way that we can condemn errors. Those who boldly and heroically kept faith with their truth, without compromise and without sparing themselves, those whose zeal roused whole generations and indirectly gave the Church countless creative impulses, are men to whom there is one thing we cannot deny—for all their exaggerations and stubbornness, their errors and their biases, for all the disastrous consequences they brought upon the Church—and that is their good faith.

(*b*) The establishing of the State Church from the time of Constantine brought with it a time of *violent opposition* to heretics. It had become increasingly the custom to measure heresy not primarily against the message of the Gospel, but against particular theological doctrines and systems, against "orthodoxy". And yet during the years of persecution the Fathers of the Church (Cyprian, Origen, Tertullian, Lactantius and others) had been prepared to stand up to the powerful opposition of Christians with different views. It is true that the opponents of heresy in the Church had from early times abandoned the prime commandments of love in their settling of questions of faith, and had abused and reviled those who held different notions and beliefs. The sowing of hatred was bound to lead to a bloody harvest. The Church in power soon abandoned the tolerance for which the persecuted Church had pleaded and with the help of the "Christian" State it began to persecute those who pleaded with it for tolerance. Centuries of Church history prepared the way for one of the most terrible phenomena of Church history, one of the most incomprehensible disfigurements of the body of Christ: the

Inquisition. The problems raised by the existence of the Inquisition were not extinguished with the last of the grisly flames it kindled at the stake.

There is no need to list here the innumerable trinitarian and christological heresies of the Greek East, or the soteriological and anthropological heresies of the Latin West, which the Church staved off only with difficulty in the post-Constantinian period. Increasingly the Church turned more and more to the State and its methods in its struggles for the purity of its doctrines and for its own existence. From the time of Theodosius the Great (d. 395), heresy was regarded as a civil political crime: an enemy of the Church is an enemy of the empire and must be punished as such. In 385 the Spanish heretic Priscillian and six of his companions were executed in Trier for heresy. Martin of Tours and others raised objections; Ambrose, Pope Siricius and Christianity as a whole condemned what appears to have been the first killing by Christians of other Christians on the grounds of unorthodoxy. But the idea became accepted with time. Leo the Great expressed satisfaction at it. And in contrast with his own earlier opinions even the great Augustine in his old age, after being unsuccessful in his dispute with the Donatists, justified the use of force against heretics with reference to Luke (14:23). But he disapproved of capital punishment for heresy, which began to be executed in individual cases on Manichaeans and Donatists. Justinian I in particular extended the Roman-Byzantine laws concerning heresy. Augustine and Justinian had a very considerable influence on medieval laws on heresy. Admittedly, where the heretics were in a majority—something that became rare later on—they behaved no less violently than their orthodox brethren. The cruelty of the heretics, the Arians for example, need not concern us here, however; it cannot justify the same acts by the Church.

What had been isolated cases in the old Church—after the collapse of the empire heresy was again generally opposed with purely ecclesiastical means—became a regular institution at the height of the medieval Church's power. What had been abhorred in the fourth century was recommended in the twelfth and thirteenth centuries. Alongside the growth of the medieval power-Church the number of heretics had also grown alarmingly (besides the Waldensians, there were in particular the different kinds of Catharism in southern France and northern Italy, which gave to German the word for heretic, *"Ketzer"*). These evangelical movements were only partly absorbed into the newly-founded mendicant orders; the only means that would have served to deal with them, a fundamental reform in the Church, was not carried out. The chosen means was force. Bishops, kings and popes prepared the way for what became known as the *Inquisition* and was to fill many of the blackest pages of Church history:[40] the systematic legalized persecution of heretics by an ecclesiastic court, which enjoyed the support of the secular power (*inquisitio haereticae pravitatis*). In 1209 Innocent III proclaimed a crusade against the Catharist Albigensians of southern France, which led to the horrors of the Albigensian wars. In 1215, at his suggestion, the Fourth Lateran Council laid down harsh laws against heresy. Two figures who had a vital influence on the development of the Inquisition were the Emperor Frederick II, who had heretics murdered in cold blood for political reasons, and Pope Gregory IX, who reorganized episcopal opposition to heresy on a papal basis and in 1231 appointed papal inquisitors to hunt out heretics. Innocent IV gave the Inquisition power to force confessions by means of torture applied by the secular arm; what that meant in terms of actual suffering defies description. Soon it became an accepted custom to burn stubborn and recalcitrant heretics.

The Inquisition was much more effective in some countries than in others; it did relatively little work in Germany, where the outraged populace killed one of Gregory IX's first inquisitors, Konrad of Marburg, after two years of cruel activity, and in England it did practically nothing. In France the Inquisition was set up to deal with the order of Templars as well as Waldensians and Cathars, in Holland it was used against Béguins and Bégards and against the Brethren of the Common Life. The Inquisition's worst work was done in Spain; in forty years four thousand people were burned in Seville alone, and the number of those burned up to 1783 is given at 31,000. Particularly terrible were the results of combining the Inquisition with witch-hunts, which developed to frightening proportions both in Catholic and Protestant areas and

---

[40] Cf. J. Vinke, *Zur Vorgeschichte der spanischen Inquisition,* Bonn 1941; H. Maisonneuve, *Etudes sur les origines de l'Inquisition,* Paris 1942, ²1960; B. Llorca, *La Inquisicion en Espana,* Madrid² 1953; C. Reviglio della Veneria, *L'inquisizione medioevale ed il processo inquisitorio,* Turin 1951; M. dela Pinta Llorente, *La inquisicion espanola y los problemas de la cultura y de la intolerancia,* Madrid 1953; W. Plöchl, *Geschichte des Kirchenrechts* I–II, Vienna 1953–55; E. van der Vekene, *Versuch einer Bibliographie der Inquisition,* Luxembourg 1959; P. Mikat, art. "Inquisition", in LThK V, 698–702; H. E. Feine, *Kirchliche Rechtsgeschichte,* Cologne–Graz⁴ 1964; A. S. Turberville, *Mediaeval Heresy and the Inquisition,* London 1964–Hamden, Connecticut 1920.

did not come to an end for a very long time (real opposition to the burning of witches only started with the Jesuits Tanner and von Spee, and with Pietism and the Enlightenment in Protestant areas). The Reformation (Luther, Melanchthon and especially Calvin) pursued heretics (particularly enthusiasts) as fiercely as the Counter-Reformation. The same pope who summoned the Council of Trent, Paul III, renewed the Papal Inquisition, along Spanish lines, in 1542, and placed it under a congregation of cardinals, which had the task of acting as a central committee responsible for the purity of the faith in all countries (the *Congregatio Romanae et universalis Inquisitionis,* later called the *Sanctum Officium Sanctissimae Inquisitionis;* it passed its first death sentence in 1545).

The goal of the Inquisition was the rooting out of heresy, which was regarded as a criminal offence guilty of the most extreme punishment. The proceedings of the Inquisition were remarkable for the fact that they could be instituted not only on the basis of a formal accusation, as in an ordinary trial; the court had a duty to establish and to investigate (*inquirere*) heresy, which did not of course exclude denunciations made by heretics themselves. Two denouncers sufficed to have a man declared guilty. He had no defender. The president of the court was virtually prosecuting counsel, judge and father-confessor in one. He was answerable to no one. There was no court of appeal against sentence. To escape torture, a false confession was often the only way out. If the accused person admitted his guilt, very often under torture, various punishments could be meted out to him; he might have to do severe works of penance, have his clothes marked with yellow crosses, or even be committed to life imprisonment, and he usually had all his goods confiscated (the Inquisition lived on income obtained in this way). If he remained stubborn, even after the most terrible tortures, he was handed over to the secular arm to be burned. In the Catholic states of southern Europe the Inquisition was not abolished until the nineteenth century (not until 1870 in the Papal States). The secret proceedings of the Roman Inquisition, which could lead to bans on teaching or publishing activities or to excommunication, continued until the Second Vatican Council. Pope Paul VI had the historical distinction of turning the Holy Office into a congregation for the teaching of the faith.

There is nothing to be gained here by passing self-righteous judgment on the past. A century of concentration camps and gas chambers has no cause to despise the centuries of the stake and the rack. In our ecclesiological context an *historical* verdict on the Inquisition is not what matters. It is obvious that in passing such a verdict account would have to be taken of the whole attitude of the Middle Ages to life and society, and in particular of the identity of Church and State in the Sacrum Imperium, the general cruelty of medieval justice, the mass religious neuroses and psychopathic features of the age (terror of demons, delusions about witches, etc.). Nor can we here go into the question of the dominant motives in individual cases, whether religious and theological, political and sociological or economic and financial (confiscation of goods). In the context of an examination of the nature of the Church a *theological* verdict is what matters. Can the Gospel of Jesus Christ offer any basis for attempting to "persuade" an erring brother, if necessary by force? Can fire and sword be a means of spreading and maintaining the true faith? Does the Church possess so much divine insight or illumination or inspiration, that it can judge a man's conscience in this way? What is the proper way for the Church to confront heresy? There can be no disputing the fact that theology has on the whole failed to meet the challenge of heresy, and fulfil the rôle which it should so clearly have taken up in the matter: a critical and constructive rôle. It is humiliating to see what arguments the great medieval theologians invented, and on the basis of the Bible at that, to justify the spiritual violation, the torturing and killing of those who did not share their views. Let no one suppose there was no other way. Theologians and bishops like Martin of Tours, Ambrose and Chrysostom, and later leaders of the Cluniac reform and Francis of Assisi, recognized and stated that heresy could not be dealt with by force. A long and disastrous process of development had the effect of stifling the voice of Christian conscience, and centuries passed before it was heard again.

The question of the relationship between the Church and heretics is one that remains with us, because heretics have continued and will continue, because every Christian is potentially not only a heretic, but also an inquisitor. As Paul knew, heresies were born with the Church, and the whole life and teaching of the Church are influenced by the question as to how the Church should confront heresy. It is clear that the Church cannot simply accept heresy. But in view of all the horrors of the past, the beginnings of a debate with heresy can only lie in a liberating confession of guilt. The spectacle of burning human torches and countless broken human lives can teach the Church humility and self-awareness. From a consciousness of guilt can spring a metanoia, a turning away not just from the burning of heretics, but from the hatred of heretics, the despising and disregarding of heretics; it is not just the terrible *punishments* of the Inquisition but the *spirit* of the Inquisition which made such cruelty possible in the first place, which the Church must set aside. A metanoia of this kind, a turning from hatred to love and to the unity of the body of Christ, would involve certain practical considerations.

1. *Love must be the rule even in matters of faith.* The Gospel of Jesus Christ culminates in love, in boundless love, which excludes no one, not even one's enemies. Jesus' love is the revelation of the love of God, and a challenge to men to love. Jesus himself said that erring and sinful men were to be pursued with especial love, just as the shepherd goes out specially after the lost sheep (Mt. 18:12–14), just as the father welcomes the prodigal son with special love, while the self-righteous elder brother appears at the end of the parable to be the truly lost son (Lk. 15:11–32). Even the inhospitable Samaritan village which did not receive Jesus was not, as the deluded disciples had wished, consumed with fire from heaven (Lk. 9:51–56). In God's sight no one is fundamentally less of a sinner than others (Lk. 13:1–5). Peter is to forgive his brother seventy times seven times, which is to say without ceasing (Mt. 18:22). Even Paul, while he sternly rejects "another gospel", has this to say: "Brethren, if a man is overtaken in any trespass, you who are spiritual should restore him in a spirit of gentleness. Look to yourself, lest you too be tempted" (Gal. 6:1). Even a man who is disobedient to the apostle's words is not to be regarded as an enemy, but warned as a brother (II Thess. 3:15). If a man were to have all knowledge and all faith, and were even to give his body to be burned, but had not love, it would gain him nothing (I Cor. 13:2 f.).

The Gospel of Jesus Christ on which the Church bases itself makes it completely impossible to turn aside from love even for a moment and even for the sake of the unity of the Church; it is love, after all, which holds the body of Christ together. Anyone who is deficient in this love mars and destroys precisely the unity of the Church. Few things harmed the Church and its unity so much as the violent treatment of heretics, the evidence of a lack of love which made countless people doubt the truth and drove them out of the Church. The road to "pure doctrine" cannot be driven over corpses. Zealous faith must not be perverted into doctrinaire intolerance. It is only a little step from "orthodoxy" to that blind and ruthless fanaticism which is the very soul of all inquisitions. However many historical and psychological explanations may be found for the Inquisition, no possible justification for it can be found when we set it beside the Gospel of Jesus Christ. A Church deserts the Gospel at the point where it tries to liquidate all opposition by physical or spiritual murder, and makes a communion of love into a religion of executioners. A Church will fail if it tries to assume the functions of God's judgment on the world and anticipates the sundering of the tares from the wheat. A Church which is called to be the body of Christ in love should need no convincing of the fact that the very idea of destroying heretics, whether physically or "merely" spiritually, must be totally alien to it.

2. *Understanding and action.* The basic attitude necessary for debates in matters of faith is best summed up in St Paul's words: "Love is patient and kind; love is not jealous or boastful; it is not arrogant or rude. Love does not insist on its own way; it is not irritable or resentful; it does not rejoice at wrong, but rejoices in the right. Love bears all things, believes all things, hopes all things, endures all things" (I Cor. 13:4–7). The love of the Church towards heretics, apart from having the negative characteristic of avoiding all kinds of force and violence, must have positive aspects as well.

The one essential thing is *understanding;* the "unmasking and refuting" of heretical doctrines, which from the time of Irenaeus was always regarded as the main aim of Church heresiologists, generally makes true understanding impossible. Understanding does not begin with polemics. Too often those who seemed unorthodox were known, yet not really known; too often they were condemned on hearsay, or on the evidence of unreliable witnesses and sources; too often their books were only read and handed down in extracts, their ideas were wrenched out of context and handed on in distorted form and made the basis of false conclusions. True understanding involves working out how people reach their conclusions, finding the *punctum veritatis* in their viewpoints and establishing points of contact with them; it involves discovering the valid concerns which underlie invalid statements, and measuring discrepancies, not against one's own theology, but against the original message of the Gospel. In this way, instead of constructing and condemning a caricature of a heretic, we shall have a true picture of him, we shall understand him and—on many points at least—excuse him.

The other essential is *action;* the debate between the Church and heretics must not simply be a matter of words but must find concrete expression. The Church, in addition to getting to know and understand heretics and their valid concerns, must weigh up these concerns carefully, and be prepared to take action on them to the extent that they are justified in the light of the Gospel of Jesus Christ. Understanding someone properly involves learning from him, and learning from someone properly involves changing oneself. This is the practical side of an insight into the truth of heresy and the error of the Church: the realization of the justified claims, demands and concerns of others. The conclusions drawn above with reference to the relationship between the Church and enthusiasm apply equally here, with a particular accent on doctrine. Violent proceedings may often seem more effective—almost the entire heretical literature of the first centuries was destroyed, leaving only scrappy quotations behind in the writings of its opponents. But heresies were not rooted out in this way; they multiplied. By fulfilling the justified demands of heresies the Church, instead of treating symptoms, is combating disease at its very roots. What the Church today has to do is not merely to rehabilitate posthumously, either in part or totally, those heretics whom the results of historical research have enabled us to see in a new light; far more important than that is to fulfil, not in part but totally, their demands and concerns in the light of the Gospel of Jesus Christ.

There may of course be dangers attached to true understanding. Heretics, for all their errors, were often more intelligent and acute than their orthodox opponents, often indeed more theologically profound and more pious, and their genuine demands have taken on a fatal fascination. There may also be dangers attached to a genuine realization of justified demands. This would set the Church in motion in directions which as yet remain uncertain. A positive attitude towards heresy is therefore bound to be a risk—as so many things are in the life of the Church and of the individual. But this risk too can be overcome by the venture of love, coupled with critical thinking and the gift of discerning spirits. This makes it clear that heresy can fulfil a positive function in the life of the Church. This is what Paul suggests—we can see now that his remark is not necessarily spoken in a tone of resignation: "There must be factions among you in order that those who are genuine among you may be recognized" (I Cor. 11:19). Heresies fulfil the function of preventing the Church from becoming rigid and paralyzed in its life and its teaching; they can preserve it from idle complacency and vain self-satisfaction; they can keep it spiritually in motion, drive it forwards and challenge it to keep ever more faithful to the Gospel. How often heresies prepared the way for good new directions in the Church; and how often they pointed the way back to good old traditions! Heresies guarantee the "genuineness" of the Church. The birth of a heresy can therefore, like many other moments of danger, be a moment of grace for the Church, provided it is overcome by the power of love. In this way too the one body of Christ is finally built up.

3. *The challenge to new unity.* Heresies represent an unorthodox conception of the Gospel, one which though it may be rejected and overcome must be seriously faced up to. The Church cannot simply accept them. In some cases it can *no longer* accept them: the more highly developed sense of faith in the later Church may well find a view which was earlier tolerable and has survived, so to speak, as an heretical archaism. The legitimate diversity of doctrine was considerably greater in the early Church than later on; and what we frequently call heresy today was very often not originally a deviation from a firmly established doctrine, but the development of possibilities in a doctrine which was as yet not fully defined. On the other hand, it may be that the Church *cannot yet* accept a particular view of the Gospel; the Church's sense of faith may need time to understand a new interpretation, and the new interpretation may have first to become clearer, less extreme and less open to misunderstanding. Doctrine

develops in effect through the interdependence, the reciprocal effects of orthodox and unorthodox doctrinal opinions. There is indeed a very long list one could make of individual points on which, much later, heretics were seen to have been right; these included practical demands like those of medieval heretics for worship in the vernacular and communion under both kinds, and several statements of doctrine which later, often in different contexts, and with different phrasing and emphasis, were taken up by the Church.

As we have seen, it is not easy to distinguish absolutely between truth and error, Church and heresy in the dynamic of history. This fact must make the Church cautious and sympathetic in its dealings with heretics, for all the limits it may find it necessary to draw. So long as the heretic does not abandon his communion with the Church, the Church must not abandon communion with him. Communion in the Church is quickly dissolved, but it is hard to restore it—as the tragic histories of heresy exemplify only too well. There may of course be occasions—in the pluralistic society of today, with its religious freedom and tolerance probably less than ever before—when the life and order of the community is seriously threatened by false teachings (for example, under totalitarian political regimes). In such cases the Church, exercising the spiritual authority of its Lord, can sever communion with a heretic or heretics in order to protect and preserve the community. Excommunication[41] was known to the New Testament Church (Mt. 18:15-18; I Cor. 5:1-5; Tit. 3:10; II Jn. 10 f.; cf. Mt. 16:18 f.; Jn. 20:23), as something which applied to an individual, never to a community; in the later New Testament writings, it is referred to in connection not only with moral offences but also false doctrines. Later such bans were often limited to exclusions from the fellowship of the Lord's Supper. But the misuse of excommunication led to reprehensible actions, not only where it was used to garner money and taxes, but above all when it was applied on principal in a spirit of intolerance and exclusivity, without any respecting of the good faith of those concerned,

41 Cf. the standard works on canon law and the history of canon law (H. E. Feine, W. Plochl) as well as the exegetical literature cited at E II, 2.

and without love. If excommunication is going to be considered in individual cases today, then it can only be in a strictly limited sense.

The following conditions must be observed, from a theological standpoint: (1) Excommunication must never be mistaken for a definitive condemnation of a person; God alone can do that. (2) Excommunication must not be regarded as a total exclusion from the fellowship of the Church, for an excommunicated person remains a baptized Christian; his good faith must always be presumed, even though such evidence as is available to human judgment seems to indicate otherwise. (3) Excommunication as an exclusion from the fellowship of the Lord's Supper should only be used as an extreme measure; before that, as Matthew 18:15–17 suggests, all other possible pastoral means must be tried (brotherly discussion, pastoral admonitions, etc.). (4) The justified demands of a heretic must be recognized first of all (cf. I Cor. 9:27: "lest after preaching to others I myself should be disqualified"). (5) Excommunication must only be a temporary disciplinary measure, in anticipation of a reconciliation and the restoring of the unity of faith. (6) Excommunication must not automatically be extended to the innocent descendants of a particular excommunicant.

Heresy should be seen, not as primarily a challenge to the unity of Church fellowship, but rather as a challenge to the Church to discover a new and deeper and purer unity—however much this aspect of it may be obscured, and however much it may be open to misunderstanding and have regrettable consequences. By giving the Church pause and encouraging it in reforms, every heresy makes possible the restoration of complete unity not simply by a return to the original state, but through the discovery of something better.

(c) At this point we must return to an historical perspective, and consider those areas where the historical and systematic problems of Church and heresy are at their acutest, and where in a sense they have been left behind: the division between the Churches of East and West, and the division brought about by the Protestant Reformation. In neither case were the divisions the work of individuals, nor were they simply caused by the splitting off of relatively small heretical groups on the fringe of the Church as a whole. At this point

—however one judges the divisions—it is clear that the Church itself has become divided. This poses fundamental problems about the whole conception of Church union, which will be pursued in a later chapter in the context of the unity of the Church.

By way of transition it will be of value to look briefly at the image John uses to express the idea of the body of Christ: the vine and the branches. The burning of heretics was justified, among other ways, by the following sentence from John's gospel:[42] "If a man does not abide in me, he is cast forth as a branch and withers; and the branches are gathered, thrown into the fire and burned" (15:6). It is impossible to imagine a more flagrant abuse of the Gospel, and of this gospel especially.

The phrase "the body of Christ" is absent from Johannine writings, as "ecclesia" is (with the exception of III Jn. 6, 9 f.). But they show a lively interest in the question of the ecclesia nonetheless (I John especially, and the other two letters in a different way); and there is similarly a lively interest in the reality underlying the image of Christ's body, the communion of believers with Christ and with one another. Of course John is primarily concerned with the individual and with his decision of faith in the revealer and his word. Thus instead of the more usual singular words like ecclesia, people of God, spiritual building, body of Christ, he generally uses plural forms to describe those united in the Church—they are the "disciples" of Christ (Jn. 13:35; 15:9, etc.), his "friends" (15:13–15), "his own" (13:1). The Church is seen as the fellowship of individuals gathered together, it is a "flock" (cf. 10:1–10), made up of sheep who know the voice of the shepherd appointed by God, the true owner of the flock. Those who are his own, scattered throughout the world, must be gathered together in unity with him. They are "his own" if they follow the shepherd's call; then together— Jews and Gentiles alike—they will be one: "one flock, one shepherd" (10:16).

There is no need to discuss here whether or not John is here developing Gnostic ideas concerning pneumatics who,

[42] Cf. note 28.

filled with the Spirit, are the bearers of the pre-existent spark of light and hence already from a potential unity, and will then be gathered together by a redeemer and united with him. Several exegetes today prefer to stress the Old Testament background of John's imagery: Israel as God's vineyard (Is. 5:1–7) or as God's choice vine (Jer. 2:21; Ps. 80:9–16), and Christ as the representative of the true Israel (Christ as a "collective personality"?). Whatever the historical background to Christ's words about himself as the true and real vine, the source of true life, may be, the passage is not the expression of an individualistic mysticism but is concerned—while concentrating on the figure of Christ—with the Church as the community of salvation. For it is in this community that the disciples, through constant faith, abide in Christ, and he in them. It is in the community that the most profound communion with Christ is fulfilled, from which alone true life stems, and individuals grow and bear fruit in living faith. Hence there is such a sharp rejection of those "antichrists" who have left the community: "They went out from us, but they were not of us; for if they had been of us, they would have continued with us; but they went out, that it might be plain that they all are not of us" (I Jn. 2:19).

"Abiding" in Christ means faithfulness and perseverance in the constantly renewed decision of faith, by which man puts himself entirely in the hands of God. The branch clings to the vine, because it is entirely nourished by the vine; and so the believer remains faithful to Christ, because he is supported and embraced totally by Christ. The believers "abide" within the fellowship of the disciples, within the Church, but they do not abide *in* the Church, they abide in Christ: "Abide in me, and I in you" (15:4). Even within the Church an individual can separate himself from Christ, by still belonging to the Church while abandoning his faithfulness to Christ. The sentence which was so disastrously misused is therefore not concerned with those who are excommunicate, and certainly not with those who should be burned, but relates to a man who, even though still belonging to the Church, has broken faith and severed himself from the stem which gives him life, thereby courting his own destruction: "If a man does not abide in me, he is cast forth as a branch and withers; and the branches are gathered, thrown into the fire and burned" (Jn. 15:6). He who remains faithful has life, and bears rich fruit. He who cuts himself off from life, incurs death.

It is only possible to abide in Christ—and this is where the ultimate meaninglessness of the Inquisition and the ultimate meaning of the Church is revealed—by abiding in *love:* "As the Father has loved me, so have I loved you; abide in my love. If you keep my commandments, you will abide in my love, just as I have kept my Father's commandments and abide in his love. These things I have spoken to you, that my joy may be in you, and that your joy may be full. This is my commandment, that you love one another as I have loved you. Greater love has no man than this, that a man lay down his life for his friends. You are my friends if you do what I command you. No longer do I call you servants, for the servant does not know what his master is doing; but I have called you friends, for all that I have heard from the Father I have made known to you. You did not choose me, but I chose you and appointed you that you should go and bear fruit and that your fruit should abide; so that whatever you ask the Father in my name, he may give it to you. This I command you, to love one another" (Jn. 15:9–17).

This then is the commandment, anticipated in the example of the washing of the feet (cf. 13:1–35), which should prevail in the Church and embrace all other commandments: love, not hatred. The faith of Christ's friends is not to be isolated and loveless, but a faith which is true in love, is vigorous and bears fruit; neither they nor the community are to enjoy existence for themselves but they are to devote their whole life to others; they are not to take the lives of others, but give their own lives for others. Love is the power of unity which binds the Church together. The love of the Father, which is given entirely to the Son, is given also to all who are in fellowship with the Son (cf. 16:27). The Father's love, which unites Father and Son, unites all and will unite all in the Church who believe in the Son: "I do not pray for these only, but also for those who are to believe in me through their word, that they may all be one; even as thou, Father, art in me, and I in thee, that they also may be in us, so that the world may believe that thou hast sent me. The glory which thou hast given me I have given to them, that they may be one even as we are one. I in them and thou in me, that they may become perfectly one, so that the world may know that thou hast sent me and hast loved them even as thou hast loved me. Father, I desire that they also, whom thou hast given me, may be with me where I am, to behold my glory which thou hast given me in thy love for me before the foundation of the world. O righteous Father, the world has not known thee, but I have known thee; and these know that thou hast sent me. I made known to them thy name, and I will make it known, that the love with which thou hast loved me may be in them, and I in them" (Jn. 17:20–26).

This concludes our study of the fundamental structure of the Church. By seeing the ecclesia as the people of God, as a spiritual creation and as the body of Christ—in concrete historical terms, with reference to the New Testament and an eye to the present, rather than in completely abstract terms—we have covered all that is fundamentally essential to an understanding of the historical nature of the Church.

What follows can therefore only be explication and exposition of what has now been stated. If in this and the preceding chapter we have principally, though not exclusively, looked at the Church from the perspective of its origins and from there looked at the Church in the present, we shall now, though again not exclusively, turn our attention to the nature of the Church from the perspective of the present, while keeping constantly in mind what we have learned about the origins of the Church.

D. *The Dimensions of the Church*

I. THE CHURCH IS ONE

1. WHAT IS THE TRUE CHURCH?

Ever since the Council of Constantinople in 381 the Church has professed the article from the Creed of Nicaea–Constantinople (D 86), reaffirmed at Ephesus and Chalcedon, that: "We believe . . . (in) the one, holy, catholic and apostolic Church" (εἰς μίαν, ἁγίαν, καθολικὴν καὶ ἀποστολικὴν ἐκκλησίαν).

The nature given to the Church through God's eschatological saving act in Christ was given it as a responsibility. This nature must be constantly realized anew and given new form in history by our personal decision of faith. The historical Church cannot do without this constant renewal of its form. Renewal of form implies change of form by means of human decision and responsibility. God does not present us with the nature of the Church as an objective fact, nor does he overwhelm it with mystic inevitability, nor work in it by organic development; he calls us constantly to new decisions of faith, to a free responsibility, to loving service. It is impossible simply to preserve the Church for all time in the original form it enjoyed as the primitive Church. Changing times demand changing forms. Yet in spite of all changes in form the basic structure of the Church given to it in Christ by God's saving act must be preserved, if it is to remain the true Church. Not every change in form is therefore in accordance with the Church's nature. Through the failure of men in their free responsibility, discrepancies between nature and form can occur: mistakes and misconceptions, errors of judgment and false developments. Thus there can be a form, an actual state, which is true to its nature or false to its nature—and therefore in this sense a true or a false Church. Here we come to the problem of what criteria we have to help us distinguish whether the Church is true or false.

(a) Can unity, holiness, catholicity and apostolicity be the marks of the true Church? In view of the many false developments, of fanaticism and heresy, even the possibility of a pseudo-Church, the question cannot be dismissed out of hand as improper. It is one that constantly confronts us and demands an answer: where and what is the Church? Certainly the true Church is a believed Church, a Church of believers and for believers; it can only be recognized for what it is through faith. But precisely this Church—and not only the universal Church, but the local Church too—has to ask itself, must ask itself, what it is that makes it legitimate. It is for the faithful themselves that the question is of real importance: is this Church or that, which calls itself the Church of Christ, really Christ's Church? The Church as the ecclesia of the faithful is, as we have seen, not simply invisible, but both visible and invisible. Precisely because it is the people of God, the Church is essentially a *people* and therefore visible. Precisely because it is a building in the Spirit it is truly a building and therefore visible. Precisely because it is the body of Christ the Church is really a body and as such visible. Faith in both the Old and New Testament senses does not exclude the visible, but proves itself in the visible. Being the people of God, a spiritual building, and the body of Christ, the Church can be recognized as the Church.

Where is the true Church? The question can be asked either of the individual in the Church or of the Church as a community. To combine these two questions leads only to confusion. For the individual the question was valid even in New Testament times, when there were false disciples, teachers and prophets, and sinners in general. Their existence makes it essential to ask: is this visible Church really the whole Church? This question is raised particularly by the existence of an established or official Church. So it is hardly surprising that it became a burning question for Augustine, at a time when the Church had begun to be an official Church, and again later, for Wyclif, Hus and the Reformers, when this official Church began to decline in the late Middle Ages. Insofar as the Church does not exist without or before or independently of its members, but *in* them, the question cannot be dismissed nor merely shifted on to an unrealistic ideal Church. But can it be answered? The answer may try to draw these or those distinctions (membership of the Church *actu* or *in potentia,* to the body or the spirit of the Church; for instance, not to the body, but to the spirit; not to the spirit, but to the body, etc.), but it finally always comes down to the fact that the concrete, empirical Church is not entirely a Church, that alongside the real members of the Church, there may be others who are only apparent, hypocritical members, so that in one way or another the concrete empirical Church is a *corpus permixtum,* a mixture of wheat and tares, good fishes and bad. External voluntary adherence to the Church and true inner membership are not necessarily synonymous.

But does this answer the question? Does this or that individual belong to the Church, really belong to the Church? There is no disputing the fact that definite signs can be recognized; the Church itself lays down external guide-lines and makes disciplinary decisions. But anything either the Church or the individual says on the subject must remain provisional and tentative. "Judge not that you be not judged" (Mt. 7:1). This is equally, in fact particularly, valid in the sphere of faith and unbelief, the basic criterion for membership of the Church. Our judgment will be not according to the canon of faith, but according to the canon of love, and in the meantime we live by the canon of hope. We do not live in a static state (faith or disbelief) but in a state of movement which is open towards the future. The final unconditional, definitive, and infallible word can only be said by him who through his grace calls, justifies and judges us. "Therefore do not pronounce judgment before the time, before the Lord comes, who will bring to light the things now hidden in darkness and will disclose the purposes of the heart. Then every man will receive his commendation from God" (I Cor. 4:5).

Where is the true Church? Our question is directed not towards the individual and his tangible membership of the Church, but to the Church as such: whether a certain given community is the true Church. God alone can know the heart of any individual but the outward form and constitution of a community is something that can be recognized. There are signs by which the Church can be recognized, signs that can be perceived by everyone. Even the non-believer is aware of them, but as a non-believer he will ultimately misinterpret them; he will recognize them and yet mistake their true significance. For him their deeper reality is veiled, not clear. He sees and yet does not see, since he does not understand what divine activity takes place in this human reality. Only for the believer do these visible signs reveal actual reality: God at work in the Church among men and through men. A recognition which is consciously critical and negative or a recognition which is neutral and indifferentist will see the signposts and the writing on them without being able to decipher what it says; for this can only be done when the recognition is positive and committed. The signs of the true Church, although they can be seen from a distance, cannot be read with objective impartiality as though they were street numbers, but only really recognized and understood in the blind leap of a trusting faith. What are these signs by which the Church can be recognized? Can unity, holiness, catholicity and apostolicity be the marks by which we can recognize it? These four credal attributes have become in our post-medieval and post-Reformation theology more and more four marks of distinction to be used apologetically.[1]

In earlier explanations of the creed the signs of the Church were commentated and explained, but not used apologetically. In combating divisions in the early Church reference was made to the apostolic commission, as in Clement's first letter (42:1–4), or to fellowship with the bishop as in Ignatius (Smyrn 8:1–2), or to the teaching tradition of the apostles as in Irenaeus,[2] guaranteed by the apostolic Church and the apostolic succession of its bishops (by which the *potentior principalitas* is the prerogative of the Roman Church) or to the collegiality of the episcopate as a whole as in Cyprian.[3] Against the Donatists Augustine emphasized the world-wide universality of the Church in addition to its sanctity,[4] against the Manicheans the consensus of nations and races in addi-

---

[1] On the individual *notae* see the manuals of fundamental theology (esp. A. Lang, M. Nicolau–J. Szlaverri, T. Zapelea) and dogmatics (esp. M. Schmaus III/1, K. Barth IV/1, E. Brunner III, O. Weber II) and the relevant encyclopaedia articles, esp. A. Kopling, art. on "Notae Ecclesiae", in LThK VII, 1044–1048 (bibli.); of the recent monographs esp. G. Thils, *Les notes de l'Eglise dans l'apologétique catholique depuis la Réforme,* Rembloux–Paris 1937.

[2] Irenaeus, *Adv. haer.* III, 3, 2; PG 7, 849.

[3] Cyprian, *Ep. 43,* 3; CSEL 3/2, 592.

[4] Augustine, *De vera religione;* PL 34, 128.

tion to its wisdom, also the authority of the Church evidenced in its miracles, nourished by hope, increased by love, and confirmed by age, then the episcopal succession and finally its undeniable epithet of catholic.[5]

On the whole, up until the late Middle Ages heresy was fought by setting out its errors. Only with the new concept of the Church introduced by Wyclif and Hus did the question of the truth of an independent Church arise. The argument used first by John of Ragusa in his *Tractatus de Ecclesia* (1431) against Hus, was developed by Juan de Torquemada in his *Summa de Ecclesia* (1486), and then used against the Reformers; unity, sanctity, catholicity and apostolicity are the four conditions of the true Church. They are, however, no longer merely characteristics (*proprietates*), but distinguishing characteristics, recognizable marks (*signa, criteria,* and from the time of Gregory of Valencia onwards, *notae*). In the *Confessio catholicae fidei* (1553) of Hosius and in the Tridentine Catechism the four characteristics constitute the principle for a division. Even more *notae* were found: Gravina found six, Pazmany seven, Suárez eight, Bellarmine fifteen, Bozi a hundred! From the seventeenth century onwards, however, apologists restricted themselves to the four classical attributes and from 1800 they were in general use. Vatican I then laid particular emphasis on the fact that the Church is in itself "a great and lasting motive for its credibility and divine mission".

The Reformers did not deny the four attributes of the Church; in fact they specifically emphasized their adherence to the creeds of the early Church. For them, however, in their concern for the people in the community and the reform of the Church, other things were decisive. They too asked the question, where is the true Church? Their answer was both theological and polemical: where the Gospel is taught in its purity and the sacraments properly administered.

Article VII of the *Confessio Augustana* 1530 teaches of the Church: "Similarly it is taught that the one holy Church will always remain. The Church is, however, the community of saints, in which the pure Gospel is preached and the sacraments properly administered". Here "pure" means according to the Scriptures, and "properly" means in accordance with their institution. This was also the teaching of the Reformed and Anglican Churches (*Con-*

[5] Augustine, *Contra ep. Manichaei; PL* 42, 175.

fessio Helvetica posterior, 1562, and Article 19 of the articles of religion of the Church of England, 1562).

These two distinguishing signs were developed and expanded. In his tract "On the Councils and Churches" (1539)[6] Luther demanded seven essential marks: (1) the preaching of the true word of God; (2) the proper administration of baptism; (3) the correct form of Lord's Supper; (4) the power of the keys; (5) the lawful vocation and ordination of ministers; (6) prayer and the singing of the psalms in the vernacular; (7) persecutions. In his violent polemic "Against Hans Worst" (1541)[7] he makes additional requirements:[7] the apostolic creed and the faith of the primitive Church, respect for the secular power, a high estimation of the married state, tolerance and prayer for persecutors (lawful vocation of ministers is omitted). At the same time he enumerates the innovations and distortions of the true Gospel perpetrated by the Roman Church in past centuries.

(*b*) Surely this exclusive way of looking at the problem is now out of date? Surely today the difficulties raised by both the Catholic and the Protestant signs have become only too obvious.

First, the problems involved in the Protestant signs. Catholic theology has never had any positive objection to raise against the two classic Protestant signs: without the preaching of the Gospel in accordance with Scripture and the administering of the sacraments as divinely ordained there can be no true Church according to the Catholic view either; both are absolute prerequisites for the Catholic Church too. The only objection is a negative one, that these two characteristics of the true Church are not truly distinguishing features. They are not visible and serve to show where the Church is hidden, rather than what it truly is. Looking at the actual state of the late medieval Church, the neglect and obscuring of the original Gospel message in preaching, theology, and the life of the Church, as well as the numerous abuses in the administration of the sacraments (Mass and confession in particular), it is clear that the two criteria of the preaching of the Gospel in accordance with Scripture and the proper administration of the sacraments are by no means so ineffective as the Catholic

[6] Luther, WA 50, 628–642.
[7] Luther, WA 51, 469–572.

side often claims; this will be more readily admitted today than it was previously. On the other hand it cannot be denied that on the basis of these two criteria alone, it became more and more difficult to distinguish the Protestant Church from the Catholic Church or from enthusiast sects. The enthusiasts made especially emphatic claims to preach the pure Gospel and administer the sacraments properly. And the Catholic Church too made it impossible to give a totally negative judgment on its preaching of the word and administration of the sacraments, first by the Tridentine reforms and even more so by more recent reforms. At any rate the question of the truth of the Catholic Church can no longer be dismissed by a reference to general principles of this sort. Equally, Protestant Churches are obliged to take a new critical and self-critical look at the original message and are arriving at a new and differentiated answer on the question of the Catholic Church.[8]

Secondly, the problems involved in the Catholic signs. As we have seen, the theology of the Reformation had no basic objections to the four classic attributes of the Church. Yet they in fact express something—not least as a defence against enthusiasm—which is omitted by the two Protestant criteria. But here we are thrown back on our question once again: how can we recognize true unity, holiness, catholicity, and apostolicity? Is it sufficient to point to the canonical legality of ecclesiastical office? The four signs, if they are genuine ones, must in any case depend upon the two others: the unity, holiness, catholicity and apostolicity of the Church do not mean anything if they are not based on the pure Gospel message, valid baptism, and the proper celebration of the Lord's Supper. Always and in every case the Church must be certain it is in essential agreement with the original New Testament message. However loudly a Church might proclaim itself one, holy, catholic and apostolic, if it did not do so in the spirit of the New Testament message it would be at best an empty and unconvincing proclamation. The individual signs may be hidden in a Church. They may exist in such a way that they are no longer seen to be convincing from outside, perhaps not even from inside, because they have lost their illuminating

---

[8] For further discussion of the problematic of the true Church, cf. *Structures*, 95–190.

power, so that men no longer believe because of the Church, but have either lost their faith because of the Church or believe in spite of it. Unity, holiness, catholicity and apostolicity are therefore not only gifts, granted to the Church by God's grace, but at the same time tasks which it is vital for the Church to fulfil in a responsible way.

What, then, is the essential thing when we are considering these signs? Not apologetical arguments, which have never led to mass conversions on either the Catholic or the Protestant side, but the living realization of the signs in the life of the Church. What use is it to a Church to "have" the holy Scriptures if the power and strength of the Gospel are not heard in it; if it "has" the sacraments only to distort them and choke them with superstition and idolatry; if its oneness, holiness, catholicity and apostolicity are firmly and visibly rooted in institutions, and yet these institutions are but hollow, lifeless forms? What is truly decisive is not the formal presence of certain characteristics, but their use and practice. The word of the Gospel must truly be preached, heard and followed, the sacraments must really be used, oneness, holiness, catholicity and apostolicity must be lived by living men in a living Church, and the *notae Ecclesiae* must become in one way or another *notae Christianorum*. To bring about the living realization of its own signs is a big enough task for each Church, whichever of them it places most emphasis on. And if every Church strives to realize its own signs in fundamental agreement with the one same New Testament message, it will in time come about that none can exclude the other as the untrue Church.

For all these reasons we have chosen to use not the apologetic term "signs of the Church", but the theologically orientated one "dimensions of the Church". Where these dimensions are realized is in the first place an open question. It will basically only be answered by the Church which proves itself in practice, whose speech and message like those of the apostle "were not in plausible words of wisdom, but in demonstration of the Spirit and power" (I Cor. 2:4).

But instead of taking it for granted that there are a number of different Churches, we must turn to the question of the unity, the oneness of the Church.

2. UNITY IN DIVERSITY

(*a*) Can it be denied that there is not one Church but many? Over two hundred Churches belong to the World Council of Churches alone, quite apart from the Catholic Church and some Protestant Churches of strict Lutheran, Reformed or Baptist persuasion which do not want to take part in the World Council. This Council has succeeded in the impressive and very valuable task of bringing together for mutual brotherly help and consultation the very great majority of non-Catholic Churches that previously were often no more than names to each other: the Orthodox Churches (Greek, Russian, even Coptic and the other autocephalous Churches) together with the Lutheran and Reformed Churches, the Anglican communion, the Old Catholics and a great number of Free Churches (Methodists, Baptists, Disciples of Christ, etc.). In this way common action by the separated Churches has been made considerably easier, common study groups and mutual assistance in evangelistic and missionary tasks throughout the world as well as a deepened ecumenical consciousness among all Christians have become a reality. The World Council of Churches deserves the active support of all Churches and all Christians.

But in spite of all this admirable work for Church unity, there is one thing that the World Council is not: it is not a Church. Nor does it wish to regard itself as one. According to the first paragraph of its constitution, it is "a fellowship of Churches, which confess our Lord Jesus Christ as God and Saviour according to the Scriptures and together endeavour to accomplish what they are called to do in the glory of God the Father, the Son and the Holy Spirit". This is "more than a mere formula of agreement", yet "less than a creed" (Evanston Declaration). That there are many gulfs between these Churches in matters of creed, worship and Church order, that they do in fact hold different beliefs, cannot be denied. The World Council of Churches is in no sense an amalgamation of Churches or Church unions, like the Panorthodox Conference, the Lutheran World Congress, the Reformed Churches' Alliance, the Lambeth Conference, the

World Unions of the Methodists, Baptists, etc., it is not a world Church nor a super-Church. Its declarations and decisions are not binding on its member Churches, who may adopt, reject or ignore them. The World Council may not take a stand on any particular conception of the Church, nor claim exclusive validity for any particular doctrine on the nature of Church unity. Yet all the member Churches believe on the basis of the New Testament that the Church of Christ is *one*. In short, the Churches of the World Council form a disunited plurality of Churches, which are all seeking the unity of the one Church.

The purpose of the World Council is not to negotiate union between the various Churches, but to put them into living contact with one another and to set in motion research and discussion into the problem of Church unity. Here it has had striking success—and recently with the co-operation of the Catholic Church as well. Yet in spite of all this can the world —the theologically uncommitted spectators—be blamed for seeing in it empirical proof of the divisions not only in Christianity, but in the Church of Christ itself?

The effects of this conflicting plurality of Churches, as is too well known to need setting out in detail here, are disastrous: the disunity and mutual rivairy of the Christian Churches is in part responsible for the widespread failure of the Christian mission to the world, particularly in Asia where the percentage of Christians in the population as a whole is very small. But the competing claims of rival Churches make the position difficult not only *vis-à-vis* ancient religions, but also in the confrontation with modern quasi-religions and secularisms, the different atheisms and agnosticisms: which of the many Churches is to be believed? In addition, urgently necessary internal reforms within the various Churches have been held up for centuries by entrenched confessional positions. So both inwardly and outwardly the existence of conflicting Churches has done indescribable harm to the credibility of the Church and its message. The divisions between the Churches are felt even in the everyday lives of millions of families who cannot worship and eat at the Lord's table together. Innumerable people have been alienated from the Church itself because of these divisions.

But far more decisive than any of these reasons is the fact that God, the foundation of the Church's existence, wills and decrees that this Church should be one, incontrovertibly one. It springs from one saving event and from one message, it should be one community of disciples, witnesses and ministers. Christ has not only reconciled God and man, he has also removed all opposition between man and man; he is the basis of his Church's unity. Can we suppose, after studying the original testimony of the Bible, that the Church of God could be a jostling confusion of larger and smaller ecclesiae, which accuse one another of erroneous beliefs, rites and orders? Can the one great people of God ever be split up into an ugly plurality of larger and smaller tribes, which although they have abandoned hot war and open rivalry for cold war and undercover competition, still continue to make a mockery of belief to the detriment of mankind? Can the splendid oneness of Christ's body ever be disrupted into members, which, although they only have meaning and beauty in unity, try to continue their existence, living and partly living, in separation? Can the one marvellously wrought temple of the Holy Spirit ever be dissolved into a plurality of little temples, chapels and holy places of all kinds, in which Christians compete with one another, luring adherents away from one another and bringing the truth of the one and only God and Father into discredit?

"The Church established by Christ the Lord is, indeed, one and unique. Yet many Christian communions present themselves to men as the true heritage of Jesus Christ. To be sure, all proclaim themselves to be disciples of the Lord, but their convictions clash and their paths diverge, as though Christ himself were divided. Without doubt, this discord openly contradicts the will of Christ, provides a stumbling-block to the world, and inflicts damage on the most holy cause of proclaiming the good news to every creature" (DOe 1).

No, the Church—and by this I mean as always the local Church *and* the universal Church, the local community *and* the community as a whole—is really and positively *one* Church, one people of God, one body of Christ, one spiritual creation.[9] The whole New Testament message bears witness to this. Everything which was said earlier about the basic structure of the Church authenticates this in many ways; there is little point in repeating it all here. The classic New Testament texts on the unity of the Church are well known: I Cor. 1:10–30 (a warning against divisions and an admonition to be united in Christ, the only foundation); I Cor. 12 (the unity

[9] On the unity of the Church see the exegetical and systematic literature on ecclesiology quoted at A I, 3 and A II, 2 and the dogmatics (esp. M. Schmaus III/1, 544–602 and K. Barth IV/1, 668–685), as well as the still important work by J. A. Möhler, *Die Einheit der Kirche* (edited by J. R. Geiselmann, Darmstadt 1957). Of the vast quantity of ecumenical literature, see in particular: Y. Congar, *Divided Christendom*, London 1939; J. Casper, *Um die Einheit der Kirche*, Vienna 1940; H. B. Murdoch, *Church, Continuity and Unity*, Cambridge 1945; S. Hanson, *The Unity of the Church in the NT*, Uppsala 1946; M. P. Boegner, *Le problème de l'unité chrétienne*, Paris 1937; H. R. T. Brandreth, *Unity and Reunion; a Bibliography*, Toronto 1948; I. Karrer, *Peter and the Church. An examination of Cullmann's thesis*, Edinburgh–London–New York 1963; E. Wolf, *Peregrinatio*, Munich 1954, esp. 146–182; T. Sartory, *Die ökumenische Bewegung und die Einheit der Kirche*, Meiningen 1955; H. Schlier, *Die Zeit der Kirche*, Freiburg 1956, 287–299; N. Schiffers, *Die Einheit der Kirche nach J. H. Newman*, Düsseldorf 1956; G. Baum, *That they may be one*, London–Westminster, Md. 1958; M. Roesle–O. Cullmann ed., *Begegnung der Christen*, Stuttgart–Frankfurt/Main 1959; L. Zander, *Einheit ohne Vereinigung*, Stuttgart 1959; J. Beckmann, K. G. Steck and F. Viering, *Von Einheit und Wesen der Kirche*, Göttingen 1960; H. Asmussen–A. Brandenburg, *Wege zur Einheit*, Osnabrück 1960; H. Volk, *Gott alles in allem*, Mainz 1961, 175–222; R. Slenczka, *Ostkirche und Ökumene. Die Einheit der Kirche als dogmatisches Problem in der neueren ostkirchlichen Theologie*, Göttingen 1962; J. Daniélou, *L'unité des chrétiens et l'avenir du monde*, Paris 1952; P. Brunner, *Pro Ecclesia*, Berlin–Hamburg 1962/66, I, 225–234; II, 195–322; A. Hastings, *One and Apostolic*, London–New York 1963; Y. Congar, *Dialogue between Christians*, London 1966; W. Marxsen ed., *Einheit der Kirche?*, Witten 1964 (see esp. the contributions by Marxsen, K. Aland, and E. Kinder). Also important are the many relevant documents of the World Council of Churches and the various confessional Unions, as well as the many histories of the ecumenical movement (esp. P. Conord, G. Gloege, W. R. Hoog, W. Menn, S. C. Neill, R. Rouse, G. H. Tavard, G. Thils) and the introductions to ecumenism (esp. A. Bellini, C. Boyer, C.-J. Dumont, M.-J. Le Guillou, E. F. Hanahoe, B. Lambert, W. H. van de Pol, M. Villain, G. Weigel).

of the spirit in a multiplicity of gifts, one body with many members); Gal. 3:27 f. (all are one in Christ without distinction of race, social status or sex); Rom. 12:3–8 (many in number are one in Christ); Acts 2:42 (perseverance in the teaching of the apostles and in fellowship, in the breaking of bread and in prayer); Acts 4:32 (the company of the believers are of one heart and soul); Jn. 10:16 (one shepherd and one flock); Jn. 17:20–26 (all are one like the Father and the Son). The most pertinent summary of what the unity of the Church is according to the New Testament can be shown by a quotation from Ephesians 4:1–6: "I therefore . . . beg you to lead a life worthy of the calling to which you have been called, with all lowliness and meekness, with patience, forbearing one another in love, eager to maintain the unity of the Spirit in the bond of peace. There is one body and one Spirit, just as you were called to the one hope that belongs to your call, one Lord, one faith, one baptism, one God and Father of us all, who is above all and through all and in all."

The unity of the Church has nothing to do with the mythological magic of the number one and the intrinsic fascination of oneness. The unity of the Church is not simply a natural entity, is not simply moral unanimity and harmony, is not just sociological conformity and uniformity. To judge it by externals (canon law, ecclesiastical language, Church administration, etc.) is to misunderstand it completely. The unity of the Church is a spiritual entity. It is not chiefly a unity of the members among themselves, it depends finally not on itself but on the unity of God, which is efficacious through Jesus Christ in the Holy Spirit. It is one and the same God who gathers the scattered from all places and all ages and makes them into one people of God. It is one and the same Christ who through his word and his Spirit unites all together in the same bond of fellowship. It is one and the same baptism by which all are made members of the same body of Christ, one and the same Lord's Supper, in which all are united with Christ and with one another. It is one and the same confession of faith in the Lord Jesus the same hope of blessedness, the same love, which is experienced in oneness of heart, the same service of the world. The Church *is* one and therefore *should be* one.

"What has revealed the love of God among us is that the only-begotten Son of God has been sent by the Father into the world, so that, being made man, the Son might by His redemption of the entire human race give new life to it and unify it (cf. I Jn. 4:9; Col. 1:18–20; Jn. 11:52). Before offering Himself up as a spotless victim upon the altar of the cross, He prayed to His Father for those who believe: 'That all may be one even as thou, Father in me, and I in thee; that they also may be one in us, that the world may believe that thou hast sent me' (Jn. 17:21). In His Church He instituted the wonderful sacrament of the Eucharist by which the unity of the Church is signified and brought about. He gave His followers a new commandment of mutual love (cf. Jn. 13:34), and promised the Spirit, their Advocate (cf. Jn. 16:7), who, as Lord and life-giver, would abide with them forever.—After being lifted up on the cross and glorified, the Lord Jesus poured forth the Spirit whom He had promised, and through whom He has called and gathered together the people of the New Covenant, who comprise the Church, into a unity of faith, hope, and charity. For, as the apostle teaches, the Church is: 'one body and one spirit, even as you were called in one hope of your calling; one Lord, one faith, one baptism' (Eph. 4:4–5). For 'all who have been baptized into Christ, have put on Christ . . . for you are all one in Christ Jesus' (Gal. 3:27–28). It is the Holy Spirit dwelling in those who believe, pervading and ruling over the entire Church, who brings about that marvellous communion of the faithful and joins them together so intimately in Christ that He is the principle of the Church's unity. By distributing various kinds of spiritual gifts and ministries (cf. I Cor. 12:4–11), He enriches the Church of Jesus Christ with different functions, 'in order to perfect the saints for a work of ministry, for building up the body of Christ' (Eph. 4:12)" (DOe 2).

(*b*) If, however, every local Church is a community, if every local Church is in its own way the ecclesia, the people of God, a creation of the Holy Spirit, the body of Christ, can the multiplicity of the Churches be a bad thing in itself? The unity of the Church should not be sought only outside the local gathering of the community. Precisely the unity of the local Church, which implies something self-contained but not isolated, involves a multiplicity of Churches, since this local

Church cannot be unique. The unity of the Church presupposes, therefore, a common life shared by all the local Churches. So the word ecclesia is quite naturally used in the plural in the New Testament and linked with place-names, which in some cases describe different worlds: Jerusalem and Corinth, Antioch and Rome.

There is, then, a multiplicity of local Churches (those of Ephesus, Philippi, Thessalonica, etc.) in which the one Church manifests itself: the Churches of individual towns and villages. And there is a multiplicity of regional Churches (the Church in Judaea, Galilee and Samaria, in Galatia, Macedonia, Asia, etc.) in which the one Church is also present: the Churches of individual provinces, dioceses, nations and continents. And finally there is a multiplicity of different types of Churches (the Hellenistic, the Judaeo-Christian, etc.) which often coincide with regional Churches but sometimes also, as a result of population movements, are dispersed throughout different regions: the Churches of different rites or denominations.

Thus the unity of the Church presupposes a multiplicity of Churches: the various Churches do not need to deny their origins or their specific situations; their language, their history, their customs and traditions, their way of life and thought, their personal structure will differ fundamentally, and no one has the right to take this from them. The same thing is not suitable for everyone, at every time and in every place. The unity of the Church, moreover, not only presupposes a multiplicity of Churches, but makes it flourish anew: through the diversity of God's callings, through the multiplicity of the gifts of the Spirit given to the Church, through the variety of the members of Christ and their functions. In the same way that different individuals are made one in the concepts of the people of God, the creation of the Holy Spirit and the body of Christ, so by analogy different Churches can be reconciled. No one has the right to set limits to God's vocations, to quench the Spirit, or to level out the member Churches.

In the New Testament Christ's Church is not seen as a centralized egalitarian or totalitarian monolith. The joyless constricting uniformity of a standardized institution or a standard type is foreign to it. It is not part of the nature of the

Church to have a uniform form of worship, nor uniform hierarchies, nor even a uniform theology. In the light of Ephesians 4:4–6, the opposite would seem to be true. Diversity in worship: one God, one baptism and one Lord's Supper —but different peoples, different communities, different languages, different rites and forms of devotion, different prayers, hymns and vestments, different styles of art and in this sense different Churches. Diversity in theology too: one God, one Lord, one hope and one faith—but different theologies, different systems, different styles of thought, different conceptual apparatus and terminology, different schools, traditions and areas of research, different universities and theologians, and in this sense again different Churches. Diversity finally in Church order: one God, one Lord, one Spirit and one body—but a different order of life, different laws, different nations and traditions, different customs, usages and administrative systems, and so in this sense too different Churches.

In all these spheres the "unity of the Spirit in the bond of peace" can be preserved "with all lowliness and meekness, with patience, forbearing one another in love" (Eph. 4:2 f.). It is not necessary for this diversity and variety to breed dissensions, enmity and strife. In certain cases, some characteristics or individual peculiarity can be sacrificed for the sake of peace and love, and mutual concessions made. As long as all have the one God, Lord, Spirit, and faith and not their own private God, Lord, Spirit and faith, all is in order.

From New Testament times onwards there have been fundamentally different historical forms of the one Church, which may all be legitimate: in different respects differently structured expressions and forms of the same one Church. As long as these Churches recognize one another as legitimate, as long as they see one another as part of one and the same Church, as long as they are in fellowship as Churches with one another and hold common services, and especially celebrate the Eucharist together, and as long as they are helping one another, working together and standing together in times of difficulty and persecution, there can be no objection to their diversity. All the differences, however profound, between the individual Churches are then swallowed up by the certainty that all are one in the unity of the Church of Christ. These differences, however striking and deep-rooted, need not separate the Churches. They do not mean a division in the Church.

The co-existence of different Churches does not, therefore, in itself jeopardize the unity of the Church; unity is only endangered by co-existence which is neither co-operation nor support, but basically a hostile confrontation. It is not the differences in themselves which are harmful, but only excluding and exclusive differences. Then these differences are no longer the expression of a legitimate diversity of Churches, but are used against other Churches as *notae ecclesiae*, they are endowed with an unqualified validity *vis-à-vis* other Churches, so that the latter can no longer be regarded as legitimate forms of the one Church, but must be seen as a distortion of the Church of Christ. Such differences are divisive and make Church fellowship impossible. The different local Churches, regional Churches and rites become different confessions: Churches no longer simply of another place, another region, another rite, but belonging to a hostile confession. Their creeds, and therefore their worship and their fundamental order, conflict with one another, so that the unity of faith, baptism and communal meal is broken.

Are such divisions in the Church always the result of narrow-mindedness, lack of charity and selfishness? This is often, but not always, true. They can also arise from the honest conviction that anything else would be a betrayal of the Gospel of Jesus Christ. To those involved the separation seems inevitable. In this way divisions spring up which can no longer be categorized by the concepts Church and heresy, divisions where it is no longer a case of the separation of individuals or of quite small groups (which generally have no permanent character and disappear in time), but rather of the breaking up, for this is how it looks empirically, of the one great Church. Two major schisms are of this type: the schism between the Western and Eastern Churches and the schism between the (Western) Catholic Church and the Church of the Reformation.

3. REUNION OF THE CHURCHES

Is a reunion, even on a limited scale, of the separated Christian Churches a real possibility? We are in the midst of an unprecedented and seemingly irresistible movement towards unity not only in the world, but also in the Church. The work of the World Council of Churches on the one hand and the Second Vatican Council on the other is bearing fruit. New relations between the great ecclesiastical centres of Christianity, between Rome, Constantinople, Moscow, Geneva and Canterbury, have been established, and close contacts have been achieved between all the Christian Churches. Churches which thought of themselves as being of different "confessions", and so mutually exclusive, have come to see themselves as only of different denominations and have united or at any rate planned the union of their Churches. As far as the great schisms are concerned—between East and West, and Catholic and Protestant—any union is in the more distant future.

(*a*) Precisely these fundamental schisms, which have led to different permanent forms of Christianity, force us to think beyond what has already been said about the Church and heretics. Here too it is important not to talk simply in abstract theoretical terms, but to keep in mind the historical background of these fundamental schisms. A reunion of the separated Christian Churches is impossible without critical historical analysis and a willingness to accept the responsibility of our own Churches for the divisions. Systematic theology must take into account, as the basis for further investigation, the findings of unprejudiced academic research into Church history. This is particularly true of the schism between East and West.

What caused the schism between the Eastern and Western Churches? It is difficult to decide whether political, cultural or theological factors were the more important. Certainly it was the culmination of an extremely complex process of alienation lasting several centuries. Just as *before* the famous date of 1054, when the papal legate laid the bull of excommunication against Patriarch Cerularius on the altar of Hagia Sophia in Constantinople, various abrogations of the communion between Rome and Constantinople had taken place (as in 484–589 and from 867 under Photius), so relations were not entirely broken off even *after* 1054. What factors prepared the way for the schism and finally brought it about? Only brief indications can be given here.[10]

1. *Factors in Church politics:* First, the transfer of the imperial capital from Rome to "New Rome" (Constantinople) and the widespread identification of the Eastern Churches with the Byzantine Empire under Basil, as the ruler and law-giver (though not an absolute one) of the Church, particularly after the time of Justinian ("imperial papism"); simultaneously in the West the foundation of a single organized Latin Church system under the primacy of the bishop of the old imperial capital ("papalism"). Then the conversion of the barbarian kings and their peoples, on whom the Western Church came to lean more and more (Pepin and the Church-State), the idea (based on a forgery) of the Donation of Constantine to the popes and in particular the crowning of Charlemagne in 800 as Holy Roman (in fact German) Emperor, which strengthened the feeling in the East that they had been betrayed by the Latins; on the other hand the systematic building up of the ascendancy of the Patriarch of Constantinople, now called the ecumenical Patriarch. Then the conquests of Islam, which fostered the nationalism of the individual Churches in the East, complicated the relationship between the Eastern and Western Churches and led to political and ecclesiastical rigidity in Byzantium. Finally the ill-fated crusades which led in 1182 to a massacre among the Latins in Constantinople and in 1204 to their conquest of Constantinople, the institution of a Latin emperor, a Latin patriarch and Latin archbishops and to extensive latinization of the conquered territories (all Greek clergy taking an oath of obedience to the Roman Church). By 1204 the schism was complete and any thought of reunion destroyed; the subsequent politically orientated attempts at union (Second Council of Lyons in 1274, Council of Florence in 1439) came to nothing. When Constantinople fell to

---

[10] The most comprehensive introduction to the historico-theological problematic is in Y. Congar, *After Nine Hundred Years,* New York 1959. Also the general works on the Eastern schism (esp. L. Bréhier, F. Dvornik, J. Gay, M. Jugie, C. Lagier, B. Leib, A. Michel, W. Norden, S. Runciman), as well as those on the Eastern Churches in general, esp.: P. Bratsiotis, ed., *Die Orthodoxe Kirche in griechischer Sicht I–II,* Stuttgart 1960; B. Spuler, *Die Morgenländischen Kirchen,* Leiden–Cologne 1964.

the Turks in 1453, the mistrust and dislike of the Orientals for the Latins was complete. Even centuries later, in the face of Latin proselytizing, the cry was raised: "Rather death than Rome! Rather the turban than the mitre!"

2. *Cultural and religious factors:* The different languages of the Eastern and Western Churches, which frequently led to intellectual and cultural isolationism on both sides and innumerable misunderstandings even in matters of theological terminology; the different cultures which meant that the Greeks saw the Latins as cunning casuists and the Latins dismissed the Greeks as uncultured barbarians; the different rites which for the Orientals were not merely a different liturgical ceremonial, but rather a complete, independent and equally legitimate way of life and faith in the Church (theology, worship, piety, constitution and organization).

3. *Theological factors:* In contrast to the Platonism and individualism of the East were the different theological methods which became important in the West particularly from the eleventh century onwards: the trend towards the natural and the empirical, towards rational analysis and scholarly research; contrasted with the mainly contemplative and monastic theology of the East, the rational theology of the schools of the West (scholasticism); contrasted with the indecisiveness of the Orientals, and their fluidity and caution in dogmatic definitions, the Western urge to define and dogmatize; in contrast to the diversity of theology and Churches in the East, the markedly increasing conformity and centralization of the Western Church and its theology, which took place after the fall of the Empire and in particular from the twelfth century onwards (the Roman Latin liturgy, piety, canon law and administration).

Thus the doctrine of the primacy and infallibility of the pope, which was more and more stressed in theory and practice and finally promulgated as a dogma, came to embody all the differences between the Churches of East and West. The Orthodox Church still sees itself as the true Church of Christ identical with the early Church, preserving unaltered and uncontaminated the faith revealed by Christ, witnessed to by the apostles and interpreted by the Fathers of the Church (orthodox—to believe rightly). Is it right in this? The distance, in many respects considerable, of both Latin and Greek Churches and patristics from the original message and Church of the New Testament is even less widely recognized in the East than in the West; the much-vaunted continuity of the Eastern tradition with the New Testament does not stand the test of critical investigation at important points. Both Churches, the Latin and the Greek, have at any rate reason enough, as far as their past history is concerned, to take a critical look at themselves and try to find a way towards a new communion (the decree on ecumenism refers in its introductory paragraph on the Eastern Churches to their special independent history, cf. DOe 14).

No less important is the need for critical investigation of the Protestant Reformation, which was far more radical in its origins and its consequences. In spite of its internal divisions, which contrast both with the Eastern and the Western Latin Church, it constitutes a new third basic form of Christianity or of the Church.

How did the Protestant Reformation come about?[11]

1. The Reformation must be seen in historical perspective against the background of the general European upheaval which took place in the sixteenth century. To this extent it was influenced by very different factors: political (the destruction of the medieval empire by the popes and the subsequent decline of papal dominance and emergence of autonomous national states or more local princedoms; the opening-up of immense new areas by discoverers and explorers), economic (the change from a natural economy to a monetary one), cultural (the ambitions of the laity in the new and prospering towns, their new participation in intellectual life, made possible by the art of printing, and new unascetic ideals of life), intellectual (a new world-view, an atmosphere of readiness for great changes, the onset of philosophical monotheism in contrast to a naïve pragmatic polydemonism). In the centre of the general upheaval was the religio-ecclesiastical dispute, marked on the one hand by the failures of the Catholic Church, on the other by Luther's advocacy of religious reform. Here too a few brief guidelines:

2. *The failures of the Catholic Church:* The decline of the *papacy:* the Great Schism and the rule of three popes, the growing power of the conciliar movement, the secularization, moral decadence and misuse of their office by the Renaissance popes, Italian

[11] The classic Catholic work on the history of the Reformation in Germany is: J. Lortz, *Die Reformation in Deutschland I–II,* Freiburg 1948. There is an excellent bibliography; for the most recent books see the art. "Reformation" by the same author in LThK VIII, 1069–1082. From the Protestant side see W. Maurer, art. "Reformation", in RGG V, 858–873, and in particular H. Bornkamm–G. Ebeling, art. "Luther", in RGG IV, 480–520.

politics, absolutist centralism, the extravagant financial policy and immorality of the curia, the resistance to all reform. The hopeless state of the *Church in general:* the councils' lack of results and failure to carry through reforms, the retrogressive nature of Church institutions (the ban on usury, Church immunity from taxes and the secular law, monopoly of schools, encouragement of mendicants, excess of feast-days, etc.), the Church's domination by canon law, the great worldliness of the rich prince-bishops and the monasteries, the numerous uneducated and spiritually impoverished proletariat, alarming superstition, religious fearfulness often expressed in wild apocalyptic forms, an externalized liturgy and a rigid popular piety. The decadence of *theology:* endless peripheral dissensions between schools of late medieval scholasticism, complete neglect of vital theological questions (Christ and the justification of the sinner, word and sacrament, law and Gospel), not infrequent tendencies towards Pelagian errors as regards man's works, indulgences, the sacrifice of the Mass. Thus general corruption of the Catholic Church (though naturally there were positive traits too) caused criticism of the Church to rise to unprecedented proportions: the criticism of the radical thinkers of the fourteenth century (Ockham, Marsilius of Padua, the mystics); the University of Paris as a court of appeal against the papal and episcopal magisterium; the alliance of nominalism and gallicanism; individualistic mysticism; the criticism, indifference or scepticism of the humanists; but also their appeal to original sources; finally the effects of the Wycliffite and Hussite sects and the critical attitude to pope and Church among the educated in the towns as well as among the depressed peasant population. At the Diet of Nuremberg in 1523 Pope Hadrian VI had a public admission of guilt read by his legate Chieregatik, an example unfortunately not so explicitly followed by later popes.

3. *The reforms of Luther:* In his brilliant, deeply devout personality, Luther incorporated, refined and focused all the exuberant religious aspirations of the late Middle Ages, with their strong positive qualities of mysticism, nominalism and popular piety, and formulated them with an unparalleled power of language. He was not concerned simply with the fight against the indescribable abuses of the Church and with gaining independence from the papacy. His personal reforming impulse, like his explosive impact on world history, sprang from one thing: the need for the Church to return to the Gospel of Christ in its original testimony in Holy Scripture. Luther's personal starting-point was not, however, the problem of the Church as such, but the problem of salvation: whether and how a man could be certain of his own salvation.

Luther found the answer for himself and for many other searchers of the time in the epistle to the Romans: Man is justified by God's gift of righteousness from his free grace, which cannot be earned by good works, but can only be accepted in trust and faith. From this rediscovery of the Pauline doctrine of justification sprang Luther's new understanding of the Church and his radical criticism of the teaching and practice of a Church grown away from the Gospel, grown secularized and bureaucratic, his criticism of its conception of the sacraments (the sacrifice of the Mass as *earning* grace) its official hierarchy, displacing Christ, its many traditions unjustified by Scripture, the pious practices of everyday Catholic life (veneration of saints, relics, etc.). The quarrel over indulgences was only the outward sign of the fundamental disagreement with Rome which rapidly came to a head and which led to Luther's excommunication; but this was powerless to halt the advance of the Reformation movement, which demanded a radical reform of the whole of Church life according to the Gospel. Its later course, determined more by political than theological or ecclesiastical factors, need not be described here.

It is unthinkable to deny, and would today be admitted by Catholic historians and theologians too, that Luther (and accordingly the other Reformers as well) aroused a new awareness in the Church of the norm of the Gospel, of faith in the work of Christ, as the only mediator; that in his total theology he helped to revive original New Testament perspectives (the primacy of grace, the priesthood of all believers, ecclesiastical office as ministry, the importance of the word, the opposition between the law and the Gospel, the ethos of everyday life and work, etc.), and that in this way he made an important contribution to the reform of the Church—indirectly to the reform of the Catholic Church too. But the unity of the Church which Luther hoped to reform had been destroyed, and on the Protestant side further divisions followed this first great schism. It was a terrible price to pay and the Churches which have their roots in the Reformation cannot be dispensed from examining how much of the blame is theirs. Was it only Luther's violent and reckless temperament which made the break inevitable? Were not the Reformers in general often blind to what was genuinely Catholic? Were not certain aspects of the New Testament overemphasized and others neglected? Did not the stressing of the word "alone", justified in itself, lead to exaggerations in almost every sphere (Scripture alone, grace alone, faith alone), so that it was soon as liable to misinterpretation as the Catholic "and" (*and* tradition, *and* free will, *and* good works)? With the best of intentions, over-hasty conclusions were often drawn, especially with regard to the priesthood of all believers and the official priesthood, freedom of conscience and the *consensus ecclesiae.* As far as the Reformation is concerned, all Churches have good cause for self-examination and self-criticism.

(*b*) The state of separated Christendom seems so abnormal, so contradictory, and so hopeless that it is easy to understand how ways have been sought to justify the unjustifiable:

A first evasion is to retreat from the disunited visible Church to an undivided Church. But can the real Church be split up platonically into a visible empirical Church and an invisible ideal one? As we have seen, the real Church is always both in one. And if the visible Church is divided, then so is the invisible one which is identical with it. Can the unity of the Church be merely "experienced" inwardly, and not also put into practice before the world? We cannot minimize our divisions by superficial spiritualistic-dualistic solutions; we shall make them all the harder to overcome if we do not see how deep they go, if we allow unity to melt away into the invisible. It is true that no proof of this unity can be given to the unbeliever. But it can and should be given authentic witness in the world by the believer, so that the Church's unity becomes effective in the world and clearly manifested in spite of its invisibility.

A second evasion is to see the divisions in the Church as a normal divinely intended development and to postpone the reconciliation of the Church to the time of eschatological fulfilment. But is it really feasible in the light of the New Testament to regard these divisions as an organic development? Surely in the light of the New Testament they can only be seen as highly inorganic, abnormal, incongruous, a false development which any idealistic concept of development shows to be on the wrong track? Is it not simply an easy way out of our obligation to work for unity here and now, to bring in eschatological fulfilment? We know that the Church of Christ did not begin in the state of schism (we shall come back to this point later) in which, for the moment, it has ended; nor can this state of schism, which completely contradicts its mission and its origins, be regarded as an inevitable intermediate stage between the founding of the Church and the time of eschatological fulfilment. There can be no theological justification for wrong human decisions. We must not try to perpetuate the divisions in the Church, either by the speculations of theological history or the consolations of eschatology. Precisely because we are confronted by a mistaken development, the fact of eschatological fulfilment obliges us to realize what our task is *now*.

A third and related evasion is to regard the different Churches which have arisen as a result of schism as the three or four great branches of the one tree (the image has been used by Zinzendorf and by some Anglicans). There is certainly much that is true in this, provided that the different Churches are in communion with one another. But can these Churches be branches or off-shoots of the same tree when they disassociate themselves from one another, when perhaps for the sake of the Gospel they must disassociate themselves? Can contradictions in essentials co-exist in the same Church: in creed, in worship, and in the fundamental order of the Church? Can something be truth in one place and error in another, dogma here and heresy there? Can a Church which does not want simply to be absorbed into the world avoid drawing a boundary line, however vague, beyond which a Church ceases to be the true Church? If one Church can complain that another has a different spirit, there can at best be an uneasy truce and not a true peace between them. Only when we can pray together, hear the word of God together, confess our faith together and share our meal together, can we speak of one Church. Only then do we confess one Lord and not many, one Spirit and not many, one God and not many.

A fourth evasion is to explain the schism by saying that there is only one empirical Church identical with the Church of Christ, which does not recognize any of the other Churches as Churches. A determined protest against all indifferentist levelling-down inside the different Churches, for the sake of the truth of Christ's Church, will certainly always be necessary. But how justified is this protest? Is this one Church—whichever it is—with its claim to absolute identity being fair to the other Christian Churches, which, it cannot be denied, have not only valid baptism and therefore membership in the body of Christ, but also much else. Is this one Church being fair to itself if it arrogantly overlooks the fact that in some respects it is not the ecclesia but merely a *vestigium ecclesiae,* and that what is only a vestige in its own case may be fully realized in the case of other Churches? To over-estimate oneself in this way is surely a sign of pharisaical self-conceit, self-righteousness and impenitence. The Anglicans reproach the Catholics—and they could reproach the Orthodox in the same way—with claiming, so to speak, the whole of the broken plate because of possessing the piece with the monogram P, or even claiming that it has not been broken at all. Not to acknowledge the breach and to claim to be the whole (although the whole means *all*) is to be guilty in a different way of perpetuating the division in the Church.

Although there are still some ambiguities, Vatican II largely clarified the attitude of the Catholic Church to the other Christian Churches. 1. Previously the Catholic Church referred to other Churches only as heretics and schismatics (implying they were not of good faith); now it calls other Christians "separated brethren". 2. Whereas previously it only recognized individual Christians outside the Church, it now recognizes the existence of communities of Christians outside the Catholic Church (*"christianae communiones", DOe 1*). 3. It sees these communities not just as sociological groups, but as "Church communities" or "Churches" (*"ecclesiae vel communitates ecclesiasticae", CE 15, cf. DOe 3*). 4. It recognizes too the bond existing between these Churches in the ecumenical movement which has arisen outside the Catholic Church and echoes the words of the fundamental declaration of the World Council of Churches: "Everywhere, large numbers have felt the impulse of this grace, and among our separated brethren also there increases from day to day a movement, fostered by the grace of the Holy Spirit, for the restoration of unity among all Christians. Taking part in this movement, which is called ecumenical, are those who invoke the Triune God and confess Jesus as Lord and Saviour. They join in not merely as individuals but also as members of the corporate groups in which they have heard the gospel, and which each regards as his Church and, indeed, God's" (DOe 1). 5. Thus the Catholic Church does not identify itself exclusively (in spite of some formulas which seem to suggest otherwise) with the Church of Christ. At one point at any rate a striking revision took place: instead of the definitive formula originally suggested by the Commission: "the unique Church of Christ which in the creed we avow as one, holy, catholic, and apostolic . . . is (*est*) the Catholic Church, which is governed by the successor of Peter and by the bishops in union with that successor", the formulation adopted was: "subsists (*substitit*) in the Catholic Church" (CE 8). The reason given by the Commission for this important and unprecedented change in the formula was that "this expression accords better with our recognition of ecclesial elements in other Churches".[12] This refers to the "Churches or ecclesial communities" mentioned in CE 15. The new formulation was purposely left as vague as possible, so as not to stand in the way of the further theological investigation of this difficult problem, which is certainly necessary.

If we wish to avoid all these evasions, there is in fact only one alternative: not to look for any theological justifications for the divisions in the Church. We should not justify these divisions, any more than we justify sin, but "suffer" them as a dark enigma, an absurd, ridiculous, tolerable yet intolerable fact of life, that is contrary both to the will of God and the good of mankind. And in so far as it is against God's will and man's good, it is at the deepest level failure, guilt, sin—whether of individuals or of the community—and rarely of one "party" alone. However great the misunderstandings, however understandable the historical genesis of the separation and the circumstances of the break, it should never, never among Christians, have come to a division in the Church. A division in the Church is a scandal and a disgrace. Anyone who did not actively try to prevent it, anyone who furthered it in any way at all must bear part of the blame—how much it is not our place to judge. Naturally the mistakes of earlier generations cannot be attributed personally to people living today. But there is none the less a common responsibility and a common guilt not only for causing but also for perpetuating the division. This guilt weighs heavily upon the separated Churches, just as it does upon divided families who have not been reconciled.

"From her very beginnings there arose in this one and only Church of God certain rifts, which the apostle strongly censures as

[12] *Schema Constitutionis De Ecclesia*, Rome 1964, S.15,25.

damnable. But in subsequent centuries more widespread disagreements appeared and quite large communities became separated from full communion with the Catholic Church—developments for which, at times, *men of both sides were to blame.* However, one cannot impute the sin of separation to those who at present are born into these communities and are instilled therein with Christ's faith. The Catholic Church accepts them with respect and affection as brothers" (DOe 3).

The Churches themselves can do nothing to free themselves from guilt in the sight of God, they can only seek to be freed: they are dependent on forgiveness. So the first step in healing the breach must be an admission of guilt and a plea for forgiveness addressed both to God, the Lord of the Church, and to our brothers: "Forgive us our trespasses, as we forgive those who trespass against us." In asking for forgiveness, we ask for the healing of the division and in asking for forgiveness we declare that we are ready to do whatever is God's will to remove the division: Metanoia!

"There can be no ecumenism worthy of the name without a change of heart. For it is from newness of attitudes, from self-denial and unstinted love, that yearnings for unity take their rise and grow towards maturity. We should therefore pray to the divine Spirit for the grace to be genuinely self-denying, humble, gentle in the service of others, and to have an attitude of brotherly generosity towards them. . . . St John has testified: 'If we say that we have not sinned, we make him a liar, and his word is not in us' (I Jn. 1:10). This holds good for sins against unity. Thus, in humble prayer, we beg pardon of God and of our separated brethren, just as we forgive those who trespass against us. Let all Christ's faithful remember that the more purely they strive to live according to the gospel, the more they are fostering and even practising Christian unity" (DOe 7).

(*c*) Out of this self-critical investigation of the roots of the division and this common confession of our common guilt emerges clearly the task facing us. This does not mean that we should try to create unity with our own hands: through our desires and our efforts, our discussions and actions, our working-parties and commissions, conferences, congresses and councils, Church unions and alliances or even simply through our tolerance and open friendliness. If Church unity already exists and if it must be rediscovered and renewed, then this is fundamentally God's work. Unity—and this we should not forget even for a minute in all our very necessary work towards unity—has been given us by God in Christ. And this should be the point from which we start with confidence—without unnecessary thoughts about whether or to what extent our efforts will be successful—in trying to formulate briefly a few guided theological principles for the ecumenical journey of all Churches—for all of them are our concern.

1. *The existing common ecclesial reality must be recognized:* In Christ we are already united—in spite of the conflicting multiplicity of Churches. We know this by faith; the unity of the Church is a unity in faith. In him all Churches, whatever their disagreements among themselves, acknowledge the *one* Lord and at the same time in the *one* Spirit, his Spirit, the *one* Father, his Father. In him all Churches possess the one Gospel, his good news, however differently they may interpret it. And if these Churches baptize validly in his name—which is not in dispute—in which ecclesia are the baptized incorporated if not in his, the one ecclesia, of which body are they members if not the one body of Christ? And if these Churches also validly celebrate the Lord's Supper—which is only disputed in a few cases (with justice?)—what body do they receive and in what body are they united, if not in his, the one body? Is there not therefore much in common in the different faiths and hopes of the Churches, so much more in common than there is separating them? Cannot the love in the different Churches rise above, if it cannot obliterate, the differences in faith? Thus the different Churches should not search for the unity of the Church as though it had never been found, but on the broad basis of the unity which has already been found, which has indeed been given to us. The unity of the Church is not merely a goal, but is the foundation of necessary work for unity. It is not, in fact, without reason that the different Christian Churches call themselves *Churches*. And it is precisely because all Christian Churches are Churches that they are faced with the task of the unity of the Church through faith in Christ.

What is held in common among the Churches is listed in the Decree on Ecumenism as: faith in Christ, baptism and through it justification and membership of Christ's body, by which all are made true Christians and our brothers in the Lord, then the written word of God, the life of grace, faith, hope and charity, along with other interior gifts of the Holy Spirit and visible elements, finally liturgical actions, which engender a life of grace and provide access to the community of salvation. So all these Churches and ecclesial communities have importance and meaning in Christ's work of salvation (DOe 3).

The Orthodox Churches separated from Rome have always been termed Churches even in the language of the Curia (DOe refers back to the Fourth Lateran Council in 1215, the Second Council of Lyons in 1274, the Council of Florence in 1439). Vatican II fortunately avoided making the episcopal structure of the Church (or even the eucharistic sacrifice) the *criterion for the title "Church"*. Such a criterion is in fact arbitrary and does not do justice to the problematic of the Protestant Reformation. As far as many Church communities with an episcopal structure are concerned (such as the Anglican Church or the Swedish Lutheran Church) it would be difficult to say whether they should be termed "Church" or "ecclesial community" (the non-validity of Anglican orders has remained historically in question even after the decision —neither definitive nor infallible—of Leo XIII; and the invalidity of the eucharistic celebration outside the Catholic and Orthodox Churches is not so easy to prove theologically as it is from the standpoint of canon law). In the light of the New Testament, we cannot attach an unlimited number of elements and conditions to the definition of the Church, without placing limits on the concept of the Church (as happened in the case of Bellarmine, who included submission to the primacy of the pope in his definition of the Church and so could not recognize even the Orthodox Churches as Churches). We have seen in our exposition of the basic structure of the Church that it is both correct theologically and fruitful ecumenically to work outwards from a fundamental skeleton concept. If we do this we can apply the name Church to any community of baptized Christians modelled on Holy Scripture, who believe in Christ the Lord, wish to celebrate the Lord's Supper, try to live according to the Gospel, and wish to have the name of Church (not all Protestant communities would wish this; to this extent it is reasonable to distinguish between "Churches" and "ecclesial communities"). This emphasis on the fundamentals of ecclesial community challenges us to deepen our fellowship and intensify its ecclesial character.

2. *The desired common ecclesial reality must be found:* The recognition of the unity which already exists in Christ calls us to the search for unity. Since we cannot find it by our own strength alone, we need not only at the beginning but all through our search the help of prayer, to him who will give us the means and the fulfilment as well as the desire: a common prayer for redemption from the evil of divisions, from prejudices and misunderstandings, all mistrust and estrangement. Is it still necessary today to admonish the Churches to pray, not against one another (for their own victory), but for one another (in mutual love)? To pray not that their will may be done, but God's; that the reunion of the Churches may take place, not as we imagine it will, but as God wants it.

"This change of heart and holiness of life, along with public and private prayer for the unity of Christians, should be regarded as the soul of the whole ecumenical movement, and can rightly be called 'spiritual ecumenism' " (DOe 8). Not only prayer among Catholics, but also common prayer with other Christians is allowed and indeed desired; common worship within certain limitations is fundamentally possible (ibid.).

From *oratio* springs true *actio*. It is not an *actio* which dissipates itself in externals, which still perhaps hopes to achieve union through force, no longer brute force, but legal sanctions (religious unity for the sake of national unity!) or political or social pressures. In fact the State merely harms the cause of Church unity by taking sides, and a Church which used the power of the State to enforce unity of faith would merely discredit itself and its faith. Tactical or pragmatic action from non-ecclesiastical motives and interests eventually cancels out all efforts in the cause of Church unity. Many previous attempts at reunion (such as the Councils of Lyons and Florence, as well as various Protestant dialogues) finally foundered because they were politically inspired. The reunion of the Churches cannot be decreed from above, it must grow up from below, from within both communities and individuals. For this reason, the vital thing at all levels is that we should learn to accept and respect one another—something we are only now beginning to take for granted; we must come to know one another and listen to one another where what is really essential, faith, is concerned; we must feel that we are one, and work together, wherever possible, so as to affirm and witness to Christ together before the world, wherever we can do so in conscience. This *actio* will of course bring *passio* with it, the very real suffering of seeing the divisions in the Church and seeing the failures of one's own Church and of other Churches. But this apparently fruitless *passio* will, if we really persevere, be transformed into fruitful *actio*. Thus on the basis of what we already have in common, which is far more significant than anything that divides us, we must constantly try to discover common ground on which we can build.

"Concern for restoring unity pertains to the whole Church, faithful and clergy alike. It extends to everyone, according to the potential of each, whether it be exercised in daily Christian living or in theological and historical studies. This very concern already reveals to some extent the bond of brotherhood existing among all Christians, and it leads toward that full and perfect unity which God lovingly desires" (DOe 5). On the necessity of the two sides coming to know one another and of dialogue on an equal footing, cf. DOe 9; on the ecumenical orientation of theology and practical training, cf. DOe 10; on common witness of Christians before the world and practical work together in public life, cf. DOe 12.

3. *Work for unity must start in one's own Church, but with the other Churches in mind:* We will naturally start our search for common ground, if we are genuinely concerned about the divisions in the Church, by looking at the Church we belong to by baptism and in which we learned our faith: not in order to withdraw into its individuality, but to find out what elements it has in common with other Churches. It would be a mistake to try to serve the cause of unity by leaving one's own Church and joining another. Individuals may be able to solve serious crises of faith by their conversion to this or that Church, it is true; but, as we know from many centuries of experience, that will not bring about the unity of the Church of Christ we all desire. It would also be a mistake to leave one's own Church in order to try and achieve unity

from outside *any* of the present Churches. Of course, it would be possible to speak without commitment from such a "neutral" standpoint, but it would not help the cause of Church unity. This neutral position would remain a no-man's-land, a place where it would be impossible to find Church unity. Alternatively, if the task were seriously undertaken, it could only be at the cost, sooner or later, of neutrality, since what would emerge would be a new confession or a new kind of Church in opposition to all the others.

Given the present disparate Churches, we can do nothing but search, humbly, unpretentiously, soberly and clearheadedly, for common ground within our own Church, declaring our loyalty, with determination but without presumption, to the Church we belong to; this must be our starting-point. Our efforts for Church unity demand not less but more involvement in our own Church than ever; we have to discover what is sound in its roots, find out its true nature and follow its best intentions. If we become more involved in our own Church, we cannot but be aware of the other Churches as well. We must not look so hard at our own Church that we do not see the other Churches which make the same claims to be the true Church of Christ, claims which in many respects may seem more justified than our own, since in this or that respect they are more attentive to the Gospel and more conscientious in carrying out its message. It then becomes inevitable that these other Churches call our own Church in question, ask of us how we follow the Gospel in this or that respect, and explicitly or implicitly ask us to observe the Gospel in this or that respect in the same way that they do, and so find common ground with them.

Can a Church which desires the unity of the Church of Christ simply dispense itself from the need to grant the justified wishes and demands of other Churches? If we begin our ecumenical efforts by looking at our own Church, this is the acid test of a true desire for unity: the willingness to renew our own Church by fulfilling the justified request of other Churches. If this were done seriously on all sides, a rapprochement, indeed unity itself, would be inevitable. Unity cannot be achieved by looking backwards, however much we respect the past, however little we can change it. Unity is only possible on the path that leads forward. The future, to which the Church must always be open, offers us new possibilities. If every Church, rejecting that unenlightened enthusiasm which takes no account of difficulties, but also decisively rejecting all kinds of confessional indifference and sloth, were to fulfil the justified wishes and demands of the other Churches, then no Church would be the same in the future as it is today. In the process of selfless giving and taking the common elements would come to light and be able to grow.

"Every renewal of the Church essentially consists in an increase of fidelity to her own calling. Undoubtedly this explains the dynamism of the movement toward unity. Christ summons the Church, as she goes her pilgrim way, to that continual reformation of which she always has need, insofar as she is an institution of men here on earth. Therefore, if the influence of events or of the times has led to deficiencies in conduct, in Church discipline, or even in the formulation of doctrine (which must be carefully distinguished from the actual deposit of faith), these should be appropriately rectified at the proper moment. Church renewal therefore has notable ecumenical importance. Already this renewal is taking place in various spheres of the Church's life: the biblical and liturgical movements, the preaching of the word of God, catechetics, the apostolate of the laity, new forms of religious life and the spirituality of married life, and the Church's social teaching and activity. All these should be considered as favourable pledges and signs of ecumenical progress in the future" (DOe 6).

4. *Truth must not be sacrificed, but rediscovered:* The Churches cannot be unified satisfactorily on the basis of indifferentist faith and half-hearted allegiances. Diplomatic settlements and compromises in dogma are not the right way. We must be mistrustful of formulas or forms of unity which conceal our differences rather than overcoming them. If unity is to be genuine, dogmatic differences must be settled theologically. They will not be solved by pretending that they are not there or that they do not matter. Unless they are genuinely overcome, they will remain a constant source of infection, the more dangerous for being hidden. We must reject "unity at any price". A Church which abandons the truth abandons itself.

"The manner and order in which Catholic belief is expressed should in no way become an obstacle to dialogue with our brethren. It is, of course, essential that the doctrine be clearly presented in its entirety. Nothing is so foreign to the spirit of ecumenism as a false conciliatory approach which harms the purity of Catholic doctrine and obscures its assured genuine meaning" (DOe 11).

Our faith must be stronger, not weaker, our judgment must be clearer, not obscurer, our ability to draw distinctions must be truly critical, not uncritical: this must be the basis of our efforts for unity. But this implies that it is not enough simply to repeat the truth. Truth must be rediscovered, reconquered anew in every age. Truths cannot be handed on like bricks, preferably undisturbed. Truth is not like stone, it is a thing of the spirit which is lost if it is allowed to petrify. Even dogmas and articles of faith are not frozen or petrified formulas, set apart from the course of human history. They too originated in specific historical situations and must constantly be prized out of their historical setting and put in wider (but of course still finite) historical perspective, so that we can appreciate them correctly, more fully, more truly. In particular, dogmas and articles of faith which were the products of fierce confrontations with hostile heresies, ramparts against particular errors, must be dissociated from the polemical plan of campaign they supported, from the narrow limitations of a specific historical moment; we must try to reinterpret them in a more balanced and suitable way, in a better way, by seeing them in the context of the saving fullness of the Old and New Testament message, a fullness which no formulas of the Church can ever exhaust. This has always happened, and is still happening, for just as Chalcedon, in the most positive manner, corrected and improved upon Ephesus, so Vatican I was corrected and improved by Vatican II. Thus we can see that there are no areas which are irreformable, which can dispense with constant renewal. Every truth needs translating. There are irreformable *constants* of truth, given to us by the revelation of God himself; but we must be able to recognize them as such in every age, and for this very reason it is essential that the human, ecclesiastical formulations of them reflecting the thoughts and language and outlook of a particular age, are not regarded as irreformable areas.

If the *truth* of faith is to be recognizable to men of any age, the *temporal guise* of faith must change with the times. A Church which truly desires to find unity with other Churches must be a lover and follower of truth, completely devoted to truth, it must be a Church which knows in all humility that it is not the manifestation of the whole truth, that it has not fulfilled the whole truth, a Church which knows that it must be led anew by the spirit of truth into all truth. Each Church will have to make sacrifices, considerable sacrifices, in the cause of unity, it will have to sacrifice everything that has stood between it and the whole truth, everything that tempted it and which often led it into error. But truth is the one thing that the Church may not sacrifice; it is something which has constantly to be sought anew, in order that it may constantly be discovered anew under different forms.

"At the same time, Catholic belief needs to be explained more profoundly and precisely, in ways and in terminology which our separated brethren too can really understand. Furthermore, Catholic theologians engaged in ecumenical dialogue, while standing fast by the teaching of the Church and searching together with separated brethren into the divine mysteries, should act with love for truth, with charity, and with humility. When comparing doctrines, they should remember that in Catholic teaching there exists an order or 'hierarchy' of truths, since they vary in their relationship to the foundation of the Christian faith. Thus the way will be opened for this kind of fraternal rivalry to incite all to a deeper realization and a clearer expression of the unfathomable riches of Christ" (DOe 11). According to DOe 6, even the formulation of doctrine is not exempt from the principle of *"ecclesia semper reformanda"*.

Extensive exegetical studies and lengthy investigations of the history of dogma and of the Church will be necessary to reconcile under one roof theologies which have lived at enmity for many centuries, to uncover the same thing concealed behind different words, to translate concepts into and out of each other's language and to undertake a critical correction of these concepts from the viewpoint of a superior norm. Instead of concealing points of difference and in a spirit of "love" trying to gloss over the truth, we must listen to each other, cautiously suspend judgment, question with humility and interpret with understanding—and in that way we shall *discover* the truth in a spirit of love. The barriers to an ecumenical consensus in theology must be reviewed and broken down: personal objections, such as intellectual sloth, emotional positions based on ulterior motives, whether of a personal, ecclesiastico-political or theological kind, personal or confessional pride, unconscious fear of having one's own orthodoxy shaken, the reluctance to break out of the golden cage of a theological system; or intellectual barriers, such as the mistaken identification of essential Church doctrine with inessential opinions of different schools of theology—(we are not aiming at unanimity in mere opinions, and to seem to do so would put an intolerable strain on the possibility of theological agreement; what we are aiming at is a unity of the Churches in *faith*)—and so on.[13]

5. *The standard for unity must be the Gospel of Jesus Christ, taken as a whole:* What should be our guide as to what is, and what ought to be, common ground between the Churches, what should be our yardstick for the justified demands of other Churches and our measure of what is and what is not truth in theory and practice? What standard must we apply in our efforts for Church unity? The Church itself cannot be standard, nor can the individual Churches, otherwise we will merely perpetuate the divisions which exist. The only standard is the Gospel of Jesus Christ. We must not seek unity through eclectic additions, whereby something is chosen from each Church and put together to form a new whole; the fundamental differences of approach between the Churches, which are what has led to the formation of these individual elements, would remain barriers just as they were before. On the other hand, unity is not to be sought by conciliatory subtraction of any elements which divide the Churches, after which we would simply make do with what was left over: a very thin and insipid distillation. No, the different Churches must be judged according to the programme which was laid down for all of them and which each acknowledges, the message which is the real basis of their existence and hence the basis of their unity: the original message of Jesus Christ, as

[13] See H. Küng, *The Council and Reunion,* London–New York 1961, chap. D VI.

revealed in its original, unique and irreplaceable form in Scripture.

The basis for the unity of the Church, and for the unification of the Churches, lies in their obedience to this one message given by their one Lord. If therefore we begin our quest for unity by examining our own Church, we must examine it, not according to its present ecclesial reality, taking its *status quo* as an absolute norm; we must measure it against the original message of Christ which it claims as its foundation. And if similarly we find it necessary to fulfil in our own Church the justified wishes and demands of other Churches, then it will not be because they have any justification *per se,* but because after critical examination we have found that they are justified in the light of that same evangelical message on which the other Churches also base their existence. We must listen to the voice of Christ in our *own* Church, not outside it; but we must listen to the voice of *Christ*. And we will then listen to the voices from outside, to see whether or not we can hear in them the message of Christ. Under no circumstances may we contradict that Gospel or the Lord whom it reveals, the Lord who is after all the Lord of the Church, by appealing to the *status quo,* whether of our own or of another Church, as though to suggest that that which exists, by virtue of the very fact that it exists, must have a justification for its existence.

While the genuine tradition of a Church must always be respected, there is a false traditionalism in old and new Churches alike; for while the older Churches recognize the value of tradition, the younger Churches, which apparently deny tradition fundamentally, are nevertheless inextricably involved in it, through national peculiarities, certain historical or social factors, or through particular leading personalities; but any kind of traditionalism must retreat and capitulate when confronted with the Gospel of Jesus Christ. It is the teaching of our own traditions and confessions that we should not listen to those traditions and confessions, but to Christ and his message. It is the Lord and his Gospel alone which can be the measure of how much in our tradition is justified and how much is unjustified; on the basis of the Gospel alone we can judge between that which has absolute and that which has only conditional validity, between those differences that are tolerable and those that are intolerable, between the points at which we must be unconditionally unanimous and the points at which we should be broad-minded and tolerant. The road to unity is not the return of one Church to another, or the exodus of one Church to join another, but a common crossroads, the conversion of all Churches to Christ and thus to one another. Unity is not the subjection of one Church to another, but the mutual regeneration and mutual acceptance of community through mutual giving and receiving.

The fundamental and original testimony of Scripture enables us, where the question of unity in diversity is concerned, to arrive not at a diversified but at a unanimous judgment on diversity, provided of course that we give due weight to the Gospel as a whole. At the very beginning of this examination[14] we saw that the New Testament offers no systematic picture of unity, but rather that, according to the different theological positions and situations of the New Testament writers, and of their communities, very different views were presented. These differences even included direct contradictions, the most famous example of which is Paul's insistence on justification by faith alone, without works, and James's view of justification by works. This gives rise to the question: cannot *any* concept of the Church be justified by reference to the New Testament? Many Catholics hold this view and use it to infer the necessity of ecclesiastical tradition, which would give certain information as to which New Testament views should be preferred. Many Protestants also maintain the same and use it to justify the existence of many different confessions, all of which claim with justice to find their origins in the New Testament.

However, both sides overlook the following points: 1. By no means *any* concept of the Church can be justified from the New Testament. For all the diversity of views expressed there, there is unanimity in the New Testament, at least in an exclusive sense. Any Church which preaches an earthly kingdom rather than the kingdom of God, any Church which preaches instead of the Kyrios Jesus Christ another or a sec-

[14] Cf. A I, 3.

ond Kyrios, any Church which teaches that man can be saved by his own efforts rather than by the grace of God, which preaches human slavery rather than human freedom, falsehood rather than truth, egoism rather than love—any such Church would find not just individual documents, but the entire writings of the New Testament unanimously ranged against him. 2. The New Testament is not a collection of contemporary and hence contradictory documents, but a succession of documents written at different times, which for all their contradictions and despite the development of ideas witness unanimously to one and the same decisive act of salvation in Jesus Christ. Beyond all the contradictions there is a unity in the New Testament as regards its positive witness, and this could well serve as a basis for Church unity.

For example, any Church which attempted to establish a Pelagian ecclesiastical system, with a doctrine of good works and pious observance of laws, and which based its claim to orthodoxy on the Epistle of James, would not only be overlooking what James himself has to say about love, but would be ignoring the fact that the epistle, according to its historical origins, can only be regarded as a *secondary* Christian source, for the following reasons: 1. The Epistle of James was unknown for centuries in the Church, it was written in cultured Greek with quotations not from the original Hebrew text but from the Greek septuagint, and its authenticity was disputed from the first (a different story from I Corinthians, for example). By contrast with a genuine apostolic letter it can only claim derived authority. 2. The Epistle of James was written by a Jew with a hellenistic education probably several decades after the death of James, the brother of the Lord, in 62, and reflects the situation of a second-generation Christian community (again very differently from I Corinthians). So from a temporal viewpoint it does not belong to the primary writings of the New Testament. 3. The Epistle of James has inherited a tremendous amount from the Jewish ethos of the Old Testament, and on the basis of this letter alone it would be difficult to distinguish specific Christian elements (once again, in contrast to I Corinthians).

We may conclude that, while on the one hand the Epistle of James is a valid piece of testimony within the New Testament canon, and while it is clear that, given their different situations, Paul and James are not in absolute contradiction, especially since both demand faith and the expression of faith in action, on the other hand in view of the question of authenticity and in view of the distance both in time and in material which separates the writer from the original Christian message, the epistle is only secondary testimony and can only be understood with reference to the older testimonies. Thus a Church which took the message of James as the basis of its existence, whether in theory or in practice, without taking due note of the other, and more particularly the original Christian documents, would not only be contradicting all the other writings of the New Testament, but the epistle itself. Such a Church would be questioning the unity of the New Testament, and hence the unity of the Church.

Conversely, a Church which on the basis of I Corinthians attempted to set up a community without system or organization, characterized by arbitrariness and "charismatic" licence, would be ignoring what Paul has to say, in I Corinthians itself, about the foundation of apostolic authority and of order in the Church. It would also be ignoring the very emphatic exhortations of the Epistle of James and of other secondary writings within the New Testament canon, which like the Acts and the pastoral letters, based on particular historical experiences, have good reason to lay a heavier stress on Church order and the offices of the Church than we find in I Corinthians. Thus a Church which took the message of I Corinthians as the basis of its existence, whether in theory or in practice, without taking due note of other New Testament writings, including the secondary writings, would not only be contradicting all the other writings of the New Testament, but I Corinthians itself. This Church too would be questioning the unity of the New Testament and hence the unity of the Church.

There is no doubt that the Acts of the Apostles idealizes very deliberately the unity of the young Church, for we know quite well from other New Testament writings what tensions and differences there were in the Church (between Jerusalem and the Diaspora, between Jewish and Gentile Christians), what factions were formed within single communities (at Jerusalem and at Corinth, for example), and we know that there were even differences between the apostles themselves (cf. Gal. 2:11–16). The early Church was not a uniform group, but a Church which included a quite unusually wide range of very diverse expressions both in theory and in practice. On the other hand, it would be an exaggeration and an intensification of these differences in the early Church to suggest that they are evidence for a diversity

of confessional Churches in opposition to one another. Such a
suggestion would fail to take note of the fact that all these
groups, those in Jerusalem and those of the Diaspora, Jews
and Gentiles alike, Peter and Paul and even the different factions in Corinth were in *communion* with each other.

The early Church is a community of Churches which are
united in acknowledging the one Lord Jesus Christ and which
are distinct from all those who do not confess the one Lord;
they are all united in the communion of the sacred meal
through one and the same baptism; and this communion was,
so far as we know, never disputed or revoked. In Jerusalem
Paul not only received from the "pillars" there, James and
Peter and John, the "right hand of fellowship" (Gal. 2:9),
but he also, we need not doubt, shared in the Lord's Supper
with them. These Churches are conscious of being *one*
Church, they acknowledge the one "church of God which is
at Corinth" (and hence in other places as well), the Church
of "those sanctified in Christ Jesus, called to be saints together with all those who in every place call on the name of
our Lord Jesus Christ, both their Lord and ours" (I Cor.
1:2).

The Churches of the New Testament are conscious of their
unity and they practise it, as witness the big collection of alms
made by some of Paul's communities on behalf of the original community in Jerusalem, which Paul took there in person
in order to give practical expression to the idea of unity (cf.
Rom. 15:25–28). Love, which all the New Testament writers
are unanimous in calling for, was not an empty word for the
Churches; it was the force which linked them all together in
brotherly communion. During the first centuries this unity
was on the whole preserved. Evidence of this is provided not
only by the lively correspondence between the Churches (Ignatius for example is in correspondence with Churches in
Syria, Asia Minor, Greece and Italy), but also by the deliber-
ations and the measure taken by the provinces of the Church
to ward off heresy. Such divisions as there were at that time
were only temporary. Even the growing language divisions
from the third century onwards did not impair the unity of
the entire Church. Only in the fifth and sixth centuries did
more permanent divisions arise, in the form of the

monophysite national Churches of Armenia, Egypt, Syria and Abyssinia. The New Testament, then, provides no basis for justifying a diversity of conflicting confessions. The New Testament reveals the unity of the Church. If we take the New Testament as a whole, rather than making selections from it, and if instead of either attempting a superficial harmonization and levelling down of contradictory New Testament writings, or alternatively just as superficially trying to dissociate them and separate them from their context, we interpret them sensitively and alertly with regard to the central truth of the New Testament, then we can see that the New Testament as a whole precisely demonstrates the unity of the Church, a unity in plurality and diversity which is distinct from uniformity or egalitarianism, as well as from selectivity and divisions.

This first dimension of the Church is closely linked to the second, which we call catholicity. "Catholic Church": as soon as we say the words, we begin to see that the question of unity arises again here, in markedly more acute form.

II. THE CHURCH IS CATHOLIC

1. CATHOLICITY IN IDENTITY

(a) The word "catholic"—the adverb is καθ' ὅλου, or the later adjective καθολικός, rendered in Latin by the loan-word *"catholicus"* or *"universalis"*—means: referring to or directed towards the whole, general.[15] In classical Greek the

---

[15] Cf. as well as the general literature under A II, 2 and D I, 1: K. Adam, *The Spirit of Catholicism*, London–New York ²1934; H. de Lubac, *Catholicism*, London and New York 1950; Y. Congar, art. "Catholicité", in Cath. II, 722–725; A. Garciadiego, *Katholike Ekklesia*, Mexico 1953; H. Asmussen–W. Stählin, *Die Katholizität der Kirche*, Stuttgart 1957; M. Lackmann, *Credo ecclesiam catholicam*, Graz 1960; T. Sartory, *Mut zur Katholizität*, Salzburg 1962; W. Beinert, *Um das dritte Kirchenattribut. Die Katholizität der Kirche im Verständnis der evgl.-luth. u. rom.-kath. Theologie der Gegenwart I–II*, Essen 1964; this contains the most complete bibliography. Also important is the inaugural lecture at Tübingen of M. Seckler, *Katholisch als Konfessionsbezeichnung*, in: ThQ 145, 1965, 401–431.

word is used above all for general statements (universals as distinct from individuals), for universal or world history, but also, for example, for dropsy which affects the whole body. In the New Testament the word is used once (Acts 4:18) as an adverb meaning "thoroughly", "completely", "totally", but the Church is never described as "catholic". This does not of course say anything against this usage of the word, but the luxuriant growth of interpretations which has grown up around this particular attribute of the Church is undoubtedly in part due to the fact that the New Testament has nothing to say on the subject.

If we do not want to lose our way in an undergrowth of speculation, which if we are thinking about the "whole" or the "general" may well seem limitless, but prefer to begin by looking at this question historically, then we must start with the original use of the word. The word is first applied to the Church in New Testament times by Ignatius of Antioch (died *circa* 110): "Wherever the bishop is, there his people should be, just as, where Jesus Christ is, there is the Catholic Church" (*Smyrn.* 8:2). "Catholic Church" in this context means quite straightforwardly the whole Church, the complete Church, in contrast to the local episcopal Churches. This is confirmed by the second oldest reference we have, half a century later, in which we learn that shortly after the death of their bishop Polycarp in 156, "the Church of God at Smyrna" sent a report about his martyrdom to "the Church of God at Philomelion and to all communities, wherever they may be, of the holy and catholic Church" (*Martyr. Polyc.* 41). "Catholic Church", again quite unpolemically, refers here to the increasingly apparent reality of a whole Church, within which the individual Churches are bound up together, a general and all-embracing Church. The texts of the second century—among which, for example, is a fragment quoted by Eusebius[16] which probably dates from this time, directed against the teachings of Montanus and stating that the latter's doctrine was to "blaspheme against the Catholic Church, the whole Church spread out under heaven"—and the texts of the third century (Hippolytus, Tertullian, Clement of Alex-

[16] Eusebius, *Hist. Eccl.* 5, 16, 9; GCS 9/1, 464.

andria) offer no clear indications about the idea of catholicity in the sense of "fullness", "perfection", "pleroma". The highly artificial attempts to deduce these meanings from the texts are all the more unconvincing, since the word "catholic" does not have this meaning in the secular writings of the time. Historically speaking there is no bridge between the use of the word "pleroma" in Ephesians 1:23 and the *"ecclesia catholica"* of the early Christian period. The word "catholic" was not in the process of time brought down from the heights of theological speculation to the plane of the Church as empirical reality and hence "impoverished" in its significance; from the very first it was understood to mean the whole Church as it was richly experienced in reality.

However, from the third century onwards the accent shifted—an inevitable polemical consequence of disputations with various heretical groups and movements: that Church and those Christians are called "Catholic" who are united in the whole Church, and not, like the heretics, separated from it. The word "Catholic" in fact takes on the sense of "orthodox": instead of the reality of catholicity there develops the claim to catholicity. The only true Church is the "Catholic Church": the all-embracing, total orthodox Church. Other Churches are heretical or schismatic. The great turning point came with Constantine, or more precisely with Theodosius, for under the religious edict of 380 the *"ecclesia catholica"* became the only lawful national religion. Every Roman now had to be a Christian, more particularly a "Catholic" Christian. Paganism and heresy became political crimes, "catholicity" became orthodoxy, defended by law. In Justinian's *Codex Iuris Romani* and later in the legal code of the Holy Roman Empire this definition was maintained; we recall the view taken of heretics. At the same time, especially through Augustine, the theological interpretation of the catholicity of the Church was further developed. The greater extent and the numerical growth of the Church added to the senses of the words *"ecclesia catholica"* which we have noted, that is a total, all-embracing Church (the original ecclesiological meaning) and an orthodox Church (secondary polemical meaning), a new idea, that of a Church extending over the whole earth (geographical catholicity) and of a

Church much larger in numbers than any other (numerical catholicity). Vincent of Lérins gave a more precise definition of catholicity, in the sense of orthodoxy, as that "which is believed everywhere and always by all men".[17] Such statements affirm in a new way the historical continuity of tradition (temporal catholicity). Medieval theology did not make any advances upon these patristic interpretations. Even the schism between East and West did not, as it should have done, raise the question of catholicity as a fundamental problem.

Not only the unity, but also the catholicity of the Church was seriously called in question by the Protestant Reformation. Whether one wished to speak about the "Catholic Church" in the original sense of a whole, total Church, or in the secondary polemical sense as an orthodox Church, or in the wider sense of a Church which extended over all the world, was larger numerically than any other and included a variety of peoples, languages and cultures, and had survived the passage of time, in short whether one wished to refer to catholicity in its original non-polemical ecclesiological sense, or in its polemical sense, or in its geographical, numerical, cultural or temporal sense, it was impossible to overlook the fact that the "Catholic Church" was not the same as it had been before that division, and that its catholicity, in whatever sense, appeared to have been destroyed along with its unity. Unity and catholicity are obviously correlative concepts; if the one dimension is upset, the other must be too. The reformers were well aware of the threat to catholicity. Luther in particular tried his utmost, though he was doomed to failure, to prevent his name becoming one of the attributes of a new Church. From the very first, for theological and also legal reasons (because of the recognition of the Church by the Empire), the reformers stressed the fact that they belonged to the "Catholic Church". By this they meant catholicity in the sense of orthodox teaching. Catholic, as it was later formulated, is that which is believed always, everywhere and by all, *according to the Scriptures.* In this way catholicity comes increasingly to mean orthodoxy in the con-

[17] Vincent of Lérins, *Commonitorium* 1. 2; PL 50, 640.

tinuity of the Gospel faith, a faith which may exist outside the reformed Churches, and existed before they came into being as such, but which has taken on new ecclesial forms in the reformed Churches.

Catholic polemicists did not accept this interpretation. In accordance with the by now traditional concepts they required not only catholicity in teaching, but catholicity of space and time and numbers. Was not this kind of catholicity only realized in the Catholic Church? But this was not so easy to prove as it seemed at first sight. Although at first the problems were considered in a broad framework, in time apologetics required that catholicity in a spatial sense, as a geographical expanse, should join catholicity in the sense of orthodoxy in the forefront of the dispute, although it was at the same time found necessary to seek refuge in all kinds of reassuring distinctions: *catholicitas absoluta—relative, materialis—formalis, physica—moralis, iuris—facti, progressiva —instantanea, simultanea—successiva.* Had it not become just a little difficult to be "catholic"? On the other hand the Protestant theologians were not making things easy for themselves, and the most varied theories had to be produced to prove, since it was by no means obvious, that the reformed Churches were indeed, or even specially, "catholic". The most important attempts to solve this dilemma have already been discussed with reference to the unity of the Church: the resort to an invisible (catholic) Church, the "branch" theory, eschatological assurances. The argument about catholicity remained largely unresolved. Which Church now really has the right to call itself catholic?

(*b*) In the light of the biblical findings which emerged from our earlier analysis, we must now attempt a systematic clarification of the historical facts. The original use of the word "catholic" is solidly based on the New Testament. Ecclesia, as we have seen, consistently and in all places has the basic meaning of a local community, a local Church. But they are only local Churches at all, inasmuch as they are the manifestation, the representation, the realization of the one *entire*, all-embracing, universal Church, of the Church as a whole. While the individual local Church is *an* entire Church, it is not *the* entire Church. The entire Church is only made up by all the local Churches together; and not by simply being added together and associated externally, but by being inwardly at one in the same God, Lord and Spirit, through the same Gospel, the same baptism and sacred meal and the same faith. The total Church is the Church as manifested, represented and realized in the local Churches. Inasmuch as the Church in this sense of the *total* Church is the *entire* Church, it may be called, according to the original usage of the word, the *catholic,* that is the whole, universal, all-embracing Church. Catholicity is essentially a question of *totality.*

Then again, inasmuch as each local Church makes present this entire Church, it too may be called catholic. A Church does not become uncatholic by being a limited local Church, but by being a limited local Church which has cut itself off from other Churches and hence from the whole, entire Church, by concentrating solely on its own life and faith and trying to be self-sufficient. So it is not the particular Church which is uncatholic, the local or regional or denominational Church, for while it may not be *the* entire Church, it is *an* entire Church. It is the particularist Church which is uncatholic, the Church which has cut itself off from the faith and life of the entire Church ("schismatic") or excluded itself from it ("heretical") or even rebelled against it ("apostate").

What can we infer from this, if we take "Catholic Church" to mean basically the whole, entire, universal Church? First of all we can establish some negative propositions.

1. Spatial extensity alone does not make a Church catholic: catholicity is not primarily a *geographical* concept. There is no point in having a Church which is more widely spread than any other, if it has become unfaithful to its own nature. An international empire, built up by the purely secular techniques of ecclesiastical politics, or even by a kind of spiritual imperialism, may be imposing, but is not itself of value; the question is, does this universal Church still continue to make manifest the one entire Church, the Catholic Church?

2. Numerical quantity alone does not make a Church catholic: catholicity is not primarily a *statistical* concept. There is no point in having a Church with the largest number of

members, if this has resulted in its being unfaithful to its own nature. Maximal membership, bought at the price of spiritual devaluation and a resultant Christianity of tradition and convention is of no value; the question is, does this mass-Church still genuinely realize the one entire Church, the Catholic Church?

3. Cultural variety alone does not make a Church catholic: catholicity is not primarily a *sociological* concept. There is no point in having a Church which embraces the widest varieties of cultures and societies, if precisely the varieties of culture and language, or race and class have resulted in its being unfaithful to its own nature, if, instead of living in and with them, it becomes dependent on these forms and allows them to prescribe its laws, so that it develops into an instrument of power of a particular culture, race or class. The fact that it has been absorbed into a variety of communities, at the cost of degenerating into a syncretistic construction full of paganisms, is of no value; the question is, does this kind of composite Church truly represent the one entire Church, the Catholic Church?

4. Temporal continuity alone does not make a Church catholic: catholicity is not primarily an *historical* concept. There is no point in having a Church which claims to be the oldest, and can point to its "fathers", whether of the sixteenth or the thirteenth or the fifth or the second century, if throughout its long history it has betrayed its true nature, if it has become no more than a venerable memorial of a venerable tradition. Its romantic history, its restorations, its archaeology are of no value, if in its development through the centuries the Church has cut itself adrift from its origins; the question is, does this kind of traditional Church still represent the one entire Church, the Catholic Church?

The most international, the largest, the most varied, the oldest Church can in fact become a stranger to itself, can become something different, can lose touch with its own innermost nature, can deviate from its true and original course. Of course, the Church has to move with the times, has constantly to modify itself, as an historical entity it has no option. But it must on no account become something different, something estranged from its true nature. It is an all-embracing *identity* which at bottom makes a Church catholic, the fact that despite all the constant and necessary changes of the times and of varying forms, and despite its blemishes and weaknesses, the Church in every place and in every age remains unchanged in its essence, whatever form it takes: this must be its aim and its desire. In this way the unchanging essence of the Church will be credibly preserved and confirmed and activated anew "always and everywhere and by all men". Only if this identity is present does the Church appear as the undiminished entire Church, as the undiluted universal Church, as the undivided total Church, as the truly Catholic Church. If a Church at any time or place or in any form renounces this identity, if it allows itself to be absorbed into any nation, culture, race, class or social phenomenon, then it becomes uncatholic; it becomes heretical if it takes on a different, foreign nature, or apostate if it consciously rebels against its proper original nature. Catholicity is that which links together all the local Churches into one entire Church, that which distinguishes them from any debased form of Church. Identity is the *basis* of catholicity.

However, we should be putting a false interpretation on the word identity if we equated it with an absorption with self, if we confused the identity of the Church with ecclesiastical narcissism. Precisely a Church which has preserved the identity of its true nature through all changes of history and of its own forms will have remained itself for other reasons than pure self-satisfaction. A Church is never there just for itself, but by its very nature is there for others, for mankind as a whole, for the entire world. We must remember that the message of Jesus was itself quite literally universal—the prerequisites of salvation are not the fatherhood of Abraham or the confirmation of the covenant through Moses, but rather faith, metanoia, the doing of the will of God in love. On the basis of this message the early Church established, not without difficulty, the idea of universality; it was to be Jewish for the Jews, Greek for the Greek, all things to all men (cf. I Cor. 9:19–23): "For in Christ Jesus you are all sons of God, through faith . . . There is neither Jew nor Greek, there is neither slave nor free, there is neither male nor female; for you are all one in Christ Jesus" (Gal. 3:26, 28). Thus the

Church saw its calling as essentially missionary, as referring to the whole world; it was to serve the world through its proclamation of the Gospel: "Go into all the world and preach the Gospel to the whole creation" (Mk. 16:15), to "all nations" (Mt. 28:19), as "witnesses . . . to the end of the earth" (Acts 1:8), "until the end of the world" (Mt. 28:20).[18]

We can see that from its very origins and by its very nature the Church is world-wide, thinking and acting with reference to the world, to the whole inhabited earth, the *oikumene*. This universality can therefore be expressed in the word "ecumenical", "concerning the whole inhabited earth". "Ecumenical" and "catholic" are words that are closely linked not only in their original meanings but also in their Christian usage.[19] One of the two oldest references to the "Catholic Church" indicates the close association between the two words: "the Catholic Church which extends over the whole oikumene" (*Martyr. Polyc.* 8:1). Universality is a consequence of catholicity.

The original meaning of "ecumenical", "concerning the whole inhabited earth", has undergone many changes in the course of time. W. A. Visser 't Hooft has listed the following senses of the word: (1) Belonging to or representing the Roman Imperium; (2) belonging to or representing the Church as a whole ("ecumenical council"); (3) having general validity throughout the Church ("ecumenical confessions of faith"); (4) concerning the world-wide missionary calling of the Church ("ecumenical mission conference"); (5) concerning the relations between the Churches or between Christians of different confessions ("the ecumenical movement"); (6) referring to the awareness that all Churches and Christians belong to the world-wide Christian community, and to the readiness to work for the unity of the Church of Christ ("ecumenical council of Churches").[20]

The catholicity of the Church, therefore, consists in a notion of entirety, based on identity and resulting in

[18] Cf. esp. B I, 2; II, 3; C I, 1.
[19] Cf. the specialist bibliography in *Structures*, 40, esp. W. A. Visser 't Hooft and J. L. Witte.
[20] W. A. Visser 't Hooft, art. *"Ökumenisch"*, in RGG IV, 1569 f.

universality. From this it is clear that unity and catholicity go together; if the Church is one, it must be universal, if it is universal it must be one. Unity and catholicity are two interwoven dimensions of one and the same Church.

"All men are called to belong to the new People of God. Wherefore this People, while remaining one and unique, is to be spread throughout the whole world and must exist in all ages, so that the purpose of God's will may be fulfilled. In the beginning God made human nature one. After His children were scattered, He decreed that they should at length be unified again (cf. Jn. 11:52). It was for this reason that God sent His Son, whom He appointed heir of all things (cf. Heb. 1:2), that he might be Teacher, King and Priest of all, the Head of the new and universal people of the sons of God. For this God finally sent His Son's Spirit as Lord and Lifegiver. He it is who, on behalf of the whole Church and each and every one of those who believe, is the principle of their coming together and remaining together in the teaching of the apostles and in fellowship, in the breaking of bread and in prayers (cf. Acts 2:42)" (CE 13).

Spatial extensity, numerical quantity, cultural and social variety, temporal continuity do not alone make up a catholic Church. However, it would be wrong to draw the opposite conclusion and say that the Church is catholic because spatially limited, small in number, culturally and socially static, or bounded by time. This would be to suggest that the Catholic Church, instead of being a world-wide Church, could be a national Church, limited to a single people, or even an "established" Church. It would be to suggest that the Catholic Church, instead of being a mass-Church, could be a tiny local group limited to the immediate surrounding area, an ecclesiola or one of those small sects whose self-importance is often in direct inverse ratio to its size. It would be to suggest that the Catholic Church, instead of containing a variety of social forms, could be limited to a single culture, such as the Byzantine, or indissolubly wedded to a single class, upper or lower, or a single race, the whites, for example. It would be to prefer to a traditional Church one that is brand new, the latest thing, for the time being unencumbered by tradition and in its first bloom, or quite simply the most modern and up-to-date Church, which conforms to criteria of the modern contemporary world. On the contrary, any kind of limitation, whether spatial or numerical, temporal or social and cultural, so far from being a sign of catholicity is more likely to be a sign of uncatholicity. And any deliberate exclusion of even a single nation or culture, race or class or period is quite definitely a sign of uncatholicity. If the Church, according to its very origins, according to the mission which sustains it and the message which it preaches, is universal, then it is quite clearly summoned, not to deny or to ignore differences between peoples and cultures, races and classes, historical periods and their individual spirits, but to transcend them. It must demonstrate in action that these differences and frontiers are—as shown by Galatians 3:28—not in the ultimate analysis relevant. In this way the Church showed itself to be catholic from the very beginning. Provided that we can be certain that a Church has not lost contact with its original nature, has not contradicted that nature, then and only then can we affirm that world-wide extensity, large membership, social and cultural variety and great age are, not for their own sake but springing from the universal nature of the entire Church, signs and indices of catholicity.

"It follows that among all the nations of the earth there is but one People of God, which takes its citizens from every race, making them citizens of a kingdom which is of a heavenly and not an earthly nature. For all the faithful scattered throughout the world are in communion with each other in the Holy Spirit, so that "he who occupies the See of Rome knows the people of India are his members" (St John Chrysostom). Since the kingdom of God is not of this world (cf. Jn. 18:36), the Church or People of God takes nothing away from the temporal welfare of any people by establishing that kingdom. Rather does she foster and take to herself, insofar as they are good, the ability, resources and customs of each people. Taking them to herself she purifies, strengthens, and ennobles them. The Church in this is mindful that she must harvest with that King to whom the nations were given for an inheritance (cf. Ps. 2:8) and into whose city they bring gifts and presents (cf. Ps. 71 (72):10; Is. 60:4–7; Rev. 21:24). This characteristic of universality which adorns the People of God is a gift from the Lord Himself. By reason of it, the Catholic Church strives energetically and constantly to bring all humanity with all its riches back to Christ its Head in the unity of His Spirit. In virtue of this catholicity each indivdual part of the Church contributes through its special gifts to the good of the other parts and of the whole Church. Thus through the common sharing of gifts and through the common effort to attain fullness in unity, the whole and each of the parts receive increase. Not only, then, is the People of God made up of different peoples, but even in its inner structure it is composed of various ranks" (CE 13; cf. DOe 14 & 16).

(c) But does not all this point quite clearly to that Church which is commonly referred to as "The Catholic Church"? Has it deserved that title? Does this one Church not come closest to the ideal of universality? Is it not geographically the most widespread, numerically the largest, culturally and socially the most varied, in terms of age the most long-lived? And yet the other Churches would question the very fundament of the catholicity of the so-called "Catholic Church", by questioning whether it has remained true to its original nature, whether it is still supported by its original calling. In reply to this, we may well ask whether such a total judgment is possible under contemporary conditions. Can we assert that the so-called "Catholic Church" is lacking in all those features we have noted as belonging to the essence of the Church, can we say it is more lacking in them than any other Church? We ought not to judge too hastily either one way or the other; we have already encountered the difficulties of the problem in connection with the unity of the Church. But let us here consider the question of catholicity, in which, as we shall see, the problems about unity recur in even clearer form.

We cannot simply ignore one curious fact, which needs explaining: the fact that one Church, from the time of Ignatius of Antioch down to the present day, has very consistently retained as part of its title that age-old attribute which we have seen to belong to the fundamental character of the Church (cf. "Christian is my name, Catholic my surname").[21] It is true that other Churches have not only wished to be catholic, but wished to be called catholic. But they have

21 Pacian, *Ep. ad Sympron,* 1, 4; PL 13, 1055.

always found it necessary to add some further definition (Anglo-Catholic, Old Catholic, etc.), precisely in order to avoid being confused with the one Church which has remained the "Catholic Church".

Some remarks of St Augustine have a peculiarly contemporary relevance: "We must remain true to the Christian faith and to the community of that Church which is catholic and which is called the Catholic Church as well by its opponents as by all the members of it. Whether they intend to or not, even heretics and schismatics, if they are talking not among themselves but to outsiders, can only refer to one Church as catholic, namely the Catholic Church. They can only make themselves clear by giving it that name by which it is known the world over."[22]

It is true that there were attempts to rename the "Catholic Church" the "Roman Church", quite simply, as though the "Roman" Church were quite simply the "Catholic" Church! By adding this word to the usual definition and speaking of the "Roman Catholic Church", it was hoped to dismiss the "Catholic Church" as an isolated particularist confessional Church, and at the time of the Counter-Reformation some Catholics were thoughtless enough to accept this label, which threatened the whole concept of catholicity by associating the Church with local limitations and making it seem a specific confessional group. There were even attempts, beginning at the time of the Reformation, to deny to the Church the title of "catholic" altogether. And yet none of these attempts altered the fact that today as always the simple name "Catholic Church" refers to the one "Catholic Church".

"Finally the Church possesses precisely the name 'Catholic', a name which significantly and despite all heresies only this one Church has retained, so that, although all heretics would like to think of themselves as Catholic, no heretic would ever dare to answer a stranger's question as to where "the Catholics" meet together by pointing to his basilica or his house."[23]

The connection between this one Church and the name

[22] Augustine, *De vera religione* 7, 12; PL 34, 128.
[23] Augustine, *Contra ep. Manichaei* 4, 5; PL 42, 175.

"Catholic" is so strong that many Protestant Churches, out of anger, fear, resignation or thoughtlessness have given up this attribute of the Church. In the traditional creed the reference to the "Catholic" Church has in many cases been replaced by the words "universal Church", in order to avoid confusion. For many it is a real insult if they are accused of "Catholic" or even "catholicizing" tendencies. Not least for this reason the "ecumenical" movement and the "Ecumenical Council of Churches" preferred the narrower, more geographical term "ecumenical" to the wider, richer concept "catholic".

How can we explain this exclusiveness, the way in which the attribute "catholic" has become associated with just this one "Catholic Church"? Is this not an indication that this Church has something that others lack? Here I do not mean its greater extent, its larger numbers, its richer variety, its more venerable age. Nor do I wish immediately to infer that the "Catholic Church" has a unique and exclusive quality by virtue of which all other Churches become uncatholic communities; what I have said about the one Church and many Churches still applies, and this kind of apologetical approach is no use to us here. What we have to do is to analyse and understand better the historical reality. Here one thing is immediately striking: if you ask not the "Catholic Church" but the other great Christian Churches, the Orthodox Churches of the East, the Lutheran Churches, the Reformed Churches, the Anglican Churches, which are in communion with the Old Catholic Church, and indirectly all the Churches which have sprung from them—if you ask them from where they derive their name and origin and nature, they will all of course, and not without reason, refer themselves and their message, their baptism, their Lord's Supper and their ministry back to Jesus Christ and his Gospel. They do not wish in this sense to be "new" Churches, founded in 1054, 1517, 1531 or at any other date. And yet each of these Churches in defining its nature will find it necessary to distinguish itself from the so-called "Catholic Church", whether directly or indirectly, with more or with less polemical emphasis. Each of these Churches owes part of its very nature as a Church to its relationship with this one Church. To explain how its own particular existence as a Church came about, each must make direct or indirect reference to the so-called "Catholic Church". However, they seek to explain their relationship with the Church of the apostles (and some Churches of the East in particular trace their history right back to one of the apostles), none of them can deny the fact that they were once, directly or indirectly, linked to this so-called "Catholic Church" and shared with it in the community of the Church; none can deny that at that time there was no split between them, no system of more or less mutual excommunication, and each must be aware of a more or less definite historical moment when it separated itself from the "Catholic Church", or the "Catholic Church" cut itself off from it. Each is now a grown-up and self-sufficient daughter, who thinks there were very good reasons why she could no longer put up with living at home with mother.

By speaking here, as a way of approaching the problem of the relationship between the "Catholic Church" and the other Churches, of mother Church and daughter Churches, a terminology I am applying in an historical and not a dogmatic sense, I am not advocating any kind of "maternalism", I am not attempting to found any juridical claims which the mother Church might have over the daughter Churches. Legal postulates of this kind cannot help to settle historical conflicts between the Churches. Nor am I trying to claim more truth either for the mother Church or for the daughter Churches. It is precisely over the question of truth that disputes have arisen, and we shall make no progress if one side simply claims the fullness of truth, or more truth than the other side, without ever being able to persuade the other side. If we want to determine the relationship between the "Catholic Church" and other Churches, and to find some measure of agreement about it, then the question of truth will have to be put on one side for a moment, though not of course entirely forgotten. In determining this relationship we must not try to decide who is right and who is wrong, who has the truth or more of the truth. In my attempt not to evaluate but to understand the relationship between the "Catholic Church" and other Churches, I should like to consider the relationship not dogmatically, as conditioned by the measure of truth on one side or the other, but historically, as conditioned by the circumstances of its origin. And for this the distinction between mother Church and daughter Churches serves very well. One thing at least should immediately become apparent—that it is unhistorical to think of the possibility of these grown-up, self-supporting daughters re-entering their mother's womb; the laws of life do not permit of such a return.

Another point that becomes clear is that it would be equally unhistorical to consider the individual Churches as simply a long list ordered according to districts or the alphabet or some other way. It would be unjust to the mother Church as well as to the daughters or granddaughters, to consider them apart from their place and order according to their genetic origins. These origins have precisely been responsible for the difficulties of the relationship between mother Church and daughter Churches; precisely because they were once one community, a single unity, the breach made such a deep and lasting impact. What happened was not a quarrel between two strangers, but a division and opposition of flesh and blood—a wound which time alone will not heal.

Daughter Churches and mother Church: is this perhaps why these daughters fear nothing so much as the thought of coming back under their mother's wing, of being subjected to the formally strict and yet, viewed in context, all too lax control of this mother, of being taken over by her as soon as they show themselves to be more approachable? In this one point, despite all their differences and distinctions, all the daughter Churches are united. They regard their mother, for all her undeniable greatness and historical experience, as not only old and paralyzed, antiquated and hidebound, but also as too scattered and diffuse. She seems to have lost sight of essentials, of the things that matter. Her faith has become superstitious, her love too juridical, her hope too earthly. For the daughters she is not the same as she was before, as she was originally. There is only one thing that these daughters, however much they may argue, resent and complain, however much they may reject and dismiss her, can never deny: that she is their mother.

Mother Church and daughter Churches: does this perhaps explain the fact that this mother is curiously jealous of her daughters, that after such a long time apart she still announces that she has "rights" over them, that she is so reluctant to see them go their own way, that she finds it so hard to understand why they will have nothing to do with her old faith, why they do not want to live in communion with her, why they reject her, why despite all her commands and finally despite all her pleas and her appeals they will not come back to her? She regards these daughters as ungrateful, disobedient, imprudent. Indeed they have had to pay dearly enough for the freedom they chose; in some respects they have become decidedly insecure, superficial, debilitated. Having cut themselves off from their mother, they began to quarrel among themselves, often no less violently than they had quarrelled with the mother. They have gone through similar unhappy experiences with their own children as their mother did with them. In this way the whole family split up and quarrelled more and more. There is only one thing that this mother, however much she may resent and regret and pass harsh judgments, cannot deny: that these daughters, so unlike one another and often so unlike her, are still her children.

What can we conclude from all this? Can we expect the daughters simply to return to their mother, as though nothing had happened, as though time had not moved forward in the meanwhile, as though their quarrel had not been about essentials? If not, then should we perhaps expect that the mother will simply move out in the wake of her daughters, giving up everything that she embodies and has preserved, everything that so many of her daughters have lost? Up to now she has been the only constant point of orientation in all the vagaries of the history of the Church and of the Churches, the only certain stable and stabilizing factor in the whole; should she now simply renounce her own chosen role, become one among many and thus lend impetus to the process of disorientation and fragmentation? If again we answer no, what then?

Three important consequences may be noted here, in addition to what has already been said about the laity and the unification of the Churches: 1. The unification of the Churches and the restoration of complete catholicity in the Church of Christ must take account of the historical genesis and the historical context of each individual Church. 2. The Churches, apart from the so-called "Catholic Church", cannot achieve the necessary unity nor the necessary catholicity of the Church, without first sorting out their relationship to the "Catholic Church", from which directly or indirectly they all stem, and making their peace with her. All ecumenical movements, laudable in themselves, and all negotiations about unity between the other Churches among themselves will lack a firm foundation at one vital point if they exclude the question of their fundamental relationship to the "Catholic Church"; if they take positive account of this relationship, then such movements towards unity will take on a new depth and a new impetus. 3. The so-called "Catholic Church" will never achieve the necessary unity or catholicity of the Church without sorting out its relationship to the Churches which directly or indirectly have sprung from her, and on her side making peace with them. All the movements towards reform and renewal within the Church, which we must all welcome, will remain incomplete if the connections—which it has, whether it likes it or not—with the other Churches are ignored. If on the other hand these connections are examined sympathetically and taken up positively, then these movements of reform will assume new breadth and depth.

From this we can understand that every Church and more particularly the "Catholic Church" must approach the problem of how to achieve the necessary unity and catholicity of the Church from a fundamentally different viewpoint, according to its particular historical context. But each, in different ways, will have to take into account what I set out in the previous chapter: questions of the many Churches and the one Church, of inclusive and exclusive differences, of the evasions which must be avoided, of a collective affirmation of collective guilt, of recognizing the unity which already exists and searching for the unity which still has to be achieved, of the need to start from one's own Church and the need to fulfil the just demands of other Churches, of the constantly new discovery of age-old truth, and of the Gospel of Jesus Christ in its richness and its totality as a standard. Only in this way will we be able to achieve unity in catholicity and catholicity in unity.

Of course, as soon as we examine the concrete historical contexts of our divisions, we come up more sharply against concrete, particularly theological, difficulties. In connection with the Protestant Reformation these are incomparably more numerous than in connection with the schism between East and West. For this reason unity in catholicity must ultimately be achieved theologically through the discussion of concrete issues; I shall not go into details of these here.

I should like to make just three comments, without providing chapter and verse:

1. Recent progress particularly in exegesis and historio-critical theology has indicated more and more clearly fundamental areas of agreement in the classic disputed issues between Catholics and Protestants—Scripture and tradition, grace and justification, the sacraments and in particular the eucharist; such areas of agreement cannot of course cover all differences, but certainly those which have *separated* the Churches.[24]

2. The greatest difficulties lie in the teachings about the Church, and the still unclarified controversies on this issue have infected all other areas of theology. But the differences of opinion which have *separated* the Churches, at least as far as the basic structure and the basic dimensions of the Church are concerned, are, as I hope to have made a little clearer, basically not insuperable.

3. Ecclesiological difficulties are centred round the theological and practical issue of the external organization of the Church, more importantly on the Church's official ministers, particularly on the question of the primacy of Peter. The primacy and infallibility of the Pope (and in the latter connection the recent Marian dogmas) are the chief difficulty in attempts to reconcile the Catholic Church with the Churches of the East, the reformed Churches, the Anglican Churches and the Old Catholic Church. We shall have to return to these problems and difficulties.[25] But for the very reason that this basic difficulty infects all other areas, the source of infection can be precisely located. It is all too easy to diagnose wrongly from the symptoms, to mistake effects for causes and to look for points of disagreement at places where in reality agreement could be achieved. Misplaced profundity is really superficiality.

[24] On the doctrines of grace and justification see H. Küng, *Justification. The Doctrine of Karl Barth and a Catholic Reflection*, London 1962, Camden 1964; on the doctrines of baptism, the eucharist and confession, cf. C III, 1–2; D III, 2.

[25] Cf. E.

In the light of our investigation we can see that the so-called "Catholic Church", rather than being proud of its name as something with which it can challenge other Churches, would do better to accept it humbly as indicating the special responsibility that it bears. As a Catholic one will have to be especially careful and discreet when, as so often, we hear well-meaning people praising the "fullness of Catholicism", when we hear catholicity defined as "pleroma, fullness, perfection". We will be cautious not just for pragmatic reasons, because we are aware of the very considerable gap between the idea of fullness, as a claim and as a programme, and the reality of fullness in concrete form—all too often Protestantism makes Catholicism look very small intellectually! No, we will be cautious for theological reasons. It is not the Church which, according to the passage most often quoted in this context (Eph. 1:19), is in possession of this fullness. The Church itself knows no fullness by virtue of which it would be universal, perfect and "catholic", of itself, unchallenged and for all time. The Church only knows the fullness of *Christ,* he who is the fulfilment of the Church as of everything, and who allows this fullness to be present in the Church. And since the Church is not of itself fullness, it has to grow from Christ towards Christ: inwardly by faith, knowledge, love and suffering, outwardly by proclaiming the Gospel and serving the world. The Church has to *become* universal. The fullness of *Christ* in the Church does not preclude dangers and temptations, shortcomings and imperfections, error or sin on the part of the *Church.* The Church knows a "pleroma" which is promiscuity, a "perfection" which is illusion and arrogance, an "affirmation of values" which is weakness, a "breadth" which is shallowness, a "cosmopolitanism" which is integralism, an "openness to the world" which is paganism, a "catholicity" which is in fact no more than "Catholicism"—and we all know what curious things that may include. In the Church we have not to collect all possible spirits together, but to distinguish between spirits. We are to test everything, but not to retain everything.

If the Church, the "Catholic Church", wants to retain its identity with its own nature, it cannot allow itself, simply in pursuit of some supposed fullness and openness, to try to include everything within itself and become an unsatisfactory *"complexio oppositorum"*. If with justice we can accuse "Protestantism" of being too little, a heretical selection from the whole, then "Catholicism" cannot escape the accusation of being too much, a syncretistic collection of heterogeneous, misguided and even sometimes unchristian elements. There is a *peccatum per excessum,* a sin of excess, as well as a *peccatum per defectum,* a sin of shortcoming. We must constantly remember to temper our Catholic "and" with the very necessary protesting cry of "alone", a limitation which makes the "and" possible in the first place. We need to replace a short-sighted and exclusive "Protestantism" and a diffuse and confused "Catholicism" with an "evangelical catholicity", based and centred on the Gospel.

The catholicity of the Church is threatened constantly and all along the line. True catholicity is a grace given to the Church and constantly renewed by its Lord. This catholicity cannot be seen, it can only be believed, or seen with the eyes of faith. But catholicity, as glimpsed in faith, is something that we should present to the world through our lives, as something credible. At this point the question arises: can we live this catholicity in the world, as something worthy of faith, can we proclaim the universality of grace and of salvation, if on the other hand we support notions like that of "no salvation outside the Church"? Is it not the so-called "Catholic Church" which is remarkable for its extreme narrowness?

2. NO SALVATION OUTSIDE THE CHURCH?

At one time—that of the Fathers of the Church and the flowering of patristics—the *ecclesia catholica* extended more or less throughout the known world. The Church had a secure place in the whole *oikumene,* in the whole of the inhabited world; it even seemed for a period that the whole world was Christian. Given these limited geographical perspectives, it was easier to formulate an axiom like "no salvation outside the Church". It was taken for granted that more or less every human being would be brought face to face existentially with the Christian message and therefore Mark 16:16 was indiscriminately applied to all those that were not baptized. In addition there was no split, apart from the smaller heresies, in the *ecclesia catholica* of the time. So the very few living at the "ends of the earth" were not seen as a problem. Anyone who did not believe—like the Mohammedans later—was in bad faith. The axiom was therefore taken literally and it was assumed that not only the pagans outside the Church, but also Jews, heretics and schismatics would finish up in hell. Even in the development of doctrine in the early Church the dangers of such a negative formulation can be seen.

The roots of this axiom go back to Ignatius of Antioch (*Philadelph.* 3:2), Irenaeus,[26] Clement of Alexandria,[27] and others. Its first complete formulation is the negative one found in Origen: "Let no one persuade or deceive himself: outside this house, that is outside the Church, no one will be saved; for if someone leaves, he is himself guilty of death."[28] Cyprian was the first to apply the axiom—using the ark as an illustration—with juridical exclusiveness and all its consequences: "Anyone who separates himself from the Church and unites with an adulteress (schism), shuts himself off from the promises of the Church, and anyone who leaves the Church of Christ, will not deserve Christ's rewards. He is an outcast, unholy, an enemy. God is not his Father, if the Church is not his mother. If anyone outside Noah's ark had been able to escape, then so might a man outside the Church."[29] We can already see, and this was consistently confirmed, later, that when the axiom was both formulated negatively and taken literally, it led to heresy. Cyprian, for instance, deduced from the axiom, apparently logically, that baptism administered outside the Church by heretics was invalid (heretical baptism) and martyrdom outside the Church was valueless. Cyprian was, however, repudiated by the Church. Augustine too often uses the axiom,[30] and, although in contrast to Cyprian he distinguishes between grave and less grave cases of heresy, he finds no possibility of salvation even in the less grave cases. The extent to which the axiom was taken literally at this time is shown by the words of Augustine's disciple Fulgentius of Ruspe: "Of this you can be certain and convinced beyond any

[26] Irenaeus, *Adv. Haer.* III, 24, 1; PG 7, 966.

[27] Clement of Alexandria, *Paedagogus* I, 6; PG 8, 281.

[28] Origen, *In Jesu Nave* 3, 5; PG 11, 841.

[29] Cyprian, *De unitate Ecclesiae* 6; CSEL 3/1, 214.

[30] Augustine, e.g. *Sermo ad Caesariensis ecclesiae plebem* 6; CSEL 53, 174; cp. also Jerome, Ep. 15; CSEL 54, 63.

doubt: not only all pagans but also all Jews, all heretics and schismatics, who die outside the present Catholic Church, will go into the everlasting fire which has been prepared for the devil and his angels."[31]

Medieval scholasticism merely echoes Augustine. Here too the axiom led to errors which were later repudiated by the Church, for example that priests separated from the Catholic Church no longer had the power of consecration. And it was precisely that pope who formulated most vehemently the principle of "No salvation outside the papal church", namely Boniface VIII in the bull *Unam sanctam* (D. 468 f.), who brought the papacy to the verge of collapse: cf. the imprisonment of Boniface VIII and the Great Western Schism with three popes all excommunicating each other. The inflexible teaching of the bull mentioned above was not upheld by later popes.

Even in the early Church, therefore, it might with advantage have been kept in mind that the New Testament image of the ark of Noah (I Pet. 3:20), from which the axiom is derived, stresses that men are saved through baptism and not that all those outside the ark are damned: "Salvation inside the ark", but not an unqualified "no salvation outside the ark"! The text rather says that Christ who "died for sins once for all, the righteous for the unrighteous, that he might bring us to God" (3:18) went and preached after his death to the "spirits" (3:19) (the fallen angels or the godless race before the flood or both?)[32], "who formerly did not obey" and therefore were not in the ark. The text would then imply that "even the worst offenders even in the next world are not excluded from Christ's saving call".[33] If such an interpretation of this difficult text were right, it would mean instead that there *was* salvation outside the ark, but at the same time it would presuppose that there is "no salvation outside *Christ*".

None the less the tremendous historical experience of the discovery of new continents with civilized and morally good peoples had to take place before a breakthrough was

[31] Fulgentius, *De fide, ad Petrum* 38, 79; PL 65, 704.

[32] Cf. H. Windisch–H. Preisker, *Die katholischen Briefe,* Tübingen [3]1951, 7072.

[33] F. Hauck, *Die Kirchenbriefe,* Göttingen [7-8]1958, 70; for various interpretations of the difficult text cp. K. H. Schelke, *Die Petrusbriefe,* Freiburg–Basle–Vienna 1961, 104–110.

achieved. Now people did not just *know* that there were countries and races outside the Church (they had *known* that in the Middle Ages too), but they were forced to take a positive interest in them. There arose a greater understanding of what it meant to belong to a world, an *oikumene,* which did not begin and end with the Mediterranean basin and the countries immediately surrounding it. There began too to be an awareness of the fact that not only the *ecclesia catholica* but Christianity as a whole is clearly part of a diminishingly small minority when seen in the light of hundreds of thousands of years of past history, the extent of the present and the incalculability of the future of humanity, in the light, that is, of the history of man in all continents and in all millennia. With new perspectives of this kind, theology inevitably began to develop gradually away from the axiom, "no salvation outside the Church". But it was a lengthy process culminating in the Second Vatican Council's emphatic affirmation that salvation is open to all, not just to schismatics, heretics and Jews, but to non-Christians too and even to atheists if they are in good faith.

In the sixteenth century, the great age of discoveries, not only theologians such as Bellarmine and Suarez but also the Council of Trent (D 1379) taught that baptism could be received not only *in re,* as Christians received it, but also *in voto;* the *in voto* concept was then later applied directly to membership of the Church. Faced with the extreme views of the eighteenth-century Jansenists, it was necessary to refute the proposition "no grace is granted outside the Church" (*Extra ecclesiam nulla conceditur gratia.* D 1379). Finally by the nineteenth century, not only because of the unbaptized pagans but because of the Christians who had been separated from the Catholic Church for several centuries, the "outside" was interpreted in such a way that it could at the same time be clearly stated: ". . . equally it is our firm belief that those who live in ignorance of the true religion incur no guilt in the eyes of the Lord, if this ignorance is invincible. Who, however, would dare to take it upon himself to determine the limits of this ignorance according to the type and variety of peoples, regions, natural dispositions and so many other things" (Pius IX. D. 1647). When in the twentieth century the encyclical *Mystici Corporis* (1943) repeated the original axiom in a rather strict form and the Jesuit Father Feeney with a group of Catholics in Boston tried to take the words of the encyclical literally and like the early Fathers of the Church maintain the damnation of all men outside the visible Catholic Church, the Holy Office had to intervene, protest against this interpretation[34] and finally declare all those to be excommunicate and *extra ecclesiam* who maintained that *extra ecclesiam* no one could be saved.

Vatican II stated very clearly the fact that people outside the Catholic Church can be saved: "Nor is God Himself far distant from those who in shadows and images seek the unknown God, for it is He who gives to all men life and breath and every other gift (cf. Acts 17:25–28), and who as Saviour wills that all men be saved (cf. I Tim. 2:4). Those also can attain to everlasting salvation who through no fault of their own do not know the gospel of Christ or His Church, yet sincerely seek God and, moved by grace, strive by their deeds to do His will as it is known to them through the dictates of conscience. Nor does divine Providence deny the help necessary for salvation to those who, without blame on their part, have not yet arrived at an explicit knowledge of God, but who strive to live a good life, thanks to His grace." (CE 16).

What then was achieved in practice by these interpretations from Trent to Vatican II? In practice, even when the axiom "no salvation outside" was nominally retained, it was clearly stated that there *is* salvation outside the Church, outside the *ecclesia catholica*. Nevertheless, it cannot be denied that the ambiguity of expression has misled many Catholics and non-Catholics alike. They do not know today precisely what they are to understand by the words "no salvation outside the Church". On the one hand they ought to say that there is *no* salvation outside the Church, yet on the other hand they have to admit that there *is* salvation outside the Church. Is there in fact salvation outside the Church or is there not? This question can only be honestly answered with either yes or no, but not with both yes and no.

Does not this negative and exclusive axiom lead to innumerable misunderstandings which continue to recur in spite of all explanations both inside and outside the Catholic Church? Even if it were previously of help to the Church in her mission, it is certainly a

[34] Cf. the letter to Archbishop Cushing of Boston published in *American Ecclesiastical Review* 77, 1952, 307–311.

hindrance to her today. And not only because the Church no longer forces anyone to believe in Christ out of fear of hell. The words are interpreted more often as either intolerance or duplicity: as intolerance when they are understood literally and exclusively in accordance with the old tradition; as duplicity when it means on the one hand that no one will be saved outside the Catholic Church and on the other hand does not exclude the fact that people outside the Catholic Church are saved, in fact millions and billions of them, the greater part of mankind. Intolerance and duplicity are rightly deeply repulsive to modern man, who has espoused the cause of the freedom of the individual in religious matters and rejects every sort of dishonesty or duplicity.

Here too it is easy to resort to the invisible Church as a way out of the dilemma. Where it was a question of the one Church and the many Churches it was particularly Protestant theologians who sought to use this way out; faced with one Christianity and many religions, it was Catholic theologians in particular who chose it. Rather than question the validity of a dubious negative axiom, the concept of the Church was stretched by theological sleight of hand to include not only Christians but also all well-meaning pagans. As we have seen, the concept of the Church can rightly be applied to the Christian Churches which compose a community of baptized Christians united by the message of the New Testament, believing in Christ the Lord, celebrating the Lord's Supper, trying to live according to the gospels and wishing to be regarded by the world as a Church. It seems mistaken, however, to extend the concept of the Church to people who do not belong to a community believing in and publicly acknowledging Christ. What sort of a Church would it be, composed of people who know nothing and even wish to know nothing of Christ? Can a vague association of "well-meaning people" be termed a Church?

To extend the concept of the Church in this way seems unjustified on the following grounds: 1. Such a concept of the Church contradicts the understanding of the Church revealed in the New Testament, as we have already seen, and the Christian tradition formed by it. For the concept of the Church of Christ an explicit belief in Christ and acknowledgement of him is fundamental. 2. Such a concept of the Church is far from necessary, as will have been seen, in order to show that the salvation of non-Christians is also possible. 3. Such a concept of the Church also makes it unnecessarily hard for Christian missionaries to preach membership of the Church to non-Christians outside the Church if at the same time they have to preach that all men of good will are already in the Church. 4. Such a concept of the Church is rightly rejected by thinking non-Christians as a purely theological construction and speculation; they regard it as pure effrontery that we Christians should impute to them, who explicitly and deliberately do not desire to be members of the Church of Christ, an unconscious *"desiderium"* towards the Church and should try to incorporate them against their will and their express *"votum"* silently into the Church, as if it were really possible to do this over their heads anyway.

It is simply not permissible for the theologian to re-interpret reality according to apparently profound speculative constructions. The non-Catholic Christian, who in fact belongs to the Church of Christ, but who has no *"votum"* or "desire", either explicit or implicit, either conscious or unconscious, to belong to the "Catholic Church", who has if anything rather the opposite *votum* or desire, can not simply be transferred to the secret list of members of the "Catholic Church". Similarly, the non-Christian who has no desire either explicit or implicit, either conscious or unconscious, to belong to Christ's Church, who has if anything quite the opposite desire, cannot be silently adopted by Christianity. Man's free will must be respected. The sole criterion for entering the community of believers should be a profession of faith. The fact that those outside the "Catholic Church", that non-Christians too, are included in Christ's grace and so can be saved, should not lead us to the conclusion that such people can be regarded as members of a specific ecclesial community against their will.

The New Testament concept of the Church, therefore, as we have come to see it, should not be adulterated for the sake of formal adherence to the wording of an axiom, which in its negative and exclusive formulation was highly dubious right from the beginning, has resulted in more or less serious errors, and has proved open to misunderstanding in its application to non-Christians and impossible to understand at all in its application to non-Catholic Christians. If we wish to insist upon the negative axiom "no salvation outside the Church", then we must not use it to threaten or damn those outside the Church, but interpret it as a hope and a promise for ourselves and our community: it is true for me, we are able to say with joy, there is no salvation outside the Church for me personally. As far as others are concerned, we do better to use a positive formulation: "Salvation inside the Church"! and so emphasize the positive truth at the heart of the easily misunderstood negative axiom.

It seems worth making the following points as regards the use of the negative axiom in theology or in preaching. 1. In dogmatic theology the phrase should be commemorated as an expression of Catholic tradition[35] and attention drawn to the limitations and misconceptions inseparable from it. In doing this it should be emphasized that what is really vital is the fact that salvation is given to us in Christ and in him alone, whether as sincere individuals we are inside or outside the Christian community of believers. 2. In preaching the phrase should be passed over and used as little as possible, since today it is either not understood or misunderstood. We can see from the history of the ecumenical councils that this has happened before. The Council of Nicaea stated that there was only one hypostasis in God. Later ecumenical councils no longer used this formula, since it was open to misunderstanding, and talked instead of one physis and three hypostases. The same thing happened in Christology, the Council of Chalcedon deliberately avoided christological formulas used by the Council of Ephesus under the influence of Cyril of Alexandria. Even in those days the Catholic Church drew a distinction—in the words of John XXIII— between the content of faith and its outer garment. Externals may change, faith remains the same. We believe in salvation through Christ in the Church. For the sake of this very faith the formula "no salvation outside the Church", which is so open to misunderstanding and so damaging to the Church's mission in the world, should no longer be used in the preaching of the word of faith.

The catholicity of the Church has to hold good therefore for those outside the Church as well as those inside it. But the test is not whether the whole world can be brought into the

[35] Cf. D. 40. 246 f., 423, 430, 468 f., 570b, 714, 999 f., 1473, 1613 f., 1646 f., 1677, 1716 ff., 1954 ff., 2199, 2319.

Church in some way or other. Of course the whole world is in the hand of God, who is the God of all men and not just of Jews or Christians, as both the Old and the New Testaments testify. In Christ the whole world receives God's grace. If we could see God's plan of salvation there would be no outside, only an inside: "God our Saviour desires all men to be saved and to come to the knowledge of the truth. For there is one God, and there is one Mediator between God and men, the man Jesus Christ who gave himself as a ransom for all" (I Tim. 2:4–6). And yet this does not mean that the whole world or even the world of believers is part of the Church. The Church exists in the world. But it can lay no exclusive claim to certainty of salvation *vis-à-vis* the world nor to spiritual authority. What it wants is quite different: to give selfless and unpretentious service to the salvation of the world. To be truly catholic the Church must think of itself not as synonymous with the world, nor yet on the other hand as an exclusive society of those already saved, but as an open community of people dedicated to serve and work for the salvation of all, of the whole of mankind.

Here we are faced with new questions about this Catholic Church which is in the world but not synonymous with it. Instead we can also say: the Church is a holy Church. Here we turn to a third dimension which illuminates the Church's unity and catholicity: the holiness of the Church.

III. THE CHURCH IS HOLY

1. SINFUL AND YET HOLY

(*a*) Several romantic descriptions of the nature of the Church finish up by having to concede, as far as their ecclesiological idealism will allow, that the "actual form" of the Church, its concrete reality, bears little relation to the "nature" they have so enthusiastically and so lovingly described. We have attempted here to take into account from the start, with sober realism and without illusions, everything which belongs to the real nature of the Church. We have dealt with its nature as it appears in particular historical forms, indeed with its nature and "un-nature" rather than with a pure and idealized nature. We have throughout taken the real Church as our starting-point, rather than pretending it does not exist and preferring to talk about an ideal Church. The remarks above about the basic structure of the Church were intended to illuminate this real Church, taking the Church as a real people of God in the context of the reality of Israel,[36] as a real spiritual creation confronted with the reality of enthusiasm,[37] as a real body of Christ opposed to the reality of heresy.[38] Similarly, the remarks above about the Church being one although divided,[39] and being catholic although limited,[40] served to throw further light on our picture of the real Church. There is nothing then new or surprising about our next conclusion; it is rather a summary and reminder of what has already been said if we conclude that the Church is a *sinful Church*.

But this is a statement which needs qualification.[41] We cannot assume that everything in the Church which is imperfect, erroneous or misguided should simply be regarded as sinful. There can be no sin without personal responsibility, and there is much we can find in the Church and its history which cannot be laid at the door of any particular person. Several things have developed in a seemingly inevitable way, without individuals being able to do very much about it, as a simple consequence of the fact that the history of the Church is undeniably a part of the history of mankind: rich yet impoverished, wide-ranging yet narrow, grand and yet petty. Under the influence of very various problems and solutions, situations and developments, languages, cultures and intellectual attitudes, the Church has been in a constant state of re-formation throughout its two thousand years of history—and in

[36] Cf. C I.   [37] Cf. C II.
[38] Cf. C III.   [39] Cf. D I, 2–3.   [40] Cf. D II.
[41] See H. Küng, *The Council and Reunion,* London and New York 1961, 34–52. See the bibliography given there as well as the works listed at A II, 2 and D I, 1 and in particular: K. Rahner, *Die Kirche der Sünder,* Freiburg 1948; H. U. von Balthasar, *Sponsa Verbi,* Einsiedeln 1960, 203–305. For the biblical concept of sanctity, see the relevant sections of the OT and NT theologies and the biblical encyclopaedias.

many respects of de-formation as well. It has constantly been moulded and at the same time marred, enriched and then despoiled. All in all, there has been a process of formation always accompanied by deformation. The Church has suffered many injuries and losses and fatal shifts of emphasis; excessive stress has been placed on some important things at the cost of neglecting others even more important.

It is difficult to attribute personal blame to anyone for the fact that the Church, while inheriting from Judaism not only its strong faith in the one God and the Messiah, its ethic governing the whole life, and the inexhaustible treasures of the Old Testament, also inherited the menace of legalism and of an externalized ritualism. Nor can we reproach anyone personally for the fact that the Church, while taking from the Greek world, with its wisdom and its feeling for beauty and for humanity, that common language (*koine*) so important for its mission, the habit of profound philosophical reflection about its faith, new concepts and ideas, new modes of thought and expression and new perspectives, all of which enabled it to translate the original message into the terms of a new age, also took over much intellectualistic theorizing, trite rationalistic formulas, idiosyncratic conceptual casuistry as well as an anthropocentric emphasis in the doctrine of grace and an anti-materialistic and anti-physical dualism. We cannot blame anyone personally for the fact that the Church, while gaining from the Roman world a sense of form and order, of authority and tradition, of unity and practical organization, also inherited from its secular political power and authoritarian traditionalism, formalism, juridicalism and triumphalism in theology and ecclesiastical life. No personal failure underlies the fact that the Church, while taking from the Germanic world, with its feeling for subjectivity, imagination and freedom, a valuable personal inwardness, a sensitive temperament, and a healthy impatience with dullness, sloth and externalized petrifaction, also learned from it a disintegrating subjectivism, a naturalistic superstition and an unfruitful mysticism, an ecclesiastical particularism and a tendency towards revolutionary individualism. It is difficult finally to see where personal blame can be attached for the fact that in the second millennium in particular the Church grew increasingly narrow, or for the fact that in modern times the Church has signally failed to adapt to the worlds of Asia and Africa and remained by and large an American and European concern; that through its growing rigidity and inflexibility it has completely failed to find common ground with the modern world, its culture and science, and so must bear the main burden of responsibility for the rejection of the Church and of Christianity by the majority of people today.

In spite of this, the inevitability and ineluctability of this evolution should not be exaggerated. We cannot honestly regard as inevitable all the lack of feeling the Church and its representatives have shown towards the needs of mankind, their failures to adapt to the new problems and the views of different eras, to understand the changing forms and values of the world, their blindness to the signs of the times and their habit of always being behind the times. There is nothing inevitable about the Church's neglect of the Gospel and the Gospel's demands and perspectives in both theology and practical decisions; there is nothing inevitable about all the worn-out apologetics and lazy excuses, designed to maintain the *status quo*, about the Church's identification with particular systems and parties, cultures or philosophical schools, about the exaggerations of its powers and claims on the world, the disguising or suppression of past failings and errors. We are deluding ourselves about reality if we try to ignore the personal failures and the personal guilt which lies behind and beneath all the wrong decisions and false developments in the history of the Church. Behind the imperfections, defects and deformities we can discern evil, sin and vice. There is an evil at work here which is far greater than the failures of individual human beings, a force which can only be described as demonic; it is this which leads to the perversion of what is Christian. The history of the Church is not only a very human history, but a deeply sinful history, and it has always been so. We have only to read the New Testament epistles to be confronted with the sad reality of sin. Even if the worst sinners, for example those guilty of incest, were excluded from the community (cf. I Cor. 5), there still remained all kinds of uncharitableness and small-mindedness, legalism and abuses of freedom, arrogance, envy and jealousy, deceit, covetousness and pleasure-seeking dissipation; these were features of the earliest Church, even though we do not need to take the stereotyped New Testament catalogues of vices as empirical descriptions of the communities (e.g. Gal. 5:19–21;

Rom. 13:13 f.). We are forced to conclude that in this respect the Church has not progressed at all, but remains all too stationary.

(*b*) In the face of this conclusion, various excuses have been attempted; they are understandable, but not acceptable:

1. Setting apart the "holy" members. In primitive times Gnostics, Novatianists, Donatists and Montanists, in medieval times the Cathars, and in modern times various enthusiasts and sectaries have all attempted to exclude sinful members from the Church, so that only the pure and sinless and holy would remain. But who would these be? "For we all make many mistakes" (Jas. 3:2), and "if we say we have no sin, we deceive ourselves, and the truth is not in us" (I Jn. 1:8). Early councils of the Church, under the influence of Augustine particularly, resisted the idea that biblical phrases like this were only to be accepted in "humility" rather than as statements of fact (D 106), that it was for the others, for the "sinners" that one prayed "Forgive us our trespasses" (D 107) and that this prayer too was to be uttered in "humility" rather than as a matter of truth (D 108). For no one has the right to say: "God, I thank thee that I am not like other men, extortioners, unjust, adulterers, or even like this tax collector . . ." (Lk. 18:11). It is precisely those who regard themselves as righteous and think they are doing penance for other sinners who should examine themselves to see whether they are not the greater sinners. All of us are sinful, the Church is a dismal *communio peccatorum* which every day must ask God anew: "forgive us our trespasses". The Church which has no sins to confess does not exist.

2. Distinguishing between a "holy" *Church* and sinful *members:* To avoid compromising the Church, there have often been attempts to draw a distinction between the members who are sinful and the Church itself which none the less remains sinless. But it is an unreal distinction. The individual Christian never acts solely to his own advantage or disadvantage. His actions, whether good or evil, are those of a fully responsible member of the Church. In actual and real terms there is no ideal Church floating above the human world. There is no such thing as a Church without members,

a fellowship of believers without believers, a people of God with no people, a spiritual building with no building, a disembodied body of Christ. It is human beings, not God, not the Lord, not the Spirit, who make up the Church. And these men, sinners though they are, remain members of the Church —this is a principle which down the centuries has been defended again and again. It is not sin which separates the individual from the fellowship of believers; only a lack of belief can do that. The sinner who believes is not to be cast out; he is to live.

3. Distinguishing between the "holy" and the sinful *parts* of the Christian: Again, to avoid compromising the Church, there have sometimes been attempts to split up the individual Christian himself. In as far as he is pure, he belongs to the Church; in as far as he is sinful, he does not. These are the sort of notions that can be played with intellectually. But real human beings cannot be divided up in this way. It would no doubt be highly convenient if a man could simply split off his sinful self, and at least be pure within the Church. But man's wretchedness consists precisely in the fact that he cannot leave his evil, his sinful self, on one side; nothing is to be gained by this kind of quantitative separation. As Scripture constantly points out, man is evil in his heart—not at some peripheral point which he might be able to shake off, but at the very centre of his being, at the focal point from which all his existence is directed. He cannot set his better half to pray for his worse half; the whole man has to pray for forgiveness for himself as a whole. It is as a unified and undivided human being with an indivisible personality that the Christian is a sinner. And it is as a wretched sinner that he is a member of the Church.

No excuses can avail us here; we must accept the realities of the case: the Church is a Church of sinners. And because these sinners are the real members of the Church, and remain as sinners members of the Church, the ecclesia itself carries this burden. Their sinfulness sullies the body of Christ itself, shakes the spiritual building itself, wounds the people of God itself. The Church itself suffers. Because it is not an idealized and hypostatized pure element, distinct from human beings, but is a fellowship of believing men, the Church is a sinful

Church—the effect not of God or Christ or the Holy Spirit, of course, but of its sinful members. This is a disturbing yet a liberating truth. It liberates us from the need to muster a threadbare apologetic, and from the need to exclude ourselves from the Church because, if we are honest with ourselves, we know we are sinners. We can and must remain a part of the Church as it really is, in full acceptance of this reality.

(c) From this we must conclude that the holiness of the Church does not stem from its members and their moral and religious behaviour. What does "holy" mean? The Old Testament word *"kadad"* implies a separation and a cutting-off, a distinguishing and dividing of what is profane and impure from what is pure. It implies a separation for God's service; pure things become holy by being removed from their profane usage and dedicated to God. The concept has a cultic background. This sense of separation is carried on in the New Testament word ἅγιος and the Latin word *"sanctus"*, which comes from *"sancire"*, to limit, enclose, sanctify, and is the opposite of *"profanus"*, meaning that which lies outside the holy area, the *"fanum"*. The New Testament concept is almost completely dependent on Old Testament usage, where holiness is the most emphatic description of the divinity of God. Holy things are those which God has set apart. By contrast with other religions human activity is not primarily involved here; what matters is the sanctifying will and word of God. Just as God's kingdom comes to men through God himself, God's name is eschatologically hallowed in men by God himself (cf. Mt. 6:9; Lk. 11:2). This is not a blessing, but a genuine request to the Father, that he himself will reveal his holiness. God himself—in a cautious passive formulation—is the logical subject of sanctification (cf. Ez. 36:23; 20:41; 28:22; Is. 5:16). Not only justification ("It is God who justifies", Rom. 8:33) but also sanctification is the work of God, according to Paul: "God chose you from the beginning to be saved, through sanctification by the Spirit" (II Thess. 2:13; cf. Eph. 1:4); "May the God of peace himself sanctify you wholly" (I Thess. 5:23). And the sanctification of men is eschatologically achieved by God's saving act in Christ: "He (the God who chose you) is the source of your life in

Christ Jesus, whom God made our wisdom, our righteousness and sanctification and redemption" (I Cor. 1:30); "But you were sanctified, you were justified in the name of the Lord Jesus Christ and in the Spirit of our God" (I Cor. 6:11). The Spirit is the "Spirit of holiness" (Rom. 1:4); his work is the sanctification of men.

Believers are "saints" in so far as they are "sanctified". The concept of sanctification is usually passive in Paul; he speaks of those who are "sanctified in Christ Jesus" (I Cor. 1:2) and "sanctified by the Holy Spirit" (Rom. 15:16). There are no self-made saints, only those who are "called to be saints" (I Cor. 1:2; Rom. 1:7; cf. 1:6; I Cor. 1:24), "saints in Jesus Christ" (Phil. 1:1), "God's chosen ones, holy and beloved" (Col. 3:12). Only through divine sanctification can men actively become holy—holy in the ethical sense, familiar from prophetic literature and the psalms. "As he who has called you is holy, be holy yourselves in all your conduct; since it is written, 'You shall be holy, for I am holy'" (I Pet. 1:15 f.; cf. Lev. 11:44). God's will is the basis and the goal of our continuing sanctification: "For this is the will of God, your sanctification" (I Thess. 4:3; cf. 4:1–8; Rom. 6:19 and 22; I Tim. 2:15; Heb. 12:14; Rev. 22:11).

It is striking that, although Ephesians 5:27 suggests it is the duty of the Church to be "holy and without blemish", the New Testament never refers to a "holy Church". On the other hand, the communities as such are referred to as "the saints", both the primitive community at Jerusalem (Rom. 15:25 f.; I Cor. 16:1 and 15; II Cor. 8:4, etc.) and the Gentile communities (Rom. 1:7; I Cor. 1:2, etc.). The Church is also referred to as a "holy nation" (I Pet. 2:9) and as a "holy temple" with the believers as its living stones (Eph. 2:21). In comparison with Old Testament usage, the New Testament significantly leaves the material element out of account. There is no reference to holy places or objects specially set apart. Even baptism and the Lord's Supper are not referred to as "holy". They do not of themselves create holiness in a magic or automatic way, but are totally dependent on a holy God on the one hand and the human response of faith on the other. The New Testament knows nothing of in-

stitutional sanctity, of a sacred "it"; it does not speak of a
Church which invests as many of its institutions, places, times
and implements as possible with the attribute "holy". The
only kind of holiness at issue here is a completely *personal*
sanctity. It is the believers who have been set apart from the
sinful world by God's saving act in Christ and have entered a
new Christian existence who make up the original *"communio sanctorum"*; they constitute the Church of the saints
and hence the holy Church. The Church is holy by being
called by God in Christ to be the communion of the faithful,
by accepting the call to his service, by being separated from
the world and at the same time embraced and supported by
his grace.

It is *God* who distinguishes the Church, sets it apart, marks
it out for his own and makes it holy, by winning power over
the hearts of men through his Holy Spirit, by establishing his
reign, by justifying and sanctifying the sinner and thereby
founding the communion of saints. This is why we do not
simply believe *in* the holy Church, but believe in God who
makes the Church holy. In the formulation of the baptismal
question from the oldest surviving Church order, quoted in an
earlier chapter,[42] we can say: "I believe in the Holy Spirit in
the holy Church for the resurrection of the body." By believing in God as the life-giving Spirit at work among men, we
believe in his work, we believe in the existence of the holy
Church, just as we believe in the forgiveness of sins and the
resurrection of the dead. We *believe* the holiness of the
Church. This holiness, being the work of God's spirit among
men, is not accessible to us or controllable by us; it is not
something seen, but something that is revealed to those who
in faith open their hearts to the sanctifying Spirit of God. To
the believer alone is revealed the fact that this people which
looks so familiar to other peoples and communities in the
world, and yet is fundamentally so dissimilar, is illumined by
the holiness of God; he alone can know that within this externally so imperfect building the Spirit of God and his holiness
dwells, that this frail and often wounded body reflects the holiness of the Kyrios. The believer is not set apart as an indi-

[42] Cf. A II, 2.

vidual; by being justified and sanctified he is made a member of the communion of saints. And God sets the community apart as something holy by awakening faith in the individual, by justifying him.

The constitution *De Ecclesia* sums the matter up in these words: Faith teaches that the Church, whose mystery is being set forth by this sacred synod, is holy in a way which can never fail. For Christ, the Son of God, who with the Father and the Spirit is praised as being "alone holy", loved the Church as his bride, delivering himself up for her. This he did that he might sanctify her (cf. Eph. 5:25–26). He united her to himself as his own body and crowned her with the gift of the Holy Spirit, for God's glory. Therefore in the Church, everyone belonging to the hierarchy, or being cared for by it, is called to holiness, according to the saying of the apostle: "For this is the will of God, your sanctification" (I Th. 4:3; cf. Eph. 1:4). Now, this holiness of the Church is unceasingly manifested, as it ought to be, through those fruits of grace that the Spirit produces in the faithful. It is expressed in multiple ways by those individuals, who, in their walk of life, strive for the perfection of charity, and thereby help others to grow.

The Lord Jesus, the divine teacher and model of all perfection, preached holiness of life to each and every one of his disciples, regardless of their situation: "You therefore are to be perfect, even as your heavenly Father is perfect" (Mt. 5:48). He himself stands as the author and finisher of this holiness of life. For he sent the holy Spirit upon all men that he might inspire them from within to love God with their whole heart and their whole soul, with all their mind and all their strength (cf. Mk. 12:30) and that they might love one another as Christ loved them (cf. Jn. 13:34; 15:12). The followers of Christ are called by God, not according to their accomplishments, but according to his own purpose and grace. They are justified in the Lord Jesus, and through baptism sought in faith they truly become sons of God and sharers in the divine nature. In this way they are really made holy. Then too by God's gifts they must hold onto and complete in their lives this holiness which they have received. They are warned by the apostle to live "as becomes saints" (Eph. 5:3), and to put on "as God's chosen ones, holy and beloved, a heart of mercy, kindness, humility, meekness, patience" (Col. 3:12), and to possess the fruits of the Spirit unto holiness (cf. Gal. 5:22; Rom. 6:22). Since we all truly offend in many things (cf. Jas. 3:2), we all need God's mercy continuously and must daily pray: "Forgive us our debts" (Mt. 6:12) (CE 39–40).

It is God who sanctifies the Church. Men in the Church are not, any more than men in the world, holy of themselves. They cannot make the Church holy; on the contrary, they are themselves the *communio peccatorum,* totally in need of justification and sanctification. The Church cannot canonize itself, justify itself, or sanctify itself. It is all too possible to imagine baptism being a merely external ritual, the Lord's Supper being a purposeless ceremony, theology being merely a philosophy of religion, Church constitutions being merely legal statutes, missionary endeavour mere propaganda. All ecclesiastical action could be secular action dressed up, or sacral action without any meaning. None of these things in itself is holy; it may, in fact, be very worldly. Holiness is not created by an institution as such nor by good will on its own. Only he who makes us capable of meaningful intentions and actions can, through his grace, make them holy; he alone can justify the godless, and sanctify men and their acts, giving his blessing to preaching, baptism and the Lord's Supper and thereby making them into what they should be, according to the will of God who sets them apart. It is he who makes the acts of the Church into holy, though never autonomously holy, acts. The Church cannot declare these things to be holy of themselves; it can only pray for sanctification and sanctity, looking with hope and trust towards a fulfilment, the measure and the manner of which God alone can decide upon. Only at the end of time will the Church truly be revealed as a Church "without spot or wrinkle" (Eph. 5:27).

To speak of the Church in the present as being "without spot or wrinkle" is misleading. The Church is only like this as a hidden reality, a reality obscured by the miserable nature of men; it is such only like this in so far as Christ has already given himself up for it, has cleansed it in the word by the washing of water in baptism, and intends to sanctify it, so that it may be presented like a bride without spot or wrinkle, in all its splendour (cf. Eph. 5:25–27). What is referred to here is an eschatological presentation. This Church without spot or wrinkle will only be a complete and revealed reality at the end of time; this is the view not only of modern exegetes, but of many of the early Fathers (especially the Latin). To take two examples: Augustine writes: "Whenever in my books I have described the Church as being without spot or wrinkle, I have not meant to imply that it was already so, but that it should prepare itself to be so, at the time when it too will appear in its glory. In the present time, because of the inexperience and weaknesses of its members it must pray every day anew: Forgive us our trespasses. . . ."[43] And Thomas Aquinas: "That the Church will be glorious, without spot or wrinkle, is the final goal to which we are led through the sufferings of Christ. This will only be true in our eternal home, not on the way thither, for now we would deceive ourselves if we were to say we have no sin, as I John 1:8 points out."[44]

This Church composed of human beings is also, through his grace, the Church of God, it is a fellowship which, for all its sinfulness, is at the same time holy and, for all its holiness, is at the same time sinful. This is the ecclesiological *simul justus et peccator:* a *communio peccatorum* which through the forgiving grace of God is really and truly a *communio sanctorum.* Looking at the Church from below, so to speak, we see only the sinfulness of man, and we lose sight of the grace of God which surrounds and embraces the Church; in this view, the Church is no more than an all-too-human religious organization. Looking at the Church from above, so to speak, we see only the holiness of God and fail to take into account the men who compose it and who are constantly weak and tempted; in this view, the Church is a heavenly entity, idealized and lofty, far above the human realm. In reality the Church is the battleground between God's Spirit and evil; the front line does not run between the holy Church and an unholy world, but right through the middle of the sinner's heart touched by the forgiving grace of God. There are not two Churches, one holy when seen from above and one sinful when seen from below. There is only one Church, holy and sinful at the same time, *casta meretrix,* as it has often been called since patristic times, echoing the Old Testament imagery. Holiness and sinfulness are two sides of the one Church, but they are not equal sides. The holiness of the

[43] Augustine, *Retract. II,* 18; PL 32, 637 f.
[44] Thomas Aquinas, *D. th.* III, q.8, a.3 ad 2.

Church is light, revealing its true nature, the sinfulness of the Church is shadow, darkening its true nature. Sin does not arise from the nature of the Church, but breaks into it; it is a dark paradox which does not belong to the Church's nature but must be reckoned as part of its "un-nature".

But this way of looking at the matter is still much too static. The Church is in motion. Sinfulness and holiness are not simply two sides of the Church, they are the past and future of the Church in its historical existence; yet both are always present in the Church; its past continues, just as its future has already begun. The Church is conditioned by the fact that it is really and truly justified and sanctified. Through God's grace it has left its sinful past behind; sin and death are behind it, and it can never finally and completely fall back into them. This past has no future for its present existence. And yet it remains its past. The Church has been saved, but is still tempted; the holiness granted to it does not automatically make it sinless; its holiness is not a permanent possession which might be guaranteed by external means like baptism and the Lord's Supper. The Church must constantly be turning away from its past again, towards its future, that is, its sanctification. God in his mercy has already granted this future to it, as an earnest of future fulfilment, and this fact conditions its whole existence. But it must constantly continue to seize this future, it must constantly be granted to it anew. Because it is holy, it must be holy; the indicative brings an imperative with it. With both humility and joy the pilgrim Church must bear its past, as something indeed past, carrying it out of the present into the future, until finally God's new mercy will cause its past to disappear for ever and its future will become its eternal and imperishable present.

"While Christ, 'holy, innocent, undefiled' (Heb. 7:26) knew nothing of sin (II Cor. 5:21), but came to expiate only the sins of the people (cf. Heb. 2:17), the Church, embracing sinners in her bosom, is at the same time holy and always in need of being purified (*sancta simul et semper purificanda*), and incessantly pursues the path of penance and renewal. The Church, 'like a pilgrim in a foreign land, presses forward amid the persecutions of the world and the consolations of God', announcing the cross and death of the Lord until He comes (cf. I Cor. 11:26)" (CE 8).

The Church presses forward, set apart from the world, different from the other communities of the world. The Church is not like natural communities, people bound together by their way of life, like families, nations, states. Nor is it like communities of interest, like trades unions or professional associations, like economic or cultural organizations. The way of the Church must be different from those of other societies. It has a different foundation, for which there is no substitute; different means, which cannot be replaced by those borrowed from other communities; a different goal, distinct from the aims of other communities; it has a different scale of values for measuring what is important or unimportant, what should be seen as success or failure, as glory or shame; it has a different membership qualification, incomprehensible to outsiders—a single qualification: faith.

And yet this community which has been set apart must not cut itself off from the world; it must be different yet not aloof, marked out yet not isolated. It cannot cut itself off entirely, since it exists within the same areas of influence and interest as other human societies, and since its members are members of other groups. But it must not try to cut itself off; the Church has not been simply taken out of the world, it has been sent back into the world as something holy, belonging to God. The Church must not try to create "sacred" areas and confines distinct from everything "profane". As we have seen, this is precisely not the sense in which Jesus preached the reign of God which began with himself; this reign is established in the world of everyday and is to spread finally throughout the whole world. Nor is this the sense of Paul's preaching about Christian freedom; for the Christian nothing is in itself impure, in the properly understood sense of the words, all things are lawful. The Church has been set apart from the world in order to live and act in the world in a different way from those who do not believe. The holy Church exists wherever in the world of everyday life men hear the word of God's grace and love, believe it and only it by handing on the love given to them in their acts for their fellow men. But the Church, although it is holy, is constantly in need of forgiveness.

2. FORGIVENESS AND RENEWAL AS CONTINUING ASPECTS OF THE LIFE OF THE CHURCH

(*a*) In the Church there is forgiveness of sins.[45] As we have seen,[46] Jesus' message of the reign of God demands more than external penance in sackcloth and ashes. It calls for metanoia, for a radical and total inner reorientation of the whole man, and his return to God. This demand is issued not only to the pious and righteous, who do not consider themselves in need of penance, but also and particularly to those whom the righteous reject and cast out. It is for them in particular that Jesus opens the way to the reign of God, it is with them in particular, to the indignation of the pious, that he keeps company, eating and drinking with notorious sinners, with Samaritans, tax collectors and prostitutes (Mk. 2:16 par.; Mt. 11:19 par.; Lk. 19:7). And he even dares to assure men explicitly that their sins are forgiven, as all the gospel writers tell us (Mk. 2:5 par.; Lk. 7:48; Jn. 8:11). By doing this Jesus opposes the law then in force, which called for the punishment of sinners; moreover, he lays claim to what for Judaism was a prerogative of God alone: "Who can forgive sins but God alone?" (Mk. 2:7 par.; Lk. 7:49). But the crowds

---

[45] On the forgiveness of sins and confession see the NT theologies, the standard works on dogma and the history of dogma and the relevant articles in ThW and the theological encyclopaedias. Also the following monographs: B. Poschmann, *Die abendländische Kirchenbusse im frühen Mittelalter*, Breslau 1930; *Poenitentia secunda. Die kirchl. Busse im ältesten Christentum bis Cyprian und Origenes*, Bonn 1940; *Penance and Anointing of the Sick*, London–New York 1964; P. Galtier, *De poenitentia tractatus dogmatico historicus*, Rome 1931² 1950; *L'Eglise et la rémission des péchés aux premiers siècles*, Paris 1932; *Aux origines du sacrement de la Pénitence*, Rome 1951; J. A. Jungmann, *Die lat. Bussriten in ihrer geschichtlichen Entwicklung*, Innsbruck 1952; H. von Campenhausen, *Kirchliches Amt und geistliche Vollmacht in den ersten drei Jahrhunderten*, Tübingen 1953; J. Grotz, *Die Entwicklung des Busssutfenwesens in der vornicänischen Kirche*, Freiburg 1955; K. Rahner, art. *Bussdisziplin, Busse, Busssakrament*, in: LThK II, 805–815, 815–818, 826–838; here too the many historico-dogmatic works by Rahner are cited. P. Anciaux, *The Sacrament of Penance*, Tenbury Wells 1962.

[46] Cf. B I, 2.

"glorified God, who had given such authority to men" (Mt. 9:8).

This last phrase, strikingly enough, speaks of "men" in the plural, and it is quite probable that it is intended to express the conviction of the early community that Jesus' authority to forgive sins was now the possession of the whole community. At all events the community believes that its sins can be forgiven. The Christian community is the eschatological communion of "saints", called and elected by God, set apart from a godless and adulterous people.[47] Its baptism is for "forgiveness of sins".[48] But baptism, which sets the seal on metanoia and faith, does not bring magic sinlessness with it. Trials and temptations remain. We must pray daily to be delivered from evil, and pray for forgiveness. And only if we forgive others, in whom we also experience the reality of sin, can we hope for forgiveness for ourselves. In this way the believer is part of the fellowship of forgiveness of God and of the Lord, who was the friend of sinners.

This fellowship of forgiveness is the focal point of forgiveness in the Church. The Church is empowered to forgive sins by its Lord who kept company with sinners and forgave them their sins. This is a new experience which distinguishes the eschatological community from any kind of Judaism. This is what is meant by the words at Matthew 18:18 (cf. 16:19b; Jn. 20:23), which are probably not *ipsissima verba* of Jesus in this form, but presuppose the existence of a coherent and precisely defined community: "Truly I say to you, whatever you bind on earth shall be bound in heaven, and whatever you loose on earth shall be loosed in heaven."

The words "bind" and "loose" are technical rabbinical expressions for "forbid" and "declare permissible", sometimes also used for "place under an interdict" and "release from an interdict". Whether they were used more in the former or the latter sense, these words were taken by the community as the basis for the forgiveness of sins, as we can see from the variant given at John 20:22 f., where there is a specific reference to the Holy Spirit and to spiritual authority: "Receive the Holy Spirit. If you forgive the sins of any, they are forgiven;

---

[47] Cf. B III, 1.   [48] Cf. C III, 1.

if you retain the sins of any, they are retained." The Church's judgment is authorized and approved by God. God acts through the Church; his judgment is not simply indicated, it is carried out. Matthew 18:18 has been inserted into a very early instruction of the community, which lays down the three stages of dealing with sinners. Everyone has the duty of reproving the sinner, that is, pointing the way from sin to repentance (18:15); if he takes no notice, the admonition is to be made more emphatic by taking along one or two of the other members of the community (18:16); if he still takes no notice, the community as a whole is to deal with the case (18:16). If he is convinced by the community as a whole, fellowship with him is restored, if he pays no heed to them, fellowship with him is broken off. The community looses the repentant sinner whom it forgives; but it binds the unrepentant sinner, who is to be as a tax collector and a Gentile (18:17). In either case the community has God behind it (18:18). This is the new and joyful certainty which the community possesses: it is not just men, it is God who has forgiven. This underlines also the seriousness of their judgment; it is God who had judged. This admonition seems to place greater emphasis on the possible negative outcome of the case; but the object of it is not punishment, it is forgiveness. The wider context of the pericope unmistakably emphasizes this, for it is preceded by the parable of the lost sheep (18:12–14), and followed by an encouragement to forgiveness and then the parable of the generous king and his merciless servant (18:21–35).

It is the whole Church, the whole community which bears the authority to forgive sins. Matthew 18:18 itself, and the whole context of instruction to the disciples, indicates that the whole community of the disciples is addressed here. The plural "you" at verse 18, in connection with the ecclesia (verse 17) and in the context of preceding phrases addressed to a communal "you" (vv. 2, 10, 12, 13), makes it clear that final judgments, particularly negative ones, are the responsibility not of the individual but of the community. There is no mention of the "apostles" or of the "twelve" in this context. There is no indication of how the community is ordered and administered, even though we may infer that an apostle or elder may have been the leader of the community; at John 20:22 f. too, it is quite generally the "disciples" who represent the community, as in John 13–16 (cf. also the parallel narrative at Luke 24:33). The whole fellowship of Jesus' disciples considers itself empowered to forgive sins, as also to administer baptism and celebrate the Lord's Supper, since the Spirit has been given to it as a whole. It is in the community, as Matthew 18:20 goes on immediately afterwards to point out, that the Lord is present: "Where two or three are gathered in my name, there am I in the midst of them."

This is not the place to go into all the complex exegetical aspects of the problem. We shall come back in the next chapter to Matthew 16:18 f. and to the whole question of ecclesiastical office. There is only room to point out here that the power of the keys, the power to bind and loose, cannot, precisely because of the parallels in the text, be understood as referring exclusively to Peter. Augustine brings this out very clearly in his interpretation of Matthew 16:18 f.: "It is the *Church* which exercises this authority, full of blessed hope, towards man burdened with sin. For Peter had only a general representative function, because he was the first of the apostles. The special thing about Peter depended on the following three qualities: by nature he was a man, by grace a Christian, by particular election the first of the apostles. But when it was said to him: 'I will give you the keys of the kingdom of heaven' (Mt. 16:19), he became thereby merely the image of the whole visible Church. . . . The Church, founded on Christ, received from the Lord the keys of the kingdom of heaven, that is, the power to forgive and retain sins. But it received this power in Peter. What the Church possesses as its own from Christ is represented metaphorically and meaningfully in Peter. Therefore petra is the symbol of Christ; but Peter is the symbol of the Church."[49]

On the basis of II Corinthians 5:18–21, it is safe to assume that Paul exercised the "ministry of reconciliation" not only in the meetings of the community (through the sermon), but that he also spoke the "word of reconciliation" to the individual sinner who came to him. We know very little about an official and ordered discipline of penance in the first and early second centuries, apart from indications of Church discipline in the Pauline communities (cf. especially I Cor. 5). In the pastoral letters similarly, and in the

[49] Augustine, *In Jo.* 124, 5; CC 36, 684 f.

Shepherd of Hermas and Ignatius, concrete disciplinary penance—confession, excommunication and absolution—plays no part (the idea that I Timothy 5:22 is the first evidence of a formal absolution is denied by all those exegetes who take the passage to refer to ordination). It was only in the next two generations that "penance" became a disputed problem, in the Western Churches at least, particularly with regard to the role of the ecclesiastical office in the discipline of penance; in early times pneumatics, martyrs and confessors claimed the right to forgive sins. The further, highly complex development of the discipline of penance in the Church is something we cannot go into here.

The following points may briefly be made:

1. For the whole of Western patristics, as already for the Shepherd of Hermas, "penance" is something non-recurring, corresponding to the non-recurring nature of baptism. Up to the fourth century even this unique reconciliation was refused for certain mortal sins.

2. In the third century Montanism and Novatianism, with their rigorous (original?) ideas of penance, failed to gain ground in the Church. At the same time the forgiveness of sins was administered less and less by pneumatics (something which Tertullian still upheld and which lasted longer in the East, until special priests and monks took over this ministry), and more and more by bishops (cf. Cyprian), whose authority was increasing at this time. There was still no private sacramental penance, only public penance.

3. The gradual intensification of the penances imposed, including often severe punishments for life, led to a decline in the idea of penance especially from the fifth century onwards; it was often put off until old age, or shortly before death.

4. From about the sixth century in Britain and Ireland, and about the seventh century on the Continent, the idea of *recurrent* penance and at the same time of *private penance* developed; smaller sins were now also included, absolved no longer only by bishops but also by priests; penance became possible as often as necessary and the penances imposed were much less severe. This was the beginning of what we now know as confession; it became general from the eighth century, and from the ninth century was often recommended as something to be undertaken periodically; confession and absolution were now seen together, with penances to be performed afterwards; in 1215 the Fourth Lateran Council prescribed confession once a year.

5. From the middle of the twelfth century, as the number seven increasingly became attached to the sacraments, the *sacramental*

character of penance became more and more established; two areas of controversy remained: the function of the priestly absolution (declarative or effective?) and the nature of the sacramental sign (*attritio* or *contritio?*).

6. In the later Middle Ages an appalling decline set in (external penances, pious works, indulgences). The Council of Trent attempted to restore the medieval *status quo ante* (in the post-Tridentine period closed confessionals were introduced, from the seventeenth century confessionals with three divisions). This development marks an increasing narrowing down, when compared with the New Testament idea of metanoia; today there is a great need for us to reflect on this idea of metanoia and to consider various possible ways of realizing it.

Forgiveness is only possible when the sinner wants his sins to be forgiven, when he confesses them and turns away from them, when there is repentance and metanoia. Jesus' call to metanoia was not, however, directed towards special kinds of human actions, but towards the radical turning of the whole man towards God. "Penance" should not therefore be limited simply to the later idea of *"paenitentia secunda"*, to the performing of certain acts of penance. We must think of penance in its original, all-embracing and radical New Testament sense of metanoia, the turning of the whole man towards God, which he has to perform every day anew. Although he has turned his back on sin through faith, it remains a constant and recurring temptation; penance is the repeated decision to turn his back on it. Baptism itself, in which man is effectively assured of the forgiveness of sins, calls upon him to engage in a continual struggle with sin, to turn continually away from it and to pray for forgiveness. Repeated metanoia, turning to God, "penance", is a consequence of baptism. It is not that baptism loses its efficacy. "Second penance" is not therefore "the second plank after the shipwreck", as it was called in quite early times, as though the ship of baptism had really sunk. The effects of baptism are not removed by subsequent sin, and the promise of grace in baptism is not thereby withdrawn. But this grace must always be accepted afresh in faith; this is possible if a man renews his metanoia and sees himself again as the man he was at the moment of baptism. In this sense "penance" is an act of faith whereby man lays hold once again of the grace which he received in faith at his baptism.

But baptism is not an isolated action; it depends on the word, the word of the Gospel which promises forgiveness of sins to the believer. The preaching of the Gospel proclaims the forgiveness of sins which has already occurred in Christ. Any metanoia, turning to God "penance", presupposes the grace and mercy and forgiveness of God promised by Christ. God's grace precedes all human metanoia; all we have to do is to accept the offer of grace in faith. For this reason the word metanoia in the New Testament has not the gloomy and negative implications which it later took on, when subsequent ideas about penance suggested that the grace of God could only be earned by human works. The New Testament tells us that metanoia comes from that grace and forgiveness of God which has already been proclaimed. It is not the consequence of an oppressive law, able to make demands but not to promise fulfilment; it is a consequence of the Gospel, of the good and joyful news of God's revealed grace, which offers forgiveness to man and makes his metanoia possible. The preaching of the Gospel is therefore the basis for all ideas about penance, and it is in the light of this that we must look at the various historical forms under which the forgiveness of sins has been administered.

1. *The preaching of the Gospel itself:* By preaching the Gospel, whether to non-believers or to the community of believers, the Church proclaims God's mercy towards sinners. Provided that the Church is not peaching something different (Greek: *allotria*) or preaching a new "law"—a sign of sin, according to Paul—provided it is really preaching the "Gospel", it will really and truly be assuring men of God's fellowship with sinners and the forgiveness of sins, and speaking "the message of reconciliation" (II Cor. 5:19). It is after all in the preaching of the Gospel that man is confronted with the real alternatives of faith or disbelief, a decision for God or a decision for the world, a return to God in love or a return to sin. In the words of preaching the kingdom of heaven is opened or closed; he who in faith opens his heart to the word is accepted by God; he who closes his heart to the word in disbelief is excluded by the very word of grace which he rejects. It is at this fundamental level that binding and loosing occurs. This is where

grace and the forgiveness of sins is not only proclaimed, but is communicated to all who believe. The Gospel is then "the power of God for salvation to everyone who has faith, to the Jew first and also to the Greek. For in it the righteousness of God is revealed through faith for faith; as it is written 'He who through faith is righteous shall live'" (Rom. 1:16 f.). There is a very real and factual meaning in the words which are spoken in the Catholic liturgy after the reading of the Gospel: "May our sins be blotted out by these words of the Gospel" (*Per haec evangelica dicta deleantur nostra delicta*).

2. *General absolution:*[50] The forgiveness of sins promised by the preaching of the word can be concretized and applied. The general absolution given to the whole community during an act of worship—generally in connection with the preaching of the word—can be seen as a concrete and explicit application of this kind. From the tenth century there existed the "public confession", the origins and theological significance of which is not entirely clear. It was a public confessing of sins by the whole community in the vernacular, often following the preaching of the word, and itself followed by an actual absolution, often using the same formula as in private confession. These are "general absolutions", which first of all had sacramental value, generally for "venial" sins. The Reformers (Luther, Zwingli, Calvin) also speak of public confession, and the idea has been partly retained in the Reformed Churches down to the present day. The Catholic Church still retains a continuation of the idea in the general absolutions given in cases of emergency, where absolution is given to the whole community without individual confessions. This again is a fulfilment of the words at Matthew 18:18. The question arises whether this kind of general absolution ought not to be renewed today, in addition to private confession, as part of the worship of the community, whether in the context of the Lord's Supper or connected with a particular service of penance.

3. *Individual absolution by laymen:*[51] Precedents are provided here by the absolutions which charismatics, confessors and martyrs give: then later by confessions heard by monks and deacons, and also by the monastic recitation of offences, etc. Lay confession has at all events a long tradition behind it, lasting as it did up to the fourteenth century in the East and up to the time of Duns Scotus

[50] Cf. J. A. Jungmann, art. "Absolution", in LThK I, 74 f., as well as the bibliography at note 45.

[51] Cf. Y. Congar, *Lay People in the Church*, London 1957, Westminster, Md. 1965; K. Rahner, art. "Laienbeichte", in LThK VI, 741 (biblio.).

it was general in Western theology to regard lay confession in emergency as an obligation. Albert the Great considered that lay confession has a true sacramental character, Thomas Aquinas considered that it has a kind of sacramental character (Thomas draws the parallel with baptism, a sacrament which can be administered by laymen). This tradition cannot be explained away in terms of a "privilege" or by other legalistic constructions; its basis is rather biblical, as shown by exegesis (cf. especially Matthew 18:18).

4. *Individual absolution by office-bearers:* In the Catholic Church of recent centuries this kind of absolution has ousted all other forms. We shall return in the next chapter to the question of ecclesiastical office.

Where there is no visible act of "penance", the attitude of metanoia can easily become something that is passive and taken for granted. But freedom in diversity must not be lost. The assurance given to men that their sins are forgiven should be a gift and a help to them, not an oppressive law and a severe discipline. "Penance" is only meaningful on the basis of man's unconditional faith in his justification by God's grace alone, not on the basis of a Pelagian view of pious works. Finally, we must never forget the saying: "So you also, when you have done all that is commanded you, say, 'We are unworthy servants; we have only done what was our duty'" (Lk. 17:10).

But it is not only *in* the Church that "penance" is necessary. The Church itself must also be capable of "penance". Not only in the sense that it must be prepared to confess its errors and failures, and make them good, but more particularly in the sense that it must always commit itself afresh to a positive renewal.

(*b*) It has been justly maintained that every Christian must begin the metanoia, and hence the reform and renewal[52] of the Church, within himself. It is certainly true that Church reform is not a matter of abstract academic discussion. At the same time, an inner, moral reform of the heart, a renewal of attitudes, is not enough by itself. Good intentions and aspirations of the heart are not always sufficient to alter reality. The

---

[52] Cf. H. U. von Balthasar, *Schleifung der Bastionen,* Einsiedeln 1952; Y. Congar, *Vraie et fausse réforme dans l'Eglise,* Paris 1954; H. Küng, *The Council and Reunion,* London and New York 1961; and the other literature on Vatican II.

good will of the individual may indeed often be there, but may be unable to find expression. Why is this? Because the external conditions, the forms and structures of the Church hamper the carrying out of his good intentions, or even in some cases make them impossible. For centuries many Christians would gladly have received communion more often, but it was only the changes in the unnecessarily rigorous fasting laws which made this possible for them—a change in Church discipline, that is. The message of Jesus Christ challenges the Church itself to a constant metanoia, to rethink and reorientate its position according to the Gospel.

The New Testament writings are of course principally concerned with the form and with the forming of the Church, which is not to conform to the world but is to develop its own form by living in the spirit of Christ. But even in the New Testament we find reforms being called for: with regard to the liturgy (I Cor. 10–11), to Church order (Mt. 18, cf. 10), to doctrine, both in opposition to insidious Judaism (in Galatians), and to the threat of Gnosticism (in I Corinthians and Colossians particularly), and then with regard to repentance and a return to the origins of the Church in general (Rev. 2–3). The New Testament, in fact, illustrates what we have already noted: the Church, since it is always a Church composed of men, sinful men, and always being deformed by human limitations and human sinfulness, must continually reform itself, through the grace and mercy of God from whom it draws the necessary strength, according to the Gospel of Jesus Christ: *ecclesia semper reformanda.* The history of the Church illustrates this in a most emphatic way. Only a superficial observer would regard Church history as simply a decline from the New Testament, as a process of continual deformation. There has been a process of deformation, but there has also been a continual process of reformation, whether visibly or invisibly. This reformation has occurred in two ways; negatively through the discarding of deformations, mistaken attitudes and developments, and positively through beneficial developments.

Most of the movements of enthusiasm and heresy were explicitly movements of reform; this is something we must not forget, even though there is no need to rehearse the whole argument again here.[53] Some of these movements emphasized the need for a return to origins, others took as their starting-point the imminent end of the world; many of them relieved the dialectical tension of a holy Church in the world by preferring a Church of the pure and holy, quite cut off from the world; this of course necessarily led to sectarian narrowness. In this context we must refer to certain movements in the early centuries of the Church, such as Montanism and Marcionism, and later movements, important particularly in connection with the debate about penance, like Novatianism (sanctity of all the members of the community) and Donatism (sanctity of office-bearers in particular), the Melitian schisms and Priscillianism. In the medieval period these tendencies were continued by those ascetic movements, already mentioned above, which also worked through travelling preachers: the Cathars (rigorous asceticism, poverty, vernacular worship) and the Waldensians (strict adherence to the Bible, coupled with a more ecclesiastical approach). As was made clear above, the Protestant Reformation aimed at a radical and total renewal of the Church by criticizing the medieval Church and by suggesting reforms on the model of the New Testament Church; also referred to were the various radicalizations of the Reformation, the movements of enthusiasm of the time. Again in the post-Reformation period Protestantism produced a whole series of attempts at renewal. Puritanism, Pietism and Methodism aimed rather at general reforms of the whole of ecclesiastical and personal life, while the revivalist movements of the late eighteenth and early nineteenth centuries in Europe and America sought a renewal of the Church through a deeper and more vital personal life of faith, which was then to affect the social life of a "Christian" society (Disciples of Christ, Churches of God, Mormons, etc.). After both the world wars there were particularly strong impulses towards renewal within Protestantism.

What concerns us here above all, however, are the movements for reform within the Catholic Church. The basis for all subsequent movements of renewal in the Church was laid with the fundamental decision, for which Paul fought and which was approved by the "Apostolic Council", to abandon Jewish law and to adapt Christianity to the Gentile world with the idea of being "all things to all men". In the first Christian centuries reforms were principally concerned with the liturgy and, in the same connection, with preaching and catechetics (the adoption of Koine-Greek and other vernaculars; about 250 the introduction of Latin as the cult lan-

[53] Cf. C II, 4; III, 4.

guage; the somewhat questionable development from the house Mass to the basilical Mass and finally to the medieval Frankish form of the Mass). Then came the translation of the Bible (continually new translations from the original languages and revisions of the accepted translations, then the Vulgate, which was a reform, strongly attacked in its day, of the Latin Bible). Then theology (disputed and often dubious developments and reorientations of the theology in Greek and Latin patristics), finally monasticism and missionary activity (the Benedictine movement of reform). The crucial impulses of reform in the already very worldly early medieval Church came from Cluny; monastic reform became a clergy reform and finally a general reform of the Church, admittedly increasingly political in tendency. Particularly important for these reforms were the German Emperors (especially Henry III), then the Popes (Leo IX, Gregory VII, Innocent III) and finally the new orders (first of all the Cistercians with Bernard of Clairvaux, the Augustinian canons, the Premonstratensians and the various knightly orders and Hospitallers of the twelfth century; finally in the thirteenth century the Dominican and above all the Franciscan movements of reform, with the unique figure of Francis of Assisi who, at a time when the medieval Church was becoming power-conscious, attempted to bring about a general inner renewal according to the Gospel). But all this could not halt the decadence of the Church in the later Middle Ages (Avignon; Western schism; Renaissance), any more than the late medieval reforming councils, which sought to achieve a "reform of the Church in its head and members", or the countless later medieval movements of reform (especially the Brethren of the Common Life).

Luther's protest against this unreformed Church was, as we have seen, only too well founded. But despite all the achievements of the Reformation, it would be over-simplifying, and indeed inaccurate, to contrast a "reformed Protestant Church" with an "unreformed Catholic Church". Not only because the Protestant Reformation, for all its genuine reforms, led to a deformation and increasing dissolution of Church unity, but above all because the Catholic Church, while remaining in constant need of reform, by no means totally failed to carry out any reforms itself. While retaining Church continuity, it undertook a vast, even if far from completed, programme of reform. The Catholic Reformation was prepared for by small groups in pre-Reformation times, given a firm basis by the Council of Trent, and carried out by a reformed papacy, reformed bishops, priests and laity and new reforming orders, especially the Society of Jesus. At the same time, it would be idle to overlook the fact that the Counter-Reformation of the sixteenth to nineteenth centuries, despite many positive achievements, often had the appearance of a movement of reaction and restoration, bent on a negative programme of rooting out abuses. All too often the idea of reform was seen not so much as a means of reconciliation and reunification but as the basis for an aggressive campaign to maintain a *status quo,* or to recapture the lost glories of the medieval past, a campaign that was waged often enough with very unspiritual weapons. The call of the Reformers for fundamental reforms in the Lord's Supper, for example, especially the introduction of the vernacular, was answered at Trent by basically reactionary measures, the abolition of abuses. The First Vatican Council similarly was a disappointment to all hopes of reform. The change from a conservative and restorative notion of reform to a positive and creative type of reform only began with Leo XIII, and reached a high point with John XXIII and the Second Vatican Council. This council achieved a fundamental reorientation of the Church with regard to other Christian Churches, to the Jews and non-Christian religions and to the modern secular world in general, a reorientation which was based on reforms at various levels within the Church itself (the renewal of forms of worship, a renewed ecclesiology, renewal of Church offices, the laity, the orders, the missions, etc.).

A very brief survey of movements of renewal in Church history makes it clear that the Church is not only an *ecclesia semper reformanda,* but was always, despite constant shortcoming, an *ecclesia semper reformata,* a fact for which we may be grateful. In this way the demands made in the Bible for the renewal of the individual Christian life can be made fruitful in the life of the Church itself. This renewal has already fundamentally taken place in Christ: "Therefore, if anyone is in Christ, he is a new creation; the old has passed away, behold, the new has come" (II Cor. 5:17). But this renewal of the new, inward and spiritual man must constantly be effected anew: "Though our outer nature is wasting away, our inner nature is being renewed every day" (II Cor. 4:16). For this reason the community is constantly challenged to renew itself: "Do not be conformed to this world, but be transformed by the renewal of your mind, that you may prove what is the will of God, what is good and acceptable and perfect" (Rom. 12:2; cf. Eph. 4:20–24; Col. 3:10). From this it is clear that the need for reform in the

Church, for which it always has ample grounds, given that the Church is human and sinful, does not arise from any kind of opportunistic or transient reason, such as an enthusiasm for progress, the desire for modernity, an automatic conformism, fear of temporal powers and so on. It arises primarily from the demands made in the Gospel by the Lord of the Church, the call to metanoia, to new faith, to new righteousness, holiness and freedom, to new life. Church reforms are not called for simply by the whim of the Church or Church leaders. They are a continuing task and opportunity given by the Lord of the Church. Reform is a way in which the Church fulfils the will of God, following in the footsteps of Christ with its eye on the coming of the kingdom. There will always be opposition. Uncommitted indifference, an illusionary view of the Church's situation, ecclesiastical self-satisfaction, a lazy traditionalism, an apologetic attitude, a superficial, narrow or secularized ecclesiology, defeatism and lack of hope—these will always exist. But genuine distress at the permanently unreformed Church, heartfelt prayers that the Church may be delivered from evil, committed and constructive criticisms of the Church, zeal for the Lord and active love—these are the sources of a continually revived readiness for reform.

Re-formare means "to give a new form" to something, to "restore an earlier, better form" of something, to "reshape the misshapen features" of something, to "give the proper form according to its real nature" to something. Church reform must be a positive reforming of the Church in accordance with its nature. If it is a real reform, it will never spend itself in purely negative acts of abolition, rejection and prohibition. It will be a positive re-forming and re-expression of its nature. The word "renewal" is often better than the word "reform", precisely because it emphasizes this positive and creative aspect. Genuine Church reform is not the same as *revolution*. It does not aim at a violent upheaval, it is not doctrinaire, fanatical or loveless in its quest of what is new. While aiming at what is new and better, it is concerned about the continuity of historical development; it is not innovation but *renewal*. Genuine Church reform is on the other hand not the same as *restoration*. It does not aim at a contented continuation of an old system, but courageously breaks with old systems in order to find greater truth. Instead of restoring old forms, it looks for new forms fitted to the age; instead of insisting with fresh intensity on the rigid observation of laws and ordinances, canons and codes, it seeks to renew the inner life of institutions and constitutions. While retaining a sense of tradition, genuine reform is concerned with finding the new and creative forms demanded by the present time; it is not restoration, but again *renewal*.

It is not enough, as we have seen, to effect an inner reform of the heart which neglects the reform of structures, institutions and constitutions. Equally, a purely external reform, abolishing abuses and merely patching up the old structures, institutions and constitutions, is of no avail. What is constantly necessary is a creative reform of conditions and structures which, far from destroying the nature of the Church, gives it new and credible form. True, what God himself through Christ in the Spirit has instituted and constituted in the Church has a share in the holiness of God himself and needs no reform. But what men themselves have instituted and constituted in the Church is conditioned by human imperfections and sinfulness and is in constant need of reform. Since, however, nature and historical form cannot properly be separated, there are no irreformable areas in the Church; at most there are irreformable constants. There is no stone, no cloister in the building of the Church which does not need reforming again and again; but the constructional formula which is the key to the whole must not be contravened. The only measure for renewal in the Church is the original Gospel of Jesus Christ himself; the only concrete guide is the apostolic Church. The credibility of the Church depends crucially on its constantly undertaking new reforms and renewing itself afresh. An unreformed Church will fail to convince. Drawing on the forgiveness which has been granted to her, the Church must help to renew both individual and community, and so demonstrate that it is a holy Church.

Two short and fundamental sentences from the documents of Vatican II, already quoted, may be repeated here: "Christ summons the Church, as she goes her pilgrim way, to that continual reformation (*ad hanc perennem reformationem*) of which she always has need, insofar as she is an institution of men here on earth" (DOe 6). "The Church . . . is at the same time holy and always in need of being purified (*semper purificanda*), and incessantly pursues the path of penance and renewal (*poenitentiam et renovationem*)" (CE 8).

(*c*) The Church has already been set apart from the world by God as something holy; this is an effect of his grace. It must remain set apart; this is his call to metanoia and renewal. It will remain set apart; this is his faithful promise. The Church cannot maintain its course of itself; like Israel, it is supported by God's mercy and faithfulness. Its being set apart cannot be revoked; the whole New Testament message depends on this belief.

External things may threaten the Church; like Israel it may be humbled and put down in various ways and places; it may be cornered and enslaved, weakened, scorned and mutilated, suppressed and persecuted, even outwardly wiped out altogether; but "the powers of death shall not prevail against it" (Mt. 16:18). It will not succumb to death; it is indestructible. God has promised it in his faithfulness a permanent and continuous existence. Despite its failings and weaknesses, God himself will keep it alive.

Internal decay may threaten the Church; like Israel it may become weak and faint-hearted, it may become proud and imperious, or undisciplined and degenerate, it may be despoiled and violated, it may in many respects forget its true calling and turn its back on its Lord; and yet "lo, I am with you always, to the close of the age" (Mt. 28:20). The glorified Lord keeps faith with the Church, protecting and helping it. It will not capitulate to sin; it is unruinable. God has promised it in his mercy an undecaying and constant existence. Despite its sin and guilt God himself will preserve it in his mercy.

A falling-away from truth may also seriously threaten the Church in individual matters; like Israel the Church may now and then doubt and hesitate, or even err away from its true course; but "the Spirit of truth" will be "with you for ever" (Jn. 14:16 f.). The Church will not yield to untruth; it is undeceivable. God has promised and granted to it infallibility. Despite its errors and misunderstandings God will preserve it in the truth.

What "infallibility" means, as the root of the word shows (Latin *"fallere"*, lead into error, blind, deceive, disappoint), is that the Church is not deceiving or deceived. The trouble with the word "infallibility" is that it suggests that the Church is "free from error", which of course cannot apply to the Church and its representatives. It means that the Church, in so far as it is humbly obedient to the word of God, has a share in the truth of God himself, "who can neither deceive nor be deceived" (Vatican I: *Deus revelans, qui nec falli nec fallere potest*, D 1783). If it is obedient, then all lies and deceits and deceitfulness are removed from it. "Infallibility" therefore means a fundamental remaining in the truth, which is not disturbed by individual errors.

This infallibility is scriptural, and even the Reformers never questioned it. Whether on the other hand it has as a necessary consequence the *a priori*, unquestionable and *verifiable* infallibility of particular *statements* is something that is not directly demonstrable from the New Testament. This is a question which is much disputed between the individual Christian Churches, especially in connection with councils, bishops and the pope, and needs a new investigation on the basis given above.[54] Two points in particular would have to be taken into account:

1. *Binding force:* Formulations of faith which have the whole Church behind them, in one form or another, have a qualitatively higher value as testimony and a qualitatively different binding force, because they are the testimony of the whole body of the faithful, than formulations of faith made by individual Christians or theologians. The unity of faith of the fellowship of believers ought not to be lightly endangered. The individual believer, and the individual theologian too, bears the responsibility for working in all sincerity from the Gospel and with the fellowship of believers. In this way he will probably be preserved from personal narrowness, subjective arbitrariness and the tendency to regard his findings as absolute; he will find true freedom in genuine modesty and in the service of the fellowship of believers.

2. *Fragmentariness:* Every formulation of faith, whether made by an individual or by the whole Church, remains imperfect, incomplete, unclear, partial and fragmentary; these are the kind of expressions used by Paul in I Corinthians 13:9–12. This is often

[54] Cf. *Structures*, 305–352.

overlooked when the infallibility of an individual statement, where infallibility begins after a colon, is considered. The partial and incomplete nature of such statements is not only the result of the polemical bias and the narrowness of doctrinal formulations made by the Church. It is part of the necessary dialectic character of all human statements of the truth. Any human statement of truth, because of its human limitations, is very close to error, and one only has to overlook the human limitations of truth to turn truth into error. All human truth stands in the shadow of error. All error contains at least a grain of truth. What a true statement says is true; what it fails to say may also be true. What a false statement says is false; what it means but does not say may be true. It is a simplified view of the truth to suppose that every sentence in its verbal formulation must be either true or false. On the contrary, any sentence can be true *and* false, according to its purpose, its context, its underlying meaning. It is much harder to discover what is meant by it than what it says. A sincere, fearless and critical ecumenical theology, the only kind which can hope to be constructive, must give up throwing dogmas at the heads of the other side. Theology today must be actively concerned to try and see the truth in what it supposes to be the errors of the other side, and to see the possibility of error in what it itself believes. In this way we would reach the situation which it is essential we reach: the abandonment of supposed error and a meeting in common Christian truth.[55]

The Church, as promised and assured by God, remains a holy Church, set apart. We need waste no time speculating what would happen if there were no Church, or no holy Church. God will ensure that there will always be a Church and that it will be holy. It will never lose its situation of being set apart, distinct and marked out from the world. Though wounded it will remain alive, though sinning it will not fall away from grace, though erring it will never lose sight of the truth. Its faith may grow weak, its love lukewarm, its hope dim; but the foundation of its faith, the root of its love, the basis of its hope, will remain, undamaged and untouched. It will continue indestructible, unshakable and true: "the pillar and bulwark of the truth" (I Tim. 3:15). Its permanency,

[55] As well as *Structures,* see *The Theologian and the Church,* London 1965, published as Chap. 3, *Freedom Today,* New York 1966.

unshakability and infallibility are not of its own making, and no one, not even the Church itself, can take these away from it. It will never cease to be what it is: the communion of saints, the people of God, the creation of the Spirit, the body of Christ. It will never become a different Church, a pseudo-Church. As the Fathers explained, it can become a beggar-woman, set itself up as a trader, sell itself as a prostitute; but through God's preserving, saving and forgiving mercy it will always remain the bride of Christ. It may wander through the world poor, hungry and helpless, but the Father will always run to embrace and kiss it on its return. It may lose its way in the desert, but the shepherd will always go out after it. It may roam through the town, but the Bridegroom will always find it. It may desert him, but he will never desert it. The Church goes on its pilgrim way through the ages, along a road not of its own choosing, along the way to which it is irrevocably called. It may lose the way, make detours, take wrong turnings, it may stumble and fall, it may fall among thieves and lie half-dead by the roadside. But God the Lord will not pass by on the other side; he will pour oil on its wounds, lift it up, give it a lodging and provide for its healing even that which could not have been foreseen. The Church will always remain the holy Church. This we know in faith: *credo sanctam ecclesiam*.

IV. THE CHURCH IS APOSTOLIC

1. FOUNDED ON THE APOSTLES

In our search for unity in diversity, catholicity in identity, holiness in sinfulness, the question of a criterion must always be in our minds. How far can the Church be one, holy and catholic? What is true unity, true catholicity, true holiness? The crucial criterion is expressed in the fourth attribute of the Church: the Church can only be truly one, holy and catholic if it is in all things an *apostolic* Church. What is in question is not any kind of unity, holiness and catholicity, but that which is founded on the apostles and in that sense is apostolic.

The adjective "apostolic"[56] is scarcely used except in Christian context. It does not occur in the Bible. But the Fathers use it constantly; it is first used, like the adjective "catholic", by Ignatius of Antioch (*Trall, Inscript.*) and in the Martyrdom of Polycarp (16:2). Its original and most general meaning is: "having a direct link with the apostles of Christ". From the second and third centuries the word "apostolic" also takes on an ascetic meaning, in the sense of "like the apostles"; both individual sects in early times and in the Middle Ages (e.g. the "Apostolic Brethren"), and early monastic literature use the word in this sense, implying the renunciation of worldly goods and of marriage. Only at a relatively late stage did the word take on a pastoral and active sense, as opposed to pure contemplation;[57] it is in this pastoral sense that the word is often used today ("apostolate"). But rather than simply adopting this meaning of the word, we must, if we are thinking about the "apostolic Church", begin by asking: what does "apostle" mean?

If we are to avoid prejudging the issue of what the apostolicity of the Church means, we must abandon any stereotyped ideas about the "twelve apostles" who are the subject of so much legendary material and so much Christian art. The association between "twelve" and "apostles" is not without its problems. The missionary command of Christ (Mk. 16:15 f.; Mt. 28:18 f.; Ld. 24:47 f.; Acts 1:8) seems to reflect the idea and the traditions that the apostles went out into the world as missionaries. But as we have seen, even Acts relates that the apostles stayed first of all in Jerusalem (Acts 8:1) and only undertook with great reluctance the mission to

---

[56] See the general literature cited at A II, 2 and D I, 1 and esp. M. Schmaus, *Dogmatik III/1*, 623–630 and K. Barth, *Church Dogmatics IV/1*, 795–809, as well as the articles in LThK (*Apostolisch:* H. Bacht, *Apostolizität der Kirche:* O. Karrer) and RGG (*Apostolisch:* K. G. Steck); of the more recent monographs: K. E. Kirk, *The Apostolic Ministry,* New York 1946; A. Ehrhardt, *The Apostolic Succession in the first two centuries of the Church,* London 1953; J. Guyot ed., *Das apostolische Amt,* Mainz 1961; C. von Heyl, *Ordination zum hl. Predigtamt und Apostolische Sukzession,* Blekmar uber Soltau 1962; A. Hastings, *One and Apostolic,* London–New York 1963.

[57] For example Rupert of Deutz, *De vita vere apostolica;* PL 170, 611–664.

the Gentiles (cf. Acts 10:1–11 and 18). It is only said of Peter that he left Jerusalem (12:17). The only missionary journeys we hear about are those of Paul and Barnabas. According to accounts which only come down to us from the third and fourth centuries, the apostles stayed for seven, twelve or fifteen years in Jerusalem to begin with. It is only the legends of a later time which portray the twelve apostles as missionaries and founders of Churches throughout the world. What is the historical truth?[58]

Matthew, Mark and John use the word "apostle" once each only; Luke on the other hand uses it 34 times (6 times in the gospel, 28 times in Acts) and Paul (including Ephesians and Colossians) 29 times (5 times in the pastoral letters). Otherwise the word is rarely used. Its basic meaning is "ambassador" and it is used in a variety of ways. It can refer to the twelve (Mt. 10:2; Mk. 6:30 and frequently in Luke), to the ambassadors of the Church (Acts 14:4, cf. 13:3), to the authorized messenger (Jn. 13:16), to missionaries (Rev. 2:2) or to Christ himself (Heb. 3:1). Paul often refers to himself with this word, especially in the introductions to his letters; he also uses it to refer to the twelve (Gal. 1:17), or a wider circle of missionaries of the Gospel (I Cor. 12:28; 15:7; II Cor. 11:5) or "messengers of the Churches" (II Cor. 8:23; Phil. 2:25).

It is striking how important the concept of apostle is to the New Testament, even though secular Greek offers hardly any linguistic parallels. The word ἀπόστολος is virtually unknown as referring to an individual, it refers to a fleet that has been sent out, a group of colonists, or else a passport or

---

[58] See esp. the articles in LThK (Apostel: K. H. Schelkle; Zwölf: A. Vögtle), RGG (H. Riesenfeld), EKL (H. Wendland), ThW (K. H. Rengstorf). Of the more recent works: C. H. Dodd, *The Apostolic Teaching and its Developments,* London 1945, New York 1949; H. von Campenhausen, *Kirchliches Amt und geistliche Vollmacht in den ersten drei Jahrhunderten,* Tübingen 1953; K. H. Schelkle, *Discipleship and Priesthood,* London–Melbourne 1966, New York 1965; B. Rigaux, Die "Zwölf" in Geschichte und Kerygma, in: *Der historische Jesus und der kerygmatische Christus,* ed. by H. Ristow and K. Matthiae, Berlin 1960, 468–486; G. Klein, *Die zwölf Apostel,* Göttingen 1961; W. Schmithals, *Das kirchliche Apostelamt,* Göttingen 1961.

bill of delivery. In many respects the concept of apostle has been derived from the Hebrew *"schaliach"* (e.g. I Kg. 14:6, where the prophet appears as God's messenger). In the post-exilic period *schaliach* is a technical term for the envoys of Jewish authorities—the name does not appear, however, until the second century A.D.; in the case of such a man the fundamental rabbinical principle applies: that an authorized representative is the same as the person himself. The connection between the two ideas is a matter of controversy and the basic problem of the origin of the apostolic idea which we find in the New Testament remains unsolved. Two extreme positions, at any rate, seem to be untenable; the New Testament idea of apostleship is not derived either from Gnosticism, or simply from the twelve.[59]

1. Did the Christian idea of apostleship come from Jewish or Judaeo-Christian Gnosis, especially in Syria? There is no need to deny the connection between the New Testament and the Gnostic ideas of apostleship. But in the context of the idea of the body of Christ we have already seen that all the Gnostic sources presently known to us come from a much later period (the body of Christ is an idea found only in Paul and the writings dependent on him) and even those often differ from New Testament sources at certain crucial points. There is not a single early reference to Gnostic apostles. There seem certainly to have been pneumatics and seekers of wisdom, who taught others, in the Syrian diaspora communities, probably in Samaria and Jerusalem; their ideas were primarily apocalyptic in tendency. We can certainly also conclude from the New Testament that there were syncretistic pneumatics who hellenized Christian ideas. But there is no evidence for the case that there were Jews or others who proclaimed such ideas in missionary fashion. In the New Testament the threat of Gnosticism is always seen as a threat from within the Church. It is a pure hypothesis to suppose that there were Gnostic systems in existence in New Testament times, sufficiently developed to produce Gnostic communities and apostles; there is no evidence for Gnostic systems, communities or apostles in New Testament times at all.

2. Is the Christian idea of apostleship connected exclusively with the twelve chosen by Jesus? We shall have to look more closely at the relationship between the twelve and the apostles. The

[59] Cf. the critique of W. Schmithals by E. Schweizer in *Theolog. Literaturzeitung* 87, 1962, 837–840.

lists of names of the twelve show slight variations (cf. Mk. 3:16–19; Mt. 10:2–4; Lk. 6:13–16; Acts 1:13). At Mark 3:14 par. the twelve apostles are not yet referred to as apostles, and at Mark 6:30 the term apostles does not seem to be a permanent title so much as a temporary activity. It is only Luke (6:13) who reports that Jesus himself called the twelve "apostles". It is striking that it is precisely the oldest New Testament texts which refer to others than the twelve as "apostles": in addition to Paul there are the Jewish Christians Andronicus and Junias in Rome, "men of note among the apostles" (Rom. 16:7), Barnabas (cf. I Cor. 9:5 f.; Gal. 2:9; Acts 14:4 and 14) and possibly Silvanus (cf. I Thess. 1:1; 2:1 and 7) and James the brother of the Lord (cf. I Cor. 15:7; Gal. 1:19; 2:9). On the other hand the only one of the circle of twelve whose missionary activity we can be certain of beyond doubt is Peter.

Leaving aside historical speculation and dogmatic simplifications, we can establish a solid historical basis for discussing this idea by beginning with the oldest New Testament writings and with the best-known apostleship of all, that of *Paul*. Paul not only refers to the ambassadors of the Churches as apostles (II Cor. 8:23; Phil. 2:25), but, especially in the introductions to his letters (cf. the first verses of I and II Corinthians, Galatians, Romans; cf. also Ephesians, Colossians, I and II Timothy, Titus), he refers to himself as an "apostle of Jesus Christ" or simply as an "apostle". This suggests a twofold meaning of the word. Apostles are (*a*) those who are witnesses of the risen Lord, to whom the crucified Lord has revealed himself as living; (*b*) those who have been commissioned by the Lord for missionary preaching. "But when he who had set me apart before I was born and had called me through his grace, was pleased to reveal his Son to me, in order that I might preach him among the Gentiles, I did not confer with flesh and blood, but I went away into Arabia; and again I returned to Damascus" (Gal. 1:15–17; cf. 1:1 and 12; I Cor. 9:1 f.; 15:7–11). And what Paul claims for himself as the "least of the apostles" (I Cor. 15:9) applies to all to whom he gives the name "apostle" (cf. I Cor. 15:7; 9:5). He contrasts with them the "false apostles, deceitful workmen, disguising themselves as apostles of Christ" (II Cor. 11:13), who claim to be apostles without having received authorization from Christ. These were presumably Judaizing opponents of Paul from Palestine who appealed to the authority of the "superlative apostles" (cf. II Cor. 11:5; 12:11)—perhaps pneumatic travelling preachers?

It is clear from the very early evidence of Galatians 1:15–17 that Paul dates his apostleship from the Damascus experience (cf. 1:11–13) and that there were apostles in Jerusalem before Paul's calling. This must have been shortly after Jesus' death—the "Apostolic Council" took place seventeen years after Paul's calling (cf. Gal. 1:18 and 2:1). But who were these apostles in Jerusalem? "Then after three years I went up to Jerusalem to visit Cephas, and remained with him fifteen days. But I saw none of the other apostles except James the Lord's brother" (1:18 f.). Peter at all events was one of the apostles; who were the "other apostles"? At I Corinthians 15:5 Paul refers to the appearances of Jesus to Peter and the *twelve;* these are therefore the first witnesses of the resurrection. If they are so important to Paul and yet are not named in connection with his first visit to Jerusalem it can only be because they were included in the words "the other apostles".

Given that there is evidence for the existence of the twelve in the time immediately after the death of Jesus, the most convincing explanation of it remains that given in the synoptic gospels: that Jesus before his death and resurrection called and appointed the twelve (Mk. 3:14). Not that we can say much historically about the time or the process by which this circle of twelve was formed. In addition to the synoptic stories of the calling of the twelve, and Paul's reference to them, there is further evidence. There is the saying at Matthew 19:28, the general insistence on the fact that the traitor Judas was one of the twelve, and finally the post-resurrection election of Matthias (Acts 1:15–26), which can scarcely be described as totally unhistorical. No other reasonable explanation can be advanced to account for how, when and where the circle of twelve could have been formed in such a short space of time. In particular it is unthinkable that Luke, writing as late as he did, could have imposed on the whole tradition, right back to its beginnings, his own conception of the apostleship of the twelve. It is probable that the title "pillars", which occurs also in Judaism (cf. I QSa 1:12), was attached to them or at least to some of them, as also to James (cf. Gal. 2:9).

What then is the significance of this selection of the twelve who, distinguished from the other disciples as they are, are clearly intended to be more than mere "disciples"? This choice is to be understood in the light of Jesus' eschatological message.[60] The number twelve is connected, if not very precisely, with "Israel", the people of twelve tribes. The significance of the number lies not so much in Israel thought of as the object of Christian preaching, but in a renewed Israel, thought of in relation to the consummation of the kingdom of God: "Truly, I say to you, in the new world, when the Son of man shall sit on his glorious throne, you who have followed me will also sit on twelve thrones, judging the twelve tribes of Israel" (Mt. 19:28; cf. Rev. 21:24). The circle of twelve was therefore found in the light of the coming kingdom of God; they are to proclaim and represent the coming, already dawning reign of God. They represent, therefore, the full tale of both the old and the new people of God.

Did the twelve chosen by Jesus assume the leadership of the primitive community? Many commentators who accept that the circle of twelve was founded during Jesus' lifetime dispute this. Later legends about the long rule of the twelve in Jerusalem, their missionary activity and their martyrdoms provided no historical basis. In Acts, written relatively late, Luke gives an account of the beginnings of the Church which is strongly coloured by theology. For example, he makes it a condition of apostleship not only to have been a witness of the resurrection, but also to have been a witness of the earthly life of Jesus, something that must have been of consequence for Paul's position; he also reserves the name of apostle (a name given by Jesus himself to the twelve, according to his gospel) for the twelve, apart from Acts 14:4 and 14; he also makes Paul unnecessarily dependent on the twelve for the authorization and exercise of his apostleship, something which conflicts with Paul's own accounts in his letters (especially Galatians 1 and 2).

[60] Cf. B I–II.

It must be admitted that apart from Peter and the shadowy figures of the sons of Zebedee, the individual personalities of the twelve remained obscure as far as later generations were concerned. Nonetheless, the role played by the twelve in the earliest history of the Church is unmistakable. It was this role, far more than their eschatological significance, which determined the importance of the twelve. The twelve are the fundamental witnesses of Christ's resurrection. This is part of the central tradition which Paul received from the primitive community and handed on to his communities (I Cor. 15:5).

The fact that Peter and the twelve were witnesses of the risen Lord is therefore established through Paul at a very early date; so that, even if the number and title of the twelve were taken to be a post-Easter development—the early date of Paul speaks against this—at all events the twelve were individually disciples of Jesus before his death. It is then not difficult to assume that these fundamental primary witnesses of the risen Lord were also seen as his "authorized representatives" (*"scheluchim"*), responsible for looking after the community, even though we can gather nothing from Paul's letters and little that is historically verifiable from Acts about the manner of their functions. This assumption would at least explain the idea evidently current among the Q communities which finds expression in Matthew 19:28, and would explain other remarks like "He who hears you hears me" (Mt. 10:40 par.). At the same time it is noteworthy that the twelve are referred to by name for the last time in Acts when the seven are appointed (6:2), and while we may assume that it is they who are referred to generally as "apostles" in connection with the "Apostolic Council" (15:2–6 and 22 f.; 16:4), they then disappear all but completely into the obscurity of history (not even the name "apostle" appears in Acts after 16:4). The reason for this cannot simply lie in the lack of source-material, since there are another dozen chapters of Acts, and since apart from I Corinthians 15:5 neither Paul nor all the literature dependent on Paul mentions the twelve once. The reason must rather lie in the fact that the function of the twelve was apparently confined to the time of the founding of the Church, or perhaps to the evangelization of the Jews. At all events it is striking that after the martyrdom of

James (12:2) there is no attempt, as there had been in the case of Judas Iscariot, to replace him. The collegium of the twelve as such dies out. What remains fundamental is the idea of apostleship, something that is by no means confined to the twelve.

The idea of the apostle is linked with that of the missionary. The title "apostle" is almost totally lacking from the earliest synoptic tradition, and presumably was added only later when the twelve were thought of as missionaries to the Jews (Mk. 6:7–12; Mt. 10:5–16; Lk. 9:1–6) or to the Gentiles (Mt. 28:19). In all these contexts there is a reference to sending out (ἀποστέλλειν = *schalach?* cf. e.g. Mt. 10:16), although the title "apostle" is not as yet used. Only at Mark 6:30 and in the list of names at Matthew 10:2 (which, while it clearly sums up all the individual callings together, does not therefore have to be a second-century interpolation; there is not the least evidence in the texts to support that idea) is the name used. It is Luke who first attributes the use of the name to Jesus himself (6:13), and he subsequently uses it, like Paul, with different meanings (John uses it once only, at 13:16). Both before Paul and in his time the word was probably used without special theological implications for missionaries and messengers of the communities (cf. II Cor. 8:2–3; Phil. 2:25; Jn. 14:16). But it was Paul who from the first associated the word with the idea of an authorized representative, and defended it in this sense against the Galatians (Gal. 1 and 2).

Paul, with his view of the world-wide mission of the Church as an eschatological event in the background, necessarily made the notion of the apostle as the authorized representative of Jesus Christ himself central to his theology. The strictly theological concept of apostleship was founded, developed, and saved from decay by Paul above all in connection with his mission to the Gentiles, which was to have a colossal impact. It was Paul who made the Church conscious of what it meant when it spoke of men like Peter and himself as "apostles", and what a great and fundamental thing it was. In consequence, the twelve chosen by Jesus during his lifetime, who may well have previously been referred to as apostles, but not in a strict sense, became known as apostles in the full

Pauline sense of the word. In time, indeed, the notion of apostleship in this sense was precisely limited to the twelve; this is where Luke, combating the possible decay of the whole apostolic idea, played a vital part. The result is that by contrast with Paul's view only the twelve are considered as "apostles"—paradoxically enough even Paul himself, apart from Acts 14:4 and 14, is not described as an "apostle" by Luke; hence "the twelve apostles". The development of the strictly theological concept of apostleship occurred not through a narrower notion (the twelve) becoming widened (all the authorized representatives of Jesus Christ), but by the limiting of the wider idea to the twelve alone, with the possible addition of Paul.

The *fundamental* significance of the apostles for the Church is clearly expressed in Paul's interpretation, along with the synoptic gospels and Acts. An apostle is the messenger of another. If the apostle is not simply the messenger of a community, but has been appointed by Christ (Gal. 1:15 f.; Acts 9:27; Mk. 3:4 par.; Mt. 28:19), and through him by the Father (cf. Mt. 10:40; Jn. 13:20), then to this extent he stands above the Church. He is not subject to its choice: "Paul an apostle—not from men nor through men, but through Jesus Christ" (Gal. 1:1). He is also not subject to its judgment: "But with me it is a very small thing that I should be judged by you or by any human court" (I Cor. 4:3). The apostle is the authorized representative of Christ. He is therefore not just a witness to the crucified and risen Lord—this would apply, as I Corinthians 15:6 indicates, to "more than five hundred brethren", but someone who has been sent and authorized by the Lord himself. His authority is not of course, like that of Jesus, derived from himself; he has received it in Christ's name and can only exercise it in his spirit. As an authorized ambassador of his Lord his own person is worthless. The apostle is not a hero or a genius but a justified sinner among other sinners. In himself he is nothing but a weak and frail man who has his treasure in earthen vessels (II Cor. 4:7); apart from Christ he can do nothing (Jn. 15:5).

The synoptic gospels are at pains to illustrate the truth of these Pauline and Johannine statements by stories which point concretely to the weakness, lack of understanding and failings of the disciples of Jesus. But it is precisely in his full humanity that the apostle is chosen, called and sent out, to be the tool of God's grace (I Cor. 15:10; Rom. 1:5) and a witness appointed by Christ (Lk. 24:48; Acts 1:8; 13:31). His primary task is the preaching of the Gospel: "For Christ did not send me to baptize but to preach the gospel" (I Cor. 1:17). His preaching is not that of his own message, but the message that has been committed to him (II Cor. 2:17; 4:2; Mk. 3:14). He can similarly expect that his work will be received and accepted as the word of God (I Thess. 2:13; II Cor. 5:20); in this respect he will be received like Christ (Gal. 4:14). By preaching the Gospel, marked out by steadfast patience and by signs and wonders (II Cor. 12:12; cf. Rom. 15:19; Mk. 3:15; 6:7 par.; Acts 2:43; 5:12; Heb. 2:4), he is a minister of Christ Jesus (Rom. 15:15 f.; cf. Rom. 1:9; Phil. 2:17) and a servant of God (I Thess. 3:2; 1:3–9).

By preaching the Gospel, the apostle arouses the response of faith and gathers together the fellowship of believers. By virtue of his message, therefore, he is also authorized to found and to lead Churches (II Cor. 10:13–16; 13:10; I Cor. 11:34; II Thess. 3:4) and to exercise discipline in the Churches (I Cor. 5:3–5; cf. I Tim. 1:20). His activity is thus not limited to preaching the Gospel and the associated work of baptizing (something which Paul rarely did, cf. I Cor. 1:14–17) and celebrating the Lord's Supper with the community (cf. I Cor. 11:17–34). He gives very precise instructions for the ordering of the life of the community, as Paul does in I Corinthians, with regard to disputes between members of the community (6:1–11), marriage, virginity and widowhood (7:1–39), the eating of food offered to idols (8:1–13; 10:14–33), the conduct of worship (11:2–34), the communal ministry of charismatics (12 and 13), preaching (14:1–40), collections for the community at Jerusalem (16:1–4). He devotes himself to the unity of communities among themselves, by journeys, sending messengers and letters, mutual intercessions.

In all these ways the apostle stands above the communities in authority and freedom, and yet at the same time he is a member of the community himself; he too is judged by the

Lord (I Cor. 4:4) and depends on his grace. He can command the obedience of the community (I Cor. 14:37; II Cor. 10:18; Rom. 15:18), and yet must be prepared to abdicate this right (I Thess. 2:7; I Cor. 9:12). His aim is not subjection, but fellowship (I Cor. 5:4; 14:37; II Cor. 2:6 and 10; Acts 15). The apostle does not act in an authoritarian manner, but with an eye to the community; he does not act in isolation but in fellowship with all the members of the community and all the gifts and ministries they have been granted; he gives his witness not on his own, but surrounded by the witness of all those who have received the Spirit. True, the members of the community need his fundamental and first-hand witness and his guidance; but he on his side needs their intercessions, their consolation and their co-operation, as all the Pauline letters emphasize. He is not to be the lord of the Church, but its servant (Rom. 12:7; I Cor. 9:19; II Cor. 1:24; 4:5; Mk. 10:44 f.; Mt. 24:45–51). His apostleship is an office of service (Rom. 11:13; 12:7; Acts 20:24), the greatness and splendour of which (II Cor. 3:7–11; 8:23) is hidden, indeed is scorned and considered disreputable by the world (I Cor. 4:8–13; II Cor. 4:8–11; 6:3–10; 11:16–33).

The apostles as the messengers, witnesses and authorized representatives of the crucified and risen Lord, as preachers, teachers, founders and leaders of the communities, are first in the Church. Paul names them emphatically in the first place in his list of charisms: "And God has appointed in the Church first apostles . . ." (I Cor. 12:28; cf. Eph. 4:11). Without the witness and ministry of these first public witnesses authorized by Christ, without the witness and ministry of Peter and the twelve, but also of James and of all the other apostles down to the last, Paul, the Church could not exist. The Church is founded on this apostolic witness and ministry, which is older than the Church itself. The apostles are the beginners, the continuing foundation-stones of the Church, the cornerstone and keystone of which is Christ himself. In this sense the Church is "built upon the foundation of the apostles and prophets, Christ Jesus himself being the chief corner-stone" (Eph. 2:20; cf. Mt. 16:18; Rev. 21:24).

The above section has outlined the extremely difficult and complex background to the remarks which Vatican II made about the calling of the twelve, or of the apostles: "The Lord Jesus, after praying to the Father and calling to Himself those whom He desired, appointed twelve men who would stay in His company, and whom He would send to preach the kingdom of God (cf. Mk. 3:13–19; Mt. 10:1–42). These apostles (cf. Lk. 6:13) He formed after the manner of a college or a fixed group, over which He placed Peter, chosen from amongst them (cf. Jn. 21:15–17). He sent them first to the children of Israel and then to all the nations (cf. Rom. 1:16), so that as sharers in His power they might make all peoples His disciples, sanctifying and governing them (cf. Mt. 28:16–20; Mk. 16:15; Lk. 24:45–48; Jn. 20:21–23). Thus they would spread His Church, and by ministering to it under the guidance of the Lord, would shepherd it all days even to the consummation of the world (cf. Mt. 28:20).

"They were fully confirmed in this mission on the day of Pentecost (cf. Acts 2:1–16) in accordance with the Lord's promise: 'You shall receive power when the Holy Spirit comes upon you, and you shall be witnesses for me in Jerusalem and in all Judaea and in Samaria and even to the very ends of the earth' (Acts 1:8). By everywhere preaching the gospel (cf. Mk. 16:20), which was accepted by their hearts under the influence of the Holy Spirit, the apostles gathered together the universal Church, which the Lord established on the apostles and built upon blessed Peter, their chief, Christ Jesus Himself remaining the supreme cornerstone (cf. Rev. 21:14; Mt. 16:18; Eph. 2:20)" (CE 19).

This then is the importance of the apostles for the Church. But what does it mean for the Church that it refers back to the apostles, that it is an apostolic Church?

2. APOSTOLICITY AND SUCCESSION

Have the apostles any successors? Can a basis, a "foundation" (Eph. 2:20) be replaced without the whole building collapsing? The apostles, who became the basis and foundation of the Church, retain this significance well beyond the first generation. They retain for the Church in all times and places their fundamental and supporting function. Since apostleship is a ministry on the basis of a particular commission, we may speak of an apostolic *office*, provided of course that it is not mistakenly seen as an hierarchic position of power, but radically as a ministry, a service. The apostolic office as a whole is unique and unrepeatable. Those members of the primitive Church to whom the risen Lord directly revealed himself and whom he personally commissioned as his messengers, cannot be replaced or represented by any successors. The decisive thing about the apostles is their personal meeting with the Lord, whom they all, in one form or another, knew as someone who had been dead and was alive again. The risen Lord's testimony to himself is a unique event; the Church of subsequent generations was not to receive new assurances through Christ's repeated appearances, but could only preach anew the tradition of the original apostolic witness. The preaching of the apostles, as it has come down to us in the writings of the New Testament, is the original, fundamental testimony of Jesus Christ, valid for all time; being unique, it cannot be replaced or made void by any later testimony. Later generations in the Church are dependent on the words, witness and ministry of the first "apostolic" generation. The apostles are and remain the original witnesses, their testimony is the original testimony and their mission the original mission.

What then can "apostolic succession" mean? As direct witnesses and messengers of the risen Lord, the apostles can have no successors. No further apostles were called. Apostleship in the sense of the original and fundamental ministry of the first witnesses and messengers died out with the death of the last apostle. Apostleship in this sense of witness and mission cannot be repeated or continued. What remains is a task and a commission. The apostolic commission is not finished, but will remain to the end of time. The apostolic task is not completed; it embraces all peoples to the ends of the earth.

The apostles are dead; there are no new apostles. But the *apostolic mission* remains. The mission of the apostles was more than the persons of the apostles themselves. The apostolic mission is now no longer instituted directly by the Lord, but indirectly by men. Since this apostolic mission remains, so too does the apostolic ministry. This apostolic ministry does not depend on further vocations to apostleship in the narrow sense, but depends on obedience to the apostles as the original witnesses and messengers of the Lord. As a result of the continuing apostolic mission there is, in the apostolic ministry, an apostolic succession: an apostolic succession of obedience. *Who* then are the followers of the apostles?

"That divine mission, entrusted by Christ to the apostles, will last until the end of the world (Mt. 28:20), since the gospel which was to be handed down by them is for all time the source of all life for the Church" (CE 20). The Constitution passes from this fundamental and general statement to considering the succession of ecclesiastical offices (cf. CE 20–29).

There can only be one basic answer: the Church. The whole Church, not just a few individuals, is the follower of the apostles. We do, after all, confess an apostolic *Church*. The *whole* Church is the new people of God, gathered by the apostles through the preaching of the Gospel of Jesus Christ. The *whole* Church is the temple of the Spirit, built on the foundation of the apostles. The *whole* Church is the body of Christ, unified by the ministry of the apostles. The authorized mission of the apostles has been handed on to the Church which the apostles summoned together; the authorized ministry of the apostles has been handed on to the Church which the apostles ministered to. The Church is the successor of the apostles in obedience, and from this obedience it derives its authority. Taking apostolicity in this sense, we can see what determines the true oneness, holiness and catholicity of the Church; it must be based on the foundations laid by the apostles. This succession must be understood in terms of substance, not just of history; there must be a real inner continuity. This continuity cannot simply be created for the Church by itself, it is something that is granted to it by the Spirit of God and Christ, the Spirit which filled the apostles and their apostolic witness, and moves and encourages the Church to follow them. The Church has only to be open to the Spirit in faith, and it will find the necessary obedience to the apostles and their witness. In this sense apostolic succession is a thing of the spirit. Apostolicity too is a gift and a requirement at the same time.

This real continuity and link with the apostles can be illustrated in two ways; the Church is apostolic, is a true follower of the apostles, when it preserves in all its members continuing agreement with the witness of the apostles, and also preserves a vital continuity with the ministry of the apostles.

1. *Agreement with the apostolic witness:* The Church does not hear its Lord and his message by direct inspiration, but only through the witness of the apostles. Of course, the Church must not simply listen to the apostles. Through their witness the Church must listen to the Lord himself, and allow him to speak in the midst of the Church through their witness; he who hears them, hears the Lord. The reverse is also true: he who does not hear the apostles, does not hear the Lord. There is no route to the Lord which bypasses the apostles. The Church can only know him through their witness. The original and fundamental witness of the apostles is the source and norm of the Church's existence in preaching, faith and action alike, in all times and places. This witness must constantly be heard anew in the Church and allowed to bear fruit in its whole life. Apostolic succession is therefore a question of a continual and living confrontation of the Church and all its members with this apostolic witness; apostolic succession is fulfilled when this witness is heard, respected, believed, confessed and followed.

The Church has been given this apostolic witness not in any abstract or indeterminate way, but in concrete historical form. The living witness of the apostles is handed down to us in the writings of the New Testament, which in turn rest on the writings of the Old Testament. The New Testament is the original, fundamental witness of the apostles, valid for the Church of all ages. Not that we must suppose all the writings of the New Testament to have been the work of apostles, in the strict sense of the word. But all these writings have been recognized and approved by the Church as a valid and original testimony (although not all writings are equally firsthand or clear testimony) of the apostolic message. This is the meaning of the New Testament canon, the means by which the Church, exercising its ministry of discerning spirits, succeeded, over a long historical period, in separating the valid apostolic testimony from the other traditions.

What testimonies to the origins of the Church can be found *outside* the New Testament? All the gospels, acts and epistles of the apostles which are not included in the New Testament, but claim to be original testimonies, are, though some of them date from the second century, apocrypha. Their slight value, by contrast with the canonical writings, can be seen at a glance; their uselessness as historical sources is generally recognized. In this sense there is no original "apostolic" tradition about the origins of the Church outside the New Testament. Valid and relevant *Church* traditions exist practically only in interpretations, explanations and applications of this original apostolic tradition as laid down in the gospels. Apostolic succession therefore entails a continuing and living confrontation of the Church with the original, fundamental testimony of Scripture; apostolic succession is achieved only if this biblical witness is faithfully followed in preaching, faith and action, if the Bible does not remain a closed book, indeed does not remain a book (a handbook, a book of laws or a history book) at all, but is a living voice of witness, to be heard and believed here and now as a message of joy, of liberation, of good news. In this sense apostolic succession means following the faith and confession of the apostles.

2. *Continuing the apostolic ministry:* The Church can only remain true to the apostolic witness, the witness of the Bible, through service. Of course, the Church is not to be the servant of the apostles, who were themselves the servants of the Church. Together with the apostles the Church must serve the Lord, the Lord of the Church and of the apostles. But the Church must do this by being drawn into the apostolic ministry, into which the apostles were themselves drawn. The Church can only be certain of its apostolic mission and authority if it is a serving Church. Apostolicity is never an unchallenged possession, a secure piece of property which the Church has at its disposal. Apostolicity can never mean power through which the Church might rule. It is not a question of others submitting to the Church; the Church must itself submit by accepting the authority of the apostles and of the Church's and the apostles' Lord.

By following the apostles, the Church can learn what real submission and real service mean. Apostolic succession entails a confrontation of the Church with the testimony of the apostles, in a living continuation of the apostolic ministries, with all their various forms of expression. There is the preaching of and testifying to the Gospel, there is the activity of baptizing which continues throughout all ages and all countries, there is the fellowship of prayer and the Lord's Supper, there is the building up of communities, the maintenance of fellowship and unity with all the Churches of the world. Every member of the Church has his own particular task, according to the charism given to him. But all this is not done for the sake of the Church itself. The apostolic Church least of all can be an end in itself. Everything the Church does must be directed towards fulfilling its apostolic mission to the outside world; it must minister to the world and to mankind. To be a Church and to have a mission are not two separate things. To be itself, the Church must follow the apostles in continually recognizing and demonstrating that it has been sent out to the world. In this sense apostolic succession not only means following the faith and confession of the apostles, it means, in consequence of that faith, following in the footsteps of the apostolic ministry.

This makes it clear that apostolicity, like unity, holiness and catholicity, is not a static attribute of the Church. Like them it is an historical dimension, a dimension which has constantly to be fulfilled anew in history. Apostolicity too must continually be achieved afresh, must be a recurring event in a living history which occurs between the Church and the apostles, between the Church's preaching and the apostles' witness, between the Church's ministry and the apostles' commission. This history is not something that can be observed neutrally from the sidelines. Apostolicity is not something that can simply be stated and proved in theory. The Church must share in this history in order to recognize and understand, to experience and discover what the apostolicity of the Church means. As an individual Christian, I must become a true successor of the apostles, I must hear their witness, believe their message, imitate their mission and ministry. I must be, and always become anew, a believing and living member of the apostolic community. Only then shall I understand what it means when I say and confess: *credo apostolicam ecclesiam.*

In this section we have tried to show what it means when the ecclesia, the fellowship of believers which is God's people, a spiritual creation, the body of Christ, sees itself as one, holy, catholic and apostolic Church. These four attributes or dimensions are far from being exclusive. A list of them would and could never end, for the mystery of the Church is not to be exhausted in this way. On the other hand, it is clear that these four dimensions are not random ones, but four essential dimensions of the Church demanded of it by the New Testament. They are dimensions which at a very deep level are interdependent; indeed, as we have often noted, they overlap and must necessarily overlap. What is ecclesiastical unity without the breadth of catholicity, the power of holiness and the original impulse of apostolicity? What is ecclesiastical catholicity without the links of unity, the distinction of holiness and the vitality of apostolicity? What is ecclesiastical holiness without the binding power of unity, the generosity of catholicity and the long roots of apostolicity? What finally is ecclesiastical apostolicity without the brotherhood of unity, the diversity of catholicity and the spirit of holiness?

Could Christians, could Christian Churches not agree on these four fundamental dimensions of the Church? Would a basic consensus not be possible, given a reasonable contribution of mutual understanding and sympathy? Not, that is, a consensus which would prohibit differences in theological interpretation and doctrine, but a consensus which would overcome the divisions in the one, holy, catholic and apostolic Church. All the more urgently at this point, in connection with apostolicity above all, but basically also in connection with unity, holiness and catholicity, we must confront the problem which, while very far from being a primary one, none the less in practice serves to divide the Churches. What should be the external constitution of this one, holy, catholic and apostolic Church, and what should ecclesiastical office mean for it?

E. The Offices of the Church

I. THE PRIESTHOOD OF ALL BELIEVERS

1. CHRIST AS THE ONLY HIGH PRIEST AND MEDIATOR

Some readers may wonder why it is only at this point that we begin to talk about those who hold office in the Church; one answer is that we have been talking about them from the first, since from the first we were talking about the fellowship of believers. The fundamental error of ecclesiologies which turned out, in fact, to be no more than hierarchologies (where *ecclesia=hierarchia*) was that they failed to realize that all who hold office are primarily (both temporally and factually speaking) not dignitaries but believers, members of the fellowship of believers; and that compared with this fundamental Christian fact any office they may hold is of secondary if not tertiary importance. Bluntly put: the believer who holds no office is a Christian and member of the Church of Christ; a man who holds office without faith is no Christian and not a member of the Church. The Church must be seen first and foremost as a fellowship of faith, and only in this light can ecclesiastical office be properly understood.

Does this mean that the community precedes ecclesiastical office, or that the community rather than the office is the higher authority? There is no question of having to make such a choice in the New Testament, where we find both community and office represented as equal authorities, both subject to a highest authority, namely Jesus Christ, the Lord of the Church, acting in time through his Spirit. With Christ come his first witnesses and heralds, whose witness is the foundation of the Church: so the apostles are superior to both community and office, and both have to prove themselves apostolic in the light of the apostles and their witness; both are responsible to the Lord and his message as it is fundamentally proclaimed by the apostles. He is the first and last authority for the whole Church and this must be our starting-point for any examination of the relationship between office and community (or Church), if we are to reach correct conclusions.

It is obvious at once that in the light of the event of Christ the usual concepts and realities attached to the idea of the priesthood, of a mediator and of office have undergone a radical "change" (cf. Heb. 7:12): "For Christ is the end of the law, that everyone who has faith may be justified" (Rom. 10:4). But the Church is in constant danger of interpreting these ideas in a different context from that of Christ, and relapsing into Judaic or pagan notions. The first terms which must be clarified in the light of the New Testament are those of "priest" and "mediator".

(a) *Priest:*[1] The modern word "priest" (Spanish *presbitero,* French *prêtre,* Italian *prete,* German and Dutch *priester*) comes via the Latin loan-word *presbyter* from the Greek πρεσβύτερος, the elder, later meaning the leader of a community. But the word priest as used today is not identical in meaning with the word presbyter as it was originally used. On the contrary, the meaning of the word priest, in the Latin language of the Church and hence in modern usage, was derived from the actual Greek word for priest, ἱερεύς, and from the Latin word *sacerdos* (Italian and Spanish *sacerdote*), for which modern languages like English, German, Dutch and French have no equivalent except the word priest (English has the adjective sacerdotal, and French has the impersonal term *le sacerdoce* for the priesthood). To understand the notion of a priest we must begin with the word ἱερεύς, which designates a priest in the historical religious sense, someone whose principal function is that of offering sacrifice. What does the New Testament have to tell us about priests in this sense of ἱερεύς?

The remarkable fact is that the word "priest" is not used once anywhere in the New Testament for someone who holds office in the Church; this applies not only to the word ἱερεύς, but also to ἀρχιερεύς, ἱεράτευμα, ἱερατεία, ἱερωσύνη,

[1] See the relevant sections on the *priesthood* in the dogmatic textbooks and esp. the art. by G. Schrenk, in ThW III, 221–284, as well as the relevant articles in other biblical and theological encyclopaedias; besides the biblical theologies see O. Cullmann, *The Christology of the New Testament,* London 1963, Philadelphia 1964, 83–107; T. F. Torrance, *Royal Priesthood,* Edinburgh–London 1955, Naperville, Illinois 1954.

ἱερατεύειν. "Priest" ("high priest") is a title given to Old Testament Judaic dignitaries (Mk. 1:44 par.; 2:26 par.; 14:53, etc.; Lk. 1:5; 19:31; Jn. 1:19; Acts 4:1 and 6), or those of the Gentiles (Acts 14:13). It is remarkable, too, that in his preaching Jesus does not use the image of the priest and the cult; his preaching, even if it is not explicitly and fundamentally critical of the cult (but cf. Mt. 12:3–8 par.; Mt. 26:61 par.), lies more in the tradition of prophecy. Jesus takes his images not from the priestly ministry but from the secular world around him (and cf. the emphatic criticism of the priestly caste, which is regarded as inferior to the heretical Samaritan, at Lk. 10:31 f.). On no occasion did Jesus describe himself or his disciples as priests.

It was only the deep impression made by Jesus' life and death, as showing a unique obedience and a devotion to God and man, that caused the community to describe Jesus' death in terms of cultic images (only one of many kinds of imagery used to describe the event of Christ); they saw his death as a sacrificial death (hence the significance of "blood" and the "lamb"), and even saw Jesus himself as the "high priest"—this is the tremendous concept, at once cultic and hostile to cult, which we find in the letter to the Hebrews.[2] This high priesthood is not thought of in terms of a static priestly cult within a sanctuary, but primarily in terms of a sacrificial way; the Son passes in obedience through the veil of his flesh, of his death, in order that the community of the new covenant may have access to the throne of God; this historical way of sacrifice is the guarantee of Christ the high priest's present role, of his appearing in the presence of God on behalf of the brethren, until he comes again: "Jesus Christ is the same yesterday and today and for ever" (Heb. 13:8). But it is precisely in this perspective, with reference to the prophets, that we are given a fundamental criticism of the Old Testament priesthood, which makes it impossible to see the ministries in the New Testament as a continuation of the Old Testament priesthood. The writer of the letter makes it unmistakably clear to any who might hanker after the ritual of the past that Christ has fulfilled and done away with the priesthood of the Old Testament. The fulfilling, superseding

[2] See bibliography under C I, 2d.

and abandoning of the priesthood of the Old Testament is shown from three points of view:

1. Like the priests of the Old Testament Christ is a priest not through taking the honour upon himself, but through God's appointing him (5:4-6). But as God's Son he makes a total break with the established idea of the priesthood; it is not inherited, since he is descended from Judah, not from Levi; and it is not traditional, since he is a priest after the order of the mysterious Melchizedek, not after the order of Aaron (7:1-28).

2. Like the priests of the Old Testament Christ represented before God a people oppressed by sin and unable to sacrifice and pray effectively, yet at the same time he is like them, sharing their weakness, feeling with them and for them in compassion, helping them (2:17 f.; 5:1-3). But the decisive difference which goes far beyond any similarity is the sin with which the Old Testament priesthood is itself burdened and which in the last resort it cannot of itself remove (7:11 and 19; 9:9; 10:2 f.); the sin which Jesus as high priest overcame, not by any static attribute, but by proving himself to be sinless through his battle against temptation and his obedience, so that he had no need to sacrifice for his own sins (7:26; 4:15; 5:7-9; 2:18).

3. Like the priests of the Old Testament Christ has to make bloody and unbloody sacrifices of atonement for sins (5:1; 8:3; 10:11). But these sacrifices are no longer objects, the blood of goats and bulls, alien blood and imperfect offerings which have constantly to be renewed and yet can never bring reconciliation and perfect fellowship with God (9:6 f.; 10:1 f.). In Christ there is the total offering of the person who offers, sacrificing himself totally through giving up his own blood, his own life. By sacrificing himself this high priest made the perfect offering which needs no renewal, but is performed once and for all: "He has no need, like those high priests, to offer sacrifices daily, first for his own sins and then for those of the people; he did this once for all when he offered up himself" (7:27; cf. 9:24-28; 10:19).

It is this unique sacrifice—ἐφάπαξ (ἅπαξ) in contrast to the daily repeated or annual sacrifices formerly offered—this "single sacrifice" (10:12), "single offering" (10:14), made by the new, unique and eternal high priest of the eschatological age, which has finally overcome sin by fulfilling the will of God in obedience, and has thus brought about complete fellowship with God once and for all: "And by that will we have been sanctified through the offering of the body of Jesus Christ once for all. And every high priest stands daily at his service, offering repeatedly the same sacrifices, which can never take away sins. But when Christ had offered for all time a single sacrifice for sins, he sat down at the right hand of God, then to wait until his enemies should be made a stool for his feet. For by a single offering he has perfected for all time those who are sanctified" (10:10–14).

The significance of these ideas for the New Testament is that all human priesthood has been fulfilled and finished by the unique, final, unrepeatable and hence unlimited sacrifice of the one continuing and eternal high priest. He, the new priest, has arisen (7:15), who is a priest for ever (7:17), not according to a legal requirement (7:16), since the former commandment has been set aside (7:18) and the old covenant is obsolete (8:13). Whoever wishes to be with Christ, who suffered outside the gate, must go forth to him outside the camp and join him there, leaving behind the old cult and covenant of Judaism, for its priests have nothing more to do with the real altar, with Christ (13:10–13). The perfect self-offering sacrifice replaces all cultic sacrifices offered by men; the perfect priest replaces all human priests (cf. also Apoc. 1:13; Jn. 17). Whereas all previous priests had only achieved something imperfect and unsatisfactory, he achieved once and for all something satisfactory; *satis fecit*, he did enough. This high priest can and must not be replaced by any other. His work was whole and perfect, neither needing nor capable of any additions, repetitions or improvements. This is the reason why the letter to the Hebrews does not recognize the angels as priests before God, and why the community has no priestly office: Christ has fulfilled definitively the truth of the priestly idea. Jesus Christ is *the* high priest of the new covenant, the representative, *the* vicarius of his people before God, *the* mediator—a word which we must examine before concluding our consideration of the priesthood of Christ.

(*b*) *Mediator:*[3] The Hebrew and Aramaic of the Bible have no specific word for mediator, although the idea of mediation both in a divine sense (the messenger of Yahweh, the spirit, wisdom) and in a human sense (kings, priests, especially Moses and the servant of God in the Ebed-Yahweh songs), is of the greatest importance for Old Testament religion. The Greek μεσίτης (Latin: *mediator*) comes from μέσος (*medius*) and obviously means one who stands in the middle or in between. It is used not so much in a spatial sense as in the sense of a neutral person of trust, an arbiter in legal transactions, an envoy, a guarantor who deposits a pledge, sometimes a man who negotiates a previously non-existent relationship (the verb μεσιτεύειν, to mediate, is used in an analogous way). The rabbis turned the idea of a legal mediator into that of a business and then a religious mediator, by using the Hebrew expression *"sarsor"* (that is, a broker or middleman) and making the middleman more than a mediator; he becomes an agent. This made it possible to see a mediator not simply as someone who is an ambassador or stands above and outside two parties, but as someone who is personally involved, has authority and can take initiatives.

Neither the synoptic writers nor Acts and John used the expression "mediator", although they record Jesus as fulfilling mediating functions (especially the forgiving of sins); the messianic titles and sayings such as Mark 10:45 require deeper investigation on this point. For the Christian community it is only the glorified Jesus who becomes in a full sense a mediator; and only the late New Testament writings use the expression for Christ. Paul does not apply it to Christ, and uses it only once, in a rabbinical sense, applied to Moses, not as the representative of God but as the spokesman and negotiator for his people; from the mediation of the law through a middleman Paul infers the inferior significance of the Mosaic law (Gal. 3:19 f.). In the first letter to Timothy, however, the expression "mediator" is used to refer to Christ, and indi-

[3] See the relevant sections in the standard works on dogmatics on the mediatorship of Christ. Cp. esp. the article by C. Spicq, in DBS V, 983–1083, and by A. Oepke, in ThW IV, 602–629, as well as the others on this subject in the biblical and theological encyclopaedias and biblical theologies.

cate his universal salvific will: "For there is one God, and
there is one mediator between God and men, the man Christ
Jesus, who gave himself as a ransom for all" (I Tim. 2:5
f.). Here the reference is not to a mediator between God and
Israel, but between God and all men; the fundamentally important point is Jesus' humanity, that which links him to his
human brethren and enables him to take responsibility for sin
and pay the "ransom" with his blood. Whether we think here
of a hellenistic kind of mediator, one who negotiates peace
and deposits a pledge, or a Judaic kind of mediator, the negotiator on mankind's behalf before God, the vital thing is that
there is only one *single* mediator, and that is Jesus Christ.

The fact that it is precisely in the letter to the Hebrews that
the word "mediator" is used at three important points (in a
more hellenistic sense) is not surprising in the light of what
has been said about Jesus Christ as the high priest. The high
priest Jesus Christ stands above the Levitical priests, because
he is the mediator of a better covenant, enacted on better
promises than the old (8:6). Christ replaces and surpasses
the mediator of the old covenant, Moses, and brings about the
new covenant, which he guarantees, just as he guarantees the
realization of its promises; "this makes Jesus the surety of a
better covenant" (7:22). This new and eternal covenant is
sealed and guaranteed by the highest possible price, his own
life and blood: "therefore he is the mediator of a new covenant, so that those who are called may receive the promised
eternal inheritance, since a death has occurred which redeems
them from the transgressions under the first covenant"
(9:15). The believer need only trust this mediator, this high
priest and leader of a new and redeemed humanity, in order
to come with him to the city of the living God: "you have
come to Mount Zion and to the city of the living God . . .
and to Jesus, the mediator of a new covenant, and to the
sprinkled blood that speaks more graciously than the blood of
Abel" (12:22 and 24).

What does this mean for the Church of the new covenant?
The Church is constantly in danger of making itself and its
organs into mediators. The New Testament speaks of
numerous means by which the knowledge and will of God is
revealed (angels, apostles, prophets, etc.). But they are

never called mediators. There is only one real mediator, in the fullest sense of the word, the man Christ Jesus (I Tim. 2:5). All the others are no more and no less than the witnesses and ambassadors of this one mediator, in whom—and here all the New Testament writings agree, even if they do not use the expression mediator—God's decisive eschatological saving act occurred. This is how Paul sees it: "All this is from God, who through Christ reconciled us to himself and gave us (i.e. the apostle) the ministry of reconciliation (i.e. the ministry of apostleship); that is, God was in Christ reconciling the world to himself, not counting their trespasses against them, and entrusting to us the message of reconciliation. So we (i.e. the apostle) are ambassadors for Christ, God making his appeal through us. We beseech you on behalf of Christ, be reconciled to God" (II Cor. 5:18-20). And in John Christ says: "I am the way, and the truth, and the life; no one comes to the Father, but by me" (Jn. 14:6; cf. 12:32; 17:18 f.). The aspects of Christ's mediatory role are very varied, according as to whether we adopt prophetic, priestly and atoning, or royal and cosmic perspectives, and see Christ more as revealer, or high priest, or king and lord of the cosmos or of humanity.

In the present context it is more important to note that the high priest alone opens to all the way into the holy of holies: "Therefore, brethren, since we have confidence to enter the sanctuary by the blood of Jesus, by the new and living way which he opened for us through the curtain, that is, through his flesh, and since we have a great high priest over the house of God, let us draw near with a true heart in full assurance of faith, with our hearts sprinkled clean from an evil conscience and our bodies washed with pure water. Let us hold fast the confession of our hope without wavering, for he who promised is faithful" (Heb. 10:19-23). "Let us then with confidence draw near to the throne of grace, that we may receive mercy and find grace to help in time of need" (4:6). Since Christ is the unique high priest and mediator between God and all men, all men who believe in him have immediate access to God through him. "Through him" (13:15) the faithful are to offer sacrifices. But the whole idea of sacrifice has undergone a radical change: no longer are sacrifices made by men from their own strength, but through the mediation of Christ; they are no longer sacrifices of atonement (nothing can be added to the atoning sacrifice of Christ), but sacrifices of thanks and praise for what Christ has perfected; not sacrifices of external gifts, but the offering of oneself. In this way sacrifice is a concrete act of witness and confession of faith, as well as a service of love: "Through him then let us continually offer up a sacrifice of praise to God, that is, the fruit of lips that acknowledge his name. Do not neglect to do good and to share what you have, for such sacrifices are pleasing to God" (13:15 f.).

Have sacrifices of this kind anything to do with priesthood? If then *all* believers have, in this particular way, to make sacrifices through Christ, this means that *all* believers have a priestly function, of a completely new kind, through Christ the one high priest and mediator. The abolition of a special priestly caste and its replacement by the priesthood of the *one* new and eternal high priest has as its strange and yet logical consequence the fact that *all* believers share in a universal priesthood.

2. THE ROYAL PRIESTHOOD OF ALL CHRISTIANS

The idea of the priesthood of all believers is also a logical conclusion to what has so far been said about the nature of the Church.

(a) The Church is the *people of God,* and we have seen[4] that this means that the Church is never merely a particular class or caste within the fellowship of the faithful. On the contrary, *all* believers, in fundamental equality, are the Church, are members of the people of God. They are all "elect", "saints", "disciples", "brethren". And hence they are precisely a royal priesthood. In God's revelation to his chosen people on Sinai they were told: "you shall be to me a kingdom of priests and a holy nation" (Ex. 19:6). The whole people is to be a priesthood, belonging to the God-king and sharing in his dignity: "a people holy to the Lord your God"

[4] Cf. C I.

(Dt. 7:6). The prophets promise that in the time of salvation the whole of Israel will be a nation of priests: "but you shall be called the priests of the Lord, man shall speak of you as the ministers of our God" (Is. 61:6; cf. 56:6 f.). Perhaps the reference to offering at Matthew 5:23 f. is a distant echo of that age-old universal priesthood, which had long since been replaced by the Aaronic priestly office? At all events, these are the promises which the young Church saw fulfilled in reality, yet in a completely new way: instead of the single nation of Israel, men from all the nations of the Gentiles are now called to belong to the holy and priestly people of God.

The Church is the *body of Christ,* and again, as we have seen,[5] this means that not just a few especially distinguished members, but all the members of the body of Christ are important and play their part. They all have their own dignity and their own functions, on the basis again of a fundamental equality. Not even the head can say to the feet that it has no need of them. All have a service to each other, in mutual sympathy and affection, in joy and help.

The Church is a *spiritual building,* and once again we have seen[6] that this means that *all* believers, not just a few chosen mediating figures, are filled with the Spirit. The prophets foretold the general outpouring of the Spirit on all flesh for the eschatological age (Joel 2:28 f.); the Spirit is to be given to the hearts of all the children of the people (cf. Is. 44:3; 63:14; Ez. 36:27; Zach. 4:6). Here too the New Testament writers see the prophecies fulfilled; the Spirit has been poured out on the whole community and on each individual (Acts 2; I Cor. 3:16). All Christians are taught and led and supported by the Spirit directly, without mediation, and they are all to live by the Spirit. This is the difference between old and new covenants: the Spirit has been given not just to a few prophets and kings, but to the whole prophetic and kingly community, composed of Jews and Gentiles alike.

The Church is a temple of the Holy Spirit, a temple which is vivified by the Spirit and filled and quickened by it in its individual members. It is this image of the temple of the Spirit, founded on a living key- and corner-stone, Jesus Christ who

[5] Cf. C III.   [6] Cf. C II.

has been raised from the dead and built out of living stones, the faithful, this image which as we have already seen introduces the further image of the temple priesthood: "Come to him, to that living stone, rejected by men but in God's sight chosen and precious; and like living stones be yourselves built into a spiritual house, to be a holy priesthood, to offer spiritual sacrifices acceptable to God through Jesus Christ" (I Pet. 2:4 f.). Here again, it is not earthly or material sacrifices which are offered, but spiritual sacrifices, prayers, praise and thanks, fruits of repentance, of faith and of love, sacrifices not made by men out of their own strength alone, but "through Jesus Christ", the one mediator and high priest. The believers themselves will therefore serve in the temple as a special "holy priesthood" (ἱεράτευμα).

The word "priest" occurs again here, not used in the sense of an official priesthood, and not in reference to the one high priest Christ, but applied through him and in him to *all* believers. The *whole* people, filled by the Spirit of Christ, becomes a priesthood set apart; all Christians are priests. It seems probable that in early times in Israel the head of each family or clan was a priest. But then a special priesthood was formed from the children of Aaron (Ex. 28 f.; Lev. 6). Later kingly and priestly office was combined in the person of the king, and the messianic saviour was once again to be both king and priest (Ps. 110). And although the reign of kings had long since passed, it remained the hope of Israel that its original calling (cf. Ex. 19:5 f.) would be realized in the eschatological age, that they would then become a priestly and kingly free nation (cf. Is. 61:6; 62:3), having access to the altar through their priestly service, for the glory of God, offering sacrifice and governing their own lives in royal freedom. This is what, so the early Christians believed, had been fulfilled in the young Church, and they were prepared to link the great words of Exodus 19:5 f. with Isaiah 43:20 and Hosea 2:23, to accumulate the titles given to Israel and then to apply them, with unparalleled emphasis, precisely to the Church of the Gentiles: "But you are a chosen race, a royal priesthood, a holy nation, God's own people, that you may declare the wonderful deeds of him who called you out of darkness into his marvellous light. Once you were no people but now you are God's people; once you had not received mercy but now you have received mercy" (I Pet. 2:9 f.).

In one of the latest New Testament writings, Revelation, it is once again clearly stated those who have been redeemed by Christ have become sharers in the royal reign of God in the world, a priesthood for the service of God: "To him who loves us and has freed us from our sins by his blood, and made us a kingdom, priests to his God and Father, to him be glory and dominion for ever and ever" (Rev. 1:5 f.). Christians are not subjects, but rulers together with Christ, are not profane men confronting the sanctuary, but priests through Christ: "Thou hast made them a kingdom and priests to our God, and they shall reign on earth" (5:10; cf. 20:6 for the Church of the future).

(*b*) However, the phrase "priesthood of all believers" can all too easily remain a negative slogan—even and indeed precisely in Protestant theology—in order to reject the idea of priestly representation and mediation. This may well be a justified reaction to centuries of clericalism in theology and in practice. But it is essential that the *positive* significance of the priesthood of all believers is realized; the positive authorization and obligation must be recognized *and* practised. It makes sense only if every member of the community can and really does exercise priestly rights and functions. Hence we must ask what the *concrete content* of this priesthood of all believers really is. How far is the whole people of the Church priestly? What we have already discovered in the New Testament can give us a lead here.

1. *Direct access to God:* In pagan cults it was often only the priests who had access to the inmost part of the temple; he mediated there between the divinity and the profane people waiting outside. In the Judaic cult too only the priests, in some cases only the high priests, had access to the inner area, the holy of holies. The priests, who formed a special class, had the task of communicating fellowship with the holy God to a people made impure by sin by the constantly repeated act of sacrificial service. In the New Testament, as we have seen, this kind of priestly mediation is superseded. By his sacrificial death, Christ perfected and finished this kind

of mediation, and thereby opened to *all* access to the holy of holies. In *faith all* have through Christ direct access to grace (Rom. 5:2; cf. Eph. 3:12; Heb. 10:22). In *baptism all* receive fellowship with Christ (Rom. 6:1–11) and *all* are washed with pure water, in order to be able to draw near to God (Heb. 10:22). In the one *Spirit all* have access to the Father (Eph. 2:18). Faith, baptism and the receiving of the Spirit together form the basis of the universal priesthood of all believers. Hence one can say, as has often been said in Christian tradition,[7] that by baptism in the Spirit received in faith all believers are consecrated as priests. Christians do not stand on the threshold of the temple like impure people begging for grace, in fear and trembling, through the priest as the holy middleman. They themselves stand in the very midst of the holy temple of God, as the holy priests chosen by God, able to communicate directly with God. The decisive thing in their new situation is not the barrier which divides them from God, but the fellowship which links them to God through Christ. The believing and baptized Christian therefore needs, in this ultimate sense, no human mediator at all in order to find and maintain fellowship with God in Christ. Every believer, as a member of the community, as a man among other men and on behalf of other men, has an ultimately direct relationship with God, which no human being even in the fellowship can take away from him and no human, nor ecclesiastical authority, can disrupt. It is in this most intimate personal sphere that ultimate decisions between an individual and God are taken, as also between an individual and his fellow men. This is where God's grace makes direct contact with man, God's Spirit guides him. This is where he finds his ultimate freedom and his ultimate responsibility. No one can judge, control or command the decisions which are made in this sphere of direct contact between God and men.

2. *Spiritual sacrifices:* The unique sacrifice of Christ fulfils all the priestly sacrifices of atonement and makes them superfluous.[8] But all believers in the new covenant have to make the sacrifices which were a part of the old covenant and

[7] Cf. H. de Lubac, *The Splendour of the Church*, London–New York 1956.
[8] See C III, 2 and E I, 1.

which the prophets regarded as higher than all the material sacrifices prescribed by the law (cf. Hos. 6:6; Mic. 6:6–8): prayer, praise and thanksgiving, penitence, justice, kindness, love, the knowledge of God. The priesthood of the believers of the new covenant is expected to make spiritual sacrifices, sacrifices wrought by the Spirit: ". . . a holy priesthood, to offer spiritual sacrifices acceptable to God through Jesus Christ" (I Pet. 2:5). According to Paul the Christian must offer his life "as a living sacrifice, holy and acceptable to God, which is your spiritual worship" (Rom. 12:1), and elsewhere he speaks of the "sacrificial offering of faith" (Phil. 2:17), and of the service of love as "a fragrant offering, a sacrifice acceptable and pleasing to God" (Phil. 4:18).

Paul also sees his preaching as a priestly ministry, an offering and self-offering (Rom. 15:16; Phil. 2:17). In other New Testament writings various kinds of sacrifices are mentioned: praise and acknowledgement of God, and the service of love to one's fellow men (Heb. 13:15 f.), the offering up of one's life (II Tim. 4:6), the prayers of the saints (Rev. 8:3 f.). In all these cases we can see that man is not to offer something external, but is to offer and sacrifice himself: not as atonement but as praise and thanksgiving for the gift of salvation. Unlike the priest of the old dispensation he need have no anxiety about whether his offering is pleasing to God, on the contrary, he can know from the first that his sacrifice will be accepted by God, since it is not made by himself alone, but "through Jesus Christ" (I Pet. 2:5), who is himself the high priest and the sacrifice pleasing to God (cf. in addition to Hebrews, Eph. 5:2). His offerings are not just spiritualized sacrifices, but sacrifices made possible by the Lord working in the present through his Spirit. This makes it clear that the priesthood of all believers is not a matter of sacralization. These offerings are not part of worship in a sanctuary, but worship in the world, in the middle of everyday life, the loving service of God, and vice versa. This is the true sacrifice of the New Testament priesthood. Any distinction between sacred and profane would be out of place here, for the consummation of the world, in which both spheres are united, is already anticipated. The apocalyptic seer expresses this in his vision of the heavenly city of Jerusalem: "And I saw no temple in the city, for its temple is the Lord God the Almighty and the Lamb" (Rev. 21:22).

3. *The preaching of the word:*[9] The priesthood of all believers includes not only the witness of actions, of one's whole life spent in loving self-sacrifice, but also the specific witness of the word (cf. Heb. 13:15). The preaching of the word of God is entrusted to all, not just to a few: "But you are . . . a royal priesthood . . . that you may declare the wonderful deeds of him who called you out of darkness into his marvellous light" (I Pet. 2:9). This preaching is not only performed in good conduct (2:12) but also in words: "Always be prepared to make a defence to anyone who calls you to account for the hope that is in you" (3:15). The reference to darkness and light recalls the saying of Jesus at Matthew 5:14, which also refers to all believers: "You are the light of the world". Although the following saying (5:15 f.) goes on to speak of good works, this first image of light primarily refers to the revelation which is given to the people who were sitting and waiting in darkness (cf. 4:15 f.). Hence the words of Jesus: "What I tell you in the dark, utter it in the light; and what you hear whispered, proclaim upon the housetops" (Mt. 10:27). The primary command which Jesus gives to his disciples is that of preaching the message of salvation (Mk. 1:35–38; 16:15; Mt. 28:18–20; Acts 1:8; I Cor. 1:17). This explains why there is such a variety of words in the New Testament, around thirty different terms, to describe the activity of preaching: proclaim, announce, preach, teach, explain, speak, say, testify, persuade, confess, charge, admonish, etc. The variety of different kinds of preaching allows each and every one to make his contribution towards the preaching of the message.

It is the word which creates the Church and constantly gathers it together again by arousing faith and obedience; the word must always go out from the Church anew (cf. Rom. 10:14–17). Because they have been "called" through the word (Rom. 1:6; I Cor. 1:24; Heb. 9:15), believers must always

---

[9] Cf. K. H. Schelkle, *Discipleship and Priesthood,* London–Melbourne 1966, New York 1965. Bibliography in H. Küng, *Justification,* London–Camden 1964, section III.

be particularly concerned about the word. All are to pray for the success of the preaching of the word, "that the word of the Lord may speed on and triumph, as it did among you" (II Thess. 3:1). But Paul is obviously not satisfied simply with "prayers for missionaries". The members of the community are not only to pray, not only to hear the word of the apostles and give a witness to the world by good deeds. They too are to proclaim and to speak even during services of worship, according to the charism given to each: "When you come together, each one has a hymn, a lesson, a revelation, a tongue, an interpretation. Let all things be done for edification" (I Cor. 14:26). By seizing their opportunity and their right to the word, in one form or another, believers as a whole bear a tremendous witness to their faith which can even persuade unbelievers: "But if all prophesy, and an unbeliever or outsider enters, he is convicted by all, he is called to account by all, the secrets of his heart are disclosed; and so, falling on his face, he will worship God and declare that God is really among you" (I Cor. 14:24 f.). At the least the community must be able to say the "Amen" to the thanksgiving of the prophet (I Cor. 14:16).

The Christian message spread with such speed from the very first because it was proclaimed by all, according to their gifts and opportunities, and not just by a few with a special commission. It spread abroad not just through the witness of apostles and evangelists, but through the preaching of merchants, soldiers and seafarers. In Acts it is stressed that "all filled with the Holy Spirit spoke the word of God with boldness" (4:31; cf. 8:4; 11:19). Paul confirms this in respect of the Church of the Thessalonians: "For not only has the word of the Lord sounded forth from you in Macedonia and Achaia, but your faith in God has gone forth everywhere, so that we need not say anything" (I Thess. 1:8). And even when Paul was in prison, the majority of the brethren proclaimed the word fearlessly and with growing courage, even if not always with the purest of motives (Phil. 1:12–18). It is true that in the New Testament period women are commanded to keep silence during the meetings of the community (I Cor. 14:33–35; cf. I Tim. 2:12); but this is something we must understand in the context of the times, not a fundamental principle; in the first letter of Peter women are charged to fulfil their own kind of preaching, by winning "without a word" (3:1). All Christians, as the letter to the Hebrews tells us, need solid food as well as milk, and they should not need to be rehearsed in the first principles of the Christian faith, but should themselves be teachers (Heb. 5:12–14).

Paul's view that the faithful are "taught by God" (I Thess. 4:9) is brought out even more strongly in the first letter of John. By contrast with Antichrists real Christians have been "anointed (i.e. given the Holy Spirit) by the Holy One", and this gives them full knowledge with regard to everything that is necessary for salvation: "And you all know" (I Jn. 2:20; cf. Jn. 14:26; some authorities have "you know everything"). This knowledge is further emphasized by the writer: "I write to you, not because you do not know the truth, but because you do know it" (I Jn. 2:21). The Spirit remains in the faithful, so that they do not need to be taught by anyone: "the anointing which you received from him abides in you, and you have no need that anyone should teach you; as his anointing teaches you about everything, and is true, and is no lie, just as it has taught you, abide in him" (2:27). This does not mean that the believers do not need the testimony which has been handed on to them by men (cf. 1:1–5; 2:7 and 24; 3:11). But it is the Spirit, the power which works within them and is independent of men, who gives them the truly convincing teaching, and their ultimate certainty. From this follows that only a man who is taught by God, by the Holy Spirit, in addition to any human testimony, can pass on the message with full authority. But on the evidence of the New Testament this applies to every Christian. Every believer can and must, having been taught by God, teach others; can and must, having received the word of God, be its herald in some form or other. Every Christian is called to be a preacher of the word, in the widest sense, even though, in view of the variety of the gifts of the Spirit, not everyone can by any means do everything. All are called to preach the Gospel in the sense of their personal Christian witness, without being all called to preach in the narrow sense of the word or to be theologians.

This theological investigation of the right and duty of all Christians to preach the word does not aim to show what may be in the realm of *practical possibilities,* given the constantly changing situations of the Church and the world—even in the New Testament Churches the extent to which the idea was put into practice varied. From the theological viewpoint it is more important to see what the New Testament sources have to tell us about what is *fundamentally possible and desirable.* We are forced to conclude that the originally rich idea of the priesthood of all believers was largely lost during centuries of clericalization and only gradually regained in very recent times. Two important aspects connected with the preaching of the word must be discussed in more detail here.

1. *Lay preaching:*[10] Whereas in primitive Christianity preaching was largely determined by the charismatic structure of the Church, we can observe how soon efforts were made—not least because of the kind of abuses which occurred in Corinth—to make preaching the privilege of holders of a particular office; this began in the second century with the institutionalization of the catechumenate. It is true that in the third century Origen, a layman, is invited by the bishops of Caesarea and Jerusalem to expound sacred Scripture in their churches, and we know of other cases; but these are all forms of teaching rather than sermons in the strict sense. At all events more and more restrictions are imposed as from the third century; Leo I and various medieval synods (Tours in 813, Aachen in 836) issued bans on lay preaching. At the same time, these bans are indirect proof of the fact that lay preaching was obviously practised and had hitherto been approved. In the twelfth century lay sermons took on increased importance, due to the movements of reform such as the Waldensians, the Humiliati (to whom Innocent III allowed a circumscribed freedom for lay preaching) and the mendicant orders, which consisted to a large extent of laymen and which were allowed to preach moral homilies and calls to repentance, to give apologetic defences and justifications of the faith (despite the ban on lay preaching throughout the whole Church given by the Fourth Lateran Synod in 1215). The Council of Trent decided that sermons in the strict sense should be reserved for bishops and their assistants; this is the origin of the general ban on lay preaching which found its way into the *Codex Iuris Canonici* (1918). And yet a layman (Lodovico Nogorola) preached at the Council of Trent itself, and at the Second Vatican Council laymen gave sermon-like addresses

[10] Cf. Y. Congar, *Lay People in the Church,* London, 1957, Westminster, Md., 1965 and K. Delahaye, art. "Laienpredigt", in LThK VI, 747 f. (bibl.).

to the Council Fathers. So much for the history of lay preaching. As far as the present time is concerned, there would seem to be very good reasons for a revival of the idea of lay preaching, provided it suited existing conditions and was properly ordered; this view is supported not only by the New Testament, but by the present situation both in the world—particularly the diminished power of the Church and the development of the secular world—and in the Church—particularly the lack of preachers and the maturity of the laity. This is especially true of the service of the word, revived by Vatican II, which may be conducted by laymen. From a theological viewpoint (and increasingly from psychological and sociological ones too), the distinction between the sexes is here irrelevant; there are absolutely no dogmatic grounds for opposing preaching by women. This does not of course mean that every Christian, while as a Christian he is called to preach the word and to give personal witness to his faith, is necessarily called to give sermons in the community. The charisms of the Spirit are various. On the other hand, charisms which have been granted to Christians ought to be acknowledged with gratitude and pressed into service. In this way sermons by lay people will be possible without specific ecclesiastical permission or training.

In Protestantism the priesthood of all believers and even lay sermons were at first not much more than a theoretical slogan. Lay preachers were an important feature of Pietism and of several nineteenth-century revivalist movements. Men and women lay preachers were systematically introduced by Methodism and the *Gemeinschaft* movement (J. H. Wichern, *Innere Mission*). Nowadays lay preaching is fairly generally recognized in the Protestant Churches and quite frequently practised, at any rate in the Free Churches. In Orthodoxy also lay people are commonly allowed to preach in church and to teach at theological colleges. Monks have especial importance in the Orthodox Church as regards teaching and the encouragement of the spiritual life.

2. *Lay theology:*[11] Whereas lay preaching was stifled at a relatively early period, lay theology lasted much longer. The first great theologians were mostly laymen: Justin, Tertullian, Pantaenus, Clement of Alexandria, Origen (who only later became a priest). Among later lay theologians were Victorinus, Pamphilus, Sextus Africanus, Lactantius, Firmicus Maternus, Prosper of Aquitaine, and in the East Socrates, Sozomen and Evagrius. A great number of theologians started at least their theological work as laymen, and were made in part against their will to become priests:

[11] Cf. Y. Congar, *op. cit.*

Cyprian, Basil, Gregory of Nyssa, Jerome, Augustine, Paulinus of
Nola, Diodore of Tarsus. Even in the Middle Ages there were still
a few isolated lay theologians—Raymond Lull is a famous example
—especially among princes—notably Henry VIII. In the patristic
period there had been no split between a religious and theological
culture reserved for the clergy and a secular lay culture in the
modern sense, and so lay theologians were taken for granted. But
as a result of the collapse of the Imperium Romanum and the
domination of the barbarians, the rich treasures of ancient cultural
tradition were maintained and preserved almost exclusively by the
clergy, especially the bishops and the monks. This in turn led to a
monopoly of education and culture reserved for the clergy, which
naturally had a vital effect on theology in particular. The position
was quite different in the East, where a cultured laity, in particular
the imperial officials, who still functioned there, were able to retain
an influential and respected position in the Church, and where in
consequence, anti-clericalism, which developed in the West from
the Middle Ages onwards, was virtually unknown. The tradition of
lay theology was thus preserved in the Eastern Churches right
down to the present day, especially in the faculty of theology at
Athens and at the Institut de Théologie Orthodoxe in Paris.

In the West the end of the Middle Ages and humanism in particular brought a limited change, and brought lay people more into
contact with theology. At the time of the Council of Basle Enea
Silvio Piccolomini (later Pius II) was a lay theologian, as were the
leaders of a constructive Catholic reform at the time of the Reformation—Gasparo Contarini, Reginald Pole and Marcello Cervini,
the two last-named both being presidents of the Council of Trent;
at that Council were also the Council Secretary Angelo Massarelli
and the Nogorola who is mentioned above. The line of lay theologians continued through the succeeding centuries (e.g. Pascal)
down to the nineteenth century (de Maistre, Veuillot, Cha-
teaubriand, Goerres, Donoso Cortes, etc.). In addition to
apologists, it was increasingly the philosophers (as in neo-
Thomism) who concerned themselves with religious questions. But
it is only in the present century, one of the most hopeful signs of
renewal, that there has come an unprecedented advance in lay
theology; in German-speaking countries this occurred long before
the Second Vatican Council, but in all countries this development
has been powerfully aided, if indirectly, by the Council. From a
theological viewpoint there is not the slightest reason why lay theologians of either sex who have doctorates in theology should not
be allowed to teach in faculties of theology. Here again not everyone can hope to do everything in the Church, but at the same time

charisms given by the Spirit should be recognized and made use of.

4. *The administering of baptism, the Lord's Supper and forgiveness of sins:* The preaching of the word of God occurs in a variety of ways in the Church. Even in formal worship it is not preached solely in the sermon. The word of God is associated with certain actions which are interpreted and decisively conditioned by the word, and thus become effective means of proclaiming God's word. As the Bible shows, the most important of these actions are baptism, the Lord's Supper, and absolution.[12] In view of what has been said above, there is no need to present a lengthy case for saying that the command to perform these three actions is addressed not just to a few select persons, but to all the disciples of Jesus, to the whole Church. The Church has always assumed, although the relevant words at Matthew 28:19 seem to have been spoken to the small circle of apostles only, that the command to baptize was addressed to the whole Church.[13] The *entire* Church is given the power to baptize; *every* Christian has the power to baptize (and to teach). The charge of forgiving sins[14] was also laid upon the Church as a whole; at Matthew 18:18 it appears as part of a general directive to the disciples, or as part of the ordering of the community. The *whole* Church has the power to forgive sins; and in communion with the Church, which exists in the communion of forgiveness of God and of Christ, *every* Christian is fundamentally empowered to take an active part in the forgiving of sins. And finally even the celebration of the Lord's Supper,[15] although it first occurred in the limited circle of the twelve, and the command "Do this in remembrance of me" (Lk. 22:19), is a charge laid upon the whole Church. The *whole* Church is given the power to eat the Lord's body and drink his blood, and *every* Christian is fundamentally empowered to take an active part in this eschatological meal of commemoration, thanksgiving and covenantal fellowship. This indicates once

---

[12] The concept of sacrament needs further examination which is outside the scope of this book.

[13] Cf. C III, 1.

[14] Cf. D III, 2a.   [15] Cf. C III, 2.

again that the priesthood of all believers even in respect of formal worship is a completely concrete reality.

It was never disputed that every Christian has a fundamental right to baptize. How far the power of loosing and binding (Mt. 18:18) is a fundamental right of the individual Christian was discussed above in connection with lay confession.[16] With regard to the Lord's Supper, the Second Vatican Council, referring to the priesthood of all believers, stated explicitly: "Mother Church earnestly desires that all the faithful be led to that full, conscious, and active participation in liturgical celebrations which is demanded by the very nature of the liturgy. Such participation by the Christian people as a 'chosen race, a royal priesthood, a holy nation, a purchased people' (I Pet. 2:9; cf. 2:4–5), is their *right* and *duty* by reason of their baptism. In the restoration and promotion of the sacred liturgy, this full and active participation by all the people is the aim to be considered before all else; for it is the primary and indispensable source from which the faithful are to derive the true Christian spirit" (*Constitutio de Sacra Liturgia* 14; cf. 26–27). The priesthood of all believers is further emphasized by the granting of the cup to the laity by the same Council—or at least the recognition of this fundamental right, which was needlessly disputed for centuries and withheld from the laity. The establishing of this fundamental right and duty to take an active part in baptism, the Lord's Supper and the forgiving of sins is not of course the same thing as determining who can and may be responsible for administering these sacraments in and for the community. We shall return to this point in the context of office in the Church.

5. *Mediating functions:* The priestly service of the community takes its origin in the community's worship, especially in the Lord's Supper. But, starting from there, it must develop outwards and become effective in the world, in service of one's fellow men in the community and, at the same time, in service to other men in the world. The priesthood of the believer is not just a private relationship between him and his God. What has been said above about direct access to God, about spiritual sacrifices made in a spirit of love and self-giving, about the preaching of the word and the administering of baptism, the Lord's Supper and the forgiving of sins, must

16 Cf. D III, 2a.

ultimately be to the advantage of all men, must always be a service of one's fellow men and of the world.

In this way all believers are absorbed into the mediating work of the one and only mediator. Their function is to mediate between God and the world, by revealing the hidden works of God and making effective his acts of power. Hence every Christian is a priest of God, by being a witness to God before the world: ". . . that you may be blameless and innocent, children of God without blemish in the midst of a crooked and perverse generation, among whom you shine as lights in the world" (Phil. 2:15; cf. I Thess. 5:5). Their function is also that of mediating between the world and God, by not only devoting themselves to their fellow men through spiritual sacrifices, but also by praying for them. Every Christian is a priest for the world, by having free access to God in faith and by being able to appear before God on behalf of others and intercede for them: "First of all, then, I urge that supplications, prayers, intercessions, and thanksgivings be made for all men" (I Tim. 2:1).

The priesthood of all believers consists in the calling of the faithful to witness to God and his will before the world, and to offer up their lives in the service of the world. It is God who creates this priesthood and hence creates fellowship among believers. Each one knows that he appears before God on behalf of others, and knows that others appear before God on his behalf. Each is responsible for his fellow men, called to share in his struggles and in his difficulties, called to bear his sins with him and to stand by him in everything. The priesthood of all believers is a fellowship in which each Christian, instead of living for himself, lives before God for others and is in turn supported by others: "Bear one another's burdens, and so fulfil the law of Christ" (Gal. 6:2). The worship of this priesthood thus develops from being worship within the community to being worship within the everyday secular world.

Our remarks about the priesthood of all believers can be best summed up in the words of the Second Vatican Council: "Christ the Lord, High Priest taken from among men (cf. Heb. 5:1–5), 'made a kingdom and priests to God his Father' (Rev. 1:6; cf. 5:9–10) out of this new people. The baptized, by regeneration and the anointing of the Holy Spirit, are consecrated into a spiritual house and a holy priesthood. Thus through all those works befitting Christian men they can offer spiritual sacrifices and proclaim the power of Him who has called them out of darkness into His marvellous light (cf. I Pet. 2:4–10). Therefore all the disciples of Christ, persevering in prayer and praising God (cf. Acts 2:42–47), should present themselves as a living sacrifice, holy and pleasing to God (cf. Rom. 12:1). Everywhere on earth they must bear witness to Christ and give an answer to those who seek an account of that hope of eternal life which is in them (cf. I Pet. 3:15)." (CE 10). For further remarks of the Council about the priesthood of all believers through the sharing of the laity in the priestly, prophetic and kingly office of Christ, cf. CE 34–36.

(c) We can now see more clearly that the priesthood of all believers is far from being just a theological slogan or an empty title. Behind the phrase there lies an extremely rich and concrete reality. One last point must be made in this context: part of this concrete reality is the *name* priesthood, which is an indissoluble part of it. Here we come back to the name *"priest"* (always in the sense of ἱερεύς or *sacerdos*). Although the New Testament insists quite unequivocally that there is no longer a priesthood in contrast to an unpriestly laity, but that the whole new people of God has become a priesthood, the name "priest" has generally been reserved for the leaders of the community in recent centuries, while the idea of the priesthood of all believers has at best, if at all, been commemorated. And yet it is very striking how slow the early Church was to use the name priest for the leader of the community at all. According to the New Testament, although Christ's sacrificial death on the cross is expressed in the Lord's Supper, the Lord's Supper itself is not regarded as a sacrifice on its own, nor even a repetition of the unique sacrificial death of Christ.[17] Thus the Lord's Supper is never referred to as a sacrifice in the New Testament. It is only in writings outside the New Testament, first of all in the Didache 14:1–3 and then in Justin and Irenaeus, that the Lord's Supper is called a sacrifice. Gradually the Lord's Supper came to be seen less and less as the communal meal of the entire priestly people, and more and more as a kind of

[17] Cf. C III, 2.

new sacrifice, offered by the leaders of the community on the community's behalf; a misunderstanding which prepared the way for calling the leaders of the community priests, and, as in pagan and Jewish tradition, distinguishing them from the rest of the people; and as time went on the ideas and images associated with the priesthood of the Old Testament were increasingly transferred to these New Testament "priests".

It is in the Didache once again (15:1) that we first come across the leaders of the community as leaders of the Lord's Supper, although they are only granted second place beside the prophets (called "your high priests" at 13:3) (cf. 15:1 f.; 10:7; 13:3). In the first letter of Clement, where similarly the leaders of the community seem to have been leaders of the Lord's Supper (44:4), the cultic arrangements of the old covenant are presented as prefiguring the cult of the community (not as in Hebrews prefiguring the cult of the high priest Christ) (40 f.). But Ignatius of Antioch still avoids using the term "priest", even when he is speaking about the worship of the community and of the bishop, to whom together with the presbyters he attaches especial importance, more than any of his predecessors (*Magn.* 7:1; *Philadelph.* 4:1 f.). Tertullian is the first to refer to the bishop as *"summus sacerdos"* (and that only once),[18] and Hippolytus speaks of the "high priesthood" of the apostles (ἀρχιερατεία).[19] Eusebius is the first, in a ceremonial address, to speak of the clergy as "priests".[20]

The rapidly increasing clericalization of the Church meant that it became more and more customary to use the word "priest" exclusively for those who held a particular office in the Church. The idea of the priesthood of all believers gradually came to be almost forgotten by the faithful and by most theologians. As a comment on this development, in the light of the lengthy discussion above, two observations may be made which sum up the whole issue: the fact that the leaders of the community are called "priests" is unexceptionable precisely because of the priesthood of all believers; but the fact that the leaders of the community *exclusively* are seen as

18 Tertullian, *De baptismo*, 17, 1; CC 1, 291.
19 Hippolytus, *Refutatio*, *Prooemium* I, 6; GCS 26, 3.
20 Eusebius, *Hist. eccl.* X, 4, 2; GCS 9/2, 862.

"priests", and become a separate caste, after pagan and Judaic patterns, standing *between* God and men and barring the direct access to God which the whole priestly people should enjoy—this as we have seen is contrary to the New Testament message: both the message of the *one* mediator and high priest Jesus Christ and that of the priesthood of *all* Christians.

A similar problem is associated with a second word, that is *spirituales* or pneumatics[21] (although German and Dutch have the words *Geistlicher* and *geestelijke* to denote a clergyman or priest, there is no equivalent in English or the modern Romance languages); this word too became limited to the leaders of the community, or to members of orders (or even, in the case of the word *spirituales,* to a particular branch of those orders). Before the end of the first millennium it was customary to refer to monks in particular as pneumatics. One of the greatest medieval preachers, Berthold of Regensburg (d. 1272), called religious "spiritual people" by contrast with secular clergy. But from the time of Gregory VII we can trace a definite development which led, by the fifteenth century, to the use of the word *spirituales* as a general description of all the clergy, order priests and secular clergy alike, as a distinction between clergy and laity. The denial of the body, the renunciation of women and marriage and hence celibacy, and then the renunciation of personal material possessions was the characteristic feature of the *"spirituales".* By contrast with them, the laity, involved as they were with marriage and with material possessions, became regarded as the *"carnales"*—or—a formulation which also dates from the eleventh century—as the left side of the body of Christ. We can see how the monkish idea of life, which was often based much more on Neo-Platonism than on the Gospel of Jesus Christ, and to which the secular clergy were expected to aspire, become virtually the norm of the "spiritual life". But we may well ask ourselves whether this is the true meaning of the Pauline distinction between those who follow the spirit and those who follow the flesh.

---

[21] Cf. E. Schweizer, art. "πνευμα, πνευματικός im NT", in ThW VI, 394–450; G. May, art. "Geistlich", in LThK IV, 618; K. H. Schelkle, *A Priestly People,* London–Melbourne 1965.

According to the New Testament, as we saw in connection with the Church as a spiritual creation,[22] *all* believing and baptized Christians are filled with the Spirit ("But you are . . . in the Spirit, if the Spirit of God really dwells in you" Rom. 8:9), and are hence *"spirituales": "*you who are spiritual" (Gal. 6:1); "and we impart this in words . . . taught by the Spirit, interpreting spiritual truths to those who possess the Spirit" (I Cor. 2:13). It is clearly not just a small group of ecstatics or ascetics who are filled with the Spirit, and certainly not any kind of ecclesiastical dignitaries. *All* Christians, having in faith received the Pneuma, the Spirit, in baptism, should be pneumatics and *"spirituales"*. The admonition of the apostle is addressed to all: "But I say, walk by the Spirit, and do not gratify the desires of the flesh. For the desires of the flesh are against the Spirit, and the desires of the Spirit are against the flesh" (Gal. 5:16 f.). Moreover, the word "flesh" does not mean for Paul, as he himself makes clear, marriage or material possessions, and not even "sins of the flesh" in the narrow sense of fornication, but it is a general term to describe a man who is distant from God and against God, a man who instead of being inspired and ruled by the Spirit of God is controlled by his own strivings and desires and wishes. "Works of the flesh", as Paul says, are not just immorality and licentiousness, but include also "idolatry, sorcery, enmity, strife, jealousy, anger, selfishness, dissension, party spirit, envy, drunkenness, carousing, and the like" (Gal. 5:19–21).

Elsewhere Paul even suggests that asceticism can be a work of the flesh (Col. 2:23). The fruit of the Spirit, by contrast, is "love, joy, peace, patience, kindness, goodness, faithfulness, gentleness, self-control" (Gal. 5:22 f.). A man is "spiritual" if, having died to sin, he seizes the opportunity and the freedom of living for God, and allows himself to be motivated by the Spirit, which is the spirit of sonship, not the spirit of slavery (Rom. 8:14 f.). The Spirit is not a thing to be possessed or controlled by man; the man who is filled with the Spirit is still exposed to trials and temptations and must constantly renew his decision for God, and renew his decision to live according to the Spirit rather than according to the flesh. Here,

[22] Cf. C II.

once again, an imperative arises from an indicative: *every* Christian *is* a spiritual person, a pneumatic, a *"spiritualis"*, in as far as he has died to flesh and sin and has received the Spirit of God. *Every* Christian *ought to be* a spiritual person, a pneumatic, a *"spiritualis"*, in as far as he can kill sin in his life and, by living in the Spirit, bring forth the fruit of the Spirit.

A third problematic word, which again has wrongly been limited to certain individuals in the Church, is *"clerus"*.[23] The idea of a limited office of ministry was developed from Acts 1:17 and 26. In Acts 1:26 the word ὁ κλῆρος is used in its original sense, meaning the *lot* used as an expression of the will of God to determine who should be the successor of Judas (in Mk. 15:24 par. the word is used of the soldiers casting lots for Jesus' clothes). From this original sense the word κλῆρος took on a more general sense of a share which is allotted to someone. This is how the word is used at Acts 1:17: Judas "was allotted his share in this ministry", that is, he had received his share in the apostolic ministry as something allotted to him, not something which he had earned for himself. This led to the use of the word *"clerus"* to indicate a share in the presbyterium, and finally to refer to all holders of ecclesiastical office. As early as Origen[24] the word κλῆρος has become an established term for those who hold office in the Church, as opposed to the people. *"Clerus"* for Jerome[25] are the holders of office inasmuch as they are the special property of the Lord, or the Lord is their lot, their share. In the post-Constantinian period the biblical distinction between (priestly!) "people" (λαός) and "non-people" (οὐ λαός, I Pet. 2:10) increasingly turned into a distinction between "people" (*laici*) and "priest" (*clerus*).[26]

The expression "layman" (λακϊός), which in the Greek sense meant the uneducated masses, and in the Jewish sense a man who was neither priest nor Levite, does not occur anywhere in the New Testament, though it is used in the first let-

---

[23] Cf. W. Foerster, in ThW III, 757–763; H. Flatten, in LThK VI, 336–339; Y. Congar, art. "Laie", in HTG II, 7–25.

[24] Origen, *In Jer.* 11, 3; PL 13, 370.

[25] Jerome, *Rp. 52*, 5; CSEL 54, 421.

[26] Cf. C I, 3.

ter of Clement (40:6) to refer to the simple faithful by contrast with the high priests, priests and Levites; from the third century onwards the word is in current use in the Church. In this way the tension between Church and world (which had itself now become "Christian") was transferred to within the Church itself, and became a tension between *"clerus"* (secular priests and monks) and "laity". The "clergy" was accorded an increasingly privileged position and grew into a new sociological class on its own, with its own privileges, immunities, dress, titles, duties (celibacy, breviary, etc.), and its own (Latin) culture and its own (Latin) liturgy. The *"clerici"* were the educated people, the *litterati,* who could understand Latin and therefore could read and write. On the other side were the laity, the ἰδιῶται, *idiotae, illiterati;* they were the βιωτικοί, *saeculares* or *populares, populi.* To a very large extent the conflicts within the medieval Church, the Reformation itself and numerous more recent disputes between "clericalism" and "laicism" can be traced to the long history of the conflict between clergy and laity, which Boniface VIII, in a constitution of 31 July, 1297, summed up in the curious remark: "The fact that the laity is hostile to the clergy is something which antiquity has handed on to us clearly enough (*clericis laicos infestos oppido tradit antiquitas*)".

It is obvious that this *antiquitas* cannot refer to the New Testament. How does this distinction appear in the light of New Testament terminology? We have already seen that *all* Christians belong to the new "people" (λαός). In the early Church there were differences of spiritual gifts and of tasks to fulfil, but there was no distinction between a group called clergy and a group called laity. The careless use of the term "laity" to apply to the priestly people of God, unless it held office in the Church, was matched by the taking over by the holders of office of the term *"clerus"*. This was to overlook the fact that the word κλῆρος in the New Testament cannot be identified at all with a share in the office of the Church. Indeed, in the first letter of Peter (5:2 f.) the word κλῆρος seems precisely to refer to communities as being a share allotted to the elder. The word has a much wider sense. *"Clerus"* does not, as in later Judaism, mean a "share in Moses", but a share in the word of God (cf. Philip to Simon the magician: "You have neither part nor lot in this matter [literally: word]", Acts 8:21), and especially a share in eschatological salvation: ". . . I send you to open their eyes, that they may turn from darkness to light and from the power of Satan to God, that they may receive forgiveness of sins and a place among those who are sanctified by faith in me" (Acts 26:17 f.). Again in Colossians: ". . . giving thanks to the Father, who has qualified us to share in the inheritance of the saints in light" (1:12). Ignatius of Antioch also uses the word in the sense of "lot". Of particular interest in the passage in Eph. 11:2 which makes the distinction between New Testament usage and the later usage of the term very clear: ἵνα ἐν κλήρῳ Ἐφεσίων εὑρεθῶ quite obviously does not mean: "that I may be discovered in the clergy of the Ephesians", but "that I may be discovered in the lot, the share of the Ephesians", i.e. "that I may share in the lot of the Ephesians, of Christians faithful to the apostles".

From a theological point of view, then, *"clerus"* means the share in eschatological salvation which God gives to *each* individual believer in the communion of all believers. This share is to be understood not simply as a "lot" but rather as a "good thing" prepared for the believer by God. We must then conclude, inverting Jerome's formulation, that the particular "share" (*clerus*) of the Lord is precisely not just the clergy, but the whole people of God; and Christ is the "share" (*clerus*) not just of the clergy, but of the whole people of God. The word *"clerus"* too, therefore, belongs to the whole Church, and not just to those who hold office in it; and while the New Testament can support the use of the term as applied to individuals, it is fundamentally the property of the whole Church.

Our conclusions, drawn on the basis of the New Testament, about the words "priest", *"spiritualis"* and *"clerus"*, are simply an extension and application of what was said above about the word "ecclesia", "Church": the ecclesia is not made up simply of those who in past centuries have often been collectively spoken of as "the Church", but is made up of *all* believers; and thus *all* believers are priests and clergy.

This poses the urgent question as to whether, in this radical

New Testament view of the Church, there is room for any kind of ecclesiastical office. Given that the exclusive and particular names like priests and clergy have no basis in the New Testament, is it not difficult to find a suitable name for those who hold office in the Church?

II. ECCLESIASTICAL OFFICE AS MINISTRY

1. SERVICE AS THE IMITATION OF CHRIST

What *name* are we to use for the ecclesiastical office as such, if the terms "priest" and "clergyman" are to be avoided? There is no lack of names: we speak of Church officials, Church government, Church administration, Church dignitaries, Church authorities; we speak of princes of the Church and of the hierarchy. The question of terminology is far from unimportant in establishing the nature of ecclesiastical office.

There are three reasons for the relatively brief treatment here of ecclesiastical office, in comparison with traditional ecclesiological treatises:

1. We should like to keep to the proportions in Scripture, which recognizes no hypertrophy of ecclesiastical office in relation to the Church.

2. We should like to keep to an analysis of the *nature* of ecclesiastical office historically understood, just as we have limited ourselves to an analysis of the *nature* of the Church historically understood. Most traditional treatises concern themselves not with the nature of ecclesiastical office but rather with inessential *forms* of it.

3. In *Structures of the Church,* which is the prolegomena to the present book, the longest section is devoted to the most difficult aspects of the problem of ecclesiastical office and attempts to clear up several difficulties concerning its nature and forms. Chapters VI–VIII of that book (pp. 95–352) must be presupposed here.

Secular and even New Testament Greek has various words for these modern expressions. It is important to see which words the New Testament uses, and for whom. The last word listed above, probably the most extensively used nowadays, "hierarchy", does not, as we at once discover, occur either in secular or in New Testament Greek at all. The word was first introduced, about half a millennium later, by Dionysius the Areopagite; but he used the word ἱεραρχία (holy origin, holy reign) precisely not for the holders of office, or their superior of subordinate rank in a total structure, but for the *whole* Church with all its ranks, which for Dionysius is in its entirety an image of the heavenly world of spirits and its ordering. This fact might not be so striking, were it not that all the other words in secular Greek for civil and religious authorities are consistently avoided in connection with the ministries of the Church. This is true of the basic word for hierarchy ἀρχή (ἄρχων), but also for τιμή and τέλος.[27]

1. ἀρχή, which always implies a primacy, whether in time ("beginning", "first principle") or in rank ("power", "authority", "office"), means, in connection with office, a leading, a precedence or rule. The Septuagint uses the word in secular contexts (for Egyptian court officials, for example) and in religious ones (for high priests, Levitical doorkeepers). The New Testament uses it for Jewish and Gentile authorities, and in a different sense for Christ (Col. 1:16: Christ is the beginning of all things, the creative principle of the world), but never for Church ministries of any sort. Similarly the title ἄρχων (ruler, prince) is used for demonic powers, Roman and Jewish officials, and also for Christ (Rev. 1:5: "ruler of the kings of earth"), but never for office in the Church.

2. τιμή, which means value, price, esteem, honour, respectability, is used to describe the honour and dignity of office. It is used only once in the New Testament in this way, to describe the honour of the high priestly office (Heb. 5:4).

3. τέλος, which means end, conclusion, goal, remainder, is used to describe the total power of office. Οἱ ἐν τέλει are those who wield power. The word does not occur in this sense in the New Testament at all.

Why is it that the New Testament obviously avoids using these then current and seemingly obvious terms? Clearly because despite the varieties of area they cover, they have one

[27] See the relevant articles in ThW.

common factor: all express a relationship of rulers and ruled. And it is precisely this which makes them unusable. There remained nothing else but to develop a new word. The word that was chosen was an unbiblical one, current neither in the Jewish nor the Hellenistic environment in this sense—indeed a fundamentally unreligious word. The particular place and function of the individual in the community was comprehensively described with a word which carried no overtones of authority, officialdom, rule, dignity or power: the word διακονία, service.[28]

It is significant that in order to describe the ministries of the New Testament Church, even a word which was used in a cultic sense in the Septuagint and might have seemed an obvious one to apply was avoided. λειτουργία and the verb λειτουργειν have scarcely any connection in origin with the modern word "liturgy". They took their origin from secular and political spheres, meaning the more or less voluntary carrying out of public services for the common good by those who are citizens (here again the word λαός is in the background; λήιτος means "concerning the people"). As the original meaning of any kind of service to the community became less current, the words took on the specialized sense of religious service: service to the gods. This meaning is the one we find throughout the Septuagint, where both words are technical terms for priestly and religious ministries, whereas the personal title λειτουργός, rarely used here, retains principally the secular sense of servant. None the less, to use these words to describe those who held office in the early Church might have seemed an obvious solution. But again the New Testament use of the words is striking. They are used to describe the service of Roman government officials (Rom. 13:6) and of the pre-Christian Old Testament priesthood (Lk. 1:23; Heb. 9:21; 10:11); they are occasionally used metaphorically to describe the ministry of Jesus Christ himself (Heb. 8:2 and 6); and they are applied to the ministries of the community as a whole (especially money collections, cf. Rom. 15:27; II Cor. 9:12) or of individuals (financial support: Phil. 2:25 and 30; the Christian way of life: Phil. 2:17; communal prayers: Acts 13:2)—but they are never used for any kind of Church office. One exception proves the rule: at Romans 15:16 Paul refers to himself as a "minister

[28] See H. W. Beyer, in ThW II, 81–93; K. H. Schelkle, *Discipleship and Priesthood,* London–Melbourne 1966.

(λειτουργός) of Christ Jesus to the Gentiles"; he sees his apostolic work, using the imagery of the cult, as a "priestly service of the Gospel of God, so that the offering of the Gentiles may be acceptable, sanctified by the Holy Spirit". But this "priestly" action is to be understood metaphorically, and is entirely applied to the preaching of the Gospel; Paul does not see himself as the mediator of revelation or grace, he sees himself as offering to God the faith and obedience of the Gentiles, as a metaphorical sacrifice of praise. It is significant that this "cultic" use of the term is elsewhere completely avoided, and there is no other example of the use of this or allied words to apply to those who hold office in the Church. The remarks above about sacrifice apply similarly to the cultic *"leiturgia"*: it has occurred once for all in Christ and now must be made effective by being proclaimed. Only outside the New Testament do we find these words being used to describe the Christian cult and important religious actions, especially the Lord's Supper; from here they came to be used for the corresponding holders of ecclesiastical office.

This service which is meant by the Greek word "diakonia" is in no danger, unlike words which suggest political or priestly services, of being misinterpreted as an honour or a new kind of rule. Diakonia means an activity which every Greek would recognize at once as being one of self-abasement: waiting at table, serving food and pouring wine. The distinction between master and servant was nowhere more visually apparent than at meals, where the noble masters would lie at the table in their long robes, while the servants, their clothes girded, had to wait on them. Even when diakonia (or the verb διακονειν) was used in a wider sense, meaning "to be responsible for the meal, for food and drink, for the means of subsistence", or quite generally carried the sense of "serving", it never lost its flavour of inferiority. Only the service of the statesman, which was in no way a humiliation, was free from this sense of inferiority.

This kind of service was unthinkable for a free Greek, for whom the development of his own personality and the exercise of power were supreme things. For a Jew it was not necessarily an inferior activity; service, especially of a great master and above all when it was service for God, he could see as representing something great. *Jesus*, however, gave this notion of service a radically new meaning; at the very heart of his eschatological message lies his commandment to love one's neighbour, a love in which the love of God is manifested. For him the diakonia becomes an essential characteristic of discipleship (the noun occurs once in the Septuagint, the verb not at all). In the New Testament we also find the word diakonia used in its original sense of waiting at table—the servant waits on his master (Lk. 17:8), Martha serves Jesus (Jn. 12:2)—and the word also occurs in its extended meaning of preparing meals and caring for the bodily needs of others (cf. Lk. 10:40; Acts 6:1; Mk. 1:31 par.; Mt. 4:11). In later Judaism we can find traces of the idea that service, and especially waiting at table, was something beneath the dignity of an ordinary person. At all events the very concrete secular sense of the word reveals what a tremendous impact it must have had not only on the Greeks but on all normal thinking people, when Jesus proclaimed: "Let the greatest among you become as the youngest, and the leader as one who serves. For which is the greater, one who sits at table, or one who serves? Is it not the one who sits at table? But I am among you as one who serves" (Lk. 22:26 f.).

But it is clear that Jesus is not merely concerned about service at table, or care for the bodily needs of others, as suggested by the wider use of the word (cf. Lk. 8:3; Mk. 15:41; Mt. 24:45); nor is he simply concerned about certain special acts of love, which can also be summed up in the word diakonia (cf. Mt. 25:42–44). His fundamental concern is with living for others (cf. Mk. 9:35; 10:43–45; Mt. 20:26–28); and the origins of the word diakonia, in contrast to other similar verbs, indicates that a completely personal service is implied. This is an essential element in being a disciple: a man is a disciple of Jesus through service of his fellow men. In contrast to all the concepts of office in existence at the time, Jesus chose and emphasized this new conception of service. Six times in the synoptic gospels we find the saying about service, quoted above from Luke, and with only very slight variations; it is evident what a strong impression on the disciples this particular saying must have made.

This is a point where something distinctively Christian can be discerned, as the choice of a completely new word shows.

The consequences are enormous. Is it possible for there to be among the followers of Jesus any kind of office which is based on *law* and *power* and which corresponds to the office of secular potentates? "And they came to Capernaum; and when he was in the house he asked them, 'What were you discussing on the way?' But they were silent; for on the way they had discussed with one another who was the greatest. And he sat down and called the twelve; and he said to them: 'If anyone would be first, he must be last of all and servant of all'" (Mk. 9:33–35). "You know that those who are supposed to rule over the Gentiles lord it over them, and their great men exercise authority over them. But it shall not be so among you; but whoever would be great among you must be your servant, and whoever would be first among you must be slave of all. For the Son of man also came not to be served but to serve, and to give his life as a ransom for many" (10:42–45).

Or can there be among the followers of Jesus any kind of office which is based on *knowledge* and *dignity,* and corresponds to the office of the scribes? "The scribes and the Pharisees sit on Moses' seat; so practise and observe whatever they tell you, but not what they do; for they preach, but do not practise. They bind heavy burdens, hard to bear, and lay them on men's shoulders; but they themselves will not move them with their finger. They do all their deeds to be seen by men; for they make their phylacteries broad and their fringes long, and they love the place of honour at feasts and the best seats in the synagogues, and salutations in the market places, and being called rabbi by men. But you are not to be called rabbi, for you have one teacher, and you are all brethren. And call no man your father on earth, for you have *one* Father, who is in heaven. Neither be called masters, for you have *one* master, the Christ. He who is greatest among you shall be your servant; whoever exalts himself will be humbled, and whoever humbles himself will be exalted" (Mt. 23:2–12).

It is not law or power, knowledge or dignity but *service* which is the basis of discipleship. The model for the disciples in their following of Christ is therefore not the secular ruler and not the learned scribe, nor even the priest who stands above his people (Jesus, remarkably enough, never once takes him as an example; cf. Hebrews); the only valid model is that of the man who serves at table: "But I am among you as one who serves (at table)" (Lk. 22:27). This attitude must be correctly understood. It is not just a question of a voluntary external self-abasement, as practised on certain days of the year by the leaders of some religious communities, but a total existence in a life and death of service for others, as prefigured by the service of Jesus himself (Mk. 10:45; Mt. 20:28) and as demanded by Jesus himself of those who would serve him: "He who loves his life loses it, and he who hates his life in this world will keep it for eternal life. If anyone serves me, he must follow me; and where I am, there shall my servant be also; if anyone serves me, the Father will honour him" (Jn. 12:25 f.).

The root and the goal of service is *love*. Service occurs out of love for others, as John indicates, with unparalleled emphasis, in the story which stands in his gospel in the place of an account of the Last Supper: the washing of the feet, which employs the imagery of waiting at table (13:1–17). In this way Jesus "having loved his own who were in the world, he loved them to the end". This is why he rises from supper, girds himself with a towel, and washes the disciples' feet as they lie at table. After doing this, putting on his clothes again and resuming his place once more, he speaks thus to them: "Do you know what I have done to you? You call me Teacher and Lord; and you are right, for so I am. If I then, your Lord and Teacher, have washed your feet, you also ought to wash one another's feet. For I have given you an example, that you also should do as I have done to you. Truly, truly, I say to you, a servant is not greater than his master; nor is he who is sent greater than he who sent him. If you know these things, blessed are you if you do them" (Jn. 13:12–17).

The putting together of the gospels shows that the young community recognized the central importance of Jesus' command. Not merely discipleship itself, but certain functions in the community are regarded as services. The word diakonia covers such actions of love as the collection and handing over of monies for the community at Jerusalem (cf. II Cor.

8:1–6 and 19 f.; 9:1 and 12 f.; Rom. 15:25 and 30 f.; Acts 11:29 f.; 12:25); the personal help given to the apostle by Timothy and Erastus (cf. Acts 19:22), Onesimus (Philem. 13) and Onesiphorus (cf. II Tim. 1:18); the general service of love which the Christians as saints show to one another (cf. I Cor. 16:15; Heb. 6:10; Rev. 2:19). Every action which helps towards the building up of the community is basically a service: "As each has received a gift, employ it for one another, as good stewards of God's varied grace; whoever speaks, as one who utters oracles of God; whoever renders service, as one who renders it by the strength which God supplies; in order that in everything God may be glorified through Jesus Christ" (I Pet. 4:10 f.). Service to others is not a matter of self-righteous good works; it is something that must be derived from God and directed towards God—each according to the call he has received, the charism given to him (cf. I Cor. 12:11; cf. 7).

This brings us back to a theme dealt with in a long section above, in connection with the Church as a spiritaul creation[29] and which we must now extend in another direction: the charismatic structure of the Church. A specific aspect of this charismatic structure, which we may call the special *diaconal* structure, is our next theme.

2. THE DIACONAL STRUCTURE

The Church, being a fellowship of gifts of the spirit, is also a fellowship of different ministries. Charisma and diakonia are correlative concepts. Diakonia is rooted in charisma, since every diakonia in the Church presupposes the call of God. Charisma leads to diakonia since every charisma in the Church only finds fulfilment in service. Where there is a real charisma, there will be responsible service for the edification and benefit of the community: "To each is given the manifestation of the Spirit for the common good" (I Cor. 12:7).

The variety of ministry in the Church is as unlimited as the variety of charisms in the Church: "As each has received a

[29] Cf. C II, 3.

gift, employ it for one another" (I Pet. 4:10). But whereas some gifts, like those of exhorting, giving aid, faith, the utterance of wisdom and of knowledge and the discernment of spirits, are more private gifts and virtues given by God, which must be employed in the service of others and practised as opportunity presents itself, there are other gifts—of apostles, prophets, teachers, evangelists, deacons, elders, bishops, pastors—which are public functions within the community ordained by God and which must be exercised regularly and constantly. Generally in the New Testament the gifts and their effects are mentioned first of all, and persons are referred to afterwards. The persons can be named because obviously there is no question of a vocation which comes and goes uncertainly; it remains constant and remains constantly associated with specific persons, who are then "appointed" to the Church as apostles, prophets, etc. (cf. Eph. 4:11). This second type of *especial* charismatic ministry is what constitutes the diaconal structure, a particular side and aspect of the general and fundamental charismatic structure of the Church.[30]

"For the nurturing and constant growth of the People of God, Christ the Lord instituted in His Church a variety of ministries, which work for the good of the whole body. For those ministers who are endowed with sacred power are servants of their brethren, so that all who are of the People of God, and therefore enjoy a true Christian dignity, can work toward a common goal freely and in an orderly way, and arrive at salvation". (CE 18).

[30] See the literature on the apostolate cited at D IV which is often relevant to the diaconal structure as a whole, and also the following more recent monographs: P. H. Menoud, *L'Eglise et le ministère selon le NT*, Neuchâtel 1949; H. von Campenhausen, *Kirchliches Amt und geistliche Vollmacht in den ersten drei Jahrhunderten*, Tübingen 1953; H. Schlier, *Die Zeit der Kirche*, Freiburg 1955, 129–147; G. Dix, *Le ministère dans l'église ancienne*, Neuchâtel–Paris 1955; E. Schweizer, *Church Order in the NT*, London–Naperville, Illinois 1961; E. Käsemann, *Essays on NT themes*, London 1964, 63–94; H. U. von Balthasar, *Sponsa Verbi*, Einsiedeln 1960, 80–147; for an historical and systematic bibliography on ecclesiastical office see *Structures* VI, 95–190, and also the relevant encyclopaedia articles.

(*a*) In the light of Pauline theology especially, it may be said of the diaconal structure of the Church:

1. The permanent ministries in the community have the same characteristics as charisms, inasmuch as in each case God calls a particular individual to a special ministry in the community and at the same time gives him the power to fulfil that ministry. It is God himself who creates and arouses a vocation through the Holy Spirit; each vocation is a manifestation, individuation and concretization of the one Charism of Jesus Christ, who is himself *the* apostle, prophet, teacher, evangelist, pastor and deacon. These ministries are there for the community, and the more they are of service to others the higher they will be; this kind of ministry is to be performed not only within the Church, but also on the frontier between the Church and the world. To the problem of the ordering of these charisms we can again apply the fundamental principles: to each his own; with all for all; obedience of all to the one Lord.

2. The New Testament offers no fixed and exclusive catalogue of these permanent ministries within the community which would be valid for all communities. For one thing there is no clear boundary between the permanent public ministries in the community and other charisms; the distinction between the two seems to be fairly fluid in some areas, as in the gifts of leadership (elders, superiors, pastors) and of giving aid (givers of alms, tenders of the sick, deacons). Moreover, the distinctions are not clearly drawn even within the permanent ministries in the community; the prophet can also be a teacher, the teacher a prophet; Paul himself embodies several ministries. Finally, the different lists of charisms (I Cor. 12:28–31; Rom. 12:6–8; Eph. 4:11) do not agree. From all this we may conclude that although each member of the community, in all places and at all times, will receive his own special call, there is no way of knowing in advance what ministries God in the freedom of his grace will see fit to call upon in specific places at specific times.

3. In the New Testament the foremost ministries are those of preaching: the ministry of reconciling, in which the word of reconciliation is proclaimed (II Cor. 5:18 f.; cf. Acts 6:4: the ministry of the word). The most fundamental of all

ministries is that of the apostles, whose role is always expressed in terms of ministry and ministering (cf. Rom. 11:13; II Cor. 3:6; 4:1; 6:3 f.; 11:8 and 23; Acts 1:17 and 25; 20:24; 21:19; I Tim. 1:12; cf. also the ministry of an evangelist: II Tim. 4:5). Besides the apostles two other groups are emphasized by Paul: "second prophets, third teachers" (I Cor. 12:28).

Prophets[31] and prophetesses (I Cor. 11:5; Acts 21:9) existed not only in the Pauline communities (cf. especially I Cor. 12–14) and at Rome, but also in Palestine and Syria (Synoptics, Acts) and Asia Minor (Revelation). In the list of charisms they are always mentioned immediately after the apostles and before any other ministries; alongside the apostles they are the most important members of the community. Thus the Church is not only built upon the apostles, but "upon the foundation of the apostles and prophets" (Eph. 2:20). Through them the Spirit expresses himself directly. The New Testament prophet is not characterized by visions or auditions, but by the word which God has given him to proclaim. They work as preachers of the word in the community, in a sober and level-headed manner, not like ecstatic visionaries who seem out of contact with the world around them. Since they are not beside themselves with ecstasy (Paul distinguishes prophecy very clearly from glossolaly), they can interrupt their prophetic utterance at any point or simply remain silent, as soon as another prophet has a revelation (cf. I Cor. 14:29–33). Freely, responsibly, and comprehensibly they preach Christ and light the way of individuals and the community in the present and in the future. They are appointed and empowered by God; not chosen or commissioned by the community, but called by the Spirit. They represent no hierarchical institution (cf. I Cor. 14:1 and 31–40; 11:15), but at the same time they are not simply an expression of the priesthood of all believers. Even though all believers are filled with the spirit of prophecy, not all are in the strict sense prophets (cf. I Cor. 12:6–10). The prophets are a relatively narrow circle of people within the community, and probably only in exceptional circumstances (as in Acts and in later times) did they become

[31] On the prophets in the NT see esp. the art. by H. Krämer, R. Rendtorff, R. Meyer and G. Friedrich, in ThW, VI, 833–836; also the art. in LThK (J. Schmid), RGG (P. Vielhauser and E. Fascher), as well as the OT and NT theologies; of the newer monographs see: O. T. Allis, *Prophecy and the Church*, London–Nutley, N.J. 1945.

preachers journeying from place to place. Although their work of preaching is very much like that of the apostles, they do not have the same powers as the apostles. The apostle is an original witness and messenger who has authority *vis-à-vis* the community, even though he too is subject to the authority of the message he preaches. The prophet on the other hand is subject to the authority of the apostle. He has authority *in* the community, as a member of the community in communion with the other prophets who have the same authority. He is not responsible for the original spreading of the faith. He is limited by the original apostolic witness, given once and for all, and is to speak by analogy, in proportion to his faith (Rom. 12:6), that is, in agreement with the faith laid down by the apostle. While the community is not in a position to judge the apostle, it has the right and duty of discerning between spirits. And even though the gift of distinguishing between spirits is a gift accorded to individuals (I Cor. 12:10), the whole community remains responsible for testing the genuineness of spirits (I Cor. 14:29–33; I Thess. 5:21), "to see whether they are of God" (I Jn. 4:1). Prophetic witness is only genuine when it is witness to Christ (I Cor. 12:3; cf. I Jn. 4:2 f.). At the same time, as Matthew in particular points out (7:15–23), false prophets can be recognized by their general conduct. The role of prophecy is the edification of the community by words of encouragement and consolation, by the preaching of repentance and of promise (I Cor. 14:3 f. and 12).

Teachers[32] are variously mentioned together with prophets. In I Corinthians they are expressly mentioned in the third place after apostles and prophets (12:28 f.; cf. Acts 13:1; Eph. 4:11). They work within a community (I Cor. 14:26; Rom. 12:7; cf. I Tim. 2:11 f.). They too belong to the important preachers of the word in the community. They hand on and interpret the message of Christ, and interpret the Old Testament in the light of the young Church. In the hellenistic synagogue communities the rabbis had a similar function; from the time of later Judaism the teachers were those who showed the way of God from the Torah and maintained the tradition of scriptural readings and teaching from generation to generation. Like the prophets the teachers base their words on the original testimony of the apostles and speak of the present and the future of the community. They too have authority through the particular spiritual gift accorded to them. But, more than the prophets, they are indebted to tradition. Their teaching is not like that of the prophets founded directly on revelation (I Cor.

[32] Cf. esp. K. H. Rengstorf, in ThW II, 162.

14:26–30), but on tradition. Prophecy is addressed to a particular concrete situation, "didascalia" is a kind of instruction. Rather than proclaiming intuitively, the teachers expound systematically. Their work is only meaningful on the basis laid by the apostles and prophets. In this context we should note the "evangelists", who are mentioned in Ephesians (4:11) before "pastors" and "teachers" and clearly have become the leading figures of the mission in the place of the apostles.

The teachers became indispensable in the post-apostolic age, although they were considerably different in form. Immediately after the end of the apostolic period the prophets are still held in the highest esteem. The Didache calls them "high priests" (13:3), to whom the first-fruits of the vinepress and threshing-floor, of cattle and sheep, of every baking and of every piece of cloth, indeed of all possessions, are due, so that they are free from all material needs (13:1–7); caring for the prophets appears to be even more important than caring for the poor (cf. 13:4). Even though false prophets are to be reckoned with (11:8–12; 16), prophets are not to be tested and judged when they speak in the spirit (11:7). Here we have a very high estimation of prophets not found in Paul. The reason may well lie in the fact that by this time there were no longer prophets in all communities (cf. 13:4), and therefore journeying prophets were increasing (cf. 13:1). But prophets still celebrate the eucharist (10:7), and the form and length of eucharistic prayers as laid down for other Christians (cf. 9:1–7; 10:1–6) is not binding on them: "Prophets should be allowed to give thanks (εὐχαριστεῖν) as much as they wish" (10:7). The eucharist is to be celebrated on the Lord's day (14:1–3). Where there are not sufficient prophets and teachers in a community, the community is to choose bishops and deacons, who will take over the functions of prophets and teachers: "Choose bishops and deacons, worthy of the Lord, merciful, unselfish, faithful and well-tried men; for they *too* perform for you the holy ministry (λειτουργοῦσιν τὴν λειτουργίαν) of prophets and teachers" (15:1). Apparently the changeover from prophets and teachers to the new holders of office did not occur without difficulties; at all events the admonition follows: "but do not for this reason think little of them (the bishops and deacons); for they are worthy of honour along with the prophets and teachers" (15:2).

With time the prophets increasingly lost this specially privileged position, largely because of anxiety about the numerous pseudo-prophets, and the growing importance of other ministries. Irenaeus complains that pseudo-prophets are ousting true prophets from the

Church.[33] Instead of the New Testament prophets, it is the prophets of the Old Testament who are increasingly referred to and cited. In the second century there are still people called prophets, but by the third century they have disappeared as a particular group within the communities. With the struggle against Gnosticism and the enthusiasm of Montanism and its prophets, prophecy within the community came to an end. If we look at the Churches of the New Testament we can see what a very perceptible weakening and impoverishment of the charismatic structure of the Church in general and of the diaconal structure in particular their disappearance signified.

4. In addition to ministries of preaching, there are also ministries of welfare and of guidance. For Paul the community is a communion of charisms, but this does not mean disorder, in which each can do as he chooses. While there is clearly no ruling class with absolute power and authority in his communities, there is certainly a hierarchy dictated by the different ministries which members of the community performed. There are in the communities those who "labour" and "toil" (κοπιουντες): not only Paul himself, working with his own hands (I Cor. 4:12), and performing all his apostolic work (I Cor. 15:10; II Cor. 6:5; 11:23 and 27; Gal. 4:11; Phil. 2:16; Col. 1:29), but other fellow workers in the communities, whom Paul especially recommends: "Mary, who has worked hard among you" (Rom. 16:6), Tryphaena, Tryphosa and Persis (Rom. 16:12; cf. also I Cor. 3:8; 15:58; II Cor. 10:15), men and women.

These references imply at least in part permanent ministries in the community. This is especially true of those who are referred to as being "over" the community (προϊστάμενοι) (I Thess. 5:12; cf. Rom. 12:8). These have a charism which is at least one of guidance, probably in fact a kind of leadership. Paul is probably referring to a permanent ministry in the community when he says that those who give aid (JB: officials, cf. AV "ruleth") should do so zealously (Rom. 12:8). At all events Paul commands: "We beseech you, brethren, to respect those who labour among you and are over you in the Lord (or: care for you in the Lord) and admonish you, and to esteem them very highly in love because

33 Irenaeus, *Adv. haer.* III, 11.9; PG 7, 891.

of their work. Be at peace among yourselves" (I Thess. 5:12 f.). He seems to refer here to people who consistently and especially care for the community, although no form of appointing them is apparent. Paul also calls for submission to *all* who do special work in the community: "I urge you to be subject to such men and to every fellow worker and labourer" (I Cor. 16:16). In the first part of the sentence quoted here Paul refers not to particular officials, but to the "household of Stephanas", who were the "first converts (first-fruits) in Achaia" and "have devoted themselves to the service of the saints" (I Cor. 16:15). The "household of Stephanas" is an entire family, who have taken on themselves a particular ministry in the community and can hence expect the submission of the other members of the community (an individual can also be a "first-fruit", e.g. Epaenetus, "who was the first convert in Asia for Christ", Rom. 16:5). The first Christians in any place appear to have at least an authority of precedence, if they take on themselves a particular ministry towards the community and assume especial burdens (for example using their house as a place for the community to meet, catering for the members of the community, etc.). These were not necessarily "first converts"; in Rome there were Aquila and Prisca, the "fellow workers" of Paul (Rom. 16:3), there was Phoebe, "deaconess of the Church at Cenchreae" (Rom. 16:1) and Archippus, who had received a ministry in the Lord (Col. 4:17).

In all these cases the ministries referred to are more or less permanent ones, which were assumed for life or at any rate for long periods; but about their substance and extent there is scarcely any reliable historical evidence. They are what Paul refers to in his list of charisms as "helpers" (ἀντιλήμψεις) and "administrators" (κυβερνήσεις, the art of steering or guiding)—but these terms are imprecise. It is clear that these names for functions within the community had not yet developed into general titles or indications of role, like those of apostles, prophets and teachers. Only later did technical terms for these functions spring up, probably at first limited in currency to local communities. In one of the last letters of Paul, in the opening address of Philippians (1:1)—and this is the only undisputedly genuine Pauline evidence for these terms—

the following names are used: "to all the saints in Christ Jesus who are at Philippi, with the bishops (ἐπίσκοποι) and deacons (διάκονοι)". It is highly improbable that this is an interpolation. These are clearly quite specific and permanent ministries which Paul is honouring by mentioning in his opening address. Although his is a fundamentally charismatic conception of the Church, Paul did not need to contest any further development of the Church's constitution. The ministries of these bishops and deacons were without any doubt gifts given by the Spirit, as far as he was concerned. However, it is almost impossible to determine precisely and certainly what the original functions of these two groups would have been.

1. *Bishops* (literally "overseers")[34]: The word *episkopos* is entirely secular in origin. In non-Christian usage it meant an official overseer, whether of a town, of subjects, or of slaves; it was used for officials of a community or of a group, for overseers on a building site, for the officials of religious communities (especially those responsible for administering wealth), for other kinds of functionaries like market superintendents and watchmen, finally for journeying preachers and for gods in their roles as tutelary divinities of certain people, towns or treaties. The word was used in much too various and vague a way to allow us to draw any conclusions from it as to its original use in the Christian sphere. In the Christian communities it must have designated some sort of supervisory or administrative office, but scarcely, as has often been maintained, any kind of economic function; otherwise it would not have been necessary for individual Christians in Corinth to set aside each his own contribution to the collection for Jerusalem (cf. I Cor. 16:2; II Cor. 9:3 f.), and both there and in Philippi it would not have been necessary to elect particular men to carry the gifts to Jerusalem (cf. I Cor. 16:3; II Cor. 8:19 and 23). The possibility that the ministry of overseer was a direct borrowing from the leaders in Jewish synagogues, or from the overseers referred to in the Damascus Document (9:18; 13:7–21; cf. 14:8–12) and in the Qumran texts (1 QS 6:12 and 14 and 20), can be refuted not only on account of the numerous differences between them, but on the grounds that these "bishops" at first existed only in the Greek communities. Apparently in these communities the common Greek

34 Cf. H. W. Beyer–H. Karpp, in RAC II, 394–407; J. Gewiess, in LThK II, 491 f.; H. W. Beyer, in ThW II, 604–619.

terms for various officials were taken over and given a new meaning in the context of the community. In any case the word *episkopos* only occurs five times in the whole New Testament; once referring to Christ (I Pet. 2:25); once in Paul (Phil. 1:1); once in Acts (20:28) and then at I Timothy 3:2 and Titus 1:7. The first evidence for the word as a ministry of the community shows that the word was used in the plural; there seem to have been a number of "bishops" in the communities without apparent distinction of rank. The term presumably is parallel to that of "superiors", those who are "over" the community, referred to above, and also to the term—only used in Ephesians (4:11) in the sense of a leader of the community—"pastor", although this was probably not a precise description of a ministry. But rare though it was, and imprecise though it was, the concept of *"episkopos"* was to have a significant history, to which we shall return.

2. *Deacons* (literally "servants"):[35] We possess no definite evidence for a Christian diaconate older than Philippians 1:1. What is described here would seem to be a definite and permanent ministry in the community, associated with and evidently inferior to that of the "bishops". It is probable that Phoebe in Cenchreae was a deaconess (Rom. 16:1). It is uncertain how far we should associate the "helpers" of I Corinthians 12:18 or "those who labour among you" (I Thess. 5:12) with a diaconate. If the ministries of apostles, prophets and teachers can be traced back to Jewish tradition in particular, the "bishops" and "deacons" seem to have been inspired more by hellenistic tradition. The commonly used Greek word διάκονος expresses the idea of service, though not that of slavery. Since a *"diakon"* in the technical sense was probably originally a man who served at table at Greek cultic ceremonies, and later a functionary responsible for catering at communal meals, the Christian *"diakon"* may be supposed originally to have fulfilled a similar role (the qualities required of a deacon mentioned in I Timothy 3:8 f. would seem to confirm this). The account of the appointing of the "seven" in Acts 6:1–6 does not by any means suggest that they were deacons in the same sense as Philippians 1:1 or I Timothy 3:8–13. *"Diakonia"*, as we have seen, is a central and frequently recurring concept in the New Testament, but on the whole it is used in a general sense, rather than

---

[35] Cf. T. Klauser, in RAC III, 888–909; J. Gewiess–J. A. Jungmann–K. Rahner, in LThK III, 318–322; K. H. Rengstorf, in ThW II, 138–162. For a detailed study of the diaconate, its history and present state, its theology and practical opportunities for its renewal, see the volume by K. Rahner and H. Vorgrimler, *Diaconia in Christo,* Freiburg–Basle–Vienna 1962.

being limited to a particular office. Moreover Luke seems purposely to have avoided the expression "deacon", which he must surely have known, not only in the above passage (Acts 6:1–6) but also more strikingly when speaking about Philip (Acts 21:8). The seven seem to have had a much greater authority than the deacons mentioned by Paul; in addition to caring for the poor, they preach and baptize (cf. Acts 8:16 and 40). Their greater authority is attested to by the ceremonious appointing of them, and it seems more reasonable to identify them with the later presbyters or elders than with the deacons. It is evident that we know nothing very precise about the place and circumstances of the founding of the diaconate, and cannot be certain about its original function. The only thing we can assert with conviction is that deacons existed in the Pauline communities, and numbered among their tasks were those of caring for the poor and attending to material things.

For Paul it is clearly unimportant how the various members of the community came to take on various ministries; Stephanas and his family, for example, had voluntarily offered their services, while Titus was chosen by the communities to be the fellow worker of Paul (II Cor. 8:9). Nowhere is there any suggestion that particular officials in the communities made formal appointments to such ministries. For Paul what is really important is the call of God, the charism of the Spirit. The community cannot summon up charisms of itself; they are granted to it, and the community can only test them and recognize them as the true workings of the Spirit. It is from their charisms, not from the community and not from the apostle, not even from their own decision, that the individuals responsible for all these varied ministries derive their authority. This call, this charism is recognized for what it is by the community through being exercised, and exercised in the right spirit. Submission is due to those who labour, not because of their appointment to a particular ministry, but because they are actually seen to perform that ministry. Anyone who is qualified for a particular ministry—as prophet, teacher, helper, superior, bishop or deacon, etc.—and who performs it properly, has received the call of God and the charism of the Spirit. Authority in the community is derived not from the holding of a certain rank, not

from a special tradition, not from old age or long membership of the community but from the performance of a ministry in the Spirit. The obedience of all is due to God, Christ,
the Spirit; only a limited, and never a unilateral obedience is
due to other men in the community. The consequence of the
obedience of all to God, Christ and the Spirit is voluntary and
mutual submission, the voluntary ministry of all to all, voluntary obedience to the different charisms of others. It is the
same Spirit who acts through all the various spiritual gifts, the
same Lord who acts through all the different ministries, the
same God who acts through all kinds of works, inspiring
them all in each individual (cf. I Cor. 12:4–6). The whole
life of the Church is a vital interaction of spiritual gifts and
services; order and peace are to reign in it, yet without
quenching the Spirit at all; this is the ecclesiastical order envisaged by Paul, and its fundaments can still be found, even
though the stresses may be differently placed, in Hebrews, the
Epistle to Barnabas and, as we have already seen, the
Didache.

But this imposing blueprint of the Church, for all its Christian radicalism, poses not a few problems. In the first place
there are a number of less important problems associated with
the "helpers" and "administrators" mentioned at I Corinthians
12:28. We note that they are mentioned a long way behind
apostles, prophets and teachers, next to last, just before those
who have the gift of glossolaly, which is regarded as the least
important gift. We also note that in the ensuing rhetorical
questions (12:29) as to whether all members of the community are apostles, prophets and teachers, and have this, that or
the other gift, it is precisely the "helpers" and "administrators" who are not listed (could it be that these are tasks
which indeed *anyone* could fulfil?). Finally we note that these
ministries (cf. those who give aid, Rom. 12:8) are mentioned among a number of gifts which for Paul are all given
by the freedom of the Spirit, and are not the result of a particular appointment. But the whole area only becomes fundamentally problematic when we draw the following conclusions from the letters generally acknowledged as being by
Paul:

1. There appears to have been no monarchical episcopate

in the Pauline communities at all; the only evidence for an episcopate in the Pauline letters (Phil. 1:1) speaks of "bishops" in the plural (as also Acts; contrast the pastoral letters).

2. There appears to have been no office of presbyter in the Pauline communities; neither presbyters nor presbyterium are mentioned once in Paul's letters (contrast Acts and the pastoral letters).

3. There appears to have been no ordination in the Pauline communities; there is no mention anywhere in Paul's letters of laying on of hands (again, contrast Acts and the pastoral letters).

However much Paul may have envisaged further development in the Churches (perhaps along the lines suggested in Philippians 1:1), he would certainly have objected to any suggestion that the organization of his Churches was incomplete or provisional. He would have maintained that the contrary was true, for these communities were filled with the Spirit and his gifts, and hence possessed—in the order of love —all that was necessary. For Paul the community in Corinth was already, in its own fashion, a complete and fully equipped Church. It was to this community that he wrote: ". . . in every way you were enriched in him (Christ) . . . so that you are not lacking in any spiritual gift" (I Cor. 1:5 and 7); ". . . you excel in everything . . ." (II Cor. 8:7); "God is able to provide you with every blessing in abundance, so that you may always have enough of everything" (II Cor. 9:8).

The problem becomes finally acute when we take a look at the Church which we know so much more about than any other of the New Testament Churches: the Church of Corinth. We have a reasonably good idea as to how preaching and the Lord's Supper were organized, as to what sort of ecclesiastical discipline and order there was. We know from Paul's lists exactly how many different kinds of ministries there were at Corinth—apostles, prophets, teachers, and so on. But there were no "bishops", deacons or elders. Moreover, when it is a question of restoring order in matters of preaching, the Lord's Supper and Church discipline, Paul never addresses himself to a single official or a single group of officials, responsible for all the community. He addresses himself throughout to *all* and at the same time to *each* individual. With regard to the irregularities that had occurred at the Lord's Supper, where the writer of the pastoral letters might have said to the Corinth community something like: "Timothy is to give the sign for the celebration to begin" (or perhaps even: "Timothy is to celebrate the Lord's Supper"?), what Paul in fact says to the Corinthians is: "When you come together to eat, wait for one another" (I Cor. 11:33). With regard to the confusion which had arisen through several members of the community preaching during worship, where the writer of the pastoral letters might have said something like: "Titus is to decide who shall speak" (or even perhaps: "Titus is to give the sermon"?), what Paul actually says is: ". . . let there be only two or at most three, and each in turn . . . you can all prophesy one by one" (14:27 and 31). And with regard to the incestuous man, where the writer of the pastoral letters might have said something like: "The elders are to exclude him from the community" (or even perhaps: "Let the bishop excommunicate him"?), what Paul actually says, addressing himself to the whole community is: "When you are assembled, and my spirit is present, with the power of our Lord Jesus, you are to deliver this man to Satan. . . . Drive out the wicked person from among you" (5:4 f. and 13).

All this is much more than an *argumentum e silentio*. The burden of proof lies with those who wish to assert that there existed in the Corinth community, in Paul's time, an office of leadership, whether elders or the later monarchic kind of episcopate. Faced with disorders which threatened the very existence of the Corinth community, in preaching (I Cor. 14), the Lord's Supper (11) and in Church discipline (5); faced, moreover, with divisions in the community (1–3) with regard to the settling of disputes within the community (6), and with regard to the collection for Jerusalem (16; II Cor. 8–9)—Paul would have had to address himself to the responsible leaders of the community, if such had existed. But here there is evidently no one to whom Paul could say: "Command and teach these things" (I Tim. 4:11), not even in connection with the Lord's Supper. The community at Corinth to which Paul wrote was a fellowship of charismatic Christians, in which *each* had a responsibility, a specific responsibility according to his charism, and in which *no one* (apart from the apostle) carried an exclusive responsibility for all the rest.

The situation outlined above is not only true of the Pauline communities (and in a limited sense also of those mentioned in the Didache, etc.): there is no evidence anywhere of a

monarchic episcopate existing in the primitive period, not
even in Acts (on the contrary, cf. Acts 20:28); and the
community at Antioch which was not founded by Paul, is led
not by bishops or elders but by prophets and teachers (the
basic facts in Luke's account, though not the detail with
which he embroiders it, are almost certainly historically reliable) (cf. Acts 11:27; 13:1–3; 21:10 f.). There is therefore
no basis whatever for the hypothesis that Paul deliberately instituted a system different from that of Jerusalem and the
Palestinian communities. Paul seems rather to have taken
over a Church system already familiar in Antioch. And even
the Church in Rome, which again was not founded by Paul,
seems to have been like Antioch and Corinth, at the time of
the letter to the Romans at any rate, in having no order of
elders or "bishops" who were specially appointed. At all
events Romans, despite its numerous personal greetings, is
significantly silent about such officials. The question remains
as to how the organization of the Pauline and the Gentile
Christian communities in general differed from those in
Jerusalem and Palestine.

(*b*) It would be wrong to suppose that the Pauline
Church system was originally general and widespread, and
that the notion of elders was only introduced into the
Churches later. The remarkable thing is that neither of the
two basic systems we find in the primitive Churches can be
regarded as *the* original one. Both kinds, in outline at least,
seem to have co-existed from the very beginning. While
bishops and deacons probably originated in the Gentile Christian communities, the office of elder comes from a Judaeo-
Christian, indeed from Jewish tradition.

"*Presbyter*" (*zekenim,* elder)[36] was the name for the man who
led each Jewish community—an age-old office. There are no accounts extant of the institution or composition of the councils of
elders. In all the traditional stories of the Old Testament their existence is taken for granted, so that they must have originated long

[36] As well as the general works on ecclesiastical office already
cited, see W. Michaelis, *Das Ältestenamt in der christlichen
Gemeinde,* Bern 1953; G. Bornkamm, in ThW VI, 651–683;
H. Haag, *Bibellexikon* 54–56.

before the settlement and the gathering of the tribes, as part of the
most ancient patriarchal tribal laws. After the entry into the promised land there were councils of elders with varying degrees of
influence in different localities, acting as local authorities; in the
post-exilic period they were more a familial aristocracy. In
Jerusalem the elders were, after the high-priests and scribes, the
third—and actually least influential—group in what became the
supreme council (συνέδριον), which is occasionally referred
to as πρεσβυτέριον in the New Testament (Lk. 22:66; Acts
22:5). The Qumran sects had elders who were subordinated to the
priests (I QS 6:8–10), and in Jewish colonies the administration
of communities or at least of the synagogue was under the supervi-
sion of elders. There was thus good reason for the primitive communities to organize themselves along the same lines. The Jewish
system with which the young community was so familiar would
also have suggested the idea that their own elders (presbyters)
were the representatives of tradition and responsible for the ordering of the community.

Although Acts seems to suggest that all the Christian communities had elders, references to them in Acts are strikingly late ones.
Nothing is reported about the appointing of elders, unless the
"seven" (6:1–7) were elders—and we can only presume that they
were not. They make their appearance suddenly in connection with
the bringing of the collection to Jerusalem (11:30), and at the
apostolic council (15:2 and 4 and 6 and 22 f.; 16:4), and then
again at the time of Paul's arrival in Jerusalem and his dispute
with James (21:18). Although in other New Testament passages
(cf. Acts 2:17; I Tim. 5:1 f.; Jn. 8:9) the word "presbyter" can
refer to those who are literally "elder"—the boundary-line is not
always precise—in these passages at any rate the word indicates the
holders of a particular office, analogous with the elders of the
supreme council, and the elders who had authority in local communities. The elders of the primitive Church sometimes appear in
Acts as representatives of the local Jerusalem community, after the
manner of the elders of a synagogue (11:30; gathered round
James at 21:18), and sometimes, together with the apostles, as the
highest court of authority for the whole Church, like the sanhedrin
(15:4; 16:4). It is possible that the local elders at Jerusalem had already extended their authority, in the Judaeo-Christian tradition
familiar to Luke, into a teaching and juridical authority binding on
the whole Church.

We cannot be historically certain whether or not a college
of elders, with at first local and then general authority

throughout the Church, existed in Jerusalem before the departure of Peter and the growing Judaization of the primitive community under James (cf. Acts 21:17–26). Nor can we be certain how far the development of a college of elders is connected with the growing distance between the Church and its origins, with the disappearance of the twelve, with the development of communities, with the presence in the communities of older and well-tried members, and with the increasing danger of heresy. At all events Luke is making an unhistorical addition—either theologically conditioned, or based on a tradition which had developed in the meantime—when he maintains that Paul and Barnabas "appointed elders . . . in every Church" (Acts 14:23; cf. especially 20:17–35), for this is not borne out by the letters of Paul himself. In the first generation there were no presbyters in hellenistic territories, at any rate in the Pauline communities of Greece and Macedonia, nor was there originally any kind of ordination in these areas, something that also came from Judaeo-Christian and Jewish tradition. Ordination in the Christian communities is the giving of authority and commissioning of particular members for a particular service, effected by the laying-on of hands, which serves as a public legitimation of the minister and his endowing with the charism needed for his ministry. This does not apply to all ministries in the community; we hear nothing about the laying-on of hands as necessary for prophecy, healing, glossolaly and other charisms. It applies to the particular ministry of founding and guiding missionary Churches, and the ministry of helping in that work. These ministries correspond most closely to the special ministry of the apostles; just as they were called by the Lord himself, the elders are now called by men.

Ordination[37] is not mentioned in any of the Pauline letters, nor any kind of ritual for appointing people to office. But there are several references in Acts and in the pastoral letters to the giving of

[37] Cf. E. Lohse, *Die Ordination im Spätjudentum und im NT,* Göttingen 1951; idem, art. "Ordination" in RGG; see also the art. "Handauflegung" in LThK (R. Mayer–N. Adler) and in RGG (H. D. Wendland).

office by the laying-on of hands and prayer. The idea of ordination was presumably taken over from Judaism at more or less the same time as the idea of elders. The outstanding example of this in the Old Testament was Moses laying his hands on Joshua and handing on to him the spirit of wisdom he needed for his work (Dt. 34:9). It was according to this pattern that in later Judaism the scribes, who by the second or first century B.C. had developed into a recognized class, "ordained" their pupils. After long training and preparation they laid their hands on them publicly, empowering them with the rights and duties of a rabbi, and handing on to them in this way the spirit of wisdom. At the time when Acts was written down, at the latest, there must have been some kind of practice of ordination in the Judaeo-Christian Churches in Palestine. According to Acts 13:1–3 Barnabas and Paul received the laying-on of hands before being sent out; but Paul himself makes no reference to this ceremony, any more than he does to other occasions when supposedly he laid hands on others; for him his missionary ministry is not dependent on any human appointment. Yet Acts makes it evident that the practice of ordination actually existed at least in Luke's time; the ritual associated with ordination would have been the laying-on of hands with intercessory prayers, as described in the commissioning of the seven (Acts 6:3–6).

It is the pastoral letters which reveal a close association between ordination and charism. Here, by contrast with Paul's view of charisms, a special charism of office is communicated by the laying-on of hands; the other charisms are neglected in these letters. Timothy himself was ordained according to one account by the presbyterium (I Tim. 4:14), according to another by the apostle himself (II Tim. 1:6); the contradiction can presumably be explained by the fact that in the first case the writer is invoking a rule of the community, in the second he is referring to the apostolic testament of Paul (cf. also the disputed passage at I Tim. 5:22). There is no indication in the New Testament that the authority accorded by ordination was limited to certain particular offices, but we can safely assume that the laying-on of hands was practised with regard to other callings than those with which it is explicitly associated in the New Testament. At the same time, this does not allow us to assume that in primitive Christian communities all callings were established by the laying-on of hands. The foregoing examination has made it abundantly clear how impossible it is to take New Testament evidence about the ordering of individual communities as evidence of the practice in all communities.

The office of presbyter is summed up in Acts 20:28–35 as a pastoral ministry. The presbyters or elders have to safeguard apostolic tradition against false doctrines and to lead the communities. The function of the elders is described as to rule well and to labour in preaching and teaching (I Tim. 5:17). In I Peter 5:1–4 the office of presbyter is again seen as a pastoral ministry, although here it is emphasized that it is subordinate to the exemplary "chief Shepherd", Christ (5:4), to whom alone is reserved the title of *"episkopos"* (2:25). Here too the task of the elder is seen as tending God's flock (5:2), a guiding role which evidently included the administration of monies (cf. 5:2: a warning against acquisitiveness) and disciplinary authority (cf. 5:3: a warning against being domineering). In the letter of James, in which there is no mention of bishops and deacons, the "elders of the church" are able to heal by prayer and are summoned to anoint the sick (5:14)—a different and rather more charismatic conception of the role than for example in Judaism; the letter obviously comes from a hellenistic area of Judaeo-Christianity. Whether the presbyter referred to in the second and third letters of John is an elder standing outside the community (a prophet?), or whether he holds office within the community, has been disputed. The twenty-four presbyters seen by the prophetic seer of Revelations in heaven (4:4 and 10; 5:5 f. and 6 and 8 and 11 and 14; 7:11 and 13; 11:16; 14:3; 19:4) do not enable us to draw any conclusions about the organization of the earthly community to which the seer belonged; the Apocalypse makes no mention of bishops, deacons, teachers or ordinary elders, only of apostles and prophets. It is highly improbable that the "angels of the churches" mentioned in chapters 2 and 3 refer to leaders of these Churches.

At the end of the Pauline period the two fundamental conceptions of Church organization (which may briefly be termed the Pauline-Gentile and the Palestinian) begin to influence one another to a certain degree, or at least to interlock, so that the different titles become somewhat confused. The identification of the titles "bishop" and "presbyter" was inevitable in view of the similarity of the functions they fulfilled. There may also have been certain connections, although indirect, linguistic or factual ones, between the Greek *episkopoi,* the word *episkopos,* that is, an overseer in the secular sense, as used in the Septuagint (cf. Num. 31:14; Neh. 11:9–22; I Macc. 1:51) and the Jewish synagogue overseer, although he was never described as an *episkopos,* as well as the "overseer" (*paquid* or *mebaqqer*) in the Dead Sea sects (I QS 6:12–20; cf. Dam. 9:17–22; with reference to the elders I QS 6:8). In Acts the same men are described as presbyters and *episkopoi:* for instance, the elders of Ephesus are referred to as *episkopoi* (Acts 20:17 and 28). Luke must have introduced this word (which he otherwise never uses, but which was increasingly current in the Pauline communities, cf. Phil. 1:1), on purpose, in order to equate the *episkopoi* of the Gentile communities with the presbyters in the Judaeo-Christian communities, and thus in the interests of Church unity and warding off heresy to unite two different traditions. The same kind of reason probably leads him to say that Paul and Barnabas appointed presbyters in all communities (14:23).

In the same way, at Titus 1:7, the idea of presbyter is replaced by that of *episkopos* within the same coherent train of thought. In the first letter of Clement (cf. especially chapters 42:44 and 47), where the writer, invoking the idea of Old Testament priesthood and a markedly abstract notion of order, demands that the elders dismissed by the community at Corinth should be reinstated, the same persons are referred to as presbyters and as *episkopoi;* here all *episkopoi* are presbyters, but not all presbyters *episkopoi,* who alone are able to perform the ministry of sacrifice. The equating of the two titles indicates the influence on the notion of presbyters of that of *episkopoi* which presumably existed earlier in Rome. But even in the first letter of Clement, which refers to deacons as well as *episkopoi,* there is no trace of a monarchic episcopate. But certainly the function of presbyters and *episkopoi* alike is no longer to preserve the apostolic tradition; the institution as such becomes a fundamental element of the apostolic tradition. It is only in the pastoral letters that we find the beginnings of the development towards a monarchic episcopate. Although here again the functions of the two offices are equated and the two terms are parallel (cf. Tit.

1:5–8), it is noticeable that the word *"episkopos"* is used throughout in the singular, while the presbyters together form a college.

This is where we can see the development beginning, in which terms originally used in different areas become largely identical and begin to take on different qualities within one and the same area. Different and local names for more or less the same officers and officials now become different and universal names for more or less different offices and officials. This complex development, which took place differently in different areas, and which finally ended as the modern view of the *episkopos* or bishop, went through three essential phases.[38]

1. Instead of prophets, teachers and other charismatic ministries, the *episkopoi* (or presbyter-*episkopoi*) gradually established themselves as the *chief and eventually sole leaders of the community*. We have seen what a primary role was accorded, in the Pauline communities but also in Antioch and Jerusalem, to apostles, prophets, teachers and pneumatic-charismatic ministries in general. But soon the generation of the apostles passed away, to be replaced in part by "evangelists" like Titus and Timothy. In the Didache, as we have already seen, the prophets as "high priests" together with the teachers were the most highly regarded, and took the chief parts in the eucharistic celebration. The *episkopoi* and deacons were at first less highly regarded, since they were concerned with the less important work of administering the

---

[38] See works cited in note 34, esp. H. W. Beyer-H. Karpp, in *RAC* II, 403–407. On the historical development of the episcopal office see J. Colson, *L'évêque dans les communautés primitives,* Paris 1951; *L'épiscopat catholique,* Paris 1963: varied historical and present-day problems of the episcopate are examined in: *L'épiscopat et l'Eglise universelle,* ed. by Y. Congar and B. D. Dupuy, Paris 1962; *L'évêque dans l'église du Christ,* ed. by H. Bouëssé and A. Mandouze, Bruges 1963; and *El Colegio episcopal,* ed. by J. Lopez Ortiz and D. Joaquin Blazquez, Madrid 1964. For developments at Vatican Council II see esp.: K. Rahner-J. Ratzinger, *The Episcopate and the Primacy,* London 1962; G. Alberigo, *Lo sviluppo della doctrina sui poteri nella Chiesa universale,* Rome 1964. The subject is discussed from the canon law point of view by T. J. Jiménez Urresti, *El binomio "primado-episcopado",* Bilbao 1962.

affairs of the community (including, and in particular, its financial affairs). But as we also saw, the Didache puts *episkopoi* and deacons on the same level as prophets and teachers, in as far as the former were to take over the work of prophets and teachers where needed—including the celebration of the eucharist. The other permanent ministries of the community, which were "only" based on a charismatic calling, could not really compete with the office of *episkopoi* and deacons, which had become institutionalized and was solidly founded on election by the community.

As early as the first letter of Clement prophets and teachers are passed over in pointed silence. The tasks of administering the community, of organizing worship and of teaching were increasingly entrusted to the *episkopoi* (or elders) and their deacons. In this way the *episkopoi*, as the pastoral letters and the first letter of Peter show, assumed an authority which, apart of course from the fundamental nature of apostolic witness and the directness of the apostolic mission, could only be compared with that of the apostles themselves. Thus, while the Church had been founded entirely on the apostles and prophets, and in its entirety had inherited the mantle of the apostles, the *episkopoi* or elders gradually came to be in a special degree the "successors of the apostles" within the Church. The apostolic succession of the whole Church turned more and more into the apostolic succession of a particular ministry, especially after the disappearance of the prophets towards the end of the second century, and of the free teacher of the community in the third century, and after teaching authority had become almost exclusively entrusted to the *episkopoi* and their helpers. The fellowship of believers, the collegiality of all believers, of all those who had charisms and fulfilled their own ministries, the collegiality of the whole Church, in short, gave place to the *collegiality of a special ministry* within the community: the collegiality of the leaders of the community, the *episkopoi* or elders, who increasingly began to see themselves as distinct from the community, from the "people"; this is where the division between "clergy" and "laity" begins.

2. Instead of there being a number of *episkopoi* or elders in a community, the idea of a monarchic episcopate was soon

established. As we have seen, the most ancient New Testament writings and the oldest uncanonical documents always speak of *episkopoi* or presbyters in the community in the plural; their ministry is a collective one. But already in the pastoral letters—this is clearly the sense of I Timothy 5:17—the instruction is given that those of the presbyters who "rule well", evidently in contrast to those presbyters who have no ministry of this kind, are to be worthy of double honour, and especially those "who labour in preaching and teaching". Ruling and teaching, as we know from I Timothy 3:2–5, is the function of the *episkopoi,* and hence we can conclude that only a section of the presbyters fulfils the office of *episkopoi.* At all events the *episkopoi* increasingly stand out from the ranks of the presbyters, a development which can be particularly traced in early times in Syria and Asia Minor.

Ignatius of Antioch, writing around the turn of the century, gives the first evidence, in strong terms, of a development which was to take place during the second century: instead of a number of *episkopoi* in one place, the idea begins to burgeon of a single *episkopos,* who has responsibility and powers of decision as the sole leader of the community. We can tell from the letters of Ignatius that even in the Churches of Asia Minor he was writing to, there can only have been one *episkopos;* on the other hand, his letter to the Roman Church is pointedly silent on the subject, presumably because in Rome there were still several presbyters fulfilling the office of *episkopos* (cf. I Clement 44:1–5). Ignatius gives dogmatic weight to the idea of a monarchical episcopate, despite its historical development: *"One* eucharist, *one* body of the Lord, *one* cup, *one* altar, and therefore *one* bishop together with the presbyterium and the deacons, my fellow servants" *(Philad.* 4:1). Here, for the very first time, we find a definite three-tiered hierarchical structure in the Church: bishop, presbyterium (this collective word is generally used for the presbyters) and deacons, a hierarchy which was later established in the West too. Instead of the collegiality of *various episkopoi* or presbyters, which had made up a collegium of equals within each community, we find the *collegiality of the one monarchical episkopos with his presbyterium* (and his deacons). The division between "clergy" and "laity", the "people", is complete.

All essential functions are in the hand of the bishop; the presbyters have no authority or responsibility of their own, the community has to obey. The bishop is the harp, the presbyters the strings (Eph. 4:1). Ignatius, with his pneumatic and mystical concept of the Church, takes no account of the apostolic ordering of the Church; his concept of office in the Church is cultic and pneumatic rather than legalistic, but precisely for this reason it becomes heavily emphasized: the bishop is the ruler in the place of God the Father, the presbyters replace the college of the apostles, the deacons perform the ministry of Christ (*Magn.* 6:1; cf. *Trall* 3:1). We enter a completely different world when we come from Paul the apostle to the bishop of Antioch; when, with something like the First Epistle to the Corinthians in our minds, we read the following decretal sentences about the bishop: "You should all obey the bishop as Jesus Christ obeys the Father, and the presbyterium like the apostles; but honour the deacons as appointed by God. No one must act in anything concerning the church without the bishop. Only the eucharist celebrated by the bishop or by those appointed by him counts as valid. Wherever the bishop appears, his people are there too, just as where Jesus Christ is, so also is the Catholic Church. Without the bishop there is to be no baptism and no celebration of the agape meal; but whatever he approves, is pleasing to God, about all this you can be sure and confident. Moreover, it is fitting that we should be sensible and turn our hearts to God while we yet have time. It is good to know God and the bishop. He who honours the bishop, will be honoured by God; anyone who does something without the bishop's knowledge, serves the devil" (*Smyrn.* 8, 1–9, 1). Explanations and admonitions of this kind, which run through all Ignatius' letters, indicate two things: that he is on the defensive against Gnostic heresies; and that many of the things he demands have not yet become established in reality.

The ideas of Ignatius of Antioch about the mystery of the Church and its unity are given a basis in ecclesiastical law by the Syrian Didascalia of the third century, which in turn form the basis of the, also Syrian, Apostolic Constitutions, the largest canonical and liturgical collection of the early period of the Church. The role of the bishop as the ruler of the community is now even more firmly established; he has the right to appoint presbyters and deacons himself, he has the power of the keys to include or exclude members of the community, he has to oversee all the community's charitable works and by teaching and example is their moral leader. In this way the apostolic succession became increasingly seen as confined to the monarchical episcopate.

3. Instead of being the leaders of an individual community, the *episkopoi* became increasingly the *leaders of dioceses*. As the Christian message spread from the towns into the countryside (to the *"pagani"*), the *episkopoi* of the towns began to take the countryside round their towns under their care, often covering quite a wide area. In this way, with the help of presbyters who were increasingly sent out into the country districts, they gradually built up a centralized system of mother and daughter Churches: the metropolitan system. The chief pastor of a town became the director and overseer of a whole area, the old *"episkopos"* of a Church in a town became a "bishop" in the modern sense. His territory was at first called *paroikia* in the East, then *eparchia;* in the West the two words *parochia* ("parish") and *dioecesis* were often used synonymously. In theology as well as in practice the role of the bishop became more and more important. Contradicting biblical terminology, the bishop now becomes called *"sacerdos"*, *summus sacerdos, pontifex*, and parallels are drawn between him and Old Testament priests or high priests. The consecration of a bishop is interpreted theologically as his wedding to the particular Church. Influenced no doubt by non-Christian practice, it became customary to keep a list of the successive occupants of the office (lists of bishops). In this way the apostolic succession of the bishop was formalized by the establishing of a recorded line of succession, intended to prove that the purity of the apostolic teaching tradition has been handed on unaltered.

From the middle or end of the third century, inspired in part at least by Jewish and pagan precedents, the bishops began to wear a distinctive dress of office. At the same time, in the Christianized Byzantine empire, bishops were accorded secular titles, insignia and privileges which up to then had been reserved for the emperor or high officials: candles, incense, a throne, shoes, the maniple, the pallium, and so on.

From here to the prince bishops of the Middle Ages was only a short step. In the fourth century the bishops of Rome, Alexandria, Antioch and Constantinople were given the rank of metropolitans, and the bishop of Jerusalem had a privileged position. The patriarchal system, in which Rome was accorded the primacy, was also developed, and from about this time the whole structure became known as a "hierarchy". Other factors became important. In addition to the special letters sent by several bishops to other, often far distant, Churches, there was lively correspondence between the bishops themselves; then, around the turn of the second century, there began the regional synods of bishops and, from the fourth century onwards, ecumenical councils; finally there was the collegial character of the consecration of bishops which began in the early third century and then after the Council of Nicaea was extended, so that consecration was to be administered by all the bishops of the ecclesiastical province, if possible, or at least three of them. These factors working together made the *collegiality of the monarchical bishoprics of the various Churches* (i.e. dioceses) more and more important; collegiality one with another and finally, in the West at least, as the Roman primacy became stronger, with the bishop of Rome.

A final short note about the diaconate: as we have seen, the function of deacons in the New Testament period can be traced only in outline; the origins of the office seem to have been very varied. With time the deacon came to be more and more a personal assistant of the bishop, often with very considerable influence. In addition to his original responsibility for the community agapes and the feeding of the poor, he now assumed wider responsibilities: the ministry to the community as a whole in material and spiritual things alike. The deacon in many cases became something like a manager of the community. He had various important functions connected with worship, especially in regard to baptism and the eucharist. The close co-operation of deacons with bishops often made them seem higher in rank than the presbyters, something that several synods had to oppose. The collegium of deacons in Rome was so powerful that after the death of Bishop Fabian in 250 they seem to have been the leaders of the community for a time. The early history of the diaconate suggests that the functions of deacons can only be restricted with difficulty; the conducting of the eucharistic celebration was the only thing that was generally barred to them.

This, very briefly sketched, is an indication of the tremendously complex development of the original constitution of the Church. Two basic forms, the Pauline and the Palestinian, combined, and within a remarkably short space of time, within a generation after Paul, the latter form completely obscured the former. We must now ask what this development means for the Church today.

(c) Nothing is to be gained from concealing the fact, which the brief sketch above makes amply clear, that a frightening gulf separates the Church of today from the original constitution of the Church. At the same time, the Church of the present must be able to justify itself, in this respect too, in the light of its own origins—and especially in this respect, since it is here that the decisive differences between individual Christian Churches are to be found. The question of the constitution of the Church is a special area of difficulty which cannot be overlooked. It is important to stress this, since there are various ways in which the present-day Church tries to avoid the uncomfortable and disturbing history of its developments from its origins.

A first way is to pretend ignorance about the whole matter. It is possible that there are those who do not know the facts about the origin of the Church, simply because they have never taken the trouble to find out. It may be that, overwhelmed with the activities of the Church and the quest for knowledge, they never had the time, and concerned themselves instead with the *status quo* or with the history of the Church since 1870, or since the Reformation, or since Gregory VII, or since Constantine, or even since Ignatius of Antioch and the first epistle of Clement. Often, instead of referring to the original testimony of Scripture, reference was made to "tradition", to "the Fathers", whether Greek or Latin, old or new, who were often chosen quite arbitrarily and still more arbitrarily quoted. In this way everything was made much easier. It was easier to show continuity, several lines of development could be drawn straight, several contradictions could be avoided. In this way many things appeared to have been "there from time immemorial", to have been part of tradition or even of divine institution. But invariably the first phase of this history was excluded—the absolutely decisive and fundamental phase, since it was the original one. This meant that it was easy to overlook some important considerations: the fact that *true* continuity can only be traced from the real origins, or, if it has been lost, be restored from them; the fact that we can only see in the light of the Church's origins how much in the present constitution is the work of men and how much is the work of God; the fact that only an awareness of these origins can enable us to determine what is essential and what is inessential, what is decisive and what is unimportant, what is permanent and what is transient.

Without a knowledge of the original history of the constitution of the Church, there is nothing to measure the present by; there will be a tendency to follow each new secular or ecclesiastical fashion, to adopt and become the prisoner of new systems, institutions and constitutions, forms and formulas, and hence to lose sight of Jesus Christ and his message, the foundation and the goal of the Church. On the other hand, by recognizing the importance of the original history of the constitution of the Church, we can rediscover the essential things in the Church and establish ourselves on a firm and secure footing. By recognizing and pondering the history of its origins, the Church of the present can liberate itself, in matters of Church constitution particularly, and take on a new freedom, a new truthfulness and a new life.

The second way out is to minimize the importance of the history of the Church's origins. The facts are accepted, but are then looked at through the rose-coloured spectacles of a particular theological system or a particular system of Church government and administration. This modifies the realities of the original history; not only are dark patches turned pink, but the contours are blurred, contrasts are smoothed over, striking features are evened out and various perspectives are lost. Important differences between Mark and Luke, between Paul and Acts, between Paul and the pastoral epistles, between John and Revelations and so on, are ignored; things are taken as historically certain when they are not; difficulties are resolved by speculative dialectic.

It is then easy enough to erect an imposing new building by using the individual stones of the New Testament—and not only the pastoral epistles and Acts, but Paul too, even Corinthians. And the new system solves all problems in a wonderful way. All the stones are put together according to a new design, while at the same time materials from elsewhere —from pagan Rome, Christian Byzantium, the German Middle Ages or modern philosophy—are smuggled into the building. In this way the old elements go to make up a new building, and such parts of the New Testament message which would not fit in are left on one side as a *quantité négligeable*. In the course of this demolition and rebuilding work some of the most interesting New Testament passages were overlooked, while certain passages (Matthew 16:18 for example) were drawn on time and again and allowed to dominate the whole; but this the builders failed to notice. Instead of trying to observe the fascinating history of the young Church from within, only as much was discovered in the New Testament as could be found—much more clearly and consistently expressed—in a modern book on canon law. From this viewpoint, it becomes incomprehensible why Peter and Paul should have had a very serious dispute, why there were factions in Corinth and confrontations in Jerusalem, to say nothing of less obvious contradictions. Such things were events from which the Church of the present could not learn anything, events of which it ought really to be ashamed and which it was best to pass over in silence. Not at all, of course, what the New Testament writers themselves did!

An ecclesiastical dishonesty and untruthfulness, however well-meant the purpose behind it, has almost always been the result of such an approach. By reconciling contradictory passages and by an arbitrary selection of texts, the original history of the Church's constitution can be made to seem straightforward; but this is to ignore some of the most profound and fruitful lessons of the New Testament, to bypass tensions which can be most instructive and to miss developments which can be most promising. In this way too it is difficult to come to terms with the tensions and contradictions in later Church history, or to adopt a positive attitude towards the whole dialectic of Church and constitutional history. On the other hand, by facing up to the real tensions of New Testament history, the origins and the present state of the Church alike become interesting once more, and lose the boring character of an establishment. By looking at the history of its origins the Church today can revive its appreciation of the Spirit of God, who blows where, how and when he wills, who can write straight even on crooked lines and reveal fresh ways out of apparently hopeless situations, and who, by recalling to the Church of the present its origins in the past, can point the way to new developments in the future.

The third way out is to split up the original history of the Church. There are those who are opposed to attempts to reconcile or smooth over differences, and are in favour of contrasts, sharp contours, the collision of opposites, the contradictions of life—but without in the last analysis really approving them. What people of this persuasion do is to opt firmly for one side, nearly always the side of Paul. And from this apparently secure position they snipe carefully at Luke and Acts, at James, at the anonymous writer of the pastoral epistles, indeed often at Paul himself for not being sufficiently consistent. They are on the side of the Gospel, fighting against the apostasy of the Church; they are able to discern spirits in the New Testament—the spirit of Protestant evangelicalism and the spirit of primitive Catholicism! In this way the history of the Church is disrupted from the first; from the first there were pure and impure currents in it, and its history is the story of a contradiction, of several Churches in opposition rather than of several Churches in unity. In consequence those who take this view are unable to see the post-apostolic history of the Church in a positive light, and are obliged instead to see an increasing falling away from the Gospel, a descent into institutionalism, sacramentalism and clericalism—until perhaps the age of the Reformers, or perhaps until the nineteenth century, or even right down to the present, when at last we are beginning once again to understand what *really* matters.

Those who split up the original history of the Church divide the things which united the New Testament Church, and by selecting from the New Testament in the interests of dissociation rather than harmonization, create—generally in their imaginations only—a Church of their own, which is neither the New Testament Church nor even that of Paul. By destroying the unity of the New Testament they destroy the unity of the Church. On the other hand, those who accept the unity of the original history of the Church, while not necessarily giving approval to everything, will be able to distinguish essentials from inessentials, original features from later developments, clarifications from obfuscations. They will also have an historical awareness of the fact that history continues, and that since time does not stand still not *all* developments must be regarded with suspicion; they will realize that maybe after all even Luke and the pastoral letters, rather than being altogether on a wrong course, represent a response to a different situation with its own needs and demands, and hence a legitimate development of Paul's ideas with regard to office and Church constitution—a development Paul himself might have wholeheartedly approved. As it looks back to its unified origins the Church of today can be assured in faith that God's guiding hand was over the history of *all* the New Testament Churches, and that today equally the Church despite all its backslidings has a future, a good future, ahead of it.

These negative points allow us to draw the following positive conclusion: the Church of the present must face up to the history of its origins in the matter of Church constitution as well. In order to ensure continuity it must take note of the gulf which separates it from its origins, without fuss but perhaps a little ashamed. In order to ensure its continued existence, it must constantly confront the challenge of its origins, and ask itself, in the light of its early history, and in the light of the better future it hopes for, what aspects of its present constitution are justified and what are not. A Church which is founded not on itself but on the Lord and his message need not fear these questions.

It is obvious that the *Second Vatican Council* has made a critical review of this kind much easier, by recalling some of the vital aspects of the constitution of the Church in the New Testament. As these have been dealt with in detail in earlier chapters, there is no need to do more here than list briefly the important perspectives given not only in the Constitution on the Church, but also in other documents of the Council:

1. The Church as the people of God and as the fellowship of the faithful (and in this connection the significance of collegiality).
2. The priesthood of all believers.
3. The charismatic dimension of the Church.
4. The importance of the local Church.
5. Ecclesiastical office as ministry.

The fruitfulness of these new, and yet entirely aboriginal ideas has been shown in previous chapters.

At some important points specific attention was paid to recent discoveries in exegetical and historical scholarship, especially, for example, as regards Jesus' preaching about the reign of God (CE 5). As far as the constitution of the Church is concerned, there was at one important point, again as a result of recent exegetical and historical research, an explicit correction of a canon of the Council of Trent, which said: "Whoever says that there is in the Catholic Church no hierarchy established by divine ordinance, consisting of bishops, presbyters, and deacons, let him be anathema" (D. 966; cf. 960). The Constitution on the Church (CE 28) makes obvious reference to this canon with its anathema, and corrects it in three ways:

1. While Trent uses the unbiblical word "hierarchy", Vatican II chooses at this point the phrase "ecclesiastical ministry" (*ministerium ecclesiasticum*).

2. While Trent uses the phrase "divine ordinance" (*divina ordinatio*) obviously to refer to the distinctions in office between bishops, presbyters and deacons, Vatican II unambiguously applies the words "divinely established" (*divinitus institutum*) solely to ecclesiastical ministry as such.

3. While for Trent there is a "hierarchy established by divine ordinance, *consisting of* (*constat*) bishops, presbyters and deacons", Vatican II says that the ecclesiastical ministry is *exercised* (*exercetur*) on different levels by those who *from antiquity* (*ab antiquo;* not, that is, from the very beginning) *have been called* (*vocantur*) bishops, priests (presbyters) and deacons".

The Tridentine proposition, if strictly interpreted, does not agree with historical realities, but the proposition of Vatican II does. The theological commission of the Council makes an explicit reference to the present state of research at this point[39] by citing the study

[39] *Schema Constitutionis De Ecclesia,* Rome 1964, 101.

by P. Benoît.[40] In doing this the commission did not wish to approve a specific interpretation of the historical origins of ecclesiastical offices, but clearly sought to avoid certain unhistorical assertions.

There are similar examples as regards the third chapter of the Constitution in a few places:

1. With reference to the term *"priest"* (CE 10; 28) the commission (contrast Trent D 957) specifically admits: "The word *'sacerdos'* (ἱερεύς) is in Holy Scripture used only of Christ, the priests of the Old Covenant and the whole Christian people. . . . In the New Testament the ministers are in general called *'episkopoi,* presbyters, overseers, etc.' ".[41] Elsewhere the Commission[42] is forced to correct itself by adding: "occasionally for heathen priests too (Acts 14:13)". The speculative linking of ecclesiastical office and *"sacrificium"* (and therefore also priesthood) which follows can therefore no longer invoke the New Testament in defining itself.

2. With reference to the term "deacon" (CE 29), and again in contrast with Trent (cf. D 958), the traditional text for the biblical foundation of the diaconate, namely Acts 6:1–6, is no longer quoted. The commission's reasoning runs as follows: "As far as Acts 6:1–6 is concerned, exegetes are no longer completely convinced that the men spoken of here correspond to our deacons, although they have traditionally been regarded as their forerunners. For this reason the text is not quoted in the Constitution."[43]

3. With reference to the term *"episkopoi"* (CE 21; 26): Precisely as regards the two powers of ordination and confirmation, which Trent reserved under anathema exclusively to the bishop (he does not hold them in common with the priests: D 967), the theological Commission of Vatican II makes two cautious deviations, clearly on the basis of a better insight into the historical facts. As regards ordination: "The Commission states that there is nothing to be laid down on the question of whether the bishop alone may ordain presbyters; therefore it deals neither with the *quaestio juris* nor the *quaestio facti.*"[44] As regards confirmation Trent had defined: "Whoever says that the ordinary minister of holy confirmation is not the bishop alone, but any simple priest, let him be anathema" (D 873). Vatican II replaces the decisive word and instead of the "ordinary minister" (*minister ordinarius*)

---

[40] P. Benoît, "Les origines de l'épiscopat selon le NT", in *L'évêque dans l'Eglise du Christ,* ed. by H. Bouëssé and A. Mandouze, Bruges 1963, 13–57.
[41] Schema 44.   [42] Schema 102.   [43] Schema 104.
[44] Schema 87.

speaks only of the "original minister" (*minister originarius*). This leaves the possibility open that the "simple priest" too can be the "ordinary minister" of confirmation, as has always been the case in the Eastern Churches and has been permitted for parish-priests in the Western Church in case of need since 1946. The Commission's reason here was "in order that justice might be done to the Eastern Churches".[45]

At this point the question arises whether, in view of the brief history of the original constitution of the Christian Church outlined above, other canons of Trent should not be scrutinized in a similar way, for example those on the administering of the sacraments in general (D 853, cf. 1958), on penance (D 902 and 920, cf. 670 and 753), on confirmation (D 960, cf. 608, 697, 1458 and 2147a), on extreme unction (D 910 and 929, cf. 99 and 700), on ordination (D 958, 960 and 966, cf. 305, 356, 548 and 701) and on the eucharist (D 940, cf. 424, 430 and 574a).

Two general conclusions follow from the foregoing:

1. The decisions of the Council of Trent (or of other councils) cannot be regarded as binding definitions where they concern questions which are being put differently today in the light of completely different problems. The Fathers of those days could not decide upon matters they did not know about. This applies particularly to new exegetical and historical problems, which only arose in recent times and need new solutions. No council is granted a fresh revelation; its solutions are tied to the capacities of the theology of its time. This does not mean, of course, that the conclusions of the Council of Trent on this subject are irrelevant for us today. Much is still valid, for example, the consistent stand which Trent took against all kinds of enthusiasm and its insistence on order in the Church; further, its rejection of the idea that, on the basis of the priesthood of all believers, everyone in the Church "without distinction" (*promiscue*) can do everything (cf. D 960), which would have been contrary to Paul's ideas (I Cor. 12:29), as the Council rightly pointed out. But it does mean that Trent, with its sometimes very exclusive definitions of the authority of ecclesiastical office, which scarcely take account of the priesthood of all believers (cf. D 957 and 961), cannot dispense us from the task of asking these questions again and finding new answers to them, in the light of modern exegetical, historical and systematic research and scholarship. We are on the contrary encouraged to do this by Vatican II, which had laid the preliminary foundations for this work.

2. The Second Vatican Council, in the third chapter of the Constitution on the Church, considers the "hierarchical structure of the

[45] Schema 99.

Church, with special reference to the episcopate". This chapter, a highly controversial document as far as the various Christian Churches are concerned, discusses the bishops as the successors of the apostles (CE 20), episcopal consecration as a sacrament (21), the college of bishops and its head (22), the relationship of the bishops within the college (23), the episcopal functions of preaching, sanctifying and governing (24–27), and finally goes on to speak (much more briefly) about priests (presbyters) (28) and deacons (29). Yet in all this Vatican II does not claim to give an account of office which accords with the origins of the Church, or has a solid backing of exegetical and historical scholarship. The remarks which the theological commission made concerning the central proposition from CE 28, quoted above, about the threefold structure of office in the Church, should in fact be read as a subtitle to the whole chapter III of the Constitution: "Whatever the facts may be about the historical origin of the presbyters, deacons or other ministries and also about the precise sense of the terms used in the New Testament to describe them, it is asserted that . . .". (*'Quidquid sit de historico ortu presbyterorum, diaconorum vel aliorum ministrorum necnon de sensu praeciso terminorum qui in Novo Testamento ad eos designandos adhibentur, asseritur . . .'.*) What this means is that chapter III is not analysing the *essence* of ecclesiastical ministries, that part which is historical and permanent and decisively conditioned by the origins of the Church, but merely the historical *forms* of ecclesiastical office as conditioned by changing circumstances. Chapter III accordingly gives us a theological and pastoral description of the nature, order and function of the different offices, based on the *present* order of the Church. For this reason it was especially important to go back to the historical roots of the present ordering of ecclesiastical office, as we have done above.[46]

(*d*) It is necessary to accentuate the contrasts in the New Testament constitution of the Church, and to stress certain features, in order to be able to draw important distinctions in our examination of the historical reality. But this must not lead us to establish unreal alternatives, as for example the alternative between office and charism. It would be a great mistake to take the differences between Palestinian and Pauline Church constitutions, as indicated above, as analogical with the contrast between office and charism (or a similar con-

[46] On the Tridentine decrees cf. *Structures* VI, 4.

trast, like "institution" and "event", etc.). The presbyter system may have degenerated later in many cases into an ecclesiastical bureaucracy, but it was far from being that at first. Similarly, the charismatic system may in many cases have dissolved later into a confusion of enthusiastic sectaries, but this was not so originally. There are several *common features* uniting the Jerusalemic with the Pauline order, uniting the idea of a ministry inspired by a free gift of the Spirit with that of a ministry exercised by special appointment. These features should not be overlooked:

1. Both the charism-inspired ministry and the appointed ministry presuppose the original witness and the original commission of the *apostles*. Neither kind of ministry can exist unless it is in accord with apostolic witness, unless it refers back to the message of Jesus Christ as testified to originally and fundamentally by the apostles and can justify itself in the light of that message. Neither kind of ministry can exist unless it is linked to the ministry of the apostles and represents the living continuation of the apostolic ministry in the Church and for the world. *Both* ministries must therefore, if they are to exist at all, form part of an *apostolic succession:* a succession in apostolic faith and witness, service and life. In Corinth as much as in Jerusalem this is how the apostolic succession is understood.

2. Charismatic and appointed ministries alike presuppose faith in the Gospel and the receiving of baptism. Neither ministry can exist, unless it is based on the priesthood of all believers, who *all* have direct access to God, who must all offer themselves as spiritual sacrifices in their everyday world, who are all called to preach the word and to take part in baptism, the Lord's Supper and the forgiving of sins, who are all called to serve one another and, after being called out of the world, are all sent out into the world again. This general priesthood, without which the particular ministry of the individual hangs in mid-air, exists in Corinth as much as in Jerusalem as a prerequisite of each particular ministry.

3. The ministry exercised by special commission, as much as charismatic ministries without special commission, is in its own way, a *charismatic ministry*. The special appointment by men is not simply a matter of an arbitrary decision by these

men. They cannot commission whom they wish, those they like or those who suit their purposes, but only those whom God has called. This special commission, as much as the unasked and unanticipated gift of the Spirit, takes its origins from the grace of God who has freedom to call whom he wishes; the men who commission, as much as those who are commissioned, must be the willing tools of God. The special commission, as much as the gifts of the Spirit, takes its origin from the authority of the glorified Lord; the demands of his Gospel and the call to follow him apply equally to both kinds of ministry. The special commission, as much as charismatic ministry, takes its origin from the freedom of the Spirit, which excludes any compulsion or power or enforced obedience towards other men and demands freedom, voluntary action and co-operation in mutual humility and love. The spiritual nature of *every* ministry in the Church is recognized in Corinth as much as in Jerusalem.

4. The special charismatic ministry originating in a special commission is subject, as much as the more general charismatic ministry, to the *discernment* of the community of believers as a whole, who have all received the Holy Spirit and the special gift of discerning spirits. Even a special commission does not exclude the possibility of error and of failures. The New Testament warns not only against false prophets and unbridled charisms, but also against false holders of office, who are hirelings rather than shepherds, who rule and try to make themselves rich instead of serving. On the other hand the free charisms given by the Spirit are not gifts which should produce chaos and disorder, but should strive to create *order*, through modesty, mutual loving service and subordination to a common Lord. Nor do these charisms appear inconsistently in meaningless fluctuation; they work, not solely but often primarily, through permanent ministries in the community (prophets and teachers), which are often indistinguishable in externals from those ministries which result from a special commission. In Corinth as much as in Jerusalem the discernment of spirits and the ordering of ministries within the community were of vital importance.

These are the common features which enabled Jerusalem and Corinth, the Jewish and Gentile Christian Churches to live together in one Church rather than being mutually exclusive; despite the very considerable differences in the constitutions of these Churches, they were in communion with each other through the communion of the Lord's Supper. These common features explain why, when the later Church came to decide on the New Testament canon, it accepted and included non-Pauline as well as Pauline writings (or alternatively included Pauline as well as non-Pauline writings), as a valid and genuine testimony of its own origins. Finally, these common features are the reason why the Church of the present does not have to make an exclusive choice between two alternatives. If an exclusive choice of this kind had been made by those responsible for drawing up the New Testament canon, it would have ignored the history of the Church, in which both kinds of constitution co-existed and indeed increasingly influenced one another; and to make such an exclusive choice would again be to ignore the history of the Church's origins.

(*e*) Despite these common features, however, the sharp contrasts which we have noted between the Pauline and Palestinian Church constitutions cannot be overlooked. And in the light of the Pauline view of the Church the question must have arisen then, as it certainly arises today in view of the present form of the Church, how is it possible to justify any *special commission by men,* given that each man has received his own charism, his vocation, directly from God? Is the inner impulse, the inner motivation for a concrete ministry, in which God's call will be expressed in a man's existence, not sufficient? What is the point of having a human command, a human call, appointment and authorization in addition?

An obvious answer here is the *argument from fact.* All this can be regarded as legitimate, because this was how things developed, this was the course the history of the Church took. First of all a presbyterium arose in Jerusalem, and then this form of ordering the community spread to other communities, and even established itself, after Paul's time, in the Pauline communities; so that finally the exercise of any special ecclesiastical ministry in the Church became universally regarded as dependent on a special commissioning by men. On this argument the "bureaucratization" of charisms is the necessary historical course of any religion. But this argument is scarcely convincing, and counter-arguments quickly come to mind. Surely the comparative religious argument, that this is what happens to all religions, is an argument on the other side—unless we want to maintain that the Christian faith is just one religion among many others, that the Christian community is just a religious organization like any other, that ecclesiastical ministries are merely a modified form of the priests and religious assistants we find in all religions. Surely we must infer that the increasing predominance of commissioned and appointed ministries as against the charismatic richness of the Pauline community represents a narrowing, an impoverishment; just as today the official Churches must often seem impoverished when compared with the charismatic vitality of several small priestless sects. We may conclude that the Corinthians, who introduced presbyters into Corinth shortly after Paul's death, would have done better to resist the tendency; and that the Corinthian eucharist at the time of Paul was much more vital and much closer to the original Lord's Supper of Jesus, than the highly ritualized liturgy of later times, as reflected in the writings of Justin around 150 or Hippolytus of Rome around 215.

But precisely at this point the second argument arises: the *argument from abuse.* As far as Corinthian worship is concerned, it would seem that the variety of charisms within the community led to great difficulties and necessitated the firm intervention of the apostle. According to this argument, Gnosticism and Montanism and all the enthusiasts of later centuries make it clear enough what happens if too much reliance in the Church is placed on Pneuma and charisma; there have always been too many false prophets, and even true prophets have often been too radical; it is a matter of historical experience that the freedom of charisms endangers order and unity in the Church. Here again counter-arguments come quickly to mind. Was the disorder in worship of the evidently very lively community at Corinth so much worse than the deadly fossilization and paralysis of the community, which was often the consequence, and in some cases the very rapid consequence, of divine worship controlled exclusively by appointed officials? It is not only prophets who can harm the Church. In addition to false prophets, there are also false and faithless pastors, who have often done more to harm the Church than any others. Surely the inflexibility, immobility, self-satisfaction, hard-heartedness and obtuseness of its pastors have caused easily as much harm to the order of the Church as the uncontrolled proliferation of the gifts of the Spirit? Surely the lust for power, imperial ambitions and quest for prestige on the part of its pastors, and their evident distance from the gospels were directly responsible—as witness the schisms in East and West—for dissolving the unity of the Church? It is clear that abuses can result from appointed offices as much as from free charisms.

The system of appointed holders of office in the Church can therefore be justified neither by reference to the actual development of such offices, nor by reference to the actual abuses of charisms. Two closely linked facts indicate the real answer. One is that the young Church obviously looked forward to the imminent return of the Lord, during the lifetime of the first generation. This expectation of an imminent end was not fulfilled and communities which had prayed "Lord, come quickly" had to establish themselves on a longer-term basis. The other is that the apostles died off leaving, as in the case of Paul, a tremendous gap in the Christian ranks. It had been essentially the apostles who guided the communities with the authority entrusted to them, controlling the variety of charisms by their exhortations and admonitions, by commands and warnings—even though this authority was often exercised from a distance. These two developments seem to have made it inevitable that one kind of ministry should become more important than the other. Rather than those charismatic ministries the authority of which could only be recognized *post facto* by the community, increased importance was given to those ministries which were exercised in the community on the basis of a special commission, and with an authority given in advance.

This points to the *real basis* of a justification for this new kind of order: the difference between an original period, which cannot be fixed by a date, and a time which followed and which led further and further away from the time of origins; the difference between the time of the founding of the Church, the laying of the foundations, and the time of building up and building on which followed; in short the difference between the apostolic age (taking the word in a broad sense) and the post-apostolic age. The Church saw itself, contrary to its expectations, obliged to reckon with a long period of existence and saw the gap which separated it in time from its origins, from the historical Jesus Christ, its crucified and risen Lord, continually growing. True, the Lord remained with it as the glorified Lord in the Spirit. But in order to remain with the Lord, the Church was dependent on the original witness of those who guaranteed the validity of the original message, the apostles. There came a time when one after the other these original witnesses died; the original testimony could no longer be directly heard. In this context the idea of tradition underwent a radical change. The few things that had been written down became tremendously important: in addition to the Pauline letters, such collections of sayings of the Lord which existed (sayings, parables, apophthegms, etc.), the traditional account of the passion and the other narrative material which was all used in the putting together of the gospels. All this now assumed a totally fundamental importance. If the words of the apostles could no longer be heard, the Church risked losing contact with its foundation, the Gospel of Jesus Christ himself. The danger that the young Church might lose touch with its origins, and, following a very common pattern of the time, become absorbed into the all-absorbing world of syncretistic Hellenism, could only be resisted if, despite the inevitable development of tradition in the course of its history, the Church remained determinedly faithful to the original apostolic testimony.

Any factors which could help to preserve the original tradition and to preserve contact with the origins of the Church took on a new importance in this new situation. These included not only the original gospel writings, but also the special commissioning of ministries intended to preserve the original apostolic testimony. Such ministries could make a vital contribution towards preserving and bringing to fruition in the post-apostolic communities the original tradition of the

Gospel of Jesus Christ; something which was especially important at a time when heretical confusion was widespread, when the communities were growing in size, but many of their individual members were losing their original zeal. This is something which—quite apart from the fact that pseudo-epigraphy was as common in the ancient world as the use of pseudonyms by writers is today—explains why the Church constitution envisaged by the pastoral letters, with its stress on apostolic tradition and on the laying-on of hands as a means of appointing officials who were to preserve that tradition, is linked with the name and the authority of the apostle Paul.

Nor can we be so certain that Paul, had he lived to a later age, would not have supported a development of this kind. In his letters, while regarding everything as the work of the Spirit, he lays great weight on the idea of Christian tradition; while he saw his communities and all their ministries as founded completely on a pneumatic and charismatic basis, he did not oppose, but evidently supported, the idea of *episkopoi* and deacons in Philippi. It is true that he had one fundamental concern which a later age did not share and to which we shall return; but it would be a mistake to presuppose that he objected to the appointing of presbyters or to ordination (he said nothing which might indicate this). To make such a presupposition would be to presuppose that from the very first the word and the spirit, tradition and charism, appointment to ministry and calling through the Spirit, were opposed; it would be to presuppose that the commissioning of ministers by the laying-on of hands was regarded from the first as unspiritual and legalistic, and that the authority conveyed by human appointment was regarded from the first as unspiritual and all too human. But according to the New Testament this was not, and indeed never ought to be, the case.

The danger of an external formalism of tradition is of course great. It would be a mistake on the part of one who commissioned others by human words and by the laying-on of hands, if he were to think that he alone had power to communicate this commission, this mission and this endowing of the Holy Spirit. He can only commission, if he too has received a commission to do so. Human words and the laying-on of human hands can achieve nothing if they are not the

expression of a received power. The words and hands of men
must be the tools of God who commissions men, who alone
can distribute authority in the Church. He who commissions
cannot command the Spirit, he can only pray for it; the
laying-on of hands must be associated with prayer. Such a
commissioning will often consist in turning a charism which
has already been received to a particular ministry (cf. Acts
6:3; even the pastoral letters indicate certain prerequisites). At
the same time, a charism for the exercise of a specific ministry
can be prayed for, as the pastoral letters suggest (cf. I Tim.
4:14; II Tim. 1:6). The laying-on of hands is not the chief
thing, but is merely a sign of the working of the Spirit. At the
same time, it is not an empty sign, but a sign which becomes
effective and powerful through words. It occurs according to
the promise of God not as a word of law, which can only
require without being able to give fulfilment, but as a word of
the Gospel, which gives what it demands.

The charism is an indicative which can and must be followed by an imperative. But it is not handed on from man to
man on a horizontal plain, so to speak. It is given not in the
name of the human administer, but in the name of Christ and
in the power of the Spirit. For this reason ordination can
never be a mechanical or automatic process. A prerequisite is
the faith of him who administers it, without which he cannot
achieve what he appears to be doing; also a prerequisite is the
faith of him who has been called, a faith he must now show
in his love and his self-sacrificing ministry. Ordination is not
the handing on of a complete authority which glorifies him
who receives it without binding him to any responsibilities;
the authority which is given is one of service, and it demands
from him a corresponding attitude, a corresponding life and
work.

He who has been appointed to a special ministry betrays
his commission if he puts himself in the foreground, behaves
as though his power were his own and thinks and acts high-
handedly. He then forgets that his commission is a charism, a
calling of the Spirit, who was given to him without merit on
his part and without his being able to earn it in any way. He
would be offending against the Gospel which he is called to
serve and which demands from him the service of his fellow

men. This would be error and fault on his part, and every Christian would be justified, and called by the Spirit, to register opposition to such an attitude by his public witness, provided this was done in truth and in love. If on the other hand this special commission is received in faith and practised in love, it brings to the recipient the certainty that he has truly been called and commissioned, confidence that he can live up to his calling, courage to tackle his tasks again and again, the strength to keep going in all trials, temptations and doubts: "Hence I remind you to rekindle the gift of God that is within you through the laying on of my hands; for God did not give us a spirit of timidity but a spirit of power and love and self-control. Do not be ashamed then of testifying to our Lord, nor of me his prisoner, but take your share of suffering for the gospel in the power of God, who saved us and called us with a holy calling, not in virtue of our works but in virtue of his own purpose and the grace which he gave us in Christ Jesus ages ago, and now has manifested through the appearance of our Saviour Christ Jesus" (II Tim. 1:6–10). Ordination is to equip the ordained person for his ministry, without of course taking from him his humanity and his human frailty. It also authorizes him as a special minister to those for whom he has been called. He, among all the members of the community, is the one who is marked out for special ministry by a particular word and a particular sign expressed through actions.

What general term can be used to describe the ministry which is connected with a special commission in the community? We have spoken of the laying-on of hands as a commissioning for a special ministry (the Bible also refers to the laying-on of hands as a means of blessing and healing, etc.), and this special ministry in the young Church is directed, as we have seen, towards the founding and guiding of Churches and towards associated work. The founding and the governing of Churches belong together; for the pomp of the Church's mission is to build up the Church, and the point of building up the Church is to extend the Church's mission. These are ministries which take up and extend the functions and duties of the apostles, their apostolic commission and ministry. Yet those who perform this ministry are never called apostles in the New Testament, since this would have reduced in stature the unique position of the apostles as the original witnesses and messengers of the Lord. But instead we find in the later writings of the New Testament—referring back in particular to the Old Testament—a concept which is not, like those of *episkopos,* deacon and presbyter, subsequently limited by canon law: the concept of the shepherd or pastor. In Acts 20:28 the presbyters or *episkopoi* are addressed as shepherds: "Take heed to yourselves and to all the flock, in which the Holy Spirit has made you guardians (*episkopoi*), to feed the church of the Lord which he obtained with his own blood." In I Peter 5:2, the presbyters are similarly addressed: "Tend the flock of God that is your charge, not by constraint but willingly, not for shameful gain but eagerly, not as domineering over those in your charge but being examples to the flock." In John Peter is instructed: "Feed my lambs . . . tend my sheep . . . feed my sheep" (Jn. 21:15–18; cf. the use of "flock" for "community" in John, especially chapter 10; cf. also I Clem. 4:3; 54:2; cf. 16:1). Finally in Ephesians the leaders of the communities— although the word is probably not a definite title of office— are referred to as "pastors" (4:11). For this reason it will be convenient to refer to those ministries, based on a special commission and concerned with the leading of the community, as *pastoral ministries.*

(*f*) This ministry, as far as one can see from the New Testament, was exercised in a *variety of different forms.* Quite apart from charismatic gifts (first-fruits, those who labour, those who lead, etc.) which of their nature cannot be systematized or predicted, it is not even possible to organize into a system—on the basis of the New Testament at least— those ministries which, with time, were administered by the laying-on of hands (presbyters, *episkopoi,* deacons, etc.). While Ignatius of Antioch's three-tier system may have had its roots in the origins of the Church, this system of offices is not simply *the* original way in which ministries were ordered and shared out. As we have seen, it is the result of a very complex historical development. It is impossible to draw clear theological and dogmatic lines of division between the three ministries, especially between the functions of the *episkopoi* and the presbyters. Such lines were only drawn as the ministries actually developed and their pastoral usefulness was determined. Even if we like to take this threefold division into bishops, presbyters (priests) and deacons as a reasonable development and as a sensible and practical order, these forms which have taken on canonical force, but which are generally the realization of only one possibility among many, should not be mistaken for dogmatic necessities. There are sufficiently varied kinds of Church constitution in the New Testament to suggest that there were several possibilities which might have been realized.

It would take at least another book in addition to the present one to work out all the implications for canon law which arise from the picture of the Church given here and especially from its diaconal structure. But this must be left to the experts, the canon lawyers. They will feel less able than ever today to accept a simple *positivist* interpretation of the laws currently in force, as though any canon laws were automatically good law, as though in the Church at any rate legality could be taken for legitimacy. Nor will they be able to take such a positivist interpretation one stage further and turn it into a *dogmatist* interpretation, as though law meant something different in the Church, as though canon law itself could be turned into theology, or mystification, or ideology with the help of theological terminology and imagery ("the power of jurisdiction in the mystical body of Christ"!); the end product of this approach would be to declare the canons to be dogmas or mysteries and in this way preserve even more certainly the *status quo*.

There are two things which the Church can expect of the canon lawyer, two ways in which he can perform a service to the Church by going beyond the positive if not positivist interpretation of the laws currently in force—an interpretation which is understandable enough. One would be the examination of the *historical development* of canon law, in order to ascertain where, as a whole and at individual points, the original intention and the real meaning can be found, and what parts are the result of natural development or the limitations of a particular historical situation; in order to see how the *ius conditum* always points to a better *ius condendum*. Secondly, an examination of the *theological bases* of canon law, designed to demythologize rather than to "theologize" it and to face up to the fundamental questions of canon law. Such fundamental questions would include: what is the relationship between Church and law? Are these two phenomena to be equated or separated, harmonized or isolated? What is the relationship between the law of God and the law of the Church? Is God ever bound by canon law? Is canon law higher than human law? What is the relationship between spiritual and secular, pneumatic and institutional, a Church of love and a Church of law? What is the relationship between canon law and the Gospel? In what respects are they related, and in what respects are they not identifiable? How far is a conflict between the Gospel and canon law possible? How far does the Gospel remain *norma normans* for all canon law? How far will the Gospel always "break" the law? How far can there be a correct, a less correct and an incorrect law? Can canon law simply take over secular legal terms (church "power", etc.)? How far does canon law exist not for its own sake and not for the sake of "the Church", but for the sake of individual men? In what respects is canon law not a law of domination, but always and everywhere a law of service? How far is it an expression of the brotherliness of the disciples of Jesus? In what respects is it conditioned by worship, by the confession of faith, by the baptismal, eucharistic and prayerful life of the community? How far should canon law remain living law? Can there ever be a fundamentally unchangeable and unrevisable canon law; can there ever be a definitive Church constitution? How far ought the law of the *ecclesia semper reformanda* to be itself a *ius semper reformandum?* What basic steps can be taken to prevent the constant threat of legalism, bureaucracy and clericalism in the Church? How can law help to preserve and further the freedom of the children of God? What is the ideal goal, a maximum or a minimum of legal forms? Should a distinction be drawn between a basic constitution and a more general legal code, a rule of conduct? What legal protection does the individual have within the Church? What about the principle of subsidiarity? What about human rights? How far can or should canon law be a model for the institution, execution and improvement of secular law . . . ?

There is of course today a canon law and disciplinary distinction between the functions of the bishop and those of the presbyter. A theological or dogmatic distinction is impossible to draw not only because *episkopoi* and presbyters were originally differentiated either differently from today or not at all, but because there are no specific episcopal functions which have not, in the course of Church history, been legitimately assumed by priests; this is especially true of confirmation and ordination. A distinction between local pastors and chief pastors is meaningful if their functions are distributed according to pastoral needs and requirements. But the relationship between local pastors and chief pastor must never be a one-sided relationship of obedience, a relationship of superior to inferiors. Both local and chief pastors owe their obedience to the one Lord, sharing a brotherly fellowship (collegiality) with demands working with and for each other.

Vatican II rejected, after objections had been raised to it, a formulation in the original schema on the Church, which said that priests "by receiving the sacrament became true priests of the second rank", and put in its place a formulation which left open any dogmatic distinction between bishops and priests.[47] We have already seen that, in addition, Vatican II specifically corrected the Tridentine definition about the authority to administer *confirmation*. At least from the fourth century onwards, in the Eastern Churches, the presbyters seem to have been the regular administers of confirmation (the distinction and delimitation of confirmation from baptism is anything but clear, precisely in view of Eastern theory and practice). In the Western Church too priests occasionally administered confirmation, a practice which has become more familiar again in the Catholic Church since 1946. As far as *ordination* is concerned, the situation is somewhat similar; as we have seen, Vatican II was undogmatic about this question too. From the Middle Ages we have several accounts of legitimate ordination by non-bishops; in the seventeenth century Cistercian abbots, who were not bishops, were still ordaining priests without let or hindrance. In view of these facts, which cannot be explained away as "privileges" or juridical constructions, many canonists are of the opinion that the power to confirm and ordain is basically given to every priest, but that for them it is a *potestas ligata,* which may not be exercised without the permission of the bishop. This idea has important consequences, at any rate as far as emergency situations are concerned (e.g. at times of persecution), when the exercise of this authority is obviously desirable.

It is not only the New Testament evidence about the structure of the Church, but also the evidence of Church history which justifies having freedom to reorganize in a manner which preserves continuity but is better suited to the times. Vatican II began reorganization of this kind in connection with the diaconate. But where

[47] Schema 72.

it needs above all to be put into practice is with respect to the *episcopate,* especially as far as confirmation is concerned, for this is something that takes a disproportionate amount of the bishops' time at the expense of more important duties. A meaningful reorganization should not involve the merging of smaller dioceses into bigger super-dioceses, still less the creation of titular bishoprics. In the light both of the early constitution of the Church and the needs of the modern age it would be preferable to return to the old system of *town bishops,* a system still fairly common in Italy. These town bishops, without pontifical titles or finery, would replace present administrative structures and would, in accordance with the principle of subsidiarity (decentralization), take over all necessary authority, especially the power to confirm and similar duties, within their particular regions. Titular bishops living in the same place as these bishops would become superfluous, or rather, particularly in very large cities, would exercise a real office as bishops of a particular district. At the same time, in order to avoid any fragmentation and in order to organize and co-ordinate supra-regional duties and also to look after relations with other regions and with the Church as a whole, the present bishops would remain as the superiors of the town bishops, as real *metropolitans,* archbishops in a real rather than a formal sense. If the bishop is really carrying out the tasks of proclaiming the Gospel, administering the sacraments and doing pastoral work, tasks which the documents of Vatican II so ideally prescribe for him, then his area of activity must be small, and the bishop, at any rate within specific contexts, must know his people. This is only possible if ecclesiastical districts are small and the bishops more numerous, as was customary in the early Church. It is not a fault in the Italian diocesan system that the dioceses are so small and the bishops numerous; it is precisely a criticism of other countries that the bishops are too few. With enormous areas to administer and care for, they can only be organizers and administrators; they must travel from confirmation to confirmation, from church consecration to church consecration, from reception to reception, from meeting to meeting; they not only have to neglect their real episcopal tasks, but also neglect their theological education to an extent which is often deleterious for their Churches. A system of small dioceses is only misguided if each town bishop supposes that he has to set up his own "curia" with officials, seminaries, matrimonial court and so on. Supra-regional duties would remain the affair not of town bishops but of the metropolitans or archbishops; they would have to oversee the education, distribution and rational employment of pastors, including ordination; they would also have a spiritual and pastoral care of bishops and pastors, and make visitations, etc. Not all the town bishops, only metropolitans, would have collegial responsibilities in the running of the Church as a whole, in ecumenical councils and in other ways.

(*g*) All questions of ecclesiastical organization and the demarcation of jurisdiction are far and away secondary when compared with the fundamental truth about the ordering of the Christian Church: namely that *all* members of the Church are inspired by the Spirit, *all* members of the Church have their charism, their special call and their personal ministry, and that pastoral ministries are not the only ones in the Church. The concentration in theory and in practice on the pastoral ministry and office has resulted in other gifts and ministries being neglected; it has too often been forgotten that pastors can only fulfil their true meaning and purpose in the Church when they are surrounded by those with other gifts and ministries, each having his own authority. Emphasis on the particular nature of the pastoral ministry must not lead to a division of the Church into pastors and "faithful", teachers and hearers, those who command and those who obey, "clergy" and "laity". We are all brothers under the one Lord. We are *all* "faithful", we all owe obedience to our Lord and to one another, and must listen to him and to each other.

As we have seen, the development of the Church from the constitution of the Pauline communities can be justified in terms of the growing distance between the Church and its origins, and historical and theological justifications can be found for the rise of the presbyter and *episkopos* system in the post-apostolic period. But this ought not to lead, as regrettably it increasingly did in the immediately post-Pauline period, to a loss of the general *charismatic structure* of the Church and, linked with that, the forgetting of the particular diaconal structure of *all* ministries, not just of the pastoral ministry. This after all was the starting point and the fundamental constitution of the Pauline communities. Once the real Paul is forgotten, the Spirit in the Church is very quickly limited, canalized and monopolized—even though this process is carefully covered up and given religious trappings. Then the Church becomes a hierarchy of pastors, who suppose that they alone are in possession of the Spirit, and for this very reason seek to quench the Spirit in others. It is understandable that men should feel nostalgia for the Church of Corinth, with its lack of order and organization, but with its vital and royal freedom. A nostalgia of this kind may well explain why Free Churches and sects so often seem to have more impetus than well-ordered Churches with a complete hierarchy.

Pastoral ministries, both local ones and those in larger districts, should not be regarded in isolation. It is true that the pastors are the successors of the apostles, inasmuch as they have a special commission and the special task of founding and guiding the Church. In this respect they have a special authority in the Church. But there are two things which should not be overlooked. The first point, which needs no further stressing here,[48] is that fundamentally the *whole* Church, and hence every individual member, stands in the line of succession from the apostles; provided that the Church and each individual member is concerned to be in accordance with the apostolic witness and to continue the apostolic ministry. The second point which must be strongly made, in order to avoid an exaggerated concentration on the *apostolic* succession, is this: as well as apostolic succession, there is also a *succession of prophets and teachers*—to say nothing of the other charisms. We are surely not justified in concluding that the commission and the tasks of the prophets and teachers were fulfilled in the apostolic period, any more than those of the apostles were. Are we then to conclude that the men who received this commission and exercised this role, as prophets and teachers, fell short of their calling? But surely God's Spirit would not have failed to arouse in the Church those two charisms which, according to Paul, were the two most important after that of the apostles themselves. Perhaps, on the contrary, they did not speak loudly enough!

What becomes of a Church in which the *prophets* are silent? What becomes of a Church in which there is no one who gives direct expression in words to the promptings of the Spirit, even if in a different form from the prophets of Paul's

[48] Cf. D IV, 2.

time; a Church in which there is no one with a conviction of his calling and responsibility to illuminate the Church's path in both present and future in a particular situation? A Church in which prophets have to keep silent declines, and becomes a spiritless organization. Outwardly everything may seem all right, things will run smoothly, according to plan and along ordered paths, situations will be weighed up in advance and all unforeseen things will have been allowed for or will simply be left on one side; but inwardly it will be a place where the Spirit can no longer blow when and where he wills, where the Spirit, given the smooth running machinery, is no longer needed and would be at best a disturbing influence, where the ecclesiastical way of life is a way without real life. The pastors in the Church who do not want to listen to the Church's prophets, who can indeed no longer hear them because in the midst of all their governing they have lost the knack of listening, may indeed quote the prophets of the past, now dangerous no longer, as saints in their sermons, but they will be so certain of possessing the Spirit themselves, that they will boast of him rather than listen to him, and will give out their decrees, their regulations and commands as coming from the Spirit. For all their talk of the Spirit and of service, they will be practising a form of rule in which power has replaced the Spirit, and ruling has replaced listening; their power, subtly "spiritual" though it may be, is open no less than secular power to being used in an absolutist, totalitarian or even terrorist manner. True, pastors *may* also be prophets; but in Paul's view this is the exception rather than the rule.

It is on the other hand a blessing for the Church and for its pastors if they are able, as the best of them have always been able, to hear the voice of the prophets: prophets here and now, men and women whose admonitions and demands can in certain situations be as uncomfortable for the Church and its pastors as the Old Testament prophets once were for the Temple priesthood and the people of Jerusalem, those prophets of old who had a habit of speaking so "one-sidedly", so "radically", whose sayings were apparently so "hard", so "loveless", so "uncompromising". A Church and its pastors which are not put off by false prophets from listening to the voices of true prophets will often hear unpleasant things and

rarely receive a comfortable message; they will be presented
with unexpected questions and "impossible" demands. But
they will be shaken into new life, they will be moved once
again by the Spirit of God and receive from him the strength,
the consolation and the joy which makes a new beginning and
true progress possible. What would have become of the
Church if Francis of Assisi had never been? If so many of the
saints, and even many of the prophets who were condemned
in their times as heretics, great and small, had never existed?
The Church has never lacked prophets. Paul was convinced
that they exist in every community. If men are willing to listen to them, they will speak. "Do not quench the Spirit, do
not despise prophesying, but test everything; hold fast to what
is good" (I Thess. 5:19–21).

What becomes of a Church in which the *teachers* are silent? It will be easier to understand this question if we speak
of *theologians* instead of teachers, for the position of teacher
has undergone several changes in the course of history. What
becomes of a Church in which there is no one who is concerned about the genuineness of tradition and the correct interpretation of the original message, in order to translate the
original message afresh in terms of the Church and the world
at the present time? A Church in which theologians have to
keep silent becomes an untruthful Church. Doctrine may
remain correct, unchanged in appearance, and may be
handed on securely; faith may appear to exist without doubt
and doctrine may seem to face no serious problems. But precisely in such a Church the most burning questions which
mankind needs to ask may be avoided; imperceptibly a set
theology which belonged to a particular historical period may
establish itself, inherited views and traditional but empty concepts will be handed on as truth, and a great gulf will open
up, unheeded, between the doctrine and practice of the present and the original message of the Gospel.

Pastors who do not want to listen to theologians in the
Church may ignore them because they have little time for or
interest in good theology, because they cling timidly to their
faith and do not want it to be disturbed, or because in their
naïvety they suppose they know all the essentials already.
Meanwhile in their ignorance they will continue all the more

firmly to give out their own personal doctrine as the doctrine of the Church, will confuse their own inherited ideas with real tradition, will cut themselves off all the more from instruction, and being themselves incompetent will seek to pass judgment on the truly competent. Ignoring the fact that there is a variety of gifts, they will claim not only to be the successors of the apostles, but also to be the successors of the teachers. There *may* be pastors who are also teachers, but Paul implies that this is not the rule.

On the other hand it can yield great fruit for the Church and its pastors if, as the best of them have always done, they listen to theologians, whose contribution is to subject current teaching to close scrutiny and to reflect on the original message of the Gospel, who practise their theological art not for its own sake, but for the sake of men, of the Church and the world; whose critical scrutiny of the Church's teaching in the light of the Gospel is intended not to be destructive but to build up, to encourage and inaugurate better teaching and better practice. The questions about truth which theology has to ask in the light of the original message of the Gospel are of immense value for all those who have to preach sermons, give instruction or have pastoral duties. Theology can help them and the Church in general to look back to its origins and to distinguish the great, valid and permanently true tradition from all inherited ideas, all the false and misguided ideas which have been handed down in doctrine and practice, and can help them and the Church to hear again in all its purity the original message, so that they are able to hand it on. Because it employs all the means of research and scholarship to reflect anew on the original message, theology is capable of finding old keys which the Church has mislaid, keys which can open locks which the centuries have rusted up, and thus help to find the way to renewal, liberating the Church so that in doctrine and practice it can live a life more faithful to the Gospel. What would have become of the Church if Origen and Augustine and Thomas Aquinas had never been—but also if Luther and Calvin and many other teachers of the Church, great and small, had never existed? The Church has never lacked teachers. Paul was convinced that they exist in every community. And if those in the Church are prepared to listen to the Church's teachers, then the teachers will speak. Here again the Spirit must not be quenched, but allowed to find expression.

We are speaking here of true prophets and good teachers— there are of course false prophets and bad teachers as well; there has always been deceiving prophecy and sterile theology. Prophets and teachers must, like the pastors, be tested by the whole community, to see whether they are what they ought to be: unpretentious yet courageous, modest yet determined, serving the Church yet free, exercising a ministry which can help the Church to discover in itself a new wakefulness, a new preparedness and new vitality. Through the ministry of prophets and teachers the pastors can know that they are not alone in their weighty and responsible task, of which neither prophets nor teachers can relieve them. But they can draw support from these other ministries.

(*h*) *Pastors in the community*, or in larger ecclesiastical areas, or in the Church as a whole, perform their ministry in the context of all the other charisms and free ministries. They can never be separated from their Churches or raised above them. They too share with their brothers in the Church obedience to the one Lord and his judgment. They too, and in a special way, are dependent on God's grace and on the intercessions of their brethren. And in their pastoral duties, in particular, they are dependent on the responsible co-operation and assistance of their communities, whether great or small. Therefore they must maintain fellowship (collegiality) not only among themselves, but above all with their communities, which like them are supported by the Spirit and called to a particular ministry. Pastors, as a result of their special commission, have a special ministry to fulfil, but this does not give them personally any precedence over other Christians.

Must the pastorate, with its different divisions, form a *class set apart?* For a very long time this was not the case and the idea of a separate class is not of its essence. The individual stages of its development into a separate class can be more or less accurately dated in the Latin Church; it is a product of the late classical period and of the early Middle Ages. As from the fourth century the pastorate was accorded certain State privileges, immunities and titles. As from the fifth century pastors began to wear special clothes (at first in the liturgy only, then in secular life as well), or perhaps one should say that they did not keep up with the changing fashions of secular life. At the same time one must remember that many apparently traditional forms of dress are very recent—the clerical collar and wearing black, for example. Right down to the sixteenth century the Church laid down no laws about uniform and restricted itself to forbidding too great a luxury in dress. Towards the end of the fifth century the pastors took over the tonsure from the monks; from the sixth century onwards celibacy began to be general, although for centuries it had been resisted, and it was far from universal in practice even down to post-Tridentine times. In the eighth century, since the common people no longer understood Latin, pastors began to have their own language, culture and liturgy (in later times their own compulsory "priestly prayers", the breviary).

The modern period has seen a reversal of much of this development. In most countries priests no longer have secular privileges and immunities. Latin and the culture associated with it have lost their intimate connection with the priesthood, and it has now even been abandoned as the general language of Catholic liturgy. The tonsure has all but disappeared as a mark of the clergy. The idea of a common uniform has also begun to disappear, and special clothes are now restricted increasingly to acts of worship, where they are appropriate. There is a growing aversion to special clerical titles. Celibacy—not in the biblical sense of a special charism, but in the canon law of a universal prescription—has already been abolished for one section of the pastorate, the deacons.

The disappearance of a clerical class from the world is a natural corollary of the general breakdown of social class structures. It does not indicate a hostile limitation of the power of the Church, but rather a neutral, perhaps even positive, process of secularization. At all events it need not be seen as a disadvantage for the pastorate, which functioned just as well in the first centuries of the Church's history as in later stages when it formed a particular social class. The degree of social recognition which it attained was usually purchased at the cost of considerable worldliness, and without it there is more chance for its purely spiritual nature to shine through. Pastoral ministries have undergone several changes, as we can see if we think of the very varied forms they have assumed in the course of the centuries. It is a far cry from the Corinthian pastors, who lacked any formal commission, and the elders at Jerusalem, to the ascetics and monks and the basilical clergy and court bishops of the Christian empire. It is a far cry too, from the medieval simple priests, canonists, court chaplains, spiritual princes, curiales and warring popes to the clergy and missionaries and finally the worker priests of modern times. A long and highly variegated procession comes to our eyes as we look back down the centuries; it reminds us not only of the relativity of clothes and social symbols, but also of the external and internal forms of the pastorate as such. The different forms it took were not dictated by the special commission given to the clergy, nor by the original Christian message, but by all kinds of cultural, social, political, and psychological factors. Therefore no single form can be regarded as definitive. Every form in which the pastoral ministry expresses its spiritual content, even if it is a form which has scarcely any external forms and is restricted to the sphere of spirituality, is in itself good. Any form which conceals or obscures the spiritual nature of the pastoral ministry should be revised or discarded. The extent to which old forms, both external and internal, of the pastoral ministry can be discarded, including dress, certain devotions, the breviary, etc., has been revealed by the worker priests. This admirable and heroic enterprise must make us think again about our method of training priests. Would not the primitive Church, which had no concept of a clerical class or rank, have gone about training priests in quite the opposite way from us—a way still fundamentally common in the Orthodox Church, which therefore does not suffer from the same lack of priests as we in the West? That is to say, instead of planting a young man in a seminary in an alien milieu, in order subsequently to send him out, when he has been "re-educated", into another alien milieu, would it not be more reasonable, given say the situation of the Paris suburbs, to choose a mature, suitable and committed Christian worker, train him in celebrating a simple form of worship with a simple Gospel homily, and then ordain him, without forcing on him a double change of role?

Such a view sheds important light on the relationship between *pastorate* and *community*. The authority of the community, the priesthood of all believers, cannot simply be derived from the existing pastoral ministries. Such a view would mean an unbiblical clericalization of the community, would mean separating the pastorate from the priesthood of all believers and giving the former an absolute value. On the other hand, the authority of the pastorate cannot simply be derived from the authority of the community, from the priesthood of all believers. Such a view would mean an unbiblical secularization of the community, would mean merging the pastorate into the priesthood of all believers. It is important to see how the pastorate and the community, with all its special gifts and ministries, belong together and yet can be distinguished.

We have seen how the whole Church, how all Christians form a priesthood, in the real original sense of the word, and thus have direct access to God, are called to make spiritual offerings in their everyday lives and to exercise mediating ministries on behalf of their brethren, and are empowered to share actively in baptism, the Lord's Supper and the forgiving of sins. Those who are empowered to exercise a particular pastoral ministry in the Church are not, at least as far as the New Testament tells us, a separate caste of consecrated priests, as they often are in primitive religions. They do not act as mediators between God and the people by means of ritual actions which they alone can perform, representing the people before God in sacrifice, and representing God to the people through oracular statements and lawgiving. In the Church of Jesus Christ, who is the only high priest and mediator, all the faithful are priests and clergy.

But this priesthood of all believers by no means excludes a particular pastoral ministry. No community can govern itself —this was not even true of Corinth, which was governed by Paul. But the authority of governing pastors does not simply result from the delegation of the community's authority to them as commissioned representatives. The authority of the pastors is not only the sum of the authority of all the individual members, added together and then handed over to them. It is not the community, as Ephesians 4:11 tells us, which creates pastoral ministries; it is the glorified Lord who creates them through his gifts, encouraging each to make a contribution to the community through his ministry (4:12). It is the pastoral ministry which, in the post-apostolic period, develops a new and particular feature: men receive a special call to public ministry on behalf of the community as a whole through the laying-on of hands, through ordination. The Gospel is not directed towards the individual only, it is directed also towards the community, in which the faithful together

hear the word, perform the rites of baptism and the forgiving
of sins and celebrate together the Lord's Supper. The word,
baptism, the forgiving of sins and the communal meal are
things which refer to the community, and this demands a special ministry from men who are called to fulfil a public pastoral ministry within the community. The individual Christian
must turn in the first instance to his neighbour, who has need
of his priestly ministry. The pastoral ministry is connected
with the community as a whole, which needs leadership.

It is important to distinguish between the general power
given to each individual Christian and the special authority
given to individuals who have a public ministry within the
community as a whole. All Christians have authority to
preach the word, to witness to their faith in the Church and
in the world, to "missionize". But only pastors with a special
calling, or those commissioned by them, have the particular
authority to preach in the meetings of the community. All
Christians are empowered to speak words of forgiveness to
their brethren when their consciences are troubled. But only
pastors with a special calling have the particular authority to
speak words of reconciliation and absolution to the community in the meetings of the community, and hence to the individual believer. All Christians are empowered to share in the
celebrations of baptism and the Lord's Supper. But only pastors with a special calling have the particular authority to administer baptism in the public assembly of the community
and to be responsible for leading the celebration of the Lord's
Supper in the community.

This particular authority in the Church is not the result of
the need for order or of purely human considerations of prac-
ticability. Of course, the pastor too is and must be a man
among men, one of the faithful among many, obedient like
the rest, a minister like his fellows. And yet there is something special about him, not something which gives him any
personal distinction, but something which distinguishes him
from other ministers: his ministry, in addition to being charismatic like theirs, is marked by a special commission. Free
charisms must justify themselves in action and must be recognized by the community. But pastoral ministries have a pre-
existing authority on the basis of the special commission with

which they appear before the community. The pastor is therefore from the first a special person in the community, since he is authorized as one with special powers to exercise a special ministry in the public life of the community. He has power to found and to govern communities, to call together, unite and build up the community; he has power to preach the word in the public assembly and to carry it out into the world as a missionary; he has power to lead public assemblies, to baptize and celebrate the Lord's Supper, to bind and to loose and to commission others like himself.

The community may presuppose that a man with this commission really has authority, even though they still have the duty of testing whether he fulfils his commission in the spirit of his commission and of the Gospel. If he fulfils it in this way, he is a true good shepherd, and Jesus' words, spoken to all disciples, will be especially true of him: "He who hears you hears me" (Lk. 10:16). Because of his special calling the pastor has a special rank among the other members of the community, but his authority can only be expressed through obedience to that calling. His authority is guaranteed by the gift of the Spirit, which was called down on him by his vocation and through the laying-on of hands and the praying over him; and this vocation must constantly be renewed, the gift of the Spirit must constantly be revived (II Tim. 1:6). Precisely because he has received authority in advance through his special commission, the pastor must daily assume that authority in new obedience.

The authority of the individual Christian, the extent of his responsibility, and the gravity of his ministry is not diminished by the authority of the pastor. Since they are all charismatic ministries, pastoral ministries and the other ministries in the community are all interwoven, each taking its life and meaning from the other. At the same time it is essential to remember that the Church never exists for the pastors; it is the pastors who exist for the Church. However much their relative independence (as bishops or pastors) can be justified, since their authority and responsibility does not simply stem from their appointment by the community, but comes from their special calling, the appointment of pastors in the Church must fundamentally take place in collaboration with those who are already pastors and with the community. And, besides the question of their appointment, even if the pastor has an independent responsibility in the matter of governing the community, which he needs to be able to fulfil his task well, the community being a royal priesthood must always have a voice in its own affairs, however this is expressed, whether directly or indirectly through a chosen representative. This is what is meant by the legal phrase so often quoted in ecclesiastical tradition: "Things that affect all must be dealt with by all" (*quod omnes tangit, ab omnibus tractari debet*).

The right to a say in the affairs of the community embraces the following things, as ecclesiastical tradition indicates:[49]

1. The right to a say in the election of bishops, pastors and other ministers. The principle laid down by Pope Celestine I is significant here: "No bishop is to be appointed against the will of the people"; Leo the Great was of the opinion: "He who is to be the overseer of all must be chosen by all". It is not unimportant in this context to note that even today canon law allows for the election of a layman as pope, something that has happened more than once in the history of the Church.

2. The right to a say in Councils of the Church: this we have dealt with in detail elsewhere.[50] Cf. in this connection the words of Bishop Cyprian of Carthage: "Since I have made it a rule from the beginning of my episcopate not to decide things on my own account without consulting you (the presbyters) and having the agreement of the people. . . ."

3. The right to a voice according to Church custom and common tradition—something that was created mostly "from below", from the communities themselves; just as many of the most important events in the history of the Church originated in initiatives "from below" (the founding of religious orders, like that founded by the layman Francis of Assisi, and various reforms, like the Cluniac reform which only later developed into a general reform of the clergy and of the Church as a whole).

4. The right to a say in the administration of Church goods and the distribution of aid (by individuals or by a collegium) and also in matters of spiritual jurisdiction.

[49] Cf. here Y. Congar, *Lay People in the Church,* London 1957, Westminster, Md. 1965.
[50] Cf. *Structures* V.

(*i*) Having described the nature, forms and functions of pastoral ministries against the background of the charismatic structure of the Church as a whole and having described in particular its diaconal structure, we can sum up briefly what is meant by *apostolic succession*:[51]

1. The fundamental element is the apostolic succession of the Church as a whole and of each individual member of it; the Church as a whole owes obedience to the apostles as the original witnesses and messengers of Christ.

2. The apostolic succession of the Church and of each individual consists in constantly renewing a factual concurrence with the apostolic message. The Church must remain in permanent accord with the witness of the apostles (Holy Scripture) and continue to perform the apostolic ministry (the mission to the world and the building up of the community). Apostolic succession is primarily a succession in the faith and witness of the apostles and the life and ministry of the apostles.

3. Within the apostolic succession of the Church as a whole there is a particular apostolic succession in the various pastoral ministries; the pastors, without themselves being apostles, are to continue the role and task of the apostles by founding and governing Churches.

4. Among the varied charismatic gifts of leadership which carried on the apostolic task, one kind in particular became of increasing importance in the post-apostolic period: the pastoral ministries of the presbyters (pastors), *episkopoi* (bishops) and deacons, which were based on a special commission (the laying-on of hands).

5. These pastoral ministries which are in an especial way the continuation of the work of the apostles exist in the Church surrounded by other gifts and ministries, especially by those who succeed the New Testament prophets and teachers, who in collaboration with the pastors have their own original authority.

6. The apostolic succession of pastors is not something that occurs automatically or mechanically through the laying-on of hands. Faith is a prerequisite and a condition; it must be active in the spirit of the apostles. This succession does not

[51] In connection with the previous passage, see esp. D IV, 2.

exclude the possibility of error or failure, and so must be tested by the faithful as a whole.

7. The apostolic succession of the pastors is something which must take place within the community of mutual service, of each other and of the world. Entry into the apostolic succession of the pastoral ministries usually occurs through the collaboration of pastors and community, which may take different forms.

8. In the light of the Pauline or Gentile Christian view of the Church, other ways of entry into the pastorate and into the apostolic succession of the pastors must remain open. The other view of the Church, the presbyterial and episcopal view, which rightly became established in the Church in practice, must still be basically open to other and different possibilities, such as existed in the New Testament Church.

Our examination of the Pauline constitution of the Church showed that a charismatic ordering of the community without any special appointing of ministries (such as ordination) is perfectly possible; in Corinth there were neither *episkopoi* nor presbyters, nor ordination, but, apart from the apostle, only freely expressed charisms. Despite this, the Church at Corinth was a community provided with everything that was necessary, equipped with the preaching of the word, baptism, the Lord's Supper and all kinds of ministries. At the same time, as we have seen, there are good reasons why at a relatively early stage there were *episkopoi* and deacons in the Pauline communities, and, after Paul's death, appointed presbyters, with the result that the presbyterial-episcopal Church constitution soon established itself throughout the Church as a whole. By speaking here of other ways into the pastoral ministry and into this special apostolic succession, it is not of course suggested that we should overthrow the whole existing constitution of the Church and go back to Corinth.

And yet one thing must be stressed: the later Church cannot simply and totally exclude the Pauline constitution. While it is unlikely ever to become a norm for the Church, this view of the Church might, even today, be of importance for certain missionary situations. We cannot suppose that the Church of the present time would wish or would be able to prevent a recurrence of what happened in Corinth and in other Pauline communities—the sudden outpouring of a charism of leadership through the freedom of the Spirit of God—given particular and possible situations, for instance: a concentration camp, a remote prison from which there is no possibility of escape, or an extreme missionary situation, say communist China—Japanese Christians after all lived for centuries without any ordained pastors. A theology which is as concerned as Catholic theology is about ordination and the particular apostolic succession of pastors, must do some hard thinking in the light of the exegetical discoveries outlined above—discoveries which it is perfectly evident were unknown to the Council of Trent. What happens, for example, if a Christian finds himself in an extreme missionary situation, and then, under the inspiration of the Spirit and on the basis of his priesthood as a believer, gathers together a small group, a little community, through the impact of his Christian witness, baptizes them and celebrates with them the Lord's Supper? Can such a man, even though he has received no special commission from men, not be a charismatic pastor after the pattern of the Pauline communities? Would his celebration of the eucharist not be as valid as that of the Corinthians in the absence of Paul? Should ordained pastors, if it came to an encounter, refuse to accept his authority to act in this way? These are at least debatable questions.

But quite apart from these exegetical findings, which are in the last analysis the decisive factor, we may wonder whether a dogmatic theology which recognizes a baptism *in voto* (although this did not exist for centuries) should not also consider the possibility of an ordination *in voto* and a celebration of the eucharist *in voto*. A Church in which every Christian can administer baptism in case of necessity and in which, according to the view of several theologians, every Christian can administer absolution in case of necessity, ought surely to consider whether there are not such things as ordination and eucharist in cases of necessity, with regard to which the "case of necessity" would then cease to be a limiting factor.

But what matters, as the all-important *exegetical findings* show, is not an extreme situation or a case of necessity but the incalculable free working of the Spirit and his gifts. This raises further questions, as for example whether, given the priesthood of all believers and the charismatic structure of the Church, the particular mode of apostolic succession we have, through the chain of laying-on of hands, should be regarded as exclusive. It represents the form, and can be approved without reservation; but is it the *only* way into the pastoral ministry and into this particular apostolic succession? Even if we were to take a new view, a less exclusive one, of this mode of succession, would the chain of laying-on of hands not still remain an impressive sign of the apostolic succession of the pastorate, and hence of the unity, catholicity and apostolicity of the Church? In that case, would there not be every reason to take a more positive view of the apostolic succession and the validity of eucharistic celebrations within those Churches which do not form part of this chain of ordinations? Would this not shed new light on problems such as that of Anglican ordination, quite apart from questions as to the validity or invalidity of particular words of ordination? There is surely no other way in which we can be just to the richness of the spiritual life and the fruitful activity of the pastors of other Churches outside the Catholic Church; there is surely no other way by which we can overcome the divisions of Christianity and arrive at mutual recognition. The enormous theological and, in particular, ecumenical implications of these questions is obvious. There is serious need for them to come under urgent discussion.

This brief survey has covered questions of diaconal structure in the Church and of individual ministries. Only one question was left, the most difficult one, the one which lies at the root of all the divisions in Christendom. Most Christians would be in agreement with what has been said above about the diaconal structure of the Church and about individual ministries. But one point remains definitely divisive: does the Church, in addition to all its pastoral ministries, need a pope as well? Is the papacy part of the essential nature of the Church?

3. THE PETRINE POWER AND THE PETRINE MINISTRY

(*a*) Readers who begin reading at this point are making a mistake. Some people, when reading any book about the Church, are constantly on the look-out for this one point: is the writer "for" or "against" the pope? The whole book is then judged on the answer to this one question; for some it must be a negative answer, for the others it must be positive. The "rest" of the book is for them more or less a matter of indifference or at any rate of secondary importance; at all events it can be judged by the answer to their one question. Our previous remarks have been intended to show how false this approach is. For it is evident that Christians can understand one another at many—perhaps even at most?—points connected with the Church, even if this one question shows up differences between them. It would be unfortunate, then, if they were to begin their dialogue by seizing hold of this one issue and have no time or interest for all the rest. There is another reason why we have left discussion of this point to the end of the book. If there is any point at all—something which is disputed by almost all Churches except the Catholic Church—in talking about a Petrine office, which is of course not exactly the same thing as the papacy, then we can only talk about a Petrine office within the Church, as something which can only be understood in the light of and with reference to the Church, rather than vice versa.

Since two long chapters of the book *Structures of the Church* (chapters 7 and 8, pp. 201–351) are devoted to the question of the Petrine office, the following arguments are given in abbreviated form. The other reasons for brevity in treating the question of ecclesiastical office, given above at the beginning of E II, 1, hold good here too.

There can be no disguising the fact that certain kinds of Catholic theology have dealt with the subject the wrong way round, especially that theology which, based indirectly on the first Epistle of Clement as well as Victor I and Stephen I, was developed by Damasus, Siricius, Innocent I, Boniface I and above all Leo I.[52] Two fundamental impulses conditioned the development in the course of the centuries of the doctrine and practice of a Roman primacy by divine right: the genius of Roman law and Peter the apostle. Roman law and practice was assisted by political factors: the influence of the Church in the imperial capital and the mysterious unifying power of attraction by Rome even after the collapse of the empire; and theological factors: the distinction drawn in the West between the authority of ordination and the authority of jurisdiction,

---

[52] See the histories of the popes, and for the following historical development, see esp. Y. Congar, "Geschichtliche Betrachtungen über Glaubensspaltungen und Einheitsproblematik", in *Begegnung der Christen*, ed. by M. Roesle–O. Cullmann, Stuttgart-Frankfurt/Main 1959, 405–429; and also by Y. Congar, "Conclusion", in *Le concile et les conciles*, Paris 1960, 329–334; *Lay People in the Church*, London 1957, Westminster, Md. 1965; Bulletin d'écclésiologie, 1939–1946; in *Revue des sciences philosophiques et théologiques*, 31, 1947, 77–96, 272–296.

which was the starting-point for the distinction between the particular jurisdiction of the bishops and the universal jurisdiction of the bishop of Rome. This Roman law and practice led, via some stagnation and some reverses, to the establishment of a unified Church, organized strictly along juridical lines and having a monarchical universal episcopate. The way for this was prepared under Nicholas I and John VIII in the ninth century, and then under the crucial influence of the forged Isidorian decretals, was developed in theory and practice with the greatest of energy and determination, especially after the Gregorian reforms. More and more, the Church came to be directed by the total authority of the pope. But it can scarcely have been a coincidence that it was Cardinal Humbert of Silva Candida who was the first to call for the absolute supremacy of the pope and his superiority to any secular power (the programme of the later *Dictatus papae* of Gregory VII), and who described the relationship between the Church and the pope as being that between a door and its hinge, a family and its mother, a building and its foundation, a river and its source; the same Cardinal Humbert, that is, who as papal legate in Constantinople in 1054 delivered the fatal excommunication against the patriarch Cerularius, which marked the official beginning of the schism between East and West, an excommunication, which only 900 years later, at the end of the Second Vatican Council, was removed by a courageous act of Christian reconciliation on the part of Paul VI and Patriarch Athenagoras, who mutually asked each other's forgiveness.

The East had, in fact, never basically understood and accepted the doctrine of the primacy which gradually developed in the West and which was formulated in masterly fashion by Leo I in particular. This is illustrated by the Council of Chalcedon, which was a vital council for the West too; for its famous canon 28 granted to the seat of New Rome (Constantinople) the same honours as to ancient Rome, something against which Leo I at once protested vigorously. The Roman Church was highly respected in the East, not only because it was the Church of the old imperial capital, not only because Rome, the only patriarchy, represented the whole of the Western world, but also and above all because the Church of

Rome was the Church where the two leading apostles Peter and Paul had worked and died. Even for the Council of Chalcedon the Roman bishop was the successor of Peter (Peter spoke through Leo). But what was never understood in the East was the mystical identification of Peter and the Roman bishop, which can be seen especially clearly in Leo's case. According to this view the whole responsibility and authority of Peter lived on in the Roman bishop, an idea from which, with increasing rapidity, fundamental juridical conclusions were drawn.

It is regrettable that this decisive question should never have been debated and clarified at an ecumenical council between East and West. True, the East had its own ecclesiology, which it had reshaped more than it realized under the influence of hellenistic thinking; it had partly developed an episcopalism of a Neo-Platonic kind and had become increasingly independent. But it could certainly appeal to the New Testament idea of the Church in its rejection of the monarchical, absolutist, centralized Church which had gradually developed in the West. The Eastern (and African) view of the Church did not start with a universal bishop, but with a fellowship of believers, with local Churches and their bishops, and was not so much legally as sacramentally, liturgically and symbolically orientated: a collegial, federated fellowship of Churches. But this older idea of the Church found less and less sympathy in Rome as time went on. In Rome meanwhile, Roman primacy and a centralized system was being developed with all the resources of canon law, politics and theology available: this, as we have seen, was the principal reason for the schism between East and West.[53]

This progress of centralization, which had many advantages but also some dangers, had of course already found important opponents in the West, beginning with Irenaeus and Polycrates, also Cyprian and Firmilian, and continuing with the Carolingian theologians, the pre-Gregorian canonists, and some lines of thought of the twelfth century Decretists, the corporative Decretalists of the thirteenth century, and above all the Conciliarists of the fourteenth, fifteenth and sixteenth centuries. But the development of a power structure within

[53] For the other factors in the East–West schism see D I, 3.

the Church continued, reaching its world-political zenith in the thirteenth century under Innocent III, Gregory IX and Innocent VI, despite, indeed partly because of the exile in Avignon (fiscalism), despite the Western schism, the reforming councils and the anti-papalist definitions of the ecumenical council of Constance. The warning signs flashed by the spiritualist sects, from the thirteenth century onwards in particular, were ignored, as were the anti-hierarchical criticisms of Marsilius of Padua, Wyclif and Hus. Even the first ecclesiological tracts arising from the quarrel between Boniface VIII and Philip the Fair of France were apologetic hierarchologies, which identified the Church with the hierarchy or even with the Roman curia and the pope. After the Western schism and the time of the reforming councils Juan de Torquemada had given Roman ecclesiology new foundations and during the renaissance the papacy was more absolutist and unecclesiastical than ever before. There then followed at the beginning of the sixteenth century—we have already indicated the various causes—the second great and lasting schism: the split between the papal Catholic Church and the anti-papal Churches of the Reformation.

No one would wish to deny the achievements of the papacy in preserving the unity of the Church and its faith, nor its services to Western civilization in general. One must not forget that at the time of the great migrations, when government and order generally collapsed and the old capital of the Empire decayed, the young peoples of the West were infinitely grateful for the existence of the *cathedra Petri,* which represented a secure rock, ever intact and unshaken. Only someone of the calibre of Leo could have saved Rome from Attila and Geiserich. In the storms and confusions which attended the birth of a new Europe the Roman See performed a service of incalculable value for the young Churches. This service was not simply a cultural one, the preserving of the invaluable heritage of the classical age; it was a genuine pastoral ministry, concerned with the building up and maintenance of these Churches. The Catholic Church of this time, and of later ages, could thank the papacy for the fact that the Church did not simply fall a prey to the State, but maintained its independence both against the imperial papism of the

Byzantine emperors and the attempted domination of local Churches by the German princes.

The unquestionable achievements of the papacy in respect of the unity of the Church during these periods cannot be denied. At the same time, there is no way round the depressing conclusion that the development of this centralized Church with absolutist means was only achieved at the cost of dividing Christendom, which found itself as a whole less and less in sympathy with this absolutist system and its aberrations. Again, it is regrettable that the necessary recalling and reflection upon the Church's origins called for by so many individuals, was not carried out at the right time. The necessity for this was only realized to a limited extent even by the post-Tridentine Church and the papacy of the Counter-Reformation. The bulwarks of power were by no means razed; they were extended with all the available resources. Within the walls, indeed even in Rome, there were of course dissenting voices—men like Contarini and other cardinals and the Viterbo circle. Older concepts of the Church continued to have their effect, though often in all too political a form, in the later Gallicans, the episcopalists, the Febronians, and finally in the Catholic Tübingen school, especially in J. A. Möhler. But the position of the papacy grew more entrenched, even though in modern times too the papacy must be given credit for having successfully preserved the unity and freedom of the Catholic Church, especially against secular absolutism.

From the Middle Ages onwards, and throughout modern times, the official Catholic ecclesiology was an ecclesiology of apologetics and reaction. It countered early Gallicanism and the French crown jurists with a theology of hierarchical and especially of papal power and a view of the Church as an organized empire; it countered conciliarist theories by a renewed emphasis on papal primacy; it countered the spiritualist movements of Wylif and Hus by stressing the ecclesiastical and social character of the Christian message; as against the Reformers, it stressed the objective value of the sacraments, the importance of hierarchical powers, the priestly office, the episcopal office and once again the primacy of the pope; as against Jansenism, which was connected with Gallicanism, it stressed in particular the teaching office of the papacy; as against the secular absolutism of the eighteenth and nineteenth centuries and against laicism, it produced the picture of the Church, endowed with all powers and re- sources, as the "perfect society". All this led very directly to the First Vatican Council, which took place in an atmosphere of anti-Gallicanism and anti-liberalism, and to its definition of papal primacy and papal infallibility.

The crucial sentences in the definition of the *primacy,* to which the Second Vatican Council frequently refers, read as follows: "And so, if anyone says that the Roman Pontiff has only the office of inspection or direction, but not the full and supreme power of jurisdiction over the whole Church, not only in matters that per- tain to faith and morals, but also in matters that pertain to the dis- cipline and government of the Church throughout the whole world, or if anyone says that he has only a more important part and not the complete fullness of this supreme power; or if anyone says that this power is not ordinary and immediate either over each and every Church or over each and every one of the pastors and the faithful: let him be anathema" (D 1831).

The definition of papal *infallibility* is only a special aspect of the infallibility of the Church: the pope, when he defines *ex cathedra,* possesses "the infallibility with which the divine Redeemer willed his Church to be endowed in defining doctrine concerning faith or morals" (D 1839). There is no need to go into this question again here.[54] Since 1870 it has only been invoked once, by Pius XII in 1950, when he defined as dogma the assumption of the Virgin Mary into heaven.

Since the definition of the primacy has often been misun- derstood the elucidations of it emerging from the Council docu- ments are of importance. They show that papal primacy,[55] even in the view of Vatican I, is by no means an arbitrary absolutism, but rather that:

1. The power of the popes is not absolute (*absolute monarchica*).

2. The power of the pope is not arbitrary (*arbitraria*).

3. The power of the pope has its limits (*limitatio*); it is limited actively by Christ, passively by the apostles and their successors. The pope is also limited as a matter of course by the natural law (*ius naturale*) and divine law (*ius divinum*).

4. The concrete limits of the exercise of primacy are: (*a*) the existence of the episcopate, which the pope can neither abolish nor

[54] Cf. D III, 2.   [55] Cf. *Structures,* VII, 2.

dissolve as regards its position or its rights; (*b*) the ordinary exercise of office by the bishops; in no case may the pope, being as it were another bishop, intervene in the daily exercise of office by the bishops; (*c*) the aim of the pope's exercise of office; its constant aim must be the edification and the unity of the Church; (*d*) the manner of the papal exercise of office; it must not be arbitrary, inopportune or exaggerated, but must be dictated by the needs and the evident benefit of the Church.

It may be added that between the two Vatican Councils the principle of *subsidiarity,* as laid down by Pius XI in *Quadragesimo anno* and as applied by Pius XII to the Church as well, became increasingly important. This principle, which was admittedly hardly put into practice during that period, implies that the things which individual members of the Church can do by themselves, should not be taken over by the community as a whole; and that things which smaller and lower bodies and authorities can do should not be taken over by higher bodies. The community must respect the individual, and the higher community must respect the lower community, in the light of this principle of subsidiarity. Put in another way, one could say: as much freedom as possible, curtailed only as much as is necessary. The principle of subsidiarity has since been confirmed by Vatican II in its declaration on religious freedom (article 7).

Would Vatican II have defined the primacy and infallibility of the pope if Vatican I had not already done so? John XXIII was no Pius IX. Moreover, Vatican II, unlike Vatican I, did not want to define new dogmas at all, being no doubt aware, as John XXIII put it, that new definitions of old truths would not help the Church's preaching of the Gospel in the modern world. And finally Vatican II was characterized by a vital awareness of fellowship, *communio,* collegiality, solidarity and service. This awareness was very different from the underlying mentality of the majority of the Fathers of Vatican I, a mentality understandably moulded by the political, cultural and religious atmosphere of the restoration period, of romantic traditionalism, and of political absolutism. It has also become apparent in the meantime that the definitions of Vatican I, despite the modifications which emerge from a study of all the reports of the Council, could in fact be interpreted in terms of a despotic absolutism. This was illustrated not only by the collective declaration of the German bishops in 1875, which was designed to ensure against any such interpretation, but also by the exaggerations of several popular Catholic interpretations of the primacy, and finally by the very style of government adopted by popes like Pius X (cf. his attitude towards the "modernists") and Pius XII (cf. his attitude towards theologians and bishops and especially towards the worker priests).

It was at this point that the papacy of John XXIII marked an epochmaking turning-point; he revealed a new or rather a very old ideal of Petrine ministry, and instead of seeing the primacy as a more or less dictatorial sovereignty over spiritual subjects, he saw it as a discreet call to serve his brethren inside and outside the Catholic Church, which must be inspired by love and understanding for mankind in the modern world and subject to the true Lord of the Church. His personal impact was made through his basic attitude and gestures rather than by big words; but it enabled all those theological insights and pastoral experiences of previous decades, which had hitherto found no outlet, to find expression in Rome and in the whole Catholic Church; and these insights and experiences, in part at least, were to have a decisive influence on the Second Vatican Council.

The definition of the primacy made by Vatican I was not withdrawn by Vatican II; it was confirmed. Yet in actual fact, quite consciously and with the agreement of the pope, it was corrected and modified by fundamentally "new" viewpoints which Vatican I in its definition had not taken into account and without which any definition of primacy was open to misunderstanding. The following aspects may be stressed, as helping towards a proper understanding of the Petrine ministry:

1. The Church cannot be deduced from the Petrine ministry, but the Petrine ministry from the Church.

2. The Petrine ministry is not a dominion, but a ministry.

3. The Church is not just the universal Church, but equally and validly the local Churches too.

4. The pope, instead of being referred to as the "head of the Church", is called "the pastor of the whole Church".

5. Bishops do not receive their full authority by papal appointment, but by episcopal consecration.

6. The pope and the bishops have a shared collegial responsibility for the governing of the whole Church.

7. The centralized system should be reformed by various practical measures.

On 1: The original draft of the Constitution on the Church was to begin with the "hierarchy", the pope at its head, and only then go on to talk about the "people of God or laity". This order was rightly rejected by the Council in favour of the present order: Chapter 1, the mystery of the Church; Chapter 2, the people of God; Chapter 3, the hierarchical structure of the Church and the episcopal office in particular. In this way it is made clear that ecclesiastical offices are not precedent or superior to the people of God, but a part of it.

On 2: What is generally true of ecclesiastical office (cf. E II, 1) is especially true of the Petrine ministry, since the pope is the "servant of the servants of God" (cf. also the significant address of Paul VI, opening the second session of Vatican II).

On 3: Cf. B III, 1: this presupposes that it is the local pastor, not the Petrine ministry, which is responsible for the local Church.

On 4: In this way the title which belongs to Christ alone, and which was often applied to the pope in such a way as to make the body of Christ seem a monster with two heads, can be used once again in its proper scriptural sense. On the change of title the Theological Commission has this to say: "Instead of 'head of the Church' we may say in this context 'shepherd of the whole Church', an expression more in keeping with the scriptural saying according to which Christ is the head of the body, but Peter is called the shepherd of the flock (cp. John 21:16 f.)"[56]

On 5: The question of the origin of episcopal jurisdiction, which was discussed as early as Trent, was left open by Vatican I. Pius XII in *Mystici Corporis* attempted to decide the question in favour of the pope, which would have made bishops more or less the delegates of the pope—something which has no foundation in history and which would in particular have conflicted with Eastern tradition. According to Vatican II the bishop receives his full authority through his episcopal consecration: "Episcopal consecration, together with the office of sanctifying, also confers the offices of teaching and of governing. (These, however, of their very nature, can be exercised only in hierarchical communion with the head and the members of the college.") (CE 21.)

On 6: "Just as, by the Lord's will, St Peter and the other apos-

[56] Schema 90.

tles constituted one apostolic college, so in a similar way the Roman Pontiff as the successor of Peter, and the bishops as the successors of the apostles are joined together. . . . The order of bishops is the successor to the college of the apostles in teaching authority and pastoral rule; or, rather, in the episcopal order the apostolic body continues without a break. Together with its head, the Roman Pontiff, and never without this head, the episcopal order is the subject of supreme and full power over the universal Church" (CE 22).

On 7: The reforms decided upon in Chapter I of the Decree on the Bishops' Pastoral Office in the Church are principally concerned with the following points: By setting up, or extending the competence of, national and regional episcopal conferences, there is to be a decentralization of the Church. At the same time the episcopate of the whole Church is to be represented in Rome by a Synod of Bishops, which will help the pope in the governing of the whole Church. Finally the Roman curia is to be reformed, and made more international. These reforms were set in motion immediately after the end of the Council.

The idea of the pope as the servant of the Church is one that can be supported from Catholic tradition. The Church never exists for the pope, the pope always exists for the Church. It is unthinkable that the pope could ever be right and the whole Church wrong. A pope who excommunicated the whole Church would be excommunicating himself. Like any other believer, the bishop of Rome is bound to try and avoid schism. All too often in Roman theology there has been a one-sided definition of schism. But classical Catholic tradition has always distinguished between two possible kinds of schism. Schism occurs—as the leading theologian of the Spanish Counter-Reformation, Francis Suárez, declared, with reference to Cajetan and Torquemada[57]—if someone cuts himself off from the pope as the head of the Church, or if someone cuts himself off from the body of the Church. In this second manner the pope too could be a schismatic, if he failed to maintain the necessary contact and fellowship with the whole body of the Church, or if he tried to excommunicate the whole Church, or if he attempted to overthrow all

[57] F. Suárez, *De charitate*. Disputatio XII de schismate, sectio I, *Opera omnia*, Paris 1858, 12, 733 f.

the customs of the Church which are safeguarded by apostolic tradition.

The idea that the pope is the servant of the Church must be extended to include the possibility of the pope having to resign or being deposed. That this possibility can become reality is testified to by the numerous trials and depositions of popes in the Middle Ages, which were undertaken for a variety of motives; these decisions were solemnly announced by the Roman synod, as the electoral college of the pope, and had to be confirmed by the emperor, as the representative of non-Roman Christendom. In the Carolingian period more than a dozen pontificates were contested in one way or another, and ended by the deposition of the pope or his violent removal from office; in the Ottonian period the number of papal elections just about balanced the number of papal depositions. The rise of the medieval reformed papacy began in a decisive manner with the deposition of all three rival popes at the synods of Pavia, Sutri and Rome under the emperor Henry III. The main grounds for deposition were the illegal assumption of office, simony, heresy and so on. In the twelfth and thirteenth centuries the usual way in which a pope or antipope lost his office during his lifetime was through waiving his claim to the title. The conciliarist period in the fifteenth century, which put an end to the Western schism and the rule of three popes and achieved the reunification of Western Christendom, based its papal depositions on the fact that an ecumenical council is superior to a pope. It must be recognized that the decrees of the Council of Constance have fundamentally the same authority as the decrees of other ecumenical councils; they form the opposite pole in the history of the Church from Vatican I. But even after Vatican I the canonists indicated various cases in which the pope could lose his office; in addition to death and resignation, there are above all mental illness, heresy and schism.

All these delicate but unavoidable historical and theological questions are discussed in detail in *Structures of the Church*. On the interpretation of the medieval papal depositions, and of the statement *"Prima sedes a nemine iudicatur"* which has its origins in a sixth-century forgery, was included in the Decretum Gratiani and thence found its way into canon law, and on the present canonical position, cf. *Structures* VII, 3 (pp. 223–240). On the ecclesiological significance of the decrees of Constance, both past and present, and the relationship between them and Vatican I, cf. *Structures* VII, 4, 5 (pp. 240–285). The crucial definitions of the ecumenical Council of Constance run as follows: "This synod declares first that, being legitimately convoked in the Holy Spirit, forming a general council and representing the universal Church, it has immediate power from Christ, which every state and dignity, even if it be the papal dignity, must obey in what concerns faith, the eradication of the mentioned schism and the reformation of the said Church in head and members. Likewise, it declares that whoever of whatever condition, state, dignity, even the papal one, refused persistently to obey the mandate, statutes and orders or prescripts of this sacred synod and of any other general council legitimately convened, above set out, or what pertains to them as done or to be done, will be penalised and duly punished with recourse if necessary to other means of law."[58]

On how far the convocation, direction and confirmation of ecumenical councils are questions of human law, cf. *Structures* VII, 6 (pp. 285–304). The often debated question as to who, in the event of a heretical, schismatic or mentally ill pope, should pronounce judgment (at least in the sense of a *sententia declaratoria*), is answered by theologians like Cajetan, M. Cano and D. Soto, and by Suárez with especial emphases, as follows: the Church; that is, the Council. If such a pope were to refuse to convoke a council, Suárez argues, then agreement between provincial or national councils would suffice. Alternatively, the college of cardinals or the episcopate would have to convoke an ecumenical council against the pope's will. Should the pope seek to prevent this, he should not be obeyed, for in this case he would be misusing his authority as supreme pastor against the justice and the commonwealth of the Church.[59]

These frontier incidents which history provides for us are not our chief concern here, but are cited because they shed considerable light on the fundamental relation between pope and Church, namely, that the pope exists to serve the Church.

[58] Mansi, 27, 590. In addition to the bibliography given in *Structures*, there is a new and important contribution to the debate by P. de Vooght: *Les pouvoirs du concile et l'autorité du pape au concile de Constance,* Paris 1965.

[59] F. Suárez, *De fide theologica*. Disputatio X de Summo Pontifice, sectio IV, *op. cit.,* 12, 317 f.

As we can see, it is not the case, as non-Catholics often assert, that the Catholic Church is saddled for better or worse with a pope, even if he acts in a way contrary to the Gospel. It is also clear that for this same reason the Church is not—as Catholics sometimes assume—relieved from the responsibility of acting itself; it cannot simply rely passively, and basically presumptuously, on the Holy Spirit; the Holy Spirit can never be invoked as a *deus ex machina*. Seen in this light, then, the definition of papal primacy is something much more human, or at least is much less high-flown and rigid, than might appear if we did not take the historical context into account.

The historical context also shows up the positive side of things, which there is no need to elucidate in detail here. If a pope really does exist for the Church and if he really fulfils his task of selfless pastoral service to the whole Church, then through him great things can be achieved and evils can be avoided. There is plenty of evidence for this too in the history of the Church, throughout the ages. Without the Petrine ministry many things would not have happened, the individual Churches would have left the unity of the Church to set up on their own, there would have been many more schisms and sects. Without the Petrine ministry various initiatives for reform within the Church and for the mission to the world would not have come about, or would have remained on a small scale or become bogged down. The Petrine ministry has made it possible to realize a good deal of external freedom, independence and unity. And if we look at the present time and see, for all the shortcomings, what an amazingly rapid and general change has come over the Catholic Church, turning it both towards reform of itself and towards ecumenical encounters, if we note that a council like Vatican II was possible at all, then we know how much we have to thank a man who took his Petrine ministry seriously and fulfilled it selflessly. Thus despite all the justified criticisms that are made of the present "system", one thing can be said: if the Catholic Church today, after all its difficulties and defeats still exists as it does, relatively well thought-of, unified and strengthened in faith and order, then it has to thank not least the Petrine ministry. And we are justified in asking: where would the Catholic Church, where indeed would Christendom as such be today, if throughout the centuries this Petrine ministry had not existed?

(*b*) No Catholic theologian is so naïve as to think that, by setting out these negative and positive points in the light of the two Vatican Councils—it is impossible to do more here— he would be able, significant though these points may be, to convince other Christians about papal primacy. This is because the real question is not the mode of exercising this primacy, or its actual limitations, but the very *existence* of papal primacy in the first place. This is where the real difficulties begin. And it would be impossible to sort them all out in one short chapter; to try and do so would imply a colossal underestimation of the difficulties, particularly the exegetical and historical ones. Since the time of Vatican I there has appeared an imposing collection of books for and against the justification of the primacy.[60] We shall not attempt the impossible here; rather than attempting to clear up the problems, all we can do is to shed some light on the questions at issue, with a view to an improved mutual understanding; this understanding will be aided in the future less by theoretical discus-

[60] Only the most recent literature on the Petrine question is given here. All the literature on New Testament ecclesiology (see A I, 3) should also be consulted. On the subject of Peter: C. Journet, *Primauté de Pierre*, Paris 1953; O. Karrer, *Peter and the Church, an examination of Cullmann's thesis*, Edinburgh–London–New York 1963. O. Cullmann, art. "πέτρα, Πέτρος", in ThW VI, 99–112; *Peter*, London–Philadelphia 1962; P. Gaechter, *Petrus und seine Zeit*, Innsbruck 1958; J. Perez de Urbel, *San Pedro, principe de los apostolos*, Burgos 1959; in the collection already cited: *Begegnung der Christen*, the contribution by J. Ringer and J. Schmid. Further bibliography in the important encyclopaedia articles on Peter by A. Vögtle–O. Perler, in LThK VIII, 334–341, and by E. Dinkler, in RGG V, 247–249; also the various articles on the pope and the papacy in the encyclopaedias. There are two very informative accounts of the state of studies in the interpretation of Mt. 16:18 f. both with exhaustive bibliographies: J. Ludwig, *Die Primatworte Mt 16:18f in der altkirchlichen Exegese*, Münster 1952, and F. Obrist, *Echtheitsfragen und Deutung der Primatsstelle Mt. 16:18 f. in der deutschen Theologie der letzten dreissig Jahre*, Münster 1960. From the orthodox point of view see esp. N. Afanassieff–N. Koulomzien–J. Meyendorff–A. Schmemann, *Der Primat des Petrus in der Orthodoxen Kirche*, Zurich, 1961.

sions than by the historical development of the Churches which has yet to come. All the difficulties are centred on three questions; the second and third questions depend on a positive answer being given to the preceding one. Are there grounds for assuming the primacy of Peter? Was the primacy of Peter something that was to continue? Is the bishop of Rome the successor of the primacy of Peter? All we can do here is to give a short summary of the Catholic answers to this, given at Vatican I, and of the Protestant difficulties. By doing so frankly and without beating about the bush the cause of Catholicism and the ecumenical cause may best be served. Our intention, here as elsewhere, is to go beyond criticism to a constructive position, which will, it is hoped, become clear.

1. The existence of the primacy of Peter; Vatican I (D 1822 f.), using the New Testament dogmatically rather than historically, bases its arguments for the Petrine primacy of jurisdiction on two points, (*a*) The *promise* of the primacy to Peter alone: "You shall be called Cephas" (Jn. 1:42), and "You are Peter, and on this rock I will build my church, and the powers of death shall not prevail against it. I will give you the keys of the kingdom of heaven, and whatever you bind on earth shall be bound in heaven, and whatever you loose on earth shall be loosed in heaven" (Mt. 16:18). (*b*) The *giving* of the jurisdiction to Peter alone, as supreme pastor and leader of the whole Church, by the risen Christ: "Feed my lambs, feed my sheep" (Jn. 21:15–17).

From the *historical viewpoint* we can say that at least the following points would in the main be accepted by exegetical scholars. Peter was, at all events, specially marked out from among the twelve, by being the first witness to Christ's resurrection (I Cor. 15:5; Lk. 24:34); as the first of the Easter witnesses, he may be regarded as the rock of the Church. Further, Peter was the leading figure in the community at Jerusalem. Up to the time of the "apostolic Council" he seems, in practice at least, to have governed the original Christian community and the Christian diaspora. This is confirmed by Galatians 2:7 f.; which establishes that the mission to the Jews and the Gentiles was divided up between Peter and Paul. Even though Luke had already, in his gospel, tried to give a much more idealized picture than either Mark or Matthew of this very human figure, this fisherman who was born in Bethsaida and lived, as a married man, in Capernaum, and even though an idealizing bias can be discerned in Acts 1–12, we can accept with certainty that Peter was the driving force of the young Church in its first missionary activity. And even though there is no sound historical basis for the interpretation of Petrine theology in Mark's gospel (Papias' story that Mark was Peter's interpreter is probably not reliable), nor in the letters attributed to Peter, and we can only infer it cautiously from the Pauline letters and Acts, we can at least be certain that Peter was the representative of Judaeo-Christianity, who in friendly fashion was opposed to Paul's mission to the Gentiles. He alone among the twelve definitely undertook missionary work outside Jerusalem. His stay in Antioch is testified to by Galatians 2:11 f. (cf. Acts 15:7), and a visit to Corinth is possible (cf. I Cor. 1:12). It is not possible, however, to establish a definite itinerary of his journeys, nor a precise chronology. This is about the bare minimum which must be accepted, on the evidence of the sources, with regard to Peter's position in the early Church.

The *difficulties* which arise in connection with further and more positive statements about Peter's position in the New Testament Church result from the following undeniable problem: how far are the statements about the position of Peter during Jesus' lifetime merely a reflection of the position of Peter after the resurrection? True, it cannot be denied (and the priority of Peter with regard to the post-resurrection appearances is probably connected with this fact) that Peter was one of the most intimate disciples of Jesus (Mk. 5:37; 9:2; 14:33), indeed the spokesman of the disciples (cf. Mk. 8:29; 9:5; 10:28; 11:21), and that no doubt for that reason his name always appears at the head of the list of the twelve (Mk. 3:16; Mt. 10:2; Lk. 6:14; Acts 1:13). Three questions, however, remain the subject of fierce controversy: (1) Whether the title added to his original name Simon (Mk. 1:16), the name Kephas (Aramaic *kepha*=rock=Peter) which became an additional name and finally his proper name, was given by the historical Jesus himself (as a promise for the future?) *or* whether it was given to him by the primitive Christian community (*vaticinium ex eventu?*); (2) whether the saying at Matthew 16:18 f., which in view of its Aramaic character very probably originated in Palestine, and which strikingly enough has no parallels in the other synoptic gospels, was a saying of the historical Jesus (the historical context for which may have been different from that of Caesarea Philippi), *or* whether the saying was attributed to Jesus by the primitive Christian community, in order to authorize the position of Simon in the community by the story of the change of name or by recasting accounts of the post-resurrection appearances; the answer to this question will depend on what view is taken of the relationship between the eschatological preaching of Jesus and the possible intention to found a Church; (3) whether the saying at Matthew 16:18 f. gives to Peter a genuine monarchical and legal ruling authority (jurisdiction) over the whole Church *or* whether it merely gives him a prior historical position as the first confessor of Jesus and first witness of his resurrection; as the spokesman and representative, perhaps even the leader of the twelve, who nonetheless remains on the same level as the other apostles. In the second case the word "rock" can refer to Peter as believer and confessor, or as an apostle; the "keys" can refer to a teaching authority or a governing authority, or both; finally "binding and loosing" can refer to a disciplinary power, or to the power to exclude others from the community, or to full authority over the kingdom of God and over sin, or quite generally to a juridical authority. John 21:15–17 will then be judged in an analogous way to Matthew 16:18 f.

2. The continuation of the Petrine primacy: Vatican I (D 1824 f.) deduces from the primacy of Peter the permanent continuation of this primacy. This primacy, appointed for the eternal salvation and the continuing good of the Church, must, according to the appointment made by Christ, necessarily continue. There are no quotations from Scripture in support of this, simply the declaration: "Whoever asserts that blessed Peter's permanent successors do not have the chief place in the whole Church, appointed by Christ the Lord, that is by divine right . . . let him be anathema."

From the *historical viewpoint* it is significant that Peter is not mentioned again after Antioch (cf. Acts 15:7; Gal. 2:11

f.). By contrast with the martyrdom of James, there is no mention of the death of Peter in the New Testament. On the other hand, a knowledge of his martyrdom evidently underlies the last chapter, added subsequently, of John's gospel. Nothing is reported about the appointment of a successor to Peter. Neither Matthew 16:18 f., nor John 21:15-17, nor Luke 22:32 make any special reference to a successor of Peter. On the other hand these writings, composed after Peter's death, indicate a continuing interest in Peter's special position, which is more than episodic; an interest that does not, for example, attach to James. In this connection two points are the subject of controversy: (1) Whether James, who after Peter's departure was clearly the leader of the Jerusalem community, was quite simply the leader of the local Jerusalem community and remained subject to Peter as the leader of the whole Church, *or* whether Peter, if he ever was the leader of the whole Church, was replaced in this position by James the brother of the Lord, as can be inferred from the second half of Acts (from 12:17 onwards), from Galatians 2:12 and from uncanonical sources (Ps-Clem. *Rec.* 1:17 and *Hom.* 1:20; *Ep. Pet.* 1; *Gospel of Thomas,* saying 12); (2) whether the Petrine texts imply a unique foundation *or* a continuing foundational *function;* that is, whether "rock" simply means the chronological beginning of the Christian community *or* the unique foundational element of the community *or* the continuing stabilizing fundament of the Church; and whether the "key-bearer" or representative "pastor" is a pattern for future forms of government *or* should be seen as the first incumbent of a continuing governmental authority.

3. The continuation of the Petrine primacy in the bishop of Rome. Vatican I (D 1824 f.) sees the permanent continuation of the Petrine primacy realized in the bishops of Rome: "Anyone following Peter in this episcopal see, receives from the institution of Christ himself Peter's primacy over the whole church. . . . Therefore whoever maintains . . . the bishop of Rome is not the successor in this primacy . . . let him be anathema." This statement is supported by a quotation from Irenaeus of Lyons (died *circa* 200), according to which "all Churches in all places are in agreement with the

Church of Rome concerning the *'potentior principalitas'* ". Apart from that, and an allusion in Ambrose, there are only two fifth-century references, both from the Roman side; one by the Roman legate at the Council of Ephesus in 431, the other by Leo the Great.

From the *historical viewpoint* it is incontestable that the Roman claim to primacy in the government of the Church, whatever the situation may have been with regard to its recognition in the East, was solidly established and clearly formulated in the West by the time of Leo I at the latest. The possibility that Peter may have been in Rome and been martyred there is one that has found increasing acceptance in recent times, both by Catholic and non-Catholic historians. This acceptance is not in fact founded on the archaeological evidence of a Petrine grave beneath the Vatican Basilica, which has been regarded very sceptically by leading experts even on the Catholic side. The literary evidence is, however, very impressive. On the basis of I Clement 5 f. a tradition of the martyrdom of Peter and Paul in Rome seems established with a high degree of probability for the Neronian period (does the reference to Babylon at I Peter 5:13 really mean Rome?). This Roman testimony from the end of the first century is confirmed by one from Asia Minor at the beginning of the second century, Ignatius, Rom. 4:3. It would be very difficult to challenge the credibility of a tradition which seems established from about A.D. 95, which is straightforward and undisputed at the time, and which at that time was free from any bias of ecclesiastical politics.

The *difficulties* do not therefore centre on the proof of Peter's presence in Rome; moreover, it would not be absolutely necessary to prove that Peter was martyred in Rome in order to justify the Roman primacy. The difficulties, which we must simply acknowledge without prejudice, concern the establishing of the succession of a monarchical bishopric of Rome, even assuming that there was a Petrine primacy for it to succeed to; it is difficult to establish that there was a *legitimate* succession, authorized in some way or another. The fact that Peter himself cannot possibly have been the founder of the Christian community in Rome, any more than Paul can, is irrelevant to the issue.

With regard to the early history of the Roman community there remain, despite extended discussions of the matter, certain difficulties which await solution and which can only be offered here as material for further discussion. It is not only that we have no idea what form Peter's activity in Rome took, and cannot know whether he was the leader of the Roman community at all—something we cannot simply assume for Peter any more than we can for Paul. The oldest and most important evidence for Peter's sojourn and death in Rome is a document which establishes at the same time a very strong case against the existence of a monarchical successor to Peter. In the letter of the Roman community to the community at Corinth, which according to a statement of Denis of Corinth, *circa* 170, reported by Eusebius, was composed by Clement, no single authority is obvious. At all events there is no sign of a monarchical episcopate in the first epistle of Clement, either in Corinth or in Rome. For this reason, it is difficult to see how Peter could have had a monarchical bishop as his successor. It is a peculiar fact, already referred to above, that even Ignatius, who in his letters to the communities in Asia Minor is already addressing, with some emphasis, monarchical bishops, does not address a bishop at all when he comes to write to the Romans. It is impossible to ascertain when a monarchical bishop first emerged from among the many bishops and presbyters in Rome. Details of the successors of Peter, like the oldest list of the bishops of Rome given by Irenaeus, which refers not to Peter but to Linus as the first bishop of Rome, who received his episcopal ministry from Peter *and* Paul, are second-century reconstructions, which may possibly have drawn on well-known Roman names. Our information about the Roman Church and its bishops is very fragmentary up to the middle of the third century; the first precise chronological dating of a Roman pontificate is the resignation of Pontian on 28 September 235.

It is understandable that the old-established, large and wealthy community of the capital of the world should from the first have been aware of its importance (cf. I Clem.) and could rightly enjoy a considerable reputation (as early as Rom. 1:8), not least because of the activity of Peter and Paul

(Ignatius, *Rom*. 4:3) and because of the exemplary charity of the community (cf. the opening of Ignatius' letter). But for a long time there is no sign of a claim to primacy, neither on behalf of the community nor of an individual. With the struggle against Gnosticism and the increasing importance of apostolic tradition and apostolic bishoprics, the importance of the Roman community, which could claim two apostles, the two greatest apostles, for itself, necessarily grew in stature. But even the passage in Irenaeus quoted by Vatican I (*Adv. Haer*. III, 3:1–2) does not refer to any *legal* obligation for other Churches to agree with the Roman Church. The Roman Church (there is no mention of a Roman bishop) figures not as the holder of a legal primacy, but as the most distinguished guardian of tradition, because of its double succession (Irenaeus too refers back to Peter *and* Paul); by ascertaining what *its* faith is, the faith of all the other Churches is assured.

The high repute of the Roman community is attested to in many letters and visits by bishops, theologians and heretics; and on this basis, towards the end of the second century, Bishop Victor could assert his claims against the Churches of Asia Minor in the dispute over Easter; still more clearly Stephen I appealed to this authority against the Africans in the dispute over baptism. But both of them had to face serious opposition in the Church as a whole, from the most important churchmen of the time; Victor was opposed by Irenaeus and Polycrates of Ephesus, Stephen by Cyprian and Firmilian. But the claims of the Roman bishops were greatly strengthened in this way, even though until far into the second millennium claims and theories always preceded reality. In all this development it is a remarkable fact that Matthew 16:18 f. in its complete wording is not quoted on a single occasion in all the Christian literature of the first few centuries, not even in the first epistle of Clement. The passage is first quoted by Tertullian in the second century, but not in support of Rome, merely in support of Peter. Not until the middle of the third century does a Roman bishop, Stephen I in fact, appeal to the precedence of Peter in his support of what he considers the superior tradition. And not until the fourth century is Matthew 16:18 f. used in support of a claim to primacy

(Optatus of Milevis, Jerome, Damasus, Leo I). In Eastern exegesis the situation is even more negative: right down to the eighth century and of course beyond that, Matthew 16:18 f. is thought of in connection with a personal primacy of Peter, unless the passage is quite simply thought of, as it is to some extent in the Western tradition, as referring to Christ or to faith. Matthew 16:18 is unanimously associated with the forgiveness of sins, which is not of course reserved to Peter alone (cf. Mt. 18:18). There are no signs that anyone seriously thought of a connection between the Matthew passage and Rome.

The aim of this analysis is not to give the impression that all these difficulties cannot be debated and in part at least answered. All these questions are historical ones; and unless one is going to take refuge in historically unfounded dogmatic postulates, the solving of them, as the vast amount of books on the subject makes very clear, is going to be a fairly exacting task. The difficulties of the argument about primacy can, as the foregoing summary has shown, be graded: before proving *"perpetuitas"*, it is essential to prove *"petrinitas";* and before proving *"romanitas"* it is essential to prove *"perpetuitas"*.

(c) Despite all these difficulties Catholic exegesis and theology has decided for a primacy of Peter, even if Matthew 16:18 f. is attributed not to the historical Jesus, but to the post-resurrection course of events. Catholic scholars remain convinced that the Petrine texts of the New Testament are only exhaustively interpreted if we infer that while there are not continual new foundations, there is at least a continuing foundational function; if the people of God of the new covenant, like that of the old covenant, has its divinely appointed pastor. They also hold, on the basis of subsequent history, that the bishop of Rome can exclusively lay claim to this function, and has with increasing clarity in the course of time fulfilled that function; at the same time, the *"ius divinum"* of the primacy can only be realized and fulfilled within the *"ius humanum"*.

Whatever view one takes, there is one thing that Orthodox and Protestant theologians, even if they find the Catholic arguments unconvincing, cannot dispute: the ministerial primacy of a single person is not contrary to Scripture. Whatever may be the justification for it, there is nothing in Scripture which would exclude such a ministerial primacy. A primacy of this kind is not from the very start in opposition to Scripture. Indeed, Orthodox and Protestant theologians will probably even concede that a ministerial primacy of this kind could be in accordance with Scripture, and at any rate provide that it is justifiable, and is carried out and exercised, in accordance with Scripture. Most of the Reformers from the young Luther via Melanchthon to Calvin conceded this, and many Orthodox and Protestant theologians today would concede it.

What was said above about the apostolic succession of pastoral ministries in general applies equally to an apostolic succession of the Petrine ministry. The decisive thing is not the historical aspect of a proven succession, however valuable that may be. The decisive thing is succession in the Spirit: in the Petrine mission and task, in the Petrine witness and ministry. If someone could prove conclusively that his predecessor and the predecessor of his predecessor and so on backwards were ultimately successors of Peter, even if he could prove that the original predecessor of all his predecessors had been "appointed" by Peter himself and invested as Peter's successor with all rights and duties, and yet on the other hand he completely fails to fulfil the Petrine mission, if he does not carry out the task it implies, if he does not give witness or perform his ministry, what use to him, what use to the Church is all the "apostolic succession"? Conversely, if there were someone whose succession, at least in its earliest years, was difficult to establish, whose "appointment" two thousand years ago was not at all documented, but who on the other hand fulfilled the Petrine mission as described in Scripture and performed this ministry for the Church, would it not be a secondary, if still important, question whether this real servant of the Church had a regular ancestral tree? He might not have a commission through the laying-on of hands, but he would have the charism, the charism of governing, and that would basically be enough.

The point we are trying to make is this: it is not the claims, the "rights", the "chain of succession" as such which are decisive, but the exercise and carrying out of a ministry in practice, service in action. When John XXIII began his great ecumenical work for the Church, for Christendom and for the world, mankind was not very interested in his place in a chain of succession and whether the legitimacy of his office was historically founded. What mankind saw with relief and joy was this: here was a man who for all his human weakness was a real rock in the modern age, able to give a new anchorage and a new sense of communion to Christianity (cf. Mt. 16:18). Here was a man who from his own deep sense of faith was able to strengthen and encourage the brethren (cf. Lk. 22:32). Here was a man, who was able to tend his sheep, as his Lord once did, with unselfish love (cf. Jn. 21:15–17). Not that the whole of mankind therefore became Catholic. But they felt spontaneously that these actions and this spirit had the Gospel of Christ behind them and were at all events justified by that Gospel. And this kind of legitimacy is more decisive for the Petrine ministry than any other.

This does not make discussion of the exegetical and historical problems superfluous. But this discussion must be seen in the proper light, in the proper perspective. One further point must be stressed here. Our discussion of the arguments has made it clear how much room to manoeuvre there is—not only in the historical questions (cf. Tertullian and Cyprian), but still more in the exegetical ones. There is a world of difference in interpretation between interpreting Matthew 16:18 f. in the light of Matthew 18:18, or vice versa, between putting greater emphasis on the passages about Peter or on those about James, etc.

How can we explain the fact that the same handful of words and short sentences can be interpreted by scholars, who claim to be working with the same historical and critical methods, in such diametrically opposed ways? There can be no doubt that the whole personality of the theologian is involved here, something that is determined by far more than these short passages themselves. Theologians, some admittedly more than others, quite obviously approach this question above all others with quite definite preconceived ideas, which can only be corrected to a very limited extent by the texts themselves. To put it more concretely: the view a theologian takes of the papacy today is not irrelevant to his interpretation of the problems which arise from the exegetical and historical texts. After looking at the centuries of controversy which have surrounded this point, we must conclude that it is improbable that greater agreement will be reached with regard to the interpretation of the texts unless to begin with a greater agreement is reached about the role of the papacy today. And this greater agreement about the role of the papacy today depends not least, indeed perhaps depends primarily, on the papacy itself, and its need to see itself more and more as a Petrine ministry.

It is an absurd situation that the Petrine ministry, which was intended, as Catholics in particular see it, to be a rocklike and pastoral ministry, preserving and strengthening the unity of the Church, should have become a gigantic, apparently immovable, insuperable and impassable block of stone barring the way to mutual understanding between the Christian Churches. Those of us who are convinced of the value of a Petrine ministry should be particularly taxed by this situation. How could such a situation possibly have arisen? Does it stem simply from a lack of knowledge, an undeveloped understanding or even a wicked refractoriness on the part of those who oppose the Petrine ministry? No one today would have the temerity to assert that. Even if the blame for the division between the Churches cannot be laid exclusively on one side or the other, we cannot evade the question: did this complete reversal of the function of the Petrine ministry not come partly, even particularly, from the fact that the Petrine *ministry* appeared to men to be more and more a Petrine *dominion?* There were of course very various historical reasons for this, and it was certainly not the result of bad faith on the part of one or more individuals. We have already indicated the long process by which the papacy became a world power.

As we have shown, things could have developed differently. Whatever view we take of the exegetical and historical basis for the Petrine ministry, and the divine or human authorization of a permanent Petrine ministry in the Church, it is clear that there might have been a different kind of development. The Roman community with its bishop, which in fact possessed quite outstanding gifts and capacities for service, could have become a truly pastoral primacy, in the sense of a spiritual responsibility, an inner leadership and an active caring for the welfare of the whole Church; this is a conception which in the pre-Constantinian age would have been totally acceptable. In this way the Roman bishopric would have become a general ecclesiastical court of appeal, capable of mediating and settling disputes, and had a primacy of selfless service, being responsible to the Lord of the Church and exercising humble charity towards all men; a primacy not in the spirit of Roman imperialism, but in the spirit of the Gospel.

No one will deny that the Roman Petrine ministry also fulfilled this role, indeed one can say that in the pre-Constantinian era this was its basic attitude. There was a genuine attempt to help the other Churches in a variety of ways, without ruling over them and without trying to stifle their individual natures and their independence in doctrine, liturgy and Church order. A good example is the part played by Rome in establishing Catholic norms in the second century (the rule of faith, the canon, ecclesiastical office) or in the struggle against Arianism. Only two examples from all the first three centuries have come down to us which reveal a different attitude, an attitude of rigid, impatient and aggressive authoritarianism and centralism, which was out to make the whole Church uniform and was ready to use extreme measures of force to do it, rather than working with the spiritual means of brotherly admonition and exemplary action. The first example is that of Bishop Victor, who wanted to excommunicate the whole of Asia Minor, merely in order to force on these ancient apostolic Churches the new date of Easter, which had only been introduced in Rome a generation before. The other is Bishop Stephen who, because of opposition to his view concerning the baptism of heretics, again wanted to use the powerful means of excommunication to exclude whole areas of the Church from the communion of the Church, and who accused the great Cyprian of being a pseudo-Christian and a pseudo-apostle.

This was the beginning of the road of unevangelical spiritual dominion, the course which can be illustrated from later apparently unimportant incidents. For example Damasus (d. 384) was the first to call the Roman *cathedra* the *sedes apostolica,* although in the original usage of the Church all Churches which had been founded by the apostles were called *ecclesiae apostolicae,* and although in the middle of the fourth century all episcopal sees were still called apostolic sees (in this way Rome began to monopolize titles of dignity). Then Bishop Siricius (d. 399) began to call his own statutes quite simply "apostolic", adopted the official imperial style in his writings, instead of the earlier pastoral style—a manner of approach which was to be so successful in the future and was also to cause so much damage—and began to claim for himself, in quite a different sense from Paul, the *"sollicitudo omnium ecclesiarum"* (II Cor. 11:28), in order to confuse the areas of genuine responsibility, and to extend the authority of the Roman bishop so that he became the metropolitan of central and southern Italy, and then the authority of the metropolitan so that he became the patriarch of the West, and then the authority of the Western patriarch so that he became the primate of East and West.

Then Bishop Innocent (d. 407) tried to insist that all important matters after they had been discussed by a synod of bishops should be presented to the Roman bishop for his decision, and brought about the centralization of the liturgy on the basis of historical fictions (namely that the Roman tradition was the Petrine tradition, thereby neglecting the Pauline tradition; that the Roman liturgy was the liturgy of Peter; that Peter had founded all the Churches of the West). Then subsequent bishops—Zosimus, Boniface, Celestine, Leo the Great, and then Felix II, Gelasius, Symmachus and Hormisdas—continued to develop their claims to domination and their actual power, like rulers of this world, so that with time the Roman patriarchate grew more and more powerful, and the successors of the Galilean fisherman became secular princes with extensive lands, rich sources of income and an army, a strange development which was legitimized *post hoc facto* by the influential forgery of the Donation of Constantine in the eighth to ninth centuries. Then finally in the ninth century Nicholas I imposed the ban of anathema on anyone who failed to observe a doctrinal or disciplinary decision of the pope, set himself up as the lord of the whole earth, and did not even shrink from declaring that the most scandalous forgeries of Church history, the pseudo-Isidorian decretals, a very recent work of Frankish forgery which had been handed over to him, had been preserved from earliest times in the Roman archives and were a binding and fundamental part of ecclesiastical law.

From this point the road necessarily led, despite the *saeculum obscurum,* to Humbert and to Gregory VII, whose *dictatus papae* goes far beyond even the colossal claims of the pseudo-Isidorian forgeries, both in its claims to power within the Church and its claims to worldly power. In this way a Petrine ministry which might originally have been possible turned into a papal world-domination, which celebrated the height of its triumphs at the beginning of the thirteenth century and came to a catastrophic end at the conclusion of that century.

This was all by no means necessary, but was the result of a ministry which, as has been variously stressed, on the one hand rendered great services to the Western Church, and on the other hand saw itself increasingly as a source of power and dominion. The view of the Petrine ministry as a spiritual power and dominion did not change much in subsequent times, despite all the criticisms of a Bernard of Clairvaux, despite the heretics, scholars and saints who opposed it. It continued unabated, while the power politics of the crusades and the policy of latinization definitively alienated the entire East from the bishop of Rome, while the Western schism brought the papacy itself to the brink of collapse, while the Protestant Reformation removed from the papacy the greater part of the Germanic and Anglo-Saxon area, while modern developments caused a majority of Catholics, especially the intellectuals, to undertake a silent inner exodus. The pope of the First Vatican Council was not far behind many of his medieval predecessors as far as a sense of spiritual domination was concerned; not only because he praised an anthology on the Roman Pontiff which reproduced the forged decretals as genuine testimonies of the papacy; not only because he described the abolition of the Papal States as sacrilege, appealing to the inalienable rights, sanctified by so many titles, of the apostolic see to its possessions; but particularly because in the council itself he identified himself with ecclesiastical tradition, branded the representatives of the opposition as his enemies and imposed his personal views on the Council by not precisely fastidious means. The difference between this approach and that of the popes of Vatican II is evident.

The revealing process by which titles were monopolized by Rome, with serious consequences, has already been briefly referred to, in connection with the idea of an *apostolic see*. Originally there were several *sedes apostolicae,* all those episcopal sees which could prove an historical connection with one of the apostles. From the time of Damasus onwards the title was increasingly limited to the bishop of Rome, so that finally there was only one "apostolic see", that of Rome.

"Pope": The word comes from πάππα(ς), i.e. father. From the third century "pope" was a title given to bishops, abbots and later in the East even to ordinary priests. From the fifth century the bishop of Rome is distinguished from other "popes" (especially the patriarchs of Constantinople, Alexandria, Antioch and Jerusalem), by such titles as *"papa urbis";* in the East he was known as *"papa occidentis".* From the end of ancient times, however, the title is increasingly reserved for the bishop of Rome, and from the eighth century the bishops of Rome regularly use it in referring to themselves, in preference to the simple word *"episcopus".* At the end of the first millennium Gregory V (d. 999) forced the archbishop of Milan to cease using this title. From that time onwards the title "pope" has been the exclusive privilege of the bishop of Rome. In his *dictatus papae* Gregory VII solemnly declared that no one else in the world deserved this unique name but the bishop of Rome.

"Vicar of Christ": According to the New Testament every Christian is to see Christ in his brother. The apostles were in a special way ambassadors in the place of Christ (cf. II Cor. 5:20; Lk. 10:16; Jn. 13:20). From this fact the title *"vicarius"* of Christ was restricted to the bishops, being drawn from Roman legal and military usage. During the post-Constantinian period, when their sense of primacy was gradually developing, the bishops of Rome referred to themselves as *vicarius* or successor *Petri.* It was not until the Middle Ages that the title *"vicarius Christi"* (or *"Dei"*) was restricted for the most part to a single person: namely the *emperor* (from the time of Charlemagne). Even Gregory VII did not claim this title. It seems to have been Bernard of Clairvaux who

influenced the spiritual world-ruler Innocent III to take over this medieval imperial title; for him it was the ideal expression of the unity of supreme spiritual and secular power; Thomas Aquinas introduced the title into dogmatics. From the fifteenth century onwards it appears in all important dogmatic documents of the popes.

"Pontifex Maximus": This was originally the title of the pagan Roman high priests. From the time of Augustus it was used by the Roman emperors, but was then abandoned in the Christian period by the Emperor Gratian (378). From the time of Leo I it has been a title of the popes (it was also used on occasions by some other bishops). Only since Renaissance times has it been exclusively reserved for the pope. Italian uses the expression *"sommo pontefice"*, French the more politically coloured expression *"souverain pontife"*, English "supreme pontiff"; there is no German equivalent.

These historical notes are of course one-sided and simplified; it was not our intention to sketch out a history of the papacy. But the darker and shadowy side must be brought out, especially because it has been customary in Catholic apologetics to fail to put it into context, and to concentrate on the admittedly important service the papacy has rendered to the Church; it must not be overlooked if we are to realize the extent of the problem and hope to find a possible positive solution. When we look at the lost unity of the Church of Christ and the considerable rigidity within the Catholic Church, the question arises with great force; is there a way back, which would also be a way forward, from this primacy of dominion to the old primacy of service and ministry?

Cautiously but with conviction we can give an affirmative answer to this question. Three points, the second more important than the first and the third than the second, must be taken into account:

1. Historical experience shows that the high points of papal dominion have always been followed immediately by times of outward humiliation and restrictions of power. After Leo I and his successors came the time of the emperor Justinian (527–565), who reduced Rome to a mere Western patriarchate, on the same level as Constantinople in the East, and regarded and confirmed himself as the real ruler of the whole

Church in matters both of doctrine and discipline. Again, after the spiritual *imperator* Nicholas I came the disgraceful "dark age" of Rome, in which the pope, caught between the merciless struggles of the Roman nobility, was reduced to the rank of a minor country bishop. Again, after the proud universal dominion of the popes in the Middle Ages, there came the humiliations of exile, the great schism and the conciliar era; the splendid age of the Renaissance was followed by the enormous losses of the Reformation period; the period of baroque dominion and the Counter-Reformation was followed by a time of decline with the Enlightenment and the age of revolution . . . *Historia docet*.

2. The process of the secularization of the papacy has, seen as a whole, been largely reversed; this happened for the most part under historical pressures, but it is a fact that must be taken into account. The development as a whole has been one from the loss of the papal world dominion to the loss of the Papal States; from the abandonment of a *potestas directa in temporalia*, via a *potestas indirecta*, down to a respecting of the independence of secular organizations; from a primacy in art and culture to a primacy of service, both humanitarian and missionary. Admittedly this abandoning of power has chiefly been connected with the relations between the papacy and secular powers in the widest sense. It has often, partly as a reaction, been associated with a development of power positions within the Church itself; thus after the loss of the Vatican State, Vatican I decided for a codification of Church law in a spirit of absolutism, and for an intensification of the process of centralization. In order to concentrate on this side of the problem, the question of power within the Church which is so much more important today, we have been considering earlier popes rather than the medieval popes. And for this reason a third point, the most important one, needs consideration.

3. A voluntary abandonment of spiritual power is possible; something that might seem unwise in terms of politics, and even of Church politics, may be required of the Church. Remarkably enough, and it is a very hopeful sign, this has actually happened in history. Apart from examples like Hadrian VI or Marcellus II who because of the disfavour of the time

or early death were unable to have a profound influence on history, there is the figure of Gregory the Great, who followed a series of very power-conscious popes; there is John XXIII, and the fact that Vatican I could be followed by a council like Vatican II.

For Leo the Great the central idea in his view of the Petrine ministry was that of *"plenitudo potestatis"*, which was so often quoted in later times and finally defined by Vatican I; by contrast the central idea for *Gregory the Great* was the idea immediately drawn from the New Testament that he was "the servant of the servants of God". As a Benedictine monk and as a deacon he had already used this title, and when he became pope he used it in his letters as an official description of himself. Other more pretentious titles, like that of "ecumenical patriarch", he rejected, since any title with the attribute *"universalis"* would reduce the stature of the other patriarchs. He pointed out that even the apostle Peter had not described himself as a universal apostle. It is curious that Vatican I should have quoted Gregory of all people in its definition of the primacy of jurisdiction, referring to a "supreme and *universal* pastor", who could say to the bishops, in Gregory's words: "My honour is the honour of the whole Church. My honour is the firm strength of my brethren. I am truly honoured when to each of them is not denied the honour due to him" (D 1828). The context of these words shows that their bias is precisely the opposite. In this letter to the Patriarch Eulogius of Alexandria Gregory is rejecting the title *"universalis papa"*, and is also saying that his letter is not to be regarded as a jurisdictional *"Iussio"*. The preceding sentences, which Vatican I did not quote, run as follows: "I have not commanded, but I have tried to indicate the things which seemed to me useful . . . I do not regard that as an honour, which I know robs my brothers of their honour". It is in this context that the words quoted by Vatican I then follow: "For my honour is the honour of the whole Church. . . ." As far as new titles are concerned, the following sentence, also not quoted by the council, runs: "Away with words which puff up vanity and injure love."[61]

This basic attitude of Gregory's enabled him to recast in a crucial way the view of a primacy of dominion held by his predecessors, Victor and Stephen, Damasus, Innocent, Leo and Gelasius. All of them had continually sung the praises of their own *cathedra Petri*; Gregory gave honour to the two Petrine sees of the East,

---

[61] Gregory the Great, *Ep. ad Eulogium episcopum Alexandrinum;* PG 77, 933.

Alexandria and Antioch, which he regarded as being on the same level as the Roman see. His predecessors had constantly emphasized the precedence, the splendour and the authority of Peter, Gregory frequently meditates penitently on the shortcomings and the denial of Peter. Authoritative firmness, which is by no means lacking in Gregory, is in this way combined with a humble spirit. The words of Gregory: "There will be good government from the highest place of all if he who governs rules more over his vice than over his brethren"[62] is characteristic of the man. The tendencies of his predecessors to centralize ecclesiastical administration completely was alien to Gregory. The instruction he gave to Augustine, the missionary he had sent out to the Anglo-Saxons, shows that he had no interest in establishing liturgical uniformity. He had no wish to impose on other Churches the local Roman liturgy and the local Roman customs: "Customs are not beloved for their place of origin; their places of origin are loved for the customs."[63] If the papacy had continued to develop in the evangelical and ecumenical spirit of Gregory the Great, many things would have been avoided, not least the schism between the Eastern and Western Churches.

A modern counterpart to Gregory the Great is *John XXIII*. He was a man who displayed more than just a different "temperament", amiable and kindly; more than just a new and attractive "style".

As in the case of Gregory, something much more crucial happened with John: the change from a Petrine *power* which, however spiritualized, however subtle, had been none the less tangible and sometimes cruelly hard, to a Petrine *ministry*, a ministry not merely asserted, but fulfilled in action. We are not interested here in the cult of personality which has still not died out among Catholics. John XXIII needs no idealizing. In many respects he remained all his life the very conservative peasant's son that he was, and retained a very traditional piety and theology. He himself said that he lacked many of the qualities of his predecessors. He never really mastered the machinery of the curia, and the decision which was forced upon him, a decision which went far beyond the curialism of Vatican I, to make those organs of the curia which were themselves most in need of reform into the leaders of the council's commissions, was one for which the council was to pay very dearly, right down to the drawing up of the council documents and some consequent discrepancies. But no one would be so small-minded as to hold these things against a man who inaugurated a

---

[62] Gregory the Great, *Regula pastor,* VI, 44; PL 77, 36.
[63] Gregory the Great, *Reg.* XI, 64; PL 77, 1187.

new epoch of hope for the whole of Christendom and for the Petrine ministry itself.

This pope had none of the airs of a *"pontifex maximus"*, a *"souverain pontife"*, a "supreme pontiff". He was not a new Christian kind of high priest. Anything hieratic, anything that smacked of pose or pretence or "saintliness" was alien to him; he carried out his ministry unpretentiously, avoiding as far as possible any applause or honours. He did not want to "pontificate" in fact, he wanted to help his fellow men, deeply sympathetic as he was to the anxieties as well as the successes of the modern world. He rarely made programmatic speeches, but constantly preached the Gospel anew. He did not interfere in an authoritarian manner in the life of other Churches and dioceses, but made it his very real business, like no bishop of Rome before him for a very long time, to be a bishop to his own Roman Church and to care for its pastors and its people.

In this way John XXIII not only made the Petrine ministry more human once again, and brought it closer to ordinary people, much more than all the imposing papal rulers of our century had done. Most importantly, he tried to give a new form to this Petrine ministry, which bases all its claims on the Gospel but all too often only means Matthew 16:18 f.; he tried to shape it in a new and complete way in accordance with the demands of the Gospel.

Here was a pope who to a quite unprecedented degree exercised an *evangelical renunciation of spiritual power,* so that he might serve the Church and the world better. His renunciation of spiritual power meant the renunciation of condemnations, threats, excommunications, use of the index, inquisitorial processes; it meant also a renunciation of new authoritarian regulations, definitions and dogmas. Above all the renunciation of spiritual power meant a renunciation of an absolutist one-man government and the convoking of an ecumenical council, something that might have seemed unnecessary after the definitions of Vatican I and according to the basic principles of curial politics was highly dangerous and inopportune. Finally, the renunciation of spiritual power meant that John stepped down from his throne and selflessly came to meet other Christians, the Jews and the modern world in general; in his encyclicals, calling for peace and social justice, religious freedom, human rights and a spirit of brotherliness, John did not confront the modern world with new ecclesiastical claims and demands, but expressed the sympathy of the Church and its modest desire to co-operate with it.

It is amazing, to say the very least, that a pope could make scarcely any appeal to the definitions of Vatican I, to the ideas of papal prerogatives, primacy of jurisdiction and infallibility, and yet in the space of five short years achieve such an enormous amount. Can we hope that the offensive aspects of the definitions of Vatican I might become as immaterial as, for example, the *dictatus papae* (which is not even to be found in Denzinger's *Enchiridion!*), if the successors of John XXIII, voluntarily renouncing their spiritual power, were to commit themselves to serving the Church along these lines? The voluntary laying aside of the tiara, the emblem of papal dominion, by Pope Paul VI, and other measures of reform in the same direction, show that this hope is not entirely without foundation. Such a commitment would represent an incalculable service to the cause of the Catholic Church and the cause of the reunion of the divided Churches, as well as to mankind in the modern world in general.

Is there a way back, or rather a way forward, to the original idea of a primacy of service? Only through the voluntary renunciation of that power which in practice has become associated with the Petrine ministry, through a long and problematical historical development, and has partly helped it but also seriously injured it. Without this renunciation of power the reunion of the divided Christian Churches is as impossible as a radical renewal of the Catholic Church according to the Gospel. The renunciation of power is by no means something that happens naturally. Why should any man, any authority or institution, give up something which it possesses, and without any visible sign of something being given in return?

The renunciation of power is in fact only possible for a man who has grasped something of the message of Jesus and of the Sermon on the Mount in particular; who has understood something of what is meant by the blessedness of the "meek" who *"shall* inherit the earth" and the blessedness of the "peacemakers" (Mt. 5:5 and 9); who gives his cloak as well when only his coat has been demanded, who goes two miles with his companion who only asked him to go one (5:40 f.), who does to men what he would wish them to do to him (7:12). That these demands of Jesus—and we must remember that it is not the individual examples, but the whole basic drift of a man's life which matters—are not abstract ideas, but are relevant for the Church and the governing of the Church too, is revealed by no one more clearly than by the apostle Paul in his attitude towards his Churches.

Paul knew very well that in his communities there was no higher authority than his own apostolic authority, entrusted to him by the Lord. And yet he did not try to extend or develop this authority, still less build it up into a sacral authority of jurisdiction. On the contrary, he constantly and voluntarily limited his own authority in the Church. He did this in the conviction that the apostles were not called to "lord it over your faith", but to "work with you for your joy" (II Cor. 1:24). He did this in the conviction that his Churches belonged not to him but to the Lord, and were therefore free in the spirit, "called to freedom" (Gal. 5:13) and not "slaves of men" (I Cor. 7:23). Paul is well aware that his Churches are immature in many ways and make mistakes. And yet he never behaves towards them as though he were a cautious pedagogue whose task it was to educate them for their freedom. Rather he presupposes this freedom as having been granted to them, he respects it, fights for it, so that his communities will not follow him under constraint, but in freedom. Of course, where Christ and his Gospel have been sacrificed to another gospel, he must threaten them with curses and judgment (I Cor. 16:22; Gal. 1:8 f.; 5:10). But the measures he resorted to with regard to an individual, temporary exclusion from the community until he should mend his ways (I Cor. 5), he never, so far as we can tell, applied to a whole community, not even in Galatia. He always keeps his authority in the background as much as he can; he appeals rather than commands, appeals to the judgment of others and their own sense of responsibility rather than delivering prohibitions, prefers gentle admonitions to disciplinary force, prefers hortative forms to imperatives, "we" phrases to "you" phrases; instead of punishing, he speaks words of forgiveness, instead of repressing freedom he challenges it to come alive.

Paul never abuses his authority. He does not extend his powers; on the contrary, he always restricts them. In matters of Church discipline he avoids making an authoritative decision, something he could easily have done (II Cor. 8:8–10). In moral questions, where the Lord and his word is not at stake, he prefers to leave his communities with their freedom, rather than lay any restraint on them (I Cor. 7:35). Even where there can be no question of what his decision is going to be, he does not offer a one-sided prescription, he involves the community (I Cor. 5). Even in cases where he unquestionably has authority to take strong measures, he restrains himself, he seems almost to beg his community not to oblige him to use that authority; again and again we can see that from his letters (cf. I Thess. 2:7; II Thess. 3:9; I Cor. 4:14; 9:12 and 18; II Cor. 13:10; Philem. 8 f.). In this way Paul never confronts his communities as their lord, not even as their high priest. The apostle is not the lord, Christ is the Lord, and this Lord lays down the norms both for the Churches and for him. He can never treat his Christians simply as "children", they are his "brothers", whose servant he is in patience, generosity and love. It is not politeness or human courtesy which is the reason why he is always ready to renounce the use of his authority; it is because he wants to be faithful to the Lord in his service. For this reason he uses his authority for building up, not for tearing down (II Cor. 10:8; 13:10).

It would be a tremendous gain both for the Church and for the Petrine ministry if the latter could take the reflection of this apostle as its pattern, imitating Paul, who did more than any of the other apostles, even than Peter, who was the greater theologian and who, according to the oldest Roman tradition, was always seen as founding the fame and authority of the Church in Rome together with Peter. If in the course of time the Petrine ministry has become too much of a Petrine dominion, then it is not least because Paul was not regarded as highly as Peter. Paul was only quoted in selected pericopes, and was merely, if with great solemnity, "commemorated"; Galatians 1:11–20 was still quoted, but not Galatians 2:11–14—in short, *"San Paolo"* was too far *"fuori le mure"*.

But it was not only Paul's image which was distorted. It is doubtful whether Peter would have recognized himself in the picture that was to be drawn of him. Not only because he was no prince of the apostles, but remained to the end of his life the modest fisherman, now a fisher of men, who wanted to follow and serve his Lord. But much more because he had another side, which all the gospels agree upon, a side which shows us the truly human Peter; misunderstanding, making mistakes, failing his Lord. It is little short of scandalizing that each of the three texts classically used to prove the precedence of Peter are accompanied in counter-point by three passages, the dark tones of which balance, if not obscure, the bright tones of the three Petrine texts. The three great promises are balanced by three serious failures. Anyone who wishes to base his claims upon the promises, cannot avoid applying to himself the three failures, which at least represent three possible temptations. And if the promises in large black letters on a golden background surround the Church of St Peter like a frieze, it would be only right, to avoid misunderstandings, to add to them the three contrary incidents in golden letters on a black background. Gregory the Great at least, who is buried in the church, would surely have understood that as well as John XXIII.

The first temptation (Mt. 16:18 f. is followed by Mt. 16:22 f.) is that of knowing better than the Lord, taking the master confidently on one side and telling him how he is to act and how things are going to happen. Peter, putting himself above his master, points out a way of triumphalism which will bypass the cross. These confident ideas of a *theologia gloriae* are precisely human thoughts, which stand in direct opposition to what God thinks and plans: they represent a pious *theologia satanae*, an inspiration of the tempter. Whenever Peter takes it for granted that he can think God's thoughts for him, whenever the confessing Peter of Matthew 16:16 becomes the misunderstanding Peter of Matthew 16:22, standing, perhaps without even noticing it, on the side of man rather than on the side of God, then the Lord turns his back on him, and delivers the hardest saying imaginable: "Get behind me, Satan! You are a hindrance to me; for you are not on the side of God, but of men." (16:23).

The second temptation (Lk. 22:32 is followed by Lk. 22:34) reminds us that a particular position and a particular gift imply particular responsibilities. And precisely this does not exclude trials and temptations; here again Satan appears, who has demanded the right to sift every disciple of Jesus like wheat. Peter's faith is not to fail. But as soon as he self-confidently supposes that his loyalty is beyond question and that his faith is a firm possession, beyond any temptation; as soon as he forgets that he is dependent on the prayer of the Lord and needs to receive faith and devotion over and over again; as soon as he regards his strength and his readiness to accompany the Lord as his own achievement, as soon as in his self-confidence he overestimates himself and no longer puts his whole trust in the Lord, then the hour of cock-crow is not far off. He will be ready to deny his Lord, to assert that he never knew him, not once only, but three times, that is to say, completely and totally: "I tell you, Peter, the cock will not crow this day, until you three times deny that you know me."

The third temptation (Jn. 21:15 is followed by Jn. 21:20 ff.): the Lord three times asks Peter, who had three times denied him, whether he loves him: "Do you love me more than these?" Only under this condition can he be entrusted with the leadership of the community; he must feed the lambs and tend the sheep by following Jesus in love. But Peter, when he no longer looks at Jesus, when he turns round, sees him who had always surpassed him in love. And his unsuitable question as to what is going to happen to John, receives an answer which seems to contradict his general commission as a pastor: "What is that to you?" So there are things which do not concern Peter. Whenever Peter does not concern himself with his own task, whenever he tries to concern himself with everything, whenever he fails to see that there are things in human life that he cannot assume responsibility for, whenever he forgets that there are special relations with Jesus which do not have to pass through him, whenever he fails to accept that there are other ways apart from his way, then he will hear the word, a word of stern rebuke that is at the same time a call to renewed discipleship: "What is that to you? Follow me!"

The greater the mission, the greater the temptation. The enormous burden of responsibility, of care, of suffering and anxiety which weighs upon the Petrine ministry—provided that Peter's successor is truly a rock, a key-bearer and pastor in the service of the whole Church—is surely immeasurable. For the times in which the papacy could be enjoyed, being something given by God—as Leo X is said to have remarked at the time of Luther—are long since past. The toils and tribulations associated with this ministry, the sense of being misunderstood and the sense of one's own incapacity, are enough to make faith unsure (cf. Lk. 22:32), to make love fail (cf. Jn. 21:17), to make the hope of overcoming the gates of death (cf. Mt. 16:18) seem faint. This ministry, more than any other, is dependent every day afresh upon the grace of the Lord. This ministry may also expect a great deal from the brethren, more than is often given to it, and of a helpful rather than an unhelpful kind: not servile subservience, not uncritical devotion, not sentimental idolatry, but daily intercession, loyal co-operation, constructive criticism and unfeigned love.

It is possible that even Orthodox and Protestant Christians may be able to sympathize with the Catholic in his conviction that the Church, and perhaps Christianity as a whole, would lack something if this Petrine ministry were suddenly no longer there: something that is not inessential for the Church. There is something imposing about this ministry, if it is soberly seen in the light of sacred Scripture for what it is: a ministry to the whole Church. The fully understood biblical notion of ministry goes far beyond the legal categories of Vatican I. This primacy of service is more than a primacy of honour (*primatus honoris*), which belongs to no one in a Church of service and in its passivity could help no one. This primacy of service is also more than a primacy of jurisdiction (*primatus iurisdictionis*), which, interpreted solely in terms of power and dominion, would be a fundamental misunderstanding and which, interpreted solely in terms of the words themselves, would leave out of account, if not contradict, the essential element, that of service. The Petrine ministry can be correctly and biblically described as a primacy of service, a pastoral primacy: *primatus servitii, primatus ministerialis, primatus pastoralis.*

Are we here describing an ideal? Have we finally ceased to talk about the *real* Church? Is the real Petrine ministry not still, as it has always been, a Petrine dominion? With all due caution we may answer: the primacy of service is being realized now once

again. There are grounds for hoping that through the voluntary renunciation of power in the widest sense of the word the Petrine
ministry will increasingly reveal itself as such in the near and more
distant future. The way is not easy. Some things can be done at
once, others will need time. At all events, a reform is in progress,
and we need only indicate briefly here the things that, quite independently of current fashions, seem required in the light of the
original message, in the light of the Gospel itself:

1. *Evangelical humility:* A renunciation of unbiblical titles,
which are proper only to God or Christ (*Sanctissimus Dominus,
Beatissimus Pater,* His Holiness, Holy Father, Head of the
Church)—or alternatively are proper to all Christians, or at least
to all bishops (Vicar of Christ, etc.). At the very least the title
once given to pagan high priests (Supreme Pontiff) can be
regarded as open to misinterpretation. Valid titles are: Bishop of
Rome, servant of the servants of God, chief pastor. In early times
popes never abandoned the names given to them in baptism; only
at the beginning of the present millennium did popes regularly
begin to change their names when they were elected (Hadrian VI
and Marcellus II, popes of the reform, are exceptions here). Some
discretion seems called for in the use of the words "apostolic" and
"holy" in connection with persons and institutions.

2. *Evangelical simplicity:* Without indulging in unrealistic and
romantic poverty, a renunciation of all the pomp and luxury which
stems from the early years of the Petrine dominion; above all in
clothes, servants, courtly apparatus, guards of honour, and especially at times of worship. Papal orders and Roman court titles
make no sense in a Church of service.

3. *Evangelical brotherliness:* A renunciation of anything that
savours of absolutist government, the imperial Byzantine–baroque
style of speaking and writing letters, all secret procedures, all solitary decisions without the co-operation of the Church or its representatives (collegiality, episcopate, council of bishops, council of
laity); the de-politicizing of the papacy by renouncing all secular
diplomacy (nunciatures).

4. *Evangelical freedom:* A furthering of the independence of
the Churches and their pastoral ministries according to the principle of subsidiarity; the internationalization and running down of
the curial power machinery; the involvement of the relevant
Churches in the election of their bishops (by means of representation both of the pastoral ministries and the communities); involvement of the whole Church in the election of the pope (by
means of the council of bishops or possibly of a supreme senate of
representatives of the pastoral ministries and the laity).

Much has happened in recent times, and the pope has often acted more courageously than have the bishops in individual countries in changing their episcopal dominion into an episcopal ministry. Much can be achieved by the bold initiatives of individuals. Decisive changes can, however, only be brought about by a radical reform of canon law, and this in turn will require: (1) a fundamental review of the nature and the function of canon law altogether; (2) concrete reforms made not according to a particular legal tradition, but according to the Gospel itself and according to the needs of the present time; (3) a complete overhaul of individual articles which have found their way from forgeries into official canon law.

Petrine ministry or Petrine dominion: this alternative is at least equally important for any ecumenical understanding of the future as an exegetical and historical discussion. A reunion of the divided Christian Churches is unthinkable at any time with the present still centralized Roman system, and would in any case make things much too easy for the *ecclesia catholica reformanda*. The situation would immediately be different, were the bishop of Rome to draw strict lines of division between his areas of competence, according to the variety of his ministries: if, that is to say, he were to exercise the function of a bishop within the diocese of Rome, the function of a metropolitan within the Roman province, the function of a primate within the Italian Church and the function of a servant of the servants of God, of a pope, within the Church as a whole, while respecting the functions of the other ministries. Is it mere illusion to think that in this way in some distant future fellowship could be re-established for example between the Catholic Church and the Anglican Church? The Church of England for its part would be given the guarantee that it could retain in its entirety its present autochthonous and autonomous Church order under the Primate of Canterbury (not merely, therefore, like the Eastern "rites" in communion with Rome); and on the other hand the Church of England would recognize a pastoral primacy of the Petrine ministry as the supreme court of appeal, mediating and settling disputes between the Churches. Then instead of a Roman imperium we should have a Catholic commonwealth. In the whole early period of the Church the Petrine ministry was no more than a secondary court of appeal in extreme cases, when the authority of bishops and patriarchs did not suffice to settle matters. It is not clear why in such a case any more could be asked for, either in principle (dogmatically) or in practice (from an organizational point of view). A graded exercise of the pastoral primacy according to its various spheres of activity, in the light of its particular spiritual responsibility and of its active care for the welfare of the various Churches among themselves, would not only be fundamentally and practically possible, but would also correspond far better to the constitution of the Church at the time of its origins in the New Testament.

No one today can tell how the Petrine ministry, how the whole diaconal structure of the Church, still less how the reunification of the divided Christian Churches will work out in the future. The present generation has the responsibility of doing the best it can. One final point must be made in this connection: each Church, because of its individual history, has its own peculiarities which are not accepted in the same way by the other Churches; each so to speak has its own "speciality". For the Catholics this "speciality" is the pope. But in a sense they are not alone; the Orthodox Christians too have their "pope": their "tradition"; and the Protestants too have their "Bible", and the Free Churches their "freedom". But just as the "papacy" of the Catholics is not simply the Petrine ministry of the New Testament, so too the "tradition" of the Orthodox is not simply the apostolic tradition, the "Bible" of the Protestants is not simply the Gospel, the "freedom" of the Free Churches is not simply the freedom of the children of God. Even the best solutions are abused if they become like party political programmes, and become the slogans with which one marches out to do battle for power in the Church; these programmes are usually linked with the name of a particular leader, and are programmes which necessarily excluded all others from the one Church.

In Corinth too there were feuding parties. Each had their programme—we do not possess individual details—and had attached it to a leader whom they praised above all the rest and made more important than all the rest, at the same time denying any authority to the others. "For it has been reported to me by Chloe's people that there is quarrelling among you, my brethren. What I mean is that each of you says, 'I belong to Paul', or 'I belong to Apollos', or 'I belong to Cephas', or 'I belong to Christ'" (I Cor. 1:11). If one wished to be anachronistic here, one would without hesitation identify the party of Cephas with the Catholics, who claim to be in the right or at any rate over the others, because of his primacy, his pastoral power and his power of the keys. The Orthodox would be the party of Apollos, who, coming from the great tradition of Greek thought, would expound revelation more intellectually, more thoughtfully, more profoundly and therefore more "correctly" than any other. And the Protestants would certainly be the party of Paul, the father of their Church, *the* apostle, the unique preacher of the cross of Christ, who did more work than all the other apostles. And the Free Churches would be the party of Christ himself, the party which, claiming freedom from all the limitations of these other Churches, their authority and their confessions, leans solely on Christ as the unique Lord and Master and on this basis forms the brotherly life of its communities.

And for whom does Paul decide? Of course, for Peter, since Peter is the rock on which the Church is founded? No, Paul passes over the name of Peter in silence, and equally tactfully that of Apollos too. What is most surprising is that he even disavows his own partisans. He does not wish that groups should depend on one person and make one person into their party programme—a person who was not crucified for them, in whose name they were not baptized. Paul brought baptism to the Corinthians. But they were not baptized in his name, but in the name of Jesus, the crucified; and they belong to him in whose name they were baptized. Hence even the name of Paul, the founder of the community, is not to become a party slogan.

We can learn from this that however much the Petrine ministry may be a rock for the Church, its unity and its coherence, it cannot be turned into a criterion for deciding what is Church and what is not Church. Tradition, however valuable it may be as a guideline for the Church, its continuity and its consistency, cannot be a dividing line beyond which orthodoxy ends and heterodoxy begins. The Bible, however fundamental it may be for the Church, its faith and its creed, cannot be turned into a quarry, the stones from which, instead of being used for building, are used for stoning others. But this is not all: it is no solution to appeal directly to Christ instead of appealing to the apostles. Even for this fourth party the question is still valid: "Is Christ divided?" (I Cor. 1:13).

Even Christ the Lord may not be used as a banner for a party which wants to make a frontal assault on others who belong to one and the same Church.

The Bible as a helpful and liberating message, faithful tradition of the original testimony, the Petrine ministry as selfless pastoral service of the Church, the free gathering of brothers in the Spirit: all this is good if each is not taken exclusively, to be used against the others. Each must be subordinated to the service of Christ, who is and remains the Lord of the Church and of everything which goes to make up the Church. No Church in the last analysis can judge itself. All are tested in the refining fire of the Lord. Then will be made clear what part of its peculiarities, what parts of its unique tradition, what parts of its special doctrine are wood, hay and stubble, and what are gold, silver and precious stones; it will then be made manifest what is valueless and transient, and what will survive and be saved (cf. I Cor. 3:12–15).

EPILOGUE

Has the Church a future? At all events, the Church has a *present*, and no hopeful glimpse of a future can prevent our confronting that present. The Church's present is a present in the *world*. We have tried in this book to emphasize, in a variety of different ways and from a variety of different perspectives, the same point: the real Church is not an ideal, sacral, eternal phenomenon, floating somewhere between God and men. The real Church is rather the Church of God, composed of men, existing in the world for the world.

The eschatological view of the world taken by the young Church, which was strongly influenced by the spirituality of later Judaism, was very largely negative, because it looked forward to the consummation of the reign of God in the immediate future. "This world," "this age" in Pauline and Johannine terminology and in most of the terminology of the New Testament, is a disastrous phenomenon, ruled by the powers of sin and death, in which demonic evil is effective and all-powerful. The man who is "flesh" or "darkness", with all his desires and lusts, with his wickedness of heart, is completely subject and given over to "this world", incapable of freeing and redeeming himself from his state of subjection. The Church can only exist in a negative state of tension with this dark, disastrous and demonic world of sin and death, which stands in opposition to God and is thus heading for its end. The Church must confront the wisdom of this world with the wisdom of God, which is revealed in the foolishness of the cross of Christ; it must oppose the spirit of this world with the Spirit which comes from God. On no account can the Church conform to this world; it cannot love this world. The Church confronts it, as the eschatological community of salvation called out of this world, as the chosen people of God, the holy temple of the Holy Spirit, the pure body of Jesus Christ.

But, despite all, this is only one side of the New Testament view of the world. By contrast with the Qumran community, the young ecclesia does not withdraw from the world. The solution is not simply hostility to the world, separation from the world, flight from the world. On the contrary, the young ecclesia sees itself as having been sent back into the world again. As the community of salvation, set apart from the world, it must fulfil its task in the world and for the world. As the new people of God, the Church is sent into the world to bring men from darkness to light, from sin to salvation, from death to life. The joyful message of the redemption of the world and of coming salvation, of the dawning and soon to be consummated reign of God, must be proclaimed to the world. The young ecclesia must testify to the love of God by its love for men, as it has been revealed in Jesus Christ. And in this way the preaching of the Church will make it clear that this evil world which deserted God has never been deserted by God; that God has never finally fallen away from his creation, though it has fallen away from him; that even this lost world remains a world which belongs to God, and which is now to be brought back to God in Christ through the Church.

The fact that the world belongs to God and that it has a goodness given to it by its creator is something that evil could never reverse and destroy. The "cosmos"—this is how Colossians and Ephesians especially, but also the prologue to John, refer to the world, with much more positive overtones—was from the first created in Christ, looking towards Christ's coming; this cosmos has been gathered up again anew in Christ and under his leadership brought back to God, in order that it may find consummation and its full freedom in the eschatological new creation. It is in this world, embraced by God's grace, that the Church as the eschatological community of salvation, as the people of God, the spiritual building, the body of Christ, has to fulfil its function of ministry in all its forms.

From the Church's viewpoint the world exists essentially in an ambivalence of light and darkness. It is the world of transience and vanity, and at the same time the world of goodness and of eschatological promise sustained by the creator. It is the realm in which evil, sin and death rule and attempt to dominate man, and at the same time it remains the good world created as such by God, and never deserted or denied by him, the world indeed which has been already reconciled and redeemed in Christ; it is the realm in which men live, the realm which they are to shape positively with all their resources. The Church confronts this ambivalent world with an ultimate freedom; it must not bury itself in the world nor flee from it, it must not abandon itself to the world nor be hostile to it, but it must approve while it denies, and deny while it approves, resisting it while it devotes itself to it and devoting itself to it while it resists it. In this royal freedom of the children of God the Church reveals its inner distance from the world, insofar as the world is distanced from God, and at the same time its entire and total commitment to the world, insofar as it is destined for God.

For the first generation Church the relationship between the Church as such and secular society with its groupings and institutions, its civilization and culture, was a question from time to time of a concrete relationship (for example, the question of obedience to secular powers), but on the whole it was not a regular theological problem. For a community which saw the world quickly passing away, the question of "forming the world" in any modern sense simply did not exist. But the later writings of the New Testament show that the Church of the second generation was already taking up, indeed had to take up, a different attitude towards the world, and that from this position the question of a "ministry to the world" becomes a real issue. This is where the problems of a Christian "formation of the world" begin, problems that were bound to increase with time, in connection with secular vocations, intellectual and cultural activity, and in economic, social and political life.

In the first three centuries the Church scarcely had any opportunity to make its commitment to the world effective *in society;* in the time of persecution it consistently kept aloof from any secular spheres, and indeed revealed in part a determined hostility to the world. The Constantinian period brought with it a new relationship to the world, in social, cultural and political activity. The result was that *sacralization* of the secular world which has been frequently discussed in the preceding chapters. Those in the Church today who still lament the *secularization* of the world, and are reluctant to accept the consequences of that development in various areas of life, overlook the fact that the modern process of secularization is basically no more than the consequence of that earlier process of sacralization, which reached its zenith in the

High Middle Ages and then underwent a dialectical change of direction. Today the Church lives for the most part in a secular society and in a secular world, even though this world, despite the process of secularization, has carried on, developed and transformed what are at root Christian impulses, insights and forms (e.g. the denuminization and demythologizing of nature, the value put on human work, the overcoming of a fatalistic and cyclical view of life by a type of historical thinking which includes human responsibility and the possibility of changing the world).

It would go far beyond the limits of this book if we were to attempt to indicate what life in a secular world means for the Church. There is no room here to discuss what risks and opportunities, what new dangers and great possibilities there are for the Church in this worldly world, which has become a hominized world with no numinous aura. It is a world in which man himself builds up, forms and transforms his own world. It is a world—and this applies particularly to the material world of science, but also increasingly to the biological and anthropological world of biophysics and genetics, of psychology, sociology and economic sciences—which makes up a closed system of phenomena and functional relationships, which are capable of being experienced, calculated, experimented with, predicted and manipulated, a closed system in which the entity known as God no longer appears, a system which would indeed be disturbed in its functional explanation and manipulation of individual phenomena by such an entity. It is a technological world in which the arts, law, social life and all areas of culture are no longer deduced from or positively formed according to religious interpretations and objectives, but are equally planned, constructed and realized by man in a completely secular way. It is a worldly world, finally, which can only exist as a completely and thoroughly pluralistic world. . . . This is a situation which does not primarily concern ecclesiology; but it is one which offers a challenge to the whole of theology, particularly theological anthropology and the theology of God and creation, for theology today has to rethink fundamentally for this new world its view of man, of nature and of God. In addition, it will be the task of pastoral theology to concern itself with the practical problems of the Church in a secular world (urbanization, industrialization, rationalization, socialization, etc.).

The Second Vatican Council undertook the hazardous task of setting out the place of the Church in the modern world. The Pastoral Constitution on the Church in the Modern World deals in a first and fundamental main section with "The Church and Man's Calling": (1) The dignity of the human person; (2) the community of mankind; (3) man's activity throughout the world; (4) the role of the Church in the modern world. The second main part deals with "Some problems of special urgency": (1) Fostering the nobility of marriage and the family; (2) the proper development of culture; (3) socio-economic life; (4) the life of the political communities; (5) the fostering of peace and the promotion of a community of nations.—This constitution, more than any other, reveals that in a world which is increasingly differentiated and highly specialized, the time is finally past when the Church could hope to give effective and concrete directives on all the great specific problems of mankind. As time goes on, it will become increasingly important for the Church's preaching to communicate to the individual Christian what his *basic attitude* should be in dealing with specialized problems in which the Church as such has no competence. Much more important than trying to give all possible prescriptions for all possible problems would be the attempt to make clear what the Gospel of Jesus Christ really means for a man today.

To help the Church to fulfil its role in the present time, it is of course important to offer sociological, psychological and historical analyses, and equally to examine and apply pastoral and moral theology. But the fundamental basis for such work must surely remain the theological investigation of what the Church, viewed from its origins, really and essentially is. It is of course of central importance that the Church has a present, that it faces up to this present and does not take refuge in romanticism, conservatism or utopianism. The present world is after all the place, and the present hour the time, in which it has to carry out its mission. Hence it will always have to take account of the changing world around it and in the light of the world achieve a continual *aggiornamento* in theory and practice. But such an *aggiornamento* will be no more than a following of all the latest fashions, will be no more than a drifting on the open sea according to the changing favours of the wind, unless it is anchored in the origins of the Church, and steered by the Gospel of Jesus Christ himself, the existential basis of the Church. *Aggiornamento* must therefore always be a reform, a return to the original form and to the original nature of the Church. And since the present can only be properly viewed and judged in the perspective of those origins, we have hoped to be completely modern and up to date by constantly returning to the New Testament at all points of our discussion, in order to discover there what is essential and what is inessential for the Church of today.

Seen in the light of the Gospel the relationship of the Church to the world contains only one essential aspect: its *ministry to the world*. Ministry is here once again, to put it first of all in negative terms, opposed to dominion. Ministry does not mean raising one's voice or putting an oar in all secular questions of economic, political, social, cultural, artistic and scientific life—matters in which today only the specialist can speak. Ministry on the contrary can sometimes mean being reserved and silent, admitting that one knows nothing about the matter and does not need to know anything about it, that in the modern world there are other experts in the field. Ministry means a courageous renunciation of all such social positions of power which through the favour or disfavour of history fell to the Church; the time for defending such positions is long since past and at best will arouse or intensify anti-ecclesiastical emotions. Ministry to the world means the renunciation of dominion over the world, the renunciation of power politics, of the claim to secular leadership, secular prestige, privileges and distinctions.

What does ministry to the world mean in positive terms? It will be as well not to search for lofty words here, lest we should try and attribute more to the Church than it is capable of fulfilling. The Church cannot "solve" the great problems of the world; neither the problem of hunger nor that of the population nor that of war nor that of the anonymity of power nor that of race hatred. . . . What the Church can do can be expressed quite simply in one phrase: it must exist for the world. How can this be done?

The Church exists for the world first of all, quite simply, by knowing what the world is. For all its knowledge, that is one thing the world does not know: where it comes from, where it stands, where it is going to. The world does not know the ultimate truth about God and man, about salvation and damnation. The Church in faith can know that its God is also the God of the world and that the world too proceeds from him and is moving towards him. The Church can know that the one God has made his covenant with the whole of mankind, that Jesus Christ died and rose again not just for the Church but for the world, and that therefore God's all-embracing loving-kindness shines out even through the splendours and the miseries of the world. Only because the Church in its faith in Jesus Christ knows about the origin, the way and the goal of the world, its possibilities and its limitations, is it capable of truly existing for the world. The Church has the gift and the responsibility of seeing and understanding the world as it really is: with understanding and openness, with criticism and freedom, with generosity and charity.

The Church exists for the world by being linked to the world. Precisely because the Church recognizes and understands the world for what it is, it cannot possibly cut itself off from the world. Of course, it must not simply conform to the world. Then it would itself become world and would thereby renounce the special ministry to which it has been called. But knowing as it does about the mercy of the one true God, who so loved the world that he gave his only Son for it, the Church will from the first be deeply linked with the world. Together with the world the Church makes up the whole of humanity which, though sinful as a whole, is as a whole the recipient of God's mercy. Could the Church ever forget this shared guilt and this shared mercy? The Church cannot shut itself off from the world in a ghetto and live a life of its own in splendid isolation. It must rather face up to the challenge of the world, accept it, share in its hopes and anxieties, its ventures and its failures. Not if it is unsympathetic or non-committal, only if it is a committed and loving Church can the Church oppose and contradict the world, if the Gospel of Jesus Christ demands it; and then only in order to remain with the world. The Church has the gift and the responsibility of being in the world and with the world; of thinking, speaking and acting as a part of the world. But even this ministry is not sufficient.

The Church exists for the world by being committed to the world. If the Church is really in sympathy with the world, a sympathetic attitude and sympathetic words will not be sufficient; a passive, more or less peaceful co-existence will not be sufficient. There will have to be pro-existence rather than co-existence, involvement rather than disengagement.

The Church's understanding of the world will be unfruitful and its links with it useless unless they lead to an active assumption of responsibility for the world. If it truly follows its Lord, the Church is called to active service of its brethren, who are all created by the one Father. A Church which only lived and worked for itself would not be the Church of Christ. The Church of Christ, in everything it does, no matter how purely inward-looking it may seem, must be outward-looking, turned towards mankind as a whole. The world, whether it knows it or not, is in need of the brotherly help of the Church. The Church has the gift and the responsibility of sharing in responsibility, not merely in words but in deeds also, for the world, its present and its future.

But in order to ensure that the Church's understanding of the world is on the right lines, its links with it are the correct ones, and its commitment to it is not something vague, all this must be seen in the light of its *original commission*. This original commission consists not in doing all kinds of *"allotria"*, "other things". The Church is called, is empowered and authorized by its Lord in the Spirit to confess and proclaim Christ; to be a witness to him and in this way to proclaim his Gospel, the good news of the eschatological reign of God which has begun with Jesus Christ, and the decision of faith which is required of us; the good news of God's grace and mercy, of the justification, sanctification and calling of sinful humanity, of a life according to the Spirit in a new freedom from law, sin and death; the good news of a life in faith, love and joy, which looks forward to the perfection of all things in that future which has already begun to dawn in the present.

The one and only essential commission which the Church has been given with regard to the world is to be a witness to the world. This commission can be fulfilled in a variety of forms and ways by individuals and by the community. There is basically nothing in the Church which ought not to be done with windows open to the street—while concentrating on the work in hand, not simply staring at the windows. However profound a sermon, however solemn an act of worship, however well-organized a system of pastoral care, however methodical an instruction, however ingenious a theology, however effective a charity—there is no value in all of this if it is done in the isolation of a self-congratulating community, of a Church which only lives for itself. How could any of these things be done in the Church without their being able, in one form or another, directly or indirectly, to help and assist the world? How can a Church preach, pray, sing hymns, teach, engage in theology, the pastorate or the diaconate, without thinking of those brothers and sisters who do not belong actively to the Church but who are nonetheless sons and daughters of the same Father? The Church need not decide itself, indeed it ought to realize with gladness that the world is always involved in whatever it does or does not do in the middle of a secular world. Sometimes the world will listen, sometimes it will ignore; sometimes it will be silent and sometimes it will speak; sometimes it will protest and sometimes it will be grateful. The Church can exist in no other way but in giving witness to the world.

The Church is a minority serving a majority. This fellowship of believers, this community of those who confess and bear witness is a sign among the nations, often hidden yet always becoming visible again; it is a living invitation to the world to unite itself with the Church and join in testifying to the great things the Lord has done, not only for the Church but for the whole world. The whole of mankind is called upon to share in giving praise and thanks, to hear the word of grace and to celebrate the meal of love once again, in order to bear witness to Christ in everyday life by being men who not only love each other, but all men.

The Church does not wish to remain isolated. It wishes to be a vanguard. As the vanguard of mankind the people of God journeys on its way—but where is it going? Once again the question arises: has the Church a future?

The reply to this must be: the Church has a future because it has a present in the world. On its journey out into the world it has a mission, a commission, a task, a ministry which it must fulfil in the present and which is always given to it by the present; this is what fulfils it, giving it reality and purpose. What presents itself constantly to the Church in the present is nothing other than God's grace, under which the Church lives and which every day brings anew. It is this grace which helps the Church to overcome all the anxieties of the present, all the shortcomings, all the doubts, all the cares, all the hopelessness, all its illusions that it can redeem itself, all the wretchedness of the Church and the world. The Church has a future because in the darkness of time God's grace is given to it, giving it a present full of light.

Why can this Church, which does not deserve this grace, receive it constantly anew? This assurance in the present comes from a past which is still present to it, because it is its origin. God's grace dawned for the Church in the crucified and risen Lord in whom the Church believes. This event in Christ gives the Church assurance as it journeys on its way, the assurance of faith which brings trust and hope if not fulfilment in this world. The saving act of God in Christ precedes the Church, is greater than the Church, embracing everything the Church is and does; and whatever point the Church comes to, it is there before it; for this saving act, precisely as something in the past, is a promise for the future. The Church has a future, because through God's grace it was given a beginning, which in the present is a promise and a hope for the future.

The promise for the future is not empty and false, because rather than being founded in something that is still to come, and must be hoped for like a Utopia, it is founded on something that has happened. But what has happened does not only point to itself, it points beyond itself into the future. The resurrection of the crucified Christ which the Church believes and preaches is the proclamation of the resurrection of all men and of the renewing of the world. This is the new event which is still to come, which does not come to the Church day by day but which is being prepared for it and for the world by the new creative act of God. Like the creation of the world at the beginning of time, like the resurrection of Christ at the centre of time, the new creation of God at the end of time is not described in Scripture, but is indicated in images. The pilgrim Church has this promise, given by the resurrection of Christ, of an absolute future, a promise it already knows about in the present: the final overcoming of sin, suffering and death, the revelation and consummation of the reign of God in the kingdom of God, the kingdom of perfect righteousness, eternal life, true freedom and cosmic peace, the final reconciliation of men with God in a never-ending love.

Indeed, the Church has a future; it has *the* future. This is the eighth day which passes description and cannot be foreseen, the day on which God will complete his work of creation, the Church will reach the goal of its pilgrimage and the world will recognize its Lord. "And that seventh age will be our sabbath, a day that knows no evening, but is followed by the day of the Lord, an everlasting eighth day, hallowed by the resurrection of Christ, prefiguring the eternal rest not only of the spirit, but of the body as well. Then we shall have holiday and we shall see, we shall see and we shall love, we shall love and we shall praise. Behold, this is how it shall be at the end without end. For what else is our end, but to come to that kingdom which has no end?"

Haec tamen septima erit sabbatum nostrum, cuius finis non erit vespera, sed dominicus dies velut octavus aeternus, qui Christi resurrectione sacratus est, aeternam non solum spiritus, verum etiam corporis requiem praefigurans. Ibi vacabimus et videbimus, videbimus et amabimus, amabimus et laudabimus. Ecce quod erit in fine sine fine. Nam quis alius noster est finis nisi pervenire ad regnum, cuius nullus est finis?[1]

[1] Augustine, *De civitate Dei* XXII, 30; CC 48, 866.

ABBREVIATIONS

A.V.	Authorized Version of the Bible.
Cath.	*Catholicisme* (Paris 1948 ff.).
CC	*Corpus Christianorum* (Turnhout–Paris 1953 ff.).
CE	*Constitutio de Ecclesia* of Vatican II (1964).
D	H. Denzinger, *Enchiridion Symbolorum* (Freiburg–Barcelona, 30th edn., 1955).
DBS	*Dictionnaire de la Bible,* suppl. vols. (Paris 1920 ff.).
DOe	*Decretum de Oecumenismo* of Vatican II (1964).
DR	*Declaratio de Religionibus nonchristianis* of Vatican II (1965).
DTC	*Dictionnaire de théologie catholique* (Paris 1909 ff.).
EKL	*Evangelisches Kirchenlexikon* (Göttingen 1955 ff.).
CGS	*Die griechischen christlichen Schriftsteller der ersten drei Jahrhunderte* (Leipzig 1897 ff.).
HTG	*Handbuch theologischer Grundbegriffe* (Munich 1962 f.).
JB	Jerusalem Bible.
LThK	*Lexikon für Theologie und Kirche* (Freiburg, 2nd ed., 1955 ff.).
ODCC	*The Oxford Dictionary of the Christian Church* (London, 3rd edn., 1961).
PG	*Patrologia Graeca,* ed. J. P. Migne (Paris 1857 ff.).
PL	*Patrologia Latina,* ed. J. P. Migne (Paris 1878 ff.).
RGG	*Die Religion in Geschichte und Gegenwart* (Tübingen, 3rd edn., 1956 ff.).
Structures	Hans Küng, *Structures of the Church,* London 1965; Camden, N.J. 1963.
ThQ	*Theologische Quartalschrift* (Tübingen).
ThW	*Theologisches Wörterbuch zum Neuen Testament,* ed. G. Kittel (Stuttgart 1933 ff.).

WA   M. Luther, *Werke. Kritische Gesamtausgabe*, known as *Weimarer Ausgabe* (Weimar 1883 ff.).

Since the literature on ecclesiology is virtually endless, detailed lists of the most important works have been given, with particular emphasis on separate works which have appeared since 1945, rather than giving individual references on individual problems. In these lists, books are cited in their first editions unless they have been significantly extended or altered in later editions.

[Translator's note: Books in these lists are in the same chronological order as in the original German footnotes, without reference to the various dates at which they may have been translated into English.]

The most detailed inter-confessional bibliography on ecclesiology is to be found in: U. Valeske, *Votum Ecclesiae*, Munich 1962, pp. 1–210.

Translations of Council documents are taken from *The Documents of Vatican II*, ed. Abbott and Gallagher, London –Dublin–New York 1966.

INDEX OF SCRIPTURAL REFERENCES

INDEX OF NAMES

SUBJECT INDEX

N.B. The name "Christ/Jesus" is not indexed as it can be subsumed throughout.